*Mark Twain among the Indians
and Other Indigenous Peoples*

D1715338

Mark Twain among the Indians and Other Indigenous Peoples

KERRY DRISCOLL

University of California Press

University of California Press, one of the most distinguished university presses in the United States, enriches lives around the world by advancing scholarship in the humanities, social sciences, and natural sciences. Its activities are supported by the UC Press Foundation and by philanthropic contributions from individuals and institutions. For more information, visit www.ucpress.edu.

University of California Press
Oakland, California

Library of Congress Cataloging-in-Publication Data

Names: Driscoll, Kerry, author.
Title: Mark Twain among the Indians and other indigenous peoples /
  Kerry Driscoll.
Description: Oakland, California : University of California Press, [2018] |
  Includes bibliographical references and index.
Identifiers: LCCN 2017056076 (print) | LCCN 2017059379 (ebook) |
  ISBN 9780520970663 (epub) | ISBN 9780520279421 (cloth : alk. paper)
Subjects: LCSH: Twain, Mark, 1835–1910—Characters—Indians. | Indians
  of North America—Social conditions—19th century. | Twain,
  Mark, 1835–1910—Political and social views. | Twain, Mark,
  1835–1910—Criticism and interpretation. | Indians in literature. |
  West (U.S.)—In literature. | Clemens, Orion, 1825–1897.
Classification: LCC PS1342.I53 (ebook) | LCC PS1342.I53 D75 2018 (print) |
  DDC 818/.409—dc23
LC record available at https://lccn.loc.gov/2017056076

Manufactured in the United States of America

26   25   24   23   22   21   20   19   18
10   9   8   7   6   5   4   3   2   1

For my sons, Liam and Austin
Lux et vita mea

"Listening to Her History." *Uniform Edition* of Mark Twain's Works, vol. 23. Courtesy of the Mark Twain Project, The Bancroft Library, University of California, Berkeley.

Contents

Illustrations

Acknowledgments

This book would not exist without the gift of time and generous institutional support. I would like to thank the National Endowment for the Humanities for awarding me a yearlong faculty research fellowship; the University of Saint Joseph for sabbatical leave; and the Elmira College Center for Mark Twain Studies for several residencies at "the quietest of all quiet places"—the writer's beloved summer home, Quarry Farm.

I am deeply indebted to the Mark Twain Papers and Project at the University of California, Berkeley, where the majority of this research was conducted. Bob Hirst, the project's general editor, fielded my incessant questions with patience and unfailing good cheer. His vast knowledge of Twain's life and work was integral to interpreting the documentary evidence that undergirds my analysis. Several of the project's other editors— Vic Fischer, Ben Griffin, and Harriet Elinor Smith—also provided valuable assistance, as did reference and administrative manager Melissa Martin, whose pleasant, efficient demeanor in responding to requests large and small set a very high bar indeed. In addition, the curatorial staff at the archives of Hartford's Mark Twain House & Museum, Tracy Brindle and Mallory Howard, along with former chief curator Patti Philippon, were instrumental in helping me unravel the mystery surrounding the Maori artifacts acquired by the Clemens family during the 1895–96 world lecture tour. I would also like to acknowledge the extraordinary efforts of Kathy Kelley, the University of Saint Joseph's interlibrary loan librarian, in tracking down the many obscure sources I requested over the past decade.

I am likewise deeply grateful to a number of individuals in New Zealand and Australia, who generously responded to my cold queries, often directing me to friends and associates if they themselves didn't have the information

I was seeking: Anna K.C. Petersen and Donald Kerr of the Hocken Collections at the University of Otago; Dimitri Anson, Department of Anthropology, University of Otago; Roger Fyfe, senior curator of human history at Christchurch's Canterbury Museum; Geraldine Lummis, who kindly shared her master's thesis on Joseph Kinsey with me; Allan Smith, secretary of the Christchurch Savage Club; Paul Moon, senior lecturer in Maori studies at the Auckland University of Technology; and Joanne Huxley, research officer at the Tasmanian Museum and Art Gallery. Their assistance was invaluable in piecing together the hidden details of Twain's transformative visit to the land "down under."

Closer to home, a number of people merit special recognition for bringing relevant archival information to my attention: Barb Schmidt, the creator of twainquotes.com, who shared numerous articles she recovered from the digitized databases of various nineteenth-century newspapers; Twain collector Kevin MacDonnell, who provided me with the Christie's auction catalog describing the writer's marginalia in Richard Irving Dodge's *Our Wild Indians*; Larry Berkove, who generously gifted me with a trove of microfilmed Dan DeQuille sketches he'd spent years assembling; and Mark Woodhouse, former curator of the Mark Twain Archives at Elmira College, for tracking down details concerning the September 1884 performance of Buffalo Bill's Wild West at the Elmira Driving Park. Their contributions prove that "it takes a village," not only to raise a child, but also to write a book.

In the course of this project's long gestation, numerous colleagues read draft chapters and offered strategic suggestions: Steve Courtney, whose unerring journalistic eye was quick to flag overblown academic jargon and bring my prose back down to earth; Bob Hirst; Sharon McCoy; Bruce Michelson; Ann Ryan; and Barb Schmidt. Neil Schmitz, my former dissertation director at SUNY-Buffalo, believed in the importance of this project early on and expressed his support throughout. I owe a particular debt of gratitude to Julius Rubin at the University of Saint Joseph, with whom I team taught a series of honors capstone seminars on Native American history and literature. Julius taught me a great deal about native peoples and generously shared books from his expansive personal library; over hours of conversation at Starbucks, he also listened intently and helped shape my argument by asking probing, insightful questions. When I had moments of doubt and frustration, he convinced me to persevere.

Many long-time friends in the Mark Twain Circle sustained me through their personal encouragement, chief among them Ann Ryan, John Bird,

Tom Quirk, and the late Michael J. Kiskis. Barbara Snedecor, the emerita director of Elmira College's Center for Mark Twain Studies, deserves special thanks for the warmth of her steadfast assurance. I am above all grateful for the enduring support of my family—my husband, Dan, and dearest sons, Liam and Austin.

Abbreviations

L3	*Mark Twain's Letters*, vol. 3, 1869
L4	*Mark Twain's Letters*, vol. 4, 1870–71
L5	*Mark Twain's Letters*, vol. 5, 1872–73
L6	*Mark Twain's Letters*, vol. 6, 1871–75
LM	*Life on the Mississippi*
MTA	*More Tramps Abroad*
MTHL	*Mark Twain-Howells Letters*, 1872–1910
NBJ1	*Mark Twain's Notebooks & Journals*, vol. 1 (1855–73)
NBJ2	*Mark Twain's Notebooks & Journals*, vol. 2 (1877–83)
NBJ3	*Mark Twain's Notebooks & Journals*, vol. 3 (1883–91)
PW	*Pudd'nhead Wilson* and *Those Extraordinary Twins*
RI	*Roughing It*
SNO	*Sketches, New and Old*
TS	*The Adventures of Tom Sawyer*
WIM	*What Is Man? And Other Philosophical Writings*

Introduction

On 13 January 1895, the Sunday *New York Herald* published an article entitled "Indians and Mark Twain," recounting a "good story" told by one Charles A. Davis, manager of the iconoclastic orator Colonel Robert Green Ingersoll. Davis had come to his position by a circuitous route, having spent much of the preceding decade as a press agent for the Adam Forepaugh Circus, promoting ticket sales through sensational advertisements and publicity stunts that often tested the limits of local law. Although the circumstances surrounding the article's appearance are unclear, Davis's improbable tale about once having arranged an interview between a "big Sioux chief" and America's most beloved author may have been an attempt to divert attention away from the latest controversy in which his current employer found himself embroiled. In early 1895, the efforts of an irate group of New Jersey ministers to prevent Ingersoll's forthcoming lecture in Hoboken by invoking an obscure, century-old statute against uttering blasphemy had become national headlines. Amidst the "hubbub" of pending court injunctions and civil rights attorneys decrying the violation of Ingersoll's constitutional right of free speech,[1] Davis's anecdote about "How the Humorist Was Outhumored by an Untutored Savage"—as the *Herald's* subheading phrased it—cleverly substituted one media circus for another, deflecting reporters' requests for updates on this tense situation through a touch of levity. But might this bizarre anecdote have any basis—however remote— in truth?

Surprisingly, several historical facts corroborate its feasibility. Davis alleges that the meeting occurred on a "particular," though unspecified, date when the circus appeared in Hartford, as sources confirm that it did in 1883, 1886, and 1888. Moreover, according to the show's official programs, only its 1888 iteration—rebranded the "4 Paw and Wild West Combined"—included the "greatest gathering of real blanket Indians ever seen this side of the Rocky Mountains."[2] Many of these were Lakota veterans of the 1876 Battle of the Little Bighorn, whom Forepaugh had recruited for his new finale, "Custer's Last Rally," the first dramatic reenactment of this landmark event, later adopted and made famous by Buffalo Bill Cody. These details, when set within the context of the agent's statement that "the Indians were then a feature of the circus," point to 1888 as the likely date of the purported incident.

On the morning of 12 June that year, Hartford newspapers reported that the circus announced its arrival with a "grand and gorgeous" parade—in which "delegations of Sioux, Comanche, Kiowa, and Pawnee Indians, in full war paint and feathers" rode through the streets accompanied by scouts, trappers, plainsmen, and a "cowboy brass band."[3] This "sumptuous" spectacle passed within a half mile of the Clemens mansion en route to Brown's Lot, a field on the southern edge of the city, where performances were held at 2 p.m. and 7:30 p.m.[4] Given Mark Twain's fame in the late 1880s, Davis—whom circus historian William L. Slout describes as legendary among his peers for "working up interviews with his stars and proprietors"[5]—doubtlessly recognized that securing the writer's endorsement for the "4 Paw and Wild West Combined" would be a public relations coup.[6] To this end, the *Herald* reports,

> The enterprising agent . . . called upon the humorist and laid the matter before him. Mark said he didn't care for Indians and was busy, and didn't see what the Indians had to do with him, anyhow.
>
> "Why, the fact is," replied the circus man, with a gravity worthy of a higher life, "they have heard of you and want naturally to see you."
>
> This didn't appear strange to Mr. Clemens. Still, he was indisposed to grant the request until Davis swore that a big Sioux chief had declared that he would never die happy if compelled to return to the reservation without having seen and spoken to the man whose fame was as wide as the world.
>
> "All right," said Twain. "Run 'em in at six and let us make it short."
>
> About that hour the humorist sat on his porch and saw to his astonishment an immense cavalcade of mounted warriors coming down the street. In the place of a half dozen chiefs expected there were not less than fifty savages tearing along like mad in exhibition of their horsemanship. They turned in upon the lawn and broke down the shrubbery and wore off the grass and devastated the whole place. The spokesman of the party was a mighty hunter, and had been previously informed that Twain was distinguished for the awful slaughter of wild beasts, so he laid himself out for a game of brag. The interpreter was in the deal and, instead of repeating what the chief really said, made a speech of his own, speaking of Twain's literary achievements.

"For Heaven's sake, choke him off!" said Twain once or twice.

The interpreter turned to the chief and said the white hunter wanted to hear more. And on he went. Every time the humorist cried for quarter the chief was told to give another hunting story. Finally, the Indian vocabulary becoming exhausted, the chief quit, whereupon Twain made a brief reply, which was quadrupled in length by the interpreter turning it into a marvellous hunting yarn. The chief listened with stolid indifference, but when they got away he grunted contemptuously and said:—"White hunter heap big liar."[7]

Although certain aspects of this narrative—such as the "immense cavalcade" of mounted warriors tearing up the bushes on Clemens's property—are clearly embellished, if not altogether invented, the specificity of the hour at which Davis states the interview occurred bolsters the credibility of his claim. At 6 p.m.—in other words, during the interim between the circus's afternoon and evening performances—a smaller group, consisting of the agent, interpreter, and "big Sioux chief," could conceivably have traveled across town to pay Mark Twain a discreet visit, hastily exchanging greetings and a handshake.

Despite—or perhaps because of—its sensational subject matter, the *Herald* story spread quickly through the nation's newspaper exchange system, appearing over the next several months in the *Washington Post, Philadelphia Times, Pittsburgh Dispatch, Kansas City Journal,* and *Los Angeles Herald,* as well as in a score of smaller regional publications in Texas, Kansas, Iowa, and Nebraska. In each reprinting, the body of the text remained unchanged, although its title shifted to capitalize on the author's celebrity—alternately becoming "Mark and the Redskin" or "Having Fun with Twain." The subheading varied as well, ranging from "Twain Comes across a Jocular Untutored Savage" to "The Humorist Tricked by a Showman and Misrepresented to the Warriors." The piece even resurfaced a decade later in William Carter Thompson's 1905 memoir *On the Road with a Circus*—not as a hoax but as a consummate example of the "wily," "publicity-provoking designs" used by press agents to advertise their shows.[8]

So did Sam Clemens actually ever meet a "mighty" Lakota leader who engaged him in a cross-cultural "game of brag"? Probably not; at least no evidence exists to prove it. Yet even if Davis's tale is apocryphal, one aspect of it rings profoundly and indisputably true: Mark Twain did *not* care for Indians. This book is an attempt to understand why. A curious lacuna exists in the enormous body of scholarship on Twain's life and work: studies of his views on race—among them Arthur Petit's *Mark Twain and the South,* Shelley Fisher Fiskin's *Was Huck Black?,* Jocelyn Chadwick's *The Jim*

Dilemma, Terrell Dempsey's *Searching for Jim,* and Joe Fulton's *The Reconstruction of Mark Twain*—focus overwhelmingly on African Americans and slavery. Comparatively little attention, however, has been paid to the writer's stance on nineteenth-century America's other major racial issue—the dispossession and attempted extermination of the country's indigenous population. Over the past half century, only a handful of essays have addressed this topic, in piecemeal, cursory fashion; it has also received brief mention in books such as Philip Foner's *Mark Twain: Social Critic* (1958); Louis J. Budd's *Mark Twain: Social Philosopher* (1962); Leslie Fiedler's *The Return of the Vanishing American* (1968); Maxwell Geismar's *Mark Twain: An American Prophet* (1970); Jeffrey Steinbrink's *Getting to Be Mark Twain* (1991); Joseph Coulombe's *Mark Twain and the American West* (2003); Ned Blackhawk's *Violence over the Land: Indians and Empires in the Early American West* (2006); and Harold J. Kolb's *Mark Twain: The Gift of Humor* (2015).

The paucity of critical inquiry regarding Twain's conflicted attitudes toward native peoples, as reflected in the fiction, letters, journalistic sketches, and speeches he wrote over a period of nearly sixty years, is in my estimation not a matter of oversight but deliberate avoidance. The author's status as an American cultural icon rests, in large part, on his reputation as "a champion of the oppressed of all races."[9] While Twain's views on blacks affirm that notion by demonstrating unequivocal growth away from the racism of his origins in the antebellum South, his representations of Indians do not follow a similarly redemptive arc. They are instead vexingly erratic and paradoxical, commingling antipathy and sympathy, fascination and visceral repugnance. Previous scholars seeking to explain the harshness of Twain's stance have been stymied not only by the absence of a linear trajectory but also the fact that—as Lou Budd perceptively noted—"there is no good reason why he reacted so violently."[10]

This conundrum has historically divided critics into two antithetical camps that oversimplify—and thereby inevitably distort—Twain's attitudes toward Indians by either vilifying or idealizing them. The most extreme example of the former tendency is Leslie Fiedler, whose reputation as a nonpareil literary provocateur had been cemented four decades earlier with the publication of his controversial essay "Come Back to the Raft Ag'in, Huck Honey." With characteristic bravado, Fiedler charges that Twain was "by instinct and conviction an absolute Indian hater, consumed by the desire to destroy not merely real Indians, but any image of Indian life which stands between White Americans and a total commitment to genocide. His only notable Indian character is Injun Joe, that haunter of caves and hater of white females, who stalks the underground darkness of *Tom Sawyer* and is finally imagined dying the most dreadful of deaths."[11] He offers little additional evidence in support of this sweeping claim, mentioning only Twain's satirical treatment of James Fenimore Cooper's Indians and derogatory remarks about the "Digger tribe" in *The Innocents Abroad* before rushing headlong into an equally facile discussion of Herman Melville. Similarly, Helen Harris's 1975 essay "Mark Twain's Response to the Native American" pronounces his depiction of Indians "unfailingly hostile."[12] Both scholars were apparently unaware of an 1886 letter to President Grover Cleveland, in which Clemens denounces a New Mexico bounty on Apache scalps as "scoundrelism." This document, along with a handful of others, undermines the absolutism of their stance by demonstrating that the writer's views on Indians were neither simplistic nor one-dimensional.[13]

The opposing critical viewpoint is equally problematic in its determination to absolve Twain from the charge of racism through selective use of evidence. This inspirational narrative of racial transcendence was first proposed by Philip Foner, who argued that Clemens outgrew the "disparaging references to those of alien origin" found in his early writing and ultimately embraced a vision of "men and women of all races, creeds, and colors ... uniting in a universal brotherhood of man."[14] Though Twain's response to cultural "Others" undeniably progressed over time, this conclusion is too pat—akin in some ways to the familiar contention about Huck Finn's wholesale rejection of his racist attitudes about blacks after spending time on the raft with Jim. More than a decade later, Maxwell Geismar followed Foner's lead in both his acknowledgment of the writer's "deep prejudice" against Indians and insistence that it was fully overcome. He lauds Twain's declaration that "my first American ancestor ... was an Indian" in the 1881 speech "Plymouth Rock and the Pilgrims" as "a remarkable opening up of the ignorant frontier mind"[15] but ignores his monstrous depiction of the Sioux three years later in "Huck Finn and Tom Sawyer among the Indians." Geismar also cites the presence of "billions of red angels" in the 1907 story "Extract from Captain Stormfield's Visit to Heaven" as definitive proof that Clemens's "original ingrained prejudice about the Indians of his youth ... was finally exorcised"[16]—a conclusion rendered untenable by his gruesome description of the rape, mutilation, and murder of Minnesota settlers at the hands of Indians in "Letters from the Earth," composed just months before his death.

Lynn W. Denton's 1972 essay, "Mark Twain and the American Indian," proposes an analogous paradigm—that the author's early bias against native peoples gradually "changed to toleration and then finally to idealism."[17] Like Foner and Geismar, she charts a redemptive pattern that culminates with "Stormfield," declaring that Twain "wholly renounced the prejudice . . . of [his] Nevada days" in this late text. Denton also correlates the liberalization of the writer's attitudes with a growing disenchantment about European colonizers in general and Puritans in particular, arguing that he became "more and more convinced that white-oriented civilization must receive the blame for the introduction of evil into an otherwise sinless society."[18] Her thesis concerning Twain's recognition of the "innate good-ness of the [continent's] original inhabitants" is grounded in a misreading of his allusion to Indians in *Life on the Mississippi* as "simple children of the forest" (LM, 37)—a clichéd nineteenth-century rhetorical trope that reifies their inferiority. Rather than valorizing the primitive, the writer's cynicism about civilization reflects a dim view of human nature in general, as *Following the Equator* attests: "There are many humorous things in the world; among them the white man's notion that he is less savage than the other savages" (FE, 213).

Louis J. Budd, James McNutt, Jeffrey Steinbrink, and Harold Kolb offer a more nuanced, clear-sighted perspective on the subject, arguing that while Twain's prejudice against Indians diminished over time, it did not entirely disappear. Budd, for example, asserts that "the brightest side of [the writ-er's] whole intellectual career is his progress away from racism" emphasiz-ing the dynamic, evolutionary quality of his views rather than an end result of unconditional triumph.[19] He also concedes that Twain's attitudes toward racial and ethnic minorities were not uniformly liberal. Unlike African Americans and the Chinese, Indians were relatively slow to "stalk into the circle of his sympathy"—an "ugly truth" attributable to the fact that Clemens initially had "little respect for any peoples who were outside the pattern of an industrial society."[20] Although he eventually acknowledged "how the pioneer had pre-empted [the Indians'] lands and smashed their culture," Budd notes that Clemens "was never to focus directly on the dark agony of the American Indian, a subject fit for his most trenchant insights."[21] This omission, in Budd's opinion, is both regrettable and per-plexing, particularly in light of Twain's bold critique of US imperialism in the Philippines during the last decade of his life.

James McNutt's 1978 essay "Mark Twain and the American Indian: Earthly Realism and Heavenly Idealism" similarly concludes that the sub-ject of Indian-white relations "alternately angered, baffled, and saddened [the writer] for a lifetime." He deems "Twain's resolution of the problem… ambiguous at best," in that he "never totally refrained from using the Indian's savagery as a club whenever convenient"; native peoples instead remained indelibly imprinted in his imagination as "a metaphor for violence and a symbol of uncivilized behavior."[22] Building on McNutt's assessment, Jeffrey Steinbrink characterizes Twain as "an 'unfinished' writer, philosophically undisciplined and more than occasionally inconsistent, throughout his career." He claims that much of the work Twain published in the *Galaxy* between 1868 and 1871—particularly the 1870 sketch "The Noble Red Man"—"raises the question whether, like Huck Finn, he had a sufficiently sound heart to countervail the deformed conscience society had inculcated in him" and concludes that "the American Indian [was] a lifelong blind spot in the field of Clemens' moral vision."[23] Harold Kolb's interpretation, in turn, reaffirms the notion of a linear trajectory first proposed by Foner and Geismar but stops short of complete redemption. He maintains that Twain's early references to Indians while living in the West "tend to be more negative than the later [ones]" because he "adopt[ed] the more sympathetic eastern view of natives" after relocating to New York and then Connecticut.[24] Although Kolb admits "this evolving pattern is not uniform" and that Twain only "partially transcended the race prejudice of his moment in history," his analysis of this progression is nonetheless too simplistic.

The views expressed on both sides of this critical fault line are—to a greater or lesser degree—characterized by a tendency toward overgeneralization, which has yielded a series of unsatisfying, often misleading conclusions. Twain's representations of American Indians are so checkered and convoluted that they defy easy categorization or summary—pitfalls I hope to avoid here. *Mark Twain among the Indians and Other Indigenous Peoples* is the first book-length work devoted exclusively to this subject. My title is an allusion to "Huck Finn and Tom Sawyer among the Indians," the writer's 1884 sequel to *Adventures of Huckleberry Finn*, which—though unfinished—represents his most sustained, ambitious attempt to portray what he perceived as the realities of native character. While Clemens was literally only "among" Indians for a relatively brief period during the early 1860s, he was nonetheless deeply enmeshed in—and hence metaphorically "among"— the ubiquitous, often incendiary, accounts of Indian raids and atrocities reported in the national press as well as the stereotypes of "noble" or "ignoble" savages promulgated in popular music, drama, and dime novels.

My approach is both chronological and geographical, exploring the origin and development of the writer's ideation about native peoples in relation to the various communities he inhabited, from antebellum Hannibal and the mining camps of the Sierra Nevada to the socially progressive enclave of Hartford's Nook Farm. The book is in a sense a work of literary archaeology, sifting through the strata of diverse, often obscure, primary sources in an attempt to re-create the cultural milieu of these formative local environs. In addition to Twain's manuscripts, letters, and unpublished notebooks, I have examined the official records pertaining to Orion Clemens's role as acting governor and ex officio superintendent of Indian Affairs at the Nevada State Archives and his little-known 1856 essay "The History of the Halfbreed Tract"; the tenor of contemporary reportage about Indians in regions where the writer lived; and the membership rosters, meeting minutes, and promotional pamphlets describing the philanthropic initiatives of the Connecticut Indian Association, a native rights advocacy group that flourished in Hartford throughout the 1880s—the period of his greatest literary productivity and civic engagement. I have also closely analyzed Clemens's reading, mining the extensive marginalia in works such as Francis Parkman's *The Jesuits in North America in the Seventeenth Century* and James Bonwick's *The Lost Tasmanian Race* for insight into his evolving views on "savagery," native spirituality, and the fateful extinction of American Indians and other indigenes around the globe ordained by "progress."

This documentary evidence challenges many of the claims found in the work of earlier scholars. For example, Geismar's assertion that Clemens exhibited the "deep prejudice of the frontiersman" against Indians implies that such antipathy was not merely prevalent but endemic in the West, when in fact the individuals with whom the writer was most closely associated in Nevada Territory—Orion, Governor James Warren Nye, and his fellow *Enterprise* writer Dan DeQuille, to name just a few—espoused progressive, sympathetic views of the Great Basin tribes. In order to more accurately understand the origins of Twain's literary identity, the cavalier attitudes evident in his early journalistic sketches must be reassessed within this broader spectrum of opinion. As Ned Blackhawk has observed, "While many suggest that the frenetic, atomistic world of Virginia City allowed Clemens to reinvent and imagine himself anew—to become Mark Twain—few have considered where his discourse of [native] inhumanity resides."[25] During his years in the West, Clemens was in a sense blind—or, at least, wryly indifferent—to the dispossession of the region's indigenous population, mocking their squalid appearance and living conditions as proof of intrinsic inferiority rather than a dire economic consequence of settler colonialism.

The conceptual course I chart in *Mark Twain among the Indians and Other Indigenous Peoples* differs from the trajectory proposed by previous scholars in several ways. I reject the notion of a strict linear progression in the writer's convictions; rather—as his notebooks, personal correspondence, and both published and unpublished work attest—the change was uneven, proceeding in fits and starts. Contradictions abound and are never fully reconciled. In *Roughing It*, for example, he callously dismisses the starving natives loitering at western stage stations as "a silent, sneaking, treacherous looking race . . . [of] prideless beggars," commenting, "if the beggar instinct were left out of an Indian he would not 'go,' any more than a clock without a pendulum" (RI, 127). Four years later, however, in the 1876 story "The Facts Concerning the Recent Carnival of Crime in Connecticut," the narrator's conscience—personified as a "shriveled, shabby dwarf . . . covered all over with a fuzzy, greenish mold"—reveals him to be plagued with shame and self-recrimination over "a peculiarly mean and pitiful act . . . toward a poor ignorant Indian in the wilds of the Rocky Mountains," presumably on that same historic journey (CT1, 645, 649).

Twain's expressions of sympathy for Indians tend to be discrete, short-lived epiphanies, punctuated by lapses into more regressive modes of thinking. This incongruity is reflected in the dissonance between Clemens's 1886 letter to Cleveland, often hailed as a watershed in the evolution of his racial attitudes, and the ethnocentric imagery found in *A Connecticut Yankee in King Arthur's Court*, published three years later. The writer's passionate protest against the bounty on Apache scalps is grounded in a recognition of the humanity of native peoples—the very trait denied in his characterization of the inhabitants of Camelot as unreasoning "animals" and "white Indians," and the elite Knights of the Round Table as a "polished-up court of Comanches" (CY, 129).

Additionally, my research refutes the conventional claim that Clemens's harshest attitudes about Indians coincide with his residence in the West and that their modulation is attributable to his relocation to the Northeast in 1868. While the writer's views unquestionably became more liberal during the twenty years he lived in Hartford, this growth occurred in a gradual, subtle fashion—and at least a decade later—than earlier critics have alleged. In the early 1870s, Twain's geographic distance from native peoples—along with significant changes in his personal and material circumstances—actually fueled his antipathy toward them rather than diminishing it. His description of the "Goshoot" tribe in *Roughing It* (1872) as "the wretchedest type of mankind I have ever seen . . . manifestly descended from the self-same gorilla, or kangaroo, or Norway rat, whichever animal-Adam the Darwinians trace them to" (RI, 126–127) is, for example, far harsher than any firsthand observation he made about Indians while living in Nevada Territory. At the core of my argument is "The Noble Red Man"—written in Buffalo and published just six months after his marriage to Olivia Langdon—which reveals the degree to which the writer's antagonistic attitudes are entwined with Victorian ideologies of gender, particularly the archetype of women as chaste and vulnerable "angels of the house" whose virtue must be vigilantly protected by men. This text, which ends with a horrifying vignette of "wives . . . ravished before their husbands' eyes [and] husbands . . . mutilated, tortured, and scalped, and their wives compelled to look on" (CT1, 446), also marks the inception of a pattern in which Indians are depicted as demonic sexual predators intent upon the destruction of white womanhood. Several of Twain's later female protagonists, such as the Widow Douglas in *The Adventures of Tom Sawyer* (1876), seventeen-year-old Peggy Mills in "Huck Finn and Tom Sawyer among the Indians" (1884), and the anonymous young bride in "The Californian's Tale" (1893) face the prospect of rape, captivity, or murder at the hands of Indians.

Although this trope disappears from Twain's fiction for more than a decade after 1893, it reappears in his harrowing description of an 1862 Minnesota massacre at the end of "Letters from the Earth":

> Twelve Indians broke into a farm house at daybreak and captured the family . . . They crucified the parents; that is to say, they stood them stark naked against the wall of the living room and nailed their hands to the wall. Then they stripped the daughters bare, stretched them upon the floor in front of their parents, and repeatedly ravished them. Finally they crucified the girls against the wall opposite the parents, and cut off their noses and their breasts. They also—but I will not go into that. There is a limit. There are indignities so atrocious that the pen cannot write them. (CT2, 927)

Twain's acknowledgment that the Dakota Indians who perpetrated this unspeakable crime had been "deeply wronged and treacherously treated by the government of the United States"—dispossessed from their ancestral homeland and reduced to starvation when the provisions guaranteed by federal treaty were not supplied—reflects a measure of political sympathy for their plight. His conclusion, however, reinforces an obdurate view of native barbarism and depravity: "Now you have *one* incident of the Minnesota massacre. I could give you fifty. They would cover all the different kinds of cruelty the brutal human talent has ever invented."

Mark Twain among the Indians and Other Indigenous Peoples also offers an extended analysis of several key factors—some previously unknown, others ignored or undervalued—that precipitated advances in the writer's thinking about American Indians during the 1880s and 1890s. His 1881 introduction to the tenets of traditional Iroquois spirituality in Francis Parkman's *The Jesuits in North America in the Seventeenth Century* was transformational, upending an inherited cultural bias regarding Christianity's superiority to other belief systems. Clemens's appreciation of the "good sense" manifested in the Iroquois conception of God fostered a reconsideration of native primitivism. Three years later, while doing background research for "Huck Finn and Tom Sawyer among the Indians," he was even more intrigued by a discussion of Cheyenne religion in Colonel Richard Irving Dodge's *Our Wild Indians: Thirty-Three Years' Personal Experience among the Red Men of the Great West*. His marginalia in this volume articulate various plans to incorporate these beliefs, including Huck's conversion to Cheyenne spirituality, into the unfinished sequel. Given the canonical status of *Adventures of Huckleberry Finn*, the Indianization of Twain's most beloved protagonist—if brought to fruition—might well have altered the course of American literature.

Clemens's interest in indigenous religion coincides with his exposure to the progressive ethos of the Connecticut Indian Association, a Hartford-based group of female reformers, who promoted the education and assimilation of American Indians into mainstream society. Although neither he nor Livy ever became members of this organization, many of their friends and neighbors at Nook Farm did. The group advanced its humanitarian agenda on multiple fronts, sponsoring lectures, amateur theatrical performances, and so-called butterfly teas to galvanize the interest of the city's intellectual elite. Throughout the 1880s, the association also waged an intensive public relations campaign seeking to raise public consciousness about the myriad injustices to which native peoples had been subjected. To this end, they wrote and placed hundreds of articles—including the 1886 editorial condemning the New Mexico bounty on Apache scalps—in local newspapers, where Clemens encountered them on a regular basis. Over time, the association's persistent advocacy on behalf of Indians thus exerted an indirect, but nonetheless discernible, influence in the modulation of his views.

These incremental advances in Twain's racial attitudes established the groundwork for the transformative experience of his 1895–96 world lecture tour. In observing the adverse effects of British imperialism on the indigenous populations of Australia and New Zealand, he finally understood the terrible human toll exacted by the advancement of Western civilization. His 1897 travelogue *Following the Equator* rages against the unjust dispossession of Australian Aboriginals and the genocidal efforts of colonial settlers who left arsenic-laced flour in the bush for them to eat; it also records the heartrending distress of his discovery that Tasmania's entire native population had been wiped out within a half century after the arrival of the island's first British convicts. The sobering reality of extinction—and the appallingly sadistic means by which it had been achieved—caused the writer to question both the notion of progress and long-held assumptions concerning the binaries of savagery and civilization. Twain's epiphany peaked in New Zealand, where he spent five weeks in late 1895 immersed in Maori history and culture, marveling at their art and meeting numerous representatives of local tribes. His conclusion that the Maori were "a superior breed of savages" (FE, 318) reflects the emergence of a newfound cultural relativism that would become the distinguishing feature of his later sociopolitical views.

Although the pattern of indigenous dispossession that unfolded in Australia and New Zealand—the discovery of gold followed by a massive influx of foreign fortune seekers, whose presence precipitated inevitable clashes over land use and resources—was uncannily reminiscent of recent US history, the plight of American Indians remains a largely unacknowledged subtext in *Following the Equator*. Glancing allusions, such as Twain's characterization of Aboriginal women as "wild squaws" and declaration that "Fennimore Cooper . . . wouldn't have traded the dullest [Aboriginal tracker] for the brightest Mohawk he ever invented," demonstrate his cognizance of the parallel (FE, 264, 218). But rather than exploring this correspondence, the writer suppresses it; as Peter Messent has observed, Twain's writing on race in the travelogue "operates over and over in a culturally self-reflexive manner . . . [yet] his awareness of the American racial theme is, at best, intermittent and . . . often unconscious."[26]

Twain continued to avoid the uncomfortable topic of American Indians during his last decade—at least in print. The 1902 dialogue "The Dervish and the Offensive Stranger," his most forthright admission of the wrongs that had been committed against them, remained unpublished until thirteen years after his death, when Albert Bigelow Paine included it in the anthology *Europe and Elsewhere*. In this piece, the writer acknowledges Indians as the "original owners of the soil" and describes the European colonization of the Americas as an egregious act of theft. The force of his indictment is blunted, however, by his situating these facts within an exculpatory philosophical framework that there is "no such thing as an evil deed . . . [only] good *intentions* and evil ones. . . . The *results* are not foreseeable" (CT2, 547–48). According to the Stranger's deterministic logic, "it is the law" that good intentions have produced good and evil results in equal measure throughout history. In other words, Europeans bear no culpability for driving Indians from their homes and "exterminat[ing] them, root and branch," since their conquest of the New World provided "farms and breathing-space and plenty and happiness" to the landless, "plodding poor" of the Old.

My intent in *Mark Twain among the Indians and Other Indigenous Peoples* is neither to defend nor to defame the writer but to explore the complexity of his engagement with native populations both at home and abroad. Clemens came of age during the bloodiest era of Indian-white relations, personally witnessed the devastating effects of colonization on the Great Basin tribes in 1860s Nevada Territory, and lived two decades beyond the crushing defeat of the Lakota at Wounded Knee and the official "closing" of the American frontier. While his attitudes toward Indians progressed in response to these sweeping historic changes, he never succeeded in fully exorcising this racial animus. It is perhaps unrealistic to expect such an outcome; for all of Twain's brilliance, he remained inescapably a man of his time and place. His intellectual journey—sprawling, untidy, incomplete—matters more than where he ultimately arrived.

Mark Twain is our nation's greatest storyteller; his work celebrates the American voice in its infinitely varied regional permutations. "A nation's language is a very large matter," he wrote in 1880. "It is not simply a manner of speech obtaining among the educated handful; the manner obtaining among the vast uneducated multitude must be considered also" (CT1, 831). And yet, amidst the rich, polyphonic chorus of ethnic voices heard in his work, those of Indians are absent. This is a missed opportunity with fateful, far-reaching consequences. What if young Sam Clemens, who grew up to become "the Lincoln of our literature," had played with native children rather than slaves at his Uncle Quarles's farm and been mesmerized in the firelight by tales from their ancient oral tradition instead of the ghost stories spun by Uncle Dan'l? He would then have learned firsthand about the humor and humanity of these "savages," their love of family and the moral cogency of their worldview. Ultimately, might he have also realized that the inferiority of American Indians so deeply ingrained in his imagination was, like that of African Americans, merely "a fiction of law and custom" (PW, 9)?

1. The Romance and Terror of Indians

In one of his earliest forays into print, sixteen-year-old Sam Clemens published a brief sketch of his hometown, "Hannibal, Missouri," in the Philadelphia *American Courier* on 8 May 1852. According to Edgar M. Branch and Robert H. Hirst, the editors of *Mark Twain's Early Tales and Sketches*, the significance of this juvenilia extends beyond its topicality, illustrating the writer's "constitutional drift away from mere factual reporting and toward imaginative invention and the human drama" (ETS1, 66)—dual signatures of his mature style. From a sociohistorical rather than literary perspective, however, the piece offers an instructive glimpse of Clemens's foundational views on history, place, and progress. Countering the smug eastern perception of the West as a "barren, uncultivated region, with a population consisting of heathens," the young reporter describes Hannibal as a thriving commercial hub in the throes of rapid industrial expansion. Within a year, he boasts, trade with neighboring Ralls County would be enhanced by the construction of a so-called plank road, an innovative type of highway featuring a smooth, level surface of wooden boards. Ambitious plans to build a railroad linking Hannibal with the city of St. Joseph on the state's western border were also under way. Clemens deems these developments particularly auspicious given the brevity of the town's existence:

> The first house was built in this city about sixteen years ago. Then the wild war-whoop of the Indian resounded where now rise our stately buildings, and their bark canoes were moored where now land our noble steamers; here they traded their skins for guns, powder, &c. But where now are the children of the forest? Hushed is the war-cry— no more does the light canoe cut the crystal waters of the proud Mississippi; but the remnant of those once powerful tribes are torn asunder and scattered abroad, and they now wander far, far from the homes of their childhood and the graves of their fathers. (ETS1, 67)

As both James McNutt and Joseph Coulombe have noted, Clemens's sentimental lament regarding the disappearance of these "children of the forest" from a landscape now dominated by the "stately buildings" and "noble steamers" of Anglo-American civilization echoes a familiar cultural script—the trope of the "Vanishing Indian," masterfully deconstructed in Brian W. Dippie's 1982 study, *The Vanishing American: White Attitudes and U.S. Indian Policy.*[1] This notion of inevitable doom, Dippie argues, was rooted in the belief that "a natural law was in operation, and no mortal could alter its course. The 'inexorable destiny' of the Indians, like that of the wilderness with which they shared an almost symbiotic relationship, was to recede before civilization's advance."[2]

While the romantic rhetoric of "Hannibal, Missouri" was soon supplanted by realism, Clemens's views on progress remained remarkably consistent over time. In *Life on the Mississippi*—published some three decades after the *American Courier* piece—he states that "two hundred years . . . have elapsed since the river took its place in history," implying that before the arrival of European explorers the region existed in a "slumbrous" natural state from which it was awakened by men like De Soto and La Salle (LM, 23, 25). Similarly, in a 1902 speech given at the christening of the St. Louis harbor boat Mark Twain, he reflects, "When La Salle came down this river a century and quarter ago there was nothing on its banks but savages. He opened up this great river and by his simple act was gathered in this great Louisiana territory."[3] History, in other words, begins with the era of colonization and commerce inaugurated by whites.

Despite its ethnocentrism, Clemens's 1852 statement concerning "once powerful tribes torn asunder and scattered abroad" accurately describes the process of Indian removal initiated soon after Missouri achieved statehood in 1821—a complex phenomenon that helps to explain the virtual absence of native peoples in the writer's recollections of his youth. According to John Mack Faragher, before the War of 1812 Missouri Territory was a "frontier of inclusion,"[4] marked by amicable economic and social relations—as well as extensive intermarriage—among indigenous groups such as the Missouri, Ioway, Osage, Oto, and Quapaw and the French and Spanish traders who had established small outposts along the Mississippi River. These unions produced a "syncretic society . . . a veritable melting pot of cultures and creeds"[5] that included a sizable métis or mixed-blood population. A major demographic shift occurred in the decade after the war as Anglo-American settlers—hailing, like the writer's own ancestors, primarily from Kentucky and Tennessee—flooded into the region, lured by the promise of rich soil. Rather than commingling with Indians as their

French predecessors had, these Anglo-Americans instead created a "frontier of exclusion" that confined "indigenous peoples to separate and distinct territories and eventually requir[ed] them to move further west."[6]

The abhorrence with which the new settlers viewed native peoples and their biracial progeny is illustrated in *Recollections of the Last Ten Years*, the 1826 memoir of Timothy Flint, a Massachusetts missionary who lived in Missouri from 1815 to 1825:

> I have hinted at the facility with which the French and Indians intermix. There seems to be as natural an affinity of the former people for them, as there is repulsion between the Anglo-Americans and them. . . . The antipathy between the two races seems fixed and unalterable. Peace there often is between them when they are cast in the same vicinity, but any affectionate intercourse, never. Whereas the French settle among them, learn their language, intermarry, and soon get smoked to the same copper complexion. A race of half-breeds springs up in their cabins.[7]

The racial hostility of Flint's words presaged an era of dramatic political change. In the early 1820s, close to three million acres in Missouri remained in the hands of both indigenous and emigrant tribes, such as the Shawnee, Delaware, Kickapoo, and Sac and Fox,[8] who had been relocated there from the Great Lakes region beginning in the 1780s. As settler colonialism expanded, these tribes faced mounting pressure to relinquish their lands. The removal process was formally inaugurated on 14 May 1824, when Missouri senator Thomas Hart Benton (1782–54)—whom Tom Sawyer pronounced "the greatest man in the world" (TS, 162)—introduced a "Proposition to Extinguish Indian Title to Lands" in the US Senate. Decrying the existence of separate native communities within Missouri as a "palpable evil, an anomaly in government, and a direct inconsistency with the policy and jurisdiction of a sovereign state," Benton argued that "sooner or later . . . the Indians must go to new homes."[9] The bill's paternalistic rhetoric touted removal as a "practical, economical, and humane remedy" to the anomalous existence of independent Indian polities within the state's borders. While proponents characterized the legislation as an even-handed "swap . . . requir[ing] only that Indians in Missouri exchange their lands within the state for 'equal' holdings from the public domain to the west,"[10] its actual purpose was "to secure the uncontested hegemony of the United States."[11] The economic impetus driving the proposition was simple, as Benton baldly admitted in his 1854 memoir *Thirty Years' View*: "To remove the Indians would make room for the spread of slaves."[12]

The passage of Senate bill 211 ushered in an era of ethnic cleansing so thorough that no federally recognized tribes or reservations exist within

Missouri today. Over the next decade, the government negotiated a series of treaties with the Osage, Kansa, Ioway, Sac and Fox, and other tribes formalizing their agreement to "cede, relinquish, and forever quit claim unto the United States all right, title, interest, and claim ... to lands ... within the limits of the state of Missouri."[13] These treaties also stipulated that the natives were prohibited from hunting or settling on any part of the forfeited territories "without special permission from the Superintendent of Indian Affairs"[14]—effectively banishing them from the region. This systematic process of dispossession culminated in an October 1836 treaty, with the Oto, Missouri, Omaha, and Yankton and Santee bands of the Sioux, annexing the Platte Purchase, two million acres in the state's northwest corner that had previously been set aside for the resettlement of Indians from the east. A presidential proclamation issued five months later by Martin Van Buren declared Indian title to Missouri land "entirely extinguished."[15]

The resignation and resentment with which Missouri's native peoples greeted this enforced relocation were manifested in the slow pace of their exodus. Some bands openly disavowed the treaties, lingering within the state's boundaries and continuing their seasonal hunts. Moreover, a significant number of those who resisted removal did so on the grounds that their mixed racial ancestry exempted them from expulsion. The nebulous legal status of these individuals denied them the political rights of their white fathers and simultaneously excluded them from the annuities and cash payments routinely granted to full-blood Indians in return for land cessions. Between 1824 and 1830, the government attempted redress of this issue through the creation of several so-called Half-Breed Tracts in Wisconsin, Minnesota, Iowa, and Nebraska Territory set aside for the exclusive use of mixed-blood members of the Omaha, Ioway, Oto, Sac and Fox, and Santee Sioux nations. All were short-lived, failed experiments, dissolved within a few decades of their establishment. Significantly, one such tract—a parcel of 119,000 acres located at the confluence of the Mississippi and Des Moines Rivers in Lee County, Iowa—was situated just fifty miles north of Hannibal.

These two factors—general resistance to removal as well as the proximity of the Iowa Half-Breed Tract—meant that natives and whites coexisted uneasily in northeastern Missouri during the years immediately preceding Clemens's birth. In *The Callaghan Mail,* a compilation of letters by one of Hannibal's earliest settlers, William Callaghan recounts an 1830 incident in which a drunken trader traveling through the forest happened upon a nineteen-year-old Sac and Fox woman sitting on a log and gratuitously shot her in the back; minutes later, the group he was traveling with was surrounded by "100 Indians on horses . . . [who] told the white men they would kill all of them" unless they revealed the identity of her murderer—which they promptly did.[16] Five years later, Callaghan's slave Isaac Crawford, "wearing a long red nubby scarf around his neck," encountered a band of Sac and Fox Indians "led by an old chief who wore a war bonnet of eagle feathers" in the forest near the family's cabin: "Isaac was scared, but he dared not turn his horse back so he rode past the chief, and had nearly got by all the Indians, when three or four braves grabbed for his red scarf . . . and a tug of war resulted. Suddenly the old chief up in front started waving his arms and jabbering. The Indian let go of Isaac's scarf and the tribe went down the road and meantime Isaac did not spare his horse in getting home."[17]

These encounters demonstrate that the policy of "total removal" advocated by Benton is not an accurate gauge of the region's social and demographic reality during the early years of Missouri statehood. As late as 1844, Callaghan—who incidentally "could speak and understand quite a bit of Indian language"—recalls trading a sack of corn for some native pottery at an encampment near Hannibal. He describes lingering with interest at the site, observing how the Indians ground the kernels "in a hollow stone with a stone pestle making a mixture which they cooked on a hot stone."[18]

A second source, R.I. Holcombe's 1884 *History of Marion County,* reports that during the spring and summer of 1836 a band of "Northern Indians" camped on the bluffs north of Hannibal, adding that "for a few years afterwards there were numbers of them in the place from time to time."[19] By the late 1850s, however, the presence of *any* Indians was unusual enough to be newsworthy, as illustrated in "Whoop! Big Injin!," an article published on the front page of the *Hannibal Messenger* on 28 July 1859: "For the last two or three days several warriors and a squaw of the Caw tribe of Indians, have been perambulating our streets in every direction, receiving from our citizens many small silver pieces, and a variety of [other] goods. . . . They have been followed, notwithstanding the excessive heat, most perseveringly, by a troop of boys all the while, to the frequent inconvenience of the tawny sons of the forest. They seem to have quite a penchant for 'fire-water.'"[20] The tribal affiliation of this itinerant group is noteworthy; the Caw, also known as the Kansa, were not indigenous to Missouri but to a region in central Kansas near present-day Council Grove. Although the text makes no mention of it, the novelty of the Indians' appearance in Hannibal reflects a traumatic dislocation caused by an 1859 federal treaty that greatly reduced the size of their reservation, leaving only undesirable land inadequate for the sustenance of their families. Starving and desperate, the Kaw began migrating in all directions and were eventually relocated to Oklahoma's Indian Territory in the early 1860s. The *Messenger* article, however, euphemistically characterizes the tribe's diaspora as a "perambulation"—a stroll undertaken for pleasure or leisure. The Indians themselves are deemed harmless exotic spectacles—objects of boyish fascination and adult pity—at once romanticized as "tawny sons of the forest" and alternately typecast in the familiar role of beggars and alcoholics. As such, they elicit no anxiety or trepidation in the local populace.

These sources demonstrate that while Indians were largely invisible in the Hannibal of Clemens's youth, they had not entirely disappeared. Dispossessed of their ancestral lands, they were reduced to the de facto status of vagrants—a trait the writer would later ascribe to his most infamous native character, Injun Joe. In two reminiscences composed later in life, he acknowledged—though in vexingly opaque terms—an awareness of their presence. For example, in "Random Extracts" from his *Autobiography*, composed in 1898, he recalls, "And then there was the 'Indian doctor;' a grave savage, remnant of his tribe, deeply read in the mysteries of nature and the secret properties of herbs; and most backwoodsmen had high faith in his powers and could tell of wonderful cures achieved by him" (A1, 215). More puzzling still is an anecdote recounted in an unpublished draft of "In Defense of Harriet Shelley," a scathing refutation of Matthew Arnold's 1888 characterization of Percy Bysshe Shelley as "a beautiful and ineffectual angel" in *Nineteenth Century* magazine.[21]

Twain objected to Arnold's attempted "canonization" of the Romantic poet on the grounds that "the requirements of saintship are needlessly exacting ... if you have [got] one little blemish you are eventually ruled out." To illustrate this point, he introduces the ironic analogue of an alleged historical figure named Injun Aleck—"a winning and beautiful and elegant Christian in the village where I was reared"—an exemplary gentleman who, like his British counterpart, possessed impeccable manners, grace, and refinement. Indeed, "he was all that," Twain avers, "but one day he hanged his mother": "There is the whole trouble. There was no harm in her; she hadn't done anything, [he never intimated that she had,] but he somehow lost his interest in her, so he hanged her. That was more than forty years ago; yet observe the result: every one of the forty-one attempts since made by his lamenting admirers to get the people of that village to accept him as a saint have failed. Just as success was on the point of being achieved, there was always somebody to pipe up and object, saying, 'But he hanged his mother, you know.'"[22]

Hannibal newspapers from the 1840s offer no corroboration of this incident, nor does it appear in any nineteenth-century annals of local Missouri history—a strange omission given the shocking nature of the murder. Twain's memory was of course notoriously unreliable, prompting him to quip in old age, "When I was younger I could remember anything, whether it had happened or not; but my faculties are decaying, now, and soon I shall be so I cannot remember any but the latter" (A1, 210). Yet even if the Injun Aleck story is apocryphal, it offers insight into his perceptions of native character. Outwardly, Aleck seems a paradigm of successful assimilation—from his Anglicized name and religious conversion to his embrace of the myriad social conventions of village life; this veneer of civility, however, conceals an incorrigibly savage core, which is exposed in the monstrous treachery of his crime. Although Aleck serves primarily as a foil within the essay, allowing Twain to argue that this unconscionable act of matricide was a "sunny playfulness" in comparison to Shelley's abandonment and humiliation of his first wife, the explicit racialization of his identity suggests a deeply rooted and abiding aversion toward "Injuns"—the origins of which can be traced back to the writer's own family history.

JANE CLEMENS AND THE "MONTGOMERY MASSACRE"

In *Dangerous Water: A Biography of the Boy Who Became Mark Twain*, Ron Powers characterizes the author's mother, Jane Lampton Clemens, as "the curator of family legends, going on and on in the chill Missouri night with tales of Indians wildly pursuing her grandmother . . . and breaking into a cabin and killing [her] brother, a man named John, and capturing his wife and children."[23] While Powers's version of events is skewed and somewhat sensationalized, Jane's maternal grandmother—Jane Montgomery Casey (1761–1844)—did indeed survive a 1781 Indian attack in frontier Kentucky as a young woman. According to a reminiscence composed by Orion Clemens soon after his mother's death in 1890, this incident instilled in her a lifelong antipathy toward native peoples: "On her mother's side was her grandfather, Col. Casey, who earned honorable mention in the printed history of Kentucky, as a leader of the defenders of the pioneers against the Indians. . . . His wife, Jane Casey, was a member of the Montgomery family, who also have received honorable mention in Kentucky history; and she herself shared in the perils of Indian warfare. Though a good Baptist she never could, while she lived, endure the presence of Indians because by savages five of her relations were killed."[24]

The "printed history" to which Orion alludes—Lewis Collins's two-volume *History of Kentucky*, first published in 1847—presents a detailed account of this attack derived "principally from Mrs. Jane [Montgomery]

Casey, who was an actor in the drama."[25] The raid targeted an isolated cluster of four cabins near the headwaters of the Green River (the site of present-day Stanford, Kentucky). One was inhabited by the family patriarch William Montgomery, his wife, and six children;[26] two others were occupied by the families of their adult sons William Junior and John; and the fourth housed his daughter and son-in-law, Molly and Joseph Russell, along with their three small children. Despite being situated approximately twelve miles from the nearest military outpost at Logan's Fort, the settlers naively "apprehend[ed] no danger from Indians"[27] and did not construct palisades to protect their dwellings.

Collins's account offers no motive for the ambush, simply stating that a party of some twenty-five generic "savages" surrounded the cabins at night and attacked at dawn. According to Daniel Trabue, whose 1827 memoir *Westward into Kentucky* is the earliest published report of the incident, the Indians were likely Cherokees incited to resist colonial encroachment into their hunting grounds by the British.[28] Trabue also states that the Indians "paid a visit" to the Montgomerys on 27 February 1781 but does not explain what transpired, only that "at daylight they attacked all the cabins early at the same time."[29] Jane's unsuspecting father and a young slave were shot and instantly killed as they stepped outside to retrieve some firewood; the boy's corpse sprawled backward across the sill, preventing the door from being barred. Jane sprang up, "pushed out the negro's head, shut the door,"[30] then grabbed a rifle to fend off the attackers and protect her two younger siblings. She ordered James, the youngest, to take cover, and directed her sister Betsy to scramble out a half-built chimney and run for help at Petitt's Station, some two miles distant. Pursued by Indians, the young girl ran for her life through the forest and reached the station in safety.

By the time the raid—which Jane forever after referred to as the "Montgomery Massacre"—was over, she had lost not only her father but also her brother John, who was shot dead in bed, "his door forced open, and his wife made prisoner."[31] Her brother-in-law Joseph meanwhile fled the scene fearing for his life, abandoning his wife and offspring "to the mercy of the savages," who took them into captivity as well. The settlers' children were not spared the Indians' wrath—in addition to the elder Montgomery's slave, Molly Russell's twelve-year-old daughter Flora was struck dead with a tomahawk, and a mulatto girl was scalped but miraculously recovered. Jane's narrative, as related by Collins, coincidentally includes a detail her great grandson would mock as unrealistic a century later in "Fenimore Cooper's Literary Offences"—that her imprisoned sister "had the presence of mind to make, by occasionally breaking a twig and scattering along their route pieces of a white handkerchief which she had torn into fragments,"[32] creating a marked trail that facilitated the party's rescue by nightfall.

Although Jane lived for more than a half century after this terrifying incident, in some ways she never recovered from it. Within a matter of months, she married Captain William Casey, himself an Indian fighter,[33] in the same clearing where her relatives had been slain. The couple then moved deeper into the Kentucky wilderness, establishing—and successfully defending—a homestead on the Green River from native marauders on at least three subsequent occasions. For years after the attack, Jane suffered from a variety of chronic ailments, such as insomnia and digestive issues, that are today recognized as the earmarks of post-traumatic stress disorder. She complained of a gnawing sensation like "a burning pit in [her] stomach" and subsisted for long periods on the "salvation" of milk because she could not tolerate heavier foods like meat and hominy.[34] She also believed that the fragile health of her eldest daughter, Peggy—born in 1783, just two years after the massacre—was somehow related to the havoc it had wreaked on her constitution.

Over time, Jane's courageous actions on that fateful day became a staple of family lore, recounted—and progressively mythicized—by her descendants. In 1844, her youngest daughter, Anne, provided a vivid description of the massacre to historian Lyman Draper, recalling how the Indians battered the cabin door "with their war clubs and tomahawks" after Jane secured it. In contrast to Collins, she claimed there was no rifle on the premises, insisting that the attackers retreated in "alarm and confusion" upon hearing Jane's command to her sister to retrieve one. Anne also recalled that the scalped mulatto left for dead in the clearing "was found . . . towards evening . . . by Jane Montgomery, brought in and finally recovered." In this version of events, Jane emerges as a formidable, larger-than-life figure—plucky, mettlesome, self-possessed—a worthy namesake for her eldest granddaughter.[35]

Jane Lampton was born in 1803 at the same Kentucky homestead her maternal ancestors had defended against Indians a decade earlier. She also spent much of her childhood there, developing a deep bond with her grandparents. According to biographer Rachel Varble, Jane assisted Mrs. Casey in caring for her dying husband in the final months of 1816, "help[ing] to concoct liniments and blisters to ease pain," and brewing herbal teas from recipes preserved in the family scrapbook.[36] Two years later, when Peggy Lampton died at the age of thirty-five, Mrs. Casey stepped into the quasi-maternal role of confidant and advice giver for her adolescent granddaughter. In addition to reciting passages from the Bible daily, she mesmerized Jane with stories of her pioneer past, recalling an occasion in 1783 when she saw twenty-three widows, including her own mother—"who owed their titles to the tomahawk and arrow"—assembled at Logan's Fort for the settlement of their estates.[37] In this way, Jane came not only to know the tale of the Montgomery Massacre by heart but also to share her grandmother's bitter enmity toward Indians. Varble reports that before accepting the hand of John Marshall Clemens, Jane enthralled another suitor with her graphic account of the 1781 incident: "Her manner of telling the story, now in whispers, now in a rush of terrible detail, now with somber gestures for the aftermath—all this fascinated [the young man]. It was the nearest he had ever come to attending the theatre."[38] She would later use these same dramatic techniques to imprint this bloody ancestral saga onto the minds and hearts of her own impressionable children. The iconography of the massacre—particularly Betsey Montgomery's hair-raising escape from savage pursuers in the Kentucky wilderness—suggestively resurfaces more than a half-century later in the writer's autobiographical dictation of 10 October 1907. After reading in the morning paper that the Essex County (NY) Republican Convention had unanimously passed a resolution declaring that "safety to man, humanity to deer and sport for hunters" would be furthered by establishing a two-week period each year when deer could be legally hunted with hounds, Twain erupts:

> There is something fresh and touching about that Republican Convention's idea of humanity. When we read of red Indians chasing a helpless white girl who is fleeing for her life, with bullets and arrows whizzing around her, the Indians' humanity is not apparent to us; the Indians seem to us only cruel and brutal, and all our sympathies are with the frightened girl. The fleeing deer is just as frightened . . . and it would seem to be logical that if the Republican hunter's performance is sport, and legitimate, the Indian's performance must be also regarded as sport, and legitimate. (A3, 162)

The intergenerational legacy of fear and racial enmity provoked by the Montgomery Massacre affirms historian Richard Slotkin's contention that the randomized violence of frontier conditions created an atmosphere of terror, at once real and imagined, that entrapped Anglo-American colonists in "an Indian-haunted dreamland."[39] According to Craig Thompson Friend, this phenomenon was particularly intense in the "dark and bloody ground" of eighteenth-century Kentucky, where the "unremitting possibility of losing one's family and one's life" produced endemic unease. As the nineteenth-century physician and memoirist Daniel Drake recalls in *Pioneer Life in Kentucky*, his mother Elizabeth Shotwell (1761–1821)—a contemporary of Jane Montgomery Casey—routinely tucked him and his siblings into bed throughout the 1780s with the admonition, "Lie still and go to sleep, or the Shawnees will catch you." Her unnerving words, Friend observes, "ensured that they—like all Kentucke settlers—persisted in that Indian-haunted dreamland, whether Indians lurked at their cabin doors or not."[40]

Orion's description of his mother's animus toward Indians—"whose presence . . . she could never endure"—suggests that her psyche was similarly scarred by the macabre story of the Montgomery Massacre. He, however, seems to have regarded Jane's bias as an anomaly in her otherwise exemplary Baptist character that violated the biblical command to "Love your enemies, bless them that curse you, do good to them that hate you, and pray for them that despitefully use you and persecute you."[41] Orion's own views of native peoples, developed over the course of a long, varied career in journalism, law, and politics, were far more tolerant and sympathetic. An 1892 poem he published in the *Chicago Tribune* called "The Reformed Savage" reveals that he not only considered Indians human beings but also recognized the terrible injustices they had suffered as a result of Anglo-American colonial expansion. He credits the efforts of Christian missionaries with unlocking the spiritual and intellectual potential of the "savage mind" and welcomes the prospect of the Indians' successful assimilation into mainstream society.[42]

Sam also composed a loving tribute to Jane after her death, pronouncing her both his "first and closest friend" and "the most eloquent person I have heard speak" (HFTS, 82, 84). Her heart, he declares, was "so large that everybody's griefs and everybody's joys found welcome in it and hospitable accommodation." In contrast to Orion, he cites no exceptions to the universality of his mother's sympathies, insisting "to the very day of her death she felt a strong interest in the whole world and everything and everybody in it"—including Satan himself, whom he once tricked her into defending (HFTS, 83). This divergence of perspectives is telling. Jane's aversion to Indians presumably lingered in Orion's memory as a locus of discomfort and dissension but is neither mentioned nor acknowledged by Sam. The "flash-light glimpses" he furnishes of her character are instead filled with absolutes—"always," "never," "everyone," "everything," and "all"—creating the impression that her compassion knew no bounds. "Her interest in people and the other animals was warm, personal, friendly," he declares; "She always found something to excuse, and as a rule to love, in the toughest of them."

For Twain, Jane's strong moral compass was exemplified in the "unstudied and unconscious pathos [of] her native speech," as well as in the impetuous bravery of her deeds. He recalls her seizing a whip out of the hands of a "burly cartman who was beating his horse over the head with the butt" of it and excoriating him for his cruelty, and also offering shelter to a young Corsican woman being chased through the streets by her enraged father. Standing with her arms outstretched across the doorway, Jane "did not flinch or show any sign of fear" in the face of the aggressor, but "stood straight and fine, and lashed him, shamed him, derided him, [and] defied him" until he begged her forgiveness and left (HFTS, 84–85). Through these bold "soldierly qualities," she proved herself a worthy namesake of her rifle-toting grandmother.

Twain's most poignant memory of his mother, however, concerns the way in which she used his childish annoyance with the "intolerable" singing of their young slave Sandy to teach an unforgettable lesson about compassion. After listening to his complaint, she gently reminds him of Sandy's existential isolation and loss: "Think; he is sold away from his mother; she is in Maryland, a thousand miles from here, and he will never see her again, poor thing. When he is singing it is a sign that he is not grieving; the noise of it drives me almost distracted, but I am always listening, and always thankful; it would break my heart if Sandy should stop singing" HFTS, 89). This anecdote suggests that the strong sympathies Clemens expressed for African Americans throughout his life and work were to some extent inspired by Jane's example. Conversely, the absence of any reference to Indians in this document intimates that the writer may have inherited and uncritically accepted her bias against them. As he coyly announced in the 1897 essay "Concerning the Jews," "I am quite sure that (bar one) I have no race prejudices, and I think I have no color prejudices nor caste prejudices nor creed prejudices. Indeed, I know it. I can stand any society. All that I care to know is that a man is a human being—that is enough for me; he can't be any worse" (CT2, 355). Though Twain refused to identify this "one" prejudice, the general disdain he expressed for native peoples throughout his writing has led numerous commentators to speculate that they are the group to whom he alludes. Ron Powers' 2005 biography of the writer unequivocally states, "A loathing of Indians . . . was the one racial prejudice that Mark Twain could never shake off."[43]

NATIVE AMERICANS IN POPULAR MUSIC AND LITERATURE

Jane Clemens's nightmarish vision of Indians as merciless predators bent upon the annihilation of home and family was countered by the sentimental depictions of noble savages that flourished in popular American culture during the 1840s and 50s. The dissonance of these conflicting—and equally exaggerated—images reinscribed the Otherness of native peoples and obscured their reality as human beings, no doubt posing a conundrum in the young writer's mind. In "Villagers of 1840–43," a series of fragmentary notes composed in Switzerland in 1897, Twain recalls that "any young person" in the Hannibal of his youth "would have been proud of a 'strain' of Indian blood," (HHT, 34) revealing that his hometown was by no means immune from this romantic stereotype. His statement suggests that a trace of indigenous ancestry—in contrast to the "one drop" rule pertaining to African American blood quantum—would exoticize and enhance one's social cachet without jeopardizing the security of Anglo-American racial status. Twain credits Marion Dix Sullivan's popular 1844 ballad "The Blue Juniata" as a source of this "soft, sappy, melancholy" (HHT, 35) ideation but garbles the lyrics, stating, "Bright Alforata of the blue Juniata got her strain from 'a far distant fount.'" In fact, the protagonist of Sullivan's song, "Bright Alfarata," is not a remote descendant of Indian ancestors but a full-blooded member of an unspecified eastern tribe, stereotypical in both her appearance and demeanor. She runs "swift as an antelope" through the forest, her loose "jetty locks" flowing behind her in the wind, and expertly plies the river's rapid current while singing of her bold warrior lover. The ballad's elegiac closing lines underscore the myth of the vanishing Indian, explaining that the "fleeting years have borne away the voice of Alfarata"— and by extension the indigenous peoples who formerly inhabited the region of central Pennsylvania through which the Juniata River flows—leaving only its name as mute testimony of their existence.[44]

Twain mentioned the song again in his autobiographical dictation of 30 November 1906, as part of an extended reminiscence about the minstrel shows he enjoyed during his youth: "The minstrel troupes had good voices, and both their solos and their choruses were a delight to me as long as the negro show continued in existence. In the beginning, the songs were rudely comic—such as 'Buffalo Gals,' 'Camptown Races,' 'Old Dan Tucker,' and so on; but a little later, sentimental songs were introduced—such as 'The Blue Juniata,' 'Sweet Ellen Bayne,' 'Nelly Bly,' 'A Life on the Ocean Wave,' 'The Larboard Watch,' etc." (A2, 296). That the writer recalled the song by name more than a half century after hearing it confirms its enduring imaginative resonance.

Another equally popular ballad of the period was "The Spotted Fawn," which recounts the tragic fate of its eponymous heroine, "as fair an Indian girl as ever blessed the earth."[45] Like "The Blue Juniata," the song is set on a historic, now safely colonized, frontier in the eastern United States—

on the "flowery marge" of Mahketewa, the native name of Mill Creek, which flows into the Ohio River at Cincinnati—attesting to the inexorable advances of Manifest Destiny. Spotted Fawn, cut from the same romantic cloth as "Bright Alfarata," is a prototypical Indian princess—the chief's only child, "the light and life of the forest shades," sought after by "many a brave" and successfully wooed by the "gallant White Cloud." In contrast to Sullivan's song, however, in which the destructive presence of Anglo-Americans is only implied, "The Spotted Fawn" dramatizes the violence of the colonial encounter and portrays Indians as the innocent victims of unprovoked white aggression. "Peace was in the forest ... and in the red man's heart," the lyrics proclaim, as the newlyweds settle into their wigwam, never unsuspecting that "fiery death" awaits from "encircling foes ... who come in wrath [with] blood in their path as they sleep."[46]

The ubiquity of "The Spotted Fawn" inspired the composition of a parody called "The Spotted Frog," which subverts the ballad's mawkish rhetoric through a series of clever substitutions. Its protagonist, as the title suggests, is not an Indian princess but an amphibian—"as fair and fat a frog as ever hopped on earth." Seated unglamorously upon "an old rotted log" in the industrial wasteland of "muddy Mill Creek's stagnant marge," the frog is bludgeoned to death with sticks and stones by "cruel boys in search of sport." According to William Turner Coggeshall's 1860 anthology, *The Poets and Poetry of the West*, "Everybody sang, repeated, or talked about 'The Spotted Fawn,' and everybody was shocked as well as provoked to admiration by its superior aptness of rhythm and alliteration when ["The Spotted Frog"] appeared in the *Cincinnati Enquirer*. The parody was published in all the papers and became the rage."[47] In contemporary terms, Coggeshall's description suggests that both versions of the lyric went "viral"—sweeping across the nation through a system of free newspaper exchanges. This nineteenth-century pop culture phenomenon even reached the sleepy village of Hannibal, where "The Spotted Fawn" and "The Spotted Frog" appeared side by side on the front page of a November 1846 issue of the local *Gazette*. While no evidence exists documenting Clemens's familiarity with either "The Spotted Fawn" or its satirical counterpart, such popular music reflects the broader cultural milieu in which he was raised. As an adolescent, the future creator of Tom Sawyer and Huckleberry Finn would likely have found the parody's depiction of the mayhem unleashed by a group of unsupervised boys at once relevant and intrinsically appealing; moreover, the tension between romanticism and realism reified in the juxtaposition of these two texts would prove instrumental in the formation of his mature literary voice.

Clemens also encountered stirring images of the noble savage in his child-hood reading. While his 1895 essay "Fenimore Cooper's Literary Offences" famously mocks the novelist's many stylistic shortcomings, several unpub-lished drafts of the piece at the Mark Twain Papers present a more nuanced, respectful perspective. "When I was a youth," he explains, "I read several of Cooper's ... tales & was enchanted with them, but I have forgotten their names & everything else connected with them except just the bare fact that the stories charmed me. What particular or combination of particulars the charm proceeded from, I do not now know."[48] As his memory warmed to the subject, however, Twain recalled at least one source of this alleged enchant-ment: "No impression [in *The Leatherstocking Tales*] remains steadily with us but one; that is the reality & vividness of Cooper's lakes & woods." But beyond these evocative landscapes—liminal spaces on the boundary between civilization and wilderness—he identified another element of Cooper's charm: "It seems to me that Cooper's very best piece of work is the old chief's pathetic speech over the body of his son, who has been slain in battle. It pos-sesses even the great quality of simplicity—a quality which is not to be found elsewhere in the Cooper literature, I think. It is almost worthy to take rank with the noble lament of Sir Bors over the corpse of Sir Launcelot."[49] Twain then quotes in full the Delaware chief Chingachgook's eulogy for Uncas at the end of *The Last of the Mohicans*: "I am a blazed pine, in a clearing of the palefaces. My race has gone from the shores of the salt lake, and the hills of the Delawares. But who can say that the serpent of his tribe has forgotten his wisdom? I am alone."[50] With these eloquent words, Chingachgook became— in the opinion of Brian Dippie—"fiction's most memorable Vanishing American."[51] Twain's acknowledgment of the speech's heartrending power suggests the degree to which he had internalized and embraced this cultural mythos. In addition, his comparison of Chingachgook's oration with a pas-sage from Thomas Malory's *Le Morte d'Arthur*—a book he held in high regard—suggests that his critique of Cooper's many "literary offences" was tempered by genuine admiration.

Although Twain derides Cooper's Indians as "idiots" in both the pub-lished and unpublished versions of the essay, proclaiming that "in the mat-ter of intellect, the difference between a Cooper Indian and the Indian that stands in front of the cigar shop is not spacious" (CT2, 186), he apparently found these characters compelling despite their lack of depth and credibility. In "Fenimore Cooper's Further Offenses," which Bernard DeVoto cobbled together from rejected drafts of the 1895 essay and published in 1946, he asserts, "A Cooper Indian who has been washed is a poor thing, and com-monplace; it is the Cooper Indian in his paint that thrills" (CT2, 198). This is not an ironic statement but an affirmation of the power of romantic fiction. The "thrill" of Cooper's iconic Indian in feathers, breechcloth, and paint took deep hold in Twain's imagination, jostling uncomfortably alongside his mother's representation of native peoples as murderous savages and his own later distasteful impressions of them in the West. In *Roughing It*, he disingenuously describes himself as "a disciple of Cooper and a worshipper of the Red Man" bitterly disillusioned by the disparity between the idealized Indians of *The Leatherstocking Tales* and depraved Goshoots he encountered in Nevada Territory: "The nausea which the Goshoots gave me . . . set me to examining authorities, to see if perchance I had been over-estimating the Red Man while viewing him through the mellow moonshine of romance. The revelations that came were disenchanting. It was curious to see how quickly the paint and tinsel fell away from him and left him treacherous, filthy, and repulsive" (RI, 129).

Over time, Cooper's Indians became a benchmark by which the writer gauged the incongruity between romanticized representations of all racial Others and the reality of their condition. In *The Innocents Abroad*, he frames his observations about the dirty, disheveled appearance of women in Palestine with the comment, "Commend me to Fennimore Cooper to find beauty in the Indians, and to Grimes [the pseudonym he assigns to the Victorian travel writer William H. Prime] to find it in the Arabs" (IA, 532). Similarly, in discussing the uncanny tracking ability of Australia's Aboriginals nearly three decades later in *Following the Equator* (1897), he states, "Fennimore Cooper lost his chance. He would have known how to value these people. He wouldn't have traded the dullest of them for the brightest Mohawk he ever invented" (FE, 218).

In conjunction with *The Leatherstocking Tales*, Henry Wadsworth Longfellow's 1855 epic *Hiawatha* played a key role in imprinting the idealized image of native peoples into the consciousness of mainstream American society. Twain's lifelong penchant for satirizing the exoticism of indigenous names—such as "Wawhoo-Wang-Wang of the Wack-a-Whack," a "noble Son of the Forest," whom he describes meeting in the 1869 sketch "A Day at Niagara"—likely originated in his reading of this poem, which features an array of Iroquois characters with comical tongue-wrenching appellations like Puggawaugun, Minjekawhan, and Pa-Puk-Kee-Wis. Although he does not allude to Longfellow in print nearly as often as Cooper, the poet receives prominent mention in the 1870 sketch "A Memory"—the title of which suggests an autobiographical reminiscence but instead playfully conflates fact and fiction. According to the sketch's narrative persona, *Hiawatha* was the one poem favored by his "austere father," a man not generally enamored of literature. This claim—which seems plausible enough upon first glance—dissolves into a haze of uncertainty with the realization that John Marshall Clemens died in 1847, eight years before the work's publication. Nonetheless, the father depicted in "A Memory" bears an unmistakable resemblance to the elder Clemens in several respects—both are judges whose emotionally fraught relationships with their sons are characterized by "a sort of armed neutrality." These parallels insinuate that John Marshall Clemens—like his fictional alter ego—may have harbored derogatory views about Indians akin to those espoused by his wife. In the sketch, the judge solemnly reads aloud a passage from *Hiawatha*, then peruses a warranty deed removed from his breast pocket, sighing: "If I had such a son as this poet, here were a subject worthier than the traditions of these Indians . . . in this very deed . . . there is more poetry, more romance, more sublimity, more splendid imagery hidden away . . . than could be found in all the traditions of all the savages that live" (CT1, 429). Seeking to curry favor with his father, the narrator sets about translating the document's dry legalistic prose "into Hiawathian blank verse, without altering or leaving out three words, and without transposing six," producing a travesty entitled "The Story of a Gallant Deed"—reproduced in full in the sketch—that elicits a fusillade of projectiles aimed at his head.

This humorous tale of familial acrimony contains a troubling racial subtext. The father's sweeping assertion that one "homely" legal document—a straightforward record of land transfer—contains more aesthetic merit than "all the traditions of all the savages that live" posits the inherent superiority of the written word to the rich, diverse oral traditions of indigenous peoples around the globe. Furthermore, in denying the capacity of "savages" to produce works of imagination and beauty, Twain challenges their very humanity. The author himself apparently shared this dim view of Indian legends—although as his 1882 travelogue *Life on the Mississippi* reveals, he later reconsidered that opinion. In chapter 59, which discusses the "Legends and Scenery" of the river valley, he records a conversation with an unidentified lecturer who remarks that the entire region "is blanketed with Indian tales and traditions" (LM, 579). Twain responds, "I reminded him that people usually merely mentioned this fact—doing it in a way to make a body's mouth water—and judiciously stopped there. Why? Because the impression left, was that these tales were full of incident and imagination—a pleasant impression which would be promptly dissipated if the tales were told. I showed him a lot of this sort of literature which I had been collecting, and he confessed that it was poor stuff, exceedingly poor rubbish" (LM, 579). The lecturer then encourages the narrator to "enlarge

[his] respect for the Indian imagination" by seeking out Henry Rowe Schoolcraft's *Algic Researches*, an 1839 anthology of native legends, myths, and tales that Longfellow had drawn upon in composing *Hiawatha*. Heeding this advice, he discovers, "The lecturer was right," and incorporates the story of "Peoban and Seegwun" into the chapter, explaining that despite its familiarity to readers of Longfellow's poem, "it is worth reading in the original form, if only that one may see how effective a genuine poem can be without the helps and graces of poetic measure and rhythm" (LM, 580). He also includes a second Indian legend, "The Undying Head," in one of the travelogue's many appendices, stating that it "is a rather long tale, but . . . makes up in weird conceits, fairy-tale prodigies, variety of incident, and energy of movement, for what it lacks in brevity" (LM, 581). This affirmation of the richness and aesthetic merit of the native oral tradition is, however, upended in the very next chapter, where Twain quotes "a most idiotic Indian legend" about the origins of White-bear Lake, only to conclude, "A dead man could get up a better legend than this one. I don't mean a fresh dead man either; I mean a man that's been dead for weeks and weeks" (LM, 592). This paradox betrays the ambivalence of the writer's attitudes about native peoples; as James McNutt comments, "It is almost as if Twain perversely introduced evidence to rebut his praise of the Indian's imagination in the previous chapter."[52]

ORION CLEMENS AND "THE HISTORY OF THE HALF-BREED TRACT"

Clemens's early views of American Indians were influenced not only by his parents but also by a sibling—his older brother Orion, who in 1855 moved to Keokuk, a town named for a recently deceased Sac chief that was founded on contested land that had originally been set aside for the Iowa Half-Breed Tract. There he became the proprietor of the Ben Franklin Book and Job Office, which specialized in the printing of "Cards, Circulars, Bill Heads, Bills Lading, Posters, and Colored Work," and hired Sam as an assistant, paying him five dollars a week plus board (L1, 64). Soon after arriving, Orion began assembling information for the *Keokuk City Directory*, published by his firm in July 1856. The project was ambitious in scope—in addition to offering a comprehensive listing of residents, businesses, and civic organizations, it included Mayor Samuel R. Curtis's inaugural address extolling the city's bright economic future, as well as a detailed retrospective of its past called "A Sketch of the Black Hawk War and History of the Half Breed Tract," penned by Orion himself. In 1929 Fred Lorch praised

Orion's essay as "compact, clear, and excellently written . . . an indication of [his] possibilities in literary craftsmanship";[53] however, the significance of its political content has been largely overlooked. As biographer Philip Fanning notes in his 2006 study *Mark Twain and Orion Clemens,* by the mid-1850s the elder Clemens had embarked on a "striking moral journey" spurred by growing disenchantment with the institution of slavery that would culminate in his active embrace of abolitionism.[54] The tenor of the "Sketch" suggests that the liberalization of Orion's thinking during this period also extended to the national policy of Manifest Destiny—for in preparing the essay, he discovered that the state's much-vaunted "free soil" had been acquired at great cost to its indigenous peoples.

Orion meticulously researched his topic, delving into the work of contemporary historians, such as Benjamin Drake, Thomas Ford, John Frost, and John Mason Peck, all of whom he acknowledges in a detailed footnote.[55] But rather than simply summarizing the views of these established authorities, he challenges and corrects them, formulating an original interpretation of the "true causes" of the region's volatile Indian-white relations on the basis of interviews conducted with a number of early settlers:

> The account here given of the characters of Keokuk and Black Hawk . . . as well the causes of the "Black Hawk War," differs in many essential particulars from that of Mr. Peck. This is done on the authority of Hon. D.W. Kilbourne, ex-Mayor of Keokuk, who settled at Montrose . . . in 1836. Black Hawk and Keokuk, with hundreds of their tribe, were frequently at his house, and he was often Black Hawk's guest. . . . We have also conversed with other early settlers, who agree in giving the same account of the characters of Keokuk and Black Hawk, and their relations to and standing among their tribe.[56]

Through these conversations, Orion sought to recover the native perspective on Iowa's colonization and learn the war's actual causes, creating a counterpoint to the existing published sources. While this information is necessarily mediated at second- or even thirdhand, his allusion to the "authority" of attorney David Wells Kilbourne is significant. One of Iowa's earliest Anglo-American pioneers, Kilbourne (1803–76) was an agent of the New York Land Company, whose extensive dealings with the local Sac and Fox population in the 1830s had earned him the nickname of "Native Chieftain."[57]

The diction of Orion's "Sketch" reflects the political epiphany elicited by his newfound knowledge. Writing "against the grain" of conventional western historiography, he constructs what Susan Kalter has termed "a remarkably empathetic narrative,"[58] chronicling a legacy of chicanery, greed, and exploitation that began with the US government's 1804 purchase of fifty million acres from four Sac chiefs "without authority to act for their nation" for the "trivial consideration" of several thousand dollars in goods and the vague promise of future annuities.[59] With rising indignation, Orion denounces the region's Anglo-American settlers as "strangers who had no right to the soil" and accuses them of "commit[ing] various aggressions upon the Indians, such as destroying their corn, killing their domestic animals, and whipping the women and children."[60] He also condemns the 1829 sale of land at the mouth of the Rock River, where a Sac village was located, as "an uncalled for measure" intended to "evade" the provisions of a previous treaty and "create a pretext for the immediate removal of the Indians to the west side of the Mississippi."[61]

Orion's critique of colonial duplicity is amplified by his laudatory remarks concerning the dignity, integrity, and courage of the two most prominent Sac and Fox leaders. He describes Black Hawk as the "noblest of Indians, and an able and patriotic chief . . . with the intelligence and power to plan a great project, and to execute it"—alluding to the ill-fated 1832 war waged in defense of his ancestral lands. Keokuk, in turn, is portrayed as a "man of extraordinary eloquence . . . [whose] style of thought and manner of speaking have been compared to that of a distinguished U.S. Senator from South Carolina, with gracefulness of action in [the Indian's] favor."[62] This praise unsettles the binaries of civilization and savagery and reveals Orion's moral allegiance to the native cause.

In terms of local Keokuk history, Orion's sketch performs a valuable service in explicating the convoluted history and fate of the Half-Breed Tract itself. He begins with an ontological question—"Who are the Half Breeds for whom this Tract was reserved?"—identifying them as mixed bloods "living among whites in St. Louis and other places, who did not 'wear the blanket,' and could not enjoy the annuities [provided by treaties for land cessions]; but yet had Indian blood in their veins."[63] He thus establishes three defining characteristics of this hybrid population—detribalized, partially assimilated individuals, who reside in Anglo-American cities and towns and wear modern clothing rather than traditional native garb, but are nonetheless branded "Other" because of their indigenous blood quantum. The ambiguity of their status reaffirms John Mack Faragher's thesis about the "frontier of inclusion" that existed in the Mississippi River valley of the early nineteenth century and also suggests that the tract's creation in 1824 reflected a broader cultural shift toward Indian segregation and exclusion. For the first decade of its existence, the federal government held a "reversionary interest" in the tract, meaning that mixed bloods could inhabit the land but had no right to sell it. Congress repealed this legislation in 1834, granting title to the "half breeds" as a class rather than specific individuals. Speculators moved in, purchasing so-called Blanket Claims for "a horse and a barrel of whiskey"[64] from individuals who had no legal right to the land, and then unscrupulously sold the parcels for several thousand dollars each, often to multiple parties simultaneously. Chaos ensued, resulting in a formal "Decree of Partition" issued by the Iowa territorial legislature in 1841. This document identified 101 half breeds with legitimate title to the tract but also determined that nearly half of that number (41) had previously surrendered their property rights to the New York Land Company. Through these machinations, much of the Sac and Fox métis population—for whom the tract had been expressly created—found themselves doubly dispossessed. Homeless and adrift, they became vagrants in the eyes of the Anglo-American judicial system, a condition that Twain would later ascribe to Injun Joe, the half-breed antagonist of his 1876 novel, *The Adventures of Tom Sawyer.*

While it is impossible to ascertain the extent of the writer's familiarity with the "Sketch of the Black Hawk War and History of the Half Breed Tract," he was undoubtedly aware of Orion's project as a result of his employment at the Ben Franklin printshop.[65] In a 10 June 1856 letter to Jane Clemens and his sister Pamela, he complains about setting type for the pamphlet: "The Directory is coming on finely. I have to work on it occasionally, which I don't like a particle" (L1, 63). He also appears to have written his own entry for the list of residents, identifying his profession as "Antiquarian." In an 1888 article in the *Chicago News*, Mayor Curtis's son William claimed that this humorous designation stemmed from Clemens's "researches among the ancient and venerable bugs of the hotel in which he boarded" (L1, 65); however, it may also be a subversive jab at his brother's preoccupation with local history. Certainly, the zeal with which Orion immersed himself in the essay's composition makes it likely that he informally shared some of his findings with Sam. Moreover, although twenty years separate the publication of the "Sketch" and *The Adventures of Tom Sawyer*, Orion's analysis of the dispossession of Iowa's mixed-blood population subliminally informs Twain's conceptualization of his villain.

According to Philip Fanning, the brothers were often politically at odds and openly clashed over the issue of slavery during this period: "Orion was (surprisingly) the more adventurous of the two, constantly challenging the consensus . . . politically, [he] was to the left of Sam."[66] The so-called Indian Question was apparently another issue on which they fundamentally disagreed. In contrast to Orion's progressive attitudes on native rights, Sam's aversion to Indians was firmly entrenched by the age of nineteen, as demonstrated in a February 1855 letter written from St. Louis and published in Orion's Muscatine *Tri-Weekly Journal* newspaper:

> Highly important news was received from New Mexico this morning. The Indians are becoming worse and worse, and seem to have things pretty much their own way on the frontier. Fourteen men were butchered, and a number severely wounded at the Pueblo of Arkansas, and the women and children carried off by the savages. The work was perfect, the whole settlement being broken up and the inhabitants murdered. The Utahs and Apaches, the tribe said to be the perpetrators of this massacre, seem determined upon the destruction of the whites, and unless a check is put upon them soon, terrible consequences will ensue. The people of Texas and New Mexico are greatly alarmed and excited, and a general breaking out of hostilities is anticipated. (L1, 51)

As the editors at the Mark Twain Project have noted, the substance of this report derives from two telegraphic briefs, published in the St. Louis *Missouri Republican* on 24 February, describing an Indian attack at a trading post on the Arkansas River in present-day Pueblo, Colorado (L1, 53n9). The language in which the writer couches these facts, however, is far more inflammatory and censorious than his sources. In describing the casualties of the raid, for example, he substitutes the graphic verb "butchered" for "killed" and also denounces its perpetrators as "savages," whereas the original accounts identify them simply as "Indians" or "Apaches and Utahs." Most significantly, he invests this localized racial violence with apocalyptic overtones, citing it as proof that the Indians are bent upon the annihilation of innocent whites and warning that "terrible consequences" will occur unless the endemic lawlessness they have fomented on the frontier is checked. It is not difficult to discern traces of the terror instilled by Jane Clemens's oft-repeated tale of the Montgomery Massacre in the shrill emotional register of these words. Orion's "Sketch of the Black Hawk War and History of the Half Breed Tract" inverts this familiar paradigm by representing native violence as an inevitable response to the repeated "insults and outrages" of colonial aggression rather than as evidence of innate barbarism. Sam evidently did not concur.

"THAT MURDERIN' HALF-BREED," INJUN JOE

The romance and terror Clemens associated with Indians in his youth strangely coalesce in *The Adventures of Tom Sawyer*, which celebrates the fantasy of white boys "playing Indian" while simultaneously demonizing and ultimately destroying the region's sole remaining indigenous inhabit-ant. Like Hannibal in the 1840s, the novel's setting is a postfrontier com-munity. St. Petersburg's defining institutions—church, school, jailhouse, and court of law—represent the hallmarks of Euro-American civilization, just as Aunt Polly's famously whitewashed fence and Jeff Thatcher's well-tended flower garden attest to both the privatization of property and domestication of what was once untamed wilderness. Colonial dominion over the landscape is so complete that the town's inhabitants rest securely in their beds at night, untroubled by the threat of aboriginal violence or the menace of animal predators. And yet vestiges of the past linger on its periphery—in derelict buildings like the old tannery and haunted house, where the spoils of an earlier lawless era lie buried in the form of the Murrel gang's treasure, as well as in the local cemetery—which the writer describes in terms more suited to Nevada Territory in the early 1860s than the outskirts of an established midwestern municipality:

> It was a graveyard of the old-fashioned western kind. It was on a hill, about a mile and a half from the village. It had a crazy board fence around it, which leaned inward in places, and outward the rest of the time, but stood upright nowhere. Grass and weeds grew rank over the whole cemetery. All the old graves were sunken in. There was not a tombstone on the place; round-topped, worm-eaten boards staggered over the graves, leaning for support and finding none. "Sacred to the Memory of" So-and-so had been painted on them once, but it could no longer . . . [be] read. (TS, 71–72)

In contrast to the tidy fences and manicured lawns of the village homes, everything about the burial ground bespeaks disorder and neglect. Like the tannery and haunted house, the cemetery is a liminal space—a social and geographical borderland—that functions both as a locus of covert criminal activity and an irresistible magnet for innocent, adventure-seeking boys. These marginal settings symbolically replicate the violent dynamic of the frontier, which Frederick Jackson Turner defined as the "meeting point between civilization and savagery."[67]

The most troubling and evocative remnant of St. Petersburg's past, how-ever, is not a place, but a person—Injun Joe. Twain's "murderin' half-breed" is largely a cipher—possessing no surname, no family, no tribe, no specific place of origin. Yet because the writer declared in the novel's preface that its characters are "drawn from real life" and "most of the adventures recorded . . . really occurred," it has long been believed that Injun Joe is based on a specific individual, although his prototype has never been identified. Twain confirms the historical existence of such a figure in his 1906 autobiograph-

ical dictations: "My father tried to reform [Injun Joe] once, but did not succeed. . . . It was a failure, and we boys were glad. For Injun Joe, drunk, was
interesting and a benefaction to us, but Injun Joe, sober, was a dreary spectacle. We watched my father's experiments upon him with a good deal of
anxiety, but it came out all right and we were satisfied. Injun Joe got drunk
oftener than before, and became tolerably interesting" (A1, 397).

Unlike the "bloody-minded miscreant" depicted in the pages of *Tom
Sawyer*, the Injun Joe Clemens recalls toward the end of his life is not a
menace but a harmless drunk—an object of pity and concern to the town's
leaders and exotic source of amusement for the local children. Racially
typecast as an incorrigible alcoholic, he exists on the margins of the community and is tolerated as an "interesting" spectacle. At this point, however,
Twain's reminiscence abruptly takes a dark turn in describing the preter-
naturally violent storm that occurred on the night of Injun Joe's death:

> I think that in "Tom Sawyer" I starved Injun Joe to death in the cave.
> But that may have been to meet the exigencies of romantic literature.
> I can't remember now whether he died in the cave or out of it, but I do
> remember that the news of his death reached me at a most unhappy
> time—that is to say, just at bedtime on a summer night when a
> prodigious storm of thunder and lightning accompanied by a deluging
> rain that turned the streets and lanes into rivers, caused me to repent
> and resolve to lead a better life. I can remember those awful thunder-
> bursts and the white glare of the lightning yet, and the wild lashing of
> the rain against the window-panes. By my teachings I perfectly well
> knew what all the wild riot was for—Satan had come to get Injun Joe.
> I had no shadow of doubt about it. It was the proper thing when a
> person like Injun Joe was required in the underworld, and I should have
> thought it strange and unaccountable if Satan had come for him in a
> less impressive way. (A1, 397–98)

Given the vagaries of memory, it is not surprising—particularly at a
remove of more than a half century—that Twain's recollection of the "real"
Injun Joe is overlaid with, and to some extent occluded by, the diabolical
qualities of his later fictional creation. The lies Joe imperturbably reels off
at the inquest framing Muff Potter for the murder of Doctor Robinson
convince Tom and Huck that "this miscreant had sold himself to Satan,"
prompting a resolve "to watch him, nights, when opportunity should offer,
in the hope of getting a glimpse of his dread master" (TS, 89). The "mortal
terror" Clemens experiences during the storm closely parallels the "seasons
of horror" Tom suffers at night when "Injun Joe infested all his dreams, and
always with doom in his eye" (TS, 173). Twain's unusual verb choice implies
that the menacing figure of Injun Joe infiltrates Tom's unconscious mind

FIGURE 1.   "Tom Dreams,"
The Adventures of Tom Sawyer.
Courtesy of the Mark Twain
Project, The Bancroft Library,
University of California,
Berkeley.

much in the same way that vermin overrun a house. Like so many of the
nation's frontier settlers, Tom is also trapped in an "Indian-haunted dreamland" dominated by fear of the savage Other.

The illustration True Williams created to accompany this passage, called
"Tom Dreams" (fig. 1), captures the magnitude of his dread. A larger-than-
life Injun Joe looms ominously over the defenseless sleeping boy, ready to
plunge a dagger into his heart. The variation in shading infuses the image
with iconic overtones of good and evil: Tom and the bed in which he lies are
delineated with spare, orderly vertical strokes, whereas Joe's features are
darkened by a profusion of irregular cross-hatching. The threat he poses is
not merely interpersonal but cultural—the specter of lawlessness and disorder that the continent's indigenous peoples posed to Anglo-American
civilization.

While Twain's autobiographical reminiscences strongly suggest that
Injun Joe was modeled on an actual figure, his identity and tribal affiliation
have never been determined. In *Sam Clemens of Hannibal*, Dixon Wecter
claims that he was part Osage, "in boyhood scalped by Pawnees and left for
dead, who in his teens was brought to Hannibal by cattlemen."[68] Wecter

burnishes Injun Joe's status as an icon of primitivism through the inclusion of colorful—though unsubstantiated—details, declaring that he "lived in a big hollow sycamore on Bear Creek" and "wore a red wig to conceal his horrid scar." The truth, however, is far more elusive. According to the 1923 obituary of "Indian Joe" published in the *Hannibal Courier-Post*, he was found as an infant in an abandoned encampment, reared by a white man in Callaway County, Missouri, and given the name "Joe Douglas." Kate Ray Kuhn's 1963 *A History of Marion County* in turn states that Joe was the lone survivor of a smallpox outbreak and taken in by an African American woman named Douglass.

In *Lighting Out for the Territory*, Shelley Fisher Fishkin further complicates the mystery of Indian Joe/Joe Douglas's racial identity in concluding, on the basis of a "yellowed newspaper clipping" and an accompanying photo displayed in the gift shop at Hannibal's Mark Twain Cave, "Joe Douglas was black. The 'one-drop' rule that pervaded legal racial categories in the United States would have defined him as black despite the fact that he was also part Osage Indian."[69] She expands the racial category of "half breed" beyond its common nineteenth-century usage denoting the progeny of an Anglo-American father and indigenous mother, introducing the possibility that one of Joe's forebears was a free black or escaped slave. Douglas did indeed have well-documented ties to Hannibal's African American community—he married twice, each time to a woman of color, and purchased property in a district where "Negro people built homes"[70] and that was later named "Douglasville" in his honor. These facts—while intriguing—do not constitute proof of Douglas's racial admixture but instead reify the isolation of his status as Other. Excluded from the social mainstream by his ambiguous ancestry, he seems to have established a strategic foothold in the village by forging alliances with another more populous, marginalized racial group.

As Twain's popularity rose, his "devilish half-breed" antagonist became progressively entwined with the historical figure of Joe Douglas in the community's collective imagination, despite the many blatant and irreconcilable disparities between them. First and foremost, Douglas was not a murderer but an honorable, law-abiding citizen, "peaceable as a kitten" in the words of local resident Doc Buck Brown.[71] Although he vehemently denied being the model for "Injun Joe," the superficial resemblance of their respective names inexplicably trumped logic. This misattribution dogged Douglas even in death, becoming literally etched in stone when the caretaker of Hannibal's Mount Olivet Cemetery placed a marker emblazoned with the words "Injun Joe" at his gravesite in the mid-1980s.[72]

The speculation surrounding both Joe Douglas's racial identity and his relationship to Mark Twain's mixed-blood antagonist is conclusively resolved in a long-forgotten article called "Tom Sawyer Characters in Hannibal" that was recovered by Victor Fischer, an editor at the Mark Twain Project, while preparing the explanatory notes for volume 1 of the writer's complete *Autobiography*. This piece, published 2 June 1902 in the Saint Louis *Post Dispatch*, chronicles Clemens's return to his hometown several days before being awarded an honorary degree at the University of Missouri. In addition to speaking with a number of the writer's boyhood friends, the reporter sought out and interviewed Joe Douglas, who provided the following account of his life:

> "I don't know my age but I think I was about 5 years old when the American soldiers captured me in 1847 during the Mexican War. With several other Mexican children I was brought to the United States. My mother was a Spanish woman and my father a Cherokee Indian. I was finally brought to Ralls County by the late Col. Ralls, an officer in the Mexican War. . . . I lived at Center, in that county, some years, then came to Hannibal."

> "As long as I remember I have been called Indian Jo." (He did not pronounce it Injun. Mr. Douglass uses excellent language.) . . . "If I am the book character," said Jo, "I don't see how I could still be alive. Mark Twain killed me in the cave. I came to Hannibal in November, 1862, and I think I am about 60 years old. Mark Twain left here about the time I came, if not before."[73]

This thumbnail autobiography sets the record straight on several counts: Douglas dates his birth to the early 1840s, explicitly identifies his ancestry as Spanish and Cherokee, and claims that his nickname originated long before his 1862 arrival in Hannibal. Moreover, the reporter's observation about Joe's "excellent language"—grounded in the distinction between standard and colloquial English usage ("Indian" versus "Injun")—highlights the disparaging connotations of ignorance, disreputability, and inferior social status inherent in the name Twain bestowed upon his villain. The *Oxford English Dictionary* traces the first use of "Injun" to an 1812 trans-Appalachian frontier newspaper called the *Salem Gazette*, which announces, "The people of Tennessee is antious to have orders commanded out for us to march against the injuns on the Wabash." The other nineteenth- and early twentieth-century examples cited in the entry demonstrate a link between this vernacular term and racial enmity ("Better not go *fur*. There is *Injuns* enough lying under wolf skins, or skulking on them cliffs," 1868; "No more attention was paid to the shooting of an 'Injun' than if he were a coyote," 1889).[74] Although not as incendiary

an epithet as "nigger," "Injun"—as the *Post Dispatch* reporter implies—
is unquestionably pejorative in its associations.

Later in the same article, the reporter describes sharing Douglas's story
with Clemens "as they were speeding past the mouth of the cave where the
book character perished," eliciting this response: "If this man you speak of
is Injun Jo . . . he must be about 95 years old. The half-breed Indian who
gave me the idea of the character was about 35 years old 60 years ago."[75]
The writer here flatly denies any connection between Joe Douglas and his
fictional creation on the basis of chronology—the dates simply do not align.
Injun Joe's actual precursor, he asserts, was born circa 1807—in other words,
during the period when "cultural and social mixing and . . . intermarriage"[76]
was commonplace among French and Spanish traders and the indigenous
inhabitants of Missouri Territory. This revised timeline also helps to explain
Joe's puzzling disguise as a Spaniard upon returning to Saint Petersburg
after his dramatic escape from the courtroom. The distinctive ethnic markers of his masquerade—a sombrero and serape (TS, 187)—may in fact be
oblique clues to his paternal ancestry.[77]

"IT'S BLOOD, IT'S BLOOD, THAT'S WHAT IT IS"

The identity of Injun Joe's historical antecedent—which will likely forever
remain a mystery—is in some respects a moot point. As a symbolic creation, Twain's villain represents the social stigma of miscegenation and the
"taint" of Indian blood in nineteenth-century American culture. In *The
Oregon Trail* (1847), Francis Parkman famously described half breeds as "a
race of rather extraordinary composition, being, according to the common
saying, half Indian, half white man, and half devil"[78]—in other words,
monstrous entities who are "enigmatically more than" the sum of their
two biological parts.[79] Unlike full-blooded Indians, who could be safely relegated to the nation's past, the mixed-blood "belonged very much to the
present and quite possibly to the future of America"[80] and thereby consti-
tuted a threat to the dominant social order. As William Scheick argues in his
groundbreaking study *The Half-Blood*, this fear of racial crossing is manifested in the grotesque representation of métis characters in nineteenth-
century dime novels, particularly the stereotype of the "twilight hybrid"—
"a malicious creature hovering in the shadow between the light of
civilization and the darkness of savagery, heir to the basest qualities of both
races"[81]—a figure who bears striking resemblance to Injun Joe.

At two different points in *The Adventures of Tom Sawyer*, Twain explicitly identifies Joe's criminality with his indigenous ancestry. In chapter 9,

he attempts to justify the extortion of additional money from Dr. Robinson for stealing the corpse of Hoss Williams by enumerating a series of past wrongs the physician has committed against him: "Five year ago you drove me away from your father's kitchen one night, when I come to ask for something to eat, and you said I warn't there for any good; and when I swore I'd get even with you if it took a hundred years, your father had me jailed for a vagrant. Did you think I'd forget? The Injun blood ain't in me for nothing. And now I've *got* you, and you got to *settle*, you know!" (TS, 74–75). This deterministic allusion to "Injun blood" suggests that Joe's vengefulness is a racial rather than personal trait—a view Herman Melville identifies with the "metaphysics of Indian-hating" in his 1857 novel *The Confidence Man.* "There is," Melville's narrator asserts, "an Indian nature," distinct from and inferior to that of whites, claiming on this basis that "'Indian blood is in me,' is the half-breed's threat."[82]

Similarly, when Huck informs the Welchman about the mysterious Spaniard's plan to disfigure the widow Douglas in chapter 30, the older man initially doubts its veracity. But once Huck divulges the stranger's true identity as Injun Joe, the Welchman "almost jumps out of his chair," exclaiming, "It's all plain enough, now. When you talked about notching ears and slitting noses I judged that that was your own embellishment, because white men don't take that sort of revenge. But an Injun! That's a different matter, altogether" (TS, 214). In racializing the "sociopathic sadism"[83] of Joe's plan to "spile" the widow's looks, the Welchman establishes a specious distinction between the treatment of women in Anglo-American and native cultures that reinforces his ethnocentric sense of superiority. Moreover, the disturbing details of Joe's revenge plot—tying the widow down in bed and allowing her to bleed to death—imply a metaphorical rape. This threat of sexual defilement, a trope Twain would associate with Indians in a number of later works, is the quintessential expression of Joe's savagery.

The writer described the half breed's plans even more graphically in his original manuscript draft: "When you want to get revenge on a woman you don't kill her—bosh! You go for her looks. You take her nose off—& her ears!"[84] This type of horrific mutilation had been widely reported in the popular press during the novel's composition in relation to General George Crook's 1872–73 campaign against the Arizona Apache, during which he criminalized the practice of cutting the noses off adulterous Apache women. Twain no doubt read of—and was repulsed by—the barbaric cruelty of this punishment and incorporated it into the novel, despite its obvious inapplicability to the offense for which Joe belatedly seeks redress.

In certain other respects, however, Twain's characterization of Injun Joe transcends the narrow typology of the "ignoble savage," grounding him in the specific social conditions of postremoval Missouri. His thirst for vengeance can only be satisfied by proxy, since the two individuals responsible for his imprisonment on the charge of vagrancy are now deceased. Joe's statement that Dr. Robinson's father had him jailed "five year ago" (TS, 74), when examined in conjunction with the timeframe of "thirty to forty years ago" Twain specifies in the novel's preface, places his arrest in the late 1830s—contemporaneous with the 1837 presidential decree that Indian title to land in Missouri had been "entirely extinguished." Joe's status thus emblemizes the plight of his race rather than individual misfortune; dispossessed and unforgiving, he incarnates the vengeful "Spirit of Place" discussed by D.H. Lawrence in his 1923 work, *Studies in Classic American Literature*: "He doesn't believe in us and our civilization, and so is our mystic enemy, for we push him off the face of the earth."[85]

The historical dimensions of Injun Joe's character are also clarified by the curious oath he utters in chapter 26 in response to his accomplice's suggestion that they rebury the box of treasure in the same part of the haunted house where it was initially hidden. Rather than invoking the name of a deity (Christian or native) he exclaims, "*No! by the great Sachem, no!*" (TS, 190), appealing to the secular authority of a polity established many centuries before European contact—the same type of indigenous social organization denounced as a "palpable evil" by Thomas Hart Benton in 1824. Sachems were hereditary civic leaders (as opposed to those who distinguished themselves by feats of physical prowess in war), who governed Algonquian tribes and confederacies by traditional means of diplomacy and consensus rather than punitive action. Joe's declaration harkens back to a native community in which he is neither an outcast nor a vagrant; more importantly, it signals his refusal to recognize the legitimacy of the institutions upon which Anglo-American authority is founded—namely, Christianity and European law. This allusion may offer a subtle clue to his tribal affiliation as well, since the Sac and Fox, who historical sources indicate were present in significant numbers around Hannibal between the 1820s and 1840s, were Algonquian peoples.

Joe's resistance to Anglo-American hegemony is evident in his angry denunciation of the punishment inflicted on him by Judge Douglas for the crime of vagrancy: "He had me *horsewhipped!*—horsewhipped in front of the jail, like a nigger!—with all the town looking on! HORSEWHIPPED!—do you understand?" (TS, 208). This simile not only registers Joe's refusal to be objectified—in other words, treated "like a nigger"—but also an obdurate sense of pride rooted in the autonomy of his indigenous heritage. In *Sitting in Darkness: Mark Twain's Asia and Comparative Racialization*, Hsuan Hsu contrasts Joe's flogging with that inflicted on Tom Sawyer by his irate schoolmaster, arguing that because the boy's punishment is undertaken voluntarily in order to protect Becky, it "affirms his masculinity and whiteness"[86]—and thereby becomes a marker of honor versus shame.

The gruesome death Twain fashions for Injun Joe in McDougal's Cave at the novel's end—imprisoned in the darkness of his primitive humanity, debarred from the "light and . . . cheer" of the civilized world, and reduced to eating candle stubs and bats before succumbing to starvation—symbolically parallels the historical exclusion and eventual erasure of Indians from the American landscape.[87] The half breed dies not of hunger but of thirst, unable to sustain himself by collecting the "precious drop that fell once in every three minutes with the dreary regularity of a clock-tick" from the cave's ceiling, amounting to a meager "dessert spoonful" each day (TS, 239). Twain's description of the agonizingly slow pace at which water seeps from the stalactite is both a philosophical meditation on the passage of time and a paean to the triumphant march of Western civilization: "That drop was falling when the Pyramids were new; when Troy fell; when the foundations of Rome were laid; when Christ was crucified; when the Conqueror created the British empire; when Columbus sailed; when the massacre at Lexington was 'news'" (TS, 239). These benchmarks of imperial progress— from ancient Egypt, Rome, and medieval Britain to the European conquest and colonization of the New World, culminating in the creation of the United States—represent the remote causes of Joe's demise. The very course of history, Twain intimates, makes the doom of "this flitting human insect" (TS, 240) inevitable.

As Hsuan Hsu has noted, the accidental nature of Joe's death—an inadvertent consequence of Judge Thatcher's attempt to protect the white children of St. Petersburg from harm—absolves the community of culpability for it, "despite the fact that the uneven and arbitrary criminalization of vagrancy had rendered him 'dead in law' long before the judge literalized his death."[88] According to the Osage scholar Carter Revard, however, the denouement of *Tom Sawyer* reflects Twain's personal hatred and fear of Indians rather than the inherent racial biases of nineteenth-century American law. In his provocative essay "Why Mark Twain Murdered Injun Joe—and Will Never Be Indicted," Revard accuses the writer of "mauling Red and White questions . . . by say[ing] nothing whatever about Injun Joe in relation to the Conquest of the West, Manifest Destiny, or ethnic cleansing, surely aspects of American history as crucial to [his] time as were slavery and the Civil War and Reconstruction."[89]

Indeed, the news of Joe's death elicits an "abounding sense of relief and security" (TS, 238) not only in Tom Sawyer but also in the Anglo-American community as a whole. His funeral is a communal rite of reintegration celebrating the restoration of harmony and civic order: "People flocked [to the mouth of McDougal's Cave] in boats and wagons from the town and from all the farms and hamlets for seven miles around; they brought their children, and all sorts of provisions, and confessed that they had had almost as satisfactory a time at the funeral as they could have had at the hanging" (TS, 240). Once Joe is buried and safely relegated to the past, the site of his death becomes a local tourist attraction: "It is many and many a year since the hapless half-breed scooped out the stone to catch the priceless drops, but to this day the tourist stares longest at that pathetic stone and that slow dropping water when he comes to see the wonders of McDougal's Cave. Injun Joe's Cup stands first in the list of the cavern's marvels; even 'Aladdin's Palace' cannot rival it" (TS, 240).

This geological formation, like Injun Joe himself, is a fiction. In comparing it to one of the cave's actual "marvels," however, Twain suggests that the incident commemorated by the landmark is a touchstone—a shared cultural referent—in the collective memory of St. Petersburg's citizens, in much the same way as the beloved tale of Aladdin from *The Arabian Nights*. The pathos with which the "tourist" ponders the half breed's fate parallels the sentimentality of the "Vanishing Indian" myth, evoking a sympathy for Joe's plight that was denied to him in life. As Susan Kalter remarks, "Joe's death is the disappearance of regional historical memory itself, the suppression of Creole community as a viable and sensible alternative" to the new monoracial order of Southern slave-holding society.[90]

"STRIPPED AND STRIPED . . . LIKE SO MANY ZEBRAS"

At the heart of *The Adventures of Tom Sawyer* lies an unresolved paradox between real and imagined Indians. On the one hand, Injun Joe—who is variously described as a "half-breed devil" (TS, 167), "stony-hearted liar" (TS, 89), and "bloody-minded outcast" (TS, 238)—is an anathema both to Mark Twain and the adult inhabitants of St. Petersburg, yet on the other, "playing Indian" exerts an irresistible hold on the imaginations of the village boys. According to historian Philip J. Deloria, the performance of Indianness—a trope dating back to the Boston Tea Party—has "provided

[the] impetus and precondition for the creative assembling" of national American identity from the colonial period to the present.[91] In *Tom Sawyer*, the mystique of indigenous Otherness first surfaces as a classic escape fantasy. After Becky Thatcher spurns Tom's romantic overtures in chapter 7, he retreats to the woods in despair and ponders,

> What if he turned his back, now, and disappeared mysteriously? What if he went away—ever so far away, into unknown countries beyond the seas—and never came back any more! How would she feel then! The idea of being a clown recurred to him now, only to fill him with disgust. . . . No, he would be a soldier, and return, after long years, all war-worn and illustrious. No—better still, he would join the Indians, and hunt buffaloes and go on the war-path in the mountain ranges and the trackless great plains of the Far West, and away in the future come back a great chief, bristling with feathers, hideous with paint, and prance into Sunday-school, some drowsy summer morning, with a blood-curdling war-whoop, and sear the eyeballs of all his companions with unappeasable envy. But no, there was something gaudier than this. He would be a pirate! (TS, 64)

Twain arranges Tom's flamboyant "career" options into a distinct hierarchy of preference (clown, soldier, Indian scout, and pirate) based on two key criteria: costume and image. Moreover, the allure of these professions depends not only on an abrupt separation from the community but also on the prospect of a dramatic return. In temporarily removing himself from the familiar environs of St. Petersburg, Tom hopes to achieve a transformation in status—to become the object of extravagant popular admiration and thereby reclaim his sweetheart's affections. Tom of course never enacts this fantasy, instead contenting himself by pretending to be Robin Hood valiantly facing down a foe in Sherwood Forest.

Several chapters later, returning to school after an extended illness, Tom again seeks to reingratiate himself with Becky not by running away but by showing off: "One more frock passed in at the gate, and Tom's heart gave a great bound. The next instant he was out, and 'going on' like an Indian; yelling, laughing, chasing boys, jumping over the fence at risk of life and limb, throwing hand-springs, standing on his head—doing all the heroic things he could conceive of" (TS, 96–97). In this instance, Twain equates indigeneity with wildness, impulsivity, and reckless displays of athletic prowess. Tom's disruptive behavior escalates when she refuses to acknowledge him; he "war-whoops around," stealing one boy's cap and tossing it onto the schoolhouse roof, and aggressively knocking over others, "tumbling them in every direction" before sprawling headlong "under Becky's nose, almost upsetting her" (TS, 97). The havoc this "Indian" wreaks within the rule-bound space of the schoolyard—while in some ways akin to the subversive Old World tradition of misrule—also evokes the threat of disorder that savagery poses to civilized society.

Becky's second rejection prompts Tom to take a bolder, more extreme step. Christening himself the "Black Avenger of the Spanish Main," he persuades Joe Harper (aka "The Terror of the Seas") and Huck Finn (the "Red-Handed") to join him on Jackson's Island where they will live as "pirates." After several days of swimming, exploring, and hunting for turtle eggs—distinctly unpiratical activities—Joe and Huck tire of the escapade and express a desire to return home; hoping to avert mutiny, Tom proposes that they "knock off being pirates, for a while, and be Indians for a change" (TS, 127). The boys eagerly agree to the new plan, and "it was not long before they were stripped, and striped from head to heel with black mud, like so many zebras,—all of them chiefs, of course—and then they went tearing through the woods to attack an English settlement" (TS, 127).

This "magically transfiguring mimetic play" involves a more radical transgression of cultural boundaries than pretending to be pirates; the boys do not merely imagine themselves as romantic outlaws, but imitate and appropriate Indian identity "viscerally through the medium of their bodies."[92] As primitive racial Others, they revel in a state of absolute freedom that according to Deloria "reject[s] every restraint—politics, society, language, meaning itself."[93] Twain's diction, however, subtly suggests that this exhilarating transformation also compromises the boys' humanity, reducing them to exotic wild animals. The simile "stripped and striped . . . like so many zebras" was likely inspired by William de la Montagne Cary's drawing "Scalp Dance," published in *Harper's Weekly* on 19 September 1874 (fig. 2). The legs of the three warriors foregrounded in this image are decorated with light and dark horizontal bands reminiscent of zebra skin, an association underscored by the long equine tails of their ceremonial regalia. "Terrible Slaughter," True Williams's illustration of this passage in the novel (fig. 3), visually echoes Cary's drawing in both the geometric pattern of the boys' body paint and the menacing gesture of the central knife-wielding figure poised above his intended victim—a pose he would replicate in illustrating Tom's nightmares about Injun Joe in chapter 23.

The manuscript of *Tom Sawyer* indicates that chapter 16 originally ended with the boys' dramatic transformation; then, at some later point in the text's composition, Twain inserted three additional paragraphs developing the scenario of "playing Indian" in greater detail.[94] Their initial plan to "attack an English settlement"—the foundation upon which

FIGURE 2. "Scalp Dance," *Harper's Weekly* (September 1874). Public domain.

Anglo-American society symbolically rests—proves unsatisfying in the absence of a man-made structure on the island to which they can lay siege. The boys then decide to separate "into three hostile tribes . . . kill[ing] and scalp[ing] each other by thousands. It was a gory day. Consequently it was an extremely satisfactory one" (TS, 127). In the aftermath of this cathartic slaughter, Tom, Joe, and Huck smoke a "pipe of peace" as night falls, discovering to their great delight the practice no longer sickens them. Twain announces, with mock solemnity, "They were glad they had gone into savagery, for they had gained something . . . and so they spent a jubilant evening. They were prouder and happier in their new acquirement than they would have been in the scalping and skinning of the Six Nations" (TS, 128).

Within the context of the novel's nineteenth-century midwestern setting, Twain's allusion to the "Six Nations" or Haudenosaunee (People of the Longhouse), a confederacy of six eastern woodland tribes (Seneca, Cayuga, Onondaga, Oneida, Mohawk, and Tuscarora), who allied with the British against the Continental Army during the American Revolution, is somewhat baffling. It does, however, have direct—and timely—relevance to his wife's hometown of Elmira, New York, where a monument commemorating the

FIGURE 3.   "Terrible Slaughter," *The Adventures of Tom Sawyer*. Courtesy of the Mark Twain Project, The Bancroft Library, University of California, Berkeley.

centenary of one of the war's most decisive military engagements was being planned in the mid-1870s. The Battle of Newtown took place several miles east of Elmira on 29 August 1779, when General John Sullivan attacked the Iroquois settlement of "New Town" in a "whirlwind of destruction,"[95] torching homes, orchards, and crops. This incident irreparably damaged the Haudenosaunee's strength; according to historian Morris Bishop, "The "unhappy fate of the great Iroquois Confederacy was decided at Newtown; the battle monument is the gravestone of the Iroquois civilization."[96]

When the fighting ended, Sullivan's soldiers collected trophies from their native victims, scalping at least ten men[97] and performing other, more grisly mutilations. Lieutenant William Barton matter-of-factly noted in his journal that he had "skinned two [Indians] from their hips down for boot legs [e.g., chaps], one for the Major [Daniel Platt] and the other for myself."[98] This atrocity is corroborated by the eyewitness account of a second officer, Rudolphus Hovensburgh, who reported seeing Indian corpses "Sm Skn By our S. for bts"—an abbreviation meaning "Some skinned by our own soldiers for boots."[99] Clemens likely heard (or perhaps misheard) this story from his brother-in-law General Charley Langdon, a member of the Newtown Monument Association, a group of prominent local citizens who spearheaded the fund-raising campaign to construct a stone obelisk at the battle site.

Twain's analogy between the "savages" on Jackson's Island and Sullivan's men is provocative. Despite the obvious disparities in time, place, and circumstance—not to mention the participants' respective ages—the two incidents are thematically linked by notions of conquest and gratification. Both involve vanquishing an enemy, whether in the form of tobacco or Iroquois warriors. Moreover, to succeed in these endeavors, an instinctive aversion—explicitly rendered in the nausea smoking previously induced in Tom, Joe, and Huck, though only implied in the callous brutality of Sullivan's men—must be overcome. But what is most significant about Twain's comparison is the manner in which the boy's "new acquirement"—and the maturation it signifies—effects a subtle shift in their racial identity and political allegiance: "*They* were prouder and happier in their new acquirement than *they* would have been in the scalping and skinning of the Six Nations" (TS, 128; emphasis added). Initially, "they" refers to Tom, Joe, and Huck in their imaginative guise as indigenous Others; midway through the sentence, however, the pronoun's meaning shifts. By syntactically melding the boys and eighteenth-century Indian fighters, the writer tacitly restores their subject position as Anglo-Americans. His analogy affirms Deloria's contention that the "powerful, liberating frivolity" of playing Indian is necessarily a temporary phenomenon, culminating in an inevitable return to everyday life—as indeed the boys do the very next morning, arriving back in St. Petersburg just in time to disrupt their own funeral service.[100]

Although *The Adventures of Tom Sawyer* was written some two decades after Clemens left Hannibal and the world of his childhood behind, the progression that the novel proposes from a youthful idealization of Indians to an adult state of active enmity in some ways mirrors the inherent contradictions of the writer's own stance. As the following chapters will demonstrate, Twain—like many other nineteenth-century Euro-Americans—was trapped in what Philip Deloria calls an unresolved "dialectic of simultaneous desire and repulsion" in his views of indigenous peoples.[101] Over the course of a long literary career, he vacillated between denouncing them as "vermin" and "reptiles"—even "desirable subject[s] for extermination"—and imaginatively representing himself as an Indian at others. In a jubilant letter to Joe Twichell on 28 November 1868, he announces that Olivia—after a series of rejections—had finally accepted his proposal of marriage. The Langdons, he explains, have made a "*conditional* surrender," contingent upon proof of his genteel, upright character: "Hurra! Hurricanes of applause," he writes, then adds, "But I am so happy I want to scalp somebody" (L2, 294). Similarly, in his 1871 "(Burlesque) Autobiography," the writer claims descent from both the illustrious Indian "reformer" John Morgan Twain, whose devotion to the "elevation" and civilization of native peoples was a euphemism for their imprisonment and hanging (BA, 11), and an eighteenth-century warrior, "PAH-GO-TO-WAH-WAH-PUKKETEKEEWIS," who attempted to assassinate George Washington but proved too drunk to shoot straight. This tongue-wrenching name, which Twain translates as "Mighty-Hunter-with-a-Hog-Eye," is a close variant of "Pau-Puk-Keewis," the villainous Iroquois trickster of Longfellow's *Hiawatha*—reflecting both the poem's lingering influence and Twain's efforts to exorcise the romantic archetype of the noble savage he had encountered there (BA, 14).

Clemens's lifelong ambivalence toward Indians is deeply entwined with his identity as an American writer. In a May 1907 autobiographical dictation, made just before receiving an honorary doctorate at Oxford University, he stated, "I take the same childlike delight in a new degree that an Indian takes in a fresh scalp, and I take no more pains to conceal my joy than the Indian does" (A3, 53). This strange conflation of two different types of skin—the parchment of the celebrated university's diploma with that atop the head of a vanquished enemy—equates the Oxford degree with the most

iconic trophy of savage warfare. In this respect, Twain's metaphorical declaration of Indianness becomes a defiant assertion of his national origin. A
young American poet named Ezra Pound would make a similar—albeit
more theatrical—statement a year later, wearing a single, long turquoise
earring with a formal frockcoat when being introduced to William Butler
Yeats in London.[102]

2. Blind in Nevada

Early Perceptions of Indians in the West

When Sam Clemens, aged twenty-five, left Saint Joseph, Missouri, on 26 July 1861 for Nevada Territory, he was headed toward an uncertain future. He had no real prospect of a job in the West other than serving as a clerk to his older brother Orion, the newly appointed territorial secretary. This lack of a clearly defined career path afforded the young man the freedom to pursue what he nostalgically characterized in *Roughing It* as "years of variegated vagabondizing"—traveling, silver-mining, and carousing, all the while acutely observing—before he ultimately discovered his destiny as a writer. Moreover, the frontier conditions in which Clemens found himself immersed beginning in August 1861, and out of which the persona "Mark Twain" was born some eighteen months later, were dynamic, unstable, rife with all manner of conflict—racial, political, interpersonal—and thus strangely suited to the indeterminacies of his own position.

Nevada Territory, formally organized by President Abraham Lincoln on 2 March 1861, was very much a work in progress upon the Clemens brothers' arrival; even its geographical borders were provisional and amorphous. In his first report to the US secretary of the interior that summer, Governor James Warren Nye noted with chagrin, "I have been unable to ascertain where the eastern boundary of the Territory is."[1] The western boundary was equally nebulous; according to Andrew Marsh, a reporter for the Sacramento *Daily Union*, the inhabitants of Esmeralda County, near Mono Lake, lived in a constant "state of 'betwixty'"—unsure whether the region belonged to California or Nevada. Marsh described the residents of other nearby districts as also existing "in the same state of glorious uncertainty as the Esmeralda people on the question of 'Who do you belong to?'" and warned that "unless the Sierra Summit line, or some other equally definite, be soon agreed upon, there will arise some knotty and bothersome legal questions out of the conflicting jurisdictions."[2]

One particularly "knotty" issue stemming from this confusion involved competing claims of land usage and patrimony. The rapid influx of fortune hunters into the Great Basin after the 1859 discovery of vast gold and silver deposits known as the Comstock Lode had profoundly disrupted the lives and traditional economies of the region's indigenous inhabitants. Although the establishment of Anglo-American hegemony was well under way in 1861, Indians remained a visible, unpredictable—and at times menacing—presence with whom the newly formed government had to negotiate and contend. Primary responsibility for maintaining amicable relations with the tribes and securing clear land title through treaty negotiations fell to Governor Nye, who also served in the capacity of ex officio superintendent of Indian Affairs. The absence of fixed territorial limits, as he explained to the secretary of the interior, greatly hampered the fulfillment of these duties: "This agency, as established, only included, as I have been informed, the tribes of the Pah-Utes and Washoes. It is now claimed that a large portion of the tribes of the Shoshones and Bannocks are within the jurisdiction of this Territory. . . . The surveyor general has received no instructions to ascertain any of the boundary lines. Whether the tribes last named are within this Territory, and if so, whether they fall within the scope of my superintendency, is a point upon which I desire instruction."[3]

It was in this volatile milieu that Clemens had sustained personal contact with indigenous peoples for the first time. Writing home to his mother two months after arriving in Carson City, he describes the territory as "fabulously rich" in both its natural resources and diverse population of "thieves, murderers, desperadoes, ladies, children, lawyers, Christians, gamblers, Indians, Chinamen, Spaniards, sharpers, cuyotes (pronounced ki-yo-ties), preachers, poets and jackass-rabbits" (L1, 137). This statement, while acknowledging the existence of Indians with a passing nod, reveals nothing of the frequency or extent of the writer's interactions with them. According to the Gold Hill *Daily News*, "plenty of bucks, squaws, and children"[4] inhabited the margins of the territory's settlements in the early 1860s, meaning that Clemens would have routinely encountered them in a variety of contexts—as partially acculturated woodcutters, housekeepers, laundresses, and occasional theatrical performers in places like Carson and Virginia Cities; as ranch hands and laborers in the mining camps of Humboldt, Esmeralda, and Aurora; and as nomads seeking to maintain their traditional lifeways despite the rapid encroachment of whites. Moreover, as the brother of the territorial secretary, he occupied a uniquely privileged, albeit peripheral, position among the political elite—men actively engaged in the creation of treaties and other legal protocols for dealing with the tribes. Clemens counted Governor Nye, his brother John, and nephew Tom among his friends, and often socialized with legislators, magistrates, and Indian agents such as Warren Wasson and Jacob Lockhart. His affection for the members of this influential cohort is reflected in the postscripts of several 1862 letters written from the Esmeralda mining district, in which he repeatedly enjoins Orion, "Remember me to Tom [Nye] and Lockhart" (L1, 185, 196).

Clemens's early *Enterprise* sketches also offer a suggestive glimpse of his camaraderie with Wasson and Lockhart, two well-respected individuals known for their progressive views on Indians. His 3 February 1863 "Letter from Carson"—the first piece signed with the pen name "Mark Twain"— describes the musical entertainment provided at a recent local party: "Mr. Wasson sang 'Call me pet names' with his usual excellence—(Wasson has a cultivated voice, and a refined musical taste, but like Judge Brumfield, he throws so much operatic affectation into his singing that the beauty of his performance is sometimes marred by it.)" (ETS1, 197). The writer's allusion to Wasson's "usual excellence" implies that this occasion was not the first on which he had heard and admired the agent's voice; on the contrary, these performances were apparently so familiar—and his association with the singer so cordial—that he felt comfortable critiquing the pretentions of his style. Clemens similarly touts his insider status in a January 1864 "Letter from Carson" by announcing, "Mr. Lockhart, the Indian agent, has just received a letter from Commissioner Bennet, in which he says he has been informed by Secretary Chase that no further steps will be taken toward building a mint in this region until our *State Representatives* arrive in Washington!" (ETS1, 423).[5] This casual name-dropping—from the US treasury secretary Salmon Chase and Hiram Pitt Bennet (the official charged with finding a suitable location for the proposed Nevada mint) to Jacob Lockhart—enhances the story's veracity by establishing the direct, unimpeachable authority of Twain's sources. It also bespeaks his status as the agent's confidant. Clemens's close relationships with Wasson and Lockhart make it likely—if not altogether inevitable—that he would have been cognizant of their liberal attitudes toward Indians.

But the writer's most direct line of information about Nevada's indigenous peoples was Orion, who served as acting governor and ex officio superintendent of Indian Affairs during Nye's frequent, sometimes protracted, absences from the territory. In this role, he exhibited the same humanitarian concern with native rights and welfare evident in his 1856 "Sketch of the

Black Hawk War." Now, however, the elder Clemens was not simply an amateur historian chronicling the government's past misdeeds but a policy
maker with the authority to implement measures ensuring the Indians fair
treatment. These efforts, documented in his official correspondence at the
Nevada State Archives, reveal a conscientious solicitude for native peoples
that his younger brother did not share. Despite Sam's physical proximity to
Indians and status as a political insider, he had little to say on the subject; like
the speaker in Whitman's "Song of Myself," he seems to have positioned
himself "both in and out of the game" of territorial politics—"watching and
wondering," on the one hand, yet wryly detached, seemingly immune to the
terrible human costs of Manifest Destiny on the other.

In contrast to Whitman's poetic persona, the characteristic stance of
Twain's *Enterprise* sketches is not "compassionating" but aloof and ironic,
reflecting a worldview in which everything—including the dispossession
and attempted eradication of Nevada's indigenous peoples—was potential
fodder for a joke. This cavalier mindset is illustrated in a local column, published on 29 December 1863, describing three Christmas gifts he received
as an anonymous practical joke: a wooden "watchman's rattle," "a toy rabbit, of the jackass persuasion, gifted with ears of aggravated dimensions, and
swathed in sagebrush," along with a crude effigy of an "Indian chief"
(ETS1, 421–22). This last object, he explains, was "a mere human creation—made of raisins, strung on a skeleton formed of a single knitting
needle, with a solitary fig for a body, and a chicken feather driven into the
head ... to denote its high official status." While it is impossible to know
whether Twain's story is apocryphal or has some basis in fact, its flippant
tone is noteworthy. The doll's appearance is not only slovenly, lacking in
style, grace, and attention to detail, but also characterized by unsettling
implied violence—from the skewered dried fruit making up its body to the
chicken feather "driven into" its head as a marker of rank. In contrast to
their Plains counterparts, Nevada Indians did not typically adorn themselves with elaborate feathered headdresses, suggesting that this detail
functions as a generic signifier of indigeneity and the primitivism Clemens
associates with Indians.

The local column itself is divided into two sections, the first of which
contains Twain's description of the gag gifts, followed by an alleged "committee report," prepared by one William A. Trinity, explaining both their
origin and meaning. The rabbit, according to "Trinity," represents Clemens's
irreverent "design for a seal in the Constitutional Convention"; the rattle
belatedly fulfills an appeal made to a nameless lady for the purpose of collecting the wits of an absentminded young man in attendance at a previous

party; and the Indian, sent "by request of a lady of the medical profession," is a presumptive remedy for constipation. Twain's Constitutional Convention allusion offers an important clue regarding the significance of these objects. Nevada's official seal, adopted during the first meeting of the territorial legislature in the fall of 1861, was a high-minded, patriotic image devised by Orion, featuring—as Sam complained several months later in a letter to his mother—"star-spangled banners and quartz mills . . . with a lot of barbarous latin about *'Volens and Potens'* (able and willing, you know)" (L1, 176). Having attended these legislative sessions as the secretary's clerk (earning a salary of eight dollars per day), he had witnessed the heated debate over the design, including the less lofty alternate proposed by representative William Osborn: "A Pah Utah leaning on a bottle of whisky, a jackass rabbit under a sage bush, a California sharper negotiating with an honest miner for his claim. Motto—'Monte Pio' that is, 'We've got 'em.'"[6]

When the territory's Constitutional Convention convened in late 1863 as a first step toward statehood, the seal's design was revisited, eliciting "much discussion, and more or less of merriment,"[7] according to the minutes of the proceedings. In the midst of this debate, representative Samuel Chapin of Virginia City rose to offer "an umbrageous design got up by 'Mark Twain' . . . as a substitute [to Orion's original], but subsequently withdrew it."[8] Although the details of Twain's emblem are not specified in the document, two of the three gifts anonymously delivered to him at the *Enterprise* correspond to key elements of Osborn's 1861 proposed seal, suggesting that his design was similar.[9]

In a remarkably candid 1876 letter to an old Saint Louis friend named Jacob Burrough, Clemens concedes that between the ages of nineteen and twenty, his outlook was characterized by "ignorance, intolerance, egotism, self-assertion, opaque perception, dense & pitiful chuckle-headedness—& an almost pathetic unconsciousness of it all"[10]—an impressive laundry list of negative traits he is proud to have successfully overcome—though perhaps not as early as he claims. While youth, inexperience, and immaturity were undoubtedly factors in shaping the writer's "opaque," intolerant perceptions of Nevada's native peoples, they neither fully explain nor exonerate them. In the late 1850s, Bret Harte—one year Clemens's junior—"consistently championed the rights of Native Americans in editorials" for the *Northern Californian* newspaper, insisting that "so-called 'Indian outrages' were in fact precipitated by white aggression."[11] Harte's expressions of moral indignation cost him his job in February 1860, when at the age of twenty-three he published a scathing account of the slaughter of Wiyot Indians at the hands of Anglo-American settlers on an island in Humboldt

Bay. The piece, sensationally entitled "Indiscriminate Massacre of Indians—Women and Children Butchered," undermines the ideological basis of Manifest Destiny by accusing the perpetrators of appalling savagery:

> Our Indian troubles have reached a crisis. Today we record acts of Indian aggression and white retaliation. It is a humiliating fact that the parties who may be supposed to represent white civilization have committed the greater barbarity. . . . A more shocking and revolting spectacle never was exhibited to the eyes of a Christian and civilized people [than the bodies of the native victims brought to Uniontown]. Old women wrinkled and decrepit lay weltering in blood, their brains dashed out and dabbled with their long grey hair. Infants scarce a span long, with their faces cloven with hatchets and their bodies ghastly with wounds.[12]

One looks in vain for a comparable indictment in either Clemens's private correspondence or early journalism. His representation of Indians instead tends to exploit and advance popular stereotypes of the ignoble savage—cruel, implacable, and bloodthirsty—or, conversely, to paint them in a ludicrous light. Though the writer's circumstances afforded him ample opportunity to observe native peoples firsthand, he did not—or perhaps could not—see them accurately. Appalled by the squalor in which the Paiute and Washoe lived, he averted his eyes, perfunctorily deeming their condition proof of innate racial inferiority rather than the result of complex historical circumstances. Fred W. Lorch, the first scholar to examine Twain's attitudes about Indians, questioned this cultural myopia in a 1945 essay, arguing that the author "should have observed during his residence in Nevada Territory that the rapid influx of the white settlers had greatly decreased the Indians' means of subsistence by depriving them of their most valuable hunting and fishing grounds and forcing them to seek their living in portions of the country so barren that starvation was all but inevitable,"[13] yet inexplicably did not. The contemporary Shoshone historian Ned Blackhawk makes a similar, albeit more sharply worded, claim in his 2006 study, *Violence over the Land: Indians and Empires in the Early American West*: "What America's most celebrated nineteenth-century writer failed to 'learn' was that Indian poverty—masquerad[ing] as 'wretchedness' and 'inferiority'—remained intimately linked to American colonization," instead falling back on "racial and cultural difference" as a facile explanation of their misery.[14]

The foreclosed quality of Clemens's racial thinking is illustrated by a simile used in a letter to his mother and sister, written in February 1862, just five months after he arrived in the territory: "Ma says 'it looks like a

man can't hold public office and be honest.' Why, certainly not, Madam. A
man *can't* hold public office and be honest. It is like a white man attempting
to play Washoe Injun—that is, trying to swallow cockroaches and grasshoppers alive and kicking—it can't be *did*, you know" (L1, 160). This analogy, intended to demonstrate that dishonesty is intrinsic to a politician's
nature, reduces Washoe identity to a single offensive trait and simultaneously posits an unbreachable divide between civilization and savagery.
Whites, he maintains, possess a discriminating palate that renders them
incapable of ingesting insects, thereby demonstrating their superiority to
Indians. The writer also exaggerates the facts to maximize the revulsion of
his female relations, for in truth the Washoe did not eat cockroaches, nor
did they "swallow grasshoppers . . . alive and kicking." Fish, deer, antelope,
rabbit, and waterfowl, along with pine nuts and the roots of edible plants,
such as tules and camas lilies, were the dietary staples of Great Basin tribes.
Swarms of crickets, locusts, and grasshoppers were also hunted in season,
driven into trenches filled with straw that was then set ablaze; the charred
insects were later pounded into a protein-rich meal used as a flour substitute in making bread.[15]

   In later works, such as *The Innocents Abroad, Roughing It*, and the 1870
sketch "The Noble Red Man," Clemens would ascribe the eating of grasshoppers to *all* western Indians—regardless of tribal affiliation—as proof of
their degraded condition. The disgust he expresses regarding native dietary
habits echoes a well-established literary trope dating back to America's first
bestseller—Mary Rowlandson's *The Sovereignty and Goodness of God*,
her 1682 narrative of the three month-long captivity she endured among
the Narragansett, Nipmuc, and Wampanoag Indians during King Philip's
War. A proper Puritan goodwife, Rowlandson was initially repulsed by the
"filthy trash" her captors ate; however, as the weeks passed, she relented in
the face of imminent starvation, discovering to her great surprise that raw
horse liver and bear meat "were sweet and savory to my taste."[16]
Rowlandson's remarkable adaptation—achieved under great duress—
counterpoints the insularity of Clemens's mindset.

   In an equally dismissive manner, Clemens reports to his mother in a
March 1862 letter, "Generally speaking, we call [Indians] sons of the devil,
when we can't think of anything worse" (L1, 175). His use of the plural first
person pronoun in this context implies that a consensus of antipathy
toward Nevada's indigenous peoples existed among Anglo-American settlers; while this may represent a commonly held viewpoint, close examination of the historical record reveals the existence of a broad, nuanced spectrum of opinion about the region's tribes, particularly among Clemens's

immediate associates—his brother, agents Lockhart and Wasson, as well as members of the *Territorial Enterprise* staff. Rollin Daggett (1831–1901), one of the paper's editors, was himself part Iroquois and quite "learned in savage lore."[17] On his 1850 journey westward from Ohio, he met and traded with bands of Lakota, Pawnee, and Potawatamie, and also spent several months among the Hopi, studying their lifeways and language.[18]

Clemens's fellow reporter Dan De Quille (1829–98), the mentor who Henry Nash Smith claims "taught him the craft of Comstock journalism,"[19] is a particularly important figure in this regard. He was a close friend of the Northern Paiute chief Winnemucca and staunch ally of the "red proprietors of the soil" in general;[20] according to his obituary, "In Virginia City he was loved by everyone: even the children of the hills, the Piutes, knew him as a friend, and if they had a grievance they came to him for advice, and he loved them as he loved everything in Nature."[21] In *Washoe Rambles*, a series of twelve sketches published from 28 July to 1 December 1861 in *The Golden Era*, De Quille presents a colorful account of a prospecting trip through western Nevada, during which he encountered large numbers of natives. The representation of Indians in this work as well as in *The Big Bonanza*, his 1876 history of the Comstock Lode, offers an instructive counterpoint to that of his younger colleague. While De Quille never acknowledges the Paiutes as equals, and occasionally lapses into conventional racial descriptors, referring to the "naked, ragged rabble" and "wild-looking children"[22] he meets, he also possesses the perspicacity to see beyond this impoverishment and recognize their essential humanity. Throughout *Washoe Rambles*, he displays both an insatiable curiosity about Paiute language, customs, and legends and an acute awareness of his outsider status as a "Waamoogena" or American. His recognition of indigenous patrimony is illustrated in the following conversation with one of his guides: "I asked the Captain ... what he called the spot of ground on which the village stood, and at first he said it was a valley; (*dootsee tooroop roop Awaamo poeikaya*); but at last he understood what I wished to know, and said among his people they spoke of it as the '*Tooroop Awaamo poeikaya*,' or the 'morning kissed valley.' This is quite a pretty and poetical name for these wild heathens to light upon ... but I give it as I received it: '*Awaamo*'—morning: '*poiska*'—a kiss; '*poiska-ya*'—kissed."[23]

Many of De Quille's sociological and linguistic observations about Nevada's Indians challenge the stereotype of savagery. The children he meets are impeccably well-behaved, prompting him to note that "some white children I have seen might learn a lesson of modesty from these Indian girls. They did not romp about and yell for this thing or that, pull and haul at everything within their reach, [or] disobey their parent."[24] He clearly enjoys the natives' company, and he readily shares whatever provisions he has on hand in order to learn more about them: "As to the Indian beggars, I am almost ashamed to say it,—I am afraid I am guilty of encouraging them; I rather like to have them around (that is such as are good-natured and full of fun), to study their language and characters."[25]

According to Lawrence Berkove, who has written extensively on the writers of the Sagebrush School, De Quille and Clemens were "kindred spirits" with a mutual fondness for smoking, drinking, and practical jokes. The men not only worked together but also shared lodgings—as well as "a huge double bed"[26]—in a boardinghouse on Virginia City's B Street, from the autumn of 1863 until the younger man's departure for San Francisco the following spring. While Clemens respected his friend's talent and intelligence, he nonetheless appears to have either resisted or chosen to ignore De Quille's progressive views on Indians. By juxtaposing their divergent responses to key events involving the Comstock's indigenous tribes in the early 1860s, the conservatism and intransigence of Clemens's stance becomes increasingly clear.

THE AFTERMATH OF THE PYRAMID LAKE WAR

When Orion and Sam disembarked the Overland Stage in Carson City on 14 August 1861, they stepped quite literally into the aftermath of the Pyramid Lake War, a brief but bloody conflict that had erupted between white settlers and the Northern Paiutes some fifteen months earlier. The town's only stagecoach stop was located at Ormsby House, a hotel and tavern owned by Margaret Ormsby, the grieving widow of Major William Ormsby, who had led his volunteer militia into a deadly ambush. The brothers spent their first few nights in Carson there before securing more affordable accommodations across the plaza at Mrs. Murphy's boardinghouse, during which the seeds of a warm, abiding friendship with Margaret were sown. When she remarried in February 1863, Orion officiated at the ceremony and Sam numbered among the invited guests. Twain's humorous description of the festivities, focusing on the disruptive antics of an incorrigible, uninvited guest—"The Unreliable"—was published in the *Territorial Enterprise* on 8 February and marks one of the earliest uses of his pen name.

Although the Pyramid Lake War lacks the notoriety of other nineteenth-century battles between Indians and whites, it stemmed from an all too familiar cause—competition over land and natural resources. Its origin can be traced to an incident in early May 1860, when two young Paiute women out gathering roots were kidnapped and sexually abused by traders at Williams Station, a commercial outpost located on the Big Bend of the Carson River about thirty miles northeast of Carson City. According to Sarah Winnemucca Hopkins's 1883 autobiography, *Life among the Piutes*, the traders, when questioned about the women's mysterious disappearance, disavowed any knowledge of their whereabouts. Several days later, however, a Paiute hunter visiting the station to barter for supplies made a disturbing discovery. After agreeing to trade his horse for "a gun, five cans of powder, five boxes of caps [and] five bars of lead,"[27] the Indian called off the deal when the station keepers reneged on their offer of the lead bars. Walking to a nearby barn to retrieve his horse, he heard muffled cries from beneath the floorboards and realized he had found the missing women. The hunter rode hurriedly back to camp and told the elders what he had observed; in response, Chief Moguannoga (known as Captain Soo to whites) hastily organized a rescue party of nine men, including Winnemucca's son Natchez, the father of the two kidnapped women.

On 7 May 1860, the Paiutes rode to Williams Station where they confronted the traders, who continued to avow their innocence. As the interrogation grew more heated, the station keepers panicked and tried to escape; one drowned after jumping off a bluff into the Carson River, another was strangled after brandishing a knife, and the three others were in all likelihood shot as they ran. After murdering the traders, the Paiutes went to the barn, located the trapdoor, and rescued the bound, terrified women from their subterranean prison; then, in a final act of rage, they set all of the buildings ablaze. By morning, all that remained of Williams Station was charred timbers and scattered iron tools.[28]

Widespread hysteria, fanned by newspaper reports that grossly exaggerated both the size of the native force and the degree of imminent danger to whites living in the area, prevailed among the settlers in the wake of this "massacre." In response, volunteer militias were quickly organized in the communities of Carson, Virginia City, Dayton, and Genoa to seek retribution against the perpetrators. These groups, though untrained and poorly equipped, were nonetheless supremely confident in the ease of their mission; as historian Myron Angel states in his landmark 1881 *History of Nevada*, "many started on the expedition with the watchword of 'An Indian for breakfast and a pony to ride,' contemplating the pleasure of sacking Pah-Ute villages, capturing their squaws and ponies, killing a few warriors, and running the balance out of the country."[29] Led by Major Ormsby, whom the *Enterprise* characterized as "impetuous as a torrent,"[30] this ragtag militia pursued the Paiutes northward to the vicinity of Pyramid Lake, where they were lured into a trap, surrounded, and attacked. At least sixty-six whites, including Ormsby, who was extolled in death as a valiant commander and victim of native treachery, perished in the Battle of Pyramid Lake on 12 May 1860.

While the exact circumstances of Ormsby's death remain unclear, surviving members of the expedition reported that he was killed at close range by Chief Winnemucca's nephew Numaga, whom he regarded as a friend and ally.[31] Sarah Winnemucca Hopkins, however, challenged this allegation, explaining, "My brother [meaning her cousin Numaga] had tried to save Major Ormsby's life. He met him in the fight, and as he was ahead of the other Indians, Major Ormsby threw down his arms, and implored him not to kill him. . . . My brother said, 'Drop down as if dead when I shoot, and I will shoot over you;' but in the hurry and agitation he still stood pleading, and was killed by another man's shot."[32] In the years preceding the Pyramid Lake War, Ormsby had indeed developed close relationships with the Paiute chiefs Truckee and Winnemucca; the ties of mutual trust were so strong that in 1857 the major invited two of Winnemucca's daughters, Sarah and Elma, into his home as companions for his young daughter Lizzie. The Winnemucca girls lived with the Ormsbys in Carson City for about a year, during which time they learned English and became gradually acculturated to the ways of whites. Given this blurring of racial and familial lines, the claim that Numaga had murdered Ormsby was deemed an unconscionable act of treachery by the territory's Anglo-American settlers.

A tenuous peace prevailed in the war's aftermath. Some settlers who had lost loved ones harbored murderous resentment toward those natives they deemed responsible; others acknowledged that the conflict had been precipitated by the crimes of the Williams Station traders. De Quille, who arrived on the Comstock one month after the hostilities ended in June 1860, belonged firmly in the latter camp, declaring in a "Letter from Washoe" published in the San Francisco *Golden Era* on 5 May 1861: "The trouble [between Indians and whites] all grows out of the villainy of some fellows *en route* to the Humboldt mines, who seized and misused some Indian women. The Pi-Utes are quite an intelligent race, apt to learn, and industrious. If there was plenty of work here for them at one dollar per day, and the whites would not molest their women, the whole tribe would gather here and soon become civilized and useful members of the community. I would much sooner encourage one of them by giving him work than a Chinaman. They know perfectly well that they are the rightful owners of this country, and often complain of the people taking possession of mines and ranches without consulting them."[33]

De Quille's account of the Pyramid Lake War in *The Big Bonanza,* his landmark 1876 history of the Comstock Lode, goes a step further in denouncing the behavior of "a hoodlum class" among Ormsby's volunteer militia, "who took Indian scalps after the battle" and then marched proudly from saloon to saloon in Virginia City with these grisly trophies dangling from the muzzles of their muskets. This passage is accompanied by a satirical illustration entitled "Savages" that subverts the settlers' claim of superiority in relation to their native foes (fig. 4). Clemens, in contrast, never mentioned the conflict in any of his published writings, although his cognizance of both its root causes and lethal consequences is assured by his presence at the deliberations of the first territorial legislature, which met at the Warm Springs Hotel—owned by one of Carson City's founders, Abraham Curry—from 1 October to 29 November 1861. These proceedings, recorded in lively detail by Sacramento's *Daily Union* reporter Andrew Marsh, reveal the complex underpinnings of Manifest Destiny in action: the legislators formalized Anglo-American control of the region by establishing Carson City as the official seat of territorial government, incorporated towns, authorized the construction of railroads and toll roads, and sanctioned the privatization of property by imposing steep fines for the trespass of livestock "on premises lawfully inclosed" by a fence at least "four and one-half feet high, substantially built, and if upon an embankment, three feet high, exclusive of ditch or embankment."[34] The representatives also divided the territory into nine counties, two of which were named Storey and Ormsby in honor of officers "who fell in defending the Territory against Indians"[35] in the recent war.

One of the most contentious topics discussed during the 1861 legislative session was a proposed act "to prohibit the sale of arms, munitions, and liquor to Indians." Marsh's account reveals the gamut of settler views on the local indigenous population. Representative John Mills, for example, declared, "The Indian always was and always would be the natural enemy of the white man, and was treacherous and unreliable. It was the wisest policy to deprive him of deadly weapons. If they refused to become civilized, let them have only their Indian weapons, whether for hunting or for war; and if they proposed to war on the whites, let them contend with bows and arrows against the rifles and cannon of civilized men."[36] Other legislators, such as J. C. Winters, vehemently countered this argument, insisting that "guns and ammunition were necessaries of life for the Indians.... There was not the slightest danger of having any difficulty with the Indians if white men would treat them well."[37] Samuel Youngs concurred,

FIGURE 4. "Savages," Dan De Quille, *The Big Bonanza.* Courtesy of the Mark Twain Project, The Bancroft Library, University of California, Berkeley.

reminding the assembly that "it was only by the humanity of the Indians that the first settlers of this Territory were saved from starvation."[38] The bill eventually passed on the thirty-seventh day of the session, when Nye's predecessor, Isaac Roop, who had served as governor of the provisional territory from 1859 to 1861, proposed an amendment "allow[ing] the sale of arms and munitions except when hostilities may exist between the whites and the Indians," explaining that "game had become so scarce since the influx of white men, that it was impossible for the Indians to maintain themselves with their bows and arrows, so that rifles, powder and lead were absolutely necessary to keep them from starvation." Roop concluded his appeal with the defiant assertion that if the prohibition passed, he would personally "give the Indians in his neighborhood guns and ammunition and pay the fine for it if enforced, until his last dollar was gone."[39]

Marsh's dispatches to the *Daily Union* also indicate the existence of a more personal animus against Indians in the war's wake. On 21 October, he reported the arrival of "Young Winnemucca"—as Numaga was known in the Anglo-American community—in Carson City:

> He was expected to visit the Legislature today . . . but for some reason he failed to make his appearance. . . . Everyone is impressed with the conviction that he is a man of good intelligence, and it is much better to have him for a friend than for an enemy. This chief was the leader of his powerful and warlike tribe in the Indian War in this Territory two years ago, and it is said there are a half dozen men here, whose relations were killed at that time, and who would not hesitate to shoot Winnemucca down on sight. That may be true, but no one here has shot at him yet.[40]

Three days later Marsh reported,

> There is a story about town today that Mrs. Ormsby, widow of Major Ormsby, caught sight of the chief this morning, and followed him for some distance, pistol in hand, endeavoring to get a shot at him. Mrs. Ormsby does not by any means look as if capable of such bloody intentions—"on the contrary, quite the reverse." I suspect the story is a canard, but you can have it for what it is worth.[41]

Later in the session, when an act prohibiting "the carrying and wearing of dangerous and deadly weapons" among the general populace was proposed, one representative waggishly inquired whether this "would include Mrs. Ormsby,"[42] validating her grounds for vengeance. Although the war had ended some eighteen months earlier, it remained an open wound in the hearts and minds of many settlers.

A FATEFUL PROSPECTING TRIP

Within two weeks of the closing of the first territorial legislature, Clemens set off on a prospecting trip to Humboldt County, about 175 miles northeast of Carson City, in the company of three other men—Billy Clagett, an old friend from Keokuk, Iowa, who had also emigrated West in 1861; Augustus Oliver, who had covered the recent legislative proceedings as an official correspondent for the San Francisco *Alta California*; and Cornbury Tillou, a sixty-year-old local blacksmith and "jack-of-all-trades," whom the younger members of the group nicknamed "Dad" (L1, 150n4). The expedition was not entirely a lark: Clagett and Oliver, both attorneys by training, were traveling to Humboldt to assume government posts—the former as notary public of Unionville, the county seat, and the latter as probate judge.

According to the University of California edition of *Roughing It*, Clemens's probable route both to and from the Humboldt mining district took him along the Carson River past a trading post called Honey Lake Smith's, which had been built on the site of Williams Station soon after its destruction in May 1860.[43] On his return trip to Carson City in early February, the writer was stranded at the trading post for eight days by a flash flood; although his humorous account of this incident in the published volume makes no mention of the post's grisly history, a joking, offhand remark made in a 28 February 1862 letter to Clagett offers indisputable evidence of his knowledge of the Pyramid Lake War. After inquiring about "Dad," who had apparently decided to spend the winter in Unionville, Clemens admonishes, "Keep your eye on the old man, Billy, and don't let him get too enthusiastic, because if he does, he will begin to feel young again, like he did when he fell in the river at Honey-Lake's; and being a lecherous old cuss anyhow, he might ravish one of those Pi-Utes and bring on an Indian war, you know. So, just keep an eye on him" (L1, 164).

This comment, framed as a playful acknowledgment of Tillou's lascivious nature, brims with affection for the older man; in fact, a few paragraphs later, he tells Clagett, "Convey unto Dad my most high-toned love and veneration" (L1, 166). What is most significant about Clemens's statement, however, is the cavalier allusion to the rape of a Paiute woman causing an Indian war—the very circumstances that precipitated the Pyramid Lake conflict. The dissonance between the writer's lighthearted tone and the atrocity tale invoked suggests a profound disengagement from the region's turbulent social and political realities. His remark subsumes the complex forces of history within the overriding priority of the personal. Moreover, in establishing an implicit link between Tillou's "enthusiasm" and the keepers of Williams Station, he insinuates that they too were lovable, essentially harmless, lechers, rather than reprehensible criminals.

As late as 1867, visitors to the "isolated inn" (RI, 197) at Honey Lake Smith's noted grim visual reminders of the violence that had destroyed Williams Station seven years earlier: the site remained littered with the charred sills of buildings, fragments of crockery, rusting scrap iron, and scattered horseshoes.[44] It therefore seems likely that Clemens, who stopped at the trading post—not once but twice—just a year and a half after the massacre, would have observed these same physical details yet had chosen not to mention them. Twain's entire account of his Humboldt journey in chapters 27–33 of *Roughing It* elides and distorts historical fact in a number of ways, as illustrated by the counternarrative of Judge Oliver, the expedition's last surviving member, in a 1910 letter to Albert Bigelow Paine. In contrast to Twain's bucolic description of carefree camaraderie—"pipe-smoking, song-singing and yarn-spinning around the evening camp-fire in the still solitudes of the desert" (RI, 182)—Oliver presents a stark image of their party traversing a landscape marked by the macabre traces of recent interracial violence: "An Indian war had just ended and on our journey we occasionally passed the charred ruins of a shack, and a rude cross to mark the spot where the owner was buried."[45] The sight of these burned homes and makeshift graves—mute challenges to Anglo-American settler colonialism—elicits unease among the men. Their fears culminate, and are comically resolved, in a firsthand encounter with Indians that Oliver characterizes as the single "most dramatic incident of [their] journey":

> One incident of our trip has never, so far as I know, been published. We were crossing the 40-mile desert. We had been traveling all day, and about three o'clock the next morning, thoroughly worn out, we reached the other side. The sun was high in the heavens, when we were aroused from our sleep by a band of Paiute warriors. We were upon our feet in an instant. The picture of the burned cabins and the lonely graves we had passed, were very suggestive. Our scalps were still our own and not dangling from the belts of our visitors. Sam pulled himself together, put his hands upon his head as if to make sure he had not been scalped and then in the exuberance of his gratitude and in his inimitable drawl, he turned to us, and as nearly as I can recall his words: "Boys, they have left us our scalps; let's give them all the flour and sugar they ask for." And we gave them a good supply for we were grateful. I regard this as the most dramatic incident of our journey and it has always seemed strange that he has not mentioned it.[46]

Oliver's comment about the "strangeness" of Twain's silence raises several questions. While the veracity of his tale cannot be proven, it is improbable that he fabricated the encounter nearly five decades after its alleged occurrence. At the same time, Twain's suppression of the story—presuming that the incident actually did happen—is equally puzzling, since it flatteringly depicts him as a quick-thinking cultural mediator who defuses a tense, potentially violent confrontation with strategic gifts. The men's exposed position, asleep in the wilderness without a designated watch, also epitomizes the naïve greenhorn qualities associated with the narrator of *Roughing It* and therefore seems well suited for inclusion.

An unpublished notebook entry Clemens made en route back to San Francisco from the Sandwich Islands in August 1866 suggests that Oliver's story does have some basis in fact. This version of events is "told"—among other stories of the writer's experiences in the West—in the second person by his crude traveling companion Mr. Brown for the amusement of passengers on board the *Smyrniote:* "And that time you was riding alone in Washoe—in the Humboldt Moun. & met the whole tribe of Shoshone Indians & was just on the point of destroying them when something whispered to you that they were not prepared to go to Paradise & you spared them" (NBJ1, 155). Clemens's account exaggerates both the degree of menace and the heroism of his response: traveling alone rather than in the security of a group, he chances upon an entire "tribe" of Shoshones—more daunting in size and character than the band of Paiutes mentioned by the judge. But the most telling difference is the nature of the encounter itself: according to Oliver, the men are defenseless and taken utterly by surprise, "roused" from their sleep by the Indians' appearance, whereas Twain presents himself as alert and formidable, capable of single-handedly destroying these indigenous foes but choosing instead to spare them in an act of exemplary Christian forbearance. His gift is not flour and sugar but a far more precious commodity—life itself. The mythic bravado of this stance, so at odds with Oliver's recollection of Clemens nervously checking his head to see if he'd been scalped, suggests that even five years after the supposed incident occurred, the memory still unnerved him, causing his fear to morph into swagger.

The question of the story's authenticity is further complicated by Twain's inscription of the numeral "78" across the notebook passage, part of a private "system of symbols and numbers" that the California editors believe was an attempt to classify the entries for future use: "The number 8 [is] written over examples of historical eloquence, and a 78 [is] used to designate contemporary anecdote, quotation, and other potential literary material. . . . Hackneyed ideas for a collection of eloquent public addresses and for cheap burlesques gave way to notes which anticipate passages in *Huckleberry Finn, Tom Sawyer,* and *Roughing It*" (NBJ1, 108, 102). The anecdote appears to have been flagged for incorporation in Twain's western travel book and later rejected, perhaps for reasons rooted in his aversion to Indians though ultimately inscrutable.

GOVERNOR NYE'S INFAMOUS GIFT

Whether fact or fiction, Clemens's offering of flour and sugar to a group of Paiute warriors is a familiar hallmark of nineteenth-century Anglo-American diplomatic relations with Indians. As anthropologists Martha Knack and Omer Stewart explain in *As Long as the River Shall Run: An Ethnohistory of the Pyramid Lake Indian Reservation,*

> The giving of gifts to Indians was a well-established policy in the
> United States as early as the American Revolution. Later, both settlers
> and government agents in the Northern Paiute territory found it
> expedient to give gifts periodically and to promise more if cooperative
> behavior were forthcoming from the natives. Initially, presents were
> distributed whenever and wherever travelers met groups of Paiutes.
> However, after 1870 . . . agents intentionally restricted the distribution
> of food and clothing to reservation sites . . . [in order to] encourage
> wandering families to concentrate on their reservations.[47]

The strategic importance of gift-giving was a lesson that James Nye—a former New York City police commissioner who knew virtually nothing about Indians—learned early in his tenure as governor. Within two days of arriving in the territory on 8 July 1861, he commissioned a report on current relations with the native population from Indian agent Warren Wasson, one of the region's earliest white inhabitants, specifically requesting "suggestions . . . as to the proper course to be pursued towards the tribes within the limits of the agency."[48] Wasson, known as "Long Beard" among the Paiutes, was thoroughly acquainted with their customs and culture as well as a fluent speaker of their language, and understood from experience the importance of ceremonial gift exchange. According to Thompson and West's 1881 *History of Nevada,* Wasson had earned the Paiutes' enduring trust and respect when he called the tribe together at Walker Lake reservation in December 1860—just months after the recent war—and gave

> each man a hickory shirt and pair of blue overalls, and . . . each woman
> some calico, needles, and thread. A decrepit old Indian arriving late at
> the 'potlatch,' was greatly disappointed because nothing had been saved
> for him, and all the other Pah-Utes seemed delighted at his misery and

the dilemma of the Agent. But Wasson quickly stripped himself, and gave his white linen shirt and cotton flannel drawers to the laggard savage, thus satisfying all and making a lasting impression upon the Indians.[49]

Nor was this the only instance of Wasson's selfless generosity. As he advised Nye,

In order to preserve [the Paiutes'] good will, more presents from the government [must] be issued to them before long, and I would suggest that a few ornaments to please their fancy be selected with other articles of more utility. . . . The agent [should also] be provided with a medicine chest, containing such simple remedies as their diseases require. I have heretofore been in the habit of furnishing them medicines at my own expense, and my prescriptions having been attended with great success . . . they will expect medicines of whoever resides among them hereafter.[50]

Unlike Wasson, Nye regarded the fostering of amicable relations with the Indians as a matter of political expedience rather than a moral imperative. He disliked frontier living and hoped that his governorship would prove a stepping-stone to the more prestigious national office of US senator— a position to which he was elected in 1865, one year after Nevada achieved statehood. Realizing that he could best demonstrate the efficacy of his leadership to Washington's power elite by preventing the outbreak of further racial hostilities in the aftermath of the Pyramid Lake War, Nye informed the secretary of the interior on 19 July 1861, "I deem it of the utmost importance that friendly relations should be maintained with all the tribes along the line of the telegraph, overland mail, and pony express, as they are now the only modes of communication with the States and the home government . . . I shall exert myself to the utmost to secure so desirable and necessary an object."[51]

At the end of July, Nye and Wasson set out for the Walker River and Pyramid Lake reservations, where the governor introduced himself as an emissary of "the great captain" in Washington and made speeches, informing the natives "that a government had been formed over this Territory, to govern by the same laws the white settlers and the Indians." He also "distribut[ed] such of the presents as have arrived, in such manner as will be best calculated to allay all feeling, and if possible to keep them quiet."[52] On this occasion, Nye apparently took Wasson's recommendation about giving the Indians "a few ornaments to please their fancy" to a literal extreme, for in addition to blankets, tools and a small number of steers, he dispensed a trendy fashion accessory—ladies' steel-spring hoopskirts.

These cage crinolines, also known as "skeleton petticoats," were lightweight bell-shaped armatures consisting of a graduated series of steel hoops, fastened with vertical tapes, which held women's voluminous skirts away from their legs and offered enhanced freedom of movement.

Wasson's complicity in this absurd, culturally insensitive joke is perplexing; owing to Nye's status as chief executive, however, the agent most likely stifled any overt expression of disapproval. The local newspapers, on the other hand, seized upon the gesture with unbridled glee, as illustrated by the following notice published in the *Territorial Enterprise* on 3 August: "Governor Nye brought some goods with him from New York for distribution among the Indians. Before starting out last Monday, the goods were overhauled and a very fine assortment of hoops was found among the lot. What disposition the Governor will make of them deponent saith not. The idea of an Indian maiden treading the forests in the full panoply of hoops, is a refinement on romance itself."[53] A California paper, the *Marysville Daily Appeal*, reprinted the story on 8 August with the title "Hoop-de-Dooden-Do," punning that "a full assortment of hoops . . . will not assist the wild squaws in the navigation of the sage-brush and chapparal. Probably they are of the peaceful sort, and are intended to displace the obsolete war-*whoops*."[54]

Although the Clemens brothers did not arrive in Carson City until almost two weeks after Nye's return from the Paiute reservations, they soon learned of the governor's farcical gift. Judging from the frequency with which Sam incorporated this detail into his descriptions of western Indians over the next decade, he apparently found its inanity hilarious. He even managed to trump the governor by adding a gender-bending twist—dressing esteemed chiefs in these crinolines rather than "wild squaws." They are the "crowning glory" of a costume worn by the fictitious "Hoop-de-doodle-do, head chief of the Washoes," an emblematic figure discussed at great length in a 20 March 1862 letter to Jane Lampton Clemens, which was published three months later in the Keokuk *Gate City*. This document is critically important for several reasons: it contains Twain's earliest known representation of Nevada Indians, and also introduces a trope that would become a hallmark of his later depictions—the claim of incontrovertible realism grounded in firsthand observation:

> If you want a full and correct account of these lovely Indians—not gleaned from Cooper's novels, Madam, but the result of personal observation—a strictly reliable account . . . imagine this warrior Hoop-de-doodle-do, head chief of the Washoes. He is five feet seven inches high; has a very broad face, whose coat of red paint is getting spotty and

dim in consequence of accumulating dirt and grease; his hair is black and straight, and dangles about his shoulders; his battered stove-pipe hat is trimmed all over with bits of gaudy ribbon and tarnished artificial flowers, and he wears it sometimes over his eyes, with an exceedingly gallus air, and sometimes on the back of his head; on his feet he wears one boot and one shoe—very ancient; his imperial robe, which almost drags the ground, is composed of a vast number of light-gray rabbit-skins sewed together; but the crowning glory of his costume (which he sports on great occasions in corduroy pants, and dispensing with the robe,) is a set of ladies' patent extension steel-spring hoops, presented to him by Gov. Nye—and when he gets that arrangement on, he looks like a very long and very bob-tailed bird in a cage that isn't big enough for him. . . . Follow him, too, when he goes out, and burn gun powder in his footsteps; because wherever he walks he sheds vermin of such prodigious size that the smallest specimen could swallow a grain of wheat without straining at it, and still feel hungry. You must not suppose that the warrior drops these vermin from choice, though. By no means, Madam—for he knows something about them which you don't; viz, that they are good to eat. (L1, 176–77)

This repulsive description, proposed as an antidote to the romantic "disease" of infatuation with Cooper's idealized noble savages, is an exercise in comic hyperbole. "Hoop" is a clownish figure, clad in an incongruous assortment of both men's and women's cast-off clothing; moreover, his ignorance is so profound that he dons these garments with a naively "gallus air," believing he looks stylish and attractive. This characterization ironically reverses the adage Clemens had shared with his mother a month earlier about the impossibility of a white man playing "Washoe Injun," for in seeking to appear "civilized," Hoop succeeds only in reifying his primitivism—a wild bird metaphorically entrapped within the "cage" of Western civilization.

Clemens's portrait of Hoop lacks historical context, avoiding any mention of the complex sociological factors that underlie his degraded appearance. The explosion of the territory's Anglo-American population in the early 1860s disrupted the fragile subsistence economy of Great Basin hunter-gatherer tribes; as game grew increasingly scarce, food and clothing could no longer be obtained from traditional sources. Indians survived by adapting age-old foraging techniques to new urban settings, scavenging trash heaps on the outskirts of mining communities for fuel, sustenance, building materials, and apparel. Although most of what Hoop wears—the stove-pipe hat, mismatched footwear, and corduroy pants—is Euro-American in origin, he retains two distinctive features of precontact dress:

red face paint and a rabbit-skin robe. This traditional cloak, made of "long, thin spirals of pelts twisted around a string core . . . wove[n] without a loom into thick square blankets to be worn over the shoulders of both men and women," was a by-product of the communal rabbit hunts that the tribe conducted every autumn. The robe did not reflect "imperial" status, as the writer derisively claims, but was rather a practical, ubiquitous "form of clothing for the cold winter days to come and of covering for the long bitter nights."[55] Hoop's motley attire reflects a hybrid cultural identity created in response to rapidly changing conditions that the writer refuses to acknowledge. Clemens's inclusion of these two ethnographically accurate details complicates the humor of his description, revealing the ways in which ethnocentric bias occludes his observations. He sees, in other words, but does not comprehend.

At virtually the same time as Clemens penned this letter, De Quille published a sketch in the *Golden Era* that also features a man wearing a hoop-skirt, albeit under radically different circumstances. "How Uncle Bob 'Got' His 'First Injun,'" told from the perspective of an innocent child named "Dan," is the tale of a white man who comes upon an Indian peacefully catching frogs, "transfering [them] . . . all alive and kicking [in]to his capacious mouth, and crunching [their] bones with the gusto of a gourmand."[56] Through a dubious process of rationalization, Uncle Bob surmises "any man that would eat live frogs would steal beef the first chance he found" and gratuitously shoots the Indian "on suspicion." At this moment the ground suddenly gives way and he plummets into a subterranean hut. After extricating himself with a "tremendous push" upward, Bob explains: "I bound[ed] like a deer across the level meadow with a great contrivance of basket-work suspended from my hips and extending some yards or more on every side— looking for all the world like I had come out in an immense hooped skirt."[57]

Although the parallel may be coincidental, the manner in which De Quille's story inverts Clemens's anecdote—depicting an Anglo-American hunter caught within a native armature of organic materials rather than an Indian "caged" in a technological apparatus of steel—highlights a fundamental difference in the two writers' outlooks. De Quille's nameless Indian, by virtue of both his hereditary title and long habitation, belongs in these environs, whereas Uncle Bob is an unwelcome alien presence. His destructive act of trespass—literally crashing through the willow roof of the family's home—can be read as a metaphor for Anglo-American colonization. Moreover, the Indian is not the primary target of De Quille's humor, but rather Bob himself, depicted fleeing across the meadow in this absurd, oddly feminized garb. Even the Indian's distasteful habit of eating live frogs

FIGURE 5. Washoe chief's family. Courtesy of the Library of Congress, Lawrence and Houseworth Collection. Public domain.

is depicted with gentle humor, unlike Clemens's scornful allusion to the fattened lice Hoop consumes. De Quille revised this sketch more than a quarter of a century later in order to make its pro-Indian stance more emphatic. The later version, published in the *Salt Lake City Tribune*, concludes with Uncle Bob's expression of deep remorse to his young nephew: "I by no means felt proud of what I had done; indeed, to this day I regret the killing of that poor frog-eater more than any other act of my life. . . . To many Injuns were no doubt shot on the Plains in the early days for no other reason than the boys got the drop on them."[58]

The alleged "realism" of Clemens's depiction of Chief Hoop-de-Doodle-do is challenged by an early 1860s photo of an unidentified Washoe chief and his family in the Lawrence and Houseworth Collection at the Library of Congress (fig. 5). The image illustrates the type of acculturated attire the writer might have actually observed in Nevada Territory— the woman's dress, as well as that of her daughter, are fashioned from industrially produced cloth into long, loose-fitting garments distinctively native in style. Tradition also meets improvisation in the decorative accessories respectively worn by mother and son—her necklace is fashioned of animal teeth, whereas his features an array of discarded food tins. Similarly, the chief wears a broad-brimmed hat and collared jacket; hoopskirts, however, are nowhere in sight. Despite their poverty, the family's demeanor is grave and dignified.

Twain's subsequent iterations of the hoopskirt allusion—all clustered between 1870 and 1872, after his relocation to the East—are noticeably harsher in tone than the 1862 letter. This shift is in part attributable to the writer's growing disillusionment with Nye, who had reneged on an 1867 promise to introduce his "Our Fellow Savages of the Sandwich Islands" lecture at New York City's Cooper Union. According to Paul Fatout, Nye "did not appear, offered no apology, and later said that he had never intended to do any favors for 'a damned secessionist.'"[59] Twain's grudge against the politician is evident in "The Reception at the President's"—a sketch published simultaneously in the *Buffalo Express* and October 1870 issue of *Galaxy* magazine—in which a perseverating Washoe miner stalls a White House receiving line by regaling President and Mrs. Grant with his reminiscences of "Governor Nye's Injun receptions":

> Many and many's the time I have been to them, and seen him stand up and beam and smile on his children, as he called them in his motherly way . . . and tell them anecdotes and lies, and quote Watt's hymns to them, until he just took the war spirit all out of them—and grim chiefs that came two hundred miles to tax the whites for whole wagon-loads of blankets and things or make eternal war if they didn't get them, he has sent away bewildered with his inspired mendacity and perfectly satisfied and enriched with an old hoop-skirt or two, a lot of Patent Office reports, and a few sides of condemned army bacon.[60]

While Nye's glib rhetoric is the main target of Twain's satire, he also disparages the greed and antagonism of the Indians attending these receptions, characterizing them as petulant children who threaten "eternal war" if their inordinate—and implicitly unwarranted—demands for trade goods are not met. The governor's success in mollifying native aggression through the distribution of useless gifts serves to underscore their ignorance and inferiority.

Two years later, on 24 January 1872, Twain prefaced his lecture on *Roughing It* in New York City with his most damning allusion to Governor Nye's frivolous gesture:

> He was a real father to those poor Nevada Indians. He gave them, without regard to their sex or age, blankets and hoopskirts. You

could see an Indian chief with a string of blacking boxes around his
neck, and over his red blanket four or five of those hoopskirts,
walking the streets as happy as a clam, with his hands sticking out of
the slats. And yet, notwithstanding all the efforts and civilizing
kindness of the good governor, those Indians didn't step out of their
savage condition—they were just as degraded as if they had never seen
a hoopskirt.[61]

This statement suggests that the writer viewed savagery as an ineradicable
state, impervious to change and progress. According to Dan De Quille, however, the Paiutes in and around Virginia City were the "living exemplifica-
tion of the dawn of civilization upon barbarism," and displayed a remarkable degree of acculturation:

> It is not unusual to see a Piute brave marching through [the] street . . .
> with a wood-saw and buck under his left arm, and upon his right
> shoulder an ax. . . . He is one of the civilized, and represents "labor"
> seeking "capital," [and yet] his pride still clings to the ancient insignia
> of the "brave" in his tribe. His face is painted in zigzag lines of black,
> white, and red; a necklace of bear's claws rests on his breast, and an
> eagle feather decorates his scalp-lock; but instead of bearing a bow and
> arrows, a tomahawk and scalping-knife, he carries only his [tools] and is
> only on the warpath to do battle with a woodpile. . . . He has, as we may
> say, beaten his sword into a ploughshare, but has not the heart to throw
> away the scabbard.[62]

INDIANS AS BEGGARS AND "INVETERATE GAMBLERS"

Clemens's delight in teasing his mother, whose antipathy to Indians ran
deep, is apparent in both the length and detail of his March 1862 letter. Not
content with presenting Hoop-de-doodle-doo in isolation, he also introduces three of the chief's wives—"graceful, beautiful creatures, called
respectively, Timid-Rat, Soaring Lark, and Gentle Wild-Cat (You see, like
all Indians, they glory in high-sounding names)"—constructing a story
within a story, replete with dialogue and denouement. Like their spouse,
these native women are disheveled and "dirty to the extreme of fashion":
"they wore the royal rabbit skin robe, their stringy matted hair hung
nearly to their waists, they had forgotten their shoes, and left their bonnets
at home, only one of them wore jewelry, the Timid Rat around whose leath-
ery throat was suspended a regal necklace composed of scraps of tin. Their
shapelessness caused them to resemble three great muffs. The young chief
Bottled Thunder was with the party, bottled up in a sort of long basket and
strapped to the back of the Soaring Lark" (L1, 177).

The entourage also includes "a juvenile muff" named Princess Invisible Rainbow whose toy, "a bogus infant made of rags" strapped into a cigar box slung across her back, mimics the cradleboard worn by Soaring Lark. This sight prompts Clemens to summarily observe "that a weakness for doll-babies is not a result of education, but an instinct, which comes as natural to any species of girl as keeping [a] clothing store does to a jew"—reflecting the degree to which essentialist stereotypes about gender and ethnicity informed his youthful worldview. The analogy, conflating the "natural" instincts of Jews and women, is of course hyperbolic, one of the letter's many punch lines; nonetheless, the ease with which Clemens articulates this sweeping generalization reflects the entitlement of his position as a white male as well as the intolerance and opacity of perception mentioned in his 1876 letter to Jacob Burrough.

These indigenous "Princesses" play dual roles in Clemens's letter—first, as uncouth interlopers who disrupt his breakfast with a friend, and second, as participants in a lively game of high-stakes poker. Resting their elbows on the window sill, they thrust their heads into the room where the men sit "like three very ancient and smoky portraits trying to get out of their frame." This simile evokes the cultural lens through which the writer viewed Indians—as antiquated, two-dimensional images, static and unreal—and simultaneously conveys his irritation at their refusal to remain within the parameters of this prescribed role. The ravenous women scrutinize each morsel the men ingest, while simultaneously voicing their bafflement at Anglo-American dietary habits:

> They examined the breakfast leisurely, and criticised it in their own
> tongue; they pointed at each article of food, with their long, skinny
> fingers, and asked each other's opinion about it; and they kept an
> accurate record of each mouthful we took, and figured up the total,
> occasionally. After awhile the Gentle Wild Cat remarked: "May be
> whity man no heap eat um grass-hopper?" (their principal article of
> diet, ma,) and John replied: "May be whity man no heap like um grass-
> hopper—*savvy!*" . . . We held further conversation with them, of the
> same interesting character, after which we closed the "talk" by giving
> them a bar of soap and a cup of coffee for breakfast, and requesting
> them to leave, which they did, after they had begged a few old shirts,
> boots, hats, etc., and a deck of cards. (L1, 178)

In *Washoe Rambles*, De Quille records a remarkably similar incident but from a more compassionate perspective. One evening as he and his two companions prepare dinner,

> Our Indian neighbors began to drop in: first came two old men . . . then
> three squaws—old, ugly, and ragged—with several small children. As

we eat our meal, these gather about and watch with eager, hungry eyes, each mouthful, and with their silent longing, seem to rebuke us for having such frightfully good appetites; their looks say plainer than words—"Will these selfish *Waamoogenas* devour all?" We would like to give the whole hungry crew a square meal, but it is impossible; we can only give each a small taste of bread.[63]

Unlike Clemens, De Quille regards his indigenous observers as "neighbors"; realizing their desperate hunger, his impulse is to feed them all, although the miners' limited provisions permit only a bit of bread. Citing Jesus's dictum, "It is more blessed to give than to receive," he distributes food freely, without anger or resentment, throughout the journey. In one such instance, De Quille marvels at the Indians' communal ethos, noting that when he offers a child some supper, "instead of sitting down and devouring it all himself he divided it with his friends, giving all hands, young and old, a taste, reserving but a few mouthfuls for himself. It was in vain that we gave him a fresh supply, telling him to eat it himself. As soon as he received it, it was distributed among the crowd."[64] The writers' disparate responses to Indian beggary reflect a key difference in their perception of racial Otherness. Encountering a cultural convention that he does not understand, Clemens reacts with anger and impatience, dismissing the Indians as nuisances, whereas the more inquisitive, charitably minded De Quille indulges them as "red brothers" and "friends"—perhaps because of his Quaker upbringing.

Similarly, in the close of Clemens's March 1862 letter, he characterizes the princesses' decision to "poker a little" after breakfast as proof that "these Indians are inveterate gamblers." This generalization is counterpointed by De Quille's statement in *The Big Bonanza* that some Paiutes enjoyed gaming while others did not: "Young Winnemucca [Numaga] never gambled, but old Winnemucca was an inveterate gambler—that is, among his own people. The Piutes do not gamble with white men."[65] In their pictorial history of *Virginia City and the Big Bonanza*, Comstock historians Ronald M. and Susan A. James explain that "gambling was a popular precontact diversion for [the] Northern Paiutes, and they continued the practice [after colonization] . . . even though they borrowed card playing from the newcomers."[66] These activities, as documented in an archival photograph of Paiutes playing cards in a vacant Virginia City lot (fig. 6), typically took place on the outskirts of towns and mining camps in plain view of Anglo-American passersby—suggesting that such sights would have been familiar to both Clemens and De Quille. The indigenous card players depicted are a mixed, multigenerational group, whose attire is a distinctive

FIGURE 6.   Paiutes gambling. Courtesy of the Historic Fourth Ward School Museum and Archives, Virginia City, Nevada.

blend of Western and traditional styles. While their jackets, hats, and shoes are no doubt secondhand castoffs, they seem in reasonably good repair and bear little resemblance to Clemens's exaggerated description of the decrepit garments worn by either Chief Hoop-de-Doodle-doo or his wives.

In Clemens's letter, the Euro-American clothing the Princesses acquire through begging proves most useful as ante. They divest themselves of hats, boots, socks, and shirts as the excitement of the card game mounts, and Soaring Lark—believing that her victory is assured—decides to unstrap her son from his cradleboard and add him to the pile, only to be trumped by Gentle Wild Cat, who reveals her winning hand of four aces. De Quille also acknowledges the existence of compulsive gambling among Indians but characterizes it as an individual shortcoming rather than as a universal trait: "Old Winnemucca has been known to lose all his ponies, all his blankets and arms, and in fact, everything he possessed, down to a breech-clout, at a single sitting. He is a good-natured, kind-hearted man, but not a man remarkable for either wisdom or cunning."[67] Clemens, on the other hand, turns his comic anecdote into a cautionary tale, warning his mother that the information will be useful "for future reference . . . if you ever turn Injun, for then your dusky compatriots will not think much of you if you don't gamble. Now, if you are acquainted with any romantic young ladies or gentlemen who dote on these loves of Indians, send them out here before the disease strikes in" (L1, 179). In pathologizing the romantic eastern perception of indigenous peoples, the writer legitimates his intolerance by insisting on the accuracy of his depiction.

"LO! THE POOR INDIAN"

The iconic image of the noble savage as a "natural" man, uncorrupted by science or education and living in harmony with the universe, was immortalized by Alexander Pope in his 1734 poem "An Essay on Man": "Lo! the poor Indian, whose untutor'd mind/ Sees God in clouds, or hears him in the wind; / His soul, proud science never taught to stray / Far as the solar walk or milky way; / Yet simple nature to his hope has giv'n, / Behind the cloud topp'd hill, an humbler heav'n."[68] Pope uses the archaic exclamation "Lo!" here in its conventional sense of "behold"—a command to contemplate the Indian as an extraordinary, albeit simple, being. When the epithet entered popular American consciousness more than a century later, however, it acquired a new, pejorative meaning. The phrase appeared as a chapter title in Horace Greeley 's *An Overland Journey* (1860), describing his encounters with bands of Osage, Potawatamie, and Arapaho west of the Missouri River en route to San Francisco. Invoking (though not explicitly naming) Pope, he notes that "the poetic Indian—the Indian of Cooper and Longfellow—is only visible to the poet's eye. To the prosaic observer, the average Indian of the woods and prairies is a being who does little credit to human nature—a slave of appetite and sloth, never emancipated from the tyranny of one animal passion save by the more ravenous demands of another."[69] This harsh view is tempered by a belief in the Indians' capacity for improvement through the adoption of Euro-American values and habits; within two decades, Greeley predicts, "conscientious, humane [and] capable" settlers could transform "an indolent savage tribe ... into a civilized Christian community," ominously adding that "otherwise [their] extermination is inexorably certain, and cannot long be postponed."[70]

On the western frontier, "Lo!" gradually morphed from a verb into a proper noun, becoming a generic name for an indigenous male. An 1863 clipping in one of Orion's scrapbooks concerning the first annual fair of the "Washoe Agricultural, Mining, and Mechanical Society" illustrates this shift. Beneath a list of the organization's officers—which included "Samuel L. Clemens, of Storey County" in the role of Recording Secretary—the article uses the heading "Lo! The Poor Indian" to introduce Reuben Parker, a 14-year-old boy from an unnamed California tribe, whose drawings were displayed at the event: "Here [are] the first rude efforts of the swarthy hand to shadow forth the gleams of art that struggle within the untutored mind. . . . [With] only the famous 'Mustard Liniment' label for his inspiration, with no other tutor than his own dim and dusky fancy, the result is indeed surprising. . . . These specimens are chiefly valuable for the proof they bear that the creative power born of genius is confined to no race or clime."[71]

Other frontier usages were more overtly derisive. An 1864 article published in the Galena, Kansas *Daily Gazette* states, "Well, Mr. Pope, if your man 'Lo' was a poor Indian, please show us some of the rich ones. We have never seen them. There have been some twenty or thirty Winnebago Indians, squaws, and papooses traveling about the streets . . . during the last week, looking about as poor and God-forsaken as the law allows."[72] Four years later, the *Colorado Weekly Chieftain* prefaced a report about the "devilish ingenuity [of Indians] in taking scalps from the unprotected settlers, and running off stock from the energetic and enterprising rancheros of Southern Colorado" with this parody of the poet's lines: "Lo, the poor Indian, who, untutored, feeds / On locusts, beetles, frogs, and centipedes,"[73] echoing Clemens' contemptuous remarks about Hoop's dietary habits.

Given the epithet's ubiquity, it is not surprising that both Clemens and De Quille used it, though for markedly different purposes. Clemens begins his 1862 letter to his mother with a satirical quatrain inspired by Pope: "Lo! the poor Indian, whose untutored mind, / Impels him, in order to raise the wind, / To double the pot and go it blind, / Until he's busted, you know," explaining "I wrote the three last lines of that poem, Ma, and Daniel Webster wrote the other one—which was really very good for Daniel, considering that he wasn't a natural poet" (L1, 174). The lyric, which anticipates his account of the Princesses' poker game, also frames the letter's overarching intent—to subvert the sentimental eastern tendency to portray Indians as "lordly sons of the forest" sweeping across the landscape "on their fiery steeds."

De Quille also uses Pope's exclamation as a proper noun, entitling a chapter in *The Big Bonanza* "Concerning 'Lo' and his Family." The presence of quotation marks around the name, however, suggests his awareness of the racialized stereotype it signifies. "Lo" never appears in the chapter itself; De Quille instead individuates the various natives he depicts, identifying them with nicknames assigned by the settlers such as "Smoke Creek Sam, the Piute detective" and an elderly Virginia City couple dubbed "Adam" and "Eve." According to Sarah Winnemucca's biographer, Sally Zanjani, "De Quille was a generally accurate witness"[74] of life on the Comstock; his chapter on "Lo" thus matter-of-factly reports on the urban foraging of frugal indigenous "housewives" who gather "half-rotten fruit, wilted turnips, carrots, and other vegetables good for their families." After watching a group devour this "vegetable garbage," De Quille engages in a self-styled experiment that displays a remarkable understanding of the culturally relativistic standards regarding the foods deemed edible by disparate groups. He purchases a handful of shrimp and savors them in front of the Paiutes, who react with horror:

> "Just try this one, Sam," said I.
> "No!" said Sam, decidedly; "glash-hop, purty-good; klicket, me eat um; scorpion-bug, heap no good. Scorpium make Injun man high up sick!"
> I now saw it all and was not so much surprised at the astonishment and disgust shown by the whole crowd of redskins. Knowing nothing about shrimps, all supposed that I was eating scorpions, a poisonous reptile very abundant in Nevada and closely resembling the shrimp.[75]

Through this prank, De Quille reverses the hierarchy of the ethnocentric gaze, demonstrating the logic whereby his food choice is offensive to the Paiutes. The relativism of his perspective calls the binaries of "savagery" and "civilization" into question and stands in contrast to Clemens's emphatic rejection of grasshoppers as a foodstuff in his March 1862 letter.

THE OWENS VALLEY INDIAN WAR

In early April 1862, Clemens headed southeast to Aurora, a mining camp on the territory's disputed western boundary with California. Over the next three months he found himself in close proximity to an outbreak of violence between the Owens Valley Indians and Anglo-American ranchers whose cattle herds, imported to feed the local miners, had destroyed the wild plants that the natives depended on for survival. Desperate for food, the Indians began killing the cattle during the winter, provoking a series of escalating clashes with settlers. Fears of war roiled the region, filling communities like Aurora with unease. On 25 March 1862, Warren Wasson telegraphed Governor Nye, then vacationing in San Francisco, requesting permission to travel to Owens Valley on a peacekeeping mission. Nye approved, authorizing an escort of fifty soldiers led by Lieutenant Herman Noble of Fort Churchill, along with a shipment of guns and ammunition "for the use of Aurora citizens" (L1, 198n8). On 7 April the group arrived in Owens Valley, where they encountered a militia led by a private citizen, "Colonel" William Mayfield, which had joined forces with the Second Cavalry California Volunteers, commanded by Lieutenant-Colonel George Evans;

according to Wasson's official report to Nye on 20 April, "We made known to them our business and instructions, but found little or no encouragement to make peace with the Indians, their desire being only to exterminate them."[76] Despite Wasson's best diplomatic efforts, a skirmish ensued on 9 April, in which Mayfield and a number of other whites, including Aurora sheriff N.F. Scott, were killed.

Clemens's April 1862 correspondence with his brother back in Carson City—aptly characterized as "businesslike and humorless"[77] by Orion's biographer Philip Fanning—documents a rare moment of direct, proactive engagement in territorial politics. Amidst updates about miscellaneous mining claims and insistent pleas to send money, he notifies the acting governor of breaking news concerning the Owens Valley conflict well in advance of any official communications from the field. On 13 April, four days after the so-called Battle of Mayfield Canyon, he writes,

> Wasson got here night before last, "from the wars." Tell Lockhart [the newly-commissioned Indian agent] he is not wounded and not killed— is altogether unhurt. He says the whites left their stone fort before he and Lieut. Noble got there. A large amount of provisions and ammunition which they left behind them fell into the hands of the Indians. They had a pitched battle with the savages, some fifty miles from the fort, in which Scott (sheriff,) and another man were killed. . . . Evans assumed the chief command—and the next morning the forces were divided into three parties, and marched against the enemy. Col. Mayfield was killed, and Sargeant Gillespie also. Noble's Corporal was wounded. The California troops went back home, and Noble remained, to help drive the stock over here. And, as Cousin Sally Dillard says, this is all that I know about the fight. (L1, 185)

This detailed description, deemed a "condensed, but essentially accurate account" of the battle by the editors at the Mark Twain Project, indicates that Wasson regarded Clemens as an ally and confidant, entrusting him with the responsibility of conveying this important news to his brother. Sam dispatched the task with admirable efficiency, but true to form, he could not resist introducing a touch of levity. His allusion to "Cousin Sally Dillard" refers to a popular 1840s burlesque in which an attorney attempts to solicit testimony from a wildly digressive witness, only to eventually realize that he in fact knows nothing about the case (L1, 187–88n4). In comparing himself to Sally, Clemens playfully impeaches his own reliability and also distances himself from the gravity of the conflict so that he can proceed to more pressing matters—informing Orion of investment opportunities in various local mines. Nonetheless, the spare, matter-of-fact tone of Clemens's narrative suggests a straightforward transcription of the agent's conversation, with one telling exception—the allusion to Indians as "savages." Wasson's letters and official reports scrupulously avoid this pejorative, instead using more neutral terms such as *tribes* and *people*. His respect for—and sympathy with—Indians as "a much abused race" is evident in his official report to Governor Nye on 20 April:

> The Indians have dug ditches and irrigated nearly all the arable land in [this] section of the country, and live by its products. They have been repeatedly told by officers of the government that they should have the exclusive possession of these lands, and they are now fighting to maintain that possession. . . . At a great expense to the government they were driven over the Sierra Nevadas from Tulare valley, and having taken up their abode here, along Owens River, as a place of last resort, they will fight to the extremity in defence of their homes. Lieutenant Noble conferred with me, and we had agreed as to the course to be pursued till we met Colonel Evans, who then assumed the command. This re-enforcement ruined all our plans [for peaceful negotiations]. We might have done better—we certainly could not have done worse.[78]

Understandably, these progressive views were not well received in Aurora; a local newspaper, the *Esmeralda Star*, praised the courage and leadership of Evans's men while conceding the futility of their efforts, adding that "Mr. Wasson's sentiments in many particulars cannot be corroborated—and have done great injustice to the participants of the Owens River troubles."[79] From his vantage point in Virginia City, De Quille disagreed, writing in the *Golden Era*,

> We have been trying to talk our selves into an Indian war. There has been some trouble at Owen River, though as far as I can learn, both from whites and Indians, the whites were to blame; but people won't listen to anything but shooting the first Indians they can find. People living on the outskirts of the settlements are much given to magnifying every move of the Indians which they do not comprehend into a very suspicious circumstance, indicative of a determination on the part of the Indians to kill, burn, and destroy, consequently they are continually sending in reports of impending danger. . . . The Indians say they have no wish to fight, nor do I think they have, unless crowded into it.[80]

Within a day of conversing with Clemens, Wasson set off for the Walker River reservation, where he sought to allay the Paiutes' concerns about the possible outbreak of widespread racial hostilities. Lieutenant Noble and his men meanwhile remained in Aurora for approximately two more weeks, both to oversee the safe relocation of the cattlemen and their stock and to ease tensions between Union and Confederate factions in the region. As

Sam informed Orion in a letter written on 24–25 April, he personally assisted with the latter endeavor, doing his small part to maintain social order:

> I went down with Lieut. Noble, awhile ago, to get Wasson's order conveying the guns of the "Esmeralda Rifles" [which Nye had requisitioned from Fort Churchill] to his (N's) custody. The people here regret being deprived of these arms, as the Secessionists have declared that in case Cal. accedes to the new boundaries, Gov. Nye shall not assume jurisdiction here. . . . All this has been told the Governor in a letter sent from here by mail. If that letter is still in Carson (or the P.O.,) express it to Frisco. It's in a white mail envelop thus directed: "His Excellency Gov. Nye, Carson City, Nevada Territory." (true copy: teste.) (L1, 197)

Clemens's letter is the private equivalent of a journalistic "scoop"—warning his brother of the region's volatility in advance of an official communication sent to—but not yet received by—Nye. Moreover, in ordering Orion to track down the letter and express it to San Francisco, he briefly steps out of his role as sibling and private citizen into the arena of territorial governance.

Sporadic skirmishes between the Indians and soldiers continued into the summer, casting a pall over Aurora throughout most of Clemens's stay. Only after the establishment of a permanent military installation—Camp Independence—in July 1862 was Wasson able to negotiate a temporary truce with local tribal leaders. Violence flared up in the region again the following spring; however, by that time Sam had relocated from Aurora to Virginia City, and the jurisdiction of Esmeralda County—including the Owens River Valley—had legally shifted to California, largely as the result of acting governor Orion Clemens's efforts to resolve a long-standing boundary dispute with Nevada Territory.[81] The memory of this conflict apparently lingered in the writer's mind, resurfacing as a glancing allusion in "Aurelia's Unfortunate Young Man," published in the *Californian* on 22 October 1864. This story, framed as a response to the quandary of a lovelorn woman uncertain about marrying her betrothed, chronicles the "disastrous process of reduction" whereby the hapless Williamson Breckinridge Caruthers loses one body part after another owing to a series of illnesses and accidents. Deprived of both his arms and legs, and blind in one eye, Caruthers falls victim to one last injury: "There was but one man scalped by the Owens River Indians last year. . . . He was hurrying home with happiness in his heart, when he lost his hair forever, and in that hour of bitterness he almost cursed the mistaken mercy that had spared his head" (SNO, 255).

This detail, exploited for its morbid humor, reflects the complex ambivalence of Twain's stance—his simultaneous cognizance of, and casual indifference to, the dispossession of indigenous peoples in the West.

A second, more oblique reference to the Owens Valley conflict occurs in chapter 39 of *Roughing It*, in which Twain reminisces about an excursion he and Calvin Higbie took to Mono Lake—about thirty miles southwest of the Aurora mining camp—during the summer of 1862. After days of trekking through the hot, dusty desert, the men hire a "half-tamed Indian" to launder their clothes; however, this mundane task yields unexpectedly terrifying results when the stove on which he heats the wash water explodes:

> Nearly a third of the shed roof over our heads was destroyed, and one of the stove lids, after cutting a small stanchion half in two in front of the Indian, whizzed between us and drove partly through the weatherboarding beyond. I was as white as a sheet and as weak as a kitten and speechless. But the Indian betrayed no trepidation, no distress, not even discomfort. He simply stopped washing, leaned forward and surveyed the clean, blank ground a moment, and then remarked: "Mph! Dam stove heap gone!" (RI, 254–55)

The men later identify the blast's cause as a forgotten cache of gunpowder stowed inside the oven by local citizens "at a time when an Indian attack had been expected"—a curiously generic reference given Clemens's firsthand knowledge of the racial violence that had afflicted the region only several months earlier. His recollection of the incident ignores the war's broader sociohistorical context, focusing instead on the solipsistic "fact that it came so near 'instigating' my funeral" (RI, 254).

ORION CLEMENS, EX OFFICIO SUPERINTENDENT OF INDIAN AFFAIRS

Throughout Clemens's sojourn in Nevada Territory, he remained in close—if occasionally fractious—contact with his older brother, as his 1862–63 correspondence from Aurora, Virginia City, and San Francisco demonstrates. They speculated in mining stock together, exchanged updates about the latest, most promising leads, and took turns sharing these developments with Jane Clemens and their sister Pamela back at home. Although Orion's moralistic pronouncements about Sam's "dissipation" strained their relationship, they maintained an active interest in the progress of one another's careers. Sam was doubtlessly aware of the challenges his sibling faced in the role of acting governor from December 1862 to July 1863, when James Nye abruptly left the territory for an extended stay in New York.

As ex officio superintendent of Indian affairs, Orion conscientiously sought to preserve peaceful relations between natives and whites. On 3 February 1863, he contacted the auditor of the US Treasury for advice regarding a particularly divisive issue:

> There is dissatisfaction in some localities among the Indians, caused by the whites cutting down the pine nut trees, which furnish almost the sole dependence of the Indians for food. In view of the two facts that the wood is essential for the whites, and the pine nuts essential to the Indians, I would be glad to know what are my powers and duties in the premises.
>
> I told the harmless Washoe chief who complained to me, and who said "after while Indian hungry," that I would write to the great chief at Washington, eastward over the mountains, three thousand miles away, and hear in two moons maybe three moons, and then tell him. A promise made to an Indian is expected by him to be fulfilled, and I hope to be able to do something within the specified time.
>
> I have information accompanied by a request for arms from the Humboldt mining region, that the miners are likely to come in collision with the Pah-Utes, from the same cause—cutting down the pine nut trees. This is a spirited, intelligent, fearless tribe. They are reasonably patient and willing to work, but formidable as enemies, from their number and warlike character.[82]

Despite Orion's use of almost comically clichéd paternalistic rhetoric, the letter shrewdly identifies competition over scarce natural resources as the root cause of conflict between the region's Indians and whites. He rejects the precedence of Anglo-American settlers in the hierarchy of respective needs, acknowledging that the piñon pine is equally essential to both races for different reasons. This recognition of indigenous rights stands in marked contrast to the sentiments expressed in "Our Country," an anonymous paean to Manifest Destiny published in a December 1863 issue of the Gold Hill *Daily News*. Exultantly proclaiming "It is all ours" in the opening line of each stanza, the poem hails the triumph of colonial domination "from the placid Western sea / To the emerald Eastern slopes ... by the ages' stern demand, ours by the gift of God,"[83] with no mention of the existence—let alone displacement—of the continent's aboriginal inhabitants.

Although Orion has often been characterized as "inept and pathetic"[84] by generations of literary scholars, this document attests to both his competence and proactive leadership. He refuses to dismiss the Indians as "savages," viewing them instead as people worthy of his attention and respect.

He listens sympathetically to the grievances of the "harmless" Washoe chief and seeks redress on the basis of moral principle rather than fear of retribution. Moreover, in reminding the Treasury official of the importance of fulfilling any promise made to Indians in a timely manner, Orion displays at least a rudimentary understanding of the primacy and power accorded to words in native oral culture. He also knowledgeably differentiates the Northern Paiutes and the Washoes, explaining that the former are more numerous and "warlike," while simultaneously commending their forbearance, work ethic, and intelligence—traits typically associated with civilized behavior.

Orion's quarterly report to William P. Dole, the federal commissioner of Indian affairs, written 2 July 1863, underscores his belief in the potential civilization and assimilation of Nevada's indigenous tribes:

> [Mr. Lockhart] is now preparing to teach the Indians to cultivate their reservations. They are peaceable, quiet, able, and willing to learn to work like white men. They voluntarily about our towns seek for work. Very little outlay is needed for gratuities of any kind to the Indians, and presents of any thing but food and clothing are worthless for any purpose. Give them a chance to work for themselves, with tools and instruction, and they will ask very little from the Government.[85]

This view would persist long after Orion's years in Nevada; his 1892 poem "The Reformed Savage" recalls the violence of colonial conquest through harrowing images of burning wigwams, screaming children, and soldiers "hunt[ing] human game," and explicitly condemns the corruption of federal agents "who fostered war to fatten greed," stealing Indian annuities in order to build "their own gaudy mansions . . . with marble fronts that seek the skies." Our nation's shameful "night of wrong," he declares, is now passing away due to the benevolent efforts of Christian missionaries: "They teach the heathen at our side / The scalping-knife to cast aside / The Nation pays for land with gold / That helps the savage mind unfold / And gather strength before undreamed, / Behold the savage man redeemed!"[86]

The progressive ethos that defined Orion's leadership as superintendent of Indian affairs is perhaps best illustrated in a request made to the treasury auditor on 10 March 1863: "I enclose with my vouchers and account for the month of February . . . a bill for vaccinating fifty-four Washoe Indians, which I have promised to pay if furnished with the money and instructed to do so. I hope the bill will be allowed and paid, as it was done for the purpose of preventing the spread of the disease, by vaccinating the Indians in the immediate vicinity of five Indians sick with it, several of whom died."[87]

Orion presents this petition to his superior in a deferential yet subtly asser-
tive manner; he does not seek *permission* to inoculate the Washoe, but
rather ex post facto reimbursement of the cost of administering the vaccine.
While careful not to overstep the limits of his authority—promising to pay
the bill only "if instructed to do so"—Orion is also unwavering in his conviction that inoculating the Indians was the proper course of action from
both a public health standpoint and a humanitarian one. The moral imperative underlying his actions is clear.

This incident seems to have inspired Twain's single most compassionate
statement about Indians in the *Enterprise* during his residence in Nevada
Territory. His "local column" of 25 February 1863 includes, among a series
of miscellaneous reports on the recent firemen's ball and a new addition to
"Mr. Melville's school," the following item:

> SMALL POX.—From Carson we learn, officially, that Dr. Munckton has
> been sent down to Pine Nut Springs to look after some cases of small
> pox, reported as existing among the Washoe Indians there. It is said that
> three men and a mahala are afflicted with it; the doctor intends
> vaccinating their attendants and warning the other Indians to keep
> away. Capt. Jo says one of the Indians caught the disease from a shirt
> given to him by a white man. We do not believe that any man would do
> such a thing as that maliciously, but at the same time, any man is
> censurable who is so careless as to leave infected clothing lying about
> where these poor devils can get hold of it. The commonest prudence
> ought to suggest the destruction of such dangerous articles. (ETS1, 406)

Although Twain does not identify his "official" Carson City sources,
they most likely were Orion and Jacob Lockhart. He describes the outbreak
as it unfolded in real time, identifying both its precise location and the
name of the physician sent to care for the afflicted. In contrast to his brother's request to the treasury auditor six days later, Twain reports that the
doctor "intends" to vaccinate the families of the infected individuals, indicating that this life-saving measure had not yet been implemented. His
diction is also noteworthy: rather than characterizing the sick as "savages,"
he refers to them respectfully as "men and a mahala"—a term meaning
"woman" in the language of the Yokuts tribe of central California as well as
"tender" in Hebrew and Arabic.

Twain presents Captain Jo's suspicions about the origin of the contagion
in a careful, evenhanded manner, defusing the implication of biological
warfare by focusing on the question of intentionality, thereby reframing
the issue in terms of fundamental human decency rather than race. In contrast to his satiric depiction of Chief Hoop-de-doodle-do a year earlier, he

also does not fault the natives for scavenging cast-off clothing but blames the negligence of the anonymous individual who left the shirt "lying about," deeming such irresponsible behavior "censurable." But most significantly, the emotional tug of Twain's phrase "these poor devils" bespeaks a flicker of solicitude for Indians not found elsewhere in his early sketches. For a moment, the blinders of indifference slip, allowing the writer to see— and pity—these indigenous victims of "one of the most communicable . . . and deadliest"[88] of Old World pathogens as fellow human beings.

HABITUATING RESISTANCE

Rather than signaling the onset of an epiphany in Twain's views regarding Indians, however, this 1863 expression of sympathy was unfortunately discrete and short-lived. Two months later he published a story in the *Enterprise* called "Horrible Affair" that recounted a rumor that five Indians had recently suffocated in a mining tunnel sealed up by local citizens to prevent the escape of a murderer who had hidden there. In this instance, the writer's apparent compassion—reflected in his hope that "the story may prove a fabrication . . . [rather than] a dark and terrible reality"—proves hollow, the setup for a broad punchline:

> The next day a strong posse went up, rolled away the stones from the mouth of the sepulchre, went in and found five dead Indians!—three men, one squaw and one child, who had gone in there to sleep, perhaps, and been smothered by the foul atmosphere after the tunnel had been closed up. We still hope the story may prove a fabrication, notwithstanding the positive assurance we have received that it is entirely true. The intention of the citizens was good, but the result was most unfortunate. To shut up a murderer in a tunnel was well enough, but to leave him there all night was calculated to impair his chances for a fair trial—the principle was good, but the application was unnecessarily "hefty." We have given the above story for truth—we shall continue to regard it as such until it is disproven. (ETS1, 246–47)

The biblical resonance of Twain's diction—"roll[ing] away the stones . . . from the mouth of the sepulchre"—establishes an ironic counterpoint between the empty tomb found by the apostles after Christ's resurrection and the remains discovered inside the Gold Hill tunnel. The writer amplifies the incident's magnitude only to comically subvert it several lines later by announcing that the "most unfortunate" result of the citizens' actions is not the deaths of five innocent people but rather the murderer's diminished chances for an impartial trial. Unlike the smallpox victims at Pine Nut

Springs, these Indians are not human beings but mere props, objectified and unreal, used to advance a cavalier joke. In ignoring the natives' motive for seeking shelter within this alien, unnatural space, Twain fails to recognize the desperation of their circumstances. Harried and dispossessed by the encroachments of settler colonialism, they literally have nowhere else to go. Even hidden beneath the earth's surface, they cannot escape the destructive impact of Anglo-American dominion.

Clemens's indifference—or metaphorical blindness—to the plight of western indigenous peoples was, in some respects, rooted in the squalor of their living conditions. Beginning with his 1862 description of Chief Hoop-de-doodle-doo, who sheds (then promptly eats) the prodigiously sized vermin that flourish on his unwashed body, the lack of hygiene he observed among Indians reinforced their Otherness, foreclosing any possibility of empathetic identification. Over time, this wry aversion deepened into revulsion, perhaps in response to his own rising socioeconomic status and geographic distance from the West. As Twain recalled in *Roughing It*, published nearly a decade after leaving Nevada, the filth of the "Goshoot" Indians—"hoard[ed and accumulate[ed] for months, years, and even generations, according to the age of the proprietor" (RI, 127)—filled him with "nausea" and "disgust." His loathing was, moreover, not restricted to the degraded primitivism of these so-called "Diggers," but included all native groups: "Wherever one finds an Indian tribe he has only found Goshoots more or less modified by circumstances and surroundings—but Goshoots, after all. They deserve pity, poor creatures; and they can have mine—at this distance. Nearer by, they never get anybody's" (RI, 129). The peremptory sweep of this conclusion distorts the complexity of the territory's racial climate in the 1860s, where Indians were in fact regarded with sympathy by some of Clemens's closest associates—Orion, Dan De Quille, Warren Wasson, and Jacob Lockhart. His statement is not the product of a flawed or selective memory but rather the culmination of geographical movements that took the writer progressively farther away from firsthand contact with indigenous peoples. The next chapter explores Twain's evolving representation of Indians between 1862 and 1872, a decade during which he left the Comstock, first for San Francisco and the Sandwich Islands, then eastward for Europe and the Holy Land, before settling into a respectable existence as a husband, father, and businessman in Buffalo, New York.

3. Indians Imagined, 1862–72

Mark Twain's infamous 1862 hoax, "Petrified Man," is in many respects a paradox—on the one hand, the slightest of squibs, a mere paragraph in length, yet simultaneously an urtext, the seed from which his literary career blossomed. Published anonymously some four months before the writer first used his celebrated nom du plume in the Virginia City *Territorial Enterprise* on 3 February 1863, Clemens could easily have disavowed its existence, but in fact did just the opposite—repeatedly claiming ownership of the piece both in private and public. On 21 October 1862, just two weeks after the hoax appeared, he wrote to Orion asking, "Between us now—did you see that squib of mine headed 'Petrified Man?'" (L1, 242). Far more significant, however, are three later declarations of authorship made between 1868 and 1875, published respectively in the *Territorial Enterprise* (as part of his Letters from Washington series), *Galaxy* magazine, and *Sketches, New and Old*. In each of these texts, Twain "spins" the story of the hoax's creation and reception as a means of mythicizing his western literary origins and touting his skill with language. To this end, his 1868 *Enterprise* Letter from Washington extols the imaginative license afforded by the free-wheeling atmosphere of early territorial journalism—wherein "news" was routinely invented, unencumbered by considerations of accuracy or fact: "To find a petrified man, or break a stranger's leg, or cave an imaginary mine, or discover some dead Indians in a Gold Hill tunnel, or massacre a family at Dutch Nick's, were feats and calamities that *we* never hesitated about devising when the public needed matters of thrilling interest for breakfast. The seemingly tranquil ENTERPRISE office was a ghastly factory of slaughter, mutilation and general destruction in those days."[1]

Discussing the hoax two years later in the *Galaxy*, Twain's emphasis shifts away from the circumstances of its composition to the power of the

93

written word to deceive a gullible public. Indeed, his claim about the "innocent good faith" with which "Petrified Man" was received and widely reprinted is so exaggerated that it qualifies as a metahoax:[2] "nobody ever perceived the satire . . . at all," he announces in mock despair. Instead, the story was "copied and guilelessly glorified," and the petrified man "steadily and implacably penetrated territory after territory, State after State, and land after land, till he swept the great globe and culminated in sublime and unimpeached legitimacy in the august London *Lancet*" (SNO, 240–42). This tongue-in-cheek account of the text's ostensible "failure" of course attests to its resounding success, as well as to the ingenuity of its creator.

But "Petrified Man" may reveal more about Twain's literary identity than he consciously intended. Following the author's lead, scholars have long interpreted it as an ahistorical document, testimony to the play of Clemens's rich, unfettered imagination; however, I would like to propose an alternate reading, grounded in the volatile geopolitical reality of Nevada Territory in the years immediately after the 1859 discovery of the Comstock Lode. The region was a contested landscape, rife with interracial tension over competing claims of land usage and patrimony that periodically erupted into bloodshed, most notably during the 1860 Pyramid Lake War. When contextualized within this contemporary pattern of "persistent localized violence,"[3] Twain's story of a mysterious stone man "glued . . . to the bed rock upon which he sat, as with a cement of adamant" (ETS1, 159) found by a group of silver miners who seek to blast him from his rightful place using the latest western technology, assumes an uncannily iconographic quality. His joke—no longer idle—in fact serves to dramatize and advance the cultural script of Manifest Destiny.

THE FLUID IDENTITY OF "PETRIFIED MAN"

The petrified man's identity is obscure in the original squib; the writer offers little information regarding his history other than an approximate date of death—"about a century ago" (ETS1, 159). As Bruce Michelson observes in *Mark Twain on the Loose*, the mummy has "no name, no time, neither tribe nor race."[4] Yet as Clemens revisited the hoax in print over the next thirteen years, he made a number of contradictory pronouncements about the petrifaction's age and ethnicity that suggest the figure is aboriginal. This ex post facto revision of the mummy's identity culminates in True Williams's 1875 illustration in *Sketches, New and Old*, which depicts him as unmistakably native—hawk-nosed and clad in a breechcloth, with long flowing hair held in place by a headband. The artist's engraving not only visually complements Twain's text but also exposes its underlying political meaning—a supplanting of the Indian in the landscape by symbolically relegating him to the past. Moreover, as an ossified relic—primordial and inert—this nameless individual portends the fate of his entire race. In this manner, the hoax imaginatively deprives Native Americans of agency, eliminating them as viable contenders for control of the West.

The setting in which Twain places his mummy—"the mountains south of Gravelly Ford"—is integral to this historicized reinterpretation. Situated on the Humboldt River just west of Ruby Valley near the present-day town of Beowawe (the Paiute word for "gate"), the rugged topography of Gravelly Ford marked the traditional boundary between Paiute and Shoshone hunting grounds; it was also a stop on the California Trail, one of the two major emigrant routes to the gold fields of the West. The record numbers of Anglo-Americans who passed through the area in the 1850s profoundly disrupted the subsistence economies of these tribes: "Emigrant parties, particularly their herds, consumed the grasses, seeds, and game that sustained these Great Basin Indians. Water sources also became jeopardized, not so much by outsiders' consumption as by their animals' defecation, while scarce timber and piñon pine fueled emigrant campfires."[5] This ecological devastation, as historian Ned Blackhawk has argued, unleashed "degenerate cycles of violence and reprisal" all along the overland routes. Indians "sought to keep whites from occupying their homelands [by] marauding those who ventured through them," while emigrants, in turn, often targeted approaching bands out of fear.[6] This pattern of escalating retribution is typified by a series of raids that occurred at Gravelly Ford, reaching a crisis point in September 1861, when four Anglo-American families were murdered there.[7] Bloodshed was so prevalent on this portion of the California Trail that on 2 January 1862, the inhabitants of Unionville petitioned that "a United States fort be established . . . at or near Gravelly Ford": "Numerous Indian outrages were committed on the emigrants in that vicinity last season; and the whole region up to the Humboldt and north of Oregon will be prospected and explored by small parties next Summer; and it is necessary that they as well as the emigrants should have some protection against the hostile Indians, who have driven back prospecting parties . . . every Summer for the past four years."[8]

Given the demands placed on both military manpower and the Union Treasury by the outbreak of the Civil War, the federal government was slow in responding to this grassroots appeal for protection; it was not until nine months later—in September 1862—that construction began on Fort Ruby, some forty miles east of the ford.[9] In the interim, native depredations against emigrant trains continued unchecked; thus, it was hardly surprising when the news broke in late summer that yet another "terrible massacre" had occurred at Gravelly Ford. Notwithstanding the frequency of such occurrences, this incident elicited an unusual degree of public interest because of the macabre aura of indeterminacy surrounding it. Because no emigrants survived the attack, its exact date and precipitating causes were "enveloped in mystery." The "harrowing particulars" of what had transpired could only be imperfectly deduced from the grisly evidence at the scene itself, as described by Sacramento *Daily Union* correspondent D.E. Bushnell writing from Virginia City:

> On the 23d day of August, 1862 . . . the bodies of twelve human beings [two men, two women, and eight children] were found in a small mountain ravine, through which a stream ran, horribly and frightfully mangled and cut to pieces. The cold water running over them had prevented them from decay. When removed from the ravine, by pressing upon the wounds, the blood, apparently fresh, would gush from them. . . . [Their] bodies are now quietly resting in one grave near by the bubbling brooklet in which they had been concealed by their brutal butchers. They appear to have been sleeping when murdered. . . . The bodies are supposed to have lain about eight days when found.[10]

As one of the citizens charged with "removing, examining and burying" the dead, Bushnell was troubled not only by the horrific violence that had been inflicted upon these individuals but also by their anonymity. In death, they became tragic, enigmatic ciphers, deprived of identity, kinship, and place of origin, their loss unmourned except by strangers. "How many like these ill-fated beings," he mused, "have found their resting places between the homes they left and the homes they sought—leaving no one to tell the history of their untimely end?" Hoping that readers might recognize—and thereby restore a modicum of dignity to—these nameless victims, Bushnell offered brief descriptions of the physical appearance and clothing of the party's presumed male leaders, along with the nature of his wounds: "one man, with dark hair, twenty-five years of age, cut through back part of the head and stabbed in the back, has an old scar on one leg below the knee, indicative of having been broken; another, thirty-five years of age, throat cut, bullet hole in back, dark hair, had on a blue jeans vest, checked shirt and new white woolen socks."[11]

The pathos of these meager details—an old scar, new socks—so woefully inadequate in resolving the mystery of the victims' identities—underscores both the futility of Bushnell's well-intentioned gesture and the shocking barbarity of the crime. Indeed, the massacre's inherently sensational qualities—the large number of murdered children, the uncanny preservation of corpses submerged in an icy stream for over a week, and the ghoulish marvel of "blood, apparently fresh" gushing from the wounds of the deceased—ensured widespread coverage of the incident, not only in the newspapers of Virginia City and the territorial capital, but also throughout California. Word of the attack also spread quickly through the more informal networks of communication, inciting much anger and speculation in the barrooms of local mining camps and trading posts.

By early September, reports concerning the Gravelly Ford massacre took a surreal turn when a Carson City editor published a rumor that its perpetrators were not Indians at all but rather "a large number of secessionists [who] had started across the Plains for Jefferson D's kingdom . . . and chosen to supply their smaller necessities in the same way that the said Jefferson D. supplies his larger necessities, viz., by stealing and murder."[12] Although this allegation was eventually discounted as a "fat hoax," the territorial government took the threat of Confederate guerillas fomenting mayhem in the mountains seriously. Governor James Nye sought the immediate assistance of Colonel Patrick Edward Connor, commander of the California Volunteers—a combined regiment of infantry and cavalry assigned to guard the overland mail route from Carson Valley to Salt Lake[13]—asking him to investigate the matter and punish those responsible. In mid-September, Connor dispatched an expedition to Gravelly Ford with explicit orders to "destroy every male Indian whom you may encounter in the vicinity of the late massacres. . . . *No prisoners will be taken.*"[14] This indiscriminate retaliation, resulting in the deaths of some twenty-four innocent Shoshone, was applauded in many western newspapers as "wise" and "well merited," and the Colonel himself boasted that the "lesson" administered to the natives would have "a salutary effect in checking future massacres."[15] According to Connor's biographer, Brigham D. Madsen, the genocidal policy that the officer pursued "against western Indians for the next three years was set at Gravelly Ford"[16]; in this respect, the reprisal presaged far bloodier clashes such as the 1863 Bear River massacre and disastrous Powder River expedition of 1865.

Despite its adverse implications for the US military's treatment of indigenous peoples, the Gravelly Ford incident registers today merely as a footnote in the annals of American history, eclipsed by other, more infamous atrocities like the massacres at Sand Creek and Wounded Knee. In 1862, however, the very name "Gravelly Ford"—as both a literal location and symbolic benchmark of appalling frontier violence—would have been instantly familiar to western readers in general and Sam Clemens in particular. The massacre occurred approximately eight weeks before the publication of "Petrified Man"—in other words, at the very moment he was embarking upon his career as a full-time journalist.

After months of fruitless struggle and deepening impoverishment in the southern Nevada mining camp of Aurora, Clemens informed his brother Orion on 7 August that he had accepted the post of local reporter for the *Territorial Enterprise* at twenty-five dollars a week but was uncertain about the starting date of his duties (L1, 233). While the writer's exact arrival in Virginia City cannot be pinpointed, a five-week gap in his correspondence suggests that he left Aurora soon after writing to an old Missouri friend, Billy Clagett, on 9 September and reached his destination 130 miles to the north toward the end of the month—after allegedly traversing the entire distance on foot.[17] During this time, it seems likely that he would have casually perused whatever newspapers came to hand, intent upon familiarizing himself with both the style and substance of territorial journalism before commencing his new position. Twain's cognizance of the Gravelly Ford massacre is thus virtually assured by the ubiquity with which the incident—in all its lurid detail—was reported during the late summer and fall of 1862.[18] From the quasi-miraculous liquefaction of the victims' blood to the specter of Confederate marauders disguised as Indians, the story's sensational elements would surely have piqued his imagination, unconsciously laying the conceptual foundation of the October hoax. After all, if the recent discovery of a dozen eerily preserved corpses in the mountains south of Gravelly Ford did not strain the limits of western readers' credulity, what other wonders might this remote location yield? Would the "news" that a mysterious stone mummy had been found there as well seem equally—if not more—plausible?

Beyond the common setting, "Petrified Man" shares several suggestive similarities with D. E. Bushnell's article announcing the discovery of the massacre victims' bodies. First, the factual tone and "patient belief-compelling detail" (SNO, 240) with which Twain describes the minutiae of the petrifaction's appearance—"Every limb and feature of the stony mummy was perfect, not even excepting the left leg, which has evidently been a wooden one during the lifetime of the owner"—stylistically echo the reporter's scrupulous enumeration of odd, distinguishing marks on the corpses. Also, in both accounts, water is the means of unnatural corporeal preservation, whether in the form of a frigid mountain stream in which the bodies were immersed or of a slow steady trickle that "dripped upon [the mummy] for ages from the crag above . . . coursed down his back and deposited a limestone sediment . . . which glued him to the bed rock upon which he sat."

Although the writer never mentioned the massacre in either his letters or later work, both his awareness of—and cavalier response to—the endemic violence then plaguing the western trails is illustrated by two unsigned articles published in the *Enterprise* on 1 October—just three days before the hoax's appearance. According to editors Edgar Marquess Branch and Robert H. Hirst, these pieces, "The Indian Troubles on the Overland Route" and "More Indian Troubles," along with a squib about the legendary Washoe zephyr entitled "A Gale," represent "the earliest extant articles that Clemens wrote for the newspaper" (ETS1, 389). Their composition, as the writer explained in his 1873 lecture "Roughing It on the Silver Frontier," was spurred by the absence of "real" news his first day on the job:

> Just as I was on the verge of despair . . . there came in a lot of emigrants with their wagon trains. They had been fighting with the Indians and got the worst of it. I got the names of their killed and wounded, and then . . . another train came in. They hadn't had any trouble and of course I was disappointed, but I did the best I could under the circumstances. I cross-questioned the boss emigrant and found that they were going right on through and wouldn't come back to make trouble . . . [so] I put that wagon train through the bloodiest Indian fight ever seen on the plains. They came out of that conflict covered with glory. The chief editor said he didn't want any better reporter than I was. I said: "You just bring on your Indians and fetch out your emigrants, leave me alone, and I will make the fur fly. I will hang a scalp on every sagebrush between here and the Missouri border."[19]

Twain's sketches are in fact grounded in two historical incidents that occurred in Idaho several weeks before the Gravelly Ford ambush—the 3 August attack against a so-called Methodist Train and another at "Massacre Rocks" on 9 August. His negative view of the region's indigenous inhabitants, whom he had vilified as "sons of the devil" in a letter to his mother earlier that spring (L1, 175), is reflected in the grim description of the bodies and goods left on the trail: "[The survivors] occasionally discovered the dead bodies of emigrants by the roadside; at one time twelve corpses were found, at another four, and at another two—all minus their scalps" (ETS1, 390). Twain refers to the agents of this hellish destruction as "Snake Indians"—another name for the Shoshone—perhaps to subliminally evoke biblical connotations of evil. Like serpents, these subhuman creatures strike without warning "in broad daylight," targeting unsuspecting victims who "apprehended no trouble" and therefore "made but a feeble resistance" against their attackers. Several lines later, he discusses another raid perpetrated by "the same tribe of uncivilized pirates" in which "all the men were killed except one" and "five young ladies were carried off," along with fifteen women and children. This link between Indians and pirates prefigures Tom Sawyer's fascination with such exotic outlaw figures more than a decade later.

On first glance, "Petrified Man" appears to have nothing to do with the dispossession of Native Americans; however, in examining the paradoxical statements the writer made concerning the figure's age, ethnicity, and race between 1862 and 1875, it becomes apparent that despite the stony rigidity of the mummy's pose, its identity is in fact fluid and unstable. While the mutability of the petrifaction's origins may be viewed simply as a source of amusement for its creator—a means of breathing new life into an old gag— a deeper, more troubling, cultural resonance can also be inferred from Twain's words. Approximately one month after the squib was originally published, he announced in a local column of the *Territorial Enterprise* that a "Mr. Herr Weisnicht" (know nothing) had recently "arrived in Virginia City from the Humboldt mines and regions beyond," bearing "the head and one foot of the petrified man, lately found in the mountains near Gravelly Ford" (ETS1, 392). These dismembered body parts are then submitted for the inspection of a "skillful assayer," whose analysis of "a small portion of dirt found under the nail of the great toe" expressly identifies the man as "a native of the Kingdom of New Jersey." Even more absurdly, Twain claims that a "trace of 'speculation' is still discernible" in the mummy's left eye, leading him to deduce that "the man was on his way to what is now the Washoe mining region for the purpose of locating the Comstock." In this version of the hoax, the petrified man has not only become an Anglo-American, but also an easterner—a solitary, albeit failed, pathfinder cut from the same mythic cloth as Natty Bumppo—intent upon opening the West to others who will inevitably follow in his footsteps. Although the local column specifies no date for the mummy's age, Twain's allusion to recent territorial history— namely, the discovery of the Comstock Lode—implies that the petrifaction may be far younger than the hundred years indicated in his initial 4 October publication. The figure thus silently presages the profound demographic disruption that became a reality in the early 1860s, when the trickle of fortune-seeking emigrants from the states became a flood.

The writer's next mention of the petrified man, eight months later in a 15 July 1863 letter to the *San Francisco Morning Call*, restores the intact mummy to his original position "cemented to the bed-rock" at Gravelly Ford but more than triples its age. The man, he now asserts, has "been sitting there . . . for the last three or four hundred years."[20] Although the *Call* article makes no reference to the figure's ethnicity, this chronology, circa

1462–1562, coincides with the earliest European exploration of the New World, thus precluding the possibility of Anglo-American origin. Twain, however, ignores the ramifications of his revised dating, apparently content to further obfuscate the mummy's history. In recalling the circumstances of the hoax's composition seven years later in a sketch published in the June 1870 issue of the *Galaxy*,[21] he maintained the chronology established in the *Call* rather than that reported in the original squib, reaffirming that this nameless individual had been "in a state of complete petrifaction for over ten generations ... dead and turned to everlasting stone for more than three hundred years" (SNO, 240). Whether this statement reflects the author's forgetfulness, indifference to consistency, or an evolving sense of the mummy's identity is uncertain.

By the time Clemens wrote the *Galaxy* piece, he was living in Buffalo with his new bride, distant not only in time and space from the contentious reality of Nevada Territory but also radically changed in terms of his life circumstances. And yet, as he embroidered the tale of the hoax's inception for the journal's eastern readers, he offered—for the first time—a brief description of Gravelly Ford, a place he never actually visited. Acknowledging that the setting was "notorious," Twain nonetheless displaces the source of its infamy, suppressing any mention of the Ford's violent history and instead emphasizing its remoteness and desolation: "There was not a living creature within fifty miles of there, except a few starving Indians, some crippled grasshoppers, and four or five buzzards out of meat and too feeble to get away" (SNO, 240). Turning a blind eye on the complex factors that caused native impoverishment and hunger, he depopulates the landscape, suggesting that it is empty, inhospitable, and devoid of life. Moreover, by placing Indians in the same category as "crippled" grasshoppers and "feeble" buzzards, Twain syntactically reinforces their status as weak—if not altogether powerless—subhuman beings.

In 1875, the implications of this baffling chronology became clear when Twain selected the *Galaxy* piece for inclusion in *Sketches, New and Old*. Like all volumes issued by the American Publishing Company, this one was to be lavishly illustrated; moreover, the artist chosen for the project was True Williams (1839–97), who had also produced engravings for *The Innocents Abroad, Roughing It,* and *The Gilded Age*. While Williams was typically given a free hand in selecting which characters or scenes to illustrate, in this instance, Clemens provided specific instructions, writing in the margin of the printer's copy of "The Petrified Man," "Make a picture of him" (ETS1, 641), followed by a marginal line beside the elaborated description.[22] The artist obliged, and based on details gleaned from the

THE PETRIFIED MAN.

NOW, to show how really hard it is to foist a moral or a truth upon an unsuspecting public through a burlesque without entirely and absurdly missing one's mark, I will here set down two experiences of my own in this thing. In the fall of 1862, in Nevada and California, the people got to running wild about extraordinary petrifications and other natural marvels. One could scarcely pick up a paper without finding in it one or two glorified discoveries of this

FIGURE 7.   "The Petrified Man," *Sketches, New and Old.* Courtesy of the Mark Twain Project, The Bancroft Library, University of California, Berkeley.

Galaxy text, depicted the mummy as an Indian (fig. 7). The logic underlying Williams's assumption is indisputable—whether the figure is one-hundred-, three-hundred-, or even four-hundred-years-old, commonsense dictates that he must be indigenous. How could he possibly be otherwise? Although no evidence—such as a note either to the artist or to the publisher—exists indicating the author's explicit approval of this illustration, the very fact of its appearance in *Sketches, New and Old* signifies his acquiescence, since Clemens—who was then serving on the company's board of directors[23]— could have easily vetoed the image but did not.

The remarkable degree of trust that Twain placed in Williams's ability to interpret his texts and translate them into illustrations is reflected in two letters written soon after the volume's publication. The first, dated November 5, 1875, directs publisher Elisha Bliss as follows: "You may let Williams have all of Tom Sawyer that you have received. He can of course make the pictures all the more understandingly after reading the whole story" (L6, 585). Two months later, Clemens reported to Howells that his confidence in the artist had not been misplaced: "Williams has made about 200 rattling pictures for [the novel]—some of them very dainty. Poor devil, what a genius he has, & how he does murder it with rum. He takes a book of mine, & without suggestion from anybody builds no end of pictures just from his reading of it" (MTHL, 121). If Twain had objected to the illustrator's work on *Sketches, New and Old,* it seems unlikely that he would have permitted such creative license with *Tom Sawyer* just a few months later.

Nonetheless, the relationship between "The Petrified Man" essay and Williams's illustration is complex and, to some extent, subversive. The image allows readers—at a glance—to perceive the figure in totality, rather than scrambling to assemble the oblique inventory of body parts presented in the original hoax. In this way, the engraving preempts Twain's joke and undermines his claim about the satire's "delicacy":

> I depended on the way the petrified man was *sitting* to explain to the public that he was a swindle. Yet I purposely mixed that up with other things, hoping to make it obscure—and I did. I would describe the position of one foot, and then say his right thumb was against the side of his nose; then talk about his other foot, and presently come back and say the fingers of his right hand were spread apart . . . then ramble off about something else, and by and by drift back again and remark that the fingers of the left hand were spread like that those of the right. But I was too ingenious. I mixed it up rather too much; and so all that description of the attitude, as a key to the humbuggery of the article, was entirely lost, for nobody but me ever discovered and comprehended the peculiar and suggestive position of the petrified man's hands.
> (SNO, 241)

By ascribing a fixed race and ethnicity to the mummy—making him unambiguously native—Williams's image dramatizes the latent allegory of colonization and dispossession inherent in Twain's narrative. The anonymous petrifaction is in fact a Stone Age man, stuck in place by primitivism,

custom, and long habitation. So intimate and abiding is the figure's connection with the landscape that he has literally become one with it, "cemented
... fast to the bed-rock" (SNO, 241). He is thus powerless to resist the
incursion of these technologically advanced newcomers. They are "all silver
miners," who under the guise of Christian decency, desire to give him a
proper burial but in reality seek his forcible removal—to *"blast him from
his position"*; usurp his rightful place (SNO, 241); and, as the local column
of 1–10 November 1862 indicates, transform him into a museum specimen:
"The remains brought in are to be seen in a neat glass case in the third
story of the Library Building, where they have been temporarily placed ...
for the inspection of the curious" (ETS1, 392). The lower left corner of
Williams's asymmetrical illustration depicts the implements that the miners have brought to bear in order to achieve their objective—shovel, pickax,
tamping rod, dynamite, and fuses. These accoutrements, along with the formality of their dress—hats, boots, jackets—constitute the tangible hallmarks of Anglo-American civilization and stand in contrast to the mummy's near nakedness. Outnumbered, empty-handed, and underdressed, the
petrified man can only greet these interlopers with a rude—though ultimately futile—gesture of defiance.

The figure on the far left of Williams's illustration, whose hands are
extended in an attempt to dissuade the miner on his right from detonating
his explosives, in all likelihood represents "Justice Sewell or Sowell of
Humboldt City," the coroner who conducts an absurd inquest on the
mummy and pronounces him a victim of "protracted exposure." Based on
an actual person, against whom Clemens held an unspecified grudge,[24]
Gilbert T. Sewall was the former owner of Carson City's first daily newspaper, the *Daily Silver Age,* as well as a political crony of his brother Orion's
boss, territorial governor James Nye. Not much is known about this individual, other than that Nye appointed him justice of the peace for Humboldt
County in early 1862 and that soon thereafter he established the Smithson
and Sewall Mining and Real Estate Agency in Humboldt City.

As the letterhead on his business stationery proclaims, Sewall was
actively involved in the enterprise of colonization, "buying, selling [and]
transferring mining claims"; however, a handful of surviving private letters
to Nye housed at the Nevada State Archives also reveal him to be a propo-
nent of amicable relations with the region's indigenous inhabitants. Writing
from Humboldt City on 31 January 1862, for example, he informed the
governor, "There is some talk of Indian troubles and some blankets and
food would be of great assistance to keep things quiet."[25] While Sewall's
request may be viewed as an expedient attempt at mollifying Paiute unrest,

his very mention of the need for food and blankets acknowledges the devastation that mining had wrought on native subsistence economies. Seven months later, on 30 July, he addressed this same issue in another letter to Nye: "The Honey Lake people are determined to keep us in hot water with the Indians if possible, and have I fear succeeded. Many of our citizens from Buena Vista have taken up the matter—a party went out from there and shot nine Indians. Our citizens do not agree as to the expediency of getting up a fight. I adhere to my first opinion—that there is no necessity of any trouble with the Indians. It is always commenced by whites."[26]

Sewall's sympathetic views regarding the plight of native peoples parallel those held by Warren Wasson, Dan De Quille, and Clemens's own brother. His defense of the mummy's right to remain in situ—which Twain dismisses as an absurd rhetorical gesture—has underlying political implications: "Judge S. refused to allow the charitable citizens to blast him from his position. The opinion expressed by his Honor that such a course would be little less than sacrilege, was eminently just and proper" (ETS1, 159). "Sacrilege"—the profanation, misuse, or theft of something sacred—is a peculiar word choice in this secular context, yet the writer repeats it, each time with a progressively more biting sneer, in his discussions of "Petrified Man" in both the 1863 *Morning Call* letter and the 1870 *Galaxy* essay. While Sewall's pomposity may be the primary target of Twain's satire, his diction also subtly conveys approval of the miners' destructive agenda.

"THE OLD PAH-UTES"

About five weeks after the appearance of "Petrified Man," the second session of the Nevada Territorial legislature convened in Carson City. Andrew Marsh was once again in attendance, covering the proceedings for the Sacramento *Daily Union;* also present were Clement T. Rice (the "Unreliable"), reporting for the *Silver Age,* and Sam Clemens, representing the *Territorial Enterprise.* Beyond conducting the usual business of authorizing taxes and new toll roads, a number of delegates met socially one evening to discuss the establishment of a new fraternal association, membership in which would be restricted to settlers who had arrived in the region before 1860. As Marsh notes, "The Pioneers, or 'Old Pah Utahs,' as they style themselves, held a meeting this evening [13 December] preliminary to a permanent organization. John K. Lovejoy [publisher of the *Washoe Times*] presided, and W.M. Gillespie [an editor from the Carson City *Silver Age*] acted as Secretary. Committees were appointed to prepare by-laws, etc., and the meeting adjourned till Thursday evening. Fifty or sixty 'full bloods,' and nearly as many 'half-breeds' were present."[27]

The group's appropriation of native identity exemplifies what anthropologist Patrick Wolfe has termed the "logic of elimination" at work in settler-colonial societies.[28] In claiming to be "Pah-Utes," these Anglo-American interlopers legitimize their presence by symbolically supplanting—and thereby erasing—the original owners of the land. One of the "half-breeds" present at the meeting was Clemens, who had not arrived in the West until 1861; nonetheless, he readily entered into the spirit of the occasion, publishing a mock tribute to "The Pah-Utes" in the *Enterprise* sometime between 13 and 19 December:

> Ah, well—it is touching to see these knotty and rugged old pioneers—who have beheld Nevada in her infancy . . . and camped . . . under her inhospitable sage brush; and smoked the same pipe; and imbibed lightning out of the same bottle; and eaten their regular bacon and beans from the same pot; and lain down to their rest under the same blanket—happy, and lousy and contented . . . it is touching, I say, to see these weather-beaten and blasted old patriarchs banding together like a decaying tribe, for the sake of the privations they have undergone, and the dangers they have met. . . . The Pah-Ute Association will become a high and honorable order in the land—its certificate of membership a patent of nobility. I extend unto the fraternity the right hand of a poor but honest half-breed, and say God speed your sacred enterprise. (ETS1, 170)

The writer's depiction of this "tribe" foregrounds three traits—a communal existence lived in close contact with nature, an ethos of sharing limited provisions, and the ubiquity of dirt and lice—that also inform his fundamental perception of Indianness. By virtue of omission, he also implies that these pioneers are the sole human inhabitants of a virgin landscape populated only by loathsome spiders, reptiles, and amphibians. Despite the hardship of their living conditions, Clemens asserts that the men were "happier . . . and more contented than they are this day or may be in the days that are to come," validating Philip Deloria's thesis that for Anglo-Americans "playing Indian" represented a fantasy of unfettered freedom.

When Washoe City held a raucous all-night party to welcome the return of their delegates on 22 December, Clemens again was on hand, writing to the *Enterprise* the next day: "When I went to bed this morning, Mr. Lovejoy, arrayed in fiery red night clothes, was dancing the war dance of his tribe (he is President of the Paiute Association) around a spittoon and Colonel Howard, dressed in a similar manner, was trying to convince him that he was a humbug. A suspicion crossed my mind that they were partially intoxicated, but I could not be sure about it on account of everything appearing to turn around so."[29] This racialized imagery extends the trope of ethnic imposture. As Twain notes in *Roughing It*, "Slang was the language of Nevada" (309), suggesting that his embrace of the term reflects a fascination with regional vernacular. And yet, as the writer's 5 February "Letter from Carson" reveals, he also recognized the association's divisive role in creating a nascent social hierarchy: "I did not return to Virginia yesterday, on account of the wedding. The parties were Hon. James H. Sturtevant, one of the first Pi-Utes of Nevada, and Miss Emma Curry, daughter of Hon. A. Curry, who also claims that his is a Pi-Ute family of high antiquity. Curry conducted the wedding arrangements himself and invited none but Pi-Utes. This interfered with me a good deal . . . [though] they said I might stay, as it was me" (ETS1, 203).

Like Twain's derogatory allusions to the "First Families of Virginia" decades later in *Pudd'nhead Wilson*, the repetition of "Pi-Ute" three times within the space of two sentences lampoons the settlers' pretense of elitism and exclusivity. Debarred from membership in this esteemed company, he insinuates himself into the proceedings with Curry's permission, though relegated to second-class status among the hired help: "At three o'clock in the afternoon, all the Pi-Utes went up stairs to the old Hall of Representatives in Curry's house, preceded by the bride and groom, and the bridesmaids and groomsmen . . . and followed by myself and the fiddlers."

"Pi-Ute" identity soon emerged as an instrumental force in the formation of the territory's Democratic Party. On 4 November 1863, the Gold Hill *Daily News* published an editorial called "That Piute Idea" decrying the "absolute and ridiculous absurdity" of using the term to describe "'pioneers' in a country whose Territorial existence is of the hoary age of two years." The article also warned that "The politician who takes up this 'piute' gabble for his platform will find that he is not addressing a democratic primary meeting in the Sixth Ward of New York, not a population of half-civilized, cross-breed mountain trappers and hunters—but an intelligent community, the great bulk of it . . . from the neighboring state of California, men of sense and hard-earned experience."[30]

This reference to ward politics links the "Pi-Utes" with another fraternal organization called "The Improved Order of Red Men," which was closely associated with the corrupt machine of New York's Tammany Hall. The order's members—all adult white men "of "good moral character and standing"—played Indian in a more obviously theatrical manner than their western counterparts, donning elaborate "native" costumes and performing "arcane rituals in shadowy rooms."[31] These performances, grounded in an insistence "that real Indians were disappearing or had already vanished," were, according to Philip Deloria, "possible only when Indian removal policy was widespread and advanced"[32]—conditions that did not yet exist in Nevada Territory. A week later, the *Daily News* impugned the pioneers' claim of primacy in "Original Occupants," an article discussing the region's inhabitants "previous to the advent of the white man." Directing newcomers to an unnamed Virginia City saloon where a glass urn containing "tarantulas, lizards, scorpions, centipedes, stinging ants, [and] 'snaiks' ad infinitum ... suspended in alcohol" was displayed, the piece pointedly added that "other old inhabitants, such as Pi-utes, antelopes, coyotes ... etc. can be found by hunting long enough in the mountains."[33] In acknowledging the reality of the Great Basin's indigenous population, the article undercuts the legitimacy of the frontier association's name.

Lovejoy was undeterred by such criticism. In late 1863, he established a newspaper in Washoe City called the *Old Pah-Utah,* prompting Twain to quip in the *Enterprise:*

> Why should [he] spell it Pah-Utah? That isn't right—it should be Pi-Uty, or Pi-Ute. I speak by authority. Because I have carefully noted the little speeches of self-gratulation of our noble red brother, and he always delivers himself in this wise: "Pi-Uty boy heepy work—Washoe heep lazy." But if you question his nationality, he remarks, with oppressive dignity: "Me no dam Washoe—me Pi-Ute!" Wherefore, my researches have satisfied me that one of these, or both, is right. Lovejoy ought to know this, even better than me; he came here before May, 1860, and is, consequently, a blooded Pi-Ute, while I am only an ignorant half-breed.[34]

In the year that had passed since Twain's announcement of the group's founding, his subject position shifts from an "honest half-breed" to an "ignorant" one, suggesting a change in attitude toward it. The hand initially extended in friendship now wags a finger in chastisement, faulting not only the spelling of the organization's president, but also the smug ascendancy exhibited by its "full blood" members. Despite his exclusion from their ranks, he proclaims greater knowledge of the local native population than these early settlers. Although the article's persona is fictive, his authority—rooted in observation of, and interaction with, Pi-Utes in Virginia City—may have autobiographical implications, offering insight into Clemens's ambivalent impressions of Nevada's native peoples. His description of the tension that existed between Paiutes and Washoes reflects an awareness of differences in tribal character, culture, and work ethic, while simultaneously mocking the "oppressive dignity" and "self-gratula-tion" displayed by one group of savages in asserting its superiority to another. Moreover, the writer's rendition of Paiute speech—however clichéd—represents his earliest known attempt to capture indigenous ver-nacular. In this regard, the *Enterprise* piece anticipates two vignettes in *Roughing It*: the "broken English" used to warn Anglo-American prospec-tors of an imminent flood on the Carson River—"'By'm-by, heap water!'" (RI, 197)—and the laconic response of a "half-tamed Indian" launderer to the explosion of a cooking stove in which six cans of gunpowder had been hidden: "the Indian betrayed no trepidation, no distress, not even discom-fort. He simply stopped washing, leaned forward and surveyed the clean, blank ground a moment, and then remarked: 'Mph! Dam stove heap gone!'—and resumed his scrubbing as placidly as if it were an entirely customary thing for a stove to do. I will explain, that 'heap' is 'Injun-English' for 'very much'" (RI, 255).

While Twain's characterizations of himself as a "half-breed" originate within the context of the Pah-Ute Association, they persist well beyond his years in Nevada Territory and evolve into a generic signifier of western identity. Within weeks of relocating from Virginia City to San Francisco in May 1864, he was chosen to preside at a reception honoring the efforts of Major Edward C. Perry—a marine engineer and Union veteran from New York City—in raising a steamship that had sunken a year earlier in the city's harbor. In "Parting Presentation," the speech he gave on this occasion, the writer signs himself "MARK TWAIN, High-you-muck-a-muck"[35] and claims to act as a spokesman for "the Diggers, the Pi-Utes, the Washoes, the Shoshones, and the numberless and nameless tribes of aborigines that roam the deserts of the Great Basin to the eastward of the snowy mountains further north" (ETS2, 7). On behalf of these "noble sons of the forest," he ceremoniously offers the major a "costly and beautiful *cane* . . . fashioned by their own inspired hands" in recognition of his services.

In the speech's closing lines, Twain identifies the "red men" he repre-sents as both the "savage" citizens of San Francisco and a number of actual native leaders, such as Winnemucca, "War Chief of the Pi-Utes," and Washakie, "Grand Chief of the Shoshones," known for their conciliatory attitudes towards whites—along with several more obscure figures associ-ated with violent resistance (ETS2, 8). "Buffalo Jim," for example, was a Paiute warrior, who led raids in the Reese River valley east of Virginia City during the mid-to-late 1860s,[36] and "Sioux-Sioux," Twain's curious misspelling of the name "Captain Soo," was Moguannoga, a mixed-blood Bannock and Paiute leader of the Humboldt Meadows band, who organized the bloody May 1860 attack on Williams Station that sparked the Pyramid Lake War.[37] The topicality of these references, which include the names of "friendly" as well as "hostile" Indians, reveals that the writer was well informed about the region's ongoing racial tensions. And yet, his ignorant substitution of "Sioux-Sioux" for "Soo" also indicates that he did not take these matters very seriously; in conflating tribes from distinctly different regions and cultures, he implies that all indigenous peoples are alike. This notion is reinforced by the speech's stereotypical depiction of Indians as filthy "nomads of the desert" clad in rabbit skins, who "fare sumptuously" on grasshoppers, crickets, and the lice that infest their own bodies—details that echo his 1862 description of Chief Hoop-de-doodle-do.

Most significantly, "Parting Presentation" marks the first appearance of the racial epithet "Digger" in Twain's extant publications from this period.[38] Although he includes the term among the names of other tribes like the Pi-Ute, Shoshone, and Washoe, it does not denote a specific ethnographic group. In *Ishi in Two Worlds*, anthropologist Theodora Kroeber dismissed the "Diggers" as a "frontier legend";[39] the name is a gloss, invented by Anglo-American settlers to collectively identify indigenous peoples in western mining regions, such as the Maidu, Miwok, Yokuts, and others who foraged for roots and bulbs with primitive digging sticks.[40] Historian Robert Heizer describes "Digger" as a "term of opprobrium" that was widely used in newspapers throughout the 1850s and '60s as a generic label for the "most miserable and degraded" of California Indians.[41] This "taxonomic stigma"—in many ways comparable to nigger—stereotyped Indians as "treacherous, bloodthirsty, dirty, squalid, lazy, comic, and/or pathetic as the time and place dictated."[42] Twain's use of this slur within weeks of relocating to a cosmopolitan urban center suggests that geographical distance from the Comstock created a psychic detachment that allowed the image of the "ignoble Indian" to take permanent hold in his imagination. In later writings concerning his travels outside the continental United States, "Digger" becomes convenient shorthand for describing the lowest, most repugnant primitive beings he encounters. In a March 1866 letter from the Sandwich Islands, he introduces a gratuitous racial simile into his discussion of local fauna: "the tamarind is as much more superb a tree than the locust as a beautiful white woman is more lovely than a Digger squaw who may chance to generally resemble her in shape and size."[43] The epithet also appears several times in *The Innocents Abroad* in relation to the poverty and filth of the Arabs he met in Palestine—a trope discussed more fully later in this chapter.

"PLEASE DO NOT NAME YOUR INJUN FOR ME"

In December 1864, Clemens left San Francisco for a three-month stay in the mining camps of Calaveras and Tuolumne counties. His time there, much of which was spent at Jim Gillis's cabin at Jackass Hill, was interrupted by a four-week interlude in Angel's Camp, where Gillis had a pocket mining claim (NBJ1, 66). This period, during which the writer heard the tale that would become "Jim Smiley and His Jumping Frog," also brought him back into tangential contact with American Indians. A notebook entry on 22 January quotes an unidentified native as saying, "White man heap savvy too much—Injun gone in," perhaps in reference to stakes wagered in a poker game; another, made between 6 and 20 February, refers to a "Pi Ute war dance on hills back of Angels'" (NBJ1, 71, 79) but contains no further comment. Indians also figured in the stories the men shared to pass the time when heavy, frequent rains kept them indoors. Twain mentions an occasion on which he and Gillis amused themselves by "talking like people 80 years old & toothless," donning the varied personae of a camp meeting preacher, bear hunter, Indian fighter, gambler, and stage driver; more significantly, he notes, "Boden crazy, asking after his wife, who had been dead 13 years—first knowledge of his being deranged" (NBJ1, 77–78). This entry is the seed of his 1893 story "The Californian's Tale" about a miner driven mad by the disappearance of his young wife, who was captured by Indians nineteen years earlier en route home from visiting her parents. Never seen or heard from again, she is presumed dead—"That or worse" (i.e., raped and forcibly assimilated into the tribe).[44] Each year as the anniversary of this tragedy approaches, the miner slips back into the past, reliving the anticipation and anxiety of his beloved's return. To avert his recognition of the horrific truth, the man's neighbors construct a collective fiction that the woman is still alive, decorating the cabin with flowers, playing festive music, and making repeated toasts to her "health and safety" while simultaneously doctoring his drink with a sedative, then ushering him off to bed. Boden's trauma seems to have made a lasting impression on Twain, shaping his representation of Indians as lustful, violent predators intent upon the destruction of white womanhood in later works such as "The Noble Red Man," *The Adventures of Tom Sawyer,* and "Huck Finn and Tom Sawyer among the Indians."

At some point during Clemens's visit, Gillis apparently played a practical joke on him, bribing a local Paiute woman to name her baby Mark Twain. Although his motive is unclear, it likely was intended to embarrass the writer by insinuating a dalliance across racial lines, thereby discrediting him as a suitor in the eyes of Molly and Nelly Daniels, the so-called Chapparel Quails. They were the most sought-after young women in Tuolumne County and were also being courted by Gillis's younger brother Billy.[45] Clemens makes no mention of this prank in his notebook; however, it arises as a subject of discussion twice in his later correspondence. A week before marrying Livy in February 1870, he wrote to Jim, recalling the days of "their poverty & their pocket-hunting vagabondage" during his Sierra sojourn, and inquiring in the postscript, "Do they continue to name all the young Injuns after me—when you pay them for the compliment?" (L4, 36). The story also resurfaces—in greatly exaggerated proportions—in an unsent 1887 letter to New York theatrical agent W.R. Ward, who sought permission to use the author's name in advertising his own dramatic adaptation of *Tom Sawyer*. While Clemens denied the request on 8 September 1887 in two curt sentences on formal letterhead from Charles L. Webster and Company ("Necessarily I cannot assent to so strange a proposition. And I think it but fair to warn you that if you put the piece on the stage, you must take the legal consequences."), his initial response, consigned to a file "for unmailed letters," is a long, hilarious tirade about Ward's impudence. Labeling the agent "No. 1365," the latest in a long line of individuals who had already tried and failed to dramatize *Tom Sawyer*, he declares, "That is a book, dear sir, which cannot be dramatized. One might as well try to dramatize any other hymn. Tom Sawyer is simply a hymn, put into prose form to give it a worldly air."[46] He then launches into an extended digression about how "strangely handsome" he was twenty-four years earlier (circa 1863), explaining,

> Upon one occasion I was traveling in the Sonora region, & stopped for an hour's nooning, to rest my horse & myself. All the town came out to look. The tribes of Indians gathered to look. A Pi Ute squaw named her baby for me—a voluntary compliment which pleased me greatly ... the president & faculty of Sonora University [arrived] & offered me the post of Professor of Moral Culture & the Dogmatic Humanities; which I accepted gratefully, & entered at once upon my duties. But my name had pleased the Indians, & in the deadly kindness of their hearts they went on naming their babies after me. I tried to stop it, but the Indians could not understand why I should object to so manifest a compliment. The thing grew ... & spread ... & became exceedingly embarrassing. The University stood it a couple of years; ... [but then] they felt obliged to call a halt. ... The president himself said to me, "I am as sorry as I can be for you ... but you see how it is: there are a hundred & thirty-two of them already, & fourteen precincts to hear from. The circumstances has [*sic*] brought your name into most wide & unfortunate renown ... & I am charged with the unpleasant duty of receiving your resignation."

The purpose of this tall tale only becomes clear in the letter's closing lines: "I know you only mean me a kindness, dear 1365, but it is a most deadly mistake. Please do not name your Injun for me."[47] Though framed as a joke, this metaphorical denial of paternity—equating Ward's adaptation of *Tom Sawyer* with a shameful, unwelcome offspring—shows the persistence of Twain's perception of Indians as an inferior race.

"ONCE A PIUTE, ALWAYS A PIUTE"

On 28 January 1876, more than a decade after leaving Nevada, Clemens— now ensconced in his elegant Hartford mansion—contacted his former *Enterprise* colleague Dan De Quille in Virginia City to request "a peck of your best *pine nuts* per express, at your earliest convenience, with bill for the same. I want to spread them before company for a novelty."[48] The gesture he envisions is, much like the "miracles" performed by Hank Morgan in *A Connecticut Yankee,* intended for maximum theatrical effect—an opportunity to flaunt the affluence he had achieved in the East, as well as his ongoing ties to the western frontier. The grandeur of the writer's conception is underscored by the large quantity of nuts he specifies (a peck equals approximately thirty-two cups), reflecting their status as a commodity— rare and therefore highly desirable. For the indigenous inhabitants of Nevada, however, piñons were not a luxury but a dietary staple; as the Paiute chief Numaga informed Anglo-American settlers in 1863, "pine nut groves were the Indians' orchards," threatening violent retaliation if they were destroyed for firewood.[49] De Quille's response on 7 February acknowledges the natives' hereditary title to these "orchards," indicating that his fulfillment of Clemens's request is contingent upon their cooperation: "I shall try the Indians here for those pine-nuts. If I can't get them here I shall write to some of my friends in eastern Nevada to get them for me. I think 'Capt. Bob,' 'Johnson,' 'One-eyed George' or some of the braves here will be able to produce the peck of Piute grub."[50] De Quille's naming of these men as liaisons through whom he would attempt to procure the nuts reflects his camaraderie with the local Indian population. As William Gillis—whose brother Steve served for many years as a compositor at the *Enterprise*— recalled in his 1924 memoir, the Paiutes were "always ready and willing to render" services for De Quille, who spoke their language fluently and was regarded as a trusted friend.[51]

While it is not known exactly whom Clemens sought to impress with this western delicacy, the urgency of his request is repeated in a second, more forthright appeal—this time formulated as a mock command—sent to the *Enterprise* several days after he had written De Quille. On 8 February, the editors published an excerpt of this letter—the original of which is lost—under the headline "Once a Piute, Always a Piute," playfully promoting the former "half-breed" to honorary full-blood status:

> Mark Twain has at last "soured on" such grub as New England civilization is able to spread before him. He writes to us: "For the love of Heaven get me a peck of pine-nuts at your earliest convenience and send them on here by express! I hanker after them as of old the Israelites longed for the flesh-pots of Egypt!" A man can stand it down east for a time on the kind of grub they have there—may linger along for years—but ultimately his stomach revolts and his soul cries out for that sound and satisfying fare on which he fed when he stalked the mountains a prince of nature and a man able to outstare the sun. He shall have the pine-nuts.[52]

The writer's tongue-in-cheek allusion to the Book of Exodus suggests that his longing for pine nuts is not motivated by a desire to affirm his wealth but rather by a deep emotional hunger—nostalgia for the carefree autonomy of his bachelor days in the territory. This "hankering," according to the newspaper, represents an epiphany about the superiority of frontier life to the constraints of eastern society—proof that Twain remains a "Piute" at heart despite his removal to Connecticut. In contrast to the diffidence of De Quille's response, the squib summarily announces that the writer's desire for this delicacy will be fulfilled.

EATING INDIANS FOR BREAKFAST

Although Europe and the Holy Land are the setting and subject of Twain's first and best-selling book, *The Innocents Abroad*, Indians figure into its text in significant, if rather puzzling, ways. The 1867 Quaker City excursion took place against the backdrop of Red Cloud's War, which had erupted a year earlier on the Great Plains when several bands of Lakota—the Oglala, Hunkpapa, Minneconjou, and Brulé—rose up in opposition to colonial expansion along the Bozeman Trail. The writer's awareness of this conflict is illustrated by a notation scrawled on an envelope containing a letter to his San Francisco friend Charles Warren Stoddard, sent from New York on 27 April 1867—the same day the *Tribune* reported that a "general war" with Indians was imminent: "To Postmaster—Dr. Sir: *Per Steamer*—d—n the Overland—too many Injuns" (L2, 37). A 5 June letter to the *Alta California*, written just days before the Quaker City's departure, also features an extended discussion of what he dismissively terms "The Indian Row."

In this text, Twain uses the Sioux War as a vehicle for dramatizing eastern ignorance about the geography and social conditions of the West; dividing the nation's population into camps of we and us, he rhetorically asks his readers, "I wonder if *you* are in as much distress about the Indians as *we* are? *We* talk Maximilian and his possible execution some, but *our* main dependence for solid conversation is the Indians" (emphasis added).[53] While initially appearing to speak from the perspective of a New Yorker (represented by the pronoun we), the chameleonic reporter reveals his true allegiance several paragraphs later: "It is funny, the absurd remarks people make about the Far West, and the wild questions they ask about it when they are discussing the Indian difficulties. It is humiliating to me to consider how high an opinion *we* have of our importance out there in the Pacific regions, and then to discover how very little some people know about *us*."[54]

The shifting meaning of these pronouns demonstrates the writer's stance as a culture broker, bridging the ideological divide between frontier and metropolis. He satirizes easterners' slavish adulation of European culture and their lack of familiarity with the West by relating a conversation with "an educated and highly-cultivated American lady, who speaks French and Italian, and has travelled in Europe and studied the country so faithfully that she knows it as well as another woman would know her flower-garden." This cosmopolite expresses concern over "some very dear friends in San Francisco and other parts of Idaho" confessing that "these Indian rumors gave her unspeakable uneasiness," while adding that she is not so worried about her acquaintances in Santa Fe and Los Angeles, "because she believed the Indians did not infest the Cariboo country as much as they did the Farrallone Mountains and other localities further West." In the guise of alleviating the woman's fears, Twain exposes her ignorance of American geography by absurdly jumbling places and countries abroad: "I told her I honestly believed that her friends in San Francisco and other parts of Idaho were just as safe there as they would be in Jerusalem or any other part of China." His comparisons grow increasingly ridiculous—"Damascus or any other locality in France," "Hongkong or any other place in Italy"—until the woman can no longer contain herself: "Are you so preposterously ignorant as all this amounts to, or are you trying to quiz me?" And I said, 'Don't you go to Europe any more till you know a little something about your own country.' I won."[55] This reprimand reflects the patriotic mindset with which Twain embarked upon his European tour—a belief that knowledge of one's homeland far outweighs exposure to the celebrated monuments of Old World culture.

After this exchange, Twain returns to the subject of Red Cloud's War and affirms his identification with the West:

> I am waiting patiently to hear that they have ordered General Connor out to polish off those Indians, but the news never comes. He has shown that he knows how to fight the kind of Indians that God made, but I suppose the humanitarians want somebody to fight the Indians that J. Fenimore Cooper made. There is just where the mistake is. The Cooper Indians are dead—died with their creator. The kind that are left are of altogether a different breed, and cannot be successfully fought with poetry, and sentiment, and soft soap, and magnanimity."[56]

Connor, whose brutal methods of Indian fighting originated in his retaliatory slaughter of innocent Shoshones after the 1862 Gravelly Ford massacre, had retired from active military service after the 1866 Powder River Expedition, during which he instructed his troops, "Do not receive overtures of peace or submission from the Indians, but attack and kill all males over twelve years of age."[57] While such tactics met with general approval west of the Mississippi, they provoked controversy along the Atlantic seaboard, as illustrated in "Cruelty to Indians," an 1865 editorial in the *New York Times:* "The latest reports of [General Connor's] operations . . . could hardly be explained in any other way than that he had been guilty of massacres. . . . We understand perfectly the anxiety of Western settlers to have the entire race exterminated. But a great government cannot, with impunity, permit injustice, even to the most helpless of its people."[58] Twain's desire that the general return to "polish off"—that is, exterminate—the tribes currently wreaking havoc on the Plains betrays an antagonism toward indigenous peoples more in keeping with frontier attitudes about "savages" than with the progressive views commonly held in the East. In the words of Connor's biographer Brigham Madsen, "The man from Missouri and the frontier general seemed to be of one mind about how to deal with Indians."[59]

Red Cloud's War was also instrumental in shaping both the narrative persona and imagery of *The Innocents Abroad* by depriving the Quaker City excursion of one of its most illustrious participants. In May 1867, William Tecumseh Sherman, the Union hero then serving as commander of the Military Division of the Missouri, was appointed to a presidential peace commission charged with negotiating an end to the violence engulfing the Plains. He was an unlikely choice for the assignment, since his contempt for Indians was well known; five months earlier he had written to U.S. Grant: "We must act with vindictive earnestness against the Sioux, even to their extermination, men, women and children," arguing that "nothing less" would ensure the successful completion of the Union Pacific railroad.[60] The general regretfully announced his withdrawal from the tour in a letter published in the *New York Times* on 31 May 1867, explaining, "I feel bound in duty and honor to stand by my post, and to defer to some more opportune occasion the gratification of a natural desire to see other and older countries than our own."[61]

Sherman's abrupt change of plans prompted an upgrade in the writer's accommodations; according to Dewey Ganzel, "shortly before sailing, Clemens was given No. 10, the spacious portside cabin which had originally been assigned to [the] General."[62] The heady experience of lodging in Sherman's quarters may have unconsciously inspired the writer's penchant for characterizing the culturally diverse peoples he encountered abroad as "Indians." As Hilton Obenzinger observes, "The further Twain traveled East the more insistent[ly] does the American West (either as Pacific slope or antebellum Missouri) make itself felt in his writing: in spirit, at least, he went with Sherman—or, rather, *after* Sherman, since actual rather than metaphorical Indian-killing was not his métier."[63] This imagery is especially pronounced in the chapters on the Holy Land, where—as he declared in one of the original *Alta* letters—the barren desert landscape reminded him of Washoe "all the time."[64] He depicts the darkly complected Arabs as a "tribe of hopeless, shirtless savages" (IA, 475) inhabiting "shabby villages of wigwams" (IA, 500), whose leaders are "only a parcel of petty chiefs—ill-clad and ill-conditioned savages much like our Indians" (IA, 486). Similarly, in Endor he sees "the wildest horde of half-naked savages we have found thus far," and deems the village's "dirt, degradation and savagery . . . worse than any Indian *campoodie*" (IA, 541)—the Paiute word for encampment.

While acknowledging that by 1869 the equation of Arabs and Indians was a "standard association made by other American travelers," Obenzinger claims that Twain's travelogue "reinvigorates the trope through exaggeration and parodic destruction."[65] The venom that infuses his descriptions, however, cannot be fully excused as hyperbole. As Twain observes the degraded condition of Palestine's inhabitants, time and space collapse, rekindling—and intensifying—his negative impression of native peoples in Nevada Territory. The inhabitants of Banias, for example, closely resemble the Washoes discussed in his March 1862 letter to Jane Clemens in outward appearance and demeanor—both are dirty, vermin-infested, outlandishly dressed beggars. But whereas Chief Hoop-de-doodle-do and his wives elicit wry amusement, Twain depicts their Middle Eastern counterparts with contempt:

This morning, during breakfast, the usual assemblage of squalid humanity sat patiently without the charmed circle of the camp and waited for such crumbs as pity might bestow upon their misery.... They reminded me much of Indians, did these people. They had but little clothing, but such as they had was fanciful in character and fantastic in its arrangement. Any little absurd gewgaw or gimcrack they had they disposed in such a way as to make it attract attention most readily. They sat in silence, and with tireless patience watched our every motion with that vile, uncomplaining impoliteness which is so truly Indian, and which makes a white man so nervous and uncomfortable and savage that he wants to exterminate the whole tribe. (IA, 472–73)

In contrast to the "Princesses" who interrupt Twain's Nevada breakfast, rudely pointing at his food with their "long, skinny fingers" and critiquing each mouthful ingested—"May be whity man no heap eat um grasshopper?" (L1, 177–78)—the Palestinian villagers watch silently from a distance hoping for "crumbs" from the tourists' repast. Nonetheless, the writer reacts with far greater hostility to their mute supplication than the effrontery of the Washoe women, who beg not only for food but also "a few old shirts, boots, hats, etc., and a deck of cards" before agreeing to leave. The discomfort Twain experiences in this instance—eliciting a shockingly genocidal impulse—stems from self-conscious awareness of his privileged circumstances and class. Unlike his meager Nevada breakfast of coffee and sage hen, those he eats each morning in Palestine are elaborate, multicourse affairs, consisting of "hot mutton chops, fried chicken, omelettes, fried potatoes and coffee—all excellent" (IA, 439). Yet because the "gorgeous" tent in which he dines is surrounded by a swarm of "human vermin," who "watch every bite he takes, with greedy looks, and swallow unconsciously every time he swallows, as if they half fancied the precious morsel went down their own throats," Twain finds no enjoyment in these meals but regards them as "worse punishment than riding all day in the sun" (IA, 454–55). He racializes his guilt, speaking from the vantage point of a generic "white man" whose civilized sensibility turns "savage" in the face of such deprivation.

Twain's identification of Arabs with American Indians grows more explicit as his journey proceeds. Trotting "across the Plain of Jezreel," he describes meeting "half a dozen Digger Indians (Bedouins) with very long spears in their hands, cavorting around on old crowbait horses, and spearing imaginary enemies" (IA, 546–47). Given that the Digger tribes of the Great Basin were not equestrian cultures, the metaphor is fundamentally inaccurate; nonetheless, the term would have registered with readers of the *Alta California* as a familiar signifier for the most degraded of human beings. Much in the same way that the writer's mangling of the name Captain Soo in his 1864 "Parting Presentation" conflates two native groups, this description ridicules the iconic image of the Plains warrior—the contemporary Lakota combatants of Red Cloud's War—thereby disparaging the Diggers and Sioux simultaneously. This subliminal association is made manifest in a passage Twain composed while finishing the manuscript for *Innocents* but did not intend to include in the published text:

> Seen afar off,—as far as from America to the Holy Land—the ancient children of Israel seem almost too lovely & too holy for this coarse earth; but seen face to face, in their legitimate descendants, with no haze of distance to soften their harsh features & no glamor of Sabbath-school glory to beautify them, they are like any other savages. They had a Solomon, a Joseph & a Moses, but other tribes of Indians have their two or three wise men, with similar suggestive intervals of time between—say five hundred to a thousand years. . . . But two wise men do not make a wise people, any more than two swallows make a summer. There was precious little about Israel to love, revere, or even respect. Many of them were superior to the Digger Indians of California, but not all of them could rank the Sioux of the Great Plains. If this be doubted, read the Old Testament & then go among the Arabs of to-day in Palestine.[66]

Twain here situates the inhabitants of Palestine in a relative hierarchy of savagery, declaring them less primitive than Diggers though on the whole not quite on par with the Sioux. This statement, while more measured than the reductive equation "Digger Indians (Bedouins)" that appears in the published text, may have been omitted because its allusion to God's chosen people was potentially offensive to Christian readers.

Twain's notion of the Indian as a contemptible racial Other is, however, complicated in *The Innocents Abroad* by several instances in which the term is used self-reflexively. Fuming at the injustice of the tourists' mistreatment by their unscrupulous guide "Bilfinger," he vows revenge: "I shall visit Paris again some day, and then let the guides beware! I shall go in my war-paint—I shall carry my tomahawk along" (IA 123–24). This declaration is accompanied by True Williams's illustration, captioned "Return in War-Paint," which shows the author wearing a formal frock coat atop buckskin leggings and a long breechcloth rather than the requisite matching dress pants (fig. 8). His shirt and tie are partially obscured by a large medallion ornamented with what appear to be animal teeth or claws. Similarly, Twain's brimmed felt hat features several long feathers that evoke a Plains-style headdress. The accessories he bears in each hand accentuate this hybrid ethnicity—a tomahawk emblazoned with the stars and

FIGURE 8.   "Return in War Paint," *The Innocents Abroad.* Courtesy of the Mark Twain Project, The Bancroft Library, University of California, Berkeley.

stripes, a satchel inscribed with the initials MT US, along with a bow and quiver full of arrows strapped across his back. The humor of Williams's engraving derives from the dissonance of its heterogeneous elements, which reveals the impotence of the narrator's vengeful fantasy. Rather than the visage of a menacing warrior, Twain—who wears no discernible "war paint"—appears baffled or perhaps fearful, his wide-eyed gaze riveted at some unseen enemy lurking outside the image's frame.

Williams's caricature so delighted Clemens that he mentioned it in a March 1869 letter to his fiancée, Olivia Langdon: "I like the pictures (for the book) ever so much. Only a dozen or two of them are finished, but they are very artistically engraved. . . . There is one of me 'on the war-path,' which is *good"* (L3, 139). The image's iconographic quality—representing the brash barbarism of the New World confronting the cultural monuments of the Old—favorably impressed Twain's publisher Elisha Bliss as well, who used it in the advance sales circulars promoting *The Innocents Abroad* as the "most unique and spicy volume in existence." In this regard, the initials on the figure's valise signify more than citizenship and national origin by suggesting that Mark Twain the Indian incarnates the United States. The writer's fantasy of revenge is emblematic of the nation's desire to cast off its stance of cultural obeisance to Europe, as well as its ineffectuality in doing so.

Twain's second representation of himself as Indian occurs later in the section concerning France. Explaining the leisurely pace of Continental dining, he states, "We take soup; then wait a few minutes for the fish; a few minutes more and the plates are changed, and the roast beef comes; another change and we take peas; change again and take lentils; change and take snail patties (I prefer grasshoppers;) change and take roast chicken and salad; then strawberry pie and ice cream; then green figs, pears, oranges, green almonds, &c.; finally coffee" (IA, 99). The significance of the aside does not become evident until nine chapters later when the writer explicitly identifies himself as an Indian, albeit in a more conflicted, contradictory manner. Standing on the shores of Italy's Lake Como—which a half century earlier the Romantic poet Percy Bysshe Shelley claimed "exceeds anything I ever beheld in beauty"[67]—Twain sniffs, "How dull its waters are compared with the wonderful transparence of Lake Tahoe!" (IA, 204).

This observation elicits a lengthy explanation of the name Tahoe's linguistic origins, which devolves into an ethnocentric tirade against the local indigenous peoples who conferred it. Etymologically, "Tahoe" derives from "Da ow ga," the Washoe word for lake;[68] Twain, however, manufactures an apocryphal alternative, insisting that this "unmusical cognomen," which "suggests no crystal waters, no picturesque shores, no sublimity," in fact means "grasshoppers" or "grasshopper soup, the favorite dish of the Digger tribe—and of the Pi-utes as well" (IA, 205). In professing his preference for grasshoppers over escargot, the writer paradoxically appropriates Indianness as a marker of national identity while at the same time condemning—and distancing himself from—the barbarism of actual natives: "[Tahoe] is Indian, and suggestive of Indians. They say it is Pi-ute—possibly it is Digger. I am satisfied that it was named by the Diggers—those degraded savages who roast their dead relatives, then mix the human grease and ashes of bones with tar, and 'gaum' it thick all over their heads and foreheads and ears, and go caterwauling about the hills and call it *mourning*. *These* are the gentry that named the Lake" (IA, 205).

Twain's caustic hyperbole has some basis in ethnographic fact. Alfred L. Kroeber's *Handbook of the Indians of California* indicates that a number of Great Basin tribes—including the Washoe, Pomo, Shasta, and some bands of Shoshones—traditionally cremated their dead and expressed their grief through communal "Cry" or "Wailing" ceremonies.[69] Clemens disparages these practices through his allusions to "roasting" corpses and "caterwauling." In addition, he generalizes and thereby misrepresents the nature of a related ritual in which the closest relative of the deceased—usually a widow—would cut off her hair in mourning, then anoint her head and face with resin from the burnt pine of the funeral pyre, refusing to wash or remarry until the pitch had worn away. According to Walter James Hoffman (1846–99), an army surgeon and early ethnologist who conducted fieldwork among numerous indigenous groups in the West, cremation was largely superseded by burial after Euro-American colonization in the mid-nineteenth century; however, the custom persisted among the Modocs of northeastern California as late as 1868, with one key difference—"the chief mourner would cover his (or her) face and hair with the blood and grease which ran from the burning body" instead of with pitch.[70] Twain's limited interaction with Indians in Nevada Territory means he likely never witnessed this phenomenon firsthand but learned of it from reports of local tribal customs that occasionally appeared in the pages of contemporary newspapers.[71] Another possible source is Ned Wakeman (1818–75), the colorful mariner with whom Clemens sailed down the Pacific coast from San Francisco in December 1866. Two years later, they met again in a Panama City hotel, where Wakeman told the writer a dream that became the basis of "Extract from Captain Stormfield's Visit to Heaven"—an unfinished tale begun in the late 1860s, which Twain reworked over the next four decades and published in *Harper's Monthly* in December 1907–January 1908. Upon arriving in his designated "district" of Heaven, Stormfield receives a halo, pair of wings, harp, and hymnbook from "a Pi Ute Injun I used to know in Tulare County; mighty good fellow—I remembered being at his funeral, which consisted of him being burnt and the other Injuns gauming their faces with his ashes and howling like wildcats" (CT2, 835–36). Several details of this description echo that in the travelogue; however, as James McNutt has observed, Twain's tone is far less censorious in "Stormfield."[72]

The youthful intolerance and ethnocentrism of Clemens's "cultural grammar"[73]—and his evolution toward a more mature, relativistic stance on diverse religious practices—can be gauged by comparing the *Innocents* passage with one in *Following the Equator*, written almost three decades later. Discussing the Hindu practice of suttee, according to which widows immolate themselves on the funeral pyres of their husbands, he does not rush to judgment but instead poses a series of questions that reflect his struggle to comprehend it: *"How* did people come to drift into such a strange custom? What was the origin of the idea? . . . Why was such a cruel death chosen—why wouldn't a gentle one have answered?" (FE, 452). He acknowledges the limitations of his western outlook, concluding that despite these efforts, he "can never understand it. It all seems impossible." He then recounts the story of a British colonial officer's attempt to dissuade a widow from ending her life in this fashion; unmoved, after days of fasting and prayer, she "walked up deliberately and steadily to the brink, stepped into the centre of the flame, sat down and leaning back in the midst as if reposing on a couch, was consumed without uttering a shriek or betraying one sign of agony" (FE, 456). Twain's reaction; "It is fine and beautiful. It compels one's reverence and respect—no, has it freely, and without compulsion," is antithetical to the invective voiced in his 1869 text.

Clemens's aversion to "Tahoe," which Lou Budd characterizes as a failure of his "celebrated ear,"[74] predates the publication of *Innocents* by at least six years. In "Bigler *vs.* Tahoe," an 1863 sketch published in the *Enterprise*, he denounces the name as an "offensive word" consisting of "hideous, discordant syllables" that belie the beauty of the "fairy-land forgotten and left asleep in the snowy Sierras" (ETS1, 290). Moreover, Twain's assertion that "Bigler" is preferable to the lake's indigenous appellation because it "at least has a Christian English twang about it whether it is pretty or not," reveals that his objections are not only aesthetic but also political. As with the creation of the "Pah-Ute" fraternal organization, the vagaries of Tahoe's nomenclature reflect the colonial effort to assert control over contested territory by effacing the presence of native peoples.[75] On the one hand, he concedes that "of course Indian names are more fitting than any others for our beautiful lakes and rivers," while on the other, he relegates their race—and hereditary title to those places—to a remote past, "ages ago, perhaps, in the morning of creation." Tahoe was first identified as Lake Bigler in 1853 by William Eddy, the surveyor general of California, in tribute to the state's third governor, John Bigler (1805–71); however, the name was rescinded eight years later owing to public furor over his secessionist sympathies.[76] In 1862, the US Department of the Interior substituted Tahoe for Bigler on its official maps, although the California legislature eventually restored the honorific after the Civil War. Despite this 1870 decree, Tahoe remained in more common usage.

In *The Innocents Abroad*, the malediction Twain pronounces against local lawmakers—wishing that "sorrow and misfortune" overtake them for not acting sooner to reinstate the lake's Anglo-American name—has given rise to much speculation regarding his sectional allegiances. The digression ultimately reveals more about his racial views, however, than his support of the Confederate cause. Its focus expands beyond the reviled Diggers to all Indians, while simultaneously gibing at the romantic rhetoric of Cooper's noble savages:

> People say that Tahoe means "Silver Lake"—"Limpid Water"—"Falling Leaf." Bosh . . . It isn't worth while, in these practical times, for people to talk about Indian poetry—there never was any in them—except in the Fennimore Cooper Indians. But *they* are an extinct tribe that never existed. I know the Noble Red Man. I have camped with the Indians; I have been on the warpath with them, taken part in the chase with them—for grasshoppers; helped them steal cattle; I have roamed with them, scalped them, had them for breakfast. I would gladly eat the whole race if I had a chance. (IA, 205)

The shift of perspective introduced midsentence in the passage's closing lines illustrates the "dialectic of simultaneous desire and repulsion" that Philip Deloria claims has characterized Euro-American attitudes toward indigenous peoples since the colonial era.[77] On the one hand, the writer imaginatively revels in the freedom of a nomadic native lifestyle, yet on the other he indulges a cannibalistic fantasy of devouring the entire race. Although his assertion "I have . . . had them for breakfast" is reminiscent of literary tall talk, it is in fact a deliberate echo of the 1860 rallying cry "An Indian for breakfast and a pony to ride" used by Major William Ormsby and his volunteer militia during the Pyramid Lake War against the Northern Paiute.[78] This suggests the degree to which Twain's memories of Nevada Territory continued to shape his perception of Indians even after he left the West.

Curiously, none of these allusions to Twain's "Indian" identity appear in the original *Alta California* letters, indicating that they were added during the spring of 1868, when he reworked and expanded them in order to create a coherent book-length narrative. Although the writer's reasons for introducing this imagery are unclear, his peripatetic lifestyle after the *Quaker City's* return offers some telling clues. On 22 November, three days after landing in New York, he moved to the nation's capital and began working as both the private secretary of Senator William Stewart of Nevada and an occasional correspondent for the New York *Herald* and *Tribune*. Over the next several months, he witnessed the contentious congressional debates regarding the day's "hot button" issues—among them the government's proposed resolution of the Sioux War. In "The Facts Concerning the Recent

Resignation," published in the *Tribune* on 27 December 1867, Twain satirizes the bureaucratic infrastructure of the executive branch by describing the absurd advice offered to members of the president's cabinet by the former "clerk of the Senate Committee on Conchology." After informing the secretary of the navy that his officers should be sent on a pleasure excursion "down the Mississippi on a raft," he visits U. S. Grant, then serving as secretary of war, to express disapproval of "his method of fighting the Indians on the Plains." He recommends assembling the tribes in "some convenient place" and having a "general massacre":

> I said there was nothing so convincing to an Indian as a general
> massacre. If he could not approve of the massacre, I said the next surest
> thing for an Indian was soap and education . . . [which] are more deadly
> in the long run; because a half massacred Indian may recover, but if you
> educate him and wash him, it is bound to finish him some time or other.
> It undermines his constitution; it strikes at the foundations of his being.
> "Sir," I said, "the time has come when blood-curdling cruelty has
> become necessary. Inflict soap and a spelling-book on every Indian that
> ravages the Plains, and let him die!" (CT1, 241)

Given the pervasive anti-Indian sentiment that existed in the late 1860s, this "joke" is politically fraught. In spurning the liberal reformist belief that native peoples were capable of assimilation into mainstream society, Twain's clerk suggests that savagery is an irremediable state. Education and hygiene will therefore neither elevate nor civilize Indians but "finish" them—achieving their eradication more effectively than warfare. This proposal, while extreme, apparently resonated in the popular consciousness, resurfacing nine years later as an unauthorized, stand-alone squib in the wake of General George Armstrong Custer's defeat at the Battle of the Little Big Horn on 25–26 June 1876. Its provocative new title (*not* supplied by the author), "A Cure for Indians—What Mark Twain Prescribes for the Infliction," reflects the collective rage that erupted in the massacre's aftermath, metaphorically positioning the writer as a physician and genocide as an efficacious means of healing the nation's dread "disease"—the presence of indigenous peoples.[79] The article spread quickly through the nation's newspaper exchange system, often appearing on the front page of local newspapers, and it even earned a place in the August issue of *Record of the Year*, a monthly "reference scrap-book" dedicated to reproducing in "permanent and convenient form, the most conspicuous and noteworthy articles that appear in the ephemeral press."[80]

The second session of the 40th Congress was dominated by discussion of President Andrew Johnson's probable impeachment but was also notable for the report of Sherman's Indian Peace Commission, presented on 7 January 1868. The group's findings prompted heated discussion in both the House and Senate regarding the broader issues underlying the government's "pacification" of native peoples—the exorbitant cost of recent military campaigns (estimated at approximately one million dollars for each Indian slain),[81] the logistical problems of establishing reservations, and the legitimacy of cash settlements to tribes as compensation for land loss. In his notebook, Twain interspersed observations on contemporary politics with recollections of his visit to the Holy Land; moreover, the thumbnail sketches he created of various senators include oblique references to Indians, suggesting that he may have been keeping a tally of their stance on native rights:

> Thad. Steavens [sic]—*very* deep eyes . . . whole face sunken & sharp—full of inequalities—dark wavy hair Indian—club-footed.—ablest man.
>
> Carey of O[hio] . . . —large face—a little full—unshaven—Indian—long, iron gray hair turned back & not parted—
>
> Horace Maynard Tenn[essee]—one of the purest men in Congress—very gentlemanly talented & fine speaker . . . O.S. [Old Style] look. *Indian.* (NBJ1, 492–494)

These entries, along with the December *Tribune* letter, reveal Clemens's active interest in the "Indian Problem" as he began the process of revising the *Alta* letters and generating new text to create *Innocents.*[82] On 11 March, the writer left Washington for San Francisco to arrange the republication rights for this material with the newspaper's owners and remained in the West until early July. On 14 and 15 April he spoke on the *Quaker City* excursion to capacity crowds at Platt's Hall, then embarked on a lecture tour of interior California and the Comstock. While in San Francisco, Clemens also renewed his acquaintance with James F. Bowman, one of Bret Harte's former coeditors at the *Californian*, who had enthusiastically reviewed his first Sandwich Islands lecture in October 1866. Now as local editor of the Oakland *News*, Bowman—writing under the pseudonym "Job Skae, Poet Larryat uv Goat Island"—promoted his friend's new venture by publishing "Lines Suggested by Reading Mark Twain's Letters from Pallistyne" in mid-April. This dialect poem praises both the shrewd candor and quintessentially American identity of Twain's epistolary persona:

> Here's a man that looks at things without speks;
> He looks thru his own ize; he sees what is vizib'e; . . .
> He perambulated Pallystne as he would a cattle-ranch in San
>   Bernadino. . .

He walked the streets uv Jeroosalem; he stood by the Sea uv Gallylee. . . .
    And the things that he seen, and that he thort, and that he felt,
Were the things a Digger Injun uv ordnery smartniss
Mite hev seen, and thort, and felt, ef he'd gone on a pilgrimig to
    Jeroosalem.[83]

Although Clemens never acknowledged Bowman's lyric, several features of the travelogue attest to its influence. His assertion that the book's purpose is "to suggest to the reader how *he* would be likely to see Europe and the East if he looked at them with his own eyes instead of the eyes of those who travelled in those countries before him" strongly echoes the sentiment—if not the quaint orthography—of the poem's opening lines. More importantly, Bowman's comparison of Twain to a "Digger Injun uv ordnery smartniss" extols his status as an American "savage" and may well have inspired the passages in which the writer self-identifies as an Indian, creating a paradoxical counterpoint to his representation of their Otherness.

THE LIMERICK INDIANS

About a month after *The Innocents Abroad* appeared, Clemens—who had by then relocated to the East—published "A Day at Niagara," his first sketch in the *Buffalo Express* under the byline Mark Twain. This piece also concerns tourism, though in a domestic rather than international setting, and features a naïve narrator visiting nineteenth-century America's premier attraction—Niagara Falls. This celebrated natural wonder was an icon of majestic, untamed wilderness closely associated in the popular imagination with Indians.[84] The presence of native people—and de rigueur purchase of their handicrafts—was an essential part of the tourist experience, as documented in an article published in *Harper's Weekly* on 9 June 1877 entitled, "Scene at Niagara Falls: Buying Mementos."[85] In his 1906 study *Niagara: An Aboriginal Center of Trade,* Peter Porter explains, "For many years Indian bead-work was one of the main attractions offered in the Bazaars there . . . during the season of travel, aged squaws and dusky maidens sat daily at various points along the route of the tourist—on the steep banks of the road leading up the hill to Goat Island, beneath the trees, close to the rapids, on Luna Island . . . and what is now Prospect Park—offering for sale, crude bead-work, pincushions, moccasins, etc. . . . Those 'Squaw Traders' were a most picturesque feature of the Cataract."[86]

These Indians were members of the local Tuscarora tribe, the sixth nation of the Haudenosaunee or Iroquois Confederacy, who had been

FIGURE 9.   Tuscarora vendors at Niagara Falls. Courtesy of Gerry Biron, Saxtons River, Vermont.

granted the exclusive right to sell their wares at Niagara for meritorious service to the Americans during the War of 1812.[87] An 1870 stereograph depicts a scene commonly encountered by Victorian visitors—three adult Tuscarora women and a young girl, all likely members of the same extended family, displaying their crafts in baskets and on a log "table" outdoors near the falls (fig. 9). Three face the camera; the other, in the right background, is seen from behind, head bowed in concentration over her needlework. All four wear dark kerchiefs and western-style calico dresses with plaid shawls draped across their shoulders. The figure on the left holds a typical souvenir—a beaded "barrel" purse shaped like the casks in which daredevils propelled themselves over the cataract.

Although "A Day at Niagara" is admittedly a minor work that, in the words of Jeff Steinbrink, "did little to carry [Twain] beyond the bounds of bad-boy burlesque,"[88] its representation—or, more accurately, erasure of—Indians is noteworthy. The sketch's assertion that the native vendors at the falls are in fact Irish immigrants is a subversive metonomy, substituting one group of "savages" for another. Twain's joke is highly topical, reflecting the widespread anti-Irish sentiment arising from the actions of a radical nationalist organization called the Fenian Brotherhood. Using Buffalo as a staging ground, the Fenians stockpiled a massive arsenal and launched an unsuccessful raid into Canada in 1866, hoping to force Britain to relinquish control of Ireland; the group remained entrenched in the city after this incident, holding a military parade and mass rally in 1868 attended by more than six thousand people.[89]

The narrator of "A Day at Niagara," who claims to have never before "come face to face with the Noble Red Man," is steeped in the romantic mythos of the vanishing Indian. He is therefore surprised to discover a display of indigenous crafts—"dainty Indian bead-work . . . and stunning moccasins, and equally stunning [carved] toy figures"—in a local shop and delighted to learn that "plenty" of friendly Indians were to be found nearby (CT1, 302). Approaching "the bridge leading over to Luna Island"—a spot frequented by Tuscarora vendors—he encounters his first "native," whom he addresses in a series of absurd clichés: "Is the Wawhoo-Wang-Wang of the Wack-a-Whack happy? Does the great Speckled Thunder sigh for the war-path, or is his heart contented with dreaming of his dusky maiden, the Pride of the Forest? Does the mighty sachem yearn to drink the blood of his enemies, or is he satisfied to make bead reticules for the papooses of the pale face?" (CT1, 303). His questions elicit an unexpected response: "An is it mesilf, Dinnis Hooligan, that ye'd be takin for a bloody Injin, ye drawlin' lantern-jawed spider-legged divil! By the piper that played before Moses, I'll ate ye!" Twain's parody of Irish speech and aggressive bluster—wherein the surname "Hooligan" functions as a pejorative signifier of ethnic rather than individual identity—also reveals the existence of a distinct social hierarchy. Although Dennis's status as an immigrant reduces him to a second-class citizen, he bristles at being mistaken for an Indian—a race even more reviled than his own.

Twain's narrator is similarly threatened with violence "in the neighborhood of Terrapin Tower," another location where native traders congregated. The "Indian" he meets in this instance, however, is a young female dressed in "fringed and beaded buckskin moccasins and leggins." Greeting her in the same sentimental language of his first exchange, he asks, "Is the heart of the forest maiden heavy? Is the Laughing- Tadpole lonely? Does she mourn over the extinguished council-fires of her race and the vanished glory of her ancestors?" He is once again rebuffed: "Faix, an is it Biddy Malone ye dare to be callin' names! Lave this or I'll shy your lean carcass over the catharact, ye sniveling blagyard!" (CT1, 303). The term "faix"—an oath meaning "faith" or "in truth"—is a stereotypical dialect expression known as a Paddyism, associated with the Roman Catholic peasantry who emigrated to America after the Great Famine of the 1840s. Biddy's words, like those of "Dinnis Hooligan," thus portray her as a two-dimensional ethnic caricature.

Although the narrator never questions the authenticity of the vendors' identities, these encounters do reinforce his dichotomous view of native character as either "tame" or "on the war-path." He then approaches a group "gathered in the shade of a great tree, making wampum and mocca-sins" and addresses them in the lofty paternalistic discourse of Indian-white diplomacy:

> Noble Red Men, Braves, Grand Sachems, War-Chiefs, Squaws, and
> High-you-Muck-a-Mucks. . . . You, Beneficent Polecat—you, Devourer-
> of-Mountains, you, Roaring Thundergust—you, Bullyboye-with-a-
> Glass-Eye——the pale face beyond the great waters greets you all! War
> and pestilence have thinned your ranks and destroyed your once proud
> nation. Poker, and seven-up, and a vain modern expense for soap,
> unknown to your glorious ancestors, have depleted your purses.
> Appropriating in your simplicity the property of others has gotten you
> into trouble. Misrepresenting facts, in your sinless innocence, has
> damaged your reputation with the soulless usurper. Trading for forty-
> rod whisky to enable you to get drunk and happy and tomahawk your
> families has played the everlasting mischief with the picturesque pomp
> of your dress, and here you are, in the broad light of the nineteenth
> century, gotten up like the ragtag and bobtail of the purlieus of New
> York! For shame! Remember your ancestors! Recall their might deeds!
> Remember Uncas!—and Red Jacket! and Hole-in-the-Day!—and
> Horace Greeley! Emulate their achievements! Unfurl yourselves under
> my banner, noble savages, illustrious guttersnipes. (CT1, 304)

Realism and romanticism collide in this mash-up of racial tropes. The narrator's exhortation, ostensibly intended to rekindle ancestral pride in these modern Indians, in fact portrays them as stereotypically ignoble savages—dirty, treacherous, drunken, and violent. Their "simplicity" and "sinless innocence" are ironic euphemisms for larceny and lies. The speech also mocks traditional native nomenclature by juxtaposing the ludicrous names of Beneficent Polecat, Roaring Thundergust, et al. with three well-known indigenous leaders. These alleged "ancestors," however, hail from three different tribes—once again insinuating that all Indians are alike—linked not by culture or bloodline but a conciliatory stance toward whites. Uncas (1598–1683) was a Mohegan sachem who favored collaboration with seventeenth-century British settlers; Red Jacket (1750–1830), a Revolutionary-era Seneca chief awarded a peace medal in recognition of the land cession treaties he negotiated with the federal government; and Hole-in-the-Day (1825–68), an Ojibwe leader instrumental in the creation of Minnesota's White Earth reservation, who was assassinated in 1868 by members of a rival clan. The "mighty deeds" of these individuals thus prefigure the doctrine of Manifest Destiny, which is evoked by the narrator's inclusion of a fourth "ancestor"—journalist Horace Greeley—whose 1865 editorial in the *New York Tribune* famously advised "Go West, young man . . . and grow up with the country."[90]

The narrator's speech eventually implodes under the accumulated weight of its paradoxical conceits. Rather than acknowledging that these "Indians" are imposters, he instead chides them for abandoning the "picturesque pomp" of their traditional dress in favor of the garb worn by the "ragtag and bobtail . . . of New York." In accusing the natives of masquerading as impoverished urban immigrants, he misconstrues the attempted assimilation and cultural adaptation represented by the modern clothes of the Tuscarora women in the 1870 stereograph. Moreover, his rhetorical conflation of the two groups—achieved by omitting the coordinating conjunction "and" in the phrase "noble savages, illustrious guttersnipes"—exposes the underpinnings of this association: Indians—like the "trundle-bed trash" Clemens had observed on Manhattan's streets in 1853—are a "mass of human vermin," dirty, poor, and homeless (L1, 10). The sketch disparages both groups simultaneously and altogether denies the existence of Indians in the East.

THE ECONOMICS OF ERASURE

Twain's representation of Native Americans in *Roughing It*, published eight years after he left Nevada Territory, paradoxically portrays them as murderous predators, lurking behind trees along the westward stagecoach route, objects of pity and revulsion—"the wretchedest type of mankind I have ever seen" (RI, 126)—and a convenient source of inexpensive labor. His celebration of the "wild, free, disorderly, grotesque society" of stalwart Anglo-American males who emigrated West to seek their fortunes also ignores the violent drama of indigenous dispossession that unfolded around him in the early 1860s: "No women, no children, no gray and stooping veterans,—none but erect, bright-eyed, quick-moving, strong-handed young giants—the strangest population, the finest population, the most gallant host that ever trooped down the startled solitudes of an *unpeopled land*" (RI, 392; emphasis added). This mythic vision of a landscape devoid of human inhabitants illustrates what historian Patricia Limerick calls "the powerful alchemy of selective storytelling . . . [through which] narratives of great complexity become simple stories of adventure and heroism and triumph."[91] In depicting Nevada's colonizers as dynamic agents of change who "startle" the desert solitude into life, Twain ignores the existence of native groups who had lived in the Great Basin for millennia. The fact that *Roughing It* records numerous firsthand interactions with Indians further reinforces his ethnocentric view that "savages" do not qualify as people.

Before setting out for the West, the narrator naively anticipates seeing "buffaloes and Indians, and prairie dogs, and antelopes," suggesting that Indians are an integral component of the region's indigenous fauna (RI, 2). Yet their inclusion amidst a list of animals implies a subtle dehumanization that grows more antagonistic as the text progresses. In chapter 5, he characterizes the cayote as a "first cousin" to the "desert-frequenting tribes of Indians"; both are contemptible, indiscriminate scavengers, who "live together in the waste places of the earth on terms of perfect confidence and friendship, while hating all other creatures and yearning to assist at their funerals" (RI, 34). Similarly, he asserts that Indians play a key role in the ecosystem of Mono Lake: "All things have their uses and their part and proper place in Nature's economy: the ducks eat the flies—the flies eat the worms—the Indians eat all three—the wild-cats eat the Indians—the white folks eat the wild-cats—and thus all things are lovely" (RI, 247). This humorous representation of the food chain allows the writer to not only satirize the unsavory dietary habits of Great Basin tribes but also posit Anglo-Americans as the apex of an evolutionary hierarchy.

Once the stagecoach enters "hostile Indian country" in Wyoming Territory, fear replaces novelty and the narrator's thirst for adventure. The keeper at La Prele Station informs the travelers that a Pony Express rider was shot there the night before their arrival, and that only two hours earlier he "had fired four times at an Indian" (RI, 55), to no avail. He recounts the incident as a type of sport, complaining that his target had "skipped around so's to spile everything—and ammunition's blamed skurse, too" (RI, 55). The travelers' anxiety, fueled by the foreboding prospect of the Indian's return, is exacerbated by the discovery of a "neat hole" through the front of their new stagecoach—a sobering reminder of its last trip through the region (RI, 55). That night, their sleep is "set with a hair-trigger ... seething and teeming with a weird and distressful confusion of shreds and fag-ends of dreams" (RI, 57), a description that prefigures Richard Slotkin's notion of the "Indian-haunted dreamland" in which Anglo-American colonists were trapped by the threat of frontier violence.[92]

The travelers' fears are realized when unknown perpetrators attack the stagecoach; shots are fired, screams are heard, and their inquiries to the driver about what transpired are met with silence. Left literally and figuratively in the dark, the men share their respective impressions of the event: "So we lit our pipes and ... lay there in the dark, listening to each other's story of how he first felt and how many thousand Indians he first thought had hurled themselves upon us. ... And we theorized too, but there never was a theory that would account for our driver's voice being out there, nor yet account for his Indian murderers talking such good English, if they *were* Indians" (RI, 57–58). The chagrin with which Twain acknowledges the possibility that these unseen marauders were not Indians reveals a fleeting awareness of his own racial bias; however, the most significant detail of the passage is the paranoia that underlies the men's speculation, prompting them to grossly overestimate both the size and deadly strength of their foe. This threat of unprovoked attack by "many thousand Indians" lingered in the writer's psyche, visualized in the prompt notes he prepared and then gave to his agent, Charles Warren Stoddard, for a lecture on *Roughing It* he delivered in Liverpool, England, on 9 January 1874 (L4, 18n1). The single boldest graphic on the page—accentuated by its surrounding frame—is a caricature of an indigenous warrior in profile, wild-haired and hawk-nosed, his eye narrowed in a baleful glare (fig. 10). Across the image, Clemens has scrawled "6000 Injuns," an arbitrary figure that appears nowhere in the travelogue but conveys his perception of native people as a formidable menace to the progress of civilization.

Ironically, the narrator's first personal encounter with an Indian occurs not in the wilderness but in the urban environment of Salt Lake City, where a métis bootblack offers to clean his shoes. Although this anecdote is intended to illustrate the relative worth of hard currency from East to West, Twain's conflation of economics, race, and social hierarchy complicates its meaning. Initially, the half breed is described as having a "complexion like a yellow-jacket," presumably because his sallow skin is smeared with blacking polish. In subsequent references, however, this simile is transformed into a demeaning epithet: the young man himself becomes "the yellow-jacket"—a type of wasp—a metaphor suggesting that race constitutes the sum total of his identity.

FIGURE 10.   Detail from prompt notes for "Roughing It on the Silver Frontier." Courtesy of the Mark Twain Project, The Bancroft Library, University of California, Berkeley.

When the narrator gives the bootblack a "silver five-cent piece, with the benevolent air of a person who is conferring wealth and blessedness upon poverty and suffering" (RI, 118) as payment, he experiences the painful "sting" of rejection and public humiliation: "The yellow-jacket took it with what I judged to be suppressed emotion, and laid it reverently down in the middle of his broad hand. Then he began to contemplate it, much as a philosopher contemplates a gnat's ear in the ample field of his microscope . . . [and presently] handed the half dime back to me and told me I ought to keep my money in my pocket-book instead of in my soul, and then I wouldn't get it cramped and shriveled up so!" (RI, 118). Monetary and social worth are simultaneously recalibrated in this transaction. Rejecting the subservience of his role as both a bootblack and half breed, the "yellow-jacket" insults the narrator, challenging his entitlement as an Anglo-American, much to the delight of the curious spectators: "What a roar of vulgar laughter there was! I destroyed the mongrel reptile on the spot, but I smiled and smiled all the time I was detaching his scalp, for the remark he made *was* good for an 'Injun'" (RI, 118). "Sunburnt with blushes" at the mortifying memory of this incident, the narrator—his white skin literally turned red—momentarily turns "savage," entertaining a violent fantasy of revenge while reinscribing the boot-black's inferior status as an "Injun." In this respect, the passage echoes Twain's murderous response in *The Innocents Abroad* to the "uncomplaining impoliteness" of the Palestinian beggars, "which makes a white man so nervous and uncomfortable and savage that he wants to exterminate the whole tribe" (IA, 473).

Chapter 25 of *Roughing It* describes the economics of erasure in the impersonal context of governmental bureaucracy. In Nevada Territory, the narrator explains, white laborers typically charged three or four dollars a load to saw up stove wood; the territorial secretary—seeking to impress the comptroller with his prudent fiscal management—therefore hires an Indian to do the work at 50 percent of the standard rate. Unlike the "yellow-jacket"—who openly bristles at the inadequate payment offered for his services—the woodcutter does not challenge the marginality of his position but completes the task in silence. The secretary then submits the "usual voucher, but signed no name to it—simply appended a note explaining that an Indian had done the work, and had done it in a very capable and satisfactory way, but could not sign the voucher owing to lack of ability in the necessary direction" (RI, 171). The government, however, denies the expenditure, refusing to recognize the Indian's labor—and by extension his very existence—on the basis of his illiteracy. As a result, the secretary is forced to pay the $1.50 out of pocket.

Although no such voucher has come to light in the territorial records, this anecdote nonetheless rings true. The anonymous native woodcutter was, in all likelihood, a Northern Paiute, a tribe whose work ethic Orion repeatedly commended in his reports as ex officio superintendent of Indian affairs: "They are peaceable, quiet, able and willing to learn to work like white men. They voluntarily about our towns seek for work. . . . Give them a chance to work for themselves, with tools and instruction, and they will ask very little else from the Government."[93] This emphasis on "work," repeated three times within the space of as many sentences, intimates that Orion's motive in hiring the Indian is not economic exploitation but a high-minded desire to facilitate his betterment.

Twain, in contrast, approaches the situation from a more pragmatic position of self-interest: "The next time the Indian sawed wood for us I taught him to make a cross at the bottom of the voucher—it looked like a cross that had been drunk a year—and then I 'witnessed' it and it went through all right" (RI, 171). This instruction is not a rudimentary first step toward literacy and eventual assimilation but an attempt to satisfy the government's requirement for acceptable documentation. The Indian's lack of facility with a pen, reflected in the wobbly, "drunken" quality of his mark, underscores the primitivism and outsider status of indigenous peoples, while at the same time introducing the subversive stereotype of native alcoholism. The anecdote sidesteps the Indians' capacity for civilization in favor of broad political satire: "The government of my country snubs honest simplicity but fondles artistic villainy, and I think I might have developed into a very capable pickpocket if I had remained in the public service a year or two" (RI, 171).

THE "GOSHOOTS"

Twain's harshest representation of Indians in *Roughing It* concerns the Goshoots, a band of western Shoshones who inhabited the desert on the border between Utah and Nevada. Numerous variations on the tribe's name appear in the historical record—"Gosiute," "Goship," "Go Sha Utes," and "Gosua Utes"—however, "Goshoot" is his own invention. In *The Transit of Empire*, Jodi Byrd argues that this unorthodox phonetic spelling is a genocidal homophone "through which Twain cajoles his readers to go and shoot Indians," a service "that would finally and fully trap them in a sanitized and distant past."[94] This point is provocative, if somewhat overstated; while the writer does not endorse the literal murder of Indians, his description of the Goshoots as "a thin, scattering race of almost naked black children . . . who produce nothing at all, and have no villages, and no gatherings together into strictly defined tribal communities" (RI, 127) leaves little doubt that he considered their eradication no loss.

Twain's remarks on the Goshoots conflate superficial firsthand impressions with the later, more systematic study of secondary sources concerning primitive peoples undertaken in the East, through which he intellectualizes and legitimates his indictment of the tribe as "the wretchedest type of mankind I have ever seen": "From what we could see and all we could learn, [the Goshoots] are very considerably inferior to even the despised Digger Indians of California; inferior to all races of savages on our continent; inferior to even the Terra del Fuegans; inferior to the Hottentots, and actually inferior in some respects to the Kytches of Africa" (RI, 126). He constructs a damning spectrum of cultural deficiency that ranges across three continents, dropping the names of exotic, little-known peoples, to whom the "Goshoots" are "very considerably inferior," "actually inferior," or merely "inferior." "Indeed," he declares, "I have been obliged to look the bulky volumes of Wood's 'Uncivilized Races of Men' clear through in order to find a savage tribe degraded enough to take rank with the Goshoots. I find but one people fairly open to that shameful verdict. It is the Bosjesmans (Bushmen) of South Africa" (RI, 126–27). The narrator's diction exposes his ethnocentrism; the verb "oblige," for example, suggests that his research is not motivated by idle curiosity but a sense of self-imposed duty. Moreover, in characterizing the conclusion derived from his reading—that only the Bushmen . . . are inferior to the "Goshoots"—as a "shameful verdict," he intimates that primitivism is a moral failing rather than a physical or cultural condition. He denies the humanity of Bushmen and Goshoots alike, claiming they "are manifestly descended from the self-same gorilla, or kangaroo, or Norway rat, whichever animal-Adam the Darwinians trace them to" (RI, 127).

Twain credits John George Wood (1827–89), a British minister who enjoyed a second career as an "armchair naturalist," as the source of this information. Despite his lack of formal training in science, Wood wrote a series of best-selling books on natural history, such as *The Common Objects of the Microscope* (1853), *The Common Objects of the Sea Shore* (1857) and *The Common Objects of the Country* (1858). In 1868, he published *The Uncivilized Races of Men in All Countries of the World, Being a Comprehensive Account of Their Manners, Customs, and of Their Physical, Social, Mental, Moral, and Religious Characteristics,* a two-volume ethnological study written without the benefit of any fieldwork. The text nonetheless sold well and was reprinted in the United States in 1870 by Elisha Bliss. As the editors of the California edition of *Roughing It* point out, however, Wood's study "did not mention the Goshutes or Diggers in his brief article on the Indians of North America" and his "conclusions were somewhat at variance with Mark Twain's [in that] he seems to have found the Fuegians and the Kytch more 'degraded' than the Bushmen" (RI, 605–6). Indeed, Wood's views on "The North American Indians," though imbued with the mythic trope of the "vanishing Indian," are far more positive than those expressed in *Roughing It:*

> Even though we do not form our estimate of the Indian from the romantic creations of Cooper, every right-thinking person will accord them the tribute of many qualities that constitute a real grandeur of character [as reflected in] their marvellous bravery . . . their stern, stoical endurance in misfortune, [and] disdain of death. . . . Driven from their hunting grounds and the territory of their ancestors, imbruted by drink, decimated and dying by epidemics and vices contracted from white men, the poor Indians vainly struggling to avert their doom of extermination have elicited the sympathy and commiseration of the civilized world.[95]

These discrepancies suggest that the writer's background research was more extensive than he acknowledges in the published text. In an October 1870 letter, Clemens reprimands Bliss for ignoring his request to send copies of several works in the American Publishing Company book catalog, which he needed for the travelogue's composition: "here I am suffering for the 'Col's' book [Albert Evans' *Our Sister Republic: A Gala Trip through Tropical Mexico in 1869–70*], & for [Albert Richardson's] 'Beyond the Missi[ssi]ppi,' & for the 'Indian Races' [by Charles De Wolf Brownell], & *especially* for the 'Uncivilized Races,' & [you] never say 'boo' about sending them. You must give me the 'Uncivilized Races' & the 'Col's,' any-how" (L4, 217). While Gribben indicates that Bliss did eventually fulfill his promise and provide copies of the Evans and Wood texts, Twain's remark about the inferiority of the Bosjesmans in fact derives from another source in his possession—Titus Fey Cronise's *The Natural Wealth of California*, likely purchased during his 1868 stay in San Francisco.

According to Cronise, the early Jesuit missionaries regarded the region's Indians as an "unfortunate race [that] stood at the very foot in the scale of humanity—inferior to the intelligence of the Bosjesmen of Africa, and worse in their habits than the disgusting aborigines of Australia."[96] In his determination to find an anthropological benchmark by which to measure the depravity of the "Goshoots," Clemens apparently either didn't read further in *The Natural Wealth of California* or conveniently forgot the context in which the statement was made. Rather than affirming the Jesuit perspective, Cronise refutes it, arguing that "It is unjust to charge the aborigines of California with being indolent ... and equally unjust to charge them with being stupid, and incapable of instruction. They are also [wrongly] accused of having been destitute of any conception of religion, affection, trade, art, or any of the higher attributes of humanity."[97] Twain's incorporation of this detail—despite its lack of ethnographic relevance—reflects his essentialist view of native cultures and identity: "wherever one finds an Indian tribe he has only found Goshoots more or less modified by circumstances and surroundings—but Goshoots, after all" (RI, 129).

In some respects, Twain's physical description of the "Goshoots" echoes his droll 1862 representation of Chief Hoop-de-doodle-do; like the fictitious Washoe chief, they are filthy and possess disgusting dietary habits, "never refusing anything that a hog would eat, though often eating what a hog would decline" (RI,127). His discussion of the tribe's character, however, is more closely related to the passage in *The Innocents Abroad* concerning the inhabitants of Banias, whose silence, tireless patience, and impassivity incite the narrator's desire to "exterminate the whole tribe." Twain alleges that the "Goshoots" are treacherous, devoid of religion and aspirations for a better life, and seemingly incapable of emotion—except where whiskey is involved. He also condemns them as a race of "prideless beggars," insisting that "if the beggar instinct were left out of an Indian he would not 'go,' any more than a clock without a pendulum" (RI, 127). Most significantly, however, his view of the tribe's subsistence on the "offal and refuse of the stations" as parasitism rather than an adaptive response to the cataclysmic changes caused by settler colonialism reveals the limits of his understanding.

FIGURE 11. "Goshoot Indians Hanging around Stations," *Roughing It.* Courtesy of the Mark Twain Project, The Bancroft Library, University of California, Berkeley.

The image Elisha Bliss chose to accompany this passage—captioned "Goshoot Indians Hanging around Stations"—reinforces Twain's claim regarding the depravity of all Indians (fig. 11). In order to cut production costs, the publisher simply recycled an engraving entitled "Utah Indians, Captured by United States Troops" from Richardson's *Beyond the Mississippi*, obscuring the bars and roofline of the structure where the Indians were confined through careful cropping.[98] The scene thus depicts neither stagecoach "stations" nor the "Goshoot" tribe but generic savages from Utah Territory in a radically different context. Moreover, the twelve individuals portrayed—ten adults and two children, all perhaps members of a single extended family—are not engaged in the act of "prideless" begging; instead, they cluster around a central kneeling figure, who stirs food in a communal pot. In the right foreground one man grooms another's hair, removing lice and eating them. This cavalier reuse of an existing engraving suggests that the image's primary purpose is to elicit revulsion at the Indians' impoverishment rather than any sort of ethnographic accuracy.

In the chapter's conclusion, Twain steps back and attempts—not very convincingly—to modulate his stance on the "Goshoots," declaring: "They deserve pity, poor creatures; and they can have mine—at this distance.

Nearer by, they never get anybody's" (RI, 129). The reliability of this statement is suspect in several ways. First, despite the writer's claim that compassion for Indians is contingent upon distance, his temporal and spatial remove from the West exacerbated his antipathy rather than mitigating it. Secondly, his generalization that westerners "never" expressed compassion for the plight of native peoples is flagrantly untrue; in September 1858— two years before the discovery of the Comstock Lode—Utah superintendent of Indian affairs Jacob Forney reported to his superiors in Washington: "I have visited a small tribe called the Go-sha-utes, who live about forty miles west of Salt Lake. They are, without exception, the most miserable looking set of human beings I ever beheld. I gave them some clothing and provisions. They have heretofore subsisted principally on snakes, lizards, roots &c. I made considerable effort to procure a small quantity of land for them, but could not find any with sufficient water to irrigate it."[99] The squalor Forney observes is identical to that described by Twain; however, he responds with sympathy rather than censure and proactively attempts— albeit with limited efficacy—to improve their plight.

Chapter 19 of *Roughing It* ends with a "snapper," intended to reframe the writer's rant against the "Goshoots" as a joke. He shifts the focus of his animus toward another "tribe," the employees of the Baltimore and Washington Railroad, whose degradation is rooted in incivility rather than race. The rumor that these railway workers are "Goshoots,"—that is, savages who also "hang around stations"—does not defame them, but instead "injure[s] the reputation of a class who have a hard enough time of it in the pitiless deserts of the Rocky Mountains" (RI, 129). "If we cannot find it in our hearts," he continues, "to give those poor naked creatures our Christian sympathy and compassion, in God's name let us at least not throw mud at them." Twain's quest to find a group "degraded enough to take rank with the Goshoots" thus reaches fruition not in the pages of Wood's *Uncivilized Races of Men* but much closer to home—in the civilized, technologically advanced East.

NATIVE REACTIONS—THEN AND NOW

Little is known about the response of nineteenth-century Indians to Twain's negative literary representations of them. One notable exception is a January 1891 letter from P. M. Barker, a former captain in the Canadian army, which appears in Kent Rasmussen's 2013 anthology, *Dear Mark Twain: Letters from His Readers*. Writing his letter just weeks after the Wounded Knee massacre, Barker—a self-described "great admirer" of the author—recounts a story concerning "a Hudson's Bay officer" he had recently met in Calgary. Two decades earlier, this unnamed individual, then stationed at Saskatchewan's Fort Carlton "in the neighborhood of large bands of Cree Indians . . . used to amuse himself by reading excerpts from 'Roughing It' to the Chiefs explaining the various points thru the aid of an interpreter."[100] He apparently did not share the vicious passage about the Goshoots but focused instead on the tall tale of "Bemis and the Buffalo," in which a wounded bull chases an inept Anglo-American hunter up a tree. According to Barker,

> The Chiefs three in number listened very attentively not manifesting the slightest inclination to be amused. After the story was finished they indulged in repeated grunts, lit their pipe passed it round, and with one accord turned to the head chief Mis-ta-wasis by name, for his opinion, which he did in the following words [:] "It must have been a wood Buffalo" and the others at once assented and returned to camp in possession of a greater knowledge than they possessed before.[101]

This account abounds in racial stereotypes—the taciturn chiefs passing a communal pipe, their primitive grunting, and grateful acquisition of "knowledge" from a civilized white superior. What neither Barker nor the Fort Carlton officer understood, however, is that Mis-ta-wasis's remark is a joke—told in convincing deadpan style—at the expense of author and letter writer alike. The chief's identification of the tree-climbing bull as a "wood buffalo," a subspecies of American bison indigenous to the forests of northern Saskatchewan, is a pun that mocks the anecdote's implausibility rather than affirming its acceptance "by men well acquainted with the habits and peculiarities of the Buffalo."[102] Doubly mediated by the interpreter's "translation" and Barker's desire to flatter Twain by adding these colonized racial Others to his already immense fan base, Mis-ta-wasis's meaning is muted, rendered opaque—and perhaps altogether misconstrued.

In contrast, the contemporary native reaction to Twain's western writing emerges with unambiguous clarity in the saga of "Sam Clemens Cove." Since his death in 1910, the writer's iconic status has been repeatedly imprinted on the American landscape. Streets and schools in numerous municipalities are named for him; the California town of Twain Harte, incorporated in 1924, pays homage to his early mining excursions in the Sierra Nevada region; and both a state park and bridge spanning the Mississippi bear his name in Missouri. In 2014, Robert Stewart, a retired official from the US Bureau of Land Management, approached the Nevada State Board of Geographic Names with a proposal to name a cove on Lake Tahoe's northeastern shore in his honor, noting that although *Roughing It*

"put Nevada on the map" no geographical feature in the state commemo-
rates his legacy.[103] Word of this proposition soon reached the headquarters
of the Washoe tribe—whose traditional homeland includes Lake Tahoe—
prompting a letter of protest from Darrel Cruz, the head of their Cultural
Resources Department. Citing Twain's fulmination against the name
"Tahoe," grounded in the apocryphal etymology that it means "grasshopper soup," as well as his numerous derogatory references to "Digger"
Indians in *The Innocents Abroad*, Cruz argued:

> Samuel Clemens had racist views on the native people of this country
> and has captured those views in his literature. In addition, Samuel
> Clemens was opposed to naming Lake Tahoe because the name was
> derived from the Washoe word "da ow" meaning lake. And to add the
> name Samuel Clemens to a place which he opposed is a disservice to
> Lake Tahoe. . . . Any name associated with a Native American people in
> and around Lake Tahoe refers to the Washoe people the original people
> of Lake Tahoe. Therefore we cannot support the notion of giving a place
> name in Lake Tahoe to Samuel Clemens.[104]

When the State Board on Geographic Names met on 13 May to vote on
Stewart's proposal, a letter of support from James Hulse, an emeritus professor of history at the University of Nevada, Reno, was read aloud. Hulse
maintained that Twain's disparaging statements about Indians were irrele-
vant, because "In his early days [the writer's] ironic-comic mode was
insulting to everyone, including governors, legislators, mine bosses, and
journalistic colleagues."[105] He also declared that Twain "learned and overcame his prejudices far better than most of his contemporaries and succes-
sors," but he offered no concrete evidence to document this change. Mr.
Cruz then presented a letter on the tribe's behalf outlining their objections
to the name. The extended debate that followed—chronicled in the board's
official minutes—mirrors the gamut of current scholarly opinion on this
topic. One committee member, for example, stated that because the exaggerated nature of the writer's prose made it "difficult to assess his true
personal feelings" toward native peoples, "we should forgive Clemens."
Another reminded the board that "Twain and Clemens are in effect
two different personalities," while a third reiterated the familiar bromide
that Twain was reacting to the "over-romanticization of Native Americans"
by authors like Nathaniel Hawthorne rather than critiquing Indians
themselves. Others invoked the dangers of applying contemporary standards of "political correctness" to an earlier era.[106] Eventually, Stewart
withdrew his support, citing the need for cultural sensitivity to the
Washoe tribe; the proposal then was indefinitely tabled, but not formally

defeated—creating a tactical loophole that allows its possible reintroduction in the future.

Several days after the meeting, Mr. Cruz reflected on the proceedings in a letter to the board's newly appointed chairman, Jeff Kintop. He explained, "I do not view the outcome as a victory. I view it as a discussion with an outcome that truly considered the sentiments of a Native people and honored our request. I am not sure if the public has an understanding of the injustices inflicted upon our tribal people. I have many stories of such treatment. It is my obligation to the people to do what I can."[107] Cruz reiterated this notion of obligation to his people—past and present—in conversation with me, explaining that his opposition to the board's proposal was not undertaken in self-interest but to commemorate the resilience and survival of his ancestors. Speaking without recrimination, he summarized the trauma of colonial contact in a single sentence: "The settlers came so fast, we had no time to assimilate."[108]

The Nevada State Board of Geographic Names' 2014 decision regarding "Sam Clemens Cove" in no way jeopardizes or diminishes Twain's literary reputation—the endurance of which is assured. It is, however, significant as a long-overdue historical corrective acknowledging the writer's animus regarding American Indians. The proposal to name a Lake Tahoe cove in his honor, though well intended, was justly recognized as an unconscionable affront to the people who hold the spiritual and hereditary title to that sublimely beautiful place.

4. The Roots of Racial Animus in "The Noble Red Man"

Published in the September 1870 issue of the *Galaxy* magazine, "The Noble Red Man" is without question Twain's harshest depiction of Indians—the hateful crescendo of a racial bias rooted in the tales of frontier violence his mother had told him as a child. The circumstances that prompted the writer to produce the sketch, however, along with his reasons for choosing to publish it in a New York literary periodical, have long been misunderstood. On first glance, the venom that permeates "The Noble Red Man" is perplexing. It was written neither during a time of war nor in the immediate aftermath of a horrific massacre, such as the Santee Sioux Uprising of 1862, that inflamed popular anti-Indian sentiment; indeed, Twain's invective runs counter to the assimilationist goals of the peace policy spearheaded by President Ulysses S. Grant. The sketch is nonetheless a highly topical piece, a vitriolic response to a different kind of event—the eastern media's effusive coverage of the June 1870 visit of two separate Sioux delegations—one led by the Brulé chief Spotted Tail, the other by Oglala leader Red Cloud—to Washington, DC, to discuss the terms of the Fort Laramie Treaty, signed two years earlier. By repositioning "The Noble Red Man" within the sociopolitical milieu in which Twain originally composed it, the submerged, multivalent sources of his antipathy come into clearer focus; and as a result, the essay—which has previously been dismissed as an anomaly, a discordant note of "peerless political incorrectness" in the overall symphony of the writer's oeuvre—assumes a new centrality in the development of his literary persona.[1]

Following the lead of the essay's opening line, "In books he is tall and tawny, muscular, straight, and of kingly presence; he has a beaked nose and an eagle eye" (CT1, 442), a number of scholars have argued that the primary target of Twain's critique is not native people themselves but rather their sentimentalized representation in the work of an earlier generation of romantic writers, most notably James Fenimore Cooper and Henry Wadsworth Longfellow.[2] Sydney Krause, in his 1967 book *Mark Twain as Critic*, offers the most extreme example of this stance, declaring, "We have in 'The Noble Red Man' the earliest, formally complete specimen of Twain's speaking through his fire-eating persona for the purpose of literary criticism."[3] Krause's emphasis on Cooper allows him to sidestep the issue of racism by interpreting the offensive epithets (e.g., "the scum of the earth!") hurled at Indians throughout the sketch as purely literary tropes; Twain's recommendation that Indians be exterminated is thus "no more to be taken seriously than is Swift's 'A Modest Proposal.'"[4] In contrast, Jeffrey Steinbrink's reading in *Getting to Be Mark Twain* is far more nuanced and perceptive: "'The Noble Red Man' bears relation to other instances of [Twain's] literary-social criticism in that it gets underway as an exercise in deflating sentimental excess or distortion . . . [however] the rest of the sketch is given over to invective, derogation, and manifest racism. Its intensely personal vituperation carries [the writer] far beyond the attitude of edgy candor needed to correct romantic misrepresentations."[5]

Steinbrink's point is well taken: in 2004, Stormfront.org, the world's largest white nationalist online forum, posted the sketch on its discussion board, touting it as "highly recommended" and "a good read."[6] The responses it elicited reveal that readers did not interpret Twain's text as a satire on Cooper's idealized Indians but as a diatribe against the drunkenness, ignorance, and degradation of native people themselves. One member wrote, "Been on the reservation in New Mexico, and they were pretty nasty. Friendly enough in there [*sic*] way, but dirty, nasty, smelly. None too bright either . . . [and] just don't get 'em drunk." Another recalled a childhood memory of "some squaw with a couple of little Injuns" urinating on the floor of a local grocery store, commenting, "Very noble people. Very noble indeed." For these individuals, the sketch was a touchstone that validated their belief in the racial inferiority of Indians.

Although the cultural construct of the "noble savage"—which Cooper admittedly played a central role in popularizing—had become an integral facet of the lens through which Americans viewed indigenous peoples after the Civil War, the sympathetic representation of Indians in the eastern press was not grounded exclusively in fictional antecedent. Federal Indian policy stood at a crossroads in the spring of 1870, largely owing to the fallout from a botched military operation that had occurred in Montana Territory on 23 January, when Colonel Eugene Baker—an officer whose alcoholism was well-known to his peers—mistakenly launched a surprise dawn raid against a village of friendly Piegans camped on the Marias River.[7]

Of the 173 natives killed in that incident, 33 were men, 90 were women, and 50 were children under the age of 12—many of whom, according to Montana Superintendent of Indian Affairs General Alfred Sully, were infants "in their mother's arms."[8] Outrage over this indiscriminate slaughter, derided in the *Chicago Tribune* as "the most disgraceful butchery in the annals of our dealings with the Indians,"[9] intensified when it was revealed that the Piegans were suffering from an outbreak of smallpox at the time of the attack, and thus had little capability for self-defense. Demands for an official investigation of the massacre eventually reached Congress, where they were derailed by General Philip Sheridan, who defended Baker's actions with the infamous pronouncement, "The problem to be solved is, who shall be killed, the whites or the Indians?"[10] Although Colonel Baker was never punished for the atrocities he inflicted upon the Piegans, the thoroughly "sickening details"[11] of the incident produced a groundswell of bipartisan support for "the Poor Indian" and much collective soul-searching about the military's ongoing role in managing Indian affairs.

In late May, the Indian Peace Commission convened in New York City to discuss the "Red Man's Wrongs" and issued a resolution declaring that "our Indian troubles are caused by the injustice of the Government, combined with individual injustice; that natural and conventional justice furnish the basis of a speedy and enduring peace, and the gradual and certain civilization of the Indians." The commission also argued that "the presence of the troops in Indian country tends to provoke outrages on both sides [and that] the present military policy is unwise, unjust, oppressive, extravagant and incompatible with Christian civilization."[12] This liberal view of the Indian's fundamental humanity and capacity for both civilization and citizenship was vehemently opposed by the inhabitants of many frontier communities, including those of Gallatin County, Montana, who issued their own counterproclamation in response:

> *Resolved,* That the Indian of poetry and romance is not the Indian of fact: the former is said to be noble, magnanimous, faithful, and brave; the latter we know to be possessed of every attribute of beastly depravity and ferocity.

> *Resolved,* That the mountain Indian can never understand the amenities of civilized life—he puts no faith in treaties, and makes his pledges and promises with intent to disregard them when interest and caprice shall dictate. The hospitality and kindness of the white settler he imputes to cowardice, and the largesses and annuities of the white man's government are received with the belief that the government fears him.

Resolved, That force is the only argument that will effectually persuade the Indian to peace and friendship, as the now peaceful conduct of the Bannocks, Snakes, and Utes, sufficiently attests.[13]

As these antithetical attitudes attest, geography was a key factor in shaping public opinion about how best to resolve the "Indian Problem"; those most exposed to the threat of violent depredations on the frontier favored ongoing military aggression, whereas the majority of eastern urbanites supported a more ambitious, long-range program of Christianization, education, and gradual assimilation. The incompatibility of these alternatives is epitomized by a question posed in an 1870 Nebraska editorial: "Shall we Williampennize or Sheridanize the Indians?"[14] This allusion to the founder of Pennsylvania colony refers to the Grant administration's policy of replacing military officers serving as Indian agents on reservations with clergymen, a significant number of whom were Quakers. Hoping to prevent another debacle like the Piegan Massacre, Grant also fostered the development of amicable relations with hostile tribes through diplomatic channels, instructing his commissioner of Indian affairs, Ely S. Parker, the first Native American appointed to this post, to invite key chiefs—among them, Red Cloud and Spotted Tail—to Washington for purposes of negotiation and reconciliation.

In keeping with these progressive national policies, contemporary reports of the Lakota leaders' historic visit to the East in metropolitan newspapers, like the *Washington Star, Philadelphia Evening Telegraph,* and *New York Times* (as well as the *New York Herald, Standard,* and *Evening Post*), present the Indians in lofty, idealized terms. Article after article emphasizes their imposing physical stature and striking manner of dress, their "natural" eloquence, and innate dignity—in other words, the very same traits that constitute the basis of Twain's attack in "The Noble Red Man." While skeptics might dismiss this similarity as a coincidence, the writer's personal reading habits, abiding interest in current events, and professional responsibilities as editor and co-owner of the *Buffalo Express* assure his awareness of the sentimental rhetoric used in describing Red Cloud and Spotted Tail. Moreover, it is likely that this imagery, rather than the iconic fictional figures of Uncas and Chingachgook, represents the concrete referent to which the sketch responds. According to Alan Gribben's reconstruction of Clemens's library, he regularly read a number of New York dailies over the course of his career; in addition to the *Times,* the writer claimed in 1888 that the *Evening Post* was his "favorite paper" and in 1895 that he "couldn't do without" the *New York Herald.*[15] But even if the extensive reports of the Lakotas' eastern sojourn somehow eluded him in these various metropolitan publications, the *Buffalo Express* reprinted—by telegraph—coverage from both the *Times* and *Tribune* throughout the month of June. These wire service stories were, in turn, supplemented by a series of locally produced—though unfortunately unsigned—editorials satirizing the "noble savagery" of the Lakota chiefs. Although it is tempting to speculate that Twain may have written some or all of these anonymous *Express* pieces, their authorship can never be definitively established; more likely, the dissonance created by their juxtaposition with the reports from other, larger newspapers piqued the writer's interest and supplied the underlying impetus for "The Noble Red Man."

Twain's dissatisfaction with the contemporary reportage on Indian affairs is evident in "How I Edited an Agricultural Paper Once," a sketch published in the July issue of the *Galaxy*. This issue would have reached newsstands in mid-June, just as the Lakota leaders concluded their triumphant two-week visit to Washington and New York City. The sketch's narrator—an individual with no practical knowledge of farming, who nonetheless assumes the temporary editorship of an agricultural publication—rationalizes his lack of qualifications as follows:

> I have been in the editorial business going on fourteen years, and [this] is the first time I ever heard of a man's having to know anything in order to edit a newspaper . . . Who write the dramatic critiques for the second-rate papers? Why, a parcel of promoted shoemakers and apprentice apothecaries, who know just as much about good acting as I do about good farming and no more. Who review the books? People who never wrote one . . . Who criticise the Indian campaigns? Gentlemen who do not know a war-whoop from a wigwam, and who have never had to run a footrace with a tomahawk, or pluck arrows out of the several members of their families to build the evening camp-fire with.[16]

This critique of journalistic ignorance anticipates the source of Twain's narrative authority in "The Noble Red Man": unlike most reporters, who know nothing of native ferocity and violence, *he* speaks as a westerner, someone whose firsthand observation of Indians affords privileged access into the alleged "truth" of their character. Thus, after describing the absurd, degraded appearance of a warrior bedecked in a "necklace of battered sardine-boxes and oyster-cans," wearing a "weather-beaten stove-pipe hat" and old hoop skirt," he adds a footnote explaining, "This is not a fancy picture; I have seen it many a time in Nevada, just as it is here limned" (CT1, 443–44).

Jeffrey Steinbrink characterizes the "racist virulence" of "The Noble Red Man" as a "'manly,' vaguely western" counterpoint to the "effeminate softness" Twain identified with the "effete East Coast."[17] While the speaker's regional affiliation is indisputable, the ethnocentrism of his views is by no means generically western.[18] The shrill derogation of Twain's language, particularly his use of sweeping racial generalizations—"All history and honest observation will show that the Red Man is a skulking coward and a windy braggart . . . [whose] heart is a cesspool of falsehood, of treachery, and of low and devilish instincts"—echoes the tenor of the Gallatin County resolution. The tone suggests that these are the views of a defiant, hard-line frontiersman, resolute in his conviction that the Indian is "nothing but a poor, filthy, naked scurvy vagabond, whom to exterminate were a charity to the Creator's worthier insects and reptiles which he oppresses." The speaker reiterates this view later in the same paragraph, declaring the Indian "a good, fair, desirable subject for extermination if ever there was one" (CT1, 443–44).

Twain's channeling of this venomous voice is a risky, complex gesture. By incorporating verifiable biographical detail and allusions to personal observation into the text, he blurs the already nebulous boundary between Sam Clemens and Mark Twain, simultaneously fleshing out the dimensions of his nom de plume by adding a sobering new trait—rabid Indian-hater—to his reputation as the "wild humorist of the Pacific Slope." In his 2003 study, *Mark Twain and the American West*, Joseph Coulombe describes "The Noble Red Man" as the writer's attempt to "distanc[e] his persona from potentially negative elements of the West to gain a greater readership in the East."[19] Considering both the time and place of its publication, however, the text is in fact a calculated declaration of difference—a bold, finger-wagging reproach directed at those living along "the Atlantic seaboard" who "wail" in misguided "humanitarian sympathy" over the plight of the "poor abused Indian" (CT1, 446). Such a gambit—even embedded within the broader framework of a monthly humor column—was far more likely to alienate liberal readers of the *Galaxy* than curry favor with them. Like the "Whittier Birthday Speech" delivered in Boston seven years later, "The Noble Red Man" is a veiled act of aggression, an occasion upon which Twain—adopting the guise of a brash frontiersman—defines himself in opposition to his genteel eastern audience.

The extremity of these political views can be gauged by comparing it with a *New York Times* editorial published on 13 June 1870, about midway through Red Cloud's historic visit to Washington: "We are quite aware that there is a class in the country which simply settles all such questions by saying, 'Any treatment is good enough for the Indians. They are vermin and must be exterminated.' We trust, however, that this savage theory is not accepted by the great body of the people. We ought to be desirous of keeping our engagements with the Indians, even if they *do* belong to an inferior race."[20] In its advocacy of genocide, "The Noble Red Man" is the consummate expression of the "savage theory" derided by the *Times*, thereby situating "Mark Twain" within that small, unenlightened class of (presumably western) citizens whose antipathy toward Indians was not shared by the majority of Americans. As the following analysis of contemporary reports regarding Red Cloud and Spotted Tail's diplomatic mission demonstrates, the caustic hyperbole of "The Noble Red Man" is intended to counter the romantic representation of Indians in the eastern press. Measure for measure, with equally broad, histrionic strokes, the writer refutes the notion of native "nobility"—epitomized in media depictions of Red Cloud—insisting that the Indian is instead "ignoble—base and treacherous, and hateful in every way" (CT1, 444). Ironically, despite these repeated claims of realism and accuracy, Twain succeeds merely in substituting one reductive stereotype for another. Nonetheless, in seeking to subvert the idealized image of the "good" Indian, he challenges the progressive ideology upon which the Grant peace policy was founded.

As Twain's 1885 publication of Grant's *Personal Memoirs* attests, he greatly admired the president but viewed the platform that had brought the former Union officer to the White House with ambivalence. In December 1868, he published a letter to the editor of the *New York Herald* entitled "Concerning General Grant's Intentions," spoofing the president-elect's stance on key issues. Within the context of an alleged interview, he poses a series of increasingly outrageous questions, to which Grant either makes no response or utters his infamous campaign slogan, "Let us have peace." Significantly, one of the subjects addressed is the "Indian Problem." Echoing the advice he had dispensed to Grant a year earlier in "The Facts Concerning the Recent Resignation," he inquires, "Sir, do you propose to exterminate the Indians suddenly with soap and education, or doom them to the eternal annoyance of warfare, relieved only by periodical pleasantries of glass beads and perishable treaties?" (CT1, 283). These alternatives represent a false dichotomy since "extermination" through cultural assimilation ultimately produces the same result as the literal "doom" of warfare—namely, elimination of the country's indigenous population—yet no other more humane options are mentioned. Given that these proposals occur within a broader pattern of frank absurdities—"Do you intend to do straightforwardly and unostentatiously what every true, high-minded Democrat has a right to expect . . . or will you, with accustomed obstinacy, do otherwise, and thus, by your own act, compel them to resort to assassination?" (CT1, 282–83)—they are clearly not meant to be taken seriously and lack the sting of comparable statements made two years later, without a trace of humor, in "The Noble Red Man." The tonal shift in Twain's discussion of genocide intimates that whatever misgivings he may have had about Grant's peace doctrine in 1868 intensified in response to the extravagant measures later implemented by the administration and enthusiastically endorsed by the eastern media in courting representatives of hostile western tribes.

THE LAKOTA IN THE EASTERN PRESS

Although native people had journeyed to the nation's capital for the purpose of treaty negotiation and ratification with some regularity since 1805,[21] the 1870 visit of not one, but two, Lakota delegations captivated the eastern press for several reasons—the groups' size and diverse composition, as well as the notoriety of Red Cloud's reputation. Spotted Tail arrived first, on 23 May, accompanied by four warriors and an interpreter;[22] nine days later, on 1 June, Red Cloud—the formidable chief who had succeeded in closing the Bozeman Trail in 1868—appeared, leading a "motley"[23] entourage of twenty Oglala headmen and their spouses dressed in traditional regalia, along with two mixed-blood interpreters. On the day of his arrival in Washington, the *New York Times* described the leader as "undoubtedly the most celebrated warrior now living on the American Continent . . . a man of brains, a good ruler, an eloquent speaker, an able general and fair diplomat. The friendship of Red Cloud is of more importance to the whites than that of any other ten chiefs on the plains."[24] Proceeding in this vein, the article advised, "Let every care be taken of him while in the East and no efforts spared to win his good will and create in his mind a favorable impression. He is a savage, but a powerful and wise man withal." This perception of Red Cloud's status, "celebrity," and strategic political significance, in conjunction with the theatrical spectacle of the delegation's exotic alterity, proved irresistible to both the media and local white populace.

According to D. C. Poole, the federal Indian agent who accompanied Spotted Tail's party, the sidewalk outside Pennsylvania Avenue's Washington House hotel, where the two Lakota delegations stayed, "was thronged with spectators who wished to see wild Indians, and . . . police [were often required] to clear a passage to the carriages, when they went out for an official visit or on a sight-seeing expedition."[25] Crowds assembled everywhere the natives went, hoping to catch a glimpse of the chiefs whom the *New York Herald* had dubbed the "Princes of the Prairies."[26] Reporters eagerly chronicled the groups' every movement and elicited their opinions on subjects ranging from contemporary women's fashion to ice cream. The media's fascination with the Lakota is reflected in the droll roster of delegates' names that appeared in the *New York Times* on 2 June: "The greatest chief of the Sioux nation, and commanding the largest band in the tribe, arrived in this city [yesterday] . . . accompanied by the following Chiefs: Red Dog, Brave Bear, Little Bear, Yellow Bear, Setting Bear, Bear Skin, Black Hawk, Long Wolf, Sword, Afraid, Red Fly, The One that Runs Through, Buck Bear, He Crow, Living Bear and Red Shirt."[27]

This picturesque nomenclature—which Twain had a lifelong penchant for satirizing ("Man Afraid of his Mother-in-Law," "Princess Invisible Rainbow," "Dilapidated Vengeance," and "Wawhoo-Wang-Wang of the Wack-a-Whack" are just a few of his most inspired creations)—accentuates the Indians' foreignness. The list also foregrounds the idealized physical description of the Oglala leader himself that occurs a few lines later: "Red Cloud, the greatest war Chief of them all, is a perfect Hercules. He is about six and a half feet in height, and large in proportion; indeed, there is not a small man among them. Magnificent buffalo robes, ornamented and bejeweled, are worn by them all. Red Cloud wears red leggings beautifully worked and trimmed with ribbons and beads, while his shirt has as many colors as the rainbow. His robe was trimmed and crossed with silks and seal strips."

This rhetoric presents the chief as larger than life—a demigod, whose resplendently "bejeweled" garments evoke an aura of both royalty and classical antiquity. Because Red Cloud steadfastly refused to be photographed on this first visit to Washington,[28] print journalism—the daily accounts of his appearance and demeanor published in the *New York Times* and *Tribune*, among others—offers the only documentation of his stay. These articles were subsequently used by artists to create the highly romanticized images published in *Harper's Weekly* and *Frank Leslie's Illustrated Newspaper* in late June and early July. On 18 June, the day after Red Cloud's delegation boarded a westbound train in New York City for their long trek home, *Harper's Weekly* printed an iconic engraving by staff artist Charles Stanley Reinhart[29] entitled "Let Us Have Peace," based largely on the *Times* report, which is quoted in the accompanying text (fig. 12).[30] Depicting the occasion of Red Cloud's introduction to President Grant, the illustration—far more mythic than realistic—abounds with symbolism. Savagery meets civilization in the clasped hands of the two leaders—one pale, the other swarthy. A tomahawk is strategically placed on the ground between them, its sharpened blade positioned away from the Great Father, signifying the Indians' abjuration of violence. Although Grant stood only five-foot eight, Reinhart represents him as taller than the six-and-a-half-foot Lakota leader, subtly aggrandizing the power of his office. Interior Secretary Jacob Cox stands behind

FIGURE 12. "Let Us Have Peace," *Harper's Weekly* (June 1870). Public domain.

the president, arms firmly folded across his chest; similarly, the Brulé leaders Spotted Tail and Swift Bear are positioned side-by-side, behind and slightly to Red Cloud's right. The backdrop against which the meeting occurs is a pristine forested landscape—emblematic of the vast tracts of land to which the natives held hereditary title. Most important, however, is the dramatic contrast the engraving establishes between the formal frock coat, bow tie, and shoes worn by Grant and Secretary Cox and the primitive attire of the Lakota leaders. In a flight of pure artistic fancy, Reinhart portrays Red Cloud bare chested—with rippled, well-developed musculature and powerful, sinewy arms—as a means of underscoring his impressively "Herculean" physique. His fringed breechcloth, belt, and leggings are all elaborately beaded; in addition, his body is adorned with a plumed headdress and several distinctive pieces of jewelry—large, crescent-shaped earrings, a bracelet, and a bear claw necklace. Red Cloud's appearance is rendered even more exotic by the three horizontal stripes painted just below his left eye; in the totality of these decorative details, the illustration presents, in Twain's words, "a being to fall down and worship" (CT1, 442)—a literal incarnation of the quintessential "Noble Savage."

The size and prominence of this engraving, which appeared on the front page of one of America's most popular periodicals, reinforced a stereotype that the writer considered inaccurate and dangerous. In "The Noble Red Man," he offers a corrective image of the Indian's "natural self," as he appears "out on the plains and in the mountains, not being on dress parade . . . [or] gotten up to see company": "He is little, and scrawny, and black, and dirty; and, judged by even the most charitable of our canons of human excellence, is thoroughly pitiful and contemptible. There is nothing in his eye or his nose that is attractive. . . . He wears no feathers in his hair, and no ornament or covering on his head. . . . He has no pendants in his ears. . . . He wears no bracelets on his arms or ankles. . . . He is not rich enough to possess a belt; he never owned a moccasin or wore a shoe in his life" (CT1, 443). While this litany of denunciation may be interpreted as a generic rejection of the "Noble Savage" stereotype, Reinhart's illustration, in conjunction with the *Times* article that inspired it, suggests that Twain's derisive allusion to the Indian's diminutive, "scrawny" stature may in fact represent a reaction to the media's depiction of Red Cloud.

The iconography of Reinhart's engraving also reflects the strategic political importance that the Grant administration ascribed to the Lakotas' visit. Robert Larson, one of Red Cloud's biographers, asserts that the federal government sought to aggrandize the chief's image because it "needed to believe that there was one Lakota leader who could speak for all of his people and deliver on all their treaty pledges. In short, federal authorities needed a 'head chief' with powers not customarily granted to him by his people."[31] The Indians were therefore treated with a degree of fanfare and ceremony normally reserved for foreign heads of state throughout the duration of their eastern stay. According to Larson, every detail of their Washington itinerary was a "carefully orchestrated event meant to impress the visiting Lakotas with the wealth and power of their white adversaries";[32] to this end, they were given VVIP tours of the Senate and Interior Buildings, as well as the Federal Arsenal and Navy Yard, where a fifteen-inch Parrott cannon was discharged for "their especial astonishment."[33] And yet, as reporters repeatedly noted, the Lakota reacted to these sights with indifference; at the Navy Yard, they expressed far more interest in the shiny brass tailings that fell from a manufacturing lathe than in the armaments themselves.[34]

On 6 June, the White House played its trump card, surprising the Lakota with a lavish reception in their honor, attended by members of Grant's cabinet, high-ranking military officers, selected senators and congressmen, and virtually the entire diplomatic corps—"representatives of every nation on the face of the globe, except China and Japan." The splendor of this soiree is chronicled in "The Gentle Savages," a feature published in the *New York Tribune* on 8 June and widely reprinted throughout the country—including on the front page of the *Buffalo Morning Express,* where Clemens likely encountered it the following day. Like a modern-day gossip column, "The Gentle Savages" drops the names of prominent A-list guests (e.g., "the stately Mrs. Thornton, the beautiful Madame Garcia, the accomplished Madame Gerolt and her fascinating daughters") and describes both the magnificently decorated presidential staterooms and the range of formal attire donned for the occasion. Mrs. Grant wore "full glowing pink grenadine, with flounced satin overskirt, and handsome diamond necklace and japonica hair [ornaments]," while the members of the diplomatic corps were "uniformly enclosed in swallow-tailed coats, white vests, neckties, gloves, and dark pantaloons."[35] The Lakota comparably adorned themselves with face paint, body trinkets, and feathered headdresses, though their appearance, as the *Herald* reporter patronizingly observed, stood in marked contrast to the "beauty, loveliness, and full dress" of Washington's social elite:

> Spotted Tail and his braves were dressed in blue blankets, white leggings, white shirts, and with each a single feather adorned the back of the hair. Their faces were painted with war paint. . . . Red Cloud was horribly painted, neck, face, and head. He wore a grotesque head piece, made of eagle feathers, and attached or sewed into red flannel [that] trailed down to the very ground, and was not only odd but beautiful. Red Dog, his lieutenant and orator, also had one of the eagle headdresses, as had several others of the chiefs. All kinds of grotesque shawls, blankets, and robes, with a variety of shirts, leggins, and every conceivable kind of bead and trinket adornment was brought into use by Red Cloud and his band.

Because of the limited number of translators on hand, meaningful conversation was impossible; nonetheless, a convivial spirit of mutual curiosity prevailed. The *Tribune* states that the Indians' "costumes, hair-dressing, paint on the cheeks, beads, [and] tin ornaments" were scrutinized with wonder by the other guests, as in turn were the diamonds and pearls worn by the diplomats' wives. After feasting on seasonal confections unfamiliar to the native palate—ice cream, fresh strawberries, bananas, cake, and fine wine—Red Cloud and Spotted Tail declared themselves "well-pleased" with the reception; with "big hearts," they professed to "like much great father, so much good eat, and much good squaws."

Grant's extravagant overture of friendship ultimately did little, however, to placate the Lakota; Spotted Tail, upon returning to his hotel after the reception, noted that the whites possessed many more good things to eat than they routinely provided to the Indians as rations.[36] Tensions escalated the next day when the delegations met with Interior Secretary Cox to discuss the status of their traditional hunting grounds and the continued presence of military forts along Wyoming's Powder River. On this occasion, Red Cloud defiantly seated himself cross-legged on the chamber's floor and delivered the first of two celebrated speeches, translated as follows on the front page of the *New York Times:*

> I come from where the sun sets. You were raised on chairs. I want to sit as I sit where the sun sets. The Great Spirit has raised me this way. . . . Whose voice was first heard in this land? It was the red people who used the bow. The Great Father may be good and kind, but I can't see it. I am good and kind to the white people, and have given my lands, and have now come from where the sun sets to see you. The Great Father has sent his people out there and left me nothing but an island. Our nation is melting away like the snow on the side of the hills where the sun is warm; while your people are like the blades of grass in Spring when Summer is coming. I don't want to see the white people making roads in our country. . . . I want no roads there. There have been stakes driven in that country, and I want them removed. I have told these things three times, and I now have come here to tell them for the fourth time.[37]

Many eastern commentators viewed Red Cloud's rich figurative language as an affirmation of his innate intelligence and the legitimacy of the Lakotas' political grievances. According to a *New York Times* report published on 11 June, "No amount of education could have enabled him to present his case with greater effect than he has lately done, drawing all his images and illustrations from nature. . . . Some of his remarks are even more characteristic of the red Indian than any speeches invented for the *Last of the Mohicans* by FENNIMORE COOPER. . . . 'My Father [the President] has a great many children out West with no ears, brains, or heart. The words of my Great Father never reach me, and mine never reach him. *There are too many streams between us'*—as fine an image as ever poet conceived."[38] This description is imbued with the stereotype of the noble savage; though unschooled, Red Cloud speaks with natural eloquence, spontaneously crafting a series of metonymies that convey his ideas with poetic precision. The comparison the *Times* reporter makes between the Lakota chief's words and a fictional benchmark of native oratory also reveals the extent to which the eastern media viewed him as an archetypal "red man," a genuine—albeit generic—embodiment of a vanishing race.[39]

Red Cloud readily accepted this symbolic mantle, introducing himself as "a representative of the original American race, the first people of the continent"[40] in his second address, delivered before an "eager throng" of some five thousand New Yorkers at the Cooper Institute on 16 June. He was more overtly conciliatory on this occasion, stressing the common humanity of natives and whites: "The Great Spirit made us both. . . . You have children. We, too, have children, and we wish to bring them up well. We ask you to help us do it. . . . All I want is right and justice. . . . We do not want riches, we want peace and love."[41] He also challenged the notion of Indian savagery, which he claimed was fueled by sensational media coverage of atrocities and depredations: "We are good, and not bad. The reports which you get about us are all on one side. You hear of us only as murderers and thieves. We are not so." According to the *Nation*, Red Cloud's speech was "comparable to nothing so much as the public recital of a fugitive slave in former years, and the moral effect on the audience was certainly of the same kind."[42] Similarly, the *Times* commented that the Lakota leader's presence on the lecture platform—his gravitas and theatrical gesticulations—was nothing short of mesmerizing: "Although the audience labored under the disadvantage of not knowing what Red Cloud said, until his words were filtered through an interpreter—and no doubt greatly weakened in the process—still his earnest manner, his impassioned gestures, the eloquence of his hands, and the magnetism which he evidently exercises over an audience, produced a vast effect on the dense throng which listened to him yesterday. His speech was like a poem."[43]

This praise became the basis for Charles Stanley Reinhart's most iconic image of the Lakota leader, "Red Cloud at Cooper Institute," published in *Harper's Weekly* on 2 July 1870 (fig. 13). In the engraving, the chief's apotheosis at the hands of the eastern media is complete. The blanket draping the lower half of his body evokes the flowing robes of ancient biblical times, suggesting that Red Cloud is a Christ-like figure, evangelizing a rapt multitude. As the inheritor of a rich oral tradition, the chief has no use for notes or a prepared script; thus, he symbolically turns away from the lectern positioned to his left and speaks extemporaneously, from the heart. Red Cloud's messianic aura is reinforced by both the intensity of his gaze and magisterial pose—right arm outstretched, palm philosophically turned

FIGURE 13. "Red Cloud Speaking at the Cooper Institute," *Harper's Weekly* (July 1870). Public domain.

upward. Although he is not pointing, his extended arm nonetheless directs the viewer's eye toward one particular member of the Lakota delegation wearing an oversized cross pendant. This detail affirms the leader's assertion, "we are good, not bad," by suggesting that the civilization and Christianization of the country's native population is already under way.

Even after the Indians' return to their reservation, the memory of Red Cloud's majestic deportment continued to exert a hold over the eastern imagination, as reflected in a statement published in the *Nation* on 23 June: "Public opinion was perhaps affected by [the visit of the Lakota delegations] more widely and more favorably than we can estimate. No marvel of all that the Indians saw on their way to the East would compare, if they but realized it, with the diffusion given to their speeches by the aid of the telegraph and press. It will be a peculiar disgrace if Congress alone shall show itself deaf to their just complaints, and bent on continuing the violations of treaty which are at the root of the present disturbances on the border."[44] The editors of the *Philadelphia Evening Telegraph* concurred, declaring that Red Cloud's "truly noble and manly bearing on all occasions inspired for him and his cause a respect that they have never obtained before with a majority of the people in this section of the country." The article praised the "plain, straightforward, and earnest manner" of the chief's speeches, which "won for him more favor with all right-thinking persons than if his conduct had been marked by subserviency, or by that low cunning which many persons are fond of assuming to be one of the most marked Indian traits."[45] This assertion of moral superiority—that *"all right-thinking persons"* were (or ought to be) sympathetic to the plight of indigenous peoples—colors much of the urban eastern reportage concerning Red Cloud and Spotted Tail's visits and reaffirmed the cultural hierarchies that provoked an angry backlash from inhabitants of other regions, especially the West.

HOW THE STORY PLAYED IN THE
BUFFALO MORNING EXPRESS

Not all eastern newspapers responded to the Washington visit of the Lakota delegations and the charismatic figure of Red Cloud with the same fervent approval as the *New York Times, Harper's Weekly,* and *Philadelphia Evening Telegraph.* Smaller regional dailies, such as the *Buffalo Morning Express* (in which Clemens owned a one-third interest), generally took a more conservative, skeptical view of the government's negotiations with its indigenous wards, as reflected in the wry tone of its in-house commentary. Indeed, the satirical manner in which the *Express* editors treated the June 1870 visit of the Lakota leaders seems not only to have galvanized the writer's thinking about native peoples by resuscitating old, deeply rooted prejudices but also to have found its way—quite literally—into the pages of "The Noble Red Man."

Like other newspapers of the period, the front page of the *Express* featured several columns of telegraphic briefs supplied by the major metropolitan publications; these nineteenth-century "sound bites" glossed the latest developments on the national and international scene. As a result, the Washington activities of Red Cloud and Spotted Tail received daily mention throughout the first two weeks of June 1870. The following item, published on 3 June, typifies the limitations of this coverage—a succinct presentation of outward, isolated facts, devoid of context or interpretation: "Spotted Tail and his party had a council to-day with the President, Secretary Belknap and Commissioner Parker, in which a desire for peace was mutually expressed. Red Cloud was not present. The Indians afterwards visited the Treasury Department. Spotted Tail was presented by the President with a fine meerschaum pipe, and Mrs. Grant added a box of smoking tobacco."[46]

Although this dispatch contains passing mention of a mutual "desire for peace," the relationship between Grant's small ceremonious gesture and his administration's broader agenda concerning Indian affairs is not specified, and can only be deduced in conjunction with other notices published during the same period. For even as the Lakota sought to preserve their ancestral right to the Black Hills through diplomatic means, the relentless work of dispossession proceeded apace in Congress. On 7 June, the *Express* reported that the House of Representatives had rejected two amendments "to exe-cute bonds for payment of treaty obligations to the Choctaw"; a week later, the following announcement appeared: "The whole Osage Indian reserva-tion in Kansas ... will be sold to actual settlers at $1.25 per acre if the proposition agreed to in the Senate is finally adopted in the House. The tract contains about 8,000,000 of acres ... [and] the Osage [will be relocated to] a new reservation in the Indian Territory."[47]

Far from the legislative halls of the US Capitol, however, the drama of dispossession played out not in words but in acts of unspeakable violence. Throughout the 1860s and 70s, news of the latest Indian raid on frontier homesteads or military outposts became a standard feature of the tele-graphic briefs published in eastern papers, meaning that reports of Grant's amicable overtures toward the Lakota in June of 1870 were frequently jux-taposed with stories of appalling bloodshed. The dissonance of these dis-patches—diplomacy conjoined with atrocity in narrow columns of print—underscores both the volatility and multivalence of Indian-white relations in this era. According to John Coward, author of *The Newspaper Indian: Native American Identity in the Press, 1820–1890*, bulletins from the fron-tier often bore incendiary headlines like "Indian Treachery" or "Indian Murderers," which told a "one-dimensional tale" of native misdeeds[48] while offering little or no background concerning the complex grievances precipitating them. In short, the briefs "distort[ed] the true nature of Indian-white encounters" by characterizing indigenous violence in the West as largely unprovoked. The *Express* published its share of these inflammatory reports, such as "More Indian Murders," which appeared on 8 June:

> Captain Mitchell, of the Fifth Infantry, arrived at St. Louis Monday from the Indian country. He furnishes an account of a recent attack on Bear Creek Station, forty miles south of Fort Dodge [Kansas]. Thirty-five Indians came to the station, which was guarded by Sergeant Murray and four men of the Third Infantry.... After cooking and eating some time in a friendly way, all but seven left. These remaining then shot two of Murray's men and severely wounded the Sergeant, after which they fled. Sixty mules belonging to Mr. Trainy, a trader of Camp Supply, were run off and one herder killed. Two or three other men were also killed at different places.[49]

This incident apparently caught Twain's eye and lingered in his memory, since he recounts it—albeit in somewhat garbled fashion—in "The Noble Red Man" as a paradigm of native treachery:

> When the Red Man declares war, the first intimation his friend the white man whom he supped with at twilight has of it, is when the war-whoop rings in his ears and the tomahawk sinks into his brain. In June, seven Indians went to a small station of the Plains where three white men lived, and asked for food; it was given them, and also tobacco. They stayed two hours, eating and smoking and talking, waiting with Indian patience for their customary odds of seven to one to offer, and as soon as it came they seized the opportunity; that is, when two of the men went out, they killed the other the instant he turned his back to do some solicited favor; then they caught his comrades separately, and killed one, but the other escaped. (CT1, 445)

Twain's version of the story elides some details and omits others; the nameless victims are not identified as army personnel but rather as ordinary—ostensibly innocent—civilians. He also embellishes the narrative by adding information that does not appear in the original dispatch—"they stayed two hours, eating and smoking and talking"—underscoring the camaraderie of these guileless Anglo-American hosts, whose kindness is repaid by Indian perfidy. The writer even invents a dramatic climax, claiming that the murder of one of the whites occurred at the very "instant he turned his back to do some solicited favor" for his native guests. In exercising this creative license, Twain allegorizes the incident at Bear Creek Station in "The Noble Red Man," transforming it into a racialized parable of the dastardly manner in which *all* Indians "declare war," regardless of time, place, or circumstance.

As the Lakota delegations' historic visit to the East drew to a close, the *Buffalo Morning Express* began supplementing its national wire service coverage of the story with a series of in-house articles, the majority of which spoof the poetic qualities of native rhetoric. On 10 June—three days after Red Cloud delivered his first remarks in Washington—the *Express* published "Making an Impression on the Noble Savage," an unsigned editorial that challenges the authenticity of the leader's "'big talk' with Secretary Cox" by claiming that "the composition reflects great credit upon either the interpreter or the Bohemian who put it together." The piece then offers a parodic version of "what the Indian really did say":

> I am a big Indian. I don't want to be anything else. I am going to sit on the floor to show you that I be an Indian. I won't have any nonsense. I come here to tell you what you have got to do if you don't want us to fight you. I don't want the white people to build roads in my country. . . . I have said

so three times and I want you to understand it now. I won't have any roads. You've got a fort out there, too, which you must take away if you don't want trouble. And your white fellows must quit going through my country killing game. We want to kill the game ourselves, and you must give us ammunition to kill it with. . . . You want me to go to farming and earn my own living. I shan't do it. I am a big Indian. Ugh.[50]

In this "translation," Red Cloud's eloquence devolves into a series of curt, petulant demands. No mention is made of the Lakotas' dispossession or loss of traditional lifeways; rather, the leader simply issues an ultimatum, identifying numerous unilateral concessions that the government "must" make in order to avoid the outbreak of war. Red Cloud is thus unflatteringly depicted as arrogant, unreasonable, and childish. The most salient feature of the *Express* parody, however, is the manner in which the chief's words have been systematically stripped of metaphor and imagery. While it is unlikely that Twain authored this piece in light of the terminal illness of his father-in-law, Jervis Langdon (who succumbed to stomach cancer on 6 August), its derisive representation of native oratory is consonant with the writer's assertion in "The Noble Red Man" that "there is nothing figurative, or moonshiny, or sentimental about [the Indian's] language. It is very simple and unostentatious, and consists of plain, straightforward lies. His 'wisdom' conferred upon an idiot would leave that idiot helpless indeed" (CT1, 444).

The similarities between Twain's sketch and the *Express* editorial are even more pronounced in their respective conclusions. The article's final paragraph reads, "We take it that that was probably about the real speech made by the deeply 'impressed' Red Cloud to Mr. Secretary Cox. In a few days Washington will know the distinguished orator no more, and our next news of him will no doubt be in connection with some little demonstration against the surveyors who are staking out a road in his country, by the results of which a few scalps, more or less, will be added to the adornment of his noble person." This characterization of an act of cold-blooded murder and mutilation as a "little demonstration," akin to picketing or some other equally innocuous form of social protest,[51] anticipates the tone and diction of the closing lines of "The Noble Red Man":

Whenever [the Indian] gets into trouble[,] the maids and matrons [of the Atlantic seaboard] throw up their hands in horror at the bloody vengeance wreaked upon him, and the newspapers clamor for a court of inquiry to examine into the conduct of the inhuman officer who inflicted the little pleasantry upon the "poor abused Indian." (They always look at the matter from the abused-Indian point of view, never from that of the bereaved white widow and orphan.) But it is a great and unspeakable comfort to know that, let them be as prompt about it as they may, the inquiry has always got to come *after* the good officer has administered his little admonition. (CT1, 446)

The stylistic signature of these lines—"little pleasantry," "little admonition"—parallels the euphemistic description of interracial violence in "Making an Impression on the Noble Savage" with one crucial difference. Whereas the *Express* writer's gibe reinforces a stereotype of primitive bloodlust and unredeemable savagery, the implications of Twain's phrasing are far more extreme. By figuratively equating murder with playful banter or gentle reproof, the sketch sanctions the vigilantism of the "good officer," presenting it as appropriate and justifiable redress for an unspecified prior injury. With callous indifference to the native's loss of life, the speaker exults in this deed of "bloody vengeance," deriving immense comfort from the fact that any punishment meted out against this nameless officer must inevitably occur after the Indian's death.

Within ten days of publishing "Making an Impression on the Noble Savage," the *Express* assailed both the authenticity of Red Cloud's oratorical skills and the earnestness of his diplomatic efforts on at least three other occasions. On 16 June, the paper reprinted a piece of racist doggerel from *Punchinello* called, "The Song of the Red Cloud," which features the members of the Lakota delegations brandishing tomahawks, performing a cancan, and creating "an uproar of shrill and guttural sounds"—"Ugh! Hrumph! How! Whoop, whoop, halooooooo!"—while negotiating with government officials.[52] Two days later, a lengthy feature, "'Lo' at the Capitol," appeared bearing the byline "Written for the *Express.*" Purporting to be a field report from Washington, DC, the article is signed, "Yours skeptically, Hy Slocum," the pseudonym of a local humorist, long suspected to have been Mark Twain but later identified as Frank Manly Thorn,[53] who published a number of sketches in the newspaper between 1868 and 1870.[54] Slocum recaps the highlights of the Lakota delegations' visit, claiming that their presence in the city "has provided the *blasé* society of this place with a wholesome sensation, by enabling its wearied members to hold communion with nature, in her visible forms, by means of halfbreed interpreters familiar with the Sioux." He attends President Grant's reception on 6 June, where he meets Spotted Tail (referred to as "Mr. Variegated Appendage") and tours the House of Representatives with an Indian he dubs *"He-that-scratches-his-head"*; most significantly, he avers that Red Cloud "employed me to write his little speech to Secretary Cox," which the inebriated Lakota chief then delivered "in a manner that exhibited my collection of aboriginal metaphors to excellent advantage." Like the earlier *Express* parody, Slocum's rendition of Red Cloud's speech is grounded in a presumption of plagiarism—words ghostwritten by a white man. It also inanely recasts the poetry of Red Cloud's original statement about the Lakota nation, "melting away like snow on the side of the hills where the sun is warm," to "my people are fading away like hospital patients before the fatal inroads of a medical student," deflating the eloquence of his rhetoric.

Although no proof exists that Clemens read (let alone wrote) "'Lo' at the Capitol," the 18 June issue of the *Express* contains several other items of personal and professional interest that increase its likelihood. To the right of Slocum's text was the latest installment of a serial travelogue entitled "Across the Continent," which concerns San Francisco and the so-called Chinese Problem—a topic the writer himself had addressed in the *Galaxy* in May. The same page also featured the newspaper's monthly review the New Books column, an eclectic digest of recent publications ranging from mythology and linguistics to domestic economy. Among the dozen or so titles discussed in the column was *Bound Down, or Life and Its Possibilities*, a novel by Anna M. Fitch, with whom Clemens had collaborated six years earlier in Nevada Territory on a short-lived literary periodical called the *Weekly Occidental*.[55] While these tangential associations with the writer's own life and work may have briefly captured his attention, an article printed in the center of page three, directly across the fold from "Lo," would have elicited closer scrutiny—"MARK TWAIN'S WICKED BOOK: Deacon B. Criticises the 'New Pilgrim's Progress'"—a humorous, but highly flattering discussion of *The Innocents Abroad* reprinted from the *Springfield Republican*. The presence of this review raises the possibility that Clemens not only saw the day's paper but also set it aside for safekeeping, perhaps intending to include the piece in a scrapbook of clippings.

In fact, several details in "The Noble Red Man" demonstrate that Twain had the *Express* of 18 June on hand when he was composing the sketch several weeks later and mined it for evidence in support of his argument. The closing paragraph, for example, alludes to "Dr. Keim's excellent book" as an authoritative source on the subject of native savagery but does not explicitly identify it by name. The text in question—De Benneville Randolph Keim's *Sheridan's Troopers on the Borders*, a firsthand account of General Philip Sheridan's 1868–69 winter campaign against the Cheyenne and other southern Plains tribes, which culminated in the infamous massacre on the Washita River,[56] happens to be one of the titles discussed in the New Books column. Moreover, the anonymous reviewer frames Keim's work within a specific topical context:

The recent visit of the chiefs of the greater tribes of savages of the Plains to Washington, at their own request, to lay their grievances before the President, has drawn attention to the Indians' side of the question, and we cannot see that Spotted Tail and Red Cloud have made their case any better than it was represented by General Sheridan in his reports to the War Department. From June, 1868 to October, 1869, the Indians massacred nearly 200 white persons and ravished over forty women captured in peaceful outlying settlements along the border, or belonging to emigrant trains traveling the settled routes of travel. Children were burned alive in the presence of their parents. Wives were ravished before their husbands' eyes. Husbands were mutilated, tortured and scalped, and their wives compelled to look on. . . . This book affords a lively and picturesque account of the military expedition against the Indians in the Winter of 1868–69, and fully justifies the opinions entertained by the Lieutenant General. The author, Dr. Keim, participated in the campaigns, and he presents an array of statistics, and descriptions of Indian warfare which are as valuable as they are interesting. The sentimental philanthropist will find much in these pages that will shake his faith in, and love for, the untameable savage of the far West.[57]

The reviewer's use of the honorific "Dr." in alluding to the book's author is a misnomer. De Benneville Randolph Keim was neither a physician nor a professor but rather a journalist, a former reporter for the *New York Herald,* who rode with Union troops and covered more than two dozen battles during the Civil War. Twain's replication of this error in "The Noble Red Man" suggests that his knowledge of Keim's "excellent book" was secondhand, gleaned solely from the newspaper summary rather than the actual memoir. He thus implies that the text is the source of the horrifying statistics cited in the conclusion of "The Noble Red Man" concerning Indian atrocities against whites, when in fact this information appears nowhere in *Sheridan's Troopers on the Borders.* Rather, the four sentences he incorporates into the sketch's final paragraph—and italicizes for additional emphasis—are reproduced verbatim from the *Express* review. Notwithstanding the questionable ethics of such unacknowledged borrowing, the writer utilizes this evidence as the trump card of his argument, declaring, "These facts and figures are official, and they exhibit the misunderstood Son of the Forest in his true character—as a creature devoid of brave or generous qualities, but cruel, treacherous, and brutal" (CT1, 446).

Twain's appropriation of this material not only illustrates the extent to which his political views were informed by regular reading of the *Express* but also his camaraderie with its other reporters. Though the New Books column carried no byline, it was in all likelihood authored by Josephus

Nelson Larned, a fellow editor and co-owner of the newspaper, whose vora-
cious reading habits once prompted Twain to remark that "he knows more
than Webster's Unabridged and the American Encyclopedia."[58] The two
men had a close, congenial working relationship and occasionally even collaborated on one another's pieces, as Twain famously described in an August
1869 letter to his fiancé Livy: "Larned & I sit upon opposite sides of the
same table & . . . occasionally, after biting our nails & scratching our heads
awhile, we just reach over and *swap manuscript*—& then we scribble away
without the least trouble, he finishing my article & I his. Some of our
patch-work editorials of this kind are all the better for the new life they get
by crossing the breed" (L3, 317).

The synergistic blend of diction, voice, and style produced in these
"swaps" bespeaks an extraordinary level of comfort and trust between
Clemens and Larned. Their freewheeling solution to the age-old problem of
writer's block—in which one man literally finishes the other's thoughts and
sentences, thereby blurring of the lines of authorship—is grounded in an
absence of egotism and professional rivalry. If Larned was indeed the author
of the 18 June New Books column, this precedent of "patch-work" literary
production may help to explain Twain's lack of compunction about quoting
an extended passage from the review without formal acknowledgment.

Ultimately, however, what is most important about the *Express* review is
not the identity of its author, which can never be conclusively determined,
but rather the similarity between its harsh representation of Indians and
"The Noble Red Man." The underlying ideological premises of both texts
are identical: Indians are violent "savages" incapable of civilization; the "sentimental philanthropists," overwhelmingly eastern in origin, who advocate
their eventual assimilation into mainstream American society are naïve and
deluded. Even Twain's most extreme assertion—that the Indian "is a good,
fair, desirable subject for extermination if ever there was one"—is tacitly
corroborated by the *Express* review. The article euphemizes the violence of
Sheridan's winter campaign likening his views on savagery to those of the
soldier-protagonist of Tennyson's 1842 dramatic monologue, "Locksley
Hall," who quaintly "counts the gray barbarian less than the Christian
child." The reviewer endorses this ethnocentric attitude, declaring that
Keim's narrative "fully justifies the opinions entertained by the Lieutenant
General." Among the many "opinions" Sheridan reputedly voiced during
this campaign, one has achieved particular notoriety. Presiding over the surrender of Comanche warriors at Fort Cobb, Oklahoma, in January 1869, the
commander was approached by an aged chief, who thumped his breast and
introduced himself with these words: "Me, Toch-a-way, me good Injun."

Sheridan's alleged response, "The only good Indians I ever saw were dead," has morphed over time into the quintessential expression of what Herman Melville called "the metaphysics of Indian-hating": "The only good Indian is a dead Indian."[59] The view of indigenous peoples presented in "The Noble Red Man" thus parallels not only the stance of the anonymous *Express* reviewer but also the US Army's most infamous Indian fighter.

The similarities between the newspaper review and Twain's sketch suggest that he had a like-minded colleague at the *Express*, someone who shared or was perhaps influenced by his cynicism regarding the liberal eastern perspective on native character. Nonetheless, the degree to which the writer's antipathy toward Indians mirrors the racial attitudes of the Buffalo community at large remains unclear. On 20 June, two days after the appearance of "'Lo' at the Capitol" and the Keim review, the *Express* ran an article entitled, "Red Cloud as an Orator," which begins by invoking the trope of the "vanishing Indian": "It is possible that we did injustice to the 'last of the Ogalallas' the other day, by suspicioning the genuineness of the speeches which were put into his mouth by Washington reporters. New York appears to have been excited to enthusiasm by Red Cloud's oration, at Cooper's Institute, on Thursday, albeit compelled to take what he said on trust from the interpreter."[60] The piece then quotes—with no satirical interpolations or commentary—two long, flattering descriptions of the Lakota leader's eloquence from the *New York Times* and *Tribune*. While this statement by no means constitutes a formal retraction of the allegations made in "Lo" and "Making an Impression on the Noble Savage," it is an acknowledgment by the newspaper's editors that their "joke" may have gone too far, violating professional standards of accuracy and impartiality, and potentially offending the sensibilities of some readers. Since the article concedes only the "possibility"—and not necessarily the fact—of injustice, it is an equivocal statement of contrition, which may signify begrudging deference to the authority of the *Times* and *Tribune* as official "newspapers of record" rather than any substantive revaluation of Red Cloud's character.

The ambivalence with which the *Express* staff viewed the Lakotas' diplomatic mission is reinforced by a notice, tucked between announcements of an upcoming yacht race on Lake Ontario and the YMCA's summer "Festival at the Rink," that appeared in the City and Vicinity column of the same day's paper:

RED CLOUD AND HIS PARTY.—The Indian delegation, comprising twenty-seven persons, *en route* from New York to their Western home, arrived in this city at midnight Friday [17 June] and "put up" in the Central Depot. They were unable to obtain accommodations either in a hotel or sleeping coach on account of their *untidy* proclivities and, therefore, had to make themselves as comfortable as possible in the depot for a few hours. Red Cloud and Spotted Tail stood up on their dignity, while all the rest lay down on the floor and went to sleep.[61]

Rather than objectively noting the brief—but nonetheless historic—presence of these native dignitaries, the anonymous reporter who covered the local beat (in all likelihood, Clemens's junior colleague Earl Berry) instead spins the news into a tale of exclusionary civic pride, bragging that the Lakota were unwelcome in Buffalo and denied lodging as a result of their poor hygiene. This narrative, however, does not entirely jive with historical fact and may reflect the writer's personal bias more than the xenophobia of the city's innkeepers.[62] According to the *New York Evening Post,* Red Cloud and his entourage left Manhattan Friday morning on the Hudson River Railroad with great fanfare and acclaim: "At the time of their departure from the St. Nicholas Hotel, a large crowd had gathered to see them, and as the chiefs passed into their coaches they shook hands cordially with those near them."[63] The Indians boarded a "special railroad car"[64] reserved for their private use, disembarking fourteen hours later in Buffalo to await the arrival of a second train that would carry them West to Chicago. Thus, the Lakota were technically not denied a "sleeping coach" as the article alleges; rather, their stranding at the Central Depot was more likely the result of a poor travel connection. The brevity of their layover, estimated at "a few hours," suggests that the federal agents escorting the delegation may have deemed providing overnight accommodations an unnecessary extravagance—and that they, not the city's inhospitable hoteliers, were responsible for the natives' discomfort. The most remarkable feature of the *Express* article, however, is that, while the reporter dismisses the Indians as "dirty savages," content to sleep on the station floor like dogs, even he must concede that Red Cloud is different. The chief is represented as a stately, almost regal figure who stands "up on [his] dignity"—just as he had several days earlier at the Cooper Institute—watchful and protective, a defender of his people's well-being and security. In this respect, the brief offers a befitting postscript to the satirical coverage of the Lakotas' eastern sojourn in the *Express.*

THE THOMAS FITCH FACTOR

According to Jeffrey Steinbrink's book, *Getting to Be Mark Twain,* the *Galaxy* appeared on newsstands in the middle of each month; the September 1870 issue would therefore have been published on or about 15 August. The deadline for the submission of Twain's copy would have been approximately two weeks earlier—between 1 and 3 August, indicating that the six short essays and handful of miscellaneous items that made up his September Memoranda column ("Political Economy," "John Chinaman in New York," "The Noble Red Man," "A Royal Compliment," "The Approaching Epidemic," and "Favors from Correspondents") were written sometime during the month of July—the last agonizing weeks of his father-in law's life.[65] Moreover, on the basis of Clemens's letters and two "personal notices" that appeared in the *Buffalo Express* on 18 and 25 July announcing what appeared to be a marked improvement in Langdon's condition (L4, 173–74), Steinbrink narrows this timeframe even further, surmising that the *Galaxy* pieces were written during the latter half of the month: "Luxuriating in the buoyant mood that accompanied Jervis Langdon's apparent return to health, Clemens produced his September 'Memoranda' in time to meet his early August deadline."[66]

While the copy may indeed have been finalized within this two-week period, several details in "The Noble Red Man" suggest an earlier inception. Early in July—shortly after the Lakota delegations had returned to their western home—Clemens himself undertook a visit to the nation's capital in an attempt to protect the business assets of his dying father-in-law. Specifically, his task involved lobbying for the passage of Senate Bill 1025, which proposed the judicial redistricting of Tennessee and promised to expedite resolution of Jervis Langdon's long-pending lawsuit against the city of Memphis, which owed him five hundred thousand dollars for a street-paving contract (L3, 264–65; 278–79).

During the five days he spent in Washington from 4 through 9 July, Clemens also found considerable time for hobnobbing with various elected officials, including two former acquaintances from Nevada Territory—Senator William Stewart and Congressman Thomas Fitch. As he bragged in a letter home to Livy on 6 July, his burgeoning literary reputation seemed to magically open political doors: "I have the advantage of obscure lobby-ists, because I can get any man's ear for a few moments, & also his polite attention & respectful hearing. The most of them—all of them, in fact—tacitly acknowledge an indebtedness to me for wisdom supplied to them by my pen, & it is a very influential point in one's favor, don't you see?" (L4, 165). This same letter recounts the breathless pace of his day—up at six a.m., off to the Senate by nine, calling on Vice President Schuyler Colfax and other members of the Judiciary Committee, touring the Government Printing Office, then choosing which of *five* dinner invitations to accept. As midnight approached, Clemens fought off exhaustion long enough to chronicle the evening's events for his spouse: "Dined from 6 to 8:30. Called on the Fitch's from 8:30–9:30. Then went to see Mr. and Mrs. Bennett & played euchre till 11."

Clemens's visit at the home of Thomas and Anna Fitch was likely the catalyst that spurred the composition of "The Noble Red Man." The two men had become acquainted in Nevada Territory when Fitch assumed the editorship of the Virginia City *Daily Union* in 1863. Their early relationship was fraught with acrimony; as Twain stated in his *Enterprise* column of 5 July 1863, "Thomas Fitch, Esq., delivered the [Independence Day] oration. I don't know Mr. Fitch personally, but by reputation I don't like him. He is a 'born' orator, though. If he always swings the English language as grandly as he did yesterday, I shall always be happy to hear him. He is a regular masked battery. He lulls you into a treacherous repose, with a few mild and graceful sentences, and then suddenly explodes in your midst with a bombshell of eloquence which shakes you to your very foundations" (ETS1, 257). Clemens also admired Fitch's writing skills, describing him in *Roughing It* as "a felicitous skirmisher with a pen," who expressed his opinions on the front page of the *Union* in a "crisp, neat way" (RI, 339). In late July 1863, however, Fitch's penchant for "skirmishing" took an aggressive physical turn when he challenged *Enterprise* editor Joe Goodman to a duel, claiming he had been defamed in its pages. As Twain reported on 2 August, the men's first attempt at settling the score ended in a standoff when a local constable arrived and arrested them both before a single shot could be fired; six weeks later, a second date was covertly arranged, and Goodman wounded his opponent below the right knee, crippling him for life (ETS1, 262–63).

Clemens remained suspicious of Fitch's character, warning Orion in a November 1864 letter, "Dawson says Daggett & Fitch will be likely to euchre you out of the nomination. He will if lying & swindling can do it. I know Daggett & Fitch both, & I swear a solemn oath that I believe that they would blast the characters of their own mothers & sisters to gain any great advantage in life. I know both dogs well. Look out for them. They are two-faced" (L1, 318). It was not until two years later, when the writer returned to Nevada on his inaugural lecture tour of 1866, that the enmity he harbored toward Fitch—who by this point had abandoned journalism and was now serving as the district attorney of Washoe County—finally dissipated. Fitch not only hosted Twain for several nights in his Washoe City home but also served as his impresario, securing the local courthouse as a performance venue, acting as doorkeeper for the sellout crowd, and warmly introducing him on the platform (L1, 366). This event inaugurated a new, more amicable phase of the men's relationship that would endure for more than forty years until Twain's death.

Although Fitch and Clemens rarely saw one another after 1866, their correspondence is characterized by fondness, mutual respect, and, most significantly, the exchange of small professional favors—a habitual quid pro quo. In late 1869, Clemens contacted Fitch requesting that he intercede to resolve a financial dispute Orion was then embroiled in with R. W. Taylor, an overly zealous federal comptroller. Taylor claimed that the territorial secretary had overpaid for the printing of laws and other legislative documents six years earlier and was now demanding immediate restitution in the amount of $1,330.08—"$954.43 in disallowed payments to printers; and $375.65 for the 'Balance due the United States per your last a/c'" (L3, 388n1). On 5 January 1870, Fitch wrote to Taylor, enclosing a letter from Orion explaining why it was impossible for him to repay the debt, and pleaded amnesty for the former secretary, stating, "I was editor of the Virginia City Union in 1863 and a portion of 1864 and can vouch for the accuracy of [Mr. Clemens's] representations with regard to the price of printers labor and materials. I hope that you will afford to Mr. Clemens any relief in your power not inconsistent with the interests of the department" (L4, 30n4). Although the outcome of this matter is unclear, Twain sent Fitch's note to his sister Pamela on 15 January to reassure Orion "that Tom is moving in the matter" and to indicate that some personal expression of gratitude was in order: "Let Orion drop him simply a line, thanking him" (L4, 30).

Twain did not forget Fitch's kindness either and reciprocated the congressman's favor some six months later, using his literary fame to advance Fitch's fledgling career as lecturer. On 10 July, the day after returning to Elmira from Washington, he wrote to James Redpath of the Boston Lyceum Bureau, who had recently added Fitch to his roster of speakers for the 1870–71 lecture season, praising his friend's "instinctive" oratorical skills: "He is a fascinating speaker. I pledge my word that he will hold any audience willing prisoners for two hours that can be gathered together before him, in any city of America, from Boston to New Orleans, & from Baltimore to San Francisco. . . . I have heard Mr. Fitch pretty often; & not afraid to make these strong statements" (L4, 170). Later that fall, Redpath used excerpts from the writer's letter to advertise—and fill the house—for Fitch's lecture in Boston on "The Coming Empire," a celebration of Manifest Destiny that focused on the settlement of California and Nevada. Over the next three years, the agent promoted Fitch's career largely by highlighting his association with Twain.

These two unrelated incidents—Orion's financial crisis and Tom Fitch's attempt to establish himself on the lecture circuit—likely converged during Clemens' visit with the Nevada Congressman on 6 July and sparked the genesis of "The Noble Red Man." According to the University of California editors of the writer's letters, among the topics discussed on this occasion were "Thomas's potential as a lecturer and, probably, his intercession in Orion Clemens's dispute with the Treasury Department" (L4, 166n6). If indeed Orion's monetary problems were addressed, it seems likely that Fitch would have contextualized the issue within the larger framework of other federal expenditures currently being debated in Congress. Just a few days before Clemens's arrival in Washington, Fitch had vehemently opposed the passage of Senate Resolution 217, which authorized the sum of fifty thousand dollars "to enable the Secretary of the Interior to defray the expenses of delegations of Indians visiting Washington, and to purchase presents for the members thereof."[67] Denouncing the proposal as a frivolous misuse of the "public treasury . . . [on behalf of] a lot of squalid and murderous savages," he singlehandedly blocked the House vote by causing the bill to be sent back to the Committee on Appropriations. The irony of the government's hounding Orion for repayment of a relatively small amount of money—expended on the laudable, legitimate enterprise of codifying the laws of Nevada Territory—and its simultaneous willingness to squander fifty times that amount "furnish[ing] champagne cocktails, boxes at the opera, strawberries and cream, and all the luxuries of the season"[68] to chiefs such as Red Cloud and Spotted Tail surely did not escape Fitch, and may have warranted at least passing mention in his conversation with the writer.

This conjecture is rendered more plausible by two additional factors. Fitch, realizing that his action on 29 June had merely delayed but not defeated SR 217, was actively formulating the next phase of his opposition at the time of Twain's visit. Given the congressman's desire to showcase his oratorical prowess for his influential friend, it is possible that he used the occasion to informally rehearse his intended plan of attack—pitting western knowledge of native character against eastern ignorance and sentimentality—a perspective that Clemens, eager to collect memories of Nevada Territory for the travel book about the West he had proposed to Bliss, would have been favorably predisposed to entertain. The fervor of Fitch's antipathy toward Indians may thus have served to rekindle Twain's own prejudices.

According to the *Congressional Globe*, the House debate over the Indian Appropriation Bill occurred on 11 July, two days after Clemens left Washington, and was dominated by Fitch in all his florid, loquacious glory. Decrying the "absurd and fruitless policy of bringing [Indians] to visit the Great Father at Washington," he singled out Henry Dawes, the chairman of the Appropriations Committee, for censure, claiming that the Massachusetts representative's support of the legislation was naïve and misinformed.

Three times within the space of three sentences Fitch charged that Dawes—and other eastern politicians like him—were so blinded by the myth of the "Noble Savage" that they could not comprehend the true barbarism and depravity of indigenous people:

> If the gentleman from Massachusetts had understood Indian customs he would have known that every eagle's plume in the red head-dress of Red Cloud, which attracted the attention of the country and excited the comment of the reporters of the press, signified a scalp taken perhaps from the head of some white man or woman. Had that been understood by those who waited upon these red brethren and sisters, I am sure no Senator or Secretary or Representative would have pressed forward to take the hand of the distinguished horse-beggar and scalp-gatherer, Red Cloud, or the distinguished Spotted Tail and his lovely and accomplished squaws. I know my friend from Massachusetts could not have understood that, or we would not have him here to-day pressing for an appropriation of $50,000 for the purpose indicated in this joint resolution.[69]

Fitch's argument is grounded in an assertion of superior knowledge—in his words, the incontrovertible "facts of the case"—gleaned from firsthand experience with Indians on the western frontier, which is essentially the same tack Twain employs in "The Noble Red Man." In truth, however, the congressman's knowledge of native customs was flawed, as demonstrated by his assertion that each eagle feather in Red Cloud's headdress symbolized the scalp of an Anglo-American victim. Fitch's bias becomes increasingly evident as the speech progresses, culminating in the declaration, "I have no hostility to good Indians—although I have never met any that I considered especially valuable." On these grounds, he openly—and unapologetically—sanctions vigilante violence: "I suppose the House will vote this money; but I would rather it were an appropriation to furnish rifles and ammunition to the people of Arizona, who are murdered and scalped at the very thresholds of their houses in the very capital of that Territory, while economy forbids that they should be defended by our Army and red tape refuses them an opportunity to defend themselves."[70]

Fitch concluded by affirming his loyalty to the citizens he was elected to represent: "No vote of mine shall ever be given for [this mistaken policy] ... When I go back to my constituents I shall be able to assure them that I did not participate in the general rush of Senators and Representatives who crowded forward to visit these savages and clasp hands red with the blood of the emigrants they scalped and murdered on the plains." Despite his impassioned efforts, SR 217 passed by a narrow margin of twelve votes; the official tally was ninety-one yeas, seventy-nine nays, and sixty abstentions. Support for the bill—and the broader agenda of Grant's Peace Policy—split overwhelmingly along party lines, although regional affiliation proved an important factor as well; like Fitch, the majority of other Republicans who broke ranks with the president and opposed the measure hailed from western or border states where Indian depredations were ongoing. And yet, even in the West, some inhabitants scorned the extremity of Fitch's rhetoric; on 23 July 1870, the *Sacramento Daily Union* attacked his "cruel and barbarous speeches . . . containing sentiments which ought to consign his name to the immortality of obloquy."[71]

Although Twain never acknowledged Thomas Fitch's fiercely anti-Indian stance as a source of inspiration for "The Noble Red Man," he did publicly applaud the contributions of all three of Nevada's elected representatives in a piece called "The Reception at the President's," which appeared a month later in the October issue of the *Galaxy*. In this sketch, a boorish western rough holds up a receiving line at the White House by subjecting President Grant to a rambling reminiscence about his "halcyon days" in 1860s Nevada Territory. After perseverating about his attendance at many "Injun receptions" hosted by Governor James Nye "out in the wilds" of Honey Lake and Carson City, the speaker declares,

> Between you and me that old man was a good deal of a Governor, take him all around. I don't know what for Senator he makes, though I think you'll admit that him and Bill Stewart and Tom Fitch take a bigger average of brains into that Capitol up yonder, by a hundred and fifty fold, than any other State in America, according to population. Now that is so. Those three men represent only twenty or twenty-five thousand people—bless you, the least little bit of a trifling ward in the city of New York casts two votes to Nevada's one— and yet those three men haven't their superiors in Congress for straight-out, simon pure brains and ability.[72]

In some ways, the playful tone of "The Reception at the President's" represents an antidote to the venomous rhetoric of "The Noble Red Man"— a return to equanimity in the aftermath of that cathartic eruption of racial invective. Juxtaposing the elegant formality of Grant's reception—"the women powdered, painted, jewelled, and splendidly upholstered, and many of the men gilded with the insignia of great naval, military, and ambassadorial rank"—with the "swell affairs" in the Nevada sagebrush attended by "old high-flavored Washoes and Pi-Utes, each one of them as powerful as a rag-factory on fire," Twain creates a genial contrast between East and West. Moreover, while the natives mentioned in "The Reception at the

President's"—"frowsy old bummers with nothing in the world on, in the summer time, but an old battered plug hat and a pair of spectacles"—are admittedly dirty, ignorant, and unkempt, they are more buffoonish than hateful.[73] Rather than menacing the existence of Anglo-American settlers, the Indians are portrayed as naïve, tractable, and childlike, their "war spirit" mollified by Nye's "persuasive tongue" and useless gifts of old hoopskirts and Patent Office reports.

Although several details in "The Reception at the President's," such as the absurd image of natives wearing castoff Anglo-American garb—hoopskirts, plug hats, and spectacles—echo "The Noble Red Man," the tenor of these descriptions could hardly be more different. While the unidentified Indian in the September sketch is contemptuously declared "a good, fair, desirable subject for extermination if ever there was one," the "frowsy old bummers" who appear in the *Galaxy* a month later are paternalistically described as "children." In large part, the dramatic change in Twain's attitude can be attributed to his composition of the opening chapters of *Roughing It* in late August. The writer's nostalgic evocation of his 1861 stagecoach journey to Nevada Territory was deeply indebted to Orion's diary, which he had borrowed earlier in the summer to refresh his memory of the trip. On 2 September, he wrote to his brother from Buffalo, expressing thanks for the loan: "Your little memorandum book is going to be ever so much use to me, & will enable me to make quite a coherent narrative of the Plains journey instead of slurring it over & jumping 2,000 miles at a stride."[74] Although these pleasant memories may have briefly tempered Twain's views of Native Americans, the animus would persist—waxing and waning erratically—throughout the remaining decades of his career.

"EXTRACTS FROM METHUSALEH'S DIARY"

Although Twain never mentioned the historic 1870 visit of Red Cloud and Spotted Tail to the nation's capital in his published work or correspondence, his cognizance of these events is demonstrated in "Extracts from Methuselah's Diary." This unfinished work, begun in July 1873 and revisited four years later during the fall of 1877, purports to be the journal of the long-lived biblical patriarch, but is in fact a satire on contemporary political issues, such as suffrage, women's rights, slavery, and missionary activities. One of Methuselah's entries concerns a fictitious tribe called the Jabalites, who "live not in houses, but in tents, and wander in lawless hordes," posing a "sore problem to my father and his council."[75] An entourage of twenty "greater and lesser chiefs"—similar in size and composition to the Lakota delegations—journey into the city for the diplomatic purpose of "mak[ing] submission" to Methuselah's father and "enter[ing] into a covenant of peace." These negotiations, like those between the Lakota and US government, center around the issue of territoriality; in return for "goods and trinkets and implements of husbandry," the Jabalites pledge "to make the right of way secure" and "not molest our caravans and merchants"—terms that echo the deliberations regarding Montana's Bozeman Trail, one of the primary emigrant routes to the gold regions of the West.

Like the parties of Red Cloud and Spotted Tail, the Jabalites arrive "with a fantastic sort of barbaric pomp," creating a frenzy among the inhabitants who "flock to the streets, the walls, the house-tops and all places of vantage" to catch sight of the "wild spectacle," just as crowds of curious onlookers did in Washington and New York. Similarly, Methuselah's description of the formal diplomatic overtures made to the chiefs, including sumptuous feasts, "loving speeches," and "store[s] of presents" evokes the Grant administration's lavish treatment of the Indians. But the most striking parallel Twain establishes between the Jabalites and Lakota is their stoic indifference to carefully orchestrated displays of the wealth and power of their respective hosts: "These that came to-day went about the city viewing the wonders of it, yet never exclaiming, nor betraying admiration in any way." The Indians likewise had stood impassive and unimpressed when a Parrott cannon was discharged for their benefit at the Federal Arsenal.

While Twain's imaginative association of Indians with the "ancient children of Israel" dates back to his 1867 observations of Palestinian Bedouins, this analogy is more extensively developed in "Methuselah's Diary." His working notes for the project explicitly identify the Jabalites as "savages," who "scalp & paint faces in war," and include a plan to "give them Sitting-Bull names," although that idea was never implemented.[76] The "Diary" does, however, express a far more sympathetic response toward American Indians than either *The Innocents Abroad* or "The Noble Red Man," reflecting the dynamic nature of the writer's views. Whereas the 1870 essay presents natives as perpetrators of horrific gratuitous violence, the manuscript situates—and to some extent, exonerates—this behavior as a response to the egregious injustices inflicted upon them:

> A visit like to this [the Jabalites] make to us as often as once in fifty or
> sixty years, and then go away and break the covenant and make trouble
> again. But they are not always to blame. They covenant to go apart and
> abide upon lands set apart for them, and subsist by the arts of peace; but
> the agents sent out to govern them do cheat and maltreat them,
> removing them to other stations not so good and stealing from them

their fertile lands and hunting districts, and abusing them with blows when they resist—a thing they will not abide; and so they rise by night and slaughter all that fall into their hands, revenging the agents' treachery and oppression as best they can. Then go our armies forth to try to carry desolation to their hearthstones but succeed not.[77]

Twain's emotionally charged language portrays the Jabalites as victims abused at the hands of corrupt government agents who cheat and defraud them of land that is rightfully theirs. He equates dispossession with outright theft and characterizes the tribe's vengeance as a justifiable reaction to these abuses. Thus, it is the agents, not the savage Jabalites, who are deemed "treacherous." His description of the army's retaliation as "carry[ing] desolation to their hearthstones" underscores the legitimacy of tribal patrimony through its positive connotations of domesticity and family life.

The solicitude of this perspective raises a question: what factors inspired the writer's apparently dramatic change of heart? A note appended to the end of the 1873 section of the manuscript offers a clue: "Take this up again under brief republican form of govt, when Meth about 300 or 400 old, and put in Custer and Howard and the Peace Commissioners (Quakers) and the Modoc Lava Beds, etc. and satirize freely."[78] This statement, demonstrating both Clemens's ongoing interest in Indian affairs and awareness of the intricacies, challenges, and inconsistencies that dogged Grant's peace policy, counterpoints the diplomatic skill of the one-armed "praying general," Oliver Otis Howard, who had successfully negotiated an end to hostilities with the Chiricahua Apache in October 1872, with George Armstrong Custer's brazen encroachment on Lakota land the following summer. The Seventh Cavalry's survey of the Yellowstone River region to determine an optimal route for the Northern Pacific Railroad precipitated a series of clashes with Sitting Bull, Gall, and Crazy Horse that would culminate in the Battle of the Little Bighorn three years later. Most germane to the composition of "Methuselah's Diary," however, is his allusion to the "Modoc Lava Beds" and Quaker "Peace Commissioners" which situates the manuscript within the context of the disastrous Modoc War of 1872–73.

This conflict, one of the costliest in US history, ended in June 1873—just days after Clemens's arrival in London—with the arrest of their headman Kintpuash (also known as Captain Jack) and his small band of followers. Like the Jabalites, the Modoc had been dispossessed—removed from their northern California homeland in the late 1860s and sent to live on a barren Oregon reservation created for their traditional enemies, the Klamath. When the government rations promised in return for these land cessions failed to materialize, Kintpuash led a group of about seventy families back to the Lost River region, now occupied by Anglo-American settlers. Clashes inevitably arose, and in late 1872 federal troops arrived to compel the Modocs' return to the Klamath reservation. They resisted, barricading themselves in the lava beds—a forbidding landscape of volcanic "fissures, caves, crevices, gorges, and ravines" said to resemble "hell with the fire out"—along California's northern boundary.[79]

Disappearing like "ants into a sponge," Kintpuash and fifty-two warriors thwarted the advances of at least four hundred soldiers and volunteer militiamen armed with howitzers for several months, inflicting many casualties while suffering only a handful of their own.[80] The Modocs' bravery and resourcefulness in the face of overwhelming odds riveted the nation throughout the winter and spring of 1873; however, on 11 April —Good Friday—the war suddenly became an "international sensation" when Kintpuash shot and killed peace commissioner General Edward R.S. Canby during a truce parley.[81] Amidst the furor that erupted over the treachery of this "Red Judas," Grant's peace policy collapsed; arguing that the Modocs' fate should be commensurate with their crime, the president authorized the tribe's "utter extermination."[82] On 1 June, Kintpuash and five other Modoc leaders were captured and transported to Fort Klamath, where after a month-long imprisonment, they were tried—without the benefit of legal representation—by military tribunal and sentenced to death.

As Benjamin Madley explains in *An American Genocide*, "The eyes of the world were on this last California Indian war. Correspondents writing for newspapers in Chicago, London, New York, Sacramento, San Francisco, and Yreka were onsite, thus ensuring that any violence against the surrendering Modocs would become national and even international news."[83] British coverage of the war's denouement was visual as well as textual. Within days of Canby's murder, the *Illustrated London News* dispatched veteran reporter-artist William Simpson to the scene, where he produced a series of drawings published on the paper's front page in late May and early June. Official portraits of the Modoc prisoners taken by photographer Louis Heller were also widely reproduced as woodcut engravings on both sides of the Atlantic. This expansive reportage assures that the writer was well informed of the latest developments concerning the war while abroad.

JOAQUIN MILLER AND THE "DEAR LITTLE MODOC"

Clemens's friendship with Joaquin Miller (1837–1913), the colorful "Poet of the Sierras," who had been living in London since late 1872, coincides with the arrest and trial of the Modoc leaders. This convergence, along with the imminent publication of Miller's purported autobiography, *Life amongst the Modocs*—issued by Robert Bentley and Sons in late July—suggests that the conflict was a likely topic of conversation between the two men. As Clemens wrote to Mary Mason Fairbanks on 6 July, "We see Miller every day or two, & like him better & better all the time. He is just getting out his Modoc book here & I have made him go to my publishers in America with it (by letter) & they will make some money for him" (L5, 402). The writer's generosity in urging Bliss to issue a US edition of Miller's work bespeaks the warmth of their camaraderie, as do a flurry of letters exchanged during June and early July discussing plans to meet. Although his reputation is now obscure, in 1873 Joaquin Miller was London's "literary lion" of the season,[84] a much sought-after presence in aristocratic drawing rooms and fashionable private clubs—an elite world into which he offered his compatriot entrée. Clemens's postscript to an 11 June note reflects this whirl of social engagements: "I am keeping strictly before my memory the fact that I am to call on you at 4:45 Saturday on the way to the Savage [Club]—so don't *you* forget. And Friday, remember, you are to call here with one literary friend of yours, & we are then to go together & pay our respects to another. Have I got that straight?" (L5, 376). The editors of *Mark Twain's Notebooks and Journals*, vol. 1 confirm that Miller introduced Clemens to "Lord Houghton (Richard Monckton Milnes), the poet and statesman, and to Lord and Lady Thomas Duffus Hardy . . . an archivist and popular novelist, [who] entertained a 'host of bright people' at their Saturday evening parties" (NBJ1, 519–20). Miller, for his part, later remembered Clemens being as "shy as a girl" on these occasions, so reticent that he "could hardly be coaxed to meet the learned and great who wanted to take him by the hand."[85]

According to biographer M. M. Marberry, Miller—who changed his birth name Cincinnatus to Joaquin in tribute to the legendary Mexican bandit Joaquin Murietta—was an adventurer with a histrionic flair for self-aggrandizement. He claimed to have both fought and lived among California Indians in the 1850s, fathering (and then abandoning) a daughter named Calle-Shasta with a Wintu or Modoc woman.[86] In London, he presented himself as a consummate westerner, dressing in a buckskin shirt, sombrero, and boots replete with jangling spurs, and blaming his notoriously illegible handwriting on a "terrible wound" inflicted by an Indian arrow, despite the absence of any discernible scar.[87] In a 1907 autobiographical dictation, Clemens—whose fame had by then far eclipsed that of his old acquaintance—recalled Miller's theatricality with ambivalence. The occasion was a July 1873 dinner in the poet's honor at the Garrick Club hosted by Anthony Trollope:

Miller, who was on the top wave of his English notoriety at that time
. . . did his full share of the talking, but he was a discordant note, a
disturber and degrader of the solemnities. He was affecting the
picturesque and untamed costume of the wild Sierras at the time, to the
charmed astonishment of conventional London, and was helping out the
effects with the breezy and independent and aggressive manners of that
far away and romantic region. . . . It was long ago, long ago! and not
even an echo of that turbulence was left in this room where it had once
made so much noise and display. . . . Joaquin Miller is white-headed, and
mute and quiet in his dear mountains. (A3, 103)

Beyond the flamboyant costumes, Miller's cachet in England was
enhanced by his much-vaunted, though historically dubious, association
with the Modoc; as he explains in his 1890 autobiography, *Romantic Life
among the Red Indians*, "I was living in London at the outbreak of the
Modoc War, and it having become known, through the 'Songs of the Sierras'
[his 1871 volume of poetry], that I had once lived with those people, and
neighboring tribes, the writers from the seat of war gave most wild and
romantic accounts of my early history . . . meanwhile, the demand for
books or stories about these Indians, the Modoc War, and the cause of it,
was very great in London."[88] He capitalized on this interest in the work's
introductory chapter: "As I write these opening lines here to-day in the Old
World, a war of extermination is declared against the Modoc Indians in the
New. I know these people. I know every foot of their once vast possessions,
stretching away to the north and east of Mount Shasta. I know their rights
and their wrongs. I have known them for nearly twenty years."[89] On these
grounds, Miller proposed himself as an advocate for "a race of people that
has lived centuries of history and . . . suffered nearly four hundred years of
wrong, and never yet had a historian." Acknowledging the Modocs' abiding
love for their land and homes, he valorized Kintpuash's resistance, insisting
"There is nothing nobler in all the histories of the hemispheres." The moral
imperative underlying Miller's text is evident in his passionate closing
statement: "When I die I shall take this book in my hand and hold it up in
the Day of Judgment, as a sworn indictment against the rulers of my country for the destruction of these people."[90]

Although Miller claimed that *Life amongst the Modocs* was a memoir,
the narrative is so highly romanticized it is now considered fiction; in the
afterword to a 1996 reprinting of the text, Alan Rosenus characterizes it as
a "reform novel" with the didactic intention of changing the attitude of
whites toward Indians.[91] Miller's progressive racial outlook does in fact
seem to have influenced Clemens, judging from his favorable representa-

tion of the Jabalites in "Extracts from Methuselah's Diary." Additional evidence of this newfound tolerance appears in a 4 July speech made to a group of American expatriates in London:

> This is an age of progress, and ours is a progressive land. A great and glorious land, too—a land which has developed a Washington, a Franklin, a William M. Tweed, a Longfellow, a Motley, a Jay Gould, a Samuel C. Pomeroy, a recent Congress which has never had its equal— (in some respects) and a United States Army which conquered sixty Indians in eight months by tiring them out—which is much better than uncivilized slaughter, God knows.[92]

Twain's declaration that the conquest of Indians through patience and tenacity is preferable to "uncivilized slaughter"—an unmistakable allusion to the recent months-long standoff at the Modoc lava beds—counters the harsh view, expressed in his 1867 sketch "The Facts concerning the Recent Resignation," that "nothing [is] so convincing to an Indian as a general massacre."

The liberalization of Clemens's attitudes toward Indians is most poignantly reflected in the nickname he coined for his beloved fifteen-month-old daughter in July 1873. As he explains in "A Record of the Small Foolishnesses of Susie and 'Bay' Clemens (Infants)," begun at Quarry Farm in the summer of 1876, "Susie never had but one nick-name, . . . and only kept that one a year. That was 'Modoc,' (from the cut of her hair). This was at the time of the Modoc war in the lava beds of northern California" (FS, 51–53). An August 1873 photograph of Susy taken in Edinburgh, paired below with Louis Heller's portrait of Kintpuash soon after his June arrest, affirms this uncanny likeness—both subjects have dark, straight, ear-length hair prominently parted in the middle (fig. 14). The frequency and obvious affection with which Clemens used this sobriquet, however, intimate that his imaginative association of Susy and Indians ran deeper than superficial outward appearance. Volumes 5 and 6 of his published correspondence reveal that the writer referred to her as "the Modoc" on at least sixteen different occasions between July 1873 and November 1874—not only in letters to Livy, Orion, and his mother but also to close family friends, such as Joe Twichell, Mary Mason Fairbanks, and the Edinburgh physician Dr. John Brown. He even incorporated the nickname into professional correspondence with his agent Frank Fuller; the Boston literary correspondent for the New York *Tribune*, Louise Chandler Moulton; and the proprietor of the *Belfast Whig* newspaper. With one exception, these allusions postdate the execution of Kintpuash and three other Modoc leaders on 3 October 1873—after which a belated groundswell of sympathy arose recasting the men as martyrs—

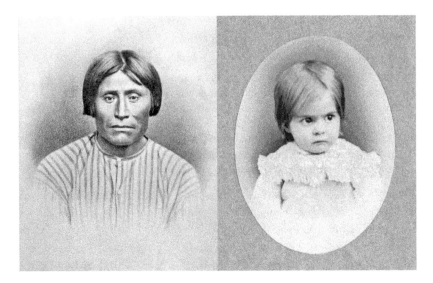

FIGURE 14.   Kintpuash and Susy Clemens. Photo of Kintpuash: Public domain. Photo of Susy Clemens: Courtesy of the Mark Twain Project, The Bancroft Library, University of California, Berkeley.

suggesting that Clemens's more charitable response to native peoples, while inspired by Miller and his London sojourn, persisted upon returning to the United States.

Clemens's first mention of Susy as "the Modoc" occurs in a 6 July 1873 letter to Mary Fairbanks, who had met and been charmed by Miller in Cleveland the previous autumn. Aware of her concerns about the poet's alleged bigamy, he teasingly reports news of her friend's impending engagement to the daughter of a local baronet, adding "Livy & the Modoc are well & they love you—so they say. The Modoc is able to stand alone, now. She is getting into a habit of swearing when things don't suit. This gives us grave uneasiness" (L5, 404). The profane outbursts Clemens humorously ascribes to his daughter characterize her as coarse and uncivilized—"wild," in other words, like an Indian. He extrapolates on this trope in a subsequent letter, regaling Fairbanks with the "savagery" of Susy's unpredictable and occasionally destructive antics: "The Modoc has just tumbled down again & smashed some more furniture—& herself. I hear an angel sing, maybe, but there's other tunes I prefer" (L6, 47). Clemens found the toddler's unruly behavior endearing, even to the point of commending (rather than reprimanding) her for scribbling on a letter to his mother in July 1874: "You see the Modoc's marks through my writing. Said *she* was writing to grandma *too"* (L6, 185). As he informed Livy, their child was "a pretty entertaining cub" (L5, 497).

Clemens's allusions to Susy as "the Modoc" reflect a romantic view of Indians completely at odds with his representation of them in *The Innocents Abroad, Roughing It,* and sketches, such as "The Noble Red Man." He portrays her in conventionally masculine terms as willful, robust, independent, and one with nature, boasting to Orion on 10 June 1874, "The Modoc is brown as an Indian, because she is seldom or never in the house, but is tramping around outside in the sun & wind, all day" (L6, 155). This ideation is developed most fully in a letter to Twichell, written soon after Clara's birth:

> The Modoc was delighted with [the baby], & gave it her doll at once. There is nothing selfish about the Modoc. She . . . rips & tears around out doors, most of the time, & consequently is hard as a pine knot & as brown as an Indian. She is bosom friend to all the chickens, ducks, turkeys & guinea hens on the place. Yesterday as she marched along the winding path that leads up the hill through the red clover beds to the summer-house, there was a long procession of these fowls stringing contentedly after her, led by a stately rooster who can look over the Modoc's head. The devotion of these vassals has been purchased with daily largess of Indian meal, & so the Modoc, attended by her body-guard, moves in state wherever she goes. (L6, 158)

Clemens's repetition of the simile "brown as an Indian" in reference to Susy's tanned complexion echoes Miller's description of his mixed-blood daughter Calle-Shasta in *Life amongst the Modocs* as not a "redskin" but a "little brown girl flitting through these forests."[93] The two children are also linked by unusually close-knit relationships with animals who protect them from harm: at one point in Miller's narrative, a "great black pet bear,"[94] who walks at Calle-Shasta's side, is given an apple after rising up on its hind legs to ward off an intruder; Susy in turn is flanked by a procession of avian bodyguards whose loyalty is repaid with generous handfuls of grain. Both writers similarly extol the confidence and ease with which the girls navigate their environs. Miller depicts Calle-Shasta as a skilled, self-sufficient equestrian, exclaiming, "How she can ride, shoot, hunt, and track the deer, and take the salmon!"[95] Susy likewise "rips & tears" through the landscape of Quarry Farm, "marching" purposefully up hills carpeted with fragrant red clover. Clemens claims, moreover, that she is "hard as a pine knot"—tough, strong, and resilient like the densely resinous heartwood at the core of a tree.

The writer's loving 1873–74 representation of Susy as "my Modoc", an epithet likely even more ubiquitous in conversation than in correspondence, seems to have produced a subtle—and presumably unconscious—modulation in his views of actual Indians. This shift, illustrated in the dissonance between his observation "there is nothing selfish about the Modoc" and statement that "the ruling trait of all savages is a greedy and consuming selfishness" in "The Noble Red Man" (CT1, 444), suggests that the emotions Clemens invested in this metaphor fostered a reconsideration of his earlier, intolerant racial attitudes. Recognizing that traditional gender roles necessitated that the "Modoc" eventually be tamed and domesticated in order to fulfill her destiny as the Victorian "angel in the house," he relinquished the nickname shortly before his daughter's third birthday. Its last recorded use accompanies the gift of a quintessentially feminine accessory: "This 'hakky' [as Susy pronounced the word handkerchief] is for the Modoc with my great love" (L6, 282). Although the writer could not have foreseen it at the time, his eldest daughter still had much more to teach him about Indians, particularly concerning their spirituality and relationship to the divine.

5. "How Much Higher and Finer Is the Indian's God"

In a 1906 autobiographical dictation, Mark Twain affectionately recalls the contemplative nature of his deceased eldest daughter, Susy. "Like other children," he asserts, "she was blithe and happy, fond of play; *unlike* the average of children she was at times much given to retiring within herself and trying to search out the hidden meanings of the deep things that make the puzzle and pathos of human existence, and in all the ages have baffled the inquirer and mocked him" (A1, 325). One such "sunless bog" into which Susy—the erstwhile "little Modoc"—descended was a spiritual crisis, precipitated by the lessons of her governess, Lilly Gillette Foote. One evening in 1880, Livy noticed Susy's difficulty in reciting her prayers and asked if something was troubling her. According to Twain,

> Susy explained that Miss Foote . . . had been teaching her about the Indians and their religious beliefs, whereby it appeared that they had not only a God, but several. This had set Susy to thinking. As a result of this thinking, she had stopped praying. She qualified this statement— that is she modified it—saying that she did not pray "in the same way" as she had formerly done. Her mother said,
>
> "Tell me about it, dear."
>
> "Well, mamma, the Indians believed they knew, but now we know they were wrong. By and by it can turn out that we are wrong. So now I only pray that there may be a God and a heaven—or something better." (A1, 326)

As this reminiscence suggests, Susy's exposure to the basic tenets of native spirituality at the tender age of eight prompted a series of disquieting realizations about the evolutionary shift from pagan pantheism to monotheism, the disparity between faith and truth, and ultimately the relativity of all belief systems. The subversive insight that "by and by, it can turn out that we are wrong" undermined her foundational belief in the inherent "truth" of Christianity, provoking a moment of existential doubt in which everything—the existence of God, the soul, and the afterlife—was called into question.

In 1880, when this incident occurred, Twain was struck by the depth and maturity of his precocious daughter's reasoning;[1] twenty-six years later, when dictating this passage of the *Autobiography*, he transformed it into an allegory of humanity's enduring quest for truth: "I wrote down this pathetic prayer in its precise wording, at the time, in a record which we kept of the children's sayings, and my reverence for it has grown with the years that have passed over my head since then. Its untaught grace and simplicity are a child's, but the wisdom of it are of all the ages that have come and gone since the race of man has lived, and longed, and hoped, and feared, and doubted" (A1, 326).

The writer's recollection of Susy's spiritual crisis is, of course, highly overdetermined in that her expression of doubt prefigures the wrenching despair he himself experienced late in life. The degree to which Twain inscribes himself in the figure of his daughter is evident in the extravagant rhetoric of the following lines:

> As a little child . . . [Susy] was oppressed and perplexed by the maddening repetition of the stock incidents of our race's fleeting sojourn here. . . . A myriad of men are born; they labor and sweat and struggle for bread; they squabble and scold and fight; they scramble for little mean advantages over each other; age creeps upon them; infirmities follow; shames and humiliations bring down their prides and their vanities; those they love are taken from them, and the joy of life is turned to aching grief. The burden of pain, care, misery, grows heavier year by year; at length ambition is dead; pride is dead; vanity is dead; longing for release is in their place. It comes at last—the only unpoisoned gift earth ever had for them—and they vanish from a world where they were of no consequence . . . Then another myriad takes their place . . . and accomplish[es] what the first myriad, and all the other myriads that came after it accomplished—nothing! (A1, 325–26)

Susy's questions about the meaning of existence become a springboard for the writer's bleak meditation on life's futility; her naïve perplexity is over-written and subsumed within the nihilism of his own views. Biographical anecdote melds into autobiography, the past becomes the present, and Susy shifts from speaking subject to tragic object lesson. While Twain never explicitly mentions his daughter's untimely death from spinal meningitis at age twenty-four in the passage, this loss—along with that of Livy in 1904—is evoked by the phrase, "those they love are taken from them, and the joy of life is turned to aching grief."

Though this memory of Susy had potent resonance for Twain in 1906—the tenth anniversary of her death—its intellectual and creative impact in fact registered much earlier. For Lilly Foote's lesson had been a revelation to Clemens as well as his eldest daughter. In "The French and the Comanches," a deleted chapter of his 1880 travelogue *A Tramp Abroad,* he states that the tribe "had no religion,"[2] reflecting a dismissive attitude about paganism's legitimacy as a belief system. Moreover, given his essentializing tendency to view all Native Americans as the same—epitomized in the passage of *Roughing It* concerning the Goshoots—this perception of the Comanches likely extended to other indigenous groups as well. Susy's interest in Indian religion, particularly in the notion that "they had not only [one] God, but several," thus served to pique the writer's own curiosity about this topic and, on at least one occasion, directly influenced both the focus of his reading and response to the information he encountered there.

In late November 1881, just a year after Miss Foote's unsettling lesson, Clemens traveled to Canada in order to secure the British copyright for *The Prince and the Pauper.* His reading material for the long rail journey was "3 volumes of Parkman . . . begin[ning] with 1498 & sketch[ing the] French, Spanish, English & Dutch occupation in America down to 1701,"[3] which proved so engrossing that he felt imaginatively transported back through history. Gazing out the train window at the wintry landscape, Twain reflected in his notebook: "Brilliant day, but snow everywhere—when sky overcast, a dreary prospect, which helped me to realize the times of Champlain & others in Canada" (NBJ2, 406). Soon after arriving in Montreal on 28 November, he wrote home informing Livy that "by [the] day after to-morrow I shall have finished" all three books—no meager feat considering that they total almost fourteen hundred pages—and declaring his eagerness to read more of the Harvard historian's work: "On the piano (I think) you will find Parkman's 'The Old Regime.' Well, won't you direct it to this hotel & send Patrick [McAleer, the family coachman] immediately to the post office with it? . . . [And] if . . . you *can* discover which volume follows The Old Regime, I would like to have *it* also."[4]

The works to which Twain refers are part of an eight-volume edition of *Parkman's Works* published in 1880 by Little, Brown, which he purchased in 1881. Although the set was dispersed in 1911, when the author's library was sold at auction, five of the titles—*The Jesuits in North America in the*

Seventeenth Century; Count Frontenac and New France under Louis XIV; The Oregon Trail; and the two-volume study, *The Conspiracy of Pontiac and the Indian War after the Conquest of Canada*—have been recovered and are currently housed at the Mark Twain Papers. The whereabouts of the remaining three books—*Pioneers of France in the New World, La Salle and the Discovery of the Great West,* and *The Old Régime in Canada*—remain unknown.[5] Clemens apparently found *The Jesuits,* the second book of the series, particularly compelling, as indicated by his remarks to Livy the following day:

> You must read about the early Jesuit missionaries in Canada. Talk about self-abnegation! heroism! fidelity to a cause! It was sublime, it was stupendous. Why what these men did & suffered, in trying to rescue the insulting & atrocious savages from the doom of hell, makes one adore & glorify human nature as exemplified in those priests—yes, & despise it at the very same time. In endurance & performance they were gods; in credulity, & in obedience to their ecclesiastical chiefs, they were swine.[6]

THE PARKMAN MARGINALIA

Twain's interest in *The Jesuits* is also demonstrated by the extensive annotations he jotted in its margins—in blue ink as well as black and purple pencil—suggesting multiple readings of the text over time. According to biographer Albert Bigelow Paine, Twain numbered Parkman's *Canadian Histories*—"especially the story of the *Old Régime* and of the *Jesuits in North America*"—among his favorite books, and returned to them periodically until the end of his life, jotting his impressions of *The Old Régime* on its title page in January 1908: "Very interesting. It tells how people religiously and otherwise insane came over from France and colonized Canada."[7] Further evidence of the writer's respect for the historian can be found in an 1897 notebook entry describing Parkman as "a man I worshiped."[8]

Since Clemens first read *The Jesuits* in the aftermath of Susy's spiritual epiphany, it is perhaps not surprising that most of his marginalia in the volume occur in the chapters discussing Iroquois religion—the animistic beliefs that the priests sought to supplant with the tenets of the "one true faith." He had been introduced to Iroquois creation stories two years earlier when the Reverend John Sanborn, an Episcopalian missionary to the Seneca tribe in western New York, sent him a copy of his monograph, *Legends, Customs, and Social Life of the Seneca Indians.* The author responded with a gracious note of thanks:

Dear Sir:

I have read the little book through, & greatly enjoyed it. I like the straightforward simplicity of its language. The Indian idea of creation is more picturesque & poetical than the Biblical one; Handsome Lake's heaven is much more attractive & reasonable than the one in Revelations; & among other striking things in the book it is curious to note that the dark-complectioned woman who descended to the watery world was provided with children by miraculous (& let us hope, immaculate) conception. It is an odd coincidence. With many thanks for the entertaining little volume.[9]

These observations concerning the superiority of native concepts of creation and heaven to those found in the Bible anticipate the tenor of Twain's marginalia in *The Jesuits*. The writer's engagement with the Parkman text is illustrated not only by the frequency of his comments but also by their self-reflexive quality; his annotations have a strongly reactive, almost dialogic quality—by turns affirming, debunking, or extrapolating upon the historian's claims. For example, Parkman's observation that "the primitive Indian was as savage in his religion as in his life" elicits an astonishing fourteen lines of commentary, covering nearly every inch of white space over two consecutive pages:

It is always held that the fact that savages the world over believe in a hereafter, is somehow or other an evidence that there must *be* a hereafter. Men who attach no value whatever to a savage's notions about astronomy, creation, the causes of thunder, lightning, the rainbow, etc., find no absurdity in attaching a value to his notion concerning a matter far more profoundly beyond his depth—viz., that there is a hereafter, & that the soul is immortal. They have also attached a value to his belief in a Supreme Being—whereas it turns out that he hadn't any.[10]

Twain's response ironizes and critiques Parkman's claim, pointing out an inconsistency in the logic of individuals who, like the historian, dismiss "savage" notions of cosmogony yet place credence in their views regarding the afterlife. Moreover, the three foundational tenets identified here—belief in a Supreme Being, the immortality of the soul, and the existence of a "hereafter"—constitute the dominant focus of his other annotations throughout the volume.

Twain's own irreligious attitudes unquestionably inform his response to Parkman's text. Next to a passage describing a Huron deity named Oscatarach, who "dwelt in a bark house beside the path, and . . . [whose] office was to remove the brains from the heads of all who went by, as a necessary preparation for immortality," he notes, "In our time this is done as a necessary preparation for the reception of religion."[11] In another instance, the writer cavalierly edits Parkman's prose—adding "Christians" to a list of so-called primitive nations, such as the Peruvians and Mexicans,[12]—subverting its original meaning. Twain also repeatedly challenges the historian's ethnocentric privileging of Christian orthodoxy over pagan "superstitions" by pointing out numerous parallels with the Bible. In discussing the Iroquois concept of the afterlife, Parkman suggests that the Indians were ignorant of morality and therefore possessed a limited understanding of good and evil:

> The primitive Indian believed in the immortality of the soul, but he did not always believe in a state of future reward and punishment. Nor, when such a belief existed, was the good to be rewarded a moral good, or the evil to be punished a moral evil. Skillful hunters, brave warriors, men of influence and consideration, went, after death to the happy hunting ground; while the slothful, the cowardly, and the weak were doomed to eat serpents and ashes in dreary regions of mist and darkness.

Unpersuaded by these specious distinctions, Twain jots in the margin: "The inventors of the Bible do not seem to have been much the superiors of the Indians in ingenuity."[13] Similarly, he counters Parkman's statement that "according to some Algonquin traditions, heaven was a scene of endless festivity, the ghosts dancing to the sound of the rattle and the drum" with the retort, "Make it a harp & musical howling, & it is Bunyan's heaven."[14]

Twain's status as a theological outlier creates an intellectual distance that allowed him to perceive similarities between Christianity and traditional Iroquois spirituality Parkman was unwilling to admit. His analogies to both the Old and New Testaments appear most frequently in the sections of *The Jesuits* discussing native concepts of God. In response to the historian's dismissive pronouncement that "the primitive Indian's idea of a Supreme Being was a conception no higher than might have been expected. . . . The [Iroquois] Creator of the World stood on the level of a barbarous and degraded humanity," Twain underscores the latter sentence and observes, "This is a conception which could have been cabbaged from the Bible."[15] A comparable assertion—that the Indian's "gods were no whit better than himself"—elicits an even stronger reaction: "The same may be said of the God invented by the Hebrews."[16]

In much the same vein, Twain assails the epistemological arrogance of the priests' conviction in the superiority of their faith, commenting that Father Le Jeune, the superior general of the Jesuit mission to New France, "sails into the poor Indian's superstitions with confidence, & never suspects that he has any himself."[17] Many of the writer's annotations indicate that he viewed Christianity and native religion as comparable mythologies; for example, next to a paragraph discussing the Catholic belief in the efficacy of holy water to drive away devils, he states, "There seems to be no valuable difference between the superstitions of the priests and those of the medicine men."[18] He seems to have been especially intrigued by the concept of novenas, described by Parkman as a "nine days' devotion" to the Virgin Mary or "some other celestial personage," undertaken with a particular intention such as curing illness or—in the case of the seventeenth-century French missionaries—ensuring their protection from hostile tribes. In several places throughout *The Jesuits,* Twain reconfigures this ritualistic petition for spiritual intercession as a commercial transaction: "Imagine the 'celestial personage' pondering the offer & finally saying reluctantly, 'It is really worth more, but never mind, I will do it for that, & make it up out of the next customer.'"[19] With each narrow escape from death, the Jesuits attribute their safety to these devotions, prompting Twain to remark, "They are going to run into debt, first they know."[20] His skepticism peaks in response to Parkman's discussion of a failed plot in which the "gift of nine French hatchets" is offered in exchange for the missionaries' murder. Noting the bizarre symmetry of this proposition, he muses, "Nine days' service to St. Joseph for their preservation, against nine French hatchets for their destruction. The values are equal; it is a close game."[21]

But the most significant insight Twain recorded in the margins of Parkman's text concerns the "appeal to fear" that the Jesuits used in their attempted conversion of the Hurons: "You do good to your friends," said Le Jeune to an Algonquin chief, "and you burn your enemies. God does the same."[22] The writer underlines this passage and marks the right margin with two vertical strokes for additional emphasis. Detecting the premises of a subliminal syllogism within the priest's proselytizing, he supplies a logical— though wildly unorthodox—conclusion, adding directly above Parkman's statement, "Therefore God is an Algonquin."[23] At first glance, this comment is nothing less than a bombshell—a bold affirmation of the universality of God; upon closer inspection, however, it proves to mean something quite different. In linking the vindictive wrath of Yahweh to the behavior of an Algonquin chief, Twain blurs the boundary between the human and divine and demolishes the hierarchical distinction between "civilized" and "primitive" religions. God, he irreverently declares, is nothing more than a savage.

At the time Clemens wrote these words in 1881, his attitude toward native peoples—whom he had described to Livy in his letter from Montreal as "insulting & atrocious savages"—could hardly be characterized as progressive. A year earlier, he had callously joked about their worthlessness in a letter to *Hartford Courant* editor Charles Hopkins Clark: "Years ago, I was accused of loading an Indian up with beans lubricated with nitroglycerine & sending him in an ox-wagon over a stumpy road. This was impossible, on its face, for no one would risk oxen in that way."[24] Lingering traces of this antagonism appear occasionally in the Parkman marginalia as well; next to a passage recounting the horrific tortures inflicted upon Father Francesco Bressani over a period of several months by his Iroquois captors, he observes, "That men should be willing to leave happy homes & endure what the missionaries endured, in order to teach the Indians the road to hell, would be rational, understandable; but why they should want to teach them the way to heaven is a thing which the mind cannot somehow grasp."[25] The perpetrators of such abominable cruelty were, in Clemens's estimation, incorrigible fiends, unworthy of the Jesuits' heroic efforts to redeem them. Despite this antipathy, the writer's introduction to indigenous religious beliefs—even through the skewed lens of Parkman's text—marks the beginning of a fundamental shift in his thinking about the nature of savagery. In refuting the historian's dogmatic claims about Christianity, he inadvertently discovered a coherence, logic, and intelligence in the Iroquois worldview that would challenge and gradually undermine his categorical rejection of Indians as "the scum of the earth" (CT1, 444).

Twain's marginalia document the incremental stages of this realization. He reacts with astonishment to Parkman's description of the joking and "incessant banter" that characterized interpersonal interaction among the Iroquois, writing next to one of the historian's footnotes, "Plainly these are not Indians of the Cooper style."[26] This acknowledgment of the disparity between actual native people and the romantic stereotypes of stoic, taciturn warriors popularized in *The Leatherstocking Tales* opened the writer's mind to a reconsideration of all his preconceptions about Indian character. More than two decades after reading *The Jesuits,* he recounted the story to a *New York Times* reporter that illustrates the cultural relativity of humor:

> You couldn't, for example, understand an English joke, yet they have their jokes—plenty of them. There's a passage in Parkman that tells of the home life of the Indian—describes him sitting at home in his wigwam with his squaw and papooses—not the stoical, icy Indian with whom we are familiar, who wouldn't make a jest for his life or notice one that anybody else made, but the real Indian that few white men ever saw—simply rocking with mirth at some tribal witticism that probably wouldn't have commended itself in the least to Parkman.[27]

Twain's realization that indigenous peoples possessed a sense of humor humanized them. A decade before reading Parkman, he had dismissed the concept of native intelligence as an oxymoron, insisting in "The Noble Red Man" that "[the Indian's] 'wisdom' conferred upon an idiot would leave that idiot helpless indeed" (CT1, 444). In *The Jesuits* marginalia, however, he commends the perspicacity and critical reasoning of the Iroquois at two different points. In one instance, he explains that while the Jesuits generally regarded the Indians as "more intelligent than the French peasantry," they also believed that "the Devil lay entrenched as behind impregnable breastworks" in their minds, citing the following speech from Lalemant's 1640 *Huron Relations:*

> At the height of the pestilence, a Huron said to one of the priests, "I see plainly that your God is angry with us because we will not believe and obey him. [The village] where you first taught his word is entirely ruined. Then you came here, and we would not listen; so [our village] is ruined too. . . . This year you have been all through our country, and found scarcely any who would do what God commands; therefore the pestilence is everywhere." After premises so hopeful, the Fathers looked for a satisfactory conclusion; but the Indian proceeded—"My opinion is, that we ought to shut you out from all the houses, and stop our ears when you speak of God, so that we cannot hear. Then we shall not be so guilty of rejecting the truth, and he will not punish us so cruelly."[28]

Impressed by the clever subversion of the Huron's logic, Twain writes "good sense" next to this passage. These same two words also occur in relation to Parkman's discussion of indigenous cosmogony. According to Iroquois oral tradition, the world began when Ataentic, a primordial female spirit, fell from the sky onto the back of an enormous turtle, upon which animals had placed a mound of mud to cushion the impact of her landing. Life on this verdant island—earth—is characterized by a dynamic balance between good and evil, which is sustained through the mediation of dichotomous spirit-beings, Ataentic and her grandson Jouskeha. As Parkman explains it,

> He is the Sun; she is the Moon. He is beneficent, but she is malignant. . . . Jouskeha raises corn for himself, and makes plentiful harvests for mankind.

> He constantly interposes between mankind and the malice of his wicked grandmother. . . . It was he who made lakes and streams; for once the earth was parched and barren, all the water being gathered under the armpit of a colossal frog; but Jouskeha pierced the armpit, and let out the water. No prayers were offered to him, his benevolent nature rendering them superfluous.[29]

The writer underscored the last sentence of this passage and jotted "good sense" next to it as well, indicating both his attraction to—and explicit approval of—the native concept of an unconditionally loving and compassionate deity, whose intercession on behalf of humanity required no supplication or entreaty. The appeal of a purely beneficent Creator such as Jouskeha, so radically different from traditional Christian notions of the Godhead, would simmer in Twain's unconscious for the next three years, resurfacing as a central plot element in "Huck Finn and Tom Sawyer among the Indians," the sequel to his masterpiece, *Adventures of Huckleberry Finn*. Although he only completed nine chapters of this narrative before abandoning it in midsentence, it nonetheless remains his most sustained and ambitious attempt to portray what he believed to be the true character of America's indigenous inhabitants. Over the years, scholars have offered a variety of explanations for the writer's failure to bring this project to fruition, ranging from Victorian "skittishness about sex"[30] to "weak characterization . . . and thematic development" (HHT, 91). The root cause, however, can be discerned in the irreconcilable traits he identified in the margins of Parkman's text—the admirable sagacity of native spiritual beliefs on the one hand and their depraved, barbarous treatment of enemies, particularly white female captives, on the other.

COLONEL RICHARD IRVING DODGE— "A MAN WHO KNOWS ALL ABOUT INDIANS"

Soon after arriving at Quarry Farm in late June 1884, Twain began sketching out the plans for his sequel. He apparently brought *The Oregon Trail* with him to Elmira from Hartford to assist with realistic representation of the Plains landscape, as well as with the appearance and customs of local tribes such as the "Ogillalah" and "Dahcotah"—two distinctive spellings which he replicates in the text. Qualitatively different from those in *The Jesuits*, his marginalia in *The Oregon Trail* note "Indian dress," "country," "Fort Laramie," "S. fork of Platte," and "interior of a lodge," evidently for handy reference during the process of composition.[31] Walter Blair's 1969 introduction to the sequel in *Hannibal, Huck, and Tom* surmises the use of Parkman's book on the basis of Twain's references to "old Vaskiss the trader" and "Robidou the blacksmith" (HFTS, 71–72), two historical figures explicitly named by the historian. Since the Mark Twain Project did not acquire Twain's copy of the volume until 2016, Blair was unable to examine it and determine the full extent of Clemens's borrowing.

As useful as *The Oregon Trail* proved in supplying basic background information, the writer soon realized that he needed additional source material to flesh out his ideas. On 6 July, he contacted his nephew Charley Webster with the following request:

> Send to me, right away, a book by *Lieut. Col. Dodge, USA,* called "25 Years on the Frontier"—or some such title—I don't remember just what. Maybe it is "25 Years Among the Indians," or maybe "25 Years in the Rocky Mountains." But the name of the *author* will guide you. I think he has written only the one book; & so any librarian can tell you the title of it.
>
> I want several other *personal narratives* of life & adventure out yonder on the Plains & in the Mountains, if you can run across them—especially life *among the Indians.* Send what you can find. I mean to take Huck Finn out there."[32]

The author in question was Richard Irving Dodge (1827–95), a seasoned army officer and former aide-de-camp to General William T. Sherman, who had served on the Plains, primarily among the Cheyenne, for over three decades. He had in fact written not one but two books—*The Plains of the Great West and their Inhabitants* (1877) and *Our Wild Indians: Thirty-Three Years' Experience among the Red Men of the Great West* (1882). Twain had read and admired Dodge's first work soon after its publication, writing to William Dean Howells on 22 February 1877, "I hope [President Hayes] will put Lt. Col. Richard Irwin [*sic*] Dodge (Author of "The Great Plains & their Inhabitants") at the head of the Indian Department. *There's* a man who knows all about Indians, & yet has some humanity in him—(knowledge of Indians, & humanity, are seldom found in the same individual)" (MTHL, 172). This remark, as Louis J. Budd observes, offers evidence that the writer's "glacial contempt for the Indian was thawing around the edges under pressure from his [Nook Farm] neighbors, who were ahead of national opinion on this score,"[33] a topic will be examined more fully in the next chapter.

According to Alan Gribben's reconstruction of the writer's library, Clemens purchased a copy of *The Plains of the Great West* on 21 January 1877, just days after it was issued.[34] He also seems to have immediately read it from cover to cover, since a note on the book's last page clearly anticipates his recommendation to Howells a month later. In his conclusion, Dodge asserts his belief that the Indian is a fundamentally "cruel inhuman savage" but simultaneously indicts the federal government for its role in perpetuating this degradation: "The Government makes three vital mistakes in dealing with Indians. 1. In not enforcing its Treaty obligations. 2. In dealing with Indians through two different Departments. 3. In yielding too much to the sentimental humanitarian element of the Country."[35] He therefore advocates the use of military force in order to accomplish the following goals:

> The Indians should be put on reservations, under the control of practical men, who have no pet theories to work out, no fortunes to make. They should be well treated, fed, clothed and induced, not forced, to work. They should be taught by precept and by experience that an Indian is no better than a white man, that comfort and plenty will be the reward of good behavior and industry and that crime of any kind will be followed by sure and immediate punishment.[36]

Twain concurred with this assessment, writing just beneath the book's closing paragraph, "Very well put forth. Such a man's relation of his experience is worth a whole winter's talk in Congress."[37] His memory of Dodge's authority as "a man who knows all about Indians" doubtlessly played a role in his request to Webster seven years later, although the book's actual title hopelessly eluded him. In fact, Clemens's recollection of the work he desired more closely resembles the title of Dodge's second book (which he had likely heard about but had not yet read) than that of his first. In light of this confusion, it is not surprising that Webster posted a copy of *Our Wild Indians* to Elmira on 9 July, along with two autobiographies—George Armstrong Custer's *My Life on the Plains* (1874) and Buffalo Bill's *The Life of the Honorable William F. Cody* (1879). Upon receiving the package, Clemens wrote his nephew again, testily informing him, "'Our Wild Indians' is Col. Dodge's *second* book. The title of his *first* one contains the words 'twenty-five years,' & you will find it in the catalogue of any big library, no doubt. The present one is useful to me, but I want *that* one also."[38] Webster's expense ledger indicates that he purchased a copy of *Life on the Plains* [sic] on 14 July, eliciting the writer's grateful response three days later: "The book you sent is the right one, even if it *hasn't* '25 years' in its title. Don't need any more Injun books."[39]

According to Walter Blair, Twain made limited use of both Custer's and Cody's memoirs in composing "Huck Finn and Tom Sawyer among the Indians" but relied "constantly—it may well be too constantly" on Dodge's work for its setting, plot, and theme (HHT, 85). While awaiting the arrival of *The Plains of the Great West*, he perused *Our Wild Indians* and discovered—to his great delight—that Dodge shared his long-standing bias against James Fenimore Cooper's romantic representation of native peoples. Dodge not only excoriated Cooper's idealized Indians, denouncing their myriad graces and virtues as "impossible in a savage,"[40] but also warned that such misrepresentation had serious—and potentially lethal—consequences for resolving the nation's so-called Indian Problem. "To the professional humanitarians

I have nothing to say," he announced in the conclusion, "except to assure them of my unalterable hostility, and determination to use every faculty with which I am endowed to wrench the Indian from their sordid grasp."[41] The fervor of Dodge's conviction allowed Twain to glimpse the dramatic potential of an incongruity he had often mined for humorous purposes— namely, that Cooper's Indians were "an extinct tribe that never existed" (IA, 205). He seized upon the interplay of Cooper's romantic construct and the deadly threat that "real" Indians posed to colonization and progress as a cornerstone of his proposed narrative, hoping to extirpate the enduring image of the "Noble Savage" from the American psyche through the dramatic arc of its plot.

But beyond its critique of Cooper, Dodge's 1882 text offered Twain an even more substantive source of inspiration—a chapter devoted to the "Religion of the Indian," which addressed many of the same aspects of indigenous spirituality that had piqued his interest in Parkman's *Jesuits*. Records from the 1911 auction at which the writer's personal library was sold indicate that *Our Wild Indians* was not only one of the most heavily annotated volumes in his collection but also that the majority of his marginalia appeared in this chapter.[42] When the volume was sold in 1995, the Christie's auction catalogue in which it was advertised contained a facsimile of two of its "most copiously annotated" pages, as well as a representative sampling of Twain's other noteworthy marginalia throughout the text. These comments reflect tremendous growth in his appreciation of native religion within the brief space of three years; rather than simply acknowledging the logic and eminent "good sense" of these concepts, his observations assert their superiority to Christian doctrine. Moreover, since spiritual beliefs are inextricably entwined with the character and culture of the group professing them, the writer's privileging of indigenous concepts of God has broader implications regarding his perception of native peoples in general.

As Twain's marginalia indicate, he adopted the stance of a comparatist in reading *Our Wild Indians*, actively engaging Dodge's ideas in much in the same way he had Parkman's. He responds to a description of the "ridiculous penances"—such as always facing a certain direction while sitting or exclusively using one's left hand—that Indians place upon themselves in order to propitiate their gods by observing that these practices are "like our fish on Fridays & lent."[43] Similarly, Dodge's example of a solemn vow to "consecrate a pony" in exchange for a warrior's successful escape from danger reminds him that in civilized society "we vow a candle"[44] in the hope of achieving an analogous outcome. This network of minor parallels between

Christian and pagan praxis irrevocably broke down, however, when the
writer encountered Dodge's detailed discussion of native notions of divinity.

Although both *The Plains of the Great West* and *Our Wild Indians* were
immensely popular and well respected in the nineteenth century, Dodge's
Eurocentric bias and essentialism make his work problematic by current
ethnographic standards. In *Our Wild Indians*, he matter-of-factly—though
erroneously—states that all indigenous groups share a single belief system:

> He believes in two gods, equals in wisdom and power. One is the Good
> God. His function is to aid the Indian in all his undertakings, to heap
> benefits upon him, to deliver his enemy into his hand, to protect him
> from danger, pain, and privation. . . . Warmth, food, joy, success in love,
> distinction in war, all come from him.
>
> The other is the Bad God. He is always the enemy of each individual red
> man, and exerts to the utmost all his powers of harm against him. From
> him proceed all the disasters, misfortunes, privations, and discomforts
> of life.[45]

Because the Good God is not "exacting or jealous," he "demands nothing
in return . . . for his unremitting labors, his devoted services, his constant
watchfulness on behalf of the Indian. . . . No prayers [or thanks] are necessary, for he does the very best he can without being asked."[46] This description of the Good God's steadfast beneficence and the unrelenting malevo-
lence of his evil counterpart strongly echoes Parkman's characterization of
Jouskeha and his grandmother Ataentic in *The Jesuits*. Twain's marginalia
reveal that the alterity of this concept intrigued him as much—if not
more—in 1884 than it had three years earlier, provoking inevitable comparison with the traditional Old Testament representation of Yahweh. As
the writer reflected on Dodge's text, he realized that the native bifurcation
of the Godhead into distinct, antithetical entities resolved a conundrum at
the heart of Christian dogma—namely, the Almighty's paradoxical capacity
for compassion *and* cruelty, comfort *and* terror, love *and* vengeance. In
Twain's estimation, this "illogical" combination of traits not only distances
humans from the divine but also disempowers them by eliciting uncertainty about their spiritual status. Conversely, by positing two separate deities conceptualized exclusively as "friend" and "foe," Indians enjoyed a
more intimate, secure connection with their Creator.

Clemens's marginalia in chapter 6 of *Our Wild Indians* not only compare the Christian image of God with the plurality of deities in native tradition but also present an unflinching assessment of their relative merits. In
four separate notes, made within the space of several pages, he pits the

foundational tenets espoused by Christians, whom he identifies by the first-person plural pronouns "we" and "our"—tacitly including himself in the fold—against the beliefs of a primitive "he." The writer subverts the biblical premise that God created man in his own image (Gen. 1:27), insisting that God is instead a human invention: "We say man made God in his own image, but the Indian has made one of his gods far better and higher than any possible man."[47] The appeal of this Good God becomes apparent when compared with the omniscient and omnipotent Creator of the Judeo-Christian tradition: "Our illogical God is all-powerful in name, but impotent in fact; the Great Spirit is not all-powerful, but does the very best he can for his injun and does it free of charge" (quoted in HHT, 90). As this statement indicates, Clemens finds the abiding, unconditional love that Indians ascribe to the Good God or Great Spirit enormously reassuring in that it does not have to be earned or sought through prayer, nor can it be capriciously revoked due to human failings. In a sense, the Great Spirit resembles an ideal parent, unwavering in his love and support for his creations. Such devotion, he suggests, is a measure of true divinity.

Through these ruminations, Twain gradually came to realize that the pagan beliefs of North America's indigenous tribes were, in many ways, superior to the Christian faith: "The Indian's bad God is the twin of our only God; his good God is better than any heretofore devised by man."[48] This conviction that the Good God is "better" than the Christian deity is grounded in the intimate and secure relationship that native peoples enjoy with their Creator: "We have to keep our God placated with prayers, & even then we are never sure of him—how much higher & finer is the Indian's God" (HHT, 90). While these encomia signal a critical breakthrough for the writer, they simultaneously present a quandary—for example, how can the preeminence of native religion be reconciled with his long-standing antipathy toward the primitives who invented it? Dodge himself acknowledges this incongruity but does not examine it in detail, simply stating, "The Indians, for so utterly savage a race, have made very remarkable progress in their religious tenets."[49] Twain concurred, marking these lines with a vertical stroke and jotting "right" in the adjacent margin. This paradox so intrigued him that he adopted it as another narrative thread of "Huck Finn and Tom Sawyer among the Indians."

In addition to providing Clemens with necessary background information about native religion, *Our Wild Indians* offered a scenario whereby this topic could be plausibly introduced into the sequel's plot. "The power of earnestness," Dodge writes, "is well exemplified in the influence that the Indian religion obtains over the white trappers and 'squaw men' who live with them. Nine-tenths are sooner or later converted to the Indian idea, and many of them have firm faith in the power of making 'medicine.'"[50] Next to this passage, Twain wrote, "H. becomes converted."[51] The initial stands for Huck Finn, who of course is neither a trapper nor a *squaw man*—a derogatory term for a non-native who marries an Indian woman and is assimilated into her tribe. Although the nine extant chapters of Twain's manuscript offer little indication of how this conversion might transpire, the prospect of an Indianized Huck—the incarnation of a hybrid cultural identity that blends red and white—invests the concept of "light[ing] out for the Territory ahead of the rest" with a new, radically subversive meaning. In the unfinished sequel, Huck encounters Indians but never comes close to integrating into their society; rather, his introduction to native religion occurs secondhand, through the agency of a scout named Brace Johnson, who spent his younger years living with the Sioux. As Huck reports,

> He didn't talk very much; and when he talked about Injuns, he talked the same as if he was talking about animals; he didn't seem to have much idea that they was men. But he had some of their ways, himself, on account of being so long amongst them; and moreover he had their religion. And one of the things that puzzled him was how such animals ever struck such a sensible religion. He said the Injuns hadn't only but two gods, a good one and a bad one, and they never paid no attention to the good one, nor ever prayed to him or worried about him at all, but only tried their level best to flatter up the bad god and keep on the good side of him; because the good one loved them and wouldn't ever think of doing them any harm. . . all the trouble come from the bad god, who was setting up nights to think up ways to bring them bad luck and bust up all their plans, and never fooled away a chance to do them all the harm he could. (HFTS, 61)

The parallels between this passage and Dodge's discussion of native religion in *Our Wild Indians* demonstrate the degree of Twain's indebtedness to it. When juxtaposed with the writer's marginalia, however, another, less obvious similarity emerges—namely, that Brace's bafflement over how savages developed "such a sensible religion" mirrors Twain's own thinking about the subject. This suggests that on some level the scout functions as a stand-in for the writer. These resemblances multiply as the sequel progresses in that Brace's values—his commitment to the preservation of family, home, and female purity—epitomize a model of genteel Victorian manhood with which Clemens closely identified.

In fact, Clemens's evolving conception of this character, whose fiancée, Peggy Mills, is taken into captivity by the Sioux, helps elucidate the motives underlying his puzzling request to Charley Webster about *The Plains of the Great West*. Considering that *Our Wild Indians* had proved such a rich source of inspiration to him, why did he still insist on obtaining a copy of Dodge's earlier book? As a result of his reading of *Plains* seven years earlier, he must have desired to retrieve a particular piece of information not found in the 1882 volume. But what? As historian Wayne Kime explains, *Our Wild Indians* was "an expanded but watered-down version of the section on Indians in *The Plains of the Great West*."[52] Whereas Dodge had "confined himself to subjects about which he or his acquaintances had direct knowledge"[53] in the earlier work, he made extensive use of work by established authorities, such as Henry R. Schoolcraft, George Catlin, and Randolph Marcy, in preparing the second. In addition, because some reviewers had expressed consternation over Dodge's graphic account of the rape of white female captives by Indians in *The Plains of the Great West*, he condensed and bowdlerized his discussion of this topic in the later book as a concession to popular taste.[54] As the trajectory of the sequel's nine extant chapters suggests, the passage Twain sought was this:

> Cooper and some other novelists knew nothing of Indians, when they put their Heroines captive in the hands of these savages . . . in the last twenty-five years, no woman has been taken prisoner by any party of Plains Indians, who did not as soon after as practicable, become a victim to the lusts of every one of her captors. . . . No words can express the horror of the situation of that most unhappy woman, who falls into the hands of these savage fiends. The husband, or other male protectors, killed or dispersed, she is borne off in triumph to where the Indians make their first camp. Here if she makes no resistance she is laid upon a buffalo robe, and each in turn violates her person, the others dancing, singing and yelling around her. If she resists at all her clothing is torn off her person, four pegs are driven into the ground and her arms and legs stretched to the utmost, are tied fast to them by thongs . . . she is [then] subjected to violation after violation, outrage after outrage, to every abuse and indignity, until not infrequently death releases her from suffering. . . . If she lives, it is to go through the same horrible ordeal in every camp until the party gets back to the home encampment.[55]

While the incidence of sexual assault among white female captives is notoriously difficult to document—and hence a topic of ongoing scholarly debate—it was hardly as ubiquitous as Dodge claims. According to ethnohistorian James Axtell, the practice was virtually nonexistent in the eastern half of the United States owing to the "ethic of strict warrior continence" and the routine adoption of captives into native families to replace lost loved ones. The rape of a female prisoner thus represented the violation of a future sister or cousin and breached the strong incest taboos of indigenous groups like the Iroquois.[56] West of the Mississippi, however, anecdotal evidence attests to the horrifying physical and sexual abuse of at least a small number of white women by Indians. Sensational accounts such as the harrowing *Narrative of the Captivity and Subsequent Sufferings of Mrs. Rachel Plummer*—a Texas teenager captured by the Comanches in 1836 and held as their prisoner for thirteen months, during which time she witnessed the murder of her two children and was herself repeatedly tortured, beaten, and raped—inflamed popular sentiment and deepened the stereotype of Indians as demonic savages.[57]

The cultural hysteria induced by even unsubstantiated allegations of interracial rape is perhaps best illustrated in the controversial legal aftermath of the 1862 Sioux Uprising, when starving, dispossessed Dakota Indians rampaged across Minnesota, murdering more than five hundred Anglo-American settlers within a six-week period in late summer. Soon thereafter, the Army hunted down and tried several hundred Dakota warriors, sentencing them all to death. In a stunning reversal, however, President Abraham Lincoln undertook a personal review of the case and issued an executive order pardoning the vast majority of those condemned. Only thirty-nine of the original three hundred native men were convicted—the majority on charges of "engaging in massacre" and a handful for the crime of "ravishing" white women—and hanged at Mankato on 26 December 1862, the largest mass execution in US history. Incensed by the president's action, several Minnesota politicians issued a vehement letter of protest highlighting the abomination of the Indians' misdeeds:

> These savages, to whom you purpose to extend your executive clemency, . . . seized nearly one hundred women and young girls and took them into a captivity which was *infinitely worse than death.* In one instance . . . these incarnate fiends . . . took a little girl outside of the lodge, removed all her clothes, and fastened her upon her back on the ground. . . . One by one they violated her person, unmoved by her cries and unchecked by evident signs of her approaching dissolution. This work was continued until her Heavenly Father relieved her from suffering. These Indians are called by some prisoners of war. There was no war about it. It was wholesale robbery, *rape,—murder.*[58]

In *Captured by Texts: Puritan to Post-modern Images of Indian Captivity,* Gary Ebersole argues that this notion of a fate "worse than death" is rooted in the "high cultural value—even sacrality—placed on female chastity and virtue" in nineteenth-century American society.[59]

"Long before the Cold War," he asserts, "the cry of 'better dead than red' (or its equivalent) was on the lips of many female captives. The reasons for this are immediately related to the larger symbolic complex of white feminine virtue, the savage sexual Other, and rape—or to put this another way, to the symbolics of racial, sexual, and gender power relations."[60] The profanation of white women through sexual contact with native men, euphemistically described as "outrages" in the mainstream press, proved such a powerful emotional trigger that it was often cited as a rationale "to justify the extermination of the Indians and the appropriation of their lands."[61] Ella Wheeler Wilcox's poem "Custer," written to commemorate the twentieth anniversary of the Battle of the Little Big Horn in 1896, reflects this racist sentiment: "If the last lone remnants of that race / Were by the white man swept from off the earth's fair face, / Were every red man slaughtered in a day, / Still would that sacrifice but poorly pay / For one insulted woman captive's woes."[62]

Victorian valorization of female purity entered the visual lexicon as well, typified in Erastus Dow Palmer's 1859 marble sculpture, "The White Captive," which depicts the daughter of a pioneer in what the artist described as "Indian bondage" (fig. 15). Stripped naked as though kidnapped from the safety of her home during the night, she stands resolutely with one hand tied to a tree, the other clenched into a fist behind her back. Gazing leftward at an unseen foe, she simultaneously turns her body away in a futile gesture of self-protection. According to Joy Kasson, the iconography of the young woman's pose invites the viewer to "contemplate the breakdown of domestic as well as sexual order";[63] the resignation with which she awaits her inevitable sexual defilement signifies the fragility of civilization in a hostile wilderness.[64]

Like many Anglo-American men of his era, Clemens revered the ideals of female purity and innocence—traits embodied in his wife Livy. Four days after their wedding on 2 February 1870, he extolled her virtues in a letter to Will Bowen, a childhood friend from Hannibal:

> She is much the most beautiful girl I ever saw . . . the sweetest, & the gentlest, & the daintiest, & the most modest and unpretentious, & the wisest in all things she should be wise in & the most ignorant in all matters it would not grace her to know . . . & her beautiful life is ordered by a religion that is all kindliness & unselfishness. Before the gentle majesty of her purity all evil things & evil ways & evil deeds stand abashed,—then surrender. (L4, 51–52)

Given this litany of superlatives, it is no coincidence that Twain's first recorded mention of the sexual threat Indians posed to white women occurs

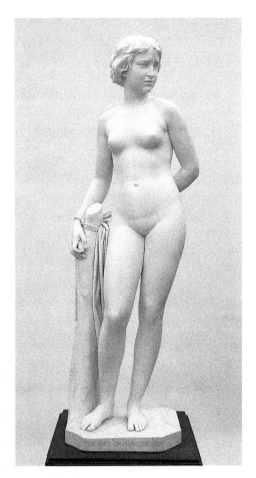

FIGURE 15.   Erastus Dow
Palmer, "The White Captive."
Metropolitan Museum of Art,
New York City. Bequest of
Hamilton Fish, 1894. Courtesy
of Creative Commons Zero/
Open Access Initiative.

in "The Noble Red Man," written six months after his marriage.
Anticipating Wilcox's poem by more than a quarter century, the sketch
describes the shocking annihilation of a prototypical Anglo-American
family—children "burned alive in the presence of their parents"; wives
"ravished before their husbands' eyes"; and husbands "mutilated, tortured,
and scalped, and their wives compelled to look on"—as proof that the
Indian is "a good, fair, desirable subject for extermination if ever there was
one" (CT1, 446). This argument reflects the degree to which the writer
subscribed to the prevailing social and moral codes of his time.

    In 1884, Clemens's role as both a husband and a father of three vulner-
able daughters, the eldest of whom—at age twelve—stood poised on the

threshold of puberty, was no doubt a subliminal factor in shaping the direction of "Huck Finn and Tom Sawyer among the Indians." Soon after embarking on its composition, he realized that the disparate ideas he had gleaned from Dodge—the deleterious effect of Fenimore Cooper's idealized Indians, the indisputable "good sense" of native religious beliefs, and the unnerving specter of their rapacious sexuality—were not only fundamentally incongruous but also elicited such deeply conflicted emotions that their coalescence into a unified narrative proved impracticable. Clemens's fascination with the indigenous notion of a good and bad god ultimately could not overcome the anathema of interracial sexual violence; by summer's end, this quandary would stall his progress on the manuscript in medias res.

THE UNFINISHED NARRATIVE

Apart from the directives Clemens fired off to Charley Webster concerning source material for his project in early July, his first formal mention of "Huck Finn and Tom Sawyer among the Indians" occurs midmonth in a letter to William Dean Howells:

> I go down [to town] every other day & have one or two teeth gouged out & stuffed. I have been in the dental chair ten days, a couple of hours a day; & shall be there 3 days this week & I suppose as many more next week. The dentist . . . gouges & digs & saws & rasps & hammers, & keeps up a steady stream of entertaining talk, all the time, like his professional ancestor the barber; & so these have been very pleasant relaxations to me, & I shall be rather sorry to see them come to an end. They have been a vast improvement to me, too—an education; I can stand the most exquisite pain, now, without outward manifestation; & indeed without any very real discomfort. The Indian has fallen in my estimation; he is no better than you or me—he is merely a product of education . . .
>
> On my off days I work at a new story (Huck Finn & Tom Sawyer among the Indians 40 or 50 years ago). (MTHL, 495–96)

This letter suggests that—in the short term, at least—the writer regarded the sequel's composition as a welcome diversion from the unpleasant business of having his teeth fixed. These activities, though seemingly unrelated, are in fact linked by the insights each affords into native character. Clemens's discovery of his capacity to withstand extreme physical discomfort provokes a reassessment of the legendary stoicism associated with the romantic image of the Noble Savage. The "education" acquired in the dentist's chair is two-fold—self-reflexive on the one hand but simultaneously directed outward, across the lines of race and culture, on the other. Realizing that the forbear-ance Indians display in response to pain is not innate but learned behavior, Clemens concludes "he is no better than you or me"—an offhanded acknowledgment of the common humanity that links savage and civilized peoples.

But Clemens's dental work influenced the conceptual genesis of "Huck Finn and Tom Sawyer among the Indians" in a more substantive way as well. The "exquisite pain" inflicted by the tools of the anonymous Elmira dentist imaginatively propelled him into the text and became its operative metaphor, shaping his representation not only of the sequel's fictional fron-tier setting but also of the major characters' responses to the horrific events that unfold there. Seated in the dentist's chair, subjected to a series of inva-sive assaults ("gouging," "digging," and the like), the writer experienced a culturally sanctioned form of torture—indeed, a kind of rape. He became a victim—passive, powerless, prostrate—experiencing a physical analogue of the psychic torment experienced by the narrative's three key male charac-ters, Huck, Tom, and Brace, in contemplating the horror of Peggy Mills's sexual defilement at the hands of her Sioux captors.

Although this dimension of the text has been largely overlooked, the concept of disabling pain lies at the heart of "Huck Finn and Tom Sawyer among the Indians." During its composition, the "howling adventures amongst the Injuns" that Tom naively envisions as a "circus" (HFTS, 37) abruptly take a dark, almost nihilistic, turn, metamorphosing into an alto-gether different kind of "howl"—one of anguished helplessness and despair. The territory to which Huck, Tom, and Jim "light out" bears no resem-blance to the Edenic wilderness of romantic fiction but is rather a place of primal terror and moral anarchy, where innocent women are raped, men go mad, families are destroyed, and civilization itself is destroyed by implaca-ble savagery. The western journey depicted in the sequel represents a night-marish descent into chaos and disorder, a plunge into the uncharted geog-raphy of Twain's psyche.

As a fragmentary and therefore provisional text, the sequel has attracted little critical attention. Among the scholars who have discussed it, the consen-sus is that the manuscript represents Twain's unsuccessful attempt to write a dime novel (HHT, 88). Although the narrative does in some respects conform to the genre's formulaic tropes—clichéd, two-dimensional characters (e.g., the innocent damsel in distress and her rugged male rescuer) and predictably vio-lent plots involving capture, pursuit, and rescue—its deviations from these conventions are far more significant. In *Reading the West*, Bill Brown traces the dime novel's evolution from its inception in the 1860s through the turn of the century, noting that by the 1870s—some fourteen years before the writer began composing his sequel—"white greed [had] replaced Indian savagery as the most familiar source of villainy."[65] At this point, the adversarial role formerly played by Indians was assumed by a variety of unscrupulous Anglo-Americans, such as swindlers, cattle rustlers, and horse thieves. In Brown's view, the beginning of the *Deadwood Dick* series in 1877 "marks the moment in the dime novel's history when the Indians, however stereotyped, no longer function to unify the white population . . . [indeed] in subsequent *Deadwood Dick* novels, the Indians join the ranks of the oppressed who need to be defended by the hero."[66] Twain's antagonistic depiction of the Sioux in "Huck Finn and Tom Sawyer among the Indians" thus distances his project from the dime novels of the period and suggests that other, perhaps unconscious, factors may have influenced the ominous direction in which it unfolded.

The sequel's dark overtones are not immediately apparent in its opening chapters. It begins at precisely the moment in which *Adventures of Huckleberry Finn* ends and promises the reader a lighthearted lark, a boyish game bred of the stifling boredom of the Missouri hemp farm where Tom, Huck, and Jim are "vacationing" with Aunt Polly. Huck and Jim are content with the ease of their existence, "plenty to eat and nothing to do" (HFTS, 34), but Tom persuades them of the desirability of spending "a couple of months or so" among the "Injuns," whom he characterizes as "the noblest human beings that's ever been in the world" (HFTS, 35)—brave, honorable, selfless, and true. Tom overcomes his friends' objections to the potential dangers of his plan by declaring Indians the "hospitablest" people in the world, among whom they will find fulfillment of two of their most fervent wishes—racial acceptance for Jim and romance for Huck: "They think just as much of niggers as they do of anybody, and the young squaws are the most beautiful be-utiful maidens that was ever in the whole world, and they love a white hunter the minute their eye falls on him" (HFTS, 36).

The childlike nature of Huck, Tom, and Jim's expedition is illustrated in their secretive preparations for the journey, carried out largely at Tom's behest. To secure a place to stash their supplies before "lighting out," they conduct a mock raid of a deserted cabin, creeping up just before dawn, "whooping and yelling, and [taking] it by surprise and never los[ing] a man" (HFTS, 38). The disparity between this game of "playing Indian," reminiscent of the antics of Tom, Huck, and Joe Harper on Jackson's Island in chapter 16 of *The Adventures of Tom Sawyer,* and the actual perils of the frontier become evident soon after the journey begins.

Within a few days of setting out, Huck, Tom, and Jim encounter a family of homesteaders bound for Oregon, who are camped on the trail awaiting the arrival of their eldest daughter's fiancée, Brace Johnson. Although Bernard DeVoto faulted Twain for what he termed the "improbable" choice having "so small a party . . . traveling alone in the Plains,"[67] the writer strategically uses the Mills family—whom Huck describes as "the simple-heartedest good-naturedest country folks in the world" (HFTS, 40)—to represent an iconic bastion of order and civility in the wilderness. Despite their lack of sophistication and formal education, each member of the family behaves in strict accordance with prescribed Victorian gender roles. Twain portrays seventeen-year-old Peggy—"the cap-sheaf of the lot . . . so gentle, she was, and so sweet" (HFTS, 41)—as an ideal of purity, delicacy, and goodness that must be vigilantly protected against the threat of evil. She is, in other words, an emblem of true womanhood, possessing many of the selfsame traits he ascribed to Livy in his 1870 letter to Will Bowen. Peggy is doted upon by her attentive male siblings, who treat her "as if she was made out of sugar or gold or something" (HFTS, 40).

Though the amenities of civilization are absent on the Plains, the young men's gallantry ensures that Peggy's status as a lady is never compromised by the physical rigors of frontier life. In the absence of a domicile where she can be ensconced as the presiding angel, they maintain the emblematic pedestal on which their sister stands through courtly deference. They rise to give her the best seat by the campfire, saddle her horse, and perform chores like gathering firewood and skinning game that would soil her delicate hands. These particular tasks, which were traditionally performed by native women and were associated in the popular consciousness with the pejorative label of "squaw," suggest that Twain's description is intended as an implicit comparison of women's place in "civilized" and "savage" societies. As he had disapprovingly commented in the margins of *Our Wild Indians*, "Indian women do all the work."[68] Peggy's selfless devotion to the well-being of others represents another hallmark of nineteenth-century femininity. This altruism extends beyond her immediate family to everyone she meets, regardless of race, class, or culture. According to Huck, she treats the Oglala warriors "as if she were their sister or their child, and they was very fond of her" (HFTS, 45). Peggy's stance toward the Indians is in fact quasi-maternal; she actively ministers to their physical and spiritual needs, bandaging their hurts and instructing them in the basic precepts of Christianity. She is so trusting of the natives that she even replaces the flintlock on one of their broken, antiquated guns—the very weapon that will be used several days later to brutally murder her father.

In contrast to his detailed representation of Peggy, Twain makes little attempt to individuate the natives in the text, to the extent that only three of the five warriors are even assigned names: Blue Fox, Hog Face, and the mysterious Man-Afraid-of-his-Mother-in-Law. And while he technically identifies them as "Ogillallahs," an unusual spelling derived from Francis Parkman's *The Oregon Trail*, they are generic Indians, "big, strong, grand looking fellows, [who] had on buckskin leggings and moccasins, and red feathers in their hair" (HFTS, 43), who outwardly conform to Tom's Cooperesque vision of the noble red man. They initially appear to be a "sociable lot," wrestling and running races with Huck, Tom, and the three Mills boys, Buck, Sam, and Bill, as well as teaching them to use tomahawks and bows and arrows. Four of the five men also perform dances with "all their fuss and feathers and war paint" (HFTS, 45), jumping, howling, and yelling about the campfire; however, one warrior refuses to participate, remaining sullen and aloof. Peggy's charitable instinct not only prompts her "to encourage him to put on his war paint . . . and dance the war dance with the others and be happy and not glum" (HFTS, 45) but also to ponder the probable cause of his unhappiness. As she tells Huck, "He's in mourning—that's what it is; he has lost a friend. And to think, here I have been hurting him, and making him remember his sorrows, when I wouldn't have done such a thing for the whole world if I had known" (HFTS, 45–46).

Peggy's solicitude is counterpointed by the Indians' callous self-interest. They demand "pretty much everything they see" (HFTS, 43), only to gamble it away, reaffirming Twain's statement in *Roughing It* that "if the beggar instinct were left out of an Indian he would not 'go,' any more than a clock without a pendulum" (RI, 127). Soon after meeting the Sioux men, Peggy gives Blue Fox a Bible and tries to "learn him some religion, but he couldn't understand, and so it didn't do him no particular good—that is, it didn't just then, but it did after a little, because when the Injuns got to gambling, same as they done every day, he put up his Bible against a tomahawk and won it" (HFTS, 45). This wager echoes Twain's 1881 marginalia equating nine novenas with nine French hatchets in Parkman's *Jesuits*: "The values are equal; it is a close game." In both instances, the incongruity of the proposed stakes serves as a synecdoche of what he perceives to be the inherent differences between native and Anglo-American cultures. Although Peggy attempts to civilize and enlighten Blue Fox through informal proselytizing, her efforts fail because he "couldn't understand." This lack of comprehension is grounded not only in linguistic difference but also—and even more profoundly—in the Indian's irredeemably savage nature. Blue Fox accepts Peggy's symbolic gift of the Word on the most literal level, viewing the Bible simply as a commodity, a pragmatic medium of exchange, which can then be traded to procure something far more useful—a weapon.

The object most coveted by the warriors is a "little dirk-knife" presented to Peggy by Brace on the eve of their separation back in Missouri. This talismanic "gift and keepsake" (HFTS, 44), which she keeps concealed next to her heart at all times, is a substitute for the protection afforded by his actual presence. When Huck inquires about its purpose, she laughingly responds, "To kill myself with," explaining that "Brace told me that if I ever fell into the hands of the savages, I mustn't stop to think about him, or the family, or anything, or wait an hour to see if I mightn't be rescued; I mustn't waste *any* time, I mustn't take any chances, I must kill myself right away" (HFTS, 44). When Huck asks why, Peggy confesses, "I don't know"; this naïveté accentuates both her unimpeachable virtue and association with Livy, whom Twain commended to Will Bowen for being "most ignorant in all matters it would not grace her to know." Similarly, Brace's gentility prohibits him from articulating the nature of his fears to Peggy; despite her cajoling, he will not relent, insisting "he *couldn't* tell me" (HFTS, 44). Within the patriarchal strictures of these gendered taboos, she must simply submit to his authority and unquestioningly accept that he knows what is "best" for her.

Because Peggy does not understand the dirk's purpose, she eventually yields to the importunate pleas of Blue Fox and relinquishes it. In return, he presents her with a bear claw necklace—a similarly talismanic object that not only attests to his prowess as a hunter but is also a symbol of good health and spiritual protection to the wearer. This offering can also be interpreted as a courtship gesture, signifying the giver's willingness to provide for the individual upon whom it is bestowed. Whether Twain understood the cultural significance of such a gift is unclear; nonetheless, the reciprocity of this exchange suggests the development of an amicable relationship between the Sioux and Anglo-American pioneers—an illusion violently shattered a few pages later.

After several days of cordial interaction with the Indians, Tom's extravagant praise of native character seems warranted. As Huck admits, "Yes, we was all stuck after the Injuns, kind of in love with them" (HFTS, 45). Indeed, Peggy is so smitten with the Sioux that she wishes Brace were present, believing that his acquaintance with these particular men would fundamentally "change his notions about Injuns, which he was down on, and hated them like snakes, and always said he wouldn't trust one any how or any where, in peace time or war time or any other time" (HFTS, 44). The ingenuousness of these views is made shockingly manifest in the sequel's third chapter when Buck, Bill, and Sam Mills are summoned to the Indian camp, ostensibly to discuss the buffalo hunt planned for the next morning with Hog Face. The other four natives meanwhile remain at the family's camp and enjoy a hearty meal prepared by Peggy and Mrs. Mills. Sensing that something is amiss, Tom and Huck set off, pretending to fetch water but in fact seeking the Mills brothers' whereabouts. Suddenly, in a single breathless sentence, Huck reports a horrifying—and apparently gratuitous—act of treachery:

> I heard a trampling like a lot of horses, and when it got pretty near, I see that other Injun coming on a pony, and driving the other ponies and all our mules and horses ahead of him, and he let off a long wild whoop, and the minute he done that, the Injun that had a gun, the one that Peggy fixed, shot her father through the head with it and scalped him, another one tomahawked her mother and scalped her, and then these two grabbed Jim and tied his hands together, and the other two grabbed Peggy, who was screaming and crying, and all of them rushed off with her and Jim and Flaxy, and as fast as I run, and as far as I run, I could still hear her, till I was a long, long ways off. (HFTS, 47–48)

The discovery subsequently awaiting the boys at the Indian camp is even more appalling—Buck, Sam, and Bill murdered, "tomahawked and scalped, and stripped; and each of them had as much as twenty-five arrows sticking in him." The particulars of "how else they had served the bodies," Huck declares, "was horrible ... [and] would not do to put in a book" (HFTS, 48). For three days after the massacre, the boys huddle together in terror, lacking food, weapons, and any means of transportation until the heroic, buckskin-clad scout Brace Johnson arrives with several fully laden pack mules. As Brace surveys the burned ruins of the camp, Huck and Tom reveal that Peggy, Flaxy, and Jim have been taken prisoner. At the mention of his beloved's name, he turns "white as milk, and the tears run down his cheeks, and he kept saying 'Oh, my God, oh my God ... I shall never see her again—never never any more—my poor little darling, so young and sweet and beautiful—but thank God, she's dead!'" (HFTS, 52).

In this scene, Twain portrays Brace as a paradoxical combination of strength and vulnerability. Outwardly, he is a paragon of virility—tall, broad-shouldered, ruggedly handsome—a marksman who is equally proficient "with a gun or bow or pistol" (HFTS, 61) and coolly courageous in the face of danger. Yet the scout is also a consummate Victorian gentleman whose valorization of female purity makes the thought of Peggy's sexual defilement unbearable. Because Huck witnessed Peggy's gift of the dirk to Blue Fox, he blurts out, "Dead? If you mean Peggy, *she's* not dead" (HFTS, 52). The explosive rage with which Brace responds to this revelation exposes the complex gender politics at work in the narrative. Whirling "like a wild-cat"—his humanity submerged in animalistic fury—he shouts in disbelief: "Not dead!

Take it back, take it back, or I'll strangle you! How do *you* know?" (HFTS, 52–53). Moments later, after recovering his equanimity, Brace explains, "You staggered me, and for a minute I believed you, and it made me most a lunatic. But it's all right—she had the dirk. Poor child, poor thing—if I had only been there!" (HFTS, 53). This loss of emotional equilibrium stems from two causes—guilt over his failure to protect Peggy and the horrific prospect of the heinous abuses she would suffer as a captive.

Twain's first draft of the manuscript contains no mention of either the dirk or the subplot involving Peggy's sexual violation. Rather, he simply acknowledges Brace's loathing of Indians but offers no explanation of its cause. At some unspecified point later in the summer, however—presumably after receiving *The Plains of the Great West* from Webster in late July— he added an eleven-page interpolation introducing these elements into chapter 3. By conjoining the violent, rapacious lust of Indians with idealized Victorian notions of gender, the writer succeeded in sharpening the narrative's focus but simultaneously preempted the development of one of its other major themes. For as the question of Peggy's fate looms larger in the text, the topic of native religion is necessarily sidelined and reduced to a minor plot device. The Sioux men, for example, never counter the young woman's gift of the Bible with any corresponding explanation of their own spiritual beliefs, nor do they engage in any ceremonial or ritualistic behaviors. They thus appear to lack—or, at the very least, profess indifference to—any creed or faith. In the absence of this mitigating cultural counterpoint, the sequel's representation of Indians grows increasingly monstrous.

Even Brace's adoption of native religion is downplayed in the manuscript. While Twain claims that the scout "thought more of the Great Spirit than he did of his own mother" (HFTS, 61), he offers no insight into the circumstances or motives underlying the scout's conversion to paganism. This omission is all the more curious in that much of the author's marginalia in *Our Wild Indians*—such as the assertion that "his Good God is better than any heretofore devised by man"—provides a strong philosophical rationale for this shift. In fact, the Indian's Good God receives only superficial mention in the sequel, which instead foregrounds Brace's fear of his malevolent counterpart. The protagonist's espousal of indigenous spiritual praxis is thus not presented as a serious or deeply informed theological decision but is equated with superstition. Many years earlier, as he explains to Huck and Tom, he had pledged never to eat meat on Fridays and Sundays in order to "perpetuate" the Bad God (HFTS, 62), whose capacity for evil and affliction is so formidable that he refuses to name him. In the aftermath of the massacre, however, the scout loses track of the days and breaks his vow by killing an antelope on Friday. Realizing his error, he fatalistically accepts the consequences that will inevitably ensue, stating, "It's my mistake, boys, and all my fault, for my carelessness. We're in for some bad luck, and we can't get around it; so the best way is to keep a sharp lookout for it and beat it if we can—I mean make it come as light as we can, for of course we can't beat it altogether" (HFTS, 62). The misfortunes stemming from what Huck terms "this blamed Friday-antelope luck" (HFTS, 73) forestall their pursuit of the Indians, First Tom is separated from his friends in a dense fog; then they encounter a murderous gang of horse-thieves; and, finally, they are stranded for eight days in a flash flood caused by a "waterspout" (HFTS, 76–77).

Despite these adversities, Brace, Huck, and Tom persist in their mission to rescue the captives. While the scout believes they are two in number (Flaxy and Jim), the boys know there are in fact three. Torn between their desire to shield Brace from the truth of Peggy's circumstances and the hope that she might still be found "alive and well" (HFTS, 54)—meaning with her virtue intact—Huck and Tom sustain the untenable illusion of the young woman's death by withholding crucial information *and* physical evidence at several points on their journey. Their alliance with Brace is progressively undermined by a well-intentioned but illogical conspiracy of silence, evasion, and outright duplicity that is destined to unravel once the rescue party reaches the Oglala men they are seeking.

This byzantine pattern of deception begins with a simple lie. In response to Brace's query about whether Peggy had the dirk when she was taken captive, Huck replies affirmatively "because it seemed the thing to say" (HFTS, 53). Soon thereafter, however, he finds the knife at the family's devastated campsite; but rather than divulging this discovery to either Brace or Tom, he conceals it in the lining of his jacket. The wisdom of withholding this tangible proof that Brace's fiancée's has survived, in Huck's estimation, is warranted because of the scout's obsessive fixation on her fate: "He seemed to be thinking about Peggy *all* the time, and never about anything else or anybody else" (HFTS, 57). While this misinformation protects Brace in the short term, it also lays the groundwork for further—and more egregious—deception. Several days later when he instructs Tom and Huck to ride ahead to the site of the Indians' most recent encampment, "look around and find [Peggy's] body . . . bury it, and be tender with it" (HFTS, 58), they play along and pretend to execute his orders. After waiting at the campsite just "long enough to dig a grave with bowie knives," the boys return and tell Brace, "It's all over—and done right" (HFTS, 59). This lie—the magnitude of which far exceeds the first—fulfills the strict conditions the scout has imposed on their mission; Huck and Tom must not reveal "how she looked, nor what the camp was like, nor anything . . . only that his orders was obeyed" (HFTS, 58). The incongruity of Brace's stance—his denial of the fact that Peggy is still alive, on the one hand and his inability to confront her corpse, on the other—reflects the degree to which he is entrapped by nineteenth-century gender constructs. Because his masculine identity is inextricably entwined with the mythos of Peggy's exalted, inviolate status, he cannot acknowledge either her rape or death without also facing the issue of his own culpability. In this respect, her ordeal becomes literally unspeakable in the text.

Twain reifies the threat that the sexual defilement of white women posed to their male protectors in chapter 7 through the figure of an anonymous stranger, broken in body and spirit, whom the scout finds wandering alone on the Plains: "He was just skin and bones and rags . . . His face . . . was baked with the sun, and was splotchy and purple, and the skin was flaked loose and curled, like old wall paper that's rotted on a damp wall. His lips was cracked and dry, and didn't cover his teeth, so he grinned very disagreeable like a steel-trap" (HFTS, 66). As Huck nurses this grotesque, tattered remnant of a human being, feeding him spoonsful of soup and explaining that he intends no harm, the man raves, "Lost, my God, lost!" while gazing longingly at a golden locket around his neck that contains an ivory portrait of "a most starchy young woman . . . dressed up regardless, and two little children in her arms" (HFTS, 66–67). Although Twain never specifies the circumstances that have reduced him to this miserable state, the iconic image ensconced within the locket—symbolizing marriage, devotion, and domesticity—intimates that he has been driven mad by the loss of his wife and children, who may well have suffered the same fate as Peggy or the other members of her family.

Twain's inspiration for this figure is cribbed directly from *The Oregon Trail*, albeit with several key differences. In Parkman's narrative—which the author marked with a vertical stroke in the margin—the skeletal man is a runaway Missouri slave, who is found after wandering on the prairie for thirty-three days: "His cheeks were shrunken in the hollow of his jaws; his eyes were unnaturally dilated, and his lips shrivelled and drawn back from his teeth like those of a corpse."[69] Like the wanderer in "Huck Finn and Tom Sawyer among the Indians," the man is too weak to walk or stand and is reduced to crawling on his hands and knees until "the bone was laid bare" (HFTS, 66). Ravenous with hunger, he too "begs eagerly for food" and devours it despite warnings that "his life was in danger if he ate so immodestly at first."[70] In desperation, both men gorge themselves in secret from their rescuers' stores; however, while the stranger, in Huck's words, "over-eat himself and died" (HFTS, 68), the escaped slave "manage[s] to survive the effects of his greediness" and leaves the Plains "in tolerable health . . . [convinced] that nothing could ever kill him."[71] Twain invents the story of the locket and lost family to underscore the menace wilderness poses to both the Anglo-American nuclear family and male sanity.

As the rescue party's proximity to the Indians increases, Huck and Tom's attempts at obfuscation grow bolder and more desperate. In chapter 9—the last, unfinished chapter of the manuscript—Brace and the two boys enter a recently vacated Indian encampment where each in turn discovers an ominous clue. Tom locates "an arrow, broke in two, which was wound with blue silk thread down by the feather, and he said he knowed it was Hog Face's, because he got the silk for him from Peggy and watched him wind it" (HFTS, 77), thereby identifying the camp's inhabitants as the perpetrators of the Mills family massacre. Because this piece of evidence offers no direct insight into Peggy's status, it can be shared, unlike Huck's simultaneous discovery of a "ragged piece of [her] dress as big as a big handkerchief . . . [with] blood on it" on the camp's periphery. Rationalizing that "if Brace was to see it he might suspicion she wasn't dead after all the pains we had took to make him believe she was," he hides the cloth beneath a buffalo chip (HFTS, 78). Brace meanwhile makes two even more disturbing findings. Calling the boys over, he points to the ground:

> "There—that's the shoe-print of a white woman. See—you can see, where she turned it down to one side, how thin the sole is. She's white, and she's a prisoner with this gang of Injuns. . . . Poor thing, it's hard luck for her," and went mumbling off, and never noticed that me and Tom was most dead with uneasiness, for we could see plain enough it was Peggy's print, and was afraid he would see it himself, or think he did, any minute. His back warn't more than turned before me and Tom had tramped on the print once or twice—just enough to take the clearness out of it, because we didn't know but he might come back for another look. (HFTS, 78)

Brace does not, however, "sing out" to inform the boys of his second finding—lifted straight from the pages of *The Plains of the Great West*—but instead stands speechless, transfixed in horror: "Pretty soon we see him yonder looking at something, and we went there, and it was four stakes drove into the ground; and he looks us very straight and steady in the eyes, first me and then Tom, and then me again, till it got pretty sultry; then he says, cold and level, but just as if he'd been asking us a question: 'Well, I believe you. Come along'" (HFTS, 78). According to Dodge, such stakes signify the fate of female prisoners who resisted the sexual advances of their captors. This circumstantial evidence, in conjunction with the footprint

Brace has just chanced upon, leads him to suspect that Peggy is not only still alive but also the victim of gang rape. Although the scene is, in Peter Stoneley's words, "fraught with prognostications of a terrible and bloody consummation,"[72] the scout resists this discomfiting possibility and instead willfully chooses to believe Huck and Tom's improbable version of events.

Panicked at the impending exposure of these prevarications, the boys struggle to formulate a rationale justifying their behavior. The explanation Tom relates to Huck—though muddled and illogical—situates their actions within a chivalric code of manliness and "honor bright" that privileges Brace's self-possession above all other considerations, including the truth:

> Wasn't you happier, when we made you think she was dead, than you
> was before? Didn't it keep you happy all this time? Of course. Well,
> wasn't it worth a little small lie like that to keep you happy instead of
> awfully miserable many days and nights? Of course. And wasn't it
> likely she would be dead before you ever run across her again?—which
> would make our lie plenty good enough. True again. And at last I would
> up and say, just you put yourself in our place, Brace Johnson: now,
> honor bright, would you have told the truth, that time, and broke the
> heart of the man that was Peggy Mills's idol? If you could, you are not
> a man, you are a devil; if you could and did, you'd be lower and hard-
> hearteder than the devils, you'd be an Injun. That's what I'll say to him,
> Huck, if the time ever comes. (HFTS, 79)

This rationale—that the boys' deceptions pay tribute to the scout's revered status as Peggy's "idol"—bespeaks the importance of preserving civilized patriarchal order amidst the moral anarchy of the wilderness. Under these circumstances, Tom argues, the mere thought of revealing Peggy's sexual defilement would be ungentlemanly, whereas actually divulging the truth would be incrementally worse, qualifying not only as evil but also as savage. Noting the dramatic change in Tom's views of Indians, Huck deems this explanation "the cleanest and slickest way out that ever was"; however, they never share it with the scout since the manuscript ends unexpectedly just a few pages later.

After the chilling discoveries at the native encampment, Brace invokes the Bad God once more, informing Huck and Tom that once they catch up with the Indians he plans to infiltrate the group disguised as a madman. He sews dried bugs, lizards, butterflies, and frogs to his coat and hat, stating, "Now if I act strange and foolish . . . I'll be safe and all right. [The Injuns] are afraid to hurt a crazy man, because they think he's under His special persecution' (he meant the Bad God, you know) 'for his sins; and they kind of avoid him, and don't much like to be around him, because they think he's bad medicine'" (HFTS, 80). Thus arrayed, he studies the trail, setting off first northward, then inexplicably turning west; whether this change of direction signaled a shift in the sequel's plot or was a device to postpone the debacle of Brace's reunion with his ruined fiancée is unclear. A few lines later, the narrative inexplicably stops in midsentence: "We struck out on this trail, and followed it a couple of days" (HFTS, 81). The absence of any closing punctuation suggests Twain's abrupt abandonment of the work— almost as if he had stood up in frustration and walked away from it at the end of August. But what exactly happened? Did the "tank" of his creativity simply run dry? In Albert Bigelow Paine's estimation, the problem lay in the infeasibility of the sequel's plot: "At the end of Chapter IX, Huck and Tom had got themselves into a predicament from which it seemed impossible to extricate them" and therefore necessitated "further inspiration, which apparently never came."[73] Walter Blair, on the other hand, suggests that Twain was stymied by his prudish inability to forthrightly address the "Indians' most horrible iniquity"—rape (HHT, 91). In *Mark Twain and the Feminine Aesthetic,* Peter Stoneley synthesizes and qualifies these perspectives, arguing that the writer was in fact capable of "entertain[ing] the idea of the act of rape, but not of the subsequent survival of the heroine as heroine": "He cannot re-introduce the ruined woman any more than he can have his characters openly discuss the likelihood of what has happened to her. . . . It seems that Twain did not complete the novel because he belatedly realized that he could not combine his ideal heroine with the realism of his portrait of life on the frontier, without a violation of one or the other."[74]

Whatever the reasons, Twain had forsaken the sequel by 1 September, when he dispiritedly informed Charley Webster "this is the first summer which I have lost. I haven't a paragraph to show for my 3-months' working-season."[75] A week later, however, a possible solution to his creative impasse presented itself in the form of a serendipitous invitation to one of the nine-teenth-century's most celebrated theatrical spectacles—Buffalo Bill's "Wild West."

WILLIAM F. CODY COMES TO TOWN

The letter, which arrived at Quarry Farm on 8 September, reads,

Samuel L. Clemens, Esq.

Dear Sir,

I should be pleased to see you at one of the entertainments of the Wild West. When you come if you will find Mr. Richmond[76]

at the judge stand, he will see that you have a good place to view the exhibition.

Very truly,
Wm. F. Cody
"Buffalo Bill"
per R.[77]

This document, as well as three complimentary tickets for grandstand seating at the show,[78] is preserved at the Mark Twain Papers in Berkeley, along with a small card on which the following words are scrawled in pencil: "Mr. Clemens [,] Mr. Cody had [sic] just gone to track—missed your card. Won't you please call at the camp & see him and Wild West."[79] Although the note is undated and unsigned, a circular stamp on the card's other side, identical to that printed on the admission ticket, bears the name of Cody's general manager, John M. Burke, suggesting that he is its author. Moreover, since performances of the Wild West began each day at 4 p.m., the information that Mr. Cody "had just gone to [the] track"—a reference to the Elmira Driving Park, a local horse-racing facility, where the exhibition was held[80]—indicates that the message was probably written in the early to midafternoon. On the basis of this evidence it can be surmised that Clemens, in his eagerness to see the show, went into town early; stopped at the Rathbun House, the elegant downtown hotel where Cody was staying; and sent up his calling card, hoping to meet the western legend in person.

Burke's note raises the possibility that Twain not only attended the Wild West but also spent some time beforehand soaking in the sights and sounds of the expansive encampment where Cody's native performers lived. Depending on the physical layout of each venue, these quarters were sometimes situated near the arena's entrance; as ticket holders strolled to their seats, they would pass through an "avenue of tepees" around which scenes of traditional Indian life unfolded, presenting them with "picturesque objects of interest until the exhibition opened."[81] Other contemporary news reports place the camp in the "back lot," adjacent to or behind the venue, and indicate that patrons were encouraged to tour it after the show's conclusion.[82] Regardless of its precise location, the camp not only entertained Anglo-American spectators but also served an important purpose for the show Indians by replicating the comforting ambience of their lost ancestral homes. As historian Louis Warren explains, "Wherever Buffalo Bill's Wild West made an appearance, a cluster of Sioux tipis soon rose on the horizon. Although most of the [Indian] performers were men, women and children also accompanied the show. . . . [the village] provided a

FIGURE 16. Indian camp, Buffalo Bill's Wild West. Courtesy of Buffalo Bill Center of the West, Cody, Wyoming. MS327.01.32.001.16.

comforting simulacrum of a real village for the performers, with meals cooking over camp fires and the familiar rhythms of Lakota language on every side" (fig. 16).[83] Within this setting, Warren claims that the Indians also "found ample means of resisting spiritual alienation," covertly performing ceremonies that the US government had banned back on the reservation. Some visitors to the camps observed what they called "Indian steam baths," which were in fact sweat lodges, "sacred structures in which Lakotas made offerings and prayers before any new endeavor."[84]

While Twain's letters and notebooks offer no evidence that he either visited Buffalo Bill's Elmira encampment or observed indigenous spiritual practices there firsthand, his idyllic description of an Indian village in the 1906 story "A Horse's Tale" may be subtly indebted to this experience. In this narrative, Buffalo Bill escorts Cathy Allison—the young female protagonist modeled after his lost daughter Susy—to the camp of "illustrious" old chief Thunder-Bird, where she sees "young Indians and girls romping and laughing and carrying on . . . and dogs fighting, and the squaws busy at work, and the bucks busy resting, and the old men sitting in a bunch smoking, and passing the pipe."[85] In many respects, this tranquil scene of intergenerational harmony parallels the picture of "domestic life, in all its romantic and stirring features"[86] that Cody promised visitors to his show camps—a reassuring counterpoint to the sensational vignettes of Indian aggression and warfare that dominated the exhibition itself. Cathy is embraced by the natives, learns "a lot of words" in their language, and receives the Indian name "Firefly" from the chief.

The details of Clemens's attendance at the Wild West have long been obscured by the fact that the dateline on Cody's letter of invitation— "Elmira, N.Y. Aug. 8 1884"—is erroneous. The postmark on the envelope in which the letter was sent reads 8 September, exactly one month later; moreover, according to the show's 1884 Route Book, the Wild West appeared in Providence, RI, from 7 to 9 August and did not reach New York State until early September.[87] Local newspapers confirm that Cody's show was booked in Elmira for four performances at the Driving Park on 6, 8, 9, and 10 September. In deference to the Sabbath, no performance was initially scheduled for Sunday, 7 September; however, the exhibition's popularity prompted Cody to add a show on that day and modify the program to include several "rare," "historically educational," and "highly instructive" features, such as "Indian Rites and Ceremonies."[88] The display ad that appeared in the Elmira *Sunday Tidings* on the day of the show proclaimed that this special iteration of the Wild West was not only "Indorsed by Pulpit, Public, and Press" but also "Wholly in Accordance with the Rational, Healthful and Moral Employment of the Day," suggesting that exposure to native religious rituals was edifying and spiritually uplifting. Despite Cody's ingenious public relations ploy, conservative members of the town clergy—most notably, one Reverend Spooner, pastor of the Lake Street Presbyterian Church—decried this "wholesale desecration of the Sabbath" in a page-long letter to the editor of the Elmira *Advertiser* that appeared on 8 September, the same day, Cody's invitation arrived at Quarry Farm.[89] Spooner's stance sparked heated debate in the community regarding individual freedom and obligatory observance of the Sabbath, prompting the *Sunday Tidings* to issue this rebuttal on 14 September: "[We] abjure all people to observe the Sabbath in their own good way, doing whatever they do unto the Lord. If it is to go to church, go; if to a picnic, go. . . . If your neighbor does not happen to observe the Sabbath, or rest day, as you do, do not be so presumptive as to point to yourself and say, 'I am holier than thou.' Do what you think is right, and that is all required of any man."[90]

While it is unclear whether Clemens was cognizant of this controversy, he was not at all ambivalent about the Wild West itself. In an effusive letter of thanks to Cody on 10 September, he informed the impresario that he had attended the show not once but twice in two consecutive days:

September 10, 1884

Dear Mr. Cody—I have now seen your Wild West show two days in succession, & have enjoyed it thoroughly. It brought vividly back the breezy, wild life of the great plains and the Rocky Mountains & stirred me like a war song. Down to its smallest details the show is genuine— cowboys, vaqueros, Indians, stage-coach, costumes & all; it is wholly free from sham and insincerity, & the effects produced upon me by its spectacles were identical with those wrought upon me a long time ago by the same spectacles on the frontier. Your pony expressman was as tremendous an interest to me yesterday as he was twenty-three years ago when he used to come whizzing by from over the desert with his war news, & your bucking horses were even painfully real to me, as I rode one of those outrages once for nearly a quarter of a minute. It is often said on the other side of the water that none of the exhibitions which we send to England are purely & distinctively American. If you will take the Wild West show over there you can remove that reproach.[91]

Twain's visceral response to the show—registered primarily as a series of involuntary somatic sensations—was no doubt magnified by the proximity of his ringside seat to the action. Cody routinely enlisted audience participation in one of its signature set-pieces, "The Deadwood Stage Coach," inviting volunteers to play passengers aboard the vehicle as Indians besieged it. Clemens thus may well have witnessed local neighbors, acquaintances, and friends portraying "victims" of this savage assault, enhancing the exhibition's realism. Indeed, the uncanny mimetic fidelity with which Buffalo Bill's "vivid scenes, incidents, and adventures"[92] reproduced "the same spectacles on the frontier" was a hallmark of the show's enduring popularity. As numerous scholars have noted, "performance and history were hopelessly intertwined" in the Wild West. Cody, a former Indian scout, also played an Indian scout, reenacting highly selective versions of events that had actually occurred, such as his famous 1876 "Duel with Chief Yellow Hand." The line "where representation stopped and lived experience began"[93] was deliberately blurred in these performances.[94] Cowboys played cowboys, and real bison charged nightly through the arenas; even the props—such as the infamous Deadwood stagecoach—were real. According to historian Philip Deloria, "The Wild West relied, not simply on the appearance of truth, but on the evocative power of actual western gear, which simultaneously signified *real* and *realistic, historical artifact* and *stage prop*."[95]

The single most important factor in affirming the show's authenticity, however, was the participation of real Indians in buckskin, feathers, and war paint: "Buffalo Bill presented actual Indians, who now inhabited their own representations. This was the most complicated kind of mimesis. Indians were imitating imitations of themselves. They re-enacted white versions of events [such as the Battle at Little Bighorn] in which some of them had actually participated."[96] In addition, native performers in the Wild West were not cast as colorful, exotic Others who danced, sang, and dressed up for the entertainment of white audiences but were instead confined to an antagonistic, one-dimensional role as ruthless murderers. Each of the show's dramatic vignettes presented "an account of Indian aggression and white defense; of Indian killers and white victims; of, in effect, badly abused conquerors."[97] Civilization's inevitable triumph over savagery was most fully epitomized in the "Attack on the Settler's Cabin," which served as the show's climactic finale from 1883 to 1906. In this emotionally charged dramatization, Cody and an entourage of mounted cowboys rescue an innocent pioneer family from death at the hands of a group of frenzied savages. The narrative of home salvation presented in this skit underscored one of the Wild West's "most persistent claims . . . that Bill Cody was the savior of the settler family."[98]

It was precisely through such mythic reenactments that the Wild West fulfilled its reputation as "America's National Entertainment." By writing "frontier history in blood," the show provided "a simplified, patriotic, and believable national epic that blended history and mythology and legitimized a view of Manifest Destiny that sanctioned the use of force."[99] Twain recognized the enormous power of this cultural script, praising the Wild West as a "purely and distinctively American" art form—a quintessential representation of the New World to the Old—and urging Cody to take it abroad. The impresario heeded this prescient advice three years later, bringing the Wild West to England in 1887, where a special performance was given for Queen Victoria and other members of the royal family. Between 1889 and 1893, the show subsequently toured France, Italy, Germany, and Spain, enjoying its greatest commercial success on the European continent.

Cody, ever the showman, realized the immense advertising value of Twain's endorsement, and repeatedly used it—without first seeking the author's permission—to promote the Wild West throughout the mid-to-late 1880s. The letter was typically published in the newspapers of cities and towns along the show's route a day or two in advance of its arrival; for example, it appeared in the *Hartford Daily Courant* on 16 July 1885 with this lead: "The following letter from Mark Twain to Buffalo Bill will be read with interest." Beneath the text, a brief advertisement was appended: "The Wild West show this season is a bigger and better show than last year. The performances in this city are given Friday and Saturday [17 and 18 July] at Charter Oak Park."[100] The frequency with which the letter was reprinted has produced considerable confusion about exactly when and where Clemens saw Cody's show; a number of reputable scholarly sources erroneously report the date as, variously, 1883, 1885, and 1886.[101] Moreover, scrapbooks of newspaper clippings at Wyoming's Buffalo Bill Historical Center indicate that Twain's testimonial remained in active circulation until at least 1893. The document's origins were further confounded by Cody's decision to use it—minus the date and salutation—in the souvenir program sold during the Wild West's first tour of England in 1887,[102] thereby creating the misleading impression that the writer attended the show then rather than three years earlier.

The question of how Buffalo Bill's Wild West might have influenced the composition of "Huck Finn and Tom Sawyer among the Indians" can of course never be fully or satisfactorily answered. If perchance Twain bought or—as Cody's distinguished guest, was given—a complimentary copy of the exhibition's program, several of its features would have eerily resonated with his own work in progress. Colonel Richard Irving Dodge's *Our Wild Indians* was featured prominently in three different sections, including a lengthy passage, entitled "An Indian's Religion," on the native concept of a Good and Bad God that had piqued his interest some weeks earlier.[103] This affirmation of Dodge's authority as an expert on indigenous spirituality, particularly from a bona fide western scout of Cody's stature, would have reminded the writer of his original intentions for the sequel, and perhaps inspired him to attempt its completion.

More importantly, the thrilling spectacle of the Wild West itself—a rich kaleidoscopic array of sights, smells, and sounds—validated the accuracy of Twain's portrayal of frontier life. The imposing figure that Cody cut in the ring—tall, athletic, dressed in fringed, beaded buckskin, his long hair billowing out from under his broad-brimmed hat—bore such a strong resemblance to the writer's description of Brace Johnson that it must have seemed the protagonist had sprung to life from the pages of his manuscript: tall, broad-shouldered, he possessed "the steadiest eye you ever see, and a handsome face. . . . His buckskin suit looked always like it was new, and it was all hung with fringes, and had a star as big as a plate between the shoulders of his coat, made of beads of all kinds of colors, and had beads on his moccasins, and a hat as broad as a barrel-head" (HFTS, 60). In addition, the show's theatrical structure interspersed dramatic reenactments of frontier violence with demonstrations of native physical prowess, such as the "Race between Sioux Boys on Bareback Indian Ponies," the "100 Yard Race between Indians on Horse and Foot," and a "Grand Quarter Mile Race between 4 Mexicans, 4 Cow Boys and 4 Indians"—feats that parallel Huck's description of the playful interaction between the Sioux warriors and the three Mills brothers in the sequel's opening chapters: "We all run foot races and horse races with them, and it was prime to see the way their ornery little ponies would split along when their pluck was up" (HFTS, 45). These similarities— and their potential to revitalize his moribund narrative—may well have inspired Twain's return to the Driving Park for an encore performance the next day.

Despite the writer's enthusiasm for the Wild West, the show ultimately seems to have thwarted rather than facilitated his completion of "Huck Finn and Tom Sawyer among the Indians." The mythic narrative Cody promulgated of civilization's triumph over savagery ran counter to the dark trajectory of the sequel's plot—the failure of Brace, Huck, and Tom to prevent the gang rape of Peggy Mills by her Sioux captors. In this regard, the "narrative of sexual danger"[104] enacted in the show's climactic finale— "Attack on the Settler's Cabin"—must have been especially problematic for Twain. Cody's vignette addresses many of the text's same themes, such as popular anxiety about the vulnerability of white women and attendant horrors of Indian captivity, albeit with a radically different denouement. "Attack on the Settler's Cabin" features a young, defenseless female—an iconic figure akin to Peggy Mills—in a remote wilderness setting anxiously awaiting the return of her hunter-husband. As he nears the family home, it is suddenly beset by a war party of yelping Indians, guns ablaze. The couple narrowly escapes indoors, where they huddle in terror with their two small children, firing shotguns through the cabin's windows in self-defense. It soon becomes evident, however, that they are surrounded and outnumbered; imminent destruction awaits—until, of course, salvation arrives in the form of Buffalo Bill and his cowboys.[105] Through the gallant intervention of these courageous white men, savagery is vanquished and home, family, and female honor are preserved. While this skit made undeniably great theater, Twain—recalling Colonel Dodge's graphic discussion of the sexual abuse of female captives in *The Plains of the Great West*—must have bristled in disbelief while viewing it, recognizing the patent oversimplification and outright falsehood of Cody's scenario. The vignette may also have triggered the more distant, troubling memory of the 1781 Montgomery Massacre in which three of Jane Clemens' Kentucky ancestors perished at Cherokee hands. In that incident, however, rescuers from Logan's Fort arrived not in the nick of time but hours too late and were therefore unable to prevent the loss of settlers' lives.

Writing to Joe Twichell on 16 September, six days after seeing the Wild West, Clemens reiterated his earlier lament to Charley Webster: "The summer has been lost time to me. I spent several weeks in the dental chair, coming down from the hill every day for [this] purpose . . . the remnant of the season I wasted in ineffectual efforts to work. I haven't a paragraph to show for my summer."[106] This harsh assessment of "Huck Finn and Tom Sawyer among the Indians" apparently abated over time, since evidence indicates he attempted to complete the text on at least two occasions several years later. In 1889 Twain arranged to have the manuscript's nine extant chapters printed on the Paige Compositor; a year later—probably in November 1890—he jotted "Tom muss die rôle Medicine Man spielen" in his notebook, suggesting a plan to have Tom rather than Brace enter the Indian camp where Peggy, Flaxy, and Jim were being held captive (NBJ3, 594). While this change would theoretically spare Brace the shock of confronting his ruined fiancée firsthand, it left the larger problem of reintegrating her into civilized society unresolved. At a loss for how to proceed, the writer appears to have abandoned the sequel forever at this point.

Although Twain failed to bring the sequel to fruition, his fascination with native spirituality—and its incongruous relation to the savage violence of Indian behavior—lingered. In a February 1894 letter to Livy, then living with the girls in Paris as he shuttled back and forth to the States, hoping to avert impending financial disaster, he writes, "Ben [Clara] & Susy must read 'Study of Indian Music' in February Century. I think it will interest them."[107] This recommendation, while grounded in his daughters' aspirations of becoming professional singers, may also have been unconsciously spurred by the memory of Susy's curiosity about Indian religion as a child. The study's author, John Comfort Fillmore, was an early pioneer in the field of ethnomusicology, who had conducted fieldwork collecting traditional songs on Nebraska's Omaha reservation. In his analysis of the formal structure of songs used in the Wawan (Sacred Pipes) Ceremony, he debunks their supposedly "primitive" character, arguing that although the melodies initially sound shrill and discordant to the western ear, their harmonies are reminiscent of "the greatest music of the modern romantic school."[108] Fillmore favorably compares the complexity of Omaha rhythms to those found in the works of Schumann, Chopin, and Mendelssohn, and also likens the "easy, smooth, [and] natural" progression of chords in one song to "numerous passages in Wagner."[109] Extrapolating from these findings, he offers a sweeping reassessment of native spirituality in the essay's conclusion, arguing "that those whom we are accustomed to despise as an inferior and barbarous race reveal, in the glimpse this music affords into their inner life, a noble religious feeling, not remotely akin to the central idea of Christianity, and expressed in music some of which is worthy of comparison with the best we ourselves possess, and incomparably superior to our worst in the same field."[110] This sentiment, which echoes the tenor of Clemens's marginalia concerning native religion in both the Dodge and Parkman texts, suggests that "A Study of Indian Music" also held intrinsic interest for him.

A year later, the writer again encountered the indigenous notion of a Good and Bad God in an unexpected transnational context. While traveling on New Zealand's North Island during the world lecture tour, the Clemenses met John Logan Campbell, the "Founding Father of Auckland." Campbell presented Livy with an autographed copy of his 1881 memoir *Poenamo*, which chronicles the months he lived among the Maori back in the 1840s. Twain incorporated a brief excerpt of this text in *Following the Equator*: "One of [the Maori] thought the missionary had got everything wrong end first and upside down. 'Why, he wants us to stop worshiping and supplicating the evil gods, and go to worshiping and supplicating the Good One! There is no sense in that. A *good* god is not going to do us any harm'" (FE, 320). Though he draws no explicit parallel between this statement and the Cheyenne beliefs discussed in *Our Wild Indians*, the coincidence is too striking to have passed unnoticed.

In a 1906 "Autobiographical Dictation," Twain posits a similar bifurcation of the Godhead between Jesus and God the Father, only to conclude that neither deity possesses much merit:

> We deal in a curiously laughable confusion of notions concerning God. We divide Him in two, bring half of Him down to an obscure and infinitesimal corner of the world to confer salvation upon a little colony of Jews—and only Jews, no one else—and leave the other half of Him throned in Heaven and looking down and eagerly and anxiously watching for results. . . . We are told that the two halves of our God are only seemingly disconnected by their separation; that in very fact the two halves remain one, and equally powerful, notwithstanding the separation. This being the case, the earthly half . . . satisfies Himself with restoring sight to a blind person, here and there, instead of restoring it to all the blind; cures a cripple, here and there, instead of curing all the cripples; furnishes to five thousand famishing persons a meal, and lets the rest of the millions that are hungry remain hungry. (A2, 129)

Twain's critique of the inadequacy of Jesus's benevolence and mercy demolishes any hopeful notion of a "good" Christian God; the "real" God, he argues, "takes no interest in man, nor in the other animals, further than to torture them, slay them, and get out of this pastime such entertainment as it may afford" (A2, 140). This despairing vision echoes and reaffirms the sentiment the writer had expressed—but could not fully explore—twenty years earlier in the margins of *Our Wild Indians:* "We have to keep our God placated with prayers, & even then we are never sure of Him—how much higher & finer is the Indian's God."

6. The Curious Tale of the Connecticut Indian Association

A year after the publication of "The Noble Red Man," Sam and Livy relocated from Buffalo to Hartford, settling in the city's "choicest residential district"[1]—Nook Farm. Their new home was a tightly knit community, wherein affluence and altruism commingled, reflecting a strong ethos of social responsibility. According to historian Kenneth Andrews, Nook Farm led the city in contributions to local charities and also championed a number of progressive causes, such as female suffrage and prison reform.[2] In October 1880, a new issue was added to this growing roster of civic concerns when five local women—Sara Thomson Kinney, Harriet Foote Hawley, Sarah Cowan, Louise Ripley, and Anna W. Riddle—met at the City Hotel to discuss "the importance of work for and among the Indians in the United States ... and [how] some effort in that direction might soon be undertaken in Connecticut."[3] Within a year of this initial meeting, these same women invited Amelia Stone Quinton, president of the Women's National Indian Association, to Hartford to explore the formation of a local branch of her organization. As a result of these deliberations, the Connecticut Indian Association was established on 15 November 1881.

Like other native rights advocacy groups in this era, the association viewed the "Americanization" of the continent's aboriginal inhabitants through detribalization, education, and Christianization as the optimal solution to the nation's so-called Indian Problem. In the words of Captain Richard H. Pratt, founder of the federal government's most infamous Indian boarding school in Carlisle, Pennsylvania, the objective of this policy was to "kill the Indian, [but] save the man," stripping native people of all vestiges of cultural identity in order to effect their assimilation into mainstream US society. The Connecticut Indian Association supported the goal of Americanization by pledging the following:

First—TO INFLUENCE THE PEOPLE,

By circulating, as widely as possible, knowledge concerning the political, financial, industrial, educational, and religious status of Indians.

Second,—TO INFLUENCE GOVERNMENT:

a, To execute all laws and fulfill all treaties and compacts which will speed Indian civilization, industrial training, self-support, education, and citizenship; and to repeal all statutes and rules which hinder these objects;

b, To grant new and better legislation for securing the above ends.

Third.—TO AID INDIANS,

In civilization, industrial training, self-support, education, citizenship, and Christianization.[4]

Connecticut's social climate in the early 1880s was clearly conducive to reform; within two years of the Indian Association's creation, it boasted a membership of 101 local women, among them Harriet Beecher Stowe, who served in the role of executive vice president. Stowe's enthusiasm for the cause is reflected in an 1883 letter to Sara Thomson Kinney, the organization's president for over thirty years, wherein she declares, "Yes always & by all means put me down for the <u>Indians</u>. I will join your society & give money & do all that I can for <u>no</u> work is more imperative than that."[5]

Like Stowe, many Christian women from across the state regarded the equitable treatment of indigenous peoples as a matter of "justice, humanity & national honor"[6] and committed themselves fervently to the achievement of that objective. By 1885, membership in the Connecticut Indian Association reached 250, more than double its size two years earlier. Over the next three years, auxiliary branches were established in New Haven, Bridgeport, Norwich, Litchfield, and a number of other towns, expanding the society's membership to 707 by 1888.[7] Although the organization's rank and file were exclusively female, its advisory board consisted of fifteen local clergymen, politicians, and businessmen, some of whom—the Reverend Joseph Twichell, *Hartford Daily Courant* owner Senator Joseph R. Hawley, the Reverend Dr. Nathaniel J. Burton, and J. Hammond Trumbull—Clemens numbered among his closest friends in Hartford. Curiously, however, the writer himself never served the association in any official capacity.

While the reasons for this are unclear, Twain's long-standing aversion to female reformers of any ilk may well have been a factor. In an 1867 sketch on "Female Suffrage," he complains that women "are always setting up sanctified confederations of all kinds, and then running for president of them"; moreover, two of the fictitious organizations he creates—the

"Pawnee Educational society" and the "Ladies' society for Dissemination of Belles Lettres among the Shoshones"—are expressly dedicated to the civilization of Indians. The absurdity of these endeavors is underscored by his enumeration of the other impractical offices, such as "State Crinoline Directress, State Superintendent of waterfalls, State Hair Oil inspectress, [and] State milliner," that he claims women would invent for themselves if enfranchised (CT1, 214).

Three years later, Twain's gentle parody of female activism assumed a darker, more vicious tone. In "The Noble Red Man," he angrily denounces the naïve, misguided efforts of the "maids and matrons...from the Atlantic seaboard," who "wail [in] humanitarian sympathy" and "throw up their hands in horror" whenever "bloody vengeance" is wreaked upon Indians in retaliation for their depredations against Anglo-American settlers (CT1, 446). This sentimental representation of natives as "poor abused" victims is, he argues, particularly dangerous in that it denies their "true" character, which is "cruel, treacherous, and brutal." Similarly, the conclusion of his 1876 novel, *The Adventures of Tom Sawyer*, states,

> The petition to the Governor for Injun Joe's pardon . . . had been largely signed; many tearful and eloquent meetings had been held, and a committee of sappy women been appointed to go into deep mourning and wail around the governor and implore him to be a merciful ass and trample his duty under foot. Injun Joe was believed to have killed five citizens of the village, but what of that? If he had been Satan himself there would have been plenty of weaklings ready to scribble their names to a pardon-petition and drip a tear on it from their permanently impaired and leaky water-works. (TS, 240–41)

While the behavior of such "sappy women" might be safely dismissed from a distance, their presence—both in Hartford and, more importantly, within the Nook Farm community itself—necessitated a more measured, tactful response. For the members of the Connecticut Indian Association were the spouses of colleagues, business associates, near neighbors and friends—in other words, people with whom the Clemenses interacted on a regular basis. Livy's dear childhood friend Alice Hooker Day enrolled as a life member soon after the organization's founding, as did Samuel Colt's widow, Elizabeth, and Susan Cheney, whose husband, Frank, owned the Cheney Silk Mills across the Connecticut River in Manchester. Despite the enthusiasm with which many of their local friends espoused this cause, the Clemenses remained steadfastly aloof. According to the association's meticulous membership rosters, Livy never officially joined its ranks, nor do any charitable contributions from the couple appear in the group's annual ledgers. The writer's skepticism about the cost and efficacy of such progressive reform movements is reflected in an October 1882 notebook entry:

> Board of Foreign Missions—I have saved a Turk's soul.
>
> What did it cost?
>
> $2,000,000.
>
> Is it worth that?
>
> U.S. Govt.—I have killed [a whole] 200 Indians.
>
> What did it cost?
>
> $2,000,000.
>
> You could have given them a college education for that. (NBJ2 500–501)

Despite this ambivalence, Clemens found himself drawn into the organization's sphere of influence at several points during the 1880s. The following account, pieced together from newspaper clippings, unpublished correspondence, and other miscellaneous documents in the Connecticut Indian Association's extensive archive, presents the previously untold narrative of the writer's ambivalent relationship with this local advocacy group.

ENTERTAINMENT AND SOCIAL REFORM

As the Connecticut Indian Association gained momentum in the mid-1880s, its members sought to increase public consciousness about the plight of native peoples and simultaneously raise money for their "practical, common-sense" objectives by sponsoring benefit lectures in the capital city on topics of general interest. These events, such as Miss Rose Cleveland's presentation on "Medieval History" in March 1884, were innocuously billed as "entertainments" in order to attract as large an audience as possible; however, the revenue generated by ticket sales (fifty cents each for general admission and seventy-five cents for reserved seating) supported the organization's first major charitable undertaking, the building of a "Connecticut Cottage" on Nebraska's Omaha reservation. The recipients of this largesse were Philip and Minnie Stabler, a young married couple then studying at Virginia's Hampton Institute, a trade school founded in 1861 to educate escaped slaves in practical skills, such as farming, carpentry, and blacksmithing. Seventeen years later, in 1878, the school expanded its mission to include Native Americans. The provision of a suitably "civilized" wood-frame home for the Stablers was intended to preclude any temptation to "go back to the blanket" upon their return to the reservation and thus regress into "savagery and degradation ... after learning the ways and customs of Christian white men."[8] The couple's inculcation into the western values of capitalism, individualism, and private property culminated in their eventual repayment of the mortgage loan and newfound status as homeowners. According to Kinney, the Stablers' "happy, well-ordered home" also served as "an object lesson and inspiration to all about them who are struggling upwards through a transition from barbarism into civilization."[9]

The association's "constant attempt to mold public opinion in its favor" was also advanced by its sponsorship of lectures by leading national advocates of indigenous rights, who were well "versed in the history of effort on behalf of that people."[10] Among the notable "Friends of the Indian"[11] who spoke at the group's annual meetings were Merrill Gates, the president of Rutgers College and a member of the Board of Indian Commissioners; Herbert Welsh, the founder of the National Indian Rights Association; Alice Fletcher, the pioneering ethnographer who spent years living among the Omaha tribe; and General Samuel Armstrong, the first principal of Hampton Institute. These events—free and open to the public—routinely attracted capacity crowds of five hundred to eight hundred people, a remarkable number considering that Hartford's population at the time was approximately forty thousand.[12]

Moreover, contemporary newspaper coverage of the Indian Association's programs, whether billed as "entertainment" or "business," invariably emphasizes the elite class of those in attendance: "the best audience Hartford can furnish," "thoughtful," "fashionable and very enthusiastic."[13] The cachet of these gatherings is exemplified by an 1889 article in the *Hartford Daily Courant:* "Unity Hall was completely filled with an audience of evident intelligence. While the ladies were in a large majority, there was present quite a number of prominent citizens of the other sex."[14] The article then names the various dignitaries present, including several clergymen—Joe Twichell and George Williamson Smith, the president of Trinity College— as well as lieutenant governor James Howard, "presid[ing] in the absence of the governor himself, who at the last moment was kept away by illness, much to his regret."[15] This quaint diction, conflating political activism with the mystique of social élan, illustrates the association's multifaceted appeal to the local citizenry.

Since Sam Clemens was, without question, Hartford's most renowned resident, Mrs. Kinney was understandably eager to enlist his support for her cause. The writer's presence at Indian Association events would not only enhance its reputation but also entice outside speakers—particularly those traveling from a great distance—to visit the city. The prospect of meeting Twain clearly intrigued General Samuel Armstrong, who asked Kinney in an

1890 letter: "I wonder if Mrs. Perkins will have that little gathering [after the annual meeting]. If she does, I hope 'Mark Twain' and his wife will be there."[16]

To Armstrong's great disappointment, they alas were not. In fact, Clemens's only documented appearance at an association function occurred in mid-1885 and was the result of a convoluted set of circumstances. The event in question was a lecture on "The Poetry and Politics of the British Isles" by the celebrated orator Chauncey Depew. A notice published in the *Hartford Times* on 15 May 1885—the day Depew delivered his address— typifies the way in which Kinney's organization harnessed the appeal of literary and historical topics to promote its agenda: "Mr. Depew's address . . . goes to the benefit of the Connecticut Indian Association, an organization which is doing some needed practical work for the too much pushed and knocked about Indians of the west; but Mr. Depew's discourse will be attractive and enjoyed for itself, regardless of the cause it is meant to aid."[17]

On 9 May 1885, approximately one week before Depew's appearance, an open letter addressed "To the Officers and Members of the Connecticut Indian Association" was circulated among and signed by twelve distinguished local men, four of whom happened to serve on its advisory board. This handwritten commendation, which I discovered in the association's archive, applauds their sponsorship of Depew's forthcoming lecture, as well as the worthiness of the progressive goals for which it had been founded:

Ladies,

We desire to congratulate the Indian Association upon the prospect of the brilliant entertainment to be given under your auspices by the Hon. Chauncey M. Depew of New York.

The object for which the Association is working is an admirable one, and far more hopeful than many in its probable good results.

We wish you every success in your effort, and if in any way we can aid you in carrying out your programme [sic] for the evening of the 15th May, we shall be happy to do so.[18]

The letter is signed "Very Respectfully Yours" by a veritable Who's Who of Hartford clergymen, business leaders, and politicians: Senator Joseph Hawley, Reverend Edwin Parker, A. P. Hyde, Mayor Henry Robinson, Francis Goodwin, J. Hammond Trumbull, Nathaniel Shipman, Charles Dudley Warner, Reverend Joseph H. Twichell, A. E. Burr, M. G. Bulkeley, and William Hamersley.

Oddly, none of the twelve signatures appended to this document matches the penmanship of the text itself; the author's identity and circumstances of its creation are deliberately effaced. More perplexingly, the men's names are not signed with the same writing implement—some appear in blue ink, others in black, and a few in pencil, suggesting that the letter was personally carried door to door rather than circulated at a venue at which all were present. But by whom? And for what reason?

The first of these questions can be answered by comparing the letter's distinctive script with other documents in Sara Kinney's hand, revealing that she was in fact its author. Thus, what initially appears to be a spontaneous expression of male support for this local female initiative proves to be a carefully orchestrated public relations ploy by the association's chief executive officer. The letter's promotional purpose became clear three days after its composition, on 12 May, when it appeared in a *Courant* article entitled "Chauncey Depew's Lecture." Lauding the event as "the chief lecture treat of the season," the piece explains that ticket sales would "aid [the Connecticut Indian Association] in their special work of erecting a cottage on the Omaha reservation, for a young married couple, who are being educated at Hampton." While the newspaper reprints the text of the letter verbatim, one salient difference occurs in the list of signatures. A thirteenth name has been added to the original twelve—that of S. L. Clemens. The article concludes with the announcement that "At the request of the association, Senator Hawley will preside at the opera house on Friday evening. Invitations have been extended to the other gentlemen to occupy seats on the platform."[19]

The disparity between the handwritten and published versions of this document is puzzling: was Clemens perhaps out of town when the petition was originally circulated on 9 May? Home, but preoccupied, indisposed, or otherwise unavailable when the request was made? Or might he have initially refused to sign the letter and later reconsidered? Both Sara Kinney's husband John and Clemens's neighbor C. D. Warner were editors at the *Courant*; Joseph Hawley, whose name tops the list of men endorsing the Indian Association's work, was the newspaper's owner and publisher. Perhaps when Mrs. Kinney submitted the article, the omission of Clemens's name caused some consternation among these men and prompted a silent emendation. The writer had, after all, a long history of civic engagement, typified in his service on the executive committee of the Union for Home Work (a local charity dedicated to providing relief for the needy), a committee that also included many of the signers of the 1885 letter—Hawley, Warner, Hamersley, Robinson, Burr, and Bulkeley.[20] Clemens's personal connection with these individuals was further cemented by his membership in Hartford's Monday Evening Club, an elite association of professionals established in 1869 to promote the free "exchange of ideas and the exercise of intellectual curiosity, "[21] which he had been invited to join in 1873.

A second possibility is that, rather than presuming Clemens's support, Warner, Hawley, or Kinney saw the writer before the 12 May issue of the *Courant* went to press, informed him of the letter's existence, and secured verbal permission to add his name. Indeed, circumstantial evidence—three letters Clemens wrote to his nephew Charley Webster on 5, 10, and 13 May—confirm his presence in Hartford during the period in question. The 13 May letter is especially intriguing in this regard, since its verso contains a cancelled message to another correspondent: "Bro Bunce: billiards tomorrow night [Thursday, 14 May] on account of Depew's lecture Friday eve. Come! Yrs truly, S L Clemens."[22] The "Bro" of the note's salutation is Ned Bunce, a Hartford banker and member of the so-called Friday Evening Club, a group of local men who convened weekly to play billiards on the third floor of Clemens's home. This club, in contrast to the decidedly more cerebral group that met on alternating Mondays, consisted of Twain's "business cronies."[23] While the note's tenor may reveal more about the writer's priorities and the relative importance of billiards than any ambivalence about attending Depew's lecture, its timing—just two days before the event—also implies a recent, rather abrupt change of plans.

A third, more likely, possibility, however, is that Clemens's name was added to the *Courant* letter for personal rather than political reasons. He had met Depew two years earlier at the New England Society's annual "Forefathers' Day" banquet in New York City, where they—along with other notable figures, such as General Ulysses S. Grant—toasted the 262nd anniversary of the Pilgrims' landing at Plymouth Rock.[24] The writer greatly admired Depew's wit, particularly his gift for crafting memorable aphorisms, and he lobbied to have Webster and Company publish a collection of his speeches in 1888.[25] But apart from their interpersonal relationship, Clemens—as a lifelong Anglophile—would surely have found Depew's topic, "The Poetry and Politics of the British Isles," intriguing in its own right. Whether the writer yielded to external pressure for the sake of social propriety or belatedly added his name to the letter of his own accord, contemporary news reports indicate that he not only attended the talk but also accepted Joseph Hawley's invitation to join him on the platform of Roberts Opera House on Friday, 15 May. A review published in the *Hartford Times* the following day indicates that he shared the spotlight with a number of other men who had signed the 9 May letter: "Wasn't it a nice audience? Fair in number, and what was probably as agreeable to Mr. Depew, of a highly intellectual stamp. On the stage were grouped Mark Twain, the divorced partner of Cable; the Reverends Twichell and Parker, Henry Robinson, Dr. Hammond Trumbull, and General Hawley. The latter introduced the lecturer in a few pregnant words."[26]

While the *Courant* and *Times* disagreed—perhaps for reasons of political partisanship (the former was staunchly Republican, whereas the latter represented Democratic views)—about the relative merits of Depew's speech, the orator fondly recalled his 1885 visit to Hartford in *My Memories of Eighty Years*, published nearly four decades later in 1921. His recollection—framed as a conversation with the dying U.S. Grant—makes no mention of either the lecture or the Connecticut Indian Association but instead focuses on the riotous dinner and after-party at which Mark Twain served as the "presiding genius."[27] This gathering finally broke up at 3 a.m.; however, even at that late hour Depew's Hartford hosts were unwilling to let the fun end. At 5 a.m., the speaker was rudely awakened by a "violent rapping" on his hotel door; answering the summons, he found a waiter bearing a silver tray upon which stood a bottle of champagne and a goblet filled with ice:

> "Who sent this?" I asked.
> "The committee, sir, with positive instructions that you should have it at five o'clock in the morning," he answered.
> "Well, my friend," I said, "is it the habit of the good people of Hartford, when they have decided to go to New York on an early train to drink a bottle of champagne at five o'clock in the morning?"
> He answered: "Most of them do, sir."[28]

Mrs. Kinney would no doubt have been deeply disheartened to learn that the "good people of Hartford" whom Depew so affectionately remembered in his memoir were not the earnest, high-minded reformers of her organization, but mischievous bon vivants and pranksters whose primary "cause"—at least on this occasion—was the sheer pleasure afforded by one another's company.

CONSCIOUSNESS RAISING AND THE POWER OF THE PRESS

Clemens's appearance at the 1885 Depew lecture seems to have been his only expression of public support for the Connecticut Indian Association; to date, no additional evidence has surfaced documenting his presence at any of their other meetings or fundraisers. Nonetheless, as an avid reader of local newspapers, he was hardly immune from the group's ubiquitous influence. According to the association's 1888 "Historical Sketch," no fewer than four standing committees—one devoted to leaflets, another to petitions, a third to the generic "distribution of literature," and the fourth to the press[29]—were charged with the dissemination of information regarding the mistreatment of Indians and the government's failure to abide by the terms of its treaties with individual tribes. The primary task of the Committee on Leaflets was the composition of a "circular" after each annual meeting, typically held in January or early February. These flyers served a twofold purpose, explaining the organization's mission—"To protect the rights [of Indians] and promote the[ir] education and civilization . . . with the view of their ultimate admission into full citizenship"[30]—and actively soliciting funds for its latest charitable undertaking. Hundreds of these circulars were distributed to churches throughout the state, where they were often read aloud from the pulpit; in addition to these general appeals, Kinney sent copies to influential private citizens personally requesting their assistance. In 1885, the cause for which the association sought funds was the building of the so-called Connecticut Cottage; a year later, at its fourth annual meeting on 1 February 1886, Kinney proudly announced the successful completion of this project as well as ambitious plans to construct additional residences on the Omaha reservation for other recent Hampton graduates.[31] Within a week, an appeal for donations to "help civilized and educated Indians . . . make civilized and Christian homes"[32] was issued: "The funds necessary for [this] purpose are earnestly solicited from the friends of the Indians. Contributions from one dollar upward will be gratefully received and acknowledged by [our] Treasurer, Miss Mary M. Vermilye, 218 Main Street, Hartford, Conn."[33]

The association's 1886 circular elicited two noteworthy—albeit antithetical—responses, now housed in the archives of the Connecticut State Library. Coincidentally, both letters are dated 13 February, suggesting that the society's flyer had arrived just a few days earlier. The first, from Governor Henry Baldwin Harrison, reads,

Dear Mrs. Kinney,

Enclosed I send, on behalf of Mrs. Harrison, a contribution [of a hundred dollars] to the funds of the Indian Rights Association. She wishes it to be used in aid of your plan of building cottages, unless you see some better use for it.[34]

The second, in contrast, states,

Dear Mrs. Kinney—

I have sworn off, in all sincerity: if this were not really & truly the case, I would say yes, at once, to your proposal. The Injun has lost a friend; but it was so ordained.

Truly yours, SL Clemens[35]

The fact that these communications are addressed to Kinney rather than the treasurer, Mary Vermilye, implies that she herself directly contacted both men. In particular, Clemens's reference to Kinney's "proposal" suggests she may have attached a note to the circular, invoking their friendship to garner support for her cause. Unfortunately, however, neither her letter (if indeed one existed) nor the pamphlet itself survives. All that remains is the writer's tantalizing reply, in which he politely but firmly declines her request. Nonetheless, the document's very existence offers insight into the dynamics of Clemens's interactions with his immediate social circle. Unlike the many brazen—and often frankly preposterous—petitions for money that routinely came his way from strangers,[36] Mrs. Kinney's solicitation was not to be ignored or discarded. Etiquette demanded a reply, expressed in the most cordial of terms, in order to avoid any breach of propriety.

Clemens thus cites extenuating—albeit unspecified—circumstances that prevent him from contributing to the association's home-building campaign. In this way, he does not dismiss the merit of her request, only its inauspicious timing. Moreover, in asserting that he has "sworn off, in all sincerity," the writer intimates he has overextended himself financially and must therefore desist from donating to *any* cause, not merely hers. Indeed, Sam and Livy had quietly undertaken a number of philanthropic enterprises in the early 1880s, such as sponsoring the Parisian education of local sculptor Karl Gerhardt between 1881 and 1884. Correspondence between Clemens and the artist indicates that he initially committed a sum of three thousand dollars to this endeavor but later revised the amount upward to forty-five hundred, a figure equivalent to approximately a hundred thousand dollars in today's currency.[37] During this same period, the couple also sent an African American painter, Charles Ethan Porter, to study art in Paris,[38] and a few years later—from 1885 to 1887—they paid the board of Warner T. McGuinn, an African American law student at Yale. In addition, though the details are somewhat sketchy, the writer apparently provided tuition assistance in the mid-1880s to A.W. Jones, an African American student of theology at Pennsylvania's Lincoln University, a historically black institution.[39] In light of these expenditures, Twain's reluctance to commit any additional monies to a new charitable cause is understandable; because of the finite nature of discretionary income, all donors must inevitably set limits and prioritize which individuals and organizations are most deserving of their support. As he had informed his neighbor Isabella Beecher Hooker in response to her 1884 solicitation for an unspecified charitable undertaking, in such matters, he and Livy were "forced to go according to our ability, not our inclinations."[40]

Significantly, three of the four beneficiaries of Clemens's generosity were young black men; in each instance, the funding was intended as symbolic reparation for the injustices inflicted upon the race during slavery. As the writer expressed it in his 1885 letter to Yale Law School dean Francis Wayland, "Do you know him [McGuinn]? And is he worthy? I do not believe I would very cheerfully help a white student who would ask a benevolence of a stranger, but I do not feel so about the other color. We have ground the manhood out of them, & the shame is ours, not theirs, & we should pay for it."[41] Similarly, when Hattie Gerhardt vaguely maligned Porter in an 1883 letter from Paris, declaring that he had "gone to the dogs," Clemens urged her not to judge him too harshly: "You must also remember . . . whenever a colored man commits an unright action, upon his head is the guilt of only about one tenth of it, and upon your heads and mine and the rest of the white race lies fairly and justly the other nine tenths of the guilt."[42]

Interpreting Clemens's note to Kinney within the context of these remarks illuminates his divergent views of blacks and Indians. As a Southerner, he had grown up in the presence of slaves and never questioned their fundamental humanity, whereas the conspicuous absence of native peoples from the Mississippi River valley of his youth meant that his formative impressions of their character came secondhand through books, newspapers, and oft-repeated tales of gruesome frontier atrocities. Although the writer's views had tempered over time from the loathing expressed in "The Noble Red Man," his representation of Indians as treacherous, remorseless murderers—"lower and hard-hearteder than the devils"—in the 1884 manuscript fragment, "Huck Finn and Tom Sawyer among the Indians" demonstrates that he had by no means relinquished his perception of them as "savages."

Clemens's skepticism about the prospect of Indians as enfranchised citizens is insinuated in the flippant tone of the note's closing line. In explaining his refusal to contribute to Kinney's cause, he parodies the rhetoric of the association's circular, which describes donors as "friends of the Indians," indicating that in his case, "the Injun has lost a friend." While this clever turn of phrase may have been intended as a joke, its connotations are unsettling. In substituting the colloquialism "Injun" for "Indian," he reinforces a popular stereotype of ignorance, enmity, and unregenerate primitivism that tacitly calls the association's goals into question. The epithet, though not as incendiary as the term *nigger*, is nonetheless demeaning and insensitive. More puzzling still is the impersonal rationale Clemens offers regarding his decision: "it was so ordained." The Calvinistic overtones of this verb—in conjunction with the passive construction of the phrase itself—syntactically absolve the writer of agency, obviating any sense of culpability in the matter. Withholding support from the Injun is therefore not a matter of personal volition but rather a fait accompli, mysteriously decreed—perhaps by some higher power—and thus irrevocable.[43]

Within ten days of declining Mrs. Kinney's request, however, Clemens was unwittingly drawn into the association's sphere of influence by means of a polemical editorial called "A Disgrace to Civilization," published in the *Courant* on 23 February. Although this text contains no explicit mention of the organization, it is unquestionably the handiwork of their indefatigable "Committee on the Press." As the association's 1888 "Historical Sketch" reports with pride, this small group of women succeeded in placing 238 articles concerning Indian affairs in newspapers throughout the state in 1885; by 1887, that number had almost tripled to 650.[44] Moreover, the group's unpublished "minute books" indicate that Mrs. Kinney herself authored most of these pieces and arranged to have them published in the *Courant* under the aegis of her husband, John. Some texts were purely informational, while others—such as "A Disgrace to Civilization"—were frankly partisan, intended to arouse impassioned public outcry:

> The *Southwest Sentinel* is the name of a neatly printed weekly paper published at Silver City, Grant county, New Mexico. . . . Among [its] official notices we find the following, displayed in prominent type and in a conspicuous position.—
>
>> $250 REWARD
>> The above reward will be paid by the Board of County Commissioners of Grant County to any citizen of said county for each and every hostile renegade Apache killed by such citizen, on presentation to said board of the scalp of such Indian.
>> By order of the Board,
>> E. STINE, clerk[45]
>
> What can be said of a people that will tolerate the publication of such an atrocious reward for murder and outrage! . . . Because there have been terrible outrages perpetrated on settlers by a handful of renegade Apaches, a notice is issued which makes the civil authorities parties to the murder of every Indian who may fall victim to the cupidity of reckless cowboys or outlaw frontiersmen. All that a brutal white man . . . has to do to secure two hundred and fifty dollars is to bring to the country commissioners' office an Indian scalp. It is true that the reward is for the killing of "hostile, renegade Apaches," but no proof of the fact is required. Every Indians scalp will secure two hundred and fifty dollars reward, to be paid by county tax.
>
> [Since] New Mexico is at present a territory . . . the United States therefore is and will remain a party to this infamous crime so long as it per-

mits such offers to be publicly made. And the whole nation is disgraced by this act of a few short-sighted men, who, under the spur of personal grief or fright, cannot see that they are taking the surest method—and the old one—of promoting Indian outbreaks.

At this point, Mrs. Kinney broadens the scope of her editorial, juxtaposing the New Mexico bounty with a horrific 1871 massacre of Aravaipa and Pinal Apaches who had sought government protection near Camp Grant, Arizona. While the men were off hunting in the mountains, over a hundred sleeping native women and children were slaughtered in the predawn hours of 30 April by a group of Tucson settlers angry over depredations against their livestock. Quoting from a "recent address" by "Professor Wayland of Yale College," she closes the editorial with these words:

> This is but a single fact [in] the history of our relations with the Apaches. Is it altogether strange that they are deficient in some of the milder gospel graces? I confess to you that words fail me; I stand in wonder that a just God could look down from heaven and see these acts, and suffer them.

> Surely, for us, standing amid the ruins of a hundred broken treaties, amid the memory of numberless murders, to discuss the Indian question is as if Ahab and Jezebel had sat down in the vineyard of Jezreel, with the smell of blood in the air, to consider the Naboth question.[46]

Wayland's allusion to King Ahab's treacherous murder of the peasant Naboth who refused to sell his vineyard because it was the inheritance of his ancestors (1 Kings 21) is a brilliant critique of Manifest Destiny, implying that the two incidents discussed in the editorial are emblematic of the entire history of native-white relations. In equating the ancient biblical "Naboth question"—namely, who holds rightful title to the land?—with the contemporary "Indian question," the text indicts all Anglo-Americans for the crime of killing "in order to take possession."

When Clemens encountered "A Disgrace to Civilization" in his morning paper, he was appalled both by the inhumanity of the New Mexico bounty and the insidious way in which it harnessed greed as a weapon of genocide. In 1886, the annual income of skilled workers ranged from three hundred to five hundred dollars (significantly less in the West, particularly among farmers and ranchers)[47]; the bounty, therefore, was a staggering sum, equivalent to almost a year's wages and an irresistible incentive to frontier settlers struggling to support their families. In essence, the "reward" declared open season on the murder of all Apaches, "hostile" or "friendly." Outraged, Clemens clipped out the editorial and enclosed it in a letter of protest to the nation's highest-ranking public official—President Grover Cleveland—asking him to stop this barbaric practice:

Hartford, Feb. 23/86

Dear Mr. President:

You not only have the power to destroy scoundrelism of many kinds in this country, but you have amply proved that you have also the unwavering disposition & purpose to do it. But for this I would be afraid to intrude upon you & ask you to read such things as this enclosure.

Most loyally yours,
S L Clemens

Although the "scoundrelism" to which the letter refers is presumably the New Mexico bounty, Clemens's nebulous neologism implicitly encompasses the broader issues of territorial conquest and imperial power raised in the editorial's latter half. In this regard, it is tempting to speculate whether the writer connected the "Professor Wayland" mentioned in the text with the individual whom he had contacted just two months earlier regarding the "worthiness" of Warner T. McGuinn. Given the uncanny correspondence of name, profession, and academic affiliation, it seems impossible that he would not have. What Clemens may not have realized in reading "A Disgrace to Civilization," however, was that Wayland numbered among Sara Kinney's staunchest allies and was a long-standing member of the Connecticut Indian Association's Advisory Board.[48] His commitment to social reform thus extended beyond the advancement of newly enfranchised blacks to the rights of other marginalized groups, such as Native Americans and prisoners. Moreover, in his role as the dean of Yale Law School, Wayland was an authoritative figure whose opinion Clemens obviously trusted and respected; for this reason, his championing of the just, humane treatment of indigenous peoples in "A Disgrace to Civilization" may well have given the writer serious pause. Wayland's graphic account of the Camp Grant massacre inverts the familiar binary of civilization and savagery that served as the cornerstone of Twain's plot in the 1884 manuscript fragment, "Huck Finn and Tom Sawyer among the Indians." Whereas the writer portrays the fictional Mills family as quintessentially innocent victims destroyed by implacable Sioux "devils," the historical circumstances of the Arizona atrocity reverse—and thereby complicate—those roles, humanizing the Indians while depicting the whites who wantonly murder and mutilate them as depraved predators.

"A Disgrace to Civilization" eventually made its way westward to New Mexico, where it incensed the citizens of Grant County. The editors of the *Southwest Sentinel* crafted a rebuttal and sent it to the *Courant*, which published it sometime in August.[49] Although Clemens probably never saw this piece, since he was in Elmira for the summer, its thesis—pitting West against East and accusing "Mr. Courant" of "false humanity, sentimentalism, and a misconception of the facts"—is useful in gauging the progression of the writer's views on indigenous peoples. Earlier in his career, most memorably in "The Noble Red Man," he had channeled the voice and antagonistic attitude of a western frontiersman, declaring the Indian "a good, fair, desirable subject for extermination if ever there was one." In contrast, his vigorous 1886 denunciation of the bounty on Apache scalps signals a gravitational shift toward a more enlightened perspective associated with the metropolitan centers of the East. Though Clemens may have chosen not to personally fund the work of the Connecticut Indian Association, the information it disseminated nonetheless proved highly effective in reshaping his understanding of the "Indian Problem."

Several months after the editorial's publication, Mrs. Kinney adopted a new, emotionally charged tactic, placing firsthand accounts of the horrific deprivations suffered by educated Indians on the front page of the *Courant*. One such article, called "About a Blackbird," appeared on 16 November bearing the subtitle "A True Story for Young People," indicating that its appeal for charitable relief was geared toward "boys and girls . . . and possibly our young gentlemen and ladies." This autobiographical sketch, written in epistolary form, tells the heart-wrenching tale of a Christianized Ottawa Indian, Andrew Blackbird (ca. 1820–1908), who was forced to abandon his "classical education" and aspirations to study medicine in order to care for his elderly father. Back on his northern Michigan reservation, Blackbird was unjustly dismissed from his position as local postmaster so that a white man could assume the job, reducing his family to a state of utter privation:

We are about out of everything, no flour nor groceries for the coming winter, nor income whereof I could depend for our existence. It is one of the darkest hours of my life. How my children are to be fed and clad this winter is a question every day with me. . . . In this cold country we would like some warm clothing, flannel or cotton flannel, thick stockings and rubber shoes. But the most I am suffering for is pants and shoes. I am not a very large man, only 5 feet and 7 inches tall and wear No. 8 shoes. I have three sons, aged 18, 16, and 9, and one little daughter of 14.[50]

As in the case of "A Disgrace to Civilization," Kinney effaces her author-ship of this article, distancing any intervention on Blackbird's behalf from the Indian Association's overarching political agenda. Nonetheless, two tell-tale details betray her involvement. First, the lead paragraph links the origins of Blackbird's letter with the Lake Mohonk Conference of the Friends of the Indian, an eclectic group of reformers, who met each October at the Mohonk Mountain House hotel in New Paltz, New York, to discuss the assimilation and eventual citizenship of Native Americans. Kinney not only regularly attended these meetings but also served as one of the organization's leaders.[51] On this basis, it can be surmised that she heard Blackbird's story at the Mohonk Conference in early October and inquired how her association might be of assistance, thus eliciting "the letter recently received [from him] in this city" mentioned in the article. Secondly, the final paragraph of the piece stipulates that donations of food, clothing, and money for the Blackbird family should be left "at Mrs. Whitman's, 70 Ann Street [Hartford]"—one of the society's vice presidents, as well as the chairwoman of its "Committee on the Distribution of Literature."[52]

Within a week, many of Hartford's citizens responded generously to Blackbird's appeal. A 23 November brief in the *Courant* updated the community on contributions received and items still needed:

> The younger children of Blackbird's family are nearly provided with clothing by the Sunday school classes of the Center [First Congregational] church, but the oldest son, Red Deer, who is lame and cannot work, and the next youngest, North Wind, who is sixteen years old, have had very little sent in for them. Possibly some of our clothing merchants might like to help them. The ladies acknowledge with thanks ten dollars from Mr. S.L. Clemens for Blackbird. Any one preferring to give money for this family, can also send that to the care of Mr. Charles F. Hurd, 231 Main Street.[53]

Clemens's contribution suggests that he may have been more comfortable donating to a needy individual (as had been the case with Gerhardt, Porter, McGuinn, and Jones) than to an incorporated group such as the Connecticut Indian Association.

Moreover, the fact that the article singles the writer out by name for special thanks bespeaks Mrs. Kinney's persistent efforts to capitalize on his celebrity in order to promote her cause—hoping that the example of his generosity might influence others to contribute as well. While Clemens's reasons for making this donation can only be conjectured, several possibilities seem likely—a lingering sense of guilt for declining Kinney's original request back in February, a growing awareness of the injustices to which native peoples had been subjected (thanks in large part to information placed in the local press at the association's behest), and a bond of personal and professional sympathy for Andrew Blackbird himself. As the Indian's letter explains, he had attempted—but failed—to support his family by lecturing and writing after losing his job with the US Postal Service. Blackbird, moreover, was a father of four, including a daughter of fourteen— the same age as his beloved Susy. These parallels—along with the Indian's poignant request for children's shoes ("His boys wear Nos. 8, 6, and 2, and his little girl 13½.")—may well have touched Clemens's heart and prompted the gift.

Over the next two years, Andrew Blackbird's plight became something of a "cause célèbre" in Hartford; the 16 November article marks the first in a series of seven features about him in the *Courant*. In January 1887, the newspaper published at the request of an anonymous "Friend of the Indian"—Kinney, no doubt—Blackbird's gracious letter of thanks (addressed "Dear Madam") for the two barrels of donations received some weeks earlier. By that May, he was actively soliciting financial assistance for a new venture—the publication of his book on the *History of the Ottawa and Chippewa Indians of Michigan, and the Grammar of Their Language*: "Although our Hartford friends have done most nobly toward getting us through the winter, I wonder if these same friends could yet do something more in this darkest hour! Say one dollar each, for which I will pledge my honor to send them each a copy of my history, as soon as it is put into book form."[54] Ten days later, the *Courant* announced that twenty dollars had been received in support of Blackbird's project but did not identify the individual contributors. It is therefore unknown whether Clemens numbered among them and would have received a copy of Blackbird's history— a unique hybrid of autobiography, tribal history, linguistics, and traditional Ottawa legends, today regarded as "one of the most important sources of information concerning the Indians in the Great Lakes region"[55]—when it arrived in early 1888.

Clemens's final interaction with the Connecticut Indian Association proved—quite literally—to be his closest encounter with the group. On 8 October 1890, a notice appeared on the front page of the *Courant*, headlined "For the Benefit of Indians," announcing a series of three "parlor lectures secured by the Indian Association of Hartford in order to raise funds for carrying on its work."[56] The topics, dates, and venues were listed as follows: "On Ibsen, October 23, at Mrs. F. Chamberlin's; on Sidney Lanier, October 31, at Mrs. W.H. Post's; on George Meredith, November 13, place to be announced." The speaker, Richard E. Burton (1859–1940), who had recently earned a doctorate in English, German, and Old Norse from Johns Hopkins University, was the only child of Clemens's "burly and magnificent" friend Reverend Dr. Nathaniel J. Burton (A1, 271). Over time, the writer had cultivated a warm, almost avuncular, relationship with the young man, who lived in close proximity to him at Nook Farm.[57] After Nathaniel's sudden death in 1887, he approached Richard and urged him to edit a selection of his father's sermons, which were published a year later by Charles Webster and Company under the title *Yale Lectures on Preaching and Other Writings*. According to Burton's 1937 reminiscence, "Mark Twain in the Hartford Days," this action not only provided the clergyman's widow (who incidentally was also a long-time member of the Connecticut Indian Association) with a royalty "ten times better than if [the book] had been brought out in the usual ten percent trade way"[58] but also helped to perpetuate his father's intellectual legacy. In this same document, Burton fondly recalls Clemens's many other acts of kindness, such as critiquing his "immature" prose with "infinite patience and good-will"[59] and assisting him in finding freelance editorial work at the *Century* magazine.

The substance of Burton's 1890 lectures—like that of Chauncey Depew's five years earlier—was reported in the *Courant* on the morning after each occurred. It is thus known that Joe Twichell ceremoniously kicked off the series on 23 October by introducing the scholar to "a large and fashionable audience," and that his address on Sidney Lanier eight days later attracted a "numerous audience that included the poet's brother. . . and his widow."[60] The newspaper's review of the final lecture, however, contains an especially intriguing detail—namely, that its location, originally listed as "to be announced," was none other than "the residence of Mrs. S. L. Clemens on Farmington Avenue." Since the series had been expressly identified and promoted in the local press as a benefit for the Connecticut Indian Association, it is not surprising that Burton's first two presentations were held at the homes of society officers, yet Livy herself had no formal ties with the organization. In light of this anomaly, what significance—if any— should be ascribed to her willingness to host a fundraiser on behalf of the assimilation and enfranchisement of native peoples? Did friendship trump politics on this occasion, or had she and her spouse perhaps grown more amenable to the association's agenda over time and therefore viewed the lecture as an opportunity to belatedly express their support?

According to the *Courant*, Burton's address on George Meredith attracted the largest audience of the series—a capacity crowd that filled the "spacious rooms" of the Clemens residence.[61] In all likelihood, this increase in attendance was not motivated by keen local interest in the topic, but curiosity—a self-serving desire to see the home's elegant interior firsthand and perhaps even catch a glimpse of its acclaimed owner. If so, the audience was not disappointed. As Burton remembers, Twain "sat in the front row . . . [at the lecture given] in his own house, and afterwards, told me what was wrong, with a judicious word of praise, when any praise was due."[62] While this statement implies that Clemens regarded the event primarily as an opportunity to mentor his young protégé, Burton's characterization of the writer as "a champion of justice, mercy, and truth" may also signal his tacit endorsement of the political cause for which the entertainment was given.

Despite the indeterminacy of Twain's motives, the very fact of his presence at the lecture—from which he could have easily recused himself and retreated to the airy isolation of the billiards room two stories above—is at once significant and deeply ironic. Seated in his library, an intimate, domestic space temporarily repurposed as a public forum, the writer found himself amidst a throng of female reformers cut from the same cloth as the "sappy women" in *Tom Sawyer* who petitioned the Missouri governor for a stay of Injun Joe's execution. Indeed, Sam and Livy's hospitality in inviting these zealous "Friends of the Indian" into their home gives profound new meaning to the Emersonian adage incised on the room's gleaming brass fire screen: "The ornament of a house is the friends who frequent it." But most importantly, the incident suggests that if the writer did harbor any lingering ambivalence about the assimilation of Native Americans in 1890, these objections were not to be voiced among the members of his immediate social circle. Instead, the enduring bonds of friendship and genteel civility—or, in the case of Burton's lecture, allegiance to the son of a dear deceased friend—prevailed over ideological difference, as they would some six months later when Clemens learned of the death of Major John C. Kinney and sent his widow the following heartfelt letter of condolence:

My Dear Mrs. Kinney:

I beg the privilege of offering my deepest sympathy in this time of your bereavement. We all loved him, and you have with you for fellow-mourners all the great host who knew him. There are those crying this morning who are unused to tears.[63]

While Clemens's tangential involvement with the Connecticut Indian Association undeniably increased his awareness of the myriad injustices to which native peoples had been subjected and elicited sporadic compassion for their plight, his racial bias against Indians diminished as a result during the 1880s but was never fully exorcised. Rather, his misgivings about the education and civilization of Indians were displaced and covertly channeled into the pages of his most ambitious novel, *A Connecticut Yankee in King Arthur's Court.*

HANK MORGAN, "MAN FACTORIES," AND THE "WHITE INDIANS" OF CAMELOT

Although *Connecticut Yankee* is set in sixth-century England, Twain's protagonist, Hank Morgan, often links the primitivism of Camelot's inhabitants with the Native Americans of his own time—coincidentally identified in chapter 2 as 1879—the same year that Captain Pratt opened the first federally sponsored Indian boarding school in Carlisle, PA (CY, 17). Moreover, Hank's project of civilizing these British "savages" closely parallels the process of "Americanizing" the country's indigenous tribes through education, the acquisition of literacy, and the introduction of basic technological proficiency. This deft interweaving of past and present expands the novel's satirical scope from a historical critique of monarchy and aristocratic privilege to the futility of his own government's attempts to assimilate and enfranchise Indians.

Like the federal boarding schools, Hank's "man factories," which he also refers to as "civilization-nurseries" (CY, 84), are located in "obscure country retreats" (CY, 81), sequestered and off-limits to the general populace. The purposes of these institutions, in his words, are metamorphosis and advancement—"to turn groping and grubbing automata into *men*" (CY 157)—a description that echoes Pratt's motto, "Kill the Indian, save the man." In addition, though the inhabitants of Camelot are already Christian, Hank undertakes their wholesale religious conversion in a manner reminiscent of the proselytizing endeavors of Pratt, Armstrong, and the other "Friends of the Indian," such as Sara Thomson Kinney. Denouncing the Roman Catholic Church as a stranglehold of ignorance, superstition, and fear (epithets also applied to the animistic beliefs of indigenous peoples), he seeks to overthrow and replace it with an enlightened Protestantism. The actions of Twain's protagonist are thus driven by the same ideology of progress that motivated Pratt and other nineteenth-century advocates of assimilation.

Hank's initial impressions of Camelot in chapter 1 establish the groundwork of this provocative atemporal analogy. Wandering through a "wilderness of thatched cabins," he encounters people with "long, coarse, uncombed hair that hung down over their faces and made them look like animals" (CY, 11). His first explicit identification of the sixth-century Britons with Indians, however, occurs in chapter 2, when he is brought, as a prisoner of

Sir Kay, to the castle where the Knights of the Round Table are feasting. This scene presents a dramatic contrast between the highest and lowest classes in Arthur's rigidly stratified kingdom—the hereditary aristocrats and powerless, disenfranchised captives. The knights, "dressed in such various and splendid colors that it hurt one's eyes to look at them" (CY, 19), are absorbed in surfeit and epicurean pleasure, oblivious to the misery and deprivation of the others who share the same room. Hank, who is of course grouped with the captives, observes,

> I was not the only prisoner present. There were twenty or more. Poor devils, many of them were maimed, hacked, carved, in a frightful way; and their hair, their faces, their clothing, were caked with black and stiffened drenchings of blood. They were suffering sharp physical pain, of course; and weariness, and hunger and thirst, no doubt . . . yet you never heard them utter a moan or a groan, or saw them show any sign of restlessness, or any disposition to complain. The thought was forced upon me: "The rascals—*they* have served other people so, in their day; it being their turn, now, they were not expecting any better treatment than this; so their philosophical bearing is not an outcome of mental training, intellectual fortitude, reasoning; it is mere animal training; they are white Indians." (CY, 20)

This passage is notable, not only for the disparaging label that Hank coins and applies to the prisoners, but also for the inexplicable abruptness with which his attitude shifts from apparent sympathy to detachment and contempt. Although Morgan's circumstances situate him squarely within this motley cohort, he nonetheless refuses to acknowledge them as peers. On the one hand, he pities the "poor devils" and expresses indignation at the appalling cruelties that have been inflicted upon them, but on the other, he stops short of empathic identification, rejecting these individuals as "Others," alien and inferior. Rather than presuming the captives' innocence, Hank—who ironically knows nothing of their character or purported crimes—instead concludes that they have been perpetrators of ruthless violence in the past and are now reaping the just consequences of these barbarous excesses. He thus dismisses the prisoners' stoic forbearance as "mere animal training," deeming them nothing more than "white Indians."

Both the syntax and substance of this passage reaffirm the critical contention that Hank's character is autobiographical in many ways. In his notebooks, Twain frequently describes the actions of his protagonist in the first person, making statements such as "I make a *peaceful* revolution and introduce advanced civilization" and "I did everything I could to bring knight-errantry into contempt."[64] This conflation of author and fictional creation demonstrates, in Everett Carter's words, that "Twain sympathized deeply with his Connecticut Yankee."[65] This identification is further underscored by two details in Hank's description of the prisoners that parallel remarks concerning Indians made by the writer himself. First, Hank's use of the passive voice in the phrase "the thought was forced upon me" echoes the closing line of Clemens's 1886 note to Sara Thomson Kinney explaining his inability to contribute to the Indian Association's home-building project on the Omaha reservation: "The Injun has lost a friend; but *it was so ordained*" (emphasis added). In both instances, the impersonal diction implies that the perspective articulated by the speaker is not his own, but inexplicably imposed from without, and therefore incontrovertible. Secondly, Hank's characterization of the captives' apparent imperviousness to pain as "mere animal training" recalls Clemens's 1884 letter to Howells describing his torturous visits to the dentist in Elmira: "I can stand the most exquisite pain, now, without outward manifestation; & indeed without any very real discomfort. The Indian has fallen in my estimation; he is no better than you or me—he is merely a product of education" (MTHL, 496).

Twain's epithet—likely inspired by Francis Parkman's reference to seventeenth-century itinerant trappers as "*coureurs de bois,* white Indians" in *Count Frontenac and New France under Louis XIV*—suggests that savagery is more a cultural condition of "manners and morals" than a strictly racial category.[66] A "white Indian" not only lacks the distinguishing outward marks of civilization, such as the ability to read and write, but is also devoid of fundamental respect for human life. The prisoners, Hank surmises, live in accordance with a primitive code of violence and revenge and are therefore deserving of the pain they suffer. The origins of this analogy can be traced back to a deleted chapter of Twain's 1880 work, *A Tramp Abroad*, entitled "The French and the Comanches," in which he argues that the "cruelty, savagery, and spirit of massacre"[67] displayed by the French throughout history prove that they exist on the "same moral and social level" as Native Americans.

Another likely source of this metaphor, discussed by Joe Fulton in *Mark Twain in the Margins*, is W. E. H. Lecky's *Spirit of Rationalism*, which the writer read and annotated during the novel's composition. A passage describing torture devices used by the Scottish clergy on suspected witches is especially relevant in this context: "We read, in a contemporary legal register, of one man who was kept for forty-eight hours in 'vehement tortour' in the caschielawis; and of another who remained in the same frightful machine <u>for eleven days and eleven nights, whose legs were broken daily for fourteen days in the boots,</u> and who was so scourged that the whole skin was torn from his body." Next to these underscored words,

Clemens notes, "These are Scotch, not Iroquois."[68] This observation is an intertextual allusion to Francis Parkman's description in *The Jesuits in North America in the Seventeenth Century*—a work he had read and greatly admired in 1881—of the "pitiless ferocity"[69] with which the Iroquois systematically burned and flayed parts of Father Francesco Bressani's body over a period of weeks in colonial Canada. Twain's analogy subversively implies that the behavior of these privileged, literate prelates, an elite minority regarded as the apex of medieval European civilization, is in fact indistinguishable from that of savages.

Moreover, Hank's perception of Sir Kay's prisoners as "white Indians" is not restricted to the lower, oppressed classes of Camelot but extends to the populace of sixth-century Britain as a whole. This ethnocentric mindset underlies his first "miracle," the act that will simultaneously free him and establish his reputation as the realm's most powerful magician: "It came into my mind, in the nick of time, how Columbus, or Cortez, or one of those people, played an eclipse as a saving trump once, on some savages, and I saw my chance. I could play it myself, now; and it wouldn't be any plagiarism, either, because I should get it in nearly a thousand years ahead of those parties" (CY, 40). Hank's recollection of this moment of early contact between the Old and New Worlds offers not only a pragmatic solution to his predicament of being burned at the stake but also an inspirational paradigm of cultural ascendancy. In claiming the power to "blot out the sun" and "smother the whole world in the dead blackness of midnight" (CY, 42), he emulates the deific stance of a celebrated European explorer, using his scientific understanding of the physical universe to manipulate and control an ignorant, primitive audience. Through the agency of time travel, Hank's "miracle," though derivative, becomes a boldly original maneuver that inverts the categories of savagery and civilization as well as the hierarchical relationship between Europe and America.

The trope of "white Indians" is also reinforced by Hank's characterization of the Knights of the Round Table as "a sort of polished-up court of Comanches," in which "there isn't a squaw... who doesn't stand ready at the dropping of a hat to desert to the buck with the biggest string of scalps at his belt" (CY, 129). While this flippant characterization of aristocratic women as "squaws" may reflect Hank's inherently democratic sensibility, the substance of his allegation—that the ladies of Arthur's court are fickle and inconstant—is rooted in ethnocentric arrogance. In Hank's estimation, such inconstancy exemplifies a debased value system wherein status, sexual allure, and the very motion of manhood are equated with barbaric violence and grisly war trophies.

Even Sandy, Hank's companion and eventual spouse, is not exempt from the pejorative label of savagery. After spending the night out of doors, he awakens "seedy, drowsy, fagged . . . and crippled with rheumatism," then asks,

> How had it fared with the nobly born, the titled aristocrat, the Demoiselle Alisande la Carteloise? Why, she was fresh as a squirrel; she had slept like the dead; and as for a bath, probably neither she nor any other noble in the land had ever had one, and so she was not missing it. Measured by modern standards, they were merely modified savages, those people. This noble lady showed no impatience to get to breakfast— and that smacks of the savage, too. On their journeys those Britons were used to long fasts, and knew how to bear them; and also how to freight-up against probable fasts before starting, after the style of the Indian and the anaconda. As like as not, Sandy was loaded for a three-day stretch. (CY, 108–9)

As this passage indicates, the pervasive lack of hygiene in Arthur's realm not only offends Hank's nineteenth-century standards and sensibilities but also strengthens the association with Indians. A key component of his grand design to civilize and uplift the nation involves the establishment of a factory to manufacture Persimmons soap and enlistment of so-called "missionaries" sent out into the countryside to "introduce a rudimentary cleanliness among the nobility" (CY, 139). As Hank proudly claims, "whenever my missionaries overcame a knight errant on the road, they washed him, and when he got well they swore him to go and get a bulletin-board and disseminate soap and civilization the rest of his days" (CY 140). Just as the "Americanized" Indians who attended government boarding schools eventually returned—radically altered in appearance and outlook—to their tribes and reservations, these knights, according to Hank's plan, will serve as role models (as well as living advertisements) for the unwashed primitives of Camelot. This conjoining of soap and civilization echoes Twain's 1867 sketch, "The Facts Concerning the Recent Resignation," written more than two decades before *A Connecticut Yankee*, in which the former clerk of the "Senate Commission on Conchology" informs the secretary of war that "soap and education are not as sudden as a massacre, but they are more deadly in the long run; because a half massacred Indian may recover, but if you educate him and wash him, it is bound to finish him some time or other" (CT1, 241).

Ironically, Hank's attempt to cleanse, educate, and civilize the inhabitants of sixth-century Britain proves a catastrophic failure that results in his own destruction, as well as that of the institution of knight-errantry itself.

While his "man-factories" and myriad technological innovations effect a striking outward transformation in the people of Arthur's realm, the change is cosmetic and illusory, a façade that crumbles before the Church's interdict. In chapter 42, when Hank learns that the legions of men trained in his schools, colleges, and "vast workshops" have turned against him and allied themselves with the Church, he is stunned. Clarence, however, is not, and pointedly questions the overweening presumption of his "Boss":

> "Did you think you had educated the superstition out of those people?"
>
> "I certainly did think it."
>
> "Well, then, you may unthink it. They stood the strain easily—until the Interdict. Since then, they merely put on a bold outside—at heart they are quaking. Make up your mind to it—when the armies come, the mask will fall." (CY, 418)

Twain's characterization of sixth-century Britons as "white Indians" culminates in the apocalyptic denouement of chapter 43, "The Battle of the Sand-Belt." Describing this military engagement as the "last stand" of chivalry, he invokes the annihilation of General George Armstrong Custer and the Seventh Cavalry by the combined forces of the Lakota, Cheyenne, and Arapaho nations at the infamous Battle of the Little Bighorn 25–26 on June 1876. Viewing the ravaged battlefield, Hank observes,

> No life was in sight, but necessarily there must have been some wounded in the rear ranks, who were carried off the field under cover of the wall of smoke; there would be sickness among the others— there always is, after an episode like that. But there would be no reinforcements; this was the last stand of the chivalry of England; it was all that was left of the order, after the recent annihilating wars. (CY, 432)

The semantics of this metaphor has long troubled scholars, who interpret the symbolic identities of the combatants in radically different ways. In *Mark Twain and West Point*, Philip Leon states that Hank's remark is "an inverted allusion to the 'last stand' of ill-fated West Pointer George Armstrong Custer and his famously unsuccessful defense against overwhelming odds."[70] Historian Richard Slotkin corroborates this assessment, arguing that Hank's role as "the commander of an elite corps of West Pointers and boys . . . links him closely to Custer . . . although this Custer has massacred all the Indians, his fate is the same: the Yankee falls into a trance caused by Merlin, and his elite corps perish of a pestilence brewed in the piled-up corpses of their slaughtered enemies."[71] The Battle of the Sand-Belt is in fact a "last stand" for both sides. Though Hank and his fifty-two young men are technically "victors," like the Native Americans who triumphed over Custer in 1876 they too are inevitably vanquished. In contrast to Leon and Slotkin, Joe Fulton argues that Twain's metaphor "identifies Hank as an Indian and hence as an uncivilized 'man of old ideas,' not the 'new man' he proclaims himself to be when first landing in Camelot . . . Hank is really *both* Custer and Sitting Bull in a history with no ultimate winners."[72]

Each of these readings, while perceptive, overlooks the larger, more significant "inversion" implied by Twain's metaphor: the Battle of the Little Big Horn predated the establishment of the federal boarding-school system (and its philosophy of assimilation through education) by three years. In a novel where the fluidity of time is a foundational premise, this reversal of causation and chronology is suggestive. The military "pacification" of hostile tribes and their containment on reservations represented the first phase of the nation's solution to the "Indian problem"; only in the aftermath of crushing defeat and forcible relocation would the government conceive of a program designed to transform indigenous peoples into useful citizens. By transposing these circumstances, Twain unhinges the logic and linear progression of history, suggesting that violence—not assimilation—is the sole means whereby savagery can be eradicated.

Twain's "last stand" allusion also resonated with Daniel Carter Beard, who illustrated *A Connecticut Yankee*. According to the artist's autobiography, *Hardly a Man Is Now Alive*, Clemens gave him a copy of the completed manuscript that he read "three times with great enjoyment."[73] Sensing the rich satirical possibilities of the parallels that Twain's text proposed between the sixth and nineteenth centuries, Beard drew a series of playful, provocative images—the most famous of which portrays the robber baron Jay Gould as a slave driver. His illustrations also pay homage to the medieval tradition of illuminated manuscripts, in that the first word of each chapter begins with a large "historiated letter"[74] containing a specific scene or individual discussed therein. For the most part, these designs present historically accurate images of both the novel's setting and diverse sixth-century characters, ranging from aristocratic gentry and clerics to peasants and prisoners.

The motif at the beginning of chapter 43, however, is a notable exception. In this instance, a capital *I*—the first letter of the opening word *in*—appears at the top of a ragged, asymmetrical rectangle featuring a chaotic jumble of dismembered men and horses, along with the phrase "A Blow-Up" (fig. 17) These figures are not Beard's own design but were in fact copied from a panel of the Bayeux Tapestry depicting the carnage at the Battle of

FIGURE 17. Initial letter, chapter 43, *A Connecticut Yankee in King Arthur's Court.* Courtesy of the Mark Twain Project, The Bancroft Library, University of California, Berkeley.

Hastings in 1066. The irregularly fringed border that frames the image, on the other hand, evokes a radically different cultural referent—the intricately painted buffalo robes created by Plains Indians to commemorate significant events in the tribe's history, including the Battle of the Little Bighorn. Beard had a lifelong fascination with native peoples and the American frontier and would therefore have been familiar with such pictographic hides. Moreover, as an artist, he would have been intrigued by the hides' stylistic similarities to the celebrated medieval tapestry, in that they display a lack of perspective and render the human form in profile. His image thus collapses time and space. Visually, it equates the preliterate knights of Arthur's realm with Indians, revealing that he—unlike later literary scholars—perceived no ambiguity in Twain's allusion to "the last stand of chivalry." Although the writer himself never explicitly mentioned this drawing, he took great delight in the illustrations for *A Connecticut Yankee* as a whole, informing one correspondent that the artist's renderings were "better than the book—which is a good deal for me to say, I reckon. I merely approved of the pictures—and very heartily, too."[75]

Among the many positive reviews *A Connecticut Yankee* garnered upon its publication in December 1889, only one apparently took note of the novel's pervasive Indian imagery. Sylvester Baxter of the *Boston Sunday Herald* discusses the metaphor in detail—not as a point of contention but of praise:

> There is a certain aspect of sober truth in this most fanciful tale, and, just as the Connecticut Yankee went back into the days of King Arthur's court, so might he go out into the world today, into Central Asia or Africa, or even into certain spots in this United States of ours, find himself amidst social conditions very similar to those of 1300 years ago, and even work his astonishing 19th century miracles with like result. For it is a fact that, when Frank Hamilton Cushing astounded the Zuni Indians with an acoustic telephone constructed of two tomato cans and a string, they deemed him a magician, and tried him for witchcraft.[76]

Baxter not only applauds the aptness of Twain's analogy but also commends his "exact perception of the essentially savage traits" of Camelot's inhabitants—their superstition, inability to reason, and resistance to new ideas. He perceives a timeless, universal truth in Hank's statement, "Whenever one of those people got a thing into his head, there was no getting it out again. I knew that, so I saved my breath, and offered no explanations." He declares that this characterization "might apply equally well to a tribe of Dakota Indians, to their hardly more civilized foes, the cowboys of the plains, to the mountaineers of Tennessee and Georgia, or even to savages in our great city slums."[77]

Baxter's attunement to this trope reflects his personal background and professional interests. In the early 1880s, he had served as a publicist for ethnographer Frank Cushing and accompanied him on the three-month-long 1886 Hemenway Southwestern Archeological Expedition to New Mexico and Arizona, organized for the purpose of tracing the prehistoric ancestry of the Zuni people. In 1888, he published *The Old New World*, a detailed account of the expedition, and authored numerous other essays on indigenous customs and cultures. Although Baxter was neither a reformer nor self-proclaimed "Friend of the Indian," this firsthand experience with native tribes instilled in him a strong sense of cultural relativism that is reflected in his comparison of the savagery of urban slum dwellers, rural southern mountaineers, and cowboys with that of the Dakota Indians. In this context, he quotes the closing paragraphs of the novel's second chapter, in which Hank declares Sir Kay's prisoners nothing more than "white Indians," citing the passage as evidence of the "scientific fidelity of . . . [Twain's] picture of medieval society." Like the writer, Baxter understood that savagery was fundamentally more a matter of manners and morals than race.[78]

KATE FOOTE: "THE INDIAN'S FRIEND"

It is unclear how the members of the Connecticut Indian Association responded to Twain's fictional representation of sixth-century Britons as "white Indians." Sara Thomson Kinney left no record of her impressions of the novel, if indeed she even read it; however, two 1890 letters to Clemens from Kate Foote, a fellow activist who would become the organization's executive vice president by the end of the decade, prove instructive in this regard. Although not a native of Hartford, Foote (1840–1923) was a cousin of the Beechers and had deep, multigenerational ties to Nook Farm. During her youth, she often stayed at the home of John and Isabella Beecher Hooker and was a boon companion of their daughters Alice and Mary; she also taught briefly at Catherine Beecher's Hartford Female Seminary in the late 1860s. Two of her older sisters, Elizabeth and Harriet (one of the original founders of the Connecticut Indian Association), married prominent Hartford men—George Warner and Joseph Hawley, respectively—and also resided at Nook Farm. But perhaps most importantly, her niece Lilly Gillette Foote worked for many years as the Clemens family's governess, and—not at all coincidentally—was also the individual responsible for Susy's unsettling introduction to the precepts of native religion. Through this expansive network of family connections, Kate enjoyed multiple avenues of access into the writer's intimate social circle.

Foote first met Clemens at a dinner given by her cousin Mary in the fall of 1868, three years before his move to Hartford, and confessed to finding him "a little peculiar" in a letter to her siblings in Guilford, a small town on the Connecticut coastline. On the basis of his "slow & labored & rather rough" speech and "familiar" conversation about a number of disreputable actors, she initially believed him to be "some green young man whom Mrs. Hooker has taken up with the benevolent design of improving." Only after learning that he was a journalist—a profession to which Kate herself aspired—did she gradually warm to the author, deciding by evening's end that she "rather lik[ed] him."[79]

By the mid-1880s Foote had fulfilled her career ambition, becoming the Washington political correspondent for the *Independent,* a weekly magazine published in New York City. Her so-called Washington Letters, though not formally syndicated, were nonetheless reprinted with some frequency in the *Courant* and kept friends and relatives at home abreast of her thinking on current topics. Around this same time, inspired by the example of her eldest sister Harriet, who had served as the president of the District of Columbia auxiliary of the Women's National Indian Association after her husband's election to the US Senate in 1881, Foote also embraced the cause of native rights. After Harriet's death in 1886, Kate succeeded her in this role and began editing the organization's newsletter, "The Indian's Friend." Soon thereafter, Foote was appointed to the Board of Indian Commissioners, chairing its committee on tribal legislation. In this capacity, she traveled throughout the western United States and Alaska from 1886 to 1895 as an "allotting agent," determining how reservations should be broken up into individual tracts of land and helping to establish schools and hospitals for Native Americans.

In 1890, Foote's professional duties took her to Southern California for three months, where she worked among the Mission Indians "study[ing] them on their reservation and in their villages"[80] in order to prepare a history of the tribe from the arrival of the Spanish missionaries to the present day. About midway through her stay, Foote wrote to Clemens:

> I wish that plaguy book of yours was not sold by subscription as I suppose it is, all your others have been & I suppose it is no use to ask at a bookseller's for it. But I want it, I mean the "Yankee at the Court of King Arthur," & so I write to you for it. I want to give it to an interesting cowboy whom I met here on a ranch in the wilds of Southern California. He was showing me his horses & his saddles & bridles & a riata & how to use it, when I thought of Merlin & the cavalry in your book & said something about it. He looked so interested that I made [a] mental vow to send him the book. Does this interest you? If so my address is care Mr. H. N. Rust. Colton, San Bernardino Co. California.
> Is it a dollar & a half book or two dollars?[81]

Foote's familiar, almost brusque, tone bespeaks her rapport with the writer, whom she had now known for more than two decades. She couches her request for the novel in forthright, decidedly unfeminine terms, asserting, "I want it"—not for herself, but an "interesting" new acquaintance. Although Foote does not specify the race or ethnicity of this individual, both the political nature of her work in Southern California and solemn pledge to acquire the book strongly suggest that he is native. In her zeal to

"Americanize" the country's indigenous inhabitants, she may well have regarded the text—so famously described by William Dean Howells as "an object-lesson in democracy"[82]—as an innovative means of fostering the young man's assimilation into mainstream society by introducing him to the virtues of republicanism, citizenship, and enfranchisement. While Foote never articulates these intentions, the rhetorical question she poses to Clemens—"Does this interest you?"—effectively enlists him as a de facto partner in her proposed social experiment. She solicits the writer's charity by appealing to his ego, hoping that the prospect of expanding his readership into "the wilds of Southern California" will entice him to send the text gratis. Anticipating the possibility that this gambit will fail, however, Foote makes an offhanded inquiry about its price in the letter's closing line, underscoring her determination to obtain the book by any means possible.

Foote's proposition apparently did interest Clemens, who immediately posted a copy of *Connecticut Yankee* to her in Colton. Her subsequent letter of thanks, dated 6 November, provides additional clues about the recipient's identity and her possible motives in offering the gift: "The book has come & I give you my thanks for it. I shall send it off in a day or two by the Doctor of the Indian agency who will go to the Thomas ranch on his route through the Indian reservation. He will tell me how the young man receives it & what effect it has on him. Then I shall either see you or tell you in a note."[83] In addition to the ranch's location on a reservation, Foote's insistence that the Indian agency physician delivering the novel inform her of its "effect" on this anonymous individual implies that the book was not provided for his idle entertainment but for an edifying—and possibly political—purpose. Judging from the comment Clemens jotted on the letter's envelope, these details led him to surmise that the recipient was native as well: "Kate Foote / About a book / sent to a boy/ (Indian?)."[84]

Unfortunately, the documentary record runs cold at this point: no letter from Foote has yet been uncovered describing *Connecticut Yankee's* impact on this young man, nor does it seem likely that the occasion ever arose for her to convey his reaction to Clemens in person. Nonetheless, valuable insights can be gleaned from this fragmentary correspondence, first and foremost that Foote herself was not at all troubled by the novel's anti-Indian rhetoric. Given her tireless work of behalf of indigenous tribes, she surely would not have recommended the text had she deemed its content objectionable. Instead, she recalls *A Connecticut Yankee* with affection, citing the humorous scene in which Hank uses a lariat to literally unseat and defeat Camelot's knights in a tournament. Secondly, despite the many similarities that exist between Twain and his fictional protagonist, he apparently did not share Hank's cynical view regarding the futility of educating "savages"; otherwise, why would he have acceded to Foote's request? Lastly, the timing of the writer's gift—just three weeks before he and Livy hosted Richard Burton's benefit lecture for the Connecticut Indian Association in their home—suggests that these apparently discrete incidents were related and heralded the emergence of a more tolerant view regarding Native Americans, facilitated in large part through the influence of female activist friends such as Kinney and Foote.

Clemens's last known communication with Foote on 16 January 1891, responding to a now-lost invitation sent two days earlier, deepens the mystery. The reformer had returned to Washington in late November upon the completion of her work among the Mission Indians and resumed her administrative role in the Women's National Indian Association. When Foote's letter arrived in Hartford on the fourteenth, Livy—noting the urgent nature of her request—immediately forwarded it to her husband, who happened to be visiting the nation's capital in an attempt to solicit financial support for the Paige compositor from Nevada's Republican senator, John Percival Jones.[85] The demands of the writer's schedule evidently did not permit him to reply to Foote in person; however, his response, written in haste just before he boarded a train for home, indicates that her invitation—whatever it may have been—was no routine matter:

> Dear Miss Foote:
>
>   Yours of day before yesterday has reached me from Hartford just as I am taking a train for home after my capitolian visit. I wish I could say yes—I would do it in a minute if the circumstances would allow it—but the recent deaths in our family circle forbid me to assist at any public function for the winter.
>
>   I wish I had time to run around & say this by word of mouth & have a glimpse of you, but train-time is too close at hand.[86]

Clemens's allusion to "assist[ing] at a public function" is intriguing, particularly when considered within the context of Foote's response to a recent horrific event. On 29 December 1890, hundreds of unarmed Lakota ghost dancers were brutally massacred by the Seventh Cavalry at Wounded Knee Creek on South Dakota's Pine Ridge reservation. Like many other native rights advocates, Foote was appalled by what the mainstream press called the "Sioux Outbreak," and devoted several of her Washington Letter editorials in the *Independent* to an examination of its complex causes. She denounced the reduction in government rations that produced widespread starvation on the reservation as well as the military's overreaction to the

Ghost Dance, concluding "if the Indians had been allowed to go on with their dance, there would have been no trouble."[87]

She also offered a sociological explanation of the Ghost Dance phenomenon itself: "Overwhelmed, stunned with the pressure of the whites upon them for their lands, dazed with the civilization, which is being forced down their throats, which it has taken us some hundreds of years to assimilate, the Indians have tried to branch out in various directions... [and seized upon] the idea of a Messiah coming to help them."[88] Although Foote's editorial makes no mention of Twain, her argument regarding the rapid, unrealistic pace at which Anglo-Americans sought to introduce their civilization among the Sioux uncannily parallels Hank Morgan's hubris in believing it was feasible to modernize the people of Camelot within a single generation; not surprisingly, these endeavors—in fact as well as fiction—end in catastrophic loss of life.

Discussion of both the Wounded Knee massacre and the news that thirty-eight Lakota leaders would soon be traveling to Washington to formally protest the government's mistreatment of their tribe dominated the annual meeting of the Women's National Indian Association, which was held in the nation's capital on 8 January 1891. Foote not only attended this conference but also spoke at it, telling the assembled crowd "about her recent visit to the Mission Indians of Southern California ... [and how] the white people of that country were beginning to show a little respect for the 'Eastern sentimentalist' on the Indian question."[89] Among the hundreds of women in the audience was Sara Thomson Kinney, one of the organization's regional vice presidents; her close relationship with Foote makes it virtually certain that they conversed privately, either during or after the conference, and may have compared notes on their recent interactions with the writer, prompting Foote to once again seek his assistance.

At the association's annual meeting, its leaders resolved to publicly support the goals of the Lakota delegation by accompanying them to their negotiations with high-ranking cabinet officials in early February. According to "The Sioux Powwow," published in the *Washington Post* on 8 February, "there was a strong desire on the part of many people to be present" at these meetings, "but the size of the room made it necessary to bring the number of spectators admitted down to a very few. The Secretary of War was present ... also Miss Kate Foote, Miss Alice Fletcher ... and others prominent in the work for Indians."[90] Despite the presence of these influential figures, the government's indifference to the Lakotas' grievances is illustrated by the anticlimactic reception arranged for them at the White House on 12 February, where the delegates had "the honor of shaking hands with the Great Father" [President Benjamin Harrison] but ironically "were not permitted to talk with him."[91]

Foote, however, was not content to merely attend these sessions as an observer but also used her influence as the president of the Association's Washington auxiliary to proactively organize a "mass meeting" on the evening of 11 February dedicated to "the education of the Anglo-Saxon on the Indian question."[92] Contemporary news reports indicate that both the floor and galleries of the city's largest Congregational church "were filled with interested auditors, and a large number were standing in the aisles and about the doors"[93] for this event. The Lakota delegates were there as well, seated on a platform in front of the pulpit, and over the course of the evening many of them rose to address the crowd through an interpreter. The keynote speaker was Thomas J. Morgan, the US commissioner on Indian affairs, who related the grisly facts of the Wounded Knee massacre in plain terms "such as no newspapers had [previously] done": "Our whole army was there, and of the Indians whom they were to meet, there were 222 lodges, which at four people in each, makes 888 men, women and children—not warriors, you observe, but all of them. The number of fighting men, you can imagine, out of that number; they were not there for war."[94] Morgan concluded his address by reaffirming the assimilationist credo that "the proper agency for cultivating the Indians is not bayonets, but books"—a belief heartily endorsed by Foote and other "Friends of the Indian."

Since the Lakota delegation arrived in Washington, DC less than three weeks after the association's annual meeting, both the recruitment of high-profile proponents and organization of the 11 February educational forum were necessarily done in haste. As such, the timing of Foote's letter to Clemens is suggestive. Might the writer's generosity in sending her a copy of *A Connecticut Yankee* two months earlier and indirectly assisting her agenda of advancing the civilization of Indians, "not [by] bayonets but books," have emboldened her to seek a more demonstrable expression of support through his presence at one of these very "public functions"?

Without question, Clemens would have been aware of both the massacre and the intense controversy that erupted in its aftermath by the time Foote's letter reached him in mid-January. News of the atrocity broke in the Eastern press on 30 December, the day after it occurred. The *New York Times* featured detailed daily coverage of the "battle" throughout the first half of the next month; the *Courant's* reportage began a bit later with the riveting eyewitness account of Dakota physician Charles Eastman on 9 January, three days before the writer left for Washington, DC. This front-page article, entitled "The Fight at Wounded Knee—What an Educated Indian Says about It," states,

> Thursday morning I visited the field of battle where those Indians were killed at Wounded Knee last Monday . . . I found eleven who were still living. Among them were two babies, about three months old, and an old woman who is totally blind, who was left for dead. Four of them were found out in the field . . . half-buried in the snow. It was a terrible and horrible sight to see women and children lie in groups dead. I suppose they were of one family. Some of the young girls [had] wrapped their heads with shawls and buried their faces in their hands. I suppose they did that so they wouldn't see the soldiers come up to shoot them. At one place there were two little children—one about one year old, the other about three—lying on their faces, dead, and about thirty yards from them a woman lay on her face dead. These were away from the camp about an eighth of a mile. In front of the tipis which were in a semi-circle lay dead most of the rest. Shells were thrown among the women and children so that they mutilated them most horribly.[95]

Extrapolating from the moral indignation Clemens had expressed five years earlier in response to the *Courant's* report about the New Mexico bounty on Apache scalps, his reaction to the even more grotesque barbarism described by Eastman is easily imagined. The sickening details of women, children, and babies indiscriminately shot in the back while fleeing for their lives may well have influenced the fervor with which he informs Foote, "I wish I could say yes—I would do it in a minute." The note expresses strong, unequivocal support for the unspecified event at which she asked him to "assist"—either as a spectator or perhaps in the more active role of speaker or toastmaster. He frames his regrets in terms of the withdrawal from public life dictated by Victorian protocols of mourning, indicating that he was not simply manufacturing an idle excuse to spare an old friend from disappointment. Clemens had in fact lost both his mother and mother-in-law the previous fall,[96] and declined a number of other social invitations during this period for presumably the same reason. His absence from the Sixth Annual Banquet of Ohio's Buckeye Society, held at Delmonico's on 6 February (about midway through the Lakota delegation's visit), was duly noted on the front page of the *New York Times:* "Letters of regret were read [at the dinner] from President Harrison, ex-President Cleveland, Governor Russell of Massachusetts and Mark Twain."[97]

The conspicuous inclusion of the writer's name among this prestigious company elucidates the possible motives underlying Foote's invitation. Knowing the expansive orbit of Twain's celebrity, she doubtlessly recognized that his presence at this (or any other) public affair would inevitably garner attention in the national press and enhance its visibility. Until Foote's original letter is recovered, however, this scenario of course remains purely—though compellingly—speculative. Nonetheless, since Twain never explicitly mentions Wounded Knee in either his published works or personal correspondence, the prospect of his willingness to take a stand—as he would so memorably at Carnegie Hall in 1906 on behalf of Booker T. Washington and the Tuskegee Institute—in support of the beleaguered Lakota is provocative.

Confirmation of this surmise would radically revise our understanding of the writer's antagonistic views toward American Indians, offering a sympathetic counterpoint to a series of oblique but troubling allusions concerning contemporary political events in *The American Claimant*. Clemens began composing this novel in early February 1891, just as the Lakota made their rounds in Washington, and may have unconsciously integrated details regarding the "Sioux Outbreak" into his narrative. In chapter 3, Washington Hawkins, currently living in Cherokee Strip—a location in Oklahoma's Indian Territory characterized by "depression, withered hopes, [and] poverty in all its varieties" (AC, 13)—visits his old friend Colonel Mulberry Sellers, whom his wife Polly describes as being much in demand at White House receptions. Sellers's latest invention—the "materialization" of departed spirits—also echoes and ironically inverts the spiritual objectives of the Ghost Dance. According to the Paiute prophet Wovoka, if enough Indians performed this ritual, a natural disaster, variously described as an earthquake or whirlwind, would cause the Anglo-American population to disappear. The natural world would then be restored to its pristine precontact state and the buffalo, along with the deceased ancestors of the tribe, would return. Sellers's "invention" reimagines this apocalyptic phenomenon as a commercial enterprise that will perpetuate the US Army's genocidal war against Indians by enlisting resurrected soldiers from classical antiquity:

> They will arise and walk. Walk?—they shall walk forever, and never die again. Walk with all the muscle and spring of their pristine vigor . . . I will dig up the Romans, I will resurrect the Greeks, I will furnish the Government, for ten millions a year, ten thousand veterans drawn from the victorious legions of all the ages—soldiers that will chase Indians year in and year out on materialized horses, and cost never a cent for rations or repairs. (AC, 28–29)

This analogy—whether intentional or otherwise—is reinforced by an early 1891 notebook entry concerning the "reduction & pacification of *all* Indian tribes" (NBJ3, 607) in reference to a book Captain John G. Bourke had written about serving in the West under General George Crook. Following Howells's recommendation that the volume was a good candidate for publication by Charles Webster and Company, Clemens sent his business partner Frederick Hall to "advance upon Captain Bourke straightway with Bible, tomahawk & scalping knife, & arrange terms—on a basis of peace or war" (MTHL, 634–35). Because the project never came to fruition, however, the potential light it might have shed on Twain's evolving attitudes toward Native Americans is indeterminate. Nonetheless, the piecemeal evidence that *does* exist from the decade between 1880 and 1890 documents a progressive—though uneven—liberalization of his racial views. As with the formative role of the Langdons in reshaping Clemens's views of African Americans, his newfound humanitarian interest in the fate of native peoples was achieved largely through the influence of Hartford friends and associates—primarily female reformers like Sara Kinney and Kate Foote but also men such as Joseph Hawley, Joe Twichell, and J. Hammond Trumbull, who enthusiastically supported the Connecticut Indian Association's assimilationist goals. The unwavering faith these individuals manifested in the Indians' capacity for integration into mainstream American society as productive, enfranchised citizens opened the writer's mind and prompted a gradual reassessment of his racial attitudes.

The ambivalence of Clemens's stance is illustrated in "The Esquimau Maiden's Romance," published in *Cosmopolitan* magazine in November 1893. Written to capitalize on popular fascination with the Chicago World's Columbian Exposition, which featured an "Eskimo Village" among its ethnological exhibits, the story centers around a conversation between the twenty-year-old Lasca, described as the "most bewitching girl of her tribe," and a first-person narrator traveling across the "lonely snow-plain" and "templed icebergs" of the polar regions, who is identified as "Mr. Twain." This fictional cross-cultural encounter is marked by mutual curiosity and respect; as "Twain" explains, "[Lasca] had been my daily comrade for a week, now, and the better I knew her the better I liked her. . . . I . . . found her company always pleasant and her conversation agreeable" (CT2, 118). He accompanies her on traditional hunts, professing admiration for her skills from a safe distance:

> I went fishing with her, but not in her perilous boat; I merely followed along on the ice and watched her strike her game with her fatally accurate spear. We went sealing together; several times I stood by while she and her family dug blubber from a stranded whale, and once I went part of the way when she was hunting a bear, but turned back before the finish, because at bottom I am afraid of bears. (CT2, 118–19)

She, in turn, is pleased by his interest, exclaiming, "Yes, I will tell you any-thing about my life that you would like to know, Mr. Twain ... for it is kind and good of you to like me and care to know about me." The intimacy of their friendship is visually represented in Francis Luis Mora's "Listening to Her History," which Frank Bliss commissioned as the frontispiece of vol-ume 23 of the *Uniform Edition of Mark Twain's Works* in 1903 (see fron-tispiece). Seated side by side on a large block of ice, their shoulders and knees touching, hands mutually extended in examination of the "jewel" suspended from Lasca's neck (in reality nothing but "a battered old N.Y. Central baggage-check" token), the camaraderie between the two figures is reflected in the ease of their physical proximity.

The narrator's affection for Lasca, whom he portrays as "honest," "sweet and natural and sincere" is nonetheless tempered by his ethnocentric con-descension toward the primitivism of her lifeways. Although she is the daughter of the tribe's wealthiest man, a "polar Vanderbilt," whose fortune consists of "*twenty-two fish-hooks—not* bone, but foreign—*made out of real iron,*" he disparages the food offered at "her father's hospitable trough" as unfit for human consumption. Throughout the story, the writer's char-acterization of Lasca utilizes stereotypical tropes of ignorance, uncleanli-ness, and disgusting dietary habits that date back to his depiction of Chief Hoop-de-doodle-do some three decades earlier. "Dreamily gnawing a candle-end" (CT2, 120), she informs the narrator, "Our tribes had a preju-dice against soap, at first, you know," to which he responds in disbelief, "'But pardon me. They *had* a prejudice against soap? Had?'—with falling inflection." The punch line is "Yes—but that was only at first; nobody would eat it." The narrator then envisions a feast of carrion, tar, turpentine, molasses, train oil, and whale blubber all "serve[d] up in a slush bucket" that prompts her to swoon with ecstasy.

The "romance" to which the story's title alludes is the tragic tale of Lasca's suitor, who was set adrift on an ice floe after being accused of steal-ing one of her father's treasured fishhooks. Nine months later, on "the day of the Great Annual Sacrifice when all the maidens of the tribe wash their faces and comb their hair" (CT2, 132), she discovers it entangled in her unkempt locks. Despite the incident's fateful outcome, it does produce a positive change in Lasca's personal hygiene: "Listen: from that day to this not a month goes by that I do not comb my hair" (CT2, 133). She thus progresses toward more acceptable Western standards of cleanliness but still falls far short of them.

According to Peter Messent, "The Esquimau Maiden's Romance" relies on "the humor of defamiliarization and incongruity" in measuring the values of Eskimo and mainstream US society against one another. "The ungrounding of the reader," he asserts, "caught in a type of cultural in-between place where neither [the] Eskimo nor American world is finally favored, is typical of one relativistic strand of Twain's comic vision."[98] This emerging sense of cultural relativism would become more pronounced during the writer's world lecture tour of 1895–96.

7. Indigenes Abroad

The Unseen Aboriginals of Australia

When Mark Twain embarked on his world lecture tour in the summer of 1895, he was a man dispossessed. Four years earlier, the looming specter of financial ruin—arising from both his investments in the ill-fated Paige Compositor and the declining revenues of his publishing firm, Charles L. Webster and Company—had caused the writer to shutter his beloved Hartford home and relocate to Europe in a desperate attempt to economize. Now, faced with the grim reality of personal bankruptcy, he made an even more painful decision to rend apart his family, leaving his oldest and youngest daughters in the care of Livy's sister Susan Crane as he undertook a grueling yearlong series of public performances on four continents in order to repay his creditors. Destitute and displaced, Clemens was, in a sense, colonized by debt—a circumstance instrumental in shaping his sympathetic response to the Aboriginal peoples he encountered while traveling through the Southern Hemisphere. Although he had witnessed the devastating effects of settler colonialism on native populations some thirty years before in Nevada Territory, he turned a blind eye to the dispossession of the Paiute, Shoshone, and Washoe at the time, viewing it with youthful indifference as an inevitable consequence of "progress." As Clemens toured Australia, Tasmania, and New Zealand in late 1895, however, the reversal of his own economic fortunes allowed him—for the very first time—to recognize and relate to the plight of indigenous peoples in imperial regimes.

Following the Equator charts the trajectory of these evolving racial views, chronicling the author's gradual shift from ideological identification with the European conqueror to the colonized "Other." In this respect, the text is more than a travelogue; it also tells a deeply personal story about the growth of his political consciousness and lays the philosophical groundwork for the fiercely anti-imperialist essays written after 1900. Clemens's peregrinations through the far-flung outposts of the British Empire caused him to question long-held assumptions about the binaries of "civilization" and "savagery" and the ethnocentric prerogative of Western nation-states to conquer less "advanced" peoples. These reflections fostered a newfound sense of cultural relativism, epitomized in his rueful pronouncement, "There are many humorous things in the world; among them the white man's notion that he is less savage than the other savages" (FE, 213).

This late-life racial epiphany—while unquestionably an important milestone in Twain's literary development—is also curiously selective, focused on the mistreatment of indigenous peoples abroad despite the many obvious links between their circumstances and those of Native Americans at the end of the nineteenth century. Indians hover at the fringes of the writer's consciousness throughout the world tour, cropping up in intermittent, offhand allusions; however, his published work never explicitly links the dispossession and attempted genocide of Aboriginal Australians and Tasmanians with their North American counterparts. Given Clemens's astute powers of observation, this omission cannot plausibly be attributed to inattention; rather, the comparison appears to have been deliberately resisted and repressed. Indeed, the paucity of information on this subject in *Following the Equator* suggests that he found it easier to critique the adverse effects of cultural hegemony overseas than to acknowledge the violent legacy of colonialism in his own land. And yet, even this claim may prove too facile considering the text's convoluted publication history and the fact that many hands—in addition to his own—played an integral role in its creation. Only by sifting through the extensive substrata of primary sources related to the book's composition—most notably, Twain's unpublished notebooks as well as drafts of both the manuscript and typescript—can the progression of these attitudes and the conundrum of his silence be accurately assessed and understood.

Following the Equator, as Dennis Welland has observed, is unique among Twain's works in that it was the only one written entirely in England.[1] Composed in a haze of grief during the months immediately after Susy's tragic death, the text was published simultaneously in London and Hartford on 12 November 1897 under two different titles, *More Tramps Abroad* and *Following the Equator*. But the disparities between the American and British editions extend far beyond their respective titles: *Following the Equator*, produced for the subscription market by the American Publishing Company, is lavishly illustrated with nearly two hundred drawings and photographs, whereas Chatto and Windus's *More Tramps Abroad*, priced at a modest six shillings, contains only three full-page illustrations and one small embedded diagram. A number of substantive differences exist in the content of the two editions as well. *Equator* comprises sixty-nine chapters versus seventy-two in *Tramps;* the maxims that head each chapter frequently vary; and occasional changes occur in wording and paragraph structure. "Each book," Welland notes, "omits substantial passages that are included in the other . . . and *More Tramps Abroad* is significantly longer than *Following the Equator.*"[2]

Additionally, since Twain was living overseas at the time of the work's publication, he more closely supervised the production of *More Tramps Abroad* than *Following the Equator.* He collaborated with editor Andrew Chatto on both the manuscript's revision and the correction of page proofs; Chatto also seems to have acted as the author's intermediary with Bliss, taking responsibility for forwarding the typescript to his American colleague.[3] Although Clemens was consulted regarding the artwork Bliss commissioned for the volume, there is no evidence that he actually saw all the illustrations before the book's publication, or that he even read—and more importantly, gave his imprimatur to—the radically altered version of the typescript Bliss prepared. On this basis, Welland argues, "There is every reason to adopt *More Tramps Abroad* as the authentic and authorised text . . . and *Following the Equator* as an abridged variant of it."[4]

Much of the material Bliss excised from *Following the Equator* consists of passages from secondary sources concerning the British mistreatment of Aboriginal peoples that Twain consulted as part of his background research. Even Chatto had balked at the excessive length of some of these quotations, as indicated in a note Clemens sent to his American publisher on 2 July 1897: "Yesterday Chatto & I ripped out a raft of reprint matter from the Australian part of the book; there is plenty of matter without it. It improves the book to leave it out. Chatto promised to write you, so that you can leave it out, too, if you like."[5] A comparison of the manuscript of *More Tramps Abroad,* housed in the Berg Collection at the New York Public Library, with the published text reveals that most of this "reprint matter" derives from *The Lost Tasmanian Race,* an 1884 work by Australian educator and historian James Bonwick (1817–1906), a self-described "friend to the poor Aborigine." Twain tore six pages out of his personal copy of Bonwick's text and inserted them wholesale into his manuscript, underlining certain sentences for emphasis and making minor changes in grammar and diction. While a small fraction of this material survives in *More Tramps Abroad* and even less in *Following the Equator,* the redacted excerpts are noteworthy for the detailed annotations Twain made in the margins. These comments, which are largely scratched out, indicating that the writer himself never intended them for publication, offer irrefutable proof that he recognized the parallels between the shameful abuses that British convicts had inflicted on Tasmanian Aboriginals and the mistreatment of American Indians by colonial settlers back home but chose not to address them in his work.

Although the exact date of this marginalia cannot be pinpointed, it seems likely that Twain acquired *The Lost Tasmanian Race* while touring Australia in September and October of 1895. He probably turned to it—along with other contemporary works like Rosa Campbell Praed's *Australian Life, Black and White* and Marcus Clarke's *For the Term of His Natural Life* on evenings when he was not lecturing, as well as during the periods of forced bed rest caused by his disabling carbuncles. The annotations are written in pencil but cancelled out in ink, revealing that he reviewed both the text and his commentary at some later point during the manuscript's composition in London. The Bonwick interpolation, therefore, offers an intriguing window into the stages of Twain's creative process, from the passionate, unbridled response of a private reader to the detached, cool-eyed assessment of a professional (and very public) writer, who delimited both the scope and tone of his work in anticipation of his audience's reaction.

Twain introduces Bonwick's work in chapter 28 of the *Tramps* manuscript with an authorial mandate, casting his readers as judges in an imaginary courtroom where the allegorical figures of "Christian" and "Savage" stand trial:

> Read the details; but read this remark of Mr. Bonwick's first and keep it in mind—for you are sitting in judgment, now, with Christian and Savage at the bar of your court: "To the great honour of these poor savages, be it recorded, they were content to fight with men. Not a single instance in early days is recorded of the outrage of a white woman, and women and children were then very rarely killed."[6]

The issue of sexual violence against white women—which the writer had long decried as the essence of savagery in works such as "The Noble Red Man," *The Adventures of Tom Sawyer*, "Huck Finn and Tom Sawyer among the Indians," and "The Californian's Tale"—recurs here with a key difference: the "savage" perpetrators of this unspeakable crime are British men, not indigenes. According to Bonwick, the Tasmanian Aboriginals displayed honor and restraint in their resistance to the incursions of European invaders—fighting male settlers but sparing women and children, whereas the behavior of the allegedly civilized convicts was indiscriminately barbaric.

The section of *The Lost Tasmanian Race* that Twain incorporated into his manuscript presents a series of atrocity tales, narrated by the convicts themselves, documenting the shocking brutality of their actions toward the island's indigenous population: "One man boasted that he had thrown an old woman upon the fire, and burnt her to death"; another confessed that "he had been in the habit of shooting the black Natives to feed his dogs"; while a third admitted to kidnapping a native woman and keeping "her chained up like wild beast, and, whenever he wanted her to do anything, [he] applied a burning stick, a firebrand snatched from the hearth, to her skin."[7] Without exception, Bonwick's stories portray the Aboriginals as innocent, unsuspecting victims, ambushed in the midst of quotidian activities like bathing and sleeping; the text presents the implacable fury of their vengeance against the colonists as a desperate—and ultimately doomed—attempt at self-preservation, rather than as evidence of innate savagery.

Twain responds to Bonwick's "catalogue of horrors" with moral outrage, denouncing the convicts as "Assassins"; however, the story that most appalled him was the unprovoked murder of a woman "far advanced in pregnancy," who had climbed a tree in order to escape pursuit by two British "sportsmen" out hunting birds. Once cornered, the "unfortunate creature" was shot at point-blank range; as Bonwick tersely reports, "A fearful scream was heard, and a premature birth took place."[8] This account, which Twain dubbed "the hideous incident of the tree," apparently reminded him of a similar, albeit unspecified, horror on the American frontier, as the note jotted alongside it suggests: "Our own modern dealings with the Indians seem to show that civilization is merely (temporarily) suppressed savagery."[9]

The significance of this marginalia cannot be overstated; in linking the British slaughter of Tasmanian Aboriginals to "our own modern dealings with the Indians," Twain acknowledges America's status as an imperial power, engaged in the same oppression and abuse of indigenous peoples as the colonial nation-states of Europe. He also expressly indicts contemporary US military policy rather than the indeterminate misdeeds of a remote past. Although the specific events to which Twain alludes are unclear, his words were written less than five years after the Wounded Knee massacre, when the Seventh Cavalry, behaving in much the same ruthless fashion as the early British settlers of Tasmania, "relentlessly hunted down and slaughtered"[10] hundreds of unarmed Lakota Ghost Dancers, the majority of them women and children. While this historical connection cannot be definitively established, the writer's cross-cultural analogy between the mistreatment of indigenes in the United States and Tasmania signals a shift in both his understanding of and sympathy for Native Americans.

When Twain revisited Bonwick's text in London a year later during the composition of *More Tramps Abroad*, he selected this annotation—to the exclusion of all others—for incorporation into the manuscript, affirming his recognition of its veracity. He did not transcribe the comment verbatim, however, but instead expanded and reframed it as a global critique of colonial conquest throughout history: "[Bonwick's] chapter is an indictment of the Human Race. Not of the English, not of the Spaniards, not of any particular group, tribe or division, but of the Race. Apparently Civilization is merely Suppressed Savagery."[11] While this revision amplifies the scope of Twain's original observation, it also paradoxically attenuates it in several ways. First, in order to make the comment more concise and aphoristic, he eliminates the parenthetical qualifier "temporarily." This change impacts the sentence's semantics by intimating that the boundary between civilized and savage behavior is less tenuous than originally alleged. Secondly, by shifting from lowercase letters to capitals, the writer reinforces the impression that "Civilization" and "Savagery" are fixed, dichotomous entities, characterized in Freudian terms by the superego's control—or lack thereof—over the primal urges of the id. But most importantly, Twain's revision obviates the sting of his original annotation by subsuming his censure of nineteenth-century US Indian policy into a condemnation of mankind's timeless capacity for violence and cruelty. This omission—a practice the writer would later refer to as "the lie of silent assertion" (CT2, 440)—minimizes the culpability of his countrymen for their abuse of Native Americans while highlighting the colonial transgressions of Britain and Spain.

Although Twain's ironic definition of civilization as "Suppressed Savagery" was eventually cut by Andrew Chatto, a fragment of the Bonwick interpolation published in chapter 28 of *More Tramps Abroad* attests to the cultural chauvinism of his stance. Seeking to explain the circumstances whereby the "pleasant," "friendly" demeanor of Tasmania's natives devolved into enmity, unleashing a deadly spiral of escalating violence and retaliation against the British colonists, the writer quotes a series of paragraphs from *The Lost Tasmanian Race*, then comments,

> The[se] incidents read like plagiarisms of our own early-day Indian tales, but not always. Very far from it.
>
> The English settlers in America were not convicts, but better men. There were a few convicts—white slaves—but so few that they hardly show in our history. In Tasmania there was a multitude of them; and they conducted themselves toward the natives after fashions which were never dreamed of by the American Englishmen. . . . Our ancestors stopped with killing; they did not deal in torture. (MTA, 172–73)

Twain's language here is fraught with unresolved tensions and contradictions. On the one hand, his curious use of the literary term "plagiarisms" acknowledges that the violent history of his own nation constitutes an antecedent for the tragedy that occurred decades later in Tasmania; the same destructive colonial paradigm plays out in both settings. And yet, having proposed this analogy, he scrambles to qualify—if not altogether deny—it, insisting, "Not always. Very far from it." Twain's evident discomfort in confronting the ignominious legacy of Indian-white relations is redoubled in the manuscript of *More Tramps Abroad*, where the phrase "very far from it" is repeated and intensified as "very, very far from it."[12] This repetition suggests a keen desire to distance the Englishmen who colonized North America from their compatriots in Tasmania. Yet in valorizing the superior moral fiber and restraint of these individuals, he rewrites—and patently falsifies—US history by insisting, "Our ancestors . . . did not deal in torture."

Frank Bliss excised this entire passage from *Following the Equator*, presumably because of practical concerns about the volume's length, rather than any qualms regarding its objectionable political content. Nonetheless, this revision, along with the other disparities between the American and British editions, raises a vexing question about the degree to which *either* published version of the text accurately reflects Twain's authorial intentions. Before peremptorily faulting the writer for overlooking the abundant parallels between the fate of Native Americans and the Aboriginal peoples of the Southern Hemisphere, the editing—and in some instances, complete elimination—of material from *The Lost Tasmanian Race* must be taken into consideration. The Bonwick marginalia document an incipient shift in Twain's racial consciousness that simmers beneath the surface of the manuscript but unfortunately never receives full expression in the finished work.

"A RED-HOT IMPERIALIST"

Although Andrew Chatto and Frank Bliss exercised considerable license in determining the amount of secondary source material incorporated into *More Tramps Abroad* and *Following the Equator*, a comparison of the manuscript and typescript reveals that they left Twain's own prose largely intact. Neither editor can therefore be held accountable for the narrative's oddly constrained political focus; that responsibility rests with Clemens alone. As Peter Messent observes in his 1993 essay, "Racial and Colonial Discourse in *Following the Equator*," the writer's "overall position on the colonial enterprise is not clear-cut," but "inconsistent" and "contradictory," vacillating between sympathy for the indigenous victims of imperialism and uncritical "hegemonic use of the rhetoric of 'progress.'"[13] The confusion Messent discerns in the text mirrors the fitful evolution of Twain's racial views over the course of his journey. Upon returning to the United States in October 1900 after a nearly decade-long absence, he informed a *New York Herald* reporter that the world lecture tour had been a profoundly transformative experience: "I left these shores, at Vancouver [in August 1895], a red-hot imperialist. I wanted the American eagle to go screaming into the Pacific. It seemed tiresome and tame for it to content itself with the Rockies."[14] While these words may seem hyperbolic, several notebook entries Clemens made during the summer of 1895, while traveling westward by rail toward his embarkation point for Australia, attest to his enthusiastic support of the doctrine of American expansionism:

> <u>Aug.</u> 6. Arrived at Spokane, Wash., 10 p.m. Full of energy & push. . . . Saw Flathead dude yesterday, on the Reservation. Every rag bran[d] new & splendid in color.
>
> <u>Aug.</u> 7. See squaws prowling about back doors & windows begging & foraging—a nuisance once familiar to me.[15]

These statements reflect a nonchalant, almost cavalier, disregard for the ways in which Native Americans had been adversely affected by colonization. At the time of Twain's visit, Spokane was a quintessential Western boomtown, the epicenter of a thriving lumber and mining industry. His thumbnail description of the city extols the capitalistic engine that drove westward expansion, then abruptly segues to the Flathead reservation, established northwest of the town some fourteen years earlier. The entry, however, does not acknowledge the complex interrelation between these two entities—namely, that Spokane's very existence is predicated upon the dispossession and displacement of the land's hereditary owners.

Moreover, Twain's flippant depiction of the young Flathead "dude" focuses on the superficial details of his garish, "bran new" western-style attire, without considering the economic and sociocultural pressures of assimilation that prompted the young man to abandon his traditional dress. This same lack of sympathy informs the writer's representation of the "begging and foraging" squaws he observes "prowling" on Spokane's perimeters, a sight that triggers unpleasant, long-forgotten associations with Nevada Territory. Twain's distaste is evident in his diction; rather than pitying the women's impoverishment or pondering its causes, he simply dismisses them as a "nuisance"—the nineteenth-century equivalent of homeless urban panhandlers.

In contrast to these notebook entries, a comment made Twain a week later suggests the emergence of a more tolerant, progressive perspective—at least on first glance: "<u>August</u> 15. 'Tacoma' is Indian & means breast (woman's) & is said to be justifiably descriptive; but the U.S., which is often an ass, has forced the dam [*sic*] French name Rainier—putting it in the maps."[16] This statement refers to a controversial 1890 decision by a federal agency, the United States Board of Geographic Names, officially replacing "Tacoma" with "Rainier," the appellation bestowed by British explorer George Vancouver in 1792 as a tribute to his friend Admiral Peter Rainier. This process of renaming epitomizes Patrick Wolfe's notion of the "logic of elimination," whereby settler colonial societies assert control over contested territory by erasing the presence of native people.[17] Twain's objection to the name change is not rooted in political indignation over the usurpation of Indian patrimony but in a pragmatic conviction that "Tacoma" is more befitting of the peak's rounded shape.[18] He remains oblivious to the underlying cultural implications of the word's etymology—that the equation of mountain and female breast reflects a traditional conception of land as an animate life source: Mother Earth.

Twain's colonial mindset is also reflected in the wry title, "At Homes," he devised to promote his lectures throughout the 1895–96 world tour. On the one hand, this oxymoron bespeaks the universality of the humorist's appeal, promising an evening of relaxed, informal entertainment, as if the genial raconteur were sharing stories with a group of intimate friends in his own parlor rather than performing in a commercial venue. On the other, it implies a linguistic definition of "home" grounded in the existence of a common language imposed through conquest. This conflation of Twain's transnational literary identity and England's dominion over its colonies is provocatively rendered in a sketch of his own hand, bearing the caption "The British Empire," which appears in both versions of the travelogue (fig. 18). As the statistics jotted at the bottom of the image indicate, the drawing's ostensible purpose is to help readers comprehend the relative vastness of the Russian and British Empires. Through a dramatic reduction in scale, the hegemony of these two world powers (which respectively controlled eleven million and eight million square miles of territory) is literally made manifest, corporealized in the shape of the writer's left hand as traced by his right. This melding of the geopolitical and personal, underscored by Twain's notation, "British Empire—the whole hand" (FE, 171), links the creative output of his pen with imperial domination.[19] The sketch—depicting the writer's empty hand, extended palm up in a gesture of expectation, waiting to be filled by the generosity of his colonial audiences—thus functions as a visual pun.

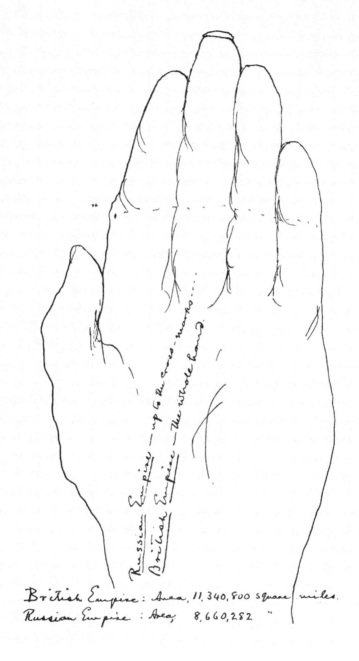

Russian Empire — up to the cross-marks.....

British Empire — the whole hand.

British Empire : Area, 11,340,800 square miles.
Russian Empire : Area; 8,660,282 "

FIGURE 18. "The British Empire," *Following the Equator*. Courtesy of the Mark Twain Project, The Bancroft Library, University of California, Berkeley.

Both versions of the published text jokingly acknowledge the grim financial impetus underlying the world lecture tour in a footnote appended to a discussion of Australia's exotic fauna: "A marsupial is a plantigrade vertebrate whose specialty is its pocket. In some countries it is extinct, in the others it is rare. The first American marsupials were Stephen Girard, Mr. Astor, and the opossum; the principal marsupials of the Southern Hemisphere are Mr. Rhodes, and the kangaroo. I, myself, am the latest marsupial. Also, I might boast that I have the largest pocket of them all. But there is nothing in that" (FE, 283).

Within the guise of this pseudoscientific explanation, the marsupial's pouch becomes a subversive metaphor for the possession of vast wealth; it is in this sense that two of the richest men in nineteenth-century America— banker Stephen Girard (1750–1831), who personally saved the US government from financial collapse during the War of 1812, and fur trader John Jacob Astor I (1763–1848)—qualify as members of the species. Twain also equates the marsupial's pocket with colonial expropriation of natural resources abroad, citing the example of British mining magnate Cecil Rhodes (1853–1902), whose fortune derived from South African diamonds. In a surprising twist, he then declares himself a marsupial "with the largest pocket of them all"—although in his case, that "pocket" is unfortunately empty. Through this ironic allusion to his personal bankruptcy, the writer admits the fundamentally imperial nature of his undertaking, capitalizing on the global reach of his celebrity in order to regain his financial footing. As his yearlong journey through Australia, New Zealand, India, and South Africa progressed, however, he would become increasingly mistrustful of colonial expansion—the tendency of "all the political establishments in the earth ... to [raid] each other's territorial-clotheslines ... and grab what they can of it as opportunity offers" (FE, 623).

THE SETTLER COLONIAL PARADIGM— AT HOME AND ABROAD

In both *More Tramps Abroad* and *Following the Equator*, Twain frequently uses the United States as a touchstone in describing Australia's size, topography, and climate. While this strategy is intended to render the exotic land "down under" more familiar to his readers, it also reveals the writer's unquestioned, and perhaps unconscious, presumption that his homeland represents the benchmark against which any modern polity is to be measured. Initially, these comparisons are grounded in objective data, such as his explanation that Australia's landmass is "about two-thirds as large as the United States was before we added Alaska" (FE, 116). Similarly, he states that Victoria, one of the provinces visited on the tour, is "80 times as large as the state of Rhode Island, and one-third as large as the State of Texas" (FE, 151). On a smaller, more comprehensible scale, he also humorously likens the distance between Melbourne and Sydney to the number of miles in a circuitous route from Boston to Buffalo (FE, 173). Even the colony's low death rate of "13 in the 1,000"—attributable, in Twain's estimation, to its mild temperatures—is characterized as "about half what it is in the city of New York" (FE, 190). These analogies suffuse the author's comments on diverse topics ranging from the architecture of Melbourne's business district, which he claims could easily pass "for a picture of the finest street in a large American city" (FE, 125), to the "dress, carriage, ways, pronunciation, inflections, [and] general appearance" of Australia's colonists. "The people have easy and cordial manners from the beginning—from the moment that the introduction is completed," he avers, insisting, "This is American" (FE, 129).[20]

As Twain's tour of New South Wales continues, these associations grow more subjective, evoking memories of people and places from his distant past; glimpsing a row of "tiny cabins" from the window of his train, he observes that the children clustered about the doorways were "rugged little simply-clad chaps that looked as if they had been imported from the banks of the Mississippi without breaking bulk" (FE, 154).[21] He also notes that a local meteorological phenomenon—the "hot wind [that] sweeps over Sydney sometimes"—has produced a rich legacy of tall tales akin to that concerning the "Washoe Zephyr" he experienced three decades earlier in the western United States: "A drawing room, the window of which has been carelessly left open during a dust-storm, is indeed an extraordinary sight. A lady who has resided in Dubbo for some years says that the dust lies so thick on the carpet that it is necessary to use a shovel to remove it." This incident, Twain remarks, "tallies very well with alkali dust-storm of Nevada, if you leave out the 'shovel' part. Still the shovel part is a pretty important part, and seems to indicate that my Nevada storm is but a poor thing, after all" (FE, 117).

This network of transnational correspondences breaks down, however, when Twain turns his attention to Australia's "picturesque" colonial past (FE, 169), despite its many striking similarities with the conquest of the American West. Both histories are quintessential examples of settler colonialism, a phenomenon in which "invasion is a structure not an event."[22] Because colonizers come to stay, they destroy in order to replace—seeking "the dissolution of native societies" in order to erect a new political order on the land base they have expropriated.²³ In Australia and the western United States, this invasion occurred precipitously and unfolded in a nearly identical pattern. For example, just as the 1859 discovery of the Comstock Lode precipitated a rapid influx of Euro-American fortune hunters into Nevada's Great Basin, displacing the indigenous population and irrevocably disrupting their traditional lifeways, the "first great gold strike" in Ballarat in 1851 also produced a flood of British emigrants to Australia. As Twain states in *Following the Equator,* "They had been coming as a stream, but they came as a flood, now. A hundred thousand people poured into Melbourne from England and other countries in a single month, and flocked away to the mines" (FE, 231).

Likewise, speculators soon "took hold" in both regions and "inaugurated a vast land scheme, [that] invited immigration, encouraging it with lurid promises of sudden wealth" (FE, 178). These "schemes" involved the frenzied extraction of natural resources through mining and caused comparable ecological devastation. The writer's description of the callous manner in which the "green and leafy paradise at Ballarat was soon ripped open, and lacerated and scarified and gutted, in the feverish search for its hidden riches" (FE, 232) uncannily evokes the "torn and guttered and disfigured" landscape of the Sierra Nevadas depicted in *Roughing It* (391), yet he draws no correlation between them. This omission is all the more perplexing in that Twain's "At Home" lectures in Australia regularly featured at least three excerpts from that text, "The Mexican Plug," "Grandfather's Old Ram," and "My Duel." His performances also often included two other sketches showcasing Western settings and themes: "Jim Baker's Blue Jay Yarn," from *A Tramp Abroad,* and "A Reminiscence of Artemus Ward," first developed as a platform piece back in 1871.²⁴ These frequent—sometimes nightly—reminders of Clemens's early prospecting days in Nevada Territory suggest that his refusal to explore these commonalities was a conscious decision, a deliberate aversion of his gaze.²⁵

Twain's silence speaks most volubly in his discussion of the appalling mistreatment of Australia's Aboriginals in *Following the Equator.* Although he vehemently critiques the colony's shameful legacy of disease, dispossession, violence, and erasure—declaring at one point, "The land belonged to *them*" (FE, 210)—he avoids any mention of the ways in which this paradigm replicates the plight of contemporary Native Americans. This curious combination of insight and blindness implies that the writer's subject position as a US citizen inhibited the development of a cross-cultural critique. The selectivity of his attention is perhaps best illustrated in the following statement: "With a country as big as the United States to live and multiply in, and with no epidemic diseases among them till the white man came with those and his other appliances of civilization, it is quite probable that there was never a day in his history when he could muster 100,000 of his race in all Australia" (FE, 207–8).

Even while acknowledging the comparable physical dimensions of the two landmasses, Twain stops short of linking the disastrous effect that so-called "virgin soil epidemics" had on American Indians, as well as on Australian natives. According to historian Alfred W. Crosby, the near absolute geographic isolation of indigenes in both the Western and Southern Hemispheres meant that they possessed no biological immunity to European diseases, such as smallpox, measles, malaria, typhus, and cholera, among others. Colonization produced an "epidemiological catastrophe"— in some cases, reducing these native populations by more than half.[26] Clemens in fact had firsthand knowledge of this problem, having reported in the *Territorial Enterprise* on a deadly 1863 outbreak of smallpox among the Washoe Indians caused by the gift of a white man's infected shirt (ETS1, 406). He also feared being a source of infection himself, musing in an 1866 notebook entry made en route to the Sandwich Islands, "15th [March] Thursday—Mumps—mumps—mumps—it was so decided to-day—a d—d disease that children have—I suppose I am to take a new disease to the Islands & depopulate them, as all white men have done heretofore" (NBJ1, 189). These personal associations are suppressed in the travelogue, which focuses exclusively on the destruction wrought in Australia by the introduction of Old World pathogens:

> The white man knew ways of reducing a native population 80 percent in 20 years. The native had never seen anything as fine as that before. . . . By the best official guess there were 4,500 aboriginals in [Victoria] when the whites came along in the middle of the 'Thirties. Of these, 1,000 lived in Gippsland, a patch of territory the size of fifteen or sixteen Rhode Islands. . . .The two Melbourne tribes could muster almost 300 when the white man came; they could muster but twenty, thirty-seven years later, in 1875. In that year there were still odds and ends of tribes scattered about the colony of Victoria, but I was told that natives of full blood are very scarce now. (FE, 208–9)

These bleak statistics evoke the popular American myth of the "Vanishing Red Man"; on both continents, European colonists believed that indigenous peoples were destined to "diminish," "fade," and ultimately disappear as the march of civilization advanced. The transnational analogy is self-evident but nonetheless remains latent; in this respect, the passage corroborates Peter Messent's observation that while Twain's writing on race in *Following the Equator* "operates over and over in a culturally self-reflexive manner . . . his awareness of the American racial theme is, at best, intermittent and . . . often unconscious."[27] The text exhibits the same "displaced expression" that Amy Kaplan identifies in Twain's 1866 letters from Hawaii, indirectly registering political parallels with US history that the author cannot bring himself to articulate.[28]

This repressed American subtext grows more insistent in Twain's discussion of the brutal means employed by British settlers to wrest territory away from Australia's Aboriginals. He traces the origins of this genocidal violence to a fundamental European misconception, explaining that since "the early whites were not used to savages," they regarded the ancient principle of collective responsibility—"if a man do you a wrong, his whole tribe is responsible"—as a "monstrous thing." On this basis, the British determined that "extermination seemed to be the proper medicine for such creatures" (FE, 209). This same argument was routinely made in frontier newspapers regarding the dispossession of American Indians; indeed, Twain himself had given voice to this racist sentiment in two early sketches. In "The Facts Concerning the Recent Resignation" (1867), a former clerk of the "Senate Committee on Conchology" cavalierly jokes about the extermination of the Plains tribes, informing the secretary of war, "Nothing [is] so convincing to an Indian as a general massacre" (CT1, 241). This indifference to the intrinsic humanity of "savages" is more starkly expressed by the narrative persona of "The Noble Red Man" (1870) who asserts—without a trace of humor—that the Indian is "nothing but a poor, filthy, naked scurvy vagabond, whom to exterminate were a charity to the Creator's worthier insects and reptiles which he oppresses" (CT1, 443).

Subliminal associations with the American frontier also inform Twain's description of the dingo he sees at the Adelaide Zoological Gardens. The fate of this wild dog, "present in great force when the whites first came to the continent . . . [which] is hunted, now, just as if he were a wolf," parallels that of his indigenous human counterparts: "He has been sentenced to extermination, and the sentence will be carried out. This is all right, and not objectionable. The world was made for man—the white man" (FE, 185–86). The writer's tacit equation of dingo and Aboriginal—categorizing them as "wild things, human or animal" (FE, 185–86)—echoes his comparison of "cayotes" and their "first cousins, the desert-frequenting tribes of Indians" in *Roughing It*, though with one crucial difference. Twain's sympathetic view of the captive Australian canine, which he deems "a beautiful creature—shapely, graceful, a little wolfish in some of his aspects, but with a most friendly eye and sociable disposition" (FE, 185), stems largely from the fact that Britain's colonization of Australia was a fait accompli by the time of his 1895 visit. The dingo's status as a zoological specimen marks it as a living relic—an impotent, iconic casualty of progress. In contrast, the free-ranging coyote, viewed from the window of Twain's Nevada-bound stagecoach in 1861, elicits visceral contempt and unease. He is a repulsive creature—"a long, slim, sick and sorry-looking skeleton . . . with a despairing expression of forsakenness and misery [and] a furtive and evil eye" (RI, 30–31).

Distance—temporal, cultural, and aesthetic—undergirds Twain's paradoxical responses to these two indigenous species (*Canis lupus* and *Canis latrans,* respectively). As a foreigner, immune from the adverse economic consequences caused by the dingo's predatory raids on colonial sheep-runs, undertaken "to appease his hunger," he can lament its captivity, diminished numbers, and impending extinction from a detached, philosophical perspective. The carrion-eating "cayote," on the other hand, subsisting "almost wholly on the carcases of oxen, mules and horses that have dropped out of emigrant trains and died, and upon windfalls of carrion, and occasional legacies of offal bequeathed to him by white men who have been opulent enough to have something better to butcher than condemned army bacon" (RI, 33), inhabits a contested landscape in the throes of active colonization. Its hunger—both for sustenance and autonomous space—is, in Twain's estimation, insatiable: "The cayote," he declares, "is a living, breathing allegory of Want." Clemens's personal involvement in the nation's westward expansion positions him as an "agent of colonialism"—albeit a relatively minor player—who simultaneously bears witness to and participates in the transformations taking place before his eyes.[29] He perceives the proximity of both cayotes and their human "relations" as a menace to the civilizing process itself: "The cayote, and the obscene bird [raven], and the Indian of the desert, testify their blood kinship with each other in that they live together in the waste places of the earth on terms of perfect confidence and friendship, while hating all other creatures and yearning to assist at their funerals" (RI, 34).

The enmity Twain ascribes to the cayote, raven, and Indian reflects the conflict and polarization inevitably arising from territoriality—access to, physical occupation of, and eventual domination over the land. These three indigenous species fiercely defend their habitat, opposing the incursion of "all other creatures," including Euro-American emigrants, with hatred and murderous rage. In this regard, territoriality—or the absence thereof—explains not only the writer's disparate responses to the dingo and cayote but also why the humanitarian concern he expresses for Australia's Aboriginals in *Following the Equator* does not extend to the comparable plight of American Indians. Even decades after his residence in the West, Twain—in keeping with his stance as a self-described "red-hot imperialist"—apparently remained so deeply enmeshed in the ideology of Manifest Destiny that he could not relinquish his youthful perceptions of Native Americans as a feared and despised enemy. The selectivity of his sympathy is reflected in a September 1895 interview with a Melbourne reporter, in which he mourns the demise of the buffalo on the Great Plains, yet makes no mention of the devastating impact this loss had on the Plains tribes, whose lives and cultural identity were inextricably intertwined with these animals: "There are no buffaloes in America now, except Buffalo Bill. . . . I can remember the time when I was a boy, when buffaloes were plentiful in America. You had only to step off the road to meet a buffalo. But now they have been all killed off. Great pity it is so. I don't like to see the distinctive animals of a country killed off."[30]

Territoriality looms especially large in Twain's discussion of the attempted extermination of Australia's Aboriginals in *Following the Equator*. He recounts this troubling history through a series of illustrative quotations from *Australian Life, Black and White*—Rosa Campbell Praed's 1885 memoir of growing up on a remote cattle station in Queensland. The writer used this work in a subtler manner than James Bonwick's *The Lost Tasmanian Race;* rather than simply pasting whole pages of uninterrupted text into his manuscript, he selected and transcribed individual paragraphs longhand, integrating them into an overarching analytical framework. The time and effort involved in this process deepened Twain's emotional response to the abuses Praed chronicles, producing a mounting crescendo of rage.

He introduces *Australian Life, Black and White* with offhanded under-statement, declaring that it provides "informing pictures of the early strug-gles of the white and the black to reform each other" (FE, 209). This euphe-mism serves to amplify the horror of the genocidal violence which the text relates. When the British first arrived in the colony, she explains, "the natives retreated before [them]"; however, "as the number of squatters increased, each one taking up miles of country," they displaced and progres-sively impoverished the local indigenous population. In order to survive, "hostile tribes" of starving Aboriginals began raiding "shepherds' huts and stockmen's camps," outposts set amidst the vast "loneliness of the Australian bush." With the inexorable growth of the colonial presence, "the Blacks' depredations became more frequent and murder was no unusual event" (FE, 209).

Although Praed's diction echoes the racial discourse of the American frontier, Twain once again avoids any comparison with the colonization and dispossession of American Indians. He dissociates himself from Praed's story by presenting the phenomenon of Australian settler colonialism as a dramatic performance, announcing that "more promising materials for a tragedy could not have been collated" (FE, 210). Australia's "primeval forest ... a solitude [alive with] the strange sounds of reptiles, birds, and insects" thus becomes a stage set—"the theater for the drama." The writer assumes the role of spectator, impassively watching the enactment of a deterministic cultural script. Once the "curtain" is raised, the action begins:

> There was a plenty of cattle, the black natives were always ill-nourished and hungry. The land belonged to *them*. The whites had not bought it, and couldn't buy it; for the tribes had no chiefs, nobody in authority, nobody competent to sell and convey; and the tribes themselves has no comprehension of the idea of transferable ownership of land. The ousted owners were despised by the white interlopers, and this opinion was not hidden under a bushel. . . . Let Mrs. Praed speak:

> > "At Nie Nie Station, one dark night, the unsuspecting hut-keeper, having, as he believed, secured himself against assault, was lying wrapped in his blankets sleeping profoundly. The Blacks crept stealthily down the chimney and battered in his skull while he slept."

> One could guess the whole drama from that little text. The curtain was up. It would not fall until the mastership of one party or the other was determined—and permanently:

> > "There was treachery on both sides. The Blacks killed the Whites when they found them defenseless, and the Whites slew the Blacks in a wholesale and promiscuous fashion which offended my childish sense of justice. . . . They were regarded as little above the level of brutes, and in some cases *were destroyed like vermin.*" (FE, 210)

Praed's description of the bloodshed that characterized the Australian colonial encounter closely parallels the degenerative cycles of violence and reprisal that occurred between Indians and whites in the West.[31] In both settings, European "interlopers" justified the expropriation of indigenous land by denouncing its "ousted owners" as "vermin." This dehumanizing simile is italicized in both *More Tramps Abroad* and *Following the Equator* but not in Praed's original, indicating that Twain himself added the typographical emphasis. Because this pejorative was commonly applied to Indians in the West—most infamously by Colonel John Chivington, who rationalized his militia's indiscriminate murder of Cheyenne women and children at the 1864 Sand Creek massacre with the statement "Nits make lice"[32]—he must have anticipated that this passage would resonate with his stateside audience.

Twain then quotes Praed's gruesome story of an anonymous squatter who invited some Aboriginals to a Christmas feast in 1856, where he poisoned them en masse with a "great pudding . . . sweetened with sugar and arsenic" (FE, 211), a toxin traditionally used to kill rats. This atrocity provokes a passionate tirade in which he argues that the squatter's unconscionable cruelty was in fact merciful, providing a "swifter and much more humane method" of death than other methods of extermination "sanctified by custom" (FE, 211). As Peter Messent has observed, this passage "reads like a direct commentary on his own country's history . . . register[ing] in a way that relates both to American Indians and to African Americans, [yet] neither group, nor America as a location, is specified."[33] His generic allusion to "many countries" offers a global indictment of colonialism rather than a critique of one particular nation-state:

> In many countries we have chained the savage and starved him to death; and this we do not care for, because custom has inured us to it; yet a quick death by poison is lovingkindness to it. In many countries we have burned the savage at the stake; and this we do not care for, because lovingkindness has inured us to it; yet a quick death is lovingkindness to it. In more than one country we have hunted the savage and his little children and their mother with dogs and guns through the woods and swamps for an afternoon's sport . . . but this method we do not mind, because custom has inured us to it; yet a quick death by poison is lovingkindness to it. In many countries we have taken the savage's land from him, and made him our slave, and lashed him every day . . . and made death his only friend . . . and this we do not care for, because custom has inured us to it; yet a quick death by poison is lovingkindness to it. (FE 212)

The key stylistic signature of this passage is Twain's repeated use of the portmanteau word "lovingkindness," coined by Bishop Miles Coverdale, who produced the first vernacular English translation of the Bible in 1535. This term, which occurs repeatedly throughout the King James version of the Old Testament, familiar to Clemens from his youth, corresponds to the Hebrew "chesed," referring to Yahweh's love for the chosen people of Israel.[34] "Lovingkindness"—in distinction to more generic notions of compassion and benevolence—denotes the divine forgiveness exhibited to, but unmerited by, sinners. It appears most memorably as a refrain in every line of Psalm 136, expressing thanks to the Lord whose "lovingkindness endures forever." Twain's usage parodies the psalm, creating a subversive analogy in which the anonymous squatter assumes the role of Yahweh, and Australia's Aboriginals represent His chosen people.

Toward the end of this passage, Twain contrasts the perverse innovation of the squatter's action with the endemic economic exploitation of native peoples by the British in South Africa and the French in the Melanesian archipelago of New Caledonia. He condemns the "Rhodes-Beit millionaires ... and Dukes in London," whose "comfortable consciences" remain untroubled by these time-honored imperial practices, then singles out the French colonial governor "M. Feillet," who "forcibly expropriated" Kanaka cultivators from New Caledonia's most fertile plantations as an incentive to potential European emigrants: "Such immigrants as could be induced to cross the seas thus found themselves in possession of thousands of coffee, cocoa, banana, and bread-fruit trees, the raising of which had cost the wretched natives years of toil, whilst the latter had a few five-franc pieces to spend in the liquor stores of Noumea" (FE, 213).

Dismissing the much-vaunted goals of "progress" and "civilization" used by Western nations to justify their conquest of less advanced societies, he denounces imperialism as "robbery, humiliation, and slow, slow murder, through poverty and the white man's whiskey. The savage's gentle friend, the savage's noble friend, the only magnanimous and unselfish friend the savage has ever had, was not there with the merciful swift release of his poisoned pudding" (FE, 213). Within the broad sweep of this censure, the writer's allusion to "the white man's whiskey" inevitably evokes the deleterious effects of alcohol on Native Americans; yet once again, by omission, the United States is tacitly exempted from his indictment. This technique, as Amy Kaplan notes, is also present in Twain's early writings on Hawaii, allowing him to "defer" troubling memories of the mistreatment of American Indians while simultaneously offering a "form for their displaced expression."[35]

THE LIMITS OF THE TOURISTIC GAZE

"The things which interest us when we travel," Twain observes in *Following the Equator* "are, first, the people; next, the novelties; and finally the history of the places and countries visited" (FE, 164). By his own admission, Australia's Aboriginals fall squarely into the second category; he deems them "marvelously interesting creatures" (FE, 221) whom he regrets— all the more acutely in retrospect—not having the opportunity to see firsthand. The writer's characterization of Aboriginals as "the prize-curiosity of all the races" (FE, 215) reflects a cultural notion of Otherness dating back to the Renaissance. During the golden age of European exploration, the term *curiosity* denoted interest in the unfamiliar without qualification or judgment; however, as Conal McCarthy explains in *Exhibiting Maori: A History of Colonial Cultures of Display,* by the mid-nineteenth century, it had acquired the pejorative connotations of "odd, bizarre, and exotic"[36] and become a signifier of the myriad deficiencies of non-European peoples in relation to the standards of western civilization. This etymology clearly informs Twain's comment that while traveling through Australia,

> We saw birds, but not a kangaroo, not an emu, not an ornithorhyncus [platypus], not a lecturer, not a native. Indeed, the land seemed quite destitute of game. But I have misused the word native. In Australia it is applied to Australian-born whites only. I should have said that we saw no Aboriginals—no "blackfellows." And to this day I have never seen one. In the great museums you will find all the other curiosities, but in the curio of chiefest interest to the stranger all of them are lacking. We have at home an abundance of museums, and not an American Indian in them. It is clearly an absurdity, but it never struck me before. (FE, 155)

In this passage, Australia's indigenous inhabitants are dehumanized and objectified as "game." Their status is further diminished through an act of linguistic preemption—the appropriation of "native" identity by the first generation of Australian-born whites. Individual birthright overrides and erases the collective patrimony of countless generations, reducing the Aboriginal population to a position of marginality as reviled "blackfellows." This clarification of nomenclature is transcribed directly from one of the writer's notebooks, suggesting that the information was supplied by one of his colonial hosts: " 'Aboriginal' means what it says. 'Native' means a <u>white</u> native-born."[37]

Although he makes no mention of it in the travelogue, Twain had reported on a similar phenomenon in a December 1862 *Enterprise* article announcing the formation of "The Pah-Utes," a fraternal association of Anglo-American pioneers who emigrated to Nevada Territory before the 1860 gold rush (ETS1, 169). In both Australia and the western United States, colonial invaders sought to legitimize their claim to territory through a symbolic—albeit spurious—assertion of indigeneity that tacitly supersedes the rights and very existence of its original inhabitants. "Pah-Utes" thus supplant Paiutes, just as the sons and daughters of the first British emigrants to Australia usurp the title of "native." The writer's off-handed reference to American Indians in the closing lines of the passage, however, indicates his awareness of the parallels between these two indigenous groups. Commenting on the "absurdity" of their absence—as stuffed taxidermic specimens—from museums on both continents, he suggests that Aboriginals and Indians are relics of a vanished past, who have no place or active role in modern society.

This linguistic distinction between "natives" and "blacks" in *Following the Equator* is a key factor in the racial epiphany Twain experienced during the world lecture tour. Before visiting Australia, he regarded these groups as separate, fixed, and mutually exclusive entities—the former, savage, wild, and menacing and the other, tractable, oppressed, and deeply sympathetic. The illustrations he encountered, however, in sources such as Robert Brough Smythe's 1878 authoritative anthology *The Aborigines of Australia* and Philip Chauncey's 1880 *Notes and Anecdotes of the Aborigines of Australia* revealed that these indigenes bore far closer physical resemblance to African Americans than Indians in terms of their complexion, physiognomy, and hair texture. This point is underscored by the dignified image of a Tasmanian woman, Truganina, that Elisha Bliss inserted into chapter 27 of the travelogue with the poignant, vaguely Cooperian caption, "The Last of her Race." The outward appearance of Australia's Aboriginals confounded the writer's racial constructs, disrupting the familiar binaries of native and black. The sympathy Clemens expresses for Australia's indigenous peoples may thus be unconsciously rooted in a compassionate view of African Americans dating back to his earliest memories. As he recalls in his *Autobiography,*

> [On the Quarles Farm] We had a faithful and affectionate good friend, ally and adviser in "Uncle Dan'l," a middle-aged slave whose head was the best one in the negro-quarter, whose sympathies were wide and warm, and whose heart was honest and simple and knew no guile. . . . It was on the farm that I got my strong liking for his race and my appreciation of certain of its fine qualities. This feeling and this estimate have stood the test of sixty years and more and have suffered no impairment. The black face is as welcome to me now as it was then. (A1, 211–12)

In addition to information culled from printed sources, Twain gained knowledge of Aboriginal habits and character from informal conversations with the so-called Old Settlers, distinguished survivors of the first generation of British emigrants from the 1830s. The elegiac tenor of their statements reflects "imperialist nostalgia," a term coined by anthropologist Renato Rosaldo to describe the "pose of innocent yearning" adopted by agents of colonialism in expressing regret for the loss of traditional cultures that they themselves have intentionally altered or destroyed in the name of "progress." This sentiment, Rosaldo explains, "revolves around a paradox: a person kills somebody, and then mourns the victim," thereby distancing—and obliquely exonerating—himself from any responsibility for the murder. "Imperialist nostalgia" serves as a mask concealing the complicity of these colonial agents with the processes of destruction[38]—a stance epitomized in the words of an Old Settler whom Twain meets at a banquet in Adelaide: "He thought [the Aboriginals] intelligent—remarkably so in some directions—and he said that along with their unpleasant qualities they had some exceedingly good ones; and he considered it a great pity that the race had died out. He instanced their invention of the boomerang and the 'weet-weet' as evidences of their brightness" (FE, 193–94).

The "great pity" expressed by the Old Settler absolves him of any role in—or responsibility for—the Aboriginals' fate. Although *Following the Equator* contains abundant evidence to the contrary, Twain nonetheless seems to embrace this premature postmortem, announcing, "To all intents and purposes [the poor creature] is dead—in the body; but he has features that will live on in literature" (FE, 215–16). Indeed, he exclaims, "why, a literature might be made out of the aboriginal all by himself, his character and ways are so freckled by varieties. . . . You do not need to invent any picturesquenesses; whatever you want in that line he can furnish you; and they will not be fancies or doubtful, but realities and authentic" (FE, 214). He views Australia's indigenous population through the culturally proscribed lens of the "picturesque," a middle ground between the beautiful and sublime. This aesthetic category was introduced in William Gilpin's 1782 book, *Observations on the River Wye*, which encouraged British tourists to cultivate an appreciation for quaint rustic scenes or "rough" objects characterized by irregular form. While Twain's familiarity with this work cannot be documented, he clearly understood—and aptly applied—Gilpin's dictum that the "picturesque" is created by "uniting in one whole a variety of parts."[39] He uses the many "freckled varieties" of Aboriginal traits to construct an archetypal "Everyman" who embodies all the contradictions of human nature—at once cowardly and brave, treacherous and loyal, cruel and kind, solitary and sociable.

This pattern of dichotomies recalls the discourse of Twain's 1870 sketch "The Noble Red Man," which counters the idealized literary image of the American Indian as "a being to fall down and worship" with his contemptible counterpart in real life. Ironically, while the writer categorically rejected the representation of Native Americans as "Noble Savages" on the basis of his limited eyewitness observation in Nevada Territory, as a tourist he uncritically accepts the existence of these paradoxical traits among Australia's indigenous peoples solely on the authority of secondhand evidence: "In his history, as preserved by the white man's official records, he is everything—everything that a human creature can be. He covers the entire ground. He is a coward—there are a thousand facts to prove it. He is brave—there are a thousand facts to prove it. He is treacherous—oh, beyond imagination! he is faithful, loyal, true—the white man's records supply you with a harvest of instances of it that are noble, worshipful, and pathetically beautiful" (FE, 214).

As in his discussion of the lovingkindness of the squatter who dispensed the poisoned Christmas pudding, Twain employs rhetorical repetition to underscore his point, insisting "there is proof of it" or "it is of record" after every antithetical attribute he identifies. Yet rather than impugning the reliability of his sources, he embraces these contradictions as further validation of the Aboriginal's status as the "prize curiosity of all the races."

The two traits Twain deems most "literary" about the Australia's indigenous population—their exceptional athletic prowess and preternatural tracking skills—also present him with a vexing conundrum. How, he wonders, can the mental acuity required to perform such acts be reconciled with the ethnocentric notion of an inferior "savage" intellect? Citing the seemingly impossible achievement of an "expert aboriginal," who threw a weet-weet (a small lightweight wooden implement traditionally used for hunting birds) an astonishing two hundred and twenty yards, he reflects, "What is the secret of the feat? No one explains. It cannot be physical strength, for that could not drive such a feather-weight any distance. It must be art" (FE, 207).

The writer is even more deeply perplexed by the Aboriginals' ability to track lost people and animals over terrain containing no discernible trace of their presence, through scrub "seamless as a blanket" and across "patches of bare rock and over alluvial ground which had to all appearance been washed clear of footprints" (FE, 174). This skill is of course identical to that displayed by the Indians of Cooper's *Leatherstocking Tales;* however, what elicits Twain's astonishment in Australia prompts only derision in the fiction of his fellow countryman. In "Fenimore Cooper's Literary Offences," published just a month before the writer departed for the Southern Hemisphere, he famously decried the myriad "crass stupidities" foisted upon readers of *The Deerslayer,* quoting a passage in which the Delaware chieftain Chingachgook "has lost the trail of a person he is tracking through the forest" as a prime example:

> Apparently that trail is hopelessly lost. Neither you nor I could ever
> have guessed out the way to find it. It was very different with
> [Chingachgook who] . . . was not stumped for long. He turned a running
> stream out of its course, and there, in the slush in its old bed, were that

person's moccasin- tracks. The current did not wash them away, as it would have done in all other like cases—no, even the eternal laws of Nature have to vacate when Cooper wants to put up a delicate job of woodcraft on the reader. (CT2, 183).

The divergence in Twain's responses—a willing suspension of disbelief regarding the abilities of Australia's indigenes, on the one hand, versus a refusal to concede even the legitimacy of Cooper's creative license (let alone the reality of this trait), on the other—stems largely from the relative intelligence he ascribed to each group. "In the matter of intellect," he remarks in the 1895 essay, "the difference between a Cooper Indian and the Indian that stands in front of the cigar shop in not spacious. . . . There was seldom a sane one among them" (CT2, 185–86). Conversely, he declares that "the aboriginal tracker's performances evince a craft, a penetration, a luminous sagacity, and a minuteness and accuracy of observation in the matter of detective-work not found in nearly so remarkable a degree in any other people, white or colored" (FE, 174). Only after describing the Aboriginal hunter's ability to examine a tree trunk covered with opossum scratches and ascertain whether the animals "*went up the night before without coming down again or not*" (FE, 218) does he acknowledge the association with American Indians, stating, "Fennimore Cooper lost his chance. He would have known how to value these people. He wouldn't have traded the dullest of them for the brightest Mohawk he ever invented" (FE, 218). This allusion—abrupt, fleeting, and undeveloped—offers yet another example of the way in which the subliminal topic of American Indians occasionally breaks through to the narrative's surface, only to be quickly resubmerged.

Twain further lauds the extraordinary intelligence of the Australian Aboriginals by relating a case in which a tracker is able to find a lost cow by identifying its hoofprint amidst a herd of others. "Wherein does one cow-track differ from another?" he asks. "There must be a difference, or the tracker could not have performed the feat; a difference minute, shadowy, and not detectible by you or me, or by the late Sherlock Holmes, and yet discernible by a member of a race charged by some people with occupying the bottom place in the gradations of human intelligence" (FE, 175). At some unspecified point after the travelogue's publication in 1897, the writer revisited this anecdote, making extensive annotations in his personal copy of *More Tramps Abroad*.[40] His marginalia—a series of brackets, strike-throughs, X marks in the margins, and occasional rewording—may represent unrealized plans for a lecture or public reading; despite the obscurity of Twain's intent, one remark is particularly germane. He underscored the last three lines quoted above beginning with the word "yet" and added a note beneath them, repudiating the assertion that the Aboriginal occupies "the bottom place in the gradations of human intelligence" in three terse monosyllables: "He does not."[41]

Regrettably, the conclusion Twain reaches in both *More Tramps Abroad* and *Following the Equator* is far less progressive than that indicated by his later commentary. After defending Australia's natives against the "low-rate intellectual reputation" ascribed to them by Westerners—insisting that "there must have been a large distribution of acuteness among those naked skinny aboriginals, or they couldn't have been such unapproachable trackers and boomerangers and weet-weeters" (FE, 207)—he then succumbs to the very "race-aversion" he critiques, declaring, "They were lazy—always lazy. . . . They went naked and houseless, and lived on fish and grubs and worms and wild fruits, and were just plain savages, for all their smartness" (FE, 207).

In dismissing Aboriginals as "just plain savages," Twain reduces them to a generic, universal type; like other primitive peoples across the globe— including American Indians—they possess the ability to "make fire by friction" and are able to stoically withstand "a good deal of physical pain." This essentialist perspective is, however, riddled with contradictions; for example, after stating that "all savages draw outline pictures on bark," the writer then singles out Aboriginal drawings for their exceptional technical accuracy and spirited expression: "As an untaught wielder of the pencil it is not likely that he has his equal among savage people" (FE, 218). A marginal note in Twain's manuscript, addressed presumably to Andrew Chatto, states, "Insert here some of his pictures from R. Brough Smythe's *Aborigines of Victoria.*" Ever wary of escalating costs, Chatto countermanded this directive, instructing his production staff, "Omit these illustrations CTW." Undeterred, Clemens added a third note—this time to Frank Bliss—offering pragmatic advice about where to secure Smythe's work in the United States: "Get it at Watkinson Library [located at Hartford's Trinity College] or Astor Library [a private research collection consolidated into the New York Public Library in 1895]."[42] Although Bliss readily acceded to a number of the writer's other recommendations regarding illustrations for *Following the Equator*,[43] he ignored this one, instead commissioning an original gouache from Daniel Carter Beard entitled "His Place in Art" (fig. 19). This decision was not dictated by cost but rather by the publisher's evident disinterest in the subject of Australia's indigenous peoples, as indicated in a snide editorial comment jotted on a small slip of paper now bound into the Berg manuscript: "Another wearisome chapter on aboriginals. All dead now. Fr B."[44]

FIGURE 19. "His Place in Art," *Following the Equator.*
Courtesy of the Mark Twain Project, The Bancroft Library,
University of California, Berkeley.

The substitution of Beard's gouache for illustrations from *The Aborigines of Victoria* realigns—and, to some extent, distorts—the text's intended focus. Rather than showcasing the indigenous drawings themselves, the image emphasizes the writer's assessment of their aesthetic merit in relation to the canon of Western art. Twain's description gleefully upends the distinction between fine and commercial art, pronouncing the work of *Punch* cartoonist George du Maurier (1834–96) superior to that of the Quattrocento master Sandro Botticelli and positioning the Aboriginal artist halfway between them:

> His art is not to be classified with savage art at all, but on a plane two degrees above it and one degree above the lowest plane of civilized art. To be exact, his place in art is between Botticelli and De Maurier [*sic*]. That is to say, he could not draw as well as De Maurier but better than Botticelli. . . . His "corrobboree" of the Australian wilds reappears in De Maurier's Belgravian ballrooms, with clothes and the smirk of civilization added; Botticelli's "Spring" is the corrobboree further idealized, but with fewer clothes and more smirk. (FE, 218–19)

In placing the figure of the Aboriginal artist at the center of his illustration, Beard literalizes Twain's ranking but simultaneously undermines it through the addition of several humorous details not found in the accompanying prose. Whereas the text stresses commonalities, the gouache highlights unmistakable markers of difference. For instance, the naked, dark-skinned native, wearing only striped body paint, presents a stark contrast to his fashionably clothed European counterparts. Faceless and symbolically "backwards," his most prominent feature—exaggeratedly rounded buttocks—accentuates a condition of crude primitivism. Moreover, the images depicted on each artist's canvas belie the writer's assertion that civilized and savage art are comparable in "feeling," "grouping," and subject matter. In keeping with his formal European training, du Maurier intently studies the small sculpture in the illustration's lower left corner and sketches two different versions of this female figure, seated and standing. Similarly, Botticelli studies the model with care but adapts it more freely, producing an image of two classically garbed women facing one another. The Aboriginal artist, however, pays the model no heed, and blithely paints what appears to be a hunter armed with a boomerang in pursuit of two kangaroos. This disparity challenges Twain's claim that the festive gatherings often painted by du Maurier and Botticelli are distinguishable from native representations of a traditional celebration called the "corrobboree" only by the addition of clothes and the superficial "smirk of civilization." Beard also subtly conveys the superiority of du Maurier's and Botticelli's draftsmanship through the relaxed position of their left hands; in contrast, the outspread fingers of the Aboriginal artist's left hand are pressed clumsily against his canvas, perhaps to steady it on the easel. In numerous ways, "His Place in Art" thus reinforces the very cultural and aesthetic hierarchies that Twain's prose attempts to dismantle.

Throughout Twain's stay in Australia, his position as a tourist paradoxically sharpened and obscured his perception of the colony's natives. Vacillating from outrage over Rosa Praed's account of the arsenic-laced Christmas pudding to complacency regarding the inevitability of their fate, the writer's inconsistent stance suggests that Aboriginals ultimately remain "novelties" for him, objectified and unreal. In this regard, it is perhaps not surprising that his discussion about them ends with a patronizing shrug:

> So much for the Aboriginals. It is difficult for me to let them alone.
> They are marvelously interesting creatures. For a quarter of a century,
> now, the several colonial governments have housed their remnants in
> comfortable stations, and fed them well and taken good care of them in
> every way. If I had found this out while I was in Australia I could have
> seen some of these people—but I didn't. I would walk thirty miles to see
> a stuffed one. (FE, 221)

The disappointment Twain expresses upon belatedly learning that Australia's Aboriginals were not extinct is grounded more in self-interest than altruism—regret over a missed opportunity to see these "creatures" firsthand. Moreover, he does not question the reasons for their invisibility but instead accepts the narrative of paternalistic benevolence promulgated by the colonial government, declaring that the "remnants" of the native population were "taken good care of . . . in every way." Although Clemens could not possibly have known otherwise, this was hardly the case: starvation, disease, and deplorable housing conditions were so commonplace at these reserves that Aboriginal mortality rates often exceeded 30 percent.[45] The flat-footed humor of his remark, "I would walk thirty miles to see a stuffed one," also bespeaks the moral myopia of his touristic gaze. If a living Aboriginal cannot be found to gratify the writer's curiosity, he flippantly declares that a stuffed taxidermic specimen will suffice in its stead. This dehumanizing joke reveals the indeterminacy of Twain's attitudes toward Australia's Aboriginals—sympathetic, on the one hand, about their exploitation and victimization, yet unable to transcend his ethnocentric impression of them as "static and unassimilatable savage Others" on the other.[46]

THE TASMANIAN TURNING POINT

After six weeks of lecturing in southeast Australia, Clemens and his family boarded a steamer in Melbourne on 31 October 1895, bound for New Zealand. As the *Mararoa* headed south toward Tasmania, the writer stood out on its deck, gazing at the desolate islands dotting the coastline. The somber reflections he jotted in his notebook on this occasion were later incorporated verbatim into both *More Tramps Abroad* and *Following the Equator*:

> Passing between Tasmania (formerly Van Diemen's Land) and neighboring islands—islands whence the poor exiled Tasmanian savages used to gaze at their lost homeland and cry; and die of broken hearts. How glad I am that all these native races are dead and gone, or nearly so. The work was mercifully swift and horrible in some portions of Australia. As far as Tasmania is concerned, the extermination was complete: not a native is left. (FE, 256)

Although Twain already knew about the tragic fate of Tasmania's Aboriginal population from his reading of Bonwick's text, it was not until this moment that the catastrophic human toll of colonialism fully registered in his consciousness. The entry's elegiac, heartfelt tone marks a watershed in his thinking—a visceral realization that racial annihilation was no laughing matter. Seeing the forbidding landscape to which the British had banished the native Tasmanians, and left them to die, reified the magnitude of their suffering and filled the writer with unbearable anguish. "Not a native is left," he states, concretizing the finality of this loss in personal terms. Moreover, his grief is commingled with—and compounded by— a vague sense of unease borne of complicity and racial guilt. The "gladness" to which he alludes is in fact an expression of relief rather than joy, suggesting that this direct confrontation with the genocidal "work" of imperialism was too painful for him to endure. To some extent, the pathos of Twain's response is grounded in imaginative projection—for like the native Tasmanians, he, Livy, and Clara were also exiles, heartsick for their lost homeland; he identifies with their plight on a personal level.

About twelve hours after Twain recorded this sentiment, the *Mararoa* docked in Hobart, Tasmania. The family disembarked and breakfasted in town with the Dobsons, friends of their long-time Hartford neighbors, John and Alice Hooker Day. Livy and Clara then set off for a "most delightful drive into the bush," while Sam toured Hobart itself, "desiring to get a glimpse of any convicts that might still remain on the island."[47] Although Tasmania's colorful history as a "convict-dump" (FE, 279) was the writer's main object of interest, his diary entry from the previous day indicates that the fate of the island's native inhabitants was also very much on his mind. Among the sites Clemens visited on his half-day excursion was the Tasmanian Museum and Art Gallery, where he received a private tour from curator Alexander Morton, an American expatriate, who had been born and raised in New Orleans. The writer's description of his visit in *Following the Equator* suggests that much of his time was spent in the museum's Tasmanian Room, which featured local natural history exhibits and a collection of Aboriginal artifacts. Morton showed his guest taxidermic specimens of the exotic indigenous fauna, including "half-a-dozen different kinds of marsupials—one the 'Tasmanian devil' . . . [and] a fish with lungs, and most curious of all . . . a parrot that kills sheep" (FE, 283).

The travelogue indicates that Twain also observed another "quite stunning" curiosity in the Tasmanian Room: "Arrow-heads and knives just like those which Primeval Man made out of flint . . . exactly duplicated in our day; and by people who have never heard of him or his works: by aborigines who lived in the islands of these seas, within our time. And they not only duplicated those works of art but did it in the brittlest and most treacherous of substances—*glass:* made them out of old brandy bottles flung out of the British camps; millions of tons of them" (FE, 284). While the writer clearly admires the artistry and technical skill required to fashion tools out of this fragile manmade substance, he remains silent on the troubling sociopolitical reality that underlies their production. Made from trash—the cast-off

FIGURE 20. "Governor Davey's Proclamation,"
More Tramps Abroad (above) and *Following the
Equator* (right). Courtesy of the Mark Twain Project,
The Bancroft Library, University of California,
Berkeley.

detritus of colonial invaders—these glass arrowheads and knives attest to
both the native population's commitment to maintaining their traditional
lifeways as well as their resourcefulness and creativity in adapting to radically changed circumstances.

Another artifact Clemens encountered in the Tasmanian Room is a
painted wooden board popularly known as "Governor Davey's Proclamation
to the Aborigines, 1816," although this title is misleading since the image
actually dates from 1829 and was produced during the administration of a
later colonial governor, Sir George Arthur. Although he discusses the
proclamation board and includes illustrations of it in both the British and
American editions of the travelogue, Twain does not specify where—or
indeed if—he saw it firsthand. Nonetheless, the significance he ascribed to
the "Governor's Proclamation" is strongly suggested by the fact that it is

"Why—Massa Guberuor"—said Black Jack—"You Proflamation all gammon, how blackfellow read him?—eh! He no read him book." "Read that then," said the Governor, pointing to a picture.

one of just three illustrations included in *More Tramps Abroad,* and the *only* one not in his own hand (fig. 20).

Twain's recognition of the image's cultural resonance was prescient, since the "Governor's Proclamation" board is today regarded as one of the most iconic documents in Australian history. In its time, however, the board was a failed instrument of diplomacy—an attempt to communicate and con-ciliate with Tasmania's preliterate natives by means of pictorial imagery.[48] The impetus for its creation came from Surveyor General George Frankland, who wrote the following in an 1829 letter to Governor Arthur:

I have lately had an opportunity of ascertaining that the aboriginal natives of van Diemen's Land are in the habit of representing events by drawings on the bark of trees. . . . In the absence of all successful communication with these unfortunate people, with whose language we are totally unacquainted, it has occurred to me that it might be possible to impart to them . . . the real wishes of the government towards them [through this visual medium]. . . . I have accordingly sketched a series of groups of figures, in which I have endeavored to represent in a manner as simple and as well adapted to their supposed ideas as possible, the actual state of things (or rather the origin of the present state), and the desired termination of hostility.[49]

About one hundred copies of Frankland's four-panel pictograph were produced on small pine boards by a local painter in Hobart and subsequently "tied to trees, passed between officials and scouts, and given to Aboriginal peoples on the frontier,"[50] promising a future of peace and justice that never materialized. Over time, the majority of these boards disappeared, although one was eventually recovered under the floorboards of Hobart's Old Government House during an 1866 renovation[51] and donated to the Tasmanian Museum and Gallery. There, in all likelihood, it was displayed among the other Aboriginal artifacts housed in the Tasmanian Room. The image was, moreover, copied and widely disseminated in a series of photographs and lithographic posters made as souvenirs of the 1866 Intercolonial Exhibition held in Melbourne and the 1867 Paris Universal Exhibition. These reproductions—also available as watercolor etchings and glass lantern slides—were commonly sold in shops catering to the colony's tourist trade throughout the nineteenth and early twentieth centuries. Images of the proclamation board were so ubiquitous that they even found their way into Victorian photo albums, such as the one now housed in the National Library of Australia commemorating the 1894–95 journey of Sir Francis J. Boileau's family from England to Australia.[52]

Clemens's interest in the proclamation board as an innovative means of cross-cultural communication and persuasion is not surprising; some fourteen years earlier, in reading Francis Parkman's *The Jesuits in North America in the Seventeenth Century,* he had marked a passage describing the "invaluable" use of pictures in converting the Iroquois to Christianity with three bold vertical strokes for emphasis. Curiously, while his description of the "Governor's Proclamation" is identical in both *More Tramps Abroad* and *Following the Equator,* the accompanying illustrations in the two editions differ in slight but significant ways. The text reads,

The governor warned these unlettered savages *by printed proclamation* that they must stay in the desolate region officially appointed for them! The proclamation was a dead letter; the savages could not read it. Afterward a *picture*-proclamation was issued. It was painted up on boards, and these were nailed to trees in the forest. Herewith is a photographic reproduction of this fashion-plate. Substantially it means:

> 1. The Governor wishes the Whites and Blacks to love each other;
> 2. He loves his black subjects;
> 3. Blacks who kill Whites will be hanged;
> 4. Whites who kill Blacks will be hanged. (MTA, 174; FE, 259)[53]

The specificity of Twain's "reading" of each panel on the proclamation board indicates that he is not recalling the image from memory; rather, his interpretation derives from careful scrutiny of a tangible artifact, sarcastically described as a "fashion-plate," while working in his London study. This speculation is corroborated by a previously unknown letter of thanks, which is preserved in a scrapbook created by curator Alexander Morton to document his tenure at the Tasmanian Museum, written on 1 December 1895 from Napier, New Zealand:

> Dear Mr. Morton:
>
> I am ever so much obliged for the pamphlets & photos. I would have written sooner to thank you for them, & for your kindnesses & courtesies conferred upon me while I was in Hobart, but we have been moving around so briskly that letter-writing was a difficult matter.
>
> I have no photographs with me, but will remember & send you one as soon as we return to Sydney toward the end of this month.[54]

Although Clemens does not specify the number or type of photographs Morton presented to him, the slight divergence in the two images of the "Governor's Proclamation" in the British and American editions of the text suggest that at least two of them depicted the board. The illustration in the former is purely pictorial, containing no title or explanatory text, whereas that in the latter includes a great deal of supplemental information. A handwritten label stating "Governor Davey's Proclamation to the Aborigines 1816" is affixed above the board's uppermost panel, along with the notation "Presented to the Museum by Mr. A. Bolter, 1867"; this provenance clearly identifies the image as the board owned by the Tasmanian Museum and Gallery.[55] The *Following the Equator* illustration also contains a number of other distinctive details that provide clues to its origin. For instance, the initials "R.S.T.," embossed above the two male figures on the top panel's left side, stand for the Royal Society of Tasmania, the colonial affiliate of

London's elite body of philosophers and research scientists, dedicated to the "Improvement of Natural Knowledge." Beneath the image is a brief excerpt from an unidentified text alluding to the political circumstances surrounding the board's creation: "'Why—Massa Gubernor'—said Black Jack—'You Proflammation all gammon, how blackfellow read him?—eh! He no read him book.' 'Read that then,' said the Governor, pointing to a picture" (fig. 20, right).

Unfortunately, Twain does not identify the source of these images in either *More Tramps Abroad* or *Following the Equator*; nonetheless, a duplicate of the illustration in the American edition—a large glass transparency owned by the State Library of Victoria—confirms that its creator was John Watt Beattie (1859–1930), whom Morton had commissioned to photograph the interior of the Tasmanian Museum and Gallery in 1895. Beattie was the island's official photographer and also the proprietor of Hobart's "Beattie Museum of Van Diemen's Land Relics," a collection of grisly artifacts, such as manacles, leg irons, cat o' nine tail whips, and orders for flogging, related to its convict history.[56] Though Twain's published work and correspondence contain no mention of Beattie or his museum, he did incorporate one of Beattie's other photographs, entitled "Relics of Convict Discipline," into chapter 29 of *Following the Equator*; this image was, in all likelihood, supplied by Morton as well. Clemens himself alludes to the collection of photographs he had acquired on the world tour in a May 1897 letter to Frank Bliss inviting him to London to finalize the details of the book's US publication: "I've got some photos somewhere—you and Mrs. Clemens can dig them out and experiment and select what you want—and London is the very place to get any others that you might need."[57] It is possible that Bliss may have chosen the more detailed image, leaving the other for Chatto, thereby accounting for the slight differences between the illustrations in the two editions.

For Clemens, the iconography of the proclamation board must have inevitably triggered associations with racial issues back in the United States; because of the prevalence of lynching during the Jim Crow era, the sight of a black man's body dangling from the limb of a tree—as depicted in the third frame of the image—would have seemed eerily familiar. Similarly, the plumed headdress of the silhouetted aboriginal chief, who is seen shaking the hand of a colonial official (possibly Governor Arthur himself) in the board's second panel, bears a striking resemblance to the traditional regalia worn by Native American leaders in their diplomatic negotiations with the federal government. But the image most likely to have given the writer pause is the idealized state of racial equality and social harmony presented in the board's topmost panel. The image depicts two multigenerational families—one black, the other white—amicably united and virtually indistinguishable from one another. The two young girls holding hands at the center of the frame are flanked by interracial pairs of adults, presumably their parents. The two men on the left, arms entwined in a gesture of fraternal affection, wear identical European garb and hold identical leashed dogs—symbols of domestication, obedience, and fidelity.[58] On the far right, their female counterparts—also dressed interchangeably—cradle one another's babies, symbolizing a relationship of deep mutual trust and intimacy that transcends race. In dress and demeanor, these Aboriginals have been thoroughly Europeanized and are prototypes of successful assimilation. As historian Penelope Edmonds points out, however, these idyllic scenes, which "apparently represent the noblest expressions of imperial endeavor," were ironically created "between two crucial moments in Indigenous/non-Indigenous relations in early Australia—the declaration of martial law in 1828 and the 'Black Line' of 1830."[59] The board's imagery is a propagandistic fabrication, concealing the fact that "Van Diemen's Land was a colony almost unprecedented in its violence towards Indigenous people."[60]

The context in which Twain situates his discussion of the "Governor's Proclamation" reflects his cognizance of this chronology. He describes the board as one of several failed "schemes" implemented by the British government to contain, pacify, and "save the Blacks from ultimate extermination, if possible" (FE, 259):

> One of its schemes was to capture [the natives] and coop them up, on a neighboring island, under guard. Bodies of Whites volunteered for the hunt, for the pay was good—£5 for each Black captured and delivered, but the success achieved was not very satisfactory. The Black was naked, and his body was greased. It was hard to get a grip on him that would hold. . . .

> Another scheme was to drive the natives into a corner of the island and fence them in by a cordon of men placed in line across the country; but the natives managed to slip through, constantly, and continue their murders and arsons. (FE, 259)

Although not identified by name, the second measure Twain discusses is the infamous Black Line, a brutal military campaign ordered by Governor Arthur in the fall of 1830. Over a period of six weeks, every able-bodied white man in the colony—convict or free—was enlisted to form a human chain for the purpose of driving the Aboriginals from their ancestral homelands, corralling them like cattle on the Forestier Peninsula at the island's extreme southeastern tip.

In many respects, the government's forcible containment of Tasmania's native population parallels the attempts of the US military to confine Indians on reservations in the latter half of the nineteenth century—both undertakings involved exorbitant expense and a significant commitment of colonial manpower yet produced largely unsatisfactory results. While Twain once again resists acknowledging these similarities, the American subtext registers clearly in his account of the colonial government's third, radically different "scheme"—the peaceful diplomatic mission of George Augustus Robinson, an uneducated Hobart bricklayer. In the early 1830s, Robinson, dubbed "The Conciliator," journeyed into the bush, "with no weapon but his tongue, and no protection but his honest eye and his humane heart" (FE, 261), and successfully negotiated the surrender of the much-feared Big River tribe. This "manifestly unconquerable" group of three hundred consisted not exclusively of warriors, as Twain explains, "but 300 men, women, and children" (FE, 260).

Twain's account of Robinson's heroic venture relies heavily on James Bonwick's *The Lost Tasmanian Race*, which he incorporated into the narrative in two distinct ways. In some instances, he cut and pasted single paragraphs from the text into his manuscript; in others, he transcribed passages longhand—as he had with Praed—silently emending them in the process. His dramatization of the climactic encounter between Robinson's party and the Big River chiefs contains two slight revisions of Bonwick's original, both of which have significant racial implications:

"Who are you?"

"We are gentlemen."

"Where are your guns?"

"We have none."

The warrior was astonished.

"Where your little guns?" (pistols).

"We have none." (FE, 263–64)

In *The Lost Tasmanian Race*, the question "Where your little guns?" reads "Where your piccaninny?"—Australian slang for an Aboriginal child. The chief's original query is a pun, figuratively conflating a child and small firearm as a means of underscoring the colonists' strong affection for, and attachment to, their weaponry. Recognizing the pejorative connotations this term possessed in relation to American slavery, Twain chose to omit it, substituting a more literal, inoffensive phrase—"little guns." While this change presumably reflects both the writer's own racial sensitivity and a desire not to offend his readers, his motive is problematized by the gratuitous introduction of another, equally objectionable racial epithet—this time in reference to Aboriginal women—in the very next sentence: "A few minutes passed—in by-play—suspense—discussion among the tribesmen—[then] Robinson's tamed squaws ventured to cross the line and begin persuasions upon the wild squaws" (FE, 264). His allusion not only implies a correlation between Aboriginal women and their indigenous North American counterparts but also considerably alters the tenor of Bonwick's original statement. In *The Lost Tasmanian Race*, these negotiations are described in a neutral, nonjudgmental manner, affirming the bond of kinship and mutual respect that exists between these two groups of women: "Some of the courageous female guides had glided around, and were holding quiet, earnest converse with their wilder sisters."[61] Twain's version, in contrast, demeans both parties by reducing them to a cultural stereotype; whether "wild" or "tamed," the women are fundamentally "squaws" all the same. This odd linguistic overlay demonstrates the writer's awareness of the abundant parallels in the settler colonial histories of Australia and the United States; however, as is so often the case in the travelogue, the allusion receives no further explication. Nonetheless, the subtle changes Twain made to Bonwick's text—suppressing a derisive term for African American children on the one hand while adding an equally disparaging one for Indian women on the other—offer compelling evidence of the ways in which the world tour destabilized his understanding of fixed racial categories.

Despite Robinson's extraordinary bloodless achievement, the surrender of the Big River tribe hastened the eradication of Tasmania's Aboriginals rather than facilitating their successful integration into colonial society. Although the travelogue makes no mention of it, subsequent British attempts to assimilate the natives closely parallel the so-called Americanization program designed to "Kill the Indian, [and] save the man," which was championed by progressive reformers, such as Sara Thomson Kinney and Kate Foote. Like the US federal boarding schools, the mission settlements established by the Tasmanian government sought to impose western beliefs and lifeways upon the natives wholesale, refashioning them as whites. As James Bonwick explains in the conclusion of *The Lost Tasmanian Race*, this ideology demanded that "They must clothe like us, eat like us, school like us, work like us, pray like us;—and all at the word of command. We treated them as marionettes. When we pulled the string, they moved; without the pull, they were still. And then, forsooth, when they did not move of themselves, we pronounced them stupid and unimprovable."[62]

Twain's discussion of the "misplaced persecutions of civilization" to which Tasmania's Aboriginals were subjected after their exile from van Diemen's land also echoes his own work. Like Huck Finn at the home of Widow Douglas, the natives were "instructed in religion and deprived of tobacco" (because smoking was considered "immoral"), forced to wear clean clothes, attend school, and keep regular hours.[63] But whereas Huck famously "lights out," donning his comfortable old rags and taking up residence in an empty sugar hogshead when the widow's "raspy" ways grow too oppressive for him, the native Tasmanians lack agency and are able to escape civilization only through death: "They pined for their lost home and their free wild life. Too late they repented that they had traded that heaven for this hell. They sat homesick on their alien crags, and day by day gazed out through their tears over the sea with unappeasable longing toward the hazy bulk which was the specter of what had been their paradise; one by one their hearts broke and they died" (FE, 265). This uncharacteristically sentimental diction—the Aboriginals' tear-stained cheeks, inconsolable "pining" for the lost homeland still within their ken, and death caused by homesickness rather than disease—is cribbed directly from the closing pages of *The Lost Tasmanian Race*. Despite mimicking Bonwick's extravagant style, Twain does not indiscriminately adopt his perspective, choosing to omit an overt comparison between the extinction of Tasmania's Aboriginals and American Indians: "It is impossible to separate the decline of the Tasmanians from the advent of the Europeans. The Indian Cacique spoke of his people melting like the snow before the sun when the pale faces came. . . . Our Aborigines have been hurried in their departure . . . by the poison of contact and the sword of destruction."[64] As the analysis of Clemens's uneasy relationship with the Connecticut Indian Association in the preceding chapter demonstrates, the writer had serious misgivings about the prospect of Native Americans as enfranchised citizens, yet paradoxically regarded the extinction of Tasmania's indigenous population as a great loss to Australian society: "These were indeed wonderful people, the natives. They ought not to have been wasted. They should have been crossed with the Whites. It would have improved the Whites and done the Natives no harm. But the Natives *were* wasted, poor heroic wild creatures" (FE, 265).

Given that official colonial records indicate the island's last indigenous man died in 1864 and the last woman twelve years later (FE, 267), Twain's retrospective advocacy of miscegenation in chapter 27 of *Following the Equator* is necessarily hypothetical and abstract—permissible because moot. As a tourist, he is able to lament a lost possibility of multiculturalism that would likely have been anathema to him at home. On a more personal level, the writer's position as an exile engenders profound sympathy for the Aboriginals' loss of their homeland as well as a new relativistic perspective on the imperialist enterprise. In the chapter's closing paragraphs, Twain playfully inverts the binaries of savagery and civilization, imagining a reversal of cultural roles—indigenous people coercing Western colonizers to adapt to their lifeways—which produces equally disastrous results:

> The Whites always mean well when they take human fish out of the ocean and try to make them dry and warm and happy and comfortable in a chicken coop; but the kindest-hearted white man can always be depended on to prove himself inadequate when he deals with savages. He cannot turn the situation around and imagine how he would like it to have a well-meaning savage transfer him from his house and his church and his clothes and his books and his choice food to a hideous wilderness of sand and rocks and snow, and ice and sleet and storm and blistering sun, with no shelter, no bed, no covering for his and his family's naked bodies, and nothing to eat but snakes and grubs and offal. This would be a hell to him; and if he had any wisdom he would know that his own civilization is a hell to the savage—but he hasn't any, and has never had any; and for lack of it he shut up those poor natives in the unimaginable perdition of his civilization, committing his crime with the very best intentions, and saw those poor creatures waste away under his tortures; and gazed at it, vaguely troubled and sorrowful, and wondered what could be the matter with them. One is almost betrayed into respecting those criminals, they were so sincerely kind, and tender, and humane, and well-meaning. (FE, 267)

This defense of the universal human right of self-determination represents a crucial epiphany for Twain; however, the sentiments expressed are not entirely his own. Although the passage makes no explicit mention of Bonwick, his influence can be detected throughout it. Key concepts and phrases regarding the "lack of wisdom" exhibited by "well-meaning" whites in imposing the standards of Western civilization upon native peoples derive from the final chapter of *The Lost Tasmanian Race*, as does the quotation Twain uses to critique the colonizers' explanation for the natives' extinction: "*They* didn't know why those exiled savaged faded away, and they did their honest best to reason it out. And one man, in a like case in New South Wales, *did* reason it out and arrive at a solution: '*It is from the wrath of God, which is revealed from heaven against all ungodliness and unrighteousness of men.*' That settles it" (FE, 267). Bonwick not only identifies the author of this statement by name and profession—the Reverend Lancelot Threlkeld, a missionary to Australia in the 1830s—but also couches it in a transnational context, specifically linking the fates of Aboriginals and American Indians:

> The Puritans of America were not alone in the belief that the Aborigines were a sort of Canaanitish people, who were doomed to be exterminated by the *peculiar people*. Even the missionary to the Black of New South Wales, Mr. Threlkeld, seems to find some comfort, in his natural astonishment at the rapid diminution of his charge, from feeling that it "is from the wrath of God, which is revealed from heaven against all ungodliness and unrighteousness of men."[65]

Although Twain does not acknowledge this cross-cultural connection, it nonetheless registers obliquely in his reference to the Tasmanian landscape as a "hideous wilderness"—an unmistakable echo of William Bradford's description of the New World as "a hideous and desolate wilderness full of wild beasts and wild men."[66] This detail encapsulates the selectivity of Twain's focus and racial sympathies during the world lecture tour. In the imaginative space created by the unseen Aboriginals of Australia lurks the liminal but irresistible trace of the indigenous peoples of his own homeland.

8. The Maori

"A Superior Breed of Savages"

Clemens's six-week sojourn in Australia simultaneously piqued and thwarted his interest in the indigenous inhabitants of the Southern Hemisphere. Both his reading and conversations with the Old Settlers raised a number of provocative questions about the legitimacy of imperial hegemony, the abrogation of hereditary land title, and the meaning of "savagery" itself. In particular, the writer's failure to encounter any Aboriginals firsthand while touring Victoria, New South Wales, and South Australia, coupled with the distressing discovery of their extinction in Tasmania, fueled a desire to learn more about, and, if at all possible, to meet and speak with native peoples on the next leg of his journey. Clemens apparently mentioned this to Malcolm Ross, a young journalist he met aboard the *Mararoa*, which left Melbourne on 31 October 1895 and arrived in Bluff, New Zealand, six days later. In "A Chat with Mark Twain," published in Dunedin's *Otago Daily Times* soon after the ship docked on 5 November, Ross described the author as "deeply interested in details connected with the discovery and early history of New Zealand; also in the Maori race," and expressed hope "that before he leaves our shores he will have an opportunity of seeing something of Maori character and customs for himself."[1]

The reporter's words proved prescient. Close examination of Clemens's New Zealand itinerary indicates that he took numerous proactive steps to learn about the colony's indigenous population—seeking out a celebrated private collector in Dunedin, touring a museum that featured displays of Maori artifacts in Christchurch, and even diverging from his established tour route to explore—and meet the inhabitants of—a traditional council house near Wanganui on the North Island. Moreover, his fascination with the Maori appears to have been contagious—as Livy announced in a letter to Susy toward the end of their five-week stay, "I have been very much interested in the Maoris since we came here."[2] Clara also participated in these outings, albeit with some ambivalence, remarking decades later in *My Father, Mark Twain* that in New Zealand she and her parents "became acquainted with a family of Maoris, one of the few groups of that race still in existence. They looked and lived like savages and their woodcarving offered specimens of primeval art. Brutal faces carved in blue and green tints."[3]

Twain's observations about the Maori in *Following the Equator* reveal a more tolerant, inquisitive mindset than that of his daughter. Indeed, much of what the writer learned about New Zealand's native peoples defied his expectations, unsettling conventional taxonomies of race and culture. As a long-time adherent of Herbert Spencer's theory of social evolution, he believed in the "beneficent necessity of Progress"[4]—that primitive races were destined to disappear in order to allow for the development of more advanced civilizations—and was therefore surprised to discover that the Maori population was "not decreasing, but actually increasing slightly" (FE, 318). His view of savagery as a static, homogeneous category was further challenged by the Maoris' skills in art, architecture, agriculture, and the military arts, which he declared "nearly approached the white man's" (FE, 319). In this respect, the Maori, so unlike any other indigenous group Clemens had previously encountered, were an enigma, resisting easy ethnographic classification: "I do not call to mind any savage race that built such good houses, or such strong and ingenious and scientific fortresses. . . . These, taken together with their high abilities in boat-building, and their tastes and capacities in the ornamental arts, modify their savagery to a semi-civilization—or at least to a quarter-civilization" (FE, 318–19). Twain's awkward parsing of percentiles—deliberating whether the Maori qualify as "semi" or merely one "quarter" civilized according to some implied evolutionary yardstick—reflects this bewilderment. By the end of the writer's stay in New Zealand, his high regard for these Aboriginals, whom he paradoxically called "a superior breed of savages" (FE, 318), would implode his rigid construct of racial binaries. This acknowledgment of Maori exceptionalism, rooted in careful study of their lifeways, stands in marked contrast to his cursory impressions of savagery as an undifferentiated, monolithic entity on his 1861 journey to the American West. In *Roughing It*, Twain expresses vehement disgust at the "treacherous, filthy and repulsive" Goshoot Indians he sees begging on the periphery of frontier stagecoach stations, concluding that "wherever one finds an Indian tribe he has only found Goshoots more or less modified by circumstances and surroundings—but Goshoots, after all" (RI, 129). The Maori—viewed from the vantage point of greater maturity and worldly experience—proved such glib essentialist generalizations untenable.

What most confounded Twain about the Maori, however, was not their advanced material culture but the fact of their enfranchisement. In contrast to American Indians, for whom suffrage remained a contentious and elusive goal in the 1890s, New Zealand's natives—men *and* women alike—had been granted the right to vote in 1867. They were also represented in the colonial legislature and cabinet by four elected members. This progressive model of governance, characterized by racial and gender equality, upended the writer's views on the immutable essence of "savagery," demonstrating that indigenous peoples could in fact be assimilated into modern settler colonial society rather than exiled or erased from it. The ways in which Twain's exposure to Maori character, customs, and culture fostered a revision of his racial attitudes can be gauged by a notebook entry made soon after he arrived in the colony. Though the passage is undated, it appears in close proximity to others made on 7 November 1895 and reflects his mindset at this early stage of the world lecture tour: "We easily perceive that the peoples furthest from civilization are the ones where equality between man and woman is furthest apart—& we consider this one of the <u>signs</u> of savagery. But we are so stupid that we can't see that we thus plainly admit that no civiliz [*sic*] can be perfect until exact equality between man & woman is included."[5]

Twain's use of the first-person plural pronoun "we" in this statement positions him squarely within the ideological framework of Western cultural privilege, according to which the radical inequality of men and women is deemed an unmistakable marker of savagery. Yet in the next sentence, he critiques the hypocrisy of industrialized societies for judging others deficient in relation to a benchmark that they themselves had not yet achieved. This irony—which he alleges most Westerners are too smug and "stupid" to see—calls into question the intrinsic distinction between civilization and savagery and reveals an emerging sense of cultural relativism. Although female suffrage is by no means synonymous with gender equality, it has historically been regarded as one important measure of it. Thus, by the terms of Twain's own definition, the enfranchisement of Maori women suggests that this allegedly primitive society was more civilized than either the United States or Great Britain. The writer's female compatriots would not receive the right to vote until twenty-five years after his visit to New Zealand; British women had to wait even longer, until Parliament passed the "Equal Franchise Act" of 1928.

Because of the brevity of Clemens's stay in New Zealand, it is doubtful that he could have acquired these rich insights into Maori culture on his own. More likely, this information was gleaned through a series of encounters with knowledgeable local hosts, who served as informal mentors to their distinguished American guest. In *Following the Equator,* Twain makes passing reference to four individuals instrumental in his tutelage— "Malcolm Ross, journalist," "Dr. Hockin," "Mr. Kinsey," and "Dr. Campbell of Auckland"—but provides little information about their identities or the extent of his interactions with them. This omission creates an odd disjuncture in the text, uncoupling effect from root cause, and allows Twain to highlight his observations about the Maori while effacing the social context out of which they emerged. By examining the travelogue in conjunction with Clemens's notebooks and the family's unpublished correspondence from the period, however, the submerged details of the writer's itinerary— where he went, what he saw, with whom, and, most importantly, how he interpreted these experiences—can be recovered. In so doing, the agency of these four remarkable figures becomes abundantly clear.

But who exactly were these men, and why was Clemens so receptive to their influence? Although their names are obscure to contemporary American readers, Malcolm Ross (1862–1930), Thomas Morland Hocken (1836–1910), Joseph Kinsey (1852–1936), and John Logan Campbell (1817–1912) were all prominent members of New Zealand's colonial elite. Hocken and Campbell were physicians; Kinsey, a shipping magnate; and Ross, as previously mentioned, a reporter. Despite their disparate ages and professions, the four shared a deep, abiding respect for Maori culture and devoted considerable time to studying it. This consensus of favorable opinion regarding the colony's indigenes, espoused not by dreamy-eyed romantics or reformers but by estimable men of science and commerce, all civic-minded pillars of their communities, seems to have surprised—and impressed—Clemens, suggesting that his deference to their authority was unconsciously aligned with issues of rank and social stature. This conjecture is corroborated by his remark in *Following the Equator* that "The highest class white men who lived among the Maoris in the earliest time had a high opinion of them and a strong affection for them. Among the whites of this sort was ... Dr. Campbell of Auckland [who] ... was a close friend of several chiefs, and [had] many pleasant things to say of their fidelity, their magnanimity, and their generosity" (FE, 319–20). The writer's Anglophilia was likely a contributing factor as well. According to his Australian lecture agent, Carlyle Smythe, Twain was "a sincere admirer of the English and a profound lover of England."[6] Hocken and Kinsey had both been born and educated in England; Campbell, in turn, hailed from Scotland, as did the parents of Malcolm Ross, the youngest of the four and the only native New Zealander among them.

Serendipitously, three of these four individuals—Ross, Hocken, and Kinsey—resided on New Zealand's South Island, where Clemens's tour of the colony began. Given that the Maori population there was historically small and largely invisible, his initial exposure to their culture came at a safe distance through the mediated study of indigenous artifacts. By the time the writer encountered natives firsthand on the North Island (where Dr. Campbell lived) several weeks later, he possessed sufficient knowledge to appreciate their customs and exotic appearance rather than dismissing them as "savages." Malcolm Ross was apparently the linchpin of this informal network, initiating Twain's entry into the inner circle of New Zealand's social elite through his extensive professional contacts.

"A JOURNALIST CANNOT LIE"

Ross began his career in his hometown of Dunedin in 1882, working as a reporter for the *Otago Daily Times*. By all accounts, he was an ambitious young man with eclectic interests, who also served for a time as private secretary to Sir James Mills, director of the Union Steamship Company, and who founded the New Zealand Alpine Club in 1891. Although Ross would later gain fame as the colony's official correspondent during World War I, reporting from the front on the disastrous 1915 Gallipoli Campaign, at the time of Twain's visit he was primarily known for his mountaineering exploits. Beginning in 1891, he and his younger brother Kenneth made no fewer than five attempts to scale the summit of New Zealand's highest—and as yet unconquered—peak, Mount Cook (12,349 feet) but were thwarted each time by inclement weather. Commissioned by the colonial government to write a guidebook describing "the scenic attractions of the Mount Cook district," Ross published *Aorangi, or the Heart of the Southern Alps*, in 1892. This title refers to a now-discredited nineteenth-century translation of the Maori name for the mountain, widely believed to mean "Cloud Piercer."[7]

  This etymology—along with the words "Alpine climbing," "Malcolm Ross," and "Mount Cook"—appears in the first notebook entry Clemens made upon arriving in New Zealand, suggesting that his initial impressions of the colony's landscape and history were filtered through a lens of information supplied by the journalist. He comments wryly on local attempts to combat the so-called rabbit plague that afflicted the South Island after British colonists introduced the species in the 1840s, joking that "the noble great range of snowy alps seen in the distance is really a pile of dead rabbits." He then explains, "Mount Cook is the highest. Strange they didn't name it Victoria or Wellington. But they will, presently. The native name of Mt. Cook is <u>Piercer of the Clouds</u>—pity they didn't leave it alone."[8]

The writer's musings on the renaming of Mount Cook, when juxtaposed with his remarks concerning Mount Rainier three months earlier, reveal a heightened sensitivity to the imperial erasure of indigenous place names. Before he departed for Australasia, his argument for preserving the name "Tacoma"—which he regarded as an apt signifier of the peak's sensuous, breast-like shape—was both pragmatic and apolitical. In this instance, however, Twain seems more acutely aware of the arbitrary exercise of power involved in replacing a native name with a colonial one. He deems it "strange," for example, that the mountain's current appellation (conferred in 1853) honors the eighteenth-century explorer Captain James Cook, who first circumnavigated and mapped New Zealand, rather than paying homage to either of the most eminent contemporary incarnations of empire: the reigning sovereign, Queen Victoria, or the duke of Wellington, arguably one of Britain's greatest nineteenth-century military commanders, who defeated Napoleon's forces at Waterloo in 1815. In predicting that the name of Mount Cook will "presently" yield to a more overtly nationalistic one, Clemens critiques the arrogance of the imperial prerogative, declaring it a "pity they didn't leave" the Maori name intact. This expression of regret signals a shift in the writer's political sensibility as the result of his travels.

Twain lectured in Invercargill on the day of his arrival in New Zealand, then traveled approximately 125 miles northeast for a two-night engagement in Dunedin. It is in this context that Ross merits his only mention in *Following the Equator*: "The [town's] population is stated at 40,000, by Malcolm Ross, journalist; stated by an M.P. at 60,000. A journalist cannot lie" (FE, 287). This tongue-in-cheek allusion to the veracity of a reporter's word reflects the camaraderie that linked the two men. According to the writer's notebook, on 7 November he met up again with Ross, who gave him a number of "very valuable books," including an 1887 edition of a memoir now regarded as a classic of New Zealand literature—*Old New Zealand: Being Incidents of Native Customs and Character in the Old Times*.[9] Published under the pseudonym "A Pakeha Maori"—a derisive term for a European turned native that describes a position analogous to "squaw man" in the American West—the author was in fact one of the colony's earliest, most notable settlers.[10] Frederick Maning (1812–83), Irish by birth, had moved to Tasmania with his family in the early 1820s. While there, he likely participated in the infamous Black Line of 1830—an experience that may well have influenced his 1832 decision to relocate to the more peaceful environs of New Zealand. Maning lived for many years among the Maoris on the North Island, working as both a trader and translator and eventually marrying a native woman with whom he had four children.

A VISIT TO ATAHAPARA

According to Allan Gribben, the writer's copy of this volume, housed at the Mark Twain Research Foundation in Perry, MO, is inscribed on the flyleaf "To Mr. Clemens, with Malcolm Ross' comps., Dunedin, 7 Nov. 1895."[11]This was the same day that the family called on one of the town's leading citizens, Dr. Thomas Morland Hocken (1836–1910). On the basis of this inscription, it may be surmised that Ross arranged the meeting and perhaps even accompanied the Clemenses to the doctor's home, named "Atahapara" after the Maori word for dawn.[12] Yet in *Following the Equator*, Twain deliberately effaces the circumstances surrounding the visit, simply announcing "to the residence of Dr. Hockin" (FE, 287) with no indication of its underlying purpose.

If Ross did in fact orchestrate this encounter, he could hardly have provided Clemens with a more expert mentor on "Maori character and customs." Hocken, who had trained as a physician in England, emigrated in 1862 to Dunedin, where he established a successful surgical practice and also worked as the local coroner. Recognizing the degree to which settler colonialism threatened the survival of indigenous culture and other historical materials, Hocken became a passionate collector in the early 1870s, acquiring old maps, sketches, photographs, and the diaries of early European explorers, as well as an array of Maori art and artifacts. He also conducted extensive fieldwork on both the North and South Islands, interviewing long-time settlers (including Frederick Maning) and Maori elders about their experiences and recording traditional tribal customs, such as war songs and dances, funeral rites, and the medicinal use of herbs.[13]

As a surgeon, Hocken was particularly fascinated with *moko*, the intricately incised style of Maori tattooing—a tradition that had fallen into decline after being denounced as a mark of "heathenism" by nineteenth-century missionaries. His collection featured many examples of what he termed "this most interesting branch of savage art," including legal deeds documenting the cession of tribal lands to European settlers that were "signed" with the distinctive *moko* of individual chiefs.[14] These elegant arabesques, symmetrically chiseled into the cheeks and forehead with tools of bone or sharks' teeth, not only indicated social rank and genealogy but also the virtuous character of the individual who bore them; each *moko* pattern, therefore, was a hallmark of personal identity.

Over time, Hocken's avocation became a cornerstone of his public reputation. Throughout the 1880s he lectured frequently about his research and published his findings in the prestigious *Transactions of the New Zealand*

Institute, which "made his name a household word throughout [the colony]."[15] The doctor's fame led to his appointment as chairman of the Early History, Maori, and South Seas Section of the *New Zealand and South Seas Exhibition,* which was held in Dunedin from 1889–90. Drawing on his own acquisitions as well as those of other like-minded collectors, Hocken assembled "the largest collection of Maori carvings and implements ever seen"[16]; he also prepared scrupulous documentation to accompany the exhibit, taking pains to provide "the native terminology for each object, correctly spelled, along with [its] relevant history."[17] He even wrote the introductory essay for the exhibition catalogue, in which he praised the Maori as "fine handsome people, brown-skinned, long-haired, intelligent, and vivacious."[18] Among the indigenous groups of the South Seas, they were, in Hocken's estimation, the "foremost of the savage race"—superior to the Australian aborigines and inhabitants of Tierra del Fuego—as demonstrated by the "remarkable beauty" of their artwork and carvings, " some . . . in scrolls and spirals, others in diamonds, squares, or inlaid and otherwise ornamented."[19]

Hocken's interest in Maori culture was abundantly reflected in the furnishings of his residence on Moray Place. Indigenous carvings adorned the home's banisters, newel posts, and doorframes, and exotic curios of feather, stone, and bone lined the walls and shelves. The décor also incorporated large native architectural elements, such as the gable end of a traditional council house, which hung over one of the fireplaces.[20] According to anthropologist Dimitri Anson, the couple's appropriation and display of these native objects alongside conventional European furnishings conveyed a political message to all who entered: "By using their home as a 'museum' the Hockens helped increase awareness and aesthetic appreciation of Maori art in Dunedin high society, where Maori otherwise had a very low profile."[21] Moreover, their showcasing of these artifacts reflects the growth of nascent nationalism among New Zealand's privileged upper classes in the closing years of the nineteenth century. As historian Anna K.C. Petersen notes, "When people . . . took the step of decorating their private homes with Maori motifs, designs and carving, they were expressing more than a nostalgia for a simpler life, identification with the land and/or interest in things Maori. Their actions represented a critical re-evaluation of Maori art" as the foundation of a unique cultural identity distinct from that of England.[22]

The brevity of Clemens's visit to Atahapara—which he aptly characterized in *Following the Equator* as a veritable "museum of Maori art and antiquities" (FE, 287)—belies the profound impact of what transpired there.

His notebook entry supplies much of the background elided in the published travelogue, beginning with the matter-of-fact assertion, "Livy, Clara & I went to Dr. Hockin's [sic] house, saw his wife & young daughter & <u>him</u>. Noble collection of books relating to N.Z. Gave me his translation of Tasman's diary."[23] The writer's underscoring of the pronoun "him" implies that his knowledge of—and evident respect for—Hocken preceded their introduction, once again pointing to the possible influence of Malcolm Ross. The subsequent details of the entry establish the doctor's status as a bona fide expert, a man whose erudition and commitment to preserving New Zealand's past prompted him not only to assemble a vast archive of primary sources on the subject but also to undertake a translation of the journal of the seventeenth-century Dutch explorer Abel Tasman, the first European to visit the North and South Islands. In this respect, the physician's gift seems more than a casual souvenir. Clemens's tour of Atahapara represents his imaginative point of entry into New Zealand history and the rich culture of its indigenous peoples; in Socratic terms, Hocken serves as an intellectual midwife assisting in the birth of his new, more relativistic racial attitudes. Within several days of their meeting, for example, the writer professed "the superiority of Maoris to Australian black-fellows" in an interview published in the *Lyttleton Times*—an opinion likely gleaned from his host.[24]

In addition to the "beautiful carvings—house-fronts, canoe-prows, 4-fingered figures, &c. Meres [short, broad-bladed war clubs] made of translucent jade"[25] that Clemens encountered in Hocken's home, he saw "pictures and prints in color of many native chiefs of the past—some of them of note in history" (FE, 287). These images were likely the work of New Zealand artist Joseph Jenner Merrett (1816–54), whose paintings—many of which portrayed high-ranking Maoris with elaborate *moko*—the physician also collected.[26] Although Twain identifies neither the artist nor the titles of the specific paintings he examined, textual clues in *Following the Equator* suggest that one of them was Merrett's "Group of Maoris" (fig. 21). The cheeks, foreheads, and chins of the three men depicted in this image are covered with *moko*, while the two women have tattoos only on and directly beneath their lips. The figures' features are gracefully rendered; their poses, likewise, are dignified and erect; and the delicate drapery of their cloaks evokes stately figures out of classical antiquity. Merrett thus represents the Maori not as savage Others but as refined and attractive human beings, whose extravagant forms of bodily adornment enhance rather than diminish their overall appearance.

Clemens had encountered facial tattooing only once before, nearly thirty years earlier during the Quaker City tour. In *The Innocents Abroad*, he

FIGURE 21.   Joseph J. Merrett, "Group of Maori," ca. 1850.
Courtesy of the Hocken Collections, Uare Taoka o Hakena,
University of Otago, New Zealand.

reports seeing—and being revolted by—"sore-eyed children and brown,
buxom girls with repulsively tattooed lips and chins" (505) in the Syrian
town of Magdala. As he scrutinizes the Merrett portraits, however, he has a
decidedly different, more favorable response:

> There is nothing of the savage in the faces; nothing could be finer than
> these men's features, nothing more intellectual than these faces,
> nothing more masculine, nothing nobler than their aspect. The
> aboriginals of Australia and Tasmania looked the savage, but these
> chiefs looked like Roman patricians. The tattooing in these portraits
> ought to suggest the savage, of course, but it does not. The designs are
> so flowing and graceful and beautiful that they are a most satisfactory
> decoration. It takes but fifteen minutes to get reconciled to the

tattooing, and but fifteen more to perceive that it is just the thing. After that, the undecorated European face is unpleasant and ignoble. (FE, 287–88)

Curiously, there is no mention of either the Merrett portraits or *moko* in Clemens's original notebook entry, indicating that this memory was reconstructed more than a year after his visit to Atahapara. Seated at his desk in London, the question of aesthetics looms large, becoming the vehicle whereby long-standing ethnocentric hierarchies are challenged and recalibrated. While admitting that the chiefs' intricate facial tattooing "ought to suggest the savage," the writer is confounded to discover that it does not. This realignment of perspective is not instantaneous, however, but rather a gradual process that unfolds in two discrete stages, each a quarter of an hour in duration. First, Clemens must overcome the cultural chauvinism inherent in his aversion to the tattoos as a signifier of primitive Otherness and "reconcile" himself to their legitimacy as an expression of ethnic identity. This realization prompts the second, more radical change in his thinking—that when compared with the beauty of the *moko* designs, the unadorned visage of the white European conqueror is not superior but in fact "unpleasant and ignoble." The binaries of civilization and savagery are inverted in this instance, producing a newfound sense of cultural relativism.

The precision with which Twain records the time spent examining these Maori portraits (repeating the phrase "but fifteen minutes. . . and but fifteen more" twice within a single sentence) suggests a genuine interest in Hocken's collection, as well as a self-conscious awareness of the portentous shift taking place. In some ways, this passage is reminiscent of the moment in chapter 15 of *Adventures of Huckleberry Finn* when Jim, after denouncing the boy's mean-spirited trick about "dreaming" their separation in the fog, turns his back on Huck and retreats to the wigwam on board the raft. Left alone to ponder the cruelty of his behavior, Huck states, "It was fifteen minutes before I could work myself up to go and humble myself to a nigger—but I done it, and I warn't ever sorry for it afterwards, neither" (HF, 105). Twain's struggle to divest himself of the ethnocentrism that is his birthright takes twice as long as Huck's—a measure of the depth and degree of his antipathy. Although the romanticized language the writer uses to describe the intelligence, virility, and innate nobility of these Maori figures (likening them to Roman aristocrats rather than plebeians) is problematic, his affirmation of their humanity nonetheless signals a moment of racial transcendence. This epiphany would, moreover, play an instrumental role in shaping Twain's response to the British domination of India and South Africa—two other colonies he later visited on his world tour. In chapter 41 of *Following the Equator*, he meditates on what he terms the "disadvantage of the white complexion," explaining that "nearly all black and brown skins are beautiful, but a beautiful white skin is rare. . . . Where dark complexions are massed, they make the whites look bleached-out, unwholesome, and sometimes frankly ghastly" (FE, 381).

Twain segues abruptly from his discussion of the Maori portraits in *Following the Equator* to a "ghastly curiosity" presented to him by Doctor Hocken—a "lignified caterpillar with a plant growing out of the back of its neck" (FE, 288). This fossil becomes the springboard for an extended meditation on Nature's cruelty in inflicting suffering on living creatures; however, the two topics are not as disparate as they initially appear. According to Major General Horatio Robley's 1896 landmark study of Maori tattooing, burnt "aweto hotete, or vegetable caterpillar" provided an "excellent black pigment" for use in creating *moko* designs.[27] Although Twain makes no mention of this fact, it is likely that the context in which Hocken shared the grisly specimen was a conversation on tattooing elicited by the Merrett portraits. His description of the process whereby the caterpillar was turned to wood also serves as an unconscious metonym of the insidious manner in which settler colonialism "destroys to replace." In preparation for its metamorphosis into a night moth, the caterpillar burrows into the soil, where the airborne "spores of a peculiar fungus" land upon its back, sprout, and grow: "The roots forced themselves down into the worm's person, and rearward along through its body, sucking up the creature's juices for sap; the worm slowly died, and turned to wood. And here he was now, a wooden caterpillar, with every detail of his former physique delicately and exactly preserved and perpetuated" (FE, 288). Inanimate yet uncannily lifelike, this artifact prefigures the effigies of "stuffed natives. . . in their proper places, and looking as natural as life" (FE, 298) that Twain would later encounter in a Christchurch museum.

"WATAPITI"

The grueling pace of Clemens's lecture schedule often necessitated traveling long distances under onerous conditions. To minimize fatigue, Livy and Clara typically traveled ahead to the next major city on the writer's itinerary, where they could relax in comfortable surroundings while he and Carlyle Smythe detoured to small towns for additional engagements. Such was the case with the family's departure from Dunedin on 9 November, when Livy and Clara boarded a train to Christchurch and the men set off for Timaru and Omaru. These sidebar excursions offered Smythe a chance to closely observe the author's proclivities and personal habits, thereby achieving a sense of "The Real Mark Twain," as he entitled an 1898 reminiscence published in *Pall Mall Magazine*. Among the many claims made in this essay, the agent states that Clemens was "addicted [to]. . . the reading of newspapers almost as much as to smoking bad cigars." Citing Twain's quip, "I'd like to see the cigar I couldn't smoke" as proof of his insatiable appetite for tobacco, Smythe comments, "Similarly I should like to see the newspaper he could not read."[28] This "devotion to newspapers" prompted Clemens to pick up the 11 November issue of the *Otago Daily Times*— presumably while in transit from one venue to the next—where his interest was piqued by an unusual item. His notebook entry for this date re-creates the occasion. Gazing out the window of his railcar, Clemens describes the landscape—"All along, going back to Omaru, we have this exquisite lightgreen brilliant sea, & the beautiful green grain—land & the snow-mountain views"—then adds the following: "Ngowhereinpatikura— mighty good imitation of Maori. Also another name—Watapiti."[29] These curious "names," which sound as though they may refer to actual New Zealand towns, are in fact humorous neologisms used in a promotional campaign for Vanity Fair cigarettes. The advertisement, presented in the guise of legitimate news, was a squib entitled "A Remarkable Bridge," which informed unsuspecting readers that

> Some "considerable distance" south of Auckland, and "quite a large number" of miles north of Wellington stands a bridge. . . . It is on the direct road to, and only a short distance from, *Ngowhereinpatikura.* When it was discovered by a party of Natives, the leader of the party exclaimed, "Homaikaraiki!" And, after many years, it is still called by the Natives "Watapiti."
>
> And so it is a pity! . . . The men who were instrumental in devoting public money to such works would look well gibbeted in chains on the same bridge, the only drawback being that no one would see them. The same amount of money, nay, half that sum, invested in Vanity Fair Cigarettes would bring happiness and enjoyment to our adult male population.[30]

Thanks in part to Clemens's meeting with Dr. Hocken, who had introduced him to the musicality of the Maori tongue a few days earlier, the writer was well positioned to understand this joke, as he recognized that the two imaginary locations mentioned in the article were a "mighty good imitation" of actual native words. But the piece likely resonated with him for another reason as well. In both its form and content, "A Remarkable Bridge" resembles a frontier hoax—the genre Twain and his colleagues at the

Virginia City *Territorial Enterprise* had mastered back in the 1860s. While lampooning the "foreignness" of indigenous place names by "translating" them into familiar English colloquialisms, the ad simultaneously satirizes corrupt politicians in much the same way that "A Bloody Massacre Near Carson" exposed the San Francisco Spring Valley Water Company's unethical practice of "cooking dividends" back in 1863. Moreover, like Twain's most famous hoax, "Petrified Man," the text can be read as an unconscious parable about territoriality. The bridge's alleged location south of Auckland and "quite a large number" of miles north of Wellington in fact encompasses nearly the entirety of New Zealand's North Island; its construction thus represents an unwelcome technological incursion into—and hegemonic possession of—the Maoris' traditional homeland. The name that the natives allegedly give to the structure—"Watapiti"—mocks their impotent distress in the face of European colonization, just as the petrified man ineffectually thumbs his nose at the miners who seek to violently displace him from the "mountains south of Gravelly Ford." Although the writer's notation offers no indication that he perceived this parallel, the fact that he considered the squib worthy of mention reflects an active interest in Maori culture.

"COSY SUPPERS" AT WARRIMOO

When Clemens and Smythe arrived at the Christchurch train station on 12 November, they were greeted by members of the local Savage Club—a colonial affiliate of the celebrated gentlemen's club founded in London in 1857—who ceremoniously escorted them to Coker's Hotel, where they were reunited with Livy and Clara. This is most likely how the writer made the acquaintance of Joseph James Kinsey, a prosperous businessman who served as the family's unofficial guide during their four-day stay in the city. Widely respected as a "man of substance and culture,"[31] Kinsey and his wife Sarah were renowned for their hospitality, welcoming dignitaries from all over the world to their home "Warrimoo," named after an Aboriginal word meaning "Place of the Eagle." Their warm reception of the Clemenses, however, stemmed not only from the writer's celebrity but also from an extensive network of interpersonal connections. Kinsey happened to be a friend of Malcolm Ross, with whom he shared a passion for mountain climbing.[32] He was, moreover, an avid collector of Maori artifacts—an avocation that brought him into close contact with Dr. Thomas Hocken. Kinsey's association with the physician can be traced back at least six years to 1889, when he served as the Canterbury commissioner of the landmark

New Zealand and South Seas Exhibition in Dunedin, which Hocken had played an instrumental role in organizing. He had in fact loaned many items from his personal collection for the exposition—"stone implements—chiefly axes and meres"[33]—where they were displayed alongside indigenous objects belonging to Hocken. Though it is unclear whether Ross or Hocken communicated with the Kinseys in advance of the Clemenses' arrival in Christchuch, their mutual acquaintance may well have arisen as a topic of conversation.

According to the effusive letters of thanks that Sam, Livy, and Clara wrote to Joseph, his wife Sarah, and his 22-year-old daughter May—Clara's exact contemporary—after their departure from Christchurch for the North Island, they enjoyed "many pleasant hours" and "cosy suppers" at Warrimoo. As Clemens remarked, "I look back with grateful pleasure upon the comfortable times spent in your hospitable house. . . . Your household made Christchurch a darling place & a charming memory for [us]."[34] No mention is made of these convivial occasions in *Following the Equator*; indeed, the text alludes to Kinsey just once in the context of an obscure joke: "*November 16.* After four pleasant days in Christchurch, we are to leave at midnight to-night. Mr. Kinsey gave me an ornithorhyncus, and I am taming it" (FE, 301). Livy's letter confirms that their host presented her husband with a stuffed platypus as an exotic parting gift, which he carried in public like a pampered pet: "Mr. Clemens does not allow the Ornithorhyncus dear to leave his arms while we are moving from boat to train and train to boat. He says it is his most treasured possession."[35]

During the family's stay in Christchurch, the Kinseys also escorted them on sightseeing excursions to the local Botanical Gardens and Canterbury Museum. Founded in 1870 and housing an impressive collection of natural history, ethnography, and fine art, the museum's most distinctive attraction was the so-called Maori House, a large, elaborately carved and vividly painted residential structure (*whare runanga*) that had been moved from the North Island and reassembled as a separate wing in 1874. Some sixty-feet long by twenty-feet wide, soaring to a height of sixteen feet at the apex of its roof, the building housed a diverse range of artifacts—"cloaks, weapons, tools, ornaments, carvings, [and] mats" intended to "evoke a mythic Maoriness"[36] for colonial audiences. When the exhibit first opened in 1875, the *Illustrated New Zealand* magazine reported,

> On entering the building . . . visitors find themselves within the walls of a genuine Maori whare, carved, painted, and embellished in the highest style of ancient Maori art. Many of the carvings are of course very grotesque—haliotis [abalone shell]-eyed monsters in every variety of

attitude, with tongues protruded, and their faces rendered more hideous by the elaborate 'tattoo' markings. . . . The building is substantially erected, on solid foundations, and may probably last long after the Maori race has become extinct.[37]

Though Twain does not name the Canterbury Museum in *Following the Equator*, his lengthy description of the exhibits he viewed in Christchurch leaves no doubt as to its identity:

> In the museum we saw many curious and interesting things; among others a fine native house of the olden time, with all the details true to the facts, and the showy colors right and in their proper places. All the details: the fine mats and rugs and things; the elaborate and wonderful wood carvings—wonderful, surely, considering who did them— wonderful in design and particularly in execution, for they were done with admirable sharpness and exactness, and yet with no better tools than flint and jade and shell could furnish; and the totem-posts were there, ancestor above ancestor, with tongues protruded and hands clasped comfortably over bellies containing other people's ancestors— grotesque and ugly devils, every one, but lovingly carved, and ably; and the stuffed natives were present, in their proper places, and looking as natural as life; and the housekeeping utensils were there, too, and close at hand the carved and finely ornamented war canoe.
>
> And we saw little jade gods, to hang around the neck—not everybody's, but sacred to the necks of natives of rank. Also jade weapons, and many kinds of jade trinkets—all made out of that excessively hard stone with- out the help of any tool of iron. And some of these things had small round holes bored through them—nobody knows how it was done; a mystery, a lost art. I think it was said that if you want such a hole bored in a piece of jade now, you must send it to London or Amsterdam where the lapidaries are. (FE, 297–98)

Several details in this passage suggest the presence of a knowledgeable, albeit invisible, guide—Joseph Kinsey—escorting the writer through the Maori House and explaining the background and significance of the arti- facts displayed, in much the same way that Dr. Hocken had done at his home in Dunedin. How otherwise would a casual tourist—a foreigner, no less—know that the carved figures on the totem poles represented canni- balistic ancestors, or that pounamu (the Maori word for local jade, also called greenstone) ornaments were sacred and therefore restricted to "natives of rank"?

Kinsey's influence can also be detected in the aplomb with which Twain proclaims the exhibit's ethnographic authenticity. "All the details" of the Maori House, he avers, are "right and in their proper places." The truth, in fact, was far more complicated. From the time the Maori House opened two decades earlier, it had elicited "much unfavorable criticism"[38] owing to the extensive alterations made in annexing the structure to the main museum building: rather than being set directly on the ground as *whare runanga* customarily were, it was instead erected on a concrete foundation; the original roof of indigenous reeds was replaced with one of corrugated metal; doors were relocated and windows added to enhance the visibility of the artifacts; and traditional native paints, made with organic pigments such as charcoal, red ochre, and poporo juice mixed with fish oil and water, were rejected in favor of commercial European products. All of these changes are documented in the *Guide to the Collections at the Canterbury Museum*, which Twain purchased on the day of his visit.[39] His insistence on the exhibit's "truth" thus strongly implies that Kinsey—rather than the printed guidebook—served as the primary source of his information.

Despite Kinsey's mentoring, Twain reacts to the Maori House with decided ambivalence. On the one hand, he genuinely admires the "elaborate and wonderful wood carvings" incorporated into its architecture, yet on the other, he feels obliged to immediately qualify that praise, adding, "wonderful, surely, considering who made them." His paternalistic tone exemplifies a colonial paradigm of "aesthetic adjudication," in which European appreciation of indigenous artifacts is inextricably conjoined with the "imputation of hierarchical difference."[40] Twain's account makes repeated reference to the primitive Stone Age implements—"no better tools than flint and jade and shell"—used by Maori artisans in executing the "admirable sharpness and exactness" of their designs. While this detail highlights the artistry of these artifacts, it simultaneously underscores the Maoris' technological inferiority to their European conquerors. Moreover, although some of the objects displayed—such as the "grotesque, ugly devils" carved onto the totem posts—offend Twain's Western sense of aesthetics, he nonetheless concedes that the figures are "lovingly carved, and ably." His recognition of the Maoris' creativity and technical skill thus represents another incremental step forward in his attempt to comprehend and accept this exotic Other.

Perhaps the most troubling aspect of Twain's account of the Maori House, however, is his allusion to the "stuffed natives . . . in their proper places, and looking as natural as life" (fig. 22). The phrase literally refers to the presence of three wax mannequins in traditional dress posed on the structure's veranda at the entrance to the exhibit. These figures, facsimiles of a display at London's Imperial Institute, were modeled on actual Maoris and represent a chief and chieftainess, along with a young girl who is

FIGURE 22. "Stuffed Native." Maori Cloak and Kete Diorama. Courtesy of the Canterbury Museum, Christchurch, New Zealand.

presumably their daughter.[41] Such wax figures, eerily "equiposed between the animate and the inanimate, the living and the dead,"[42] were displayed in a number of late nineteenth-century New Zealand museums, where—as historian Conal McCarthy argues—they served to advance a familiar colonial script: "When real Maori proved to be too much of a handful or refused to live up to their ethnic stereotype, wax models were found to be a much more malleable substitute, their mortuary pallour signifying their fate in a much more acquiescent way."[43] In describing the mannequins' lifelike appearance, Twain extends this symbolism by introducing the unsettling image of a taxidermic trophy, implying that the indigenous culture of the "olden times" is dead and relegated to the past. The phrase also echoes the terms in which the writer couched his regret at not seeing any aborigines while touring Australia: "If I had found out [they had been removed to comfortable stations].... I could have seen some of those people—but I didn't. I would walk thirty miles to see a stuffed one" (FE, 221). His insistence that the figures occupy "their proper places" thus refers not to their physical location on the veranda but more broadly to the museum exhibit as a whole. For Twain and other colonial visitors, the Maori House represents a simulacrum, a window into a doomed, rapidly vanishing past.

A SAVAGE SALUTE

Several days after visiting the Canterbury Museum, Joseph Kinsey accompanied Clemens to the Christchurch Savage Club, where a lavish banquet was given in his honor after his last "At Home" in the city. This organization, a local affiliate of the bohemian gentlemen's club established in London in 1858 for writers and artists, was named after the eighteenth-century satirical poet Richard Savage, immortalized in Samuel Johnson's *Life of the English Poets*. Its members, described in the club's literature as "warmly interested in the promotion of Christian knowledge and the sale of exciseable liquors,"[44] adopted a playful pose of primitivism, deeming themselves "Savages" to signify their lack of pretension and pride. This identity was reflected in the décor of their clubhouses, the walls of which were adorned with "old tomahawks and moccasins, spear-heads and wampum-belts, and something resembling a circular disc cut from a horsehair-bottomed chair, but which was understood to be a human scalp."[45] Dinner invitations, admissions tickets, and other promotional materials for club activities featured images of Plains Indians clad in buckskin, wearing long feathered headdresses, and clutching ceremonial rattles and war clubs. This iconography was so thoroughly woven into the fabric of the club's identity that a poem composed on the occasion of the first "Ladies' Night" proclaims to the assembled "squaws," "Behold us in our warpaint, and without! / You share our wigwam in communion sweet, / And make the pow-wow pleasant and complete."[46] Twain had been entertained at the club's original London location during his first visit to England in 1872 and was well acquainted with its bohemian ethos; he also repeatedly used the term *savage* to describe lapses in his own behavior, such as the infamous faux pas of the 1877 Whittier birthday speech. In his letter of apology to Emerson, Holmes, and Longfellow, he declared that he was "only heedlessly a savage, not premeditatively."[47]

In keeping with this tradition of ethnic imposture, the Christchurch Savages looked to New Zealand's indigenous population as the inspiration for their chapter's identity. Their gatherings, called *korero* after the Maori word for meeting, were chaired by a "Great Chief" and "Tohunga"—or master of ceremonies—both of whom wore traditional feathered cloaks over their Victorian formalwear.[48] As Paul Fatout reports in *Mark Twain Speaking*, the Christchurch Savages feted the writer with "a most *recherché* supper" featuring cleverly themed dishes, such as "Grenouille sautante a la Smiley" and "Gelée au vin Huckleberry."[49] They also elected him the first honorary member of their club, ratifying the vote with a rousing Maori salute, "Ake, ake, ake, kia kaha!" (Forever and ever be strong!).[50]

Clemens expressed his gratitude in a brief impromptu speech, stating, "I am proud to belong to this gang of Savages . . . [and] hope to learn that warwhoop of yours." The writer's unusual diction—conflating the Maori chant with a traditional Native American battle cry—suggests that Indians are an unconscious referent in his remarks on the disparity between civilization and savagery:

> Mr. Chairman and Savages, as you call yourselves, for some reason best known to yourselves, for certainly I should not have taken you for such. I have mixed a good deal with the lower order of savages, and I have seen them in all costumes and in no costumes at all—in all costumes except this one that you wear this evening. With my experience of savages, I know that however picturesque they may be in their dress, and sometimes they are very picturesque, the costume which I see before me is the best one suited to educated and cultured savages. I am glad to meet this kind of savages.[51]

In noting the incongruity between the group's imagined collective identity and the refinement of their evening dress, manners, and cuisine, Twain seems to assert the essentialist notion that all human beings—regardless of their habiliments—are fundamentally savage; and yet, in distinguishing "the lower order of savages" from the "educated and cultured" ones seated before him, he paradoxically implies the existence of an evolutionary social hierarchy. His insistence on the authority of firsthand observation—claiming to have seen savages "in all costumes and no costumes at all"—echoes a footnote appended to his description of a nameless Indian wearing an "execrable rabbit-skin robe flowing from his shoulders—an old hoop-skirt on, outside of it—[and] a necklace of battered sardine-boxes and oyster-cans reposing on his bare breast" in the 1870 essay "The Noble Red Man": "This is not a fancy picture; I have seen it many a time in Nevada, just as it is here limned" (CT1, 443–44). Twain's allusion to the "picturesque" qualities of nakedness also recalls an anecdote in an 1888 letter to his nephew, William L. Webster, a budding stamp collector. After promising to send the boy any stamps he receives, he adds, "[This] reminds me that when the first revenue stamps arrived at the post office and family grocery combined in one of the coast towns of California during the war, a squaw who liked bright colors pasted eight hundred dollars' worth of them onto her naked body before the P. Mr. noticed what she was up to. If you could but add her to your collection!"[52]

"A MOST ENVIABLE COLLECTION OF MAORI THINGS"

When the Clemenses left Christchurch for the North Island at midnight on 16 November, Joseph Kinsey and his daughter May accompanied them to the railway station and lavished many gifts upon the family as mementos of their stay. Upon their arrival in Auckland four days later, Livy sent Joseph a gracious note of thanks for "all the pleasure you gave us," stating,

> Thus Mr. Kinsey I must repeat—you see you cannot turn it off now you must read this letter—how greatly I value your most beautiful and interesting gifts to us. I feel that I have a most enviable collection of Maori things owing to your great generosity. I prize them every single one so very much. I feel when I look at them almost as if I must be a chieftainess.[53]

Although Livy's letter unfortunately does not name the "Maori things" they received, her allusion to feeling like a "chieftainess" offers a tantalizing clue, intimating that thanks to their host's tutelage, she both understood and appreciated their cultural significance. Kinsey's gifts, in fact, were not random trinkets, but *taonga* (the Maori word for treasure)—objects imbued with spiritual meaning and befitting for individuals of elevated social rank. As a collector, he was no doubt familiar—at least in some rudimentary sense—with the concept of *mana*, "that most central of Maori values, which can be understood as power, prestige, authority, influence, and control,"[54] often conveyed through the display of prized possessions. The objects he presented to the Clemenses represented tangible emblems of their *mana*. As Livy's comment indicates, these artifacts playfully "nativize" his American guests, metaphorically transforming them into "Pakeha Maori."

While the precise contents of this "most enviable collection" are presently unknown, at least two pieces of it survive in the archive of the Mark Twain House and Museum in Hartford, though neither was originally identified as Maori. The first is a pounamu pendant, approximately four and a half inches in length, with slight serrations—"a traditional Maori method of surface decoration"[55]—cut into the bottom edge. Pounamu, also known as river jade, is found only on New Zealand's South Island and is treasured by all Maoris in much the same way that Europeans value gold. In addition to having the physical properties of strength, durability, and beauty, pounamu denotes status (*mana*) and is considered sacred (*tapu*),[56] and is therefore closely associated with chieftainship and peacemaking. The amulet Kinsey gave Livy resembles a chisel, a tool used primarily for wood-carving, but probably was not functional; rather, as an item of personal adornment, it signifies her high social rank. Although the pendant's age cannot be definitively established, the distinctive hourglass-shaped hole through which the brass bail is inserted at the top indicates that it was drilled with a stone rather than metal tool, suggesting that its origin pre-dates European contact. The precision of the hole's craftsmanship thus exemplifies the "lost art" Twain extolled in the Maori ornaments displayed at the Canterbury Museum: "Some of these things had small round holes bored through them—nobody knows how it was done; a mystery . . . if you want such a hole bored in a piece of jade now, you must send it to London or Amsterdam where the lapidaries are" (FE, 298). The pendant (fig. 23) came to the Twain House as part of a 1981 bequest from Clara Clemens's longtime secretary, Phyllis Harrington, that also included several of Livy's haircombs and some coral jewelry. The presence of this anomalous item among other conventional Victorian accessories bespeaks its cherished status. Although Livy presumably never wore the piece, the fact that she saved it throughout all the family's moves in the tumultuous decade after Susy's death, and that Clara herself kept it for another half century, bespeaks the pendant's sentimental significance.

The second "Maori thing" that Kinsey presented to the Clemenses is a carved spear called a *taiaha*, which bears a faded sticker on its shaft reading, "J.J. Kinsey, Christchurch" (fig. 23). Like the greenstone pendant, this object, "a stylized representation of a human head with the tongue extended, generally accepted as part of the act of ritualized challenge,"[57] is symbolic. According to the *Guide to the Collections in the Canterbury Museum* that Twain owned, a *taiaha* was "used as a weapon, but also as a sign of office. A Maori orator speaks walking up and down, with a tai-aha in his hand."[58] What more appropriate gift could Kinsey have chosen to honor the author whose "At Home" lectures were attracting enthusiastic capacity crowds in both Australia and New Zealand? The Twain House Museum received the *taiaha*—along with a number of other souvenirs from the world lecture tour—in 1972 from a descendant of William Edgar Grumman, Twain's stenographer at Stormfield, to whom Clara donated the

FIGURE 23. Pounamu pendant and Maori *taiaha*. Gifts to Sam and Livy Clemens from Joseph J. Kinsey, 1895. Courtesy of the Mark Twain House and Museum, Hartford, Connecticut.

contents of the home's attic after her father's death in April 1910. The provenance of these objects—including a boomerang, several spears, wooden callisthenic clubs, and a carved headrest—is uncertain. They were, however, long presumed to be African, since Grumman found them inside a shipping crate labeled "Mark Twain, S.S. Damascus, Cape Town, South Africa." While the carved designs on several of the other spears suggest South Pacific origin, only the *taiaha* can be definitively traced to Kinsey.

A cryptic list of Maori words that Clemens entered into his notebook on 20 November —the date of the family's arrival in Auckland after a harrowing three-day crossing from the South Island—offers yet another clue regarding this "most enviable collection of Maori things." Bracketed by references to luggage, the list appears to have been made as the couple unpacked their bags at the Star Hotel and closely inspected Kinsey's largesse for the first time. This was possibly the occasion Livy alluded to four days later in a letter to her sister Susan Crane:

> I was counting up [the presents we have received] the other day, and in Christchurch we received *thirty-eight* gifts, that is, counting a half dozen photographs as one gift. If I had counted such little gifts separately, there would have been double the number. Boxes of bonbons, flowers, pamphlets, photographs, & c. & c. Generally I feel nothing but pleasure in them (they are usually little things), but there I felt a little burdened, there was so much.[59]

According to Robert H. Hirst, general editor of the Mark Twain Project, the handwriting in the 20 November entry belongs to both Sam and Livy, indicating that this "counting up" was not simply numerical but a collaborative process of recollection and reminiscence, during which they attempted to assign the proper indigenous names to the various objects spread out before them. Swapping the pencil back and forth, husband and wife each took turns jotting down words, which the other then modified or annotated. The entry thus presents a vignette of domestic intimacy, testimony—in oblique shorthand—to the rapport that existed between them.

The native words—all nouns, occasionally spelled incorrectly then crossed out or erased and rewritten—appear on the left side of the page with English translations on the right, as follows:

Mere—Green stone weapon

~~whare~~

whaere—Maori house

chieftain's staff

tiki

kaka—feathers[60]

The couple's uncertainty over how to spell *whare* (the first, rejected attempt is actually correct), along with its mistranslation as a "chieftain's staff," implies that these terms are being recalled from memory. Moreover, with the exception of *tiki*, which was written by Sam and not translated, the other three words are in Livy's hand; conversely, three of the four English translations are his. Of the two meanings listed for *whare*, the correct one—"Maori house"—is supplied by Livy, whereas "chieftain's staff" represents his contribution. Like the pounamu pendant and *taiaha,* the items listed have symbolic meaning in Maori culture; for example, a *mere*—a flat, broad-bladed club made of pounamu—was a traditional symbol of chieftainship, as were the prized red feathers of the *kaka* or parrot, typically woven into cloaks worn exclusively by people of high rank. The reference to *tiki,* on the other hand, is a bit more ambiguous, since the word can signify both the carved figure of a deity or an amulet representing an ancestor worn about the neck as a talisman. If in fact these words refer to some of Kinsey's other gifts, they similarly pay tribute to the family's status.

On 12 December, a second set of presents—consisting of unspecified books and more photographs—reached the Clemenses in Wellington. Although the titles of the enclosed texts are unknown, the pictures—taken by Kinsey himself—apparently documented the family's stay in Christchurch.[61] Each of the family members' thank-you notes make special note of the images. Sam, for example, comments that they are "just about perfect," while Clara states, "The photographs are beautiful with such a delightful finish and the likenesses are admirable." Livy, in turn, expresses her gratitude as well as that of tour manager Carlyle G. Smythe: "Mr. Smythe sends his kind regards . . . and thanks you for your thought of him. He likes the picture *extremely, we all do,* and will be very glad indeed to possess copies of them, when you have leisure and the new dark room ready for your work." These repeated references to "likenesses" indicate that the photos depicted members of the family and various acquaintances made during their stay in Christchurch, rather than local scenes or landmarks. This surmise is corroborated by Livy's acceptance of Kinsey's offer to supply additional photographs for use as illustrations in the forthcoming travelogue: "Mr. Clemens thinks if it will not trouble you that perhaps London would be the first place to reach us with anything that you are so good as to send us. We shall be delighted to have the slides and the views that you speak of."[62]

Unfortunately, the whereabouts of these photographs is presently unknown; however, they almost certainly numbered among those the writer mentioned as potential illustrations in a May 1897 letter to Frank Bliss: "I've got some photos somewhere—you and Mrs. Clemens can dig them out and experiment and select what you want."[63] Apparently, at least one of them met with the editor's approval and was incorporated into chapter 35 of *Following the Equator,* bearing the caption "Maori Women in Feather Robes" (fig. 24). While the reproduction in the published volume is tiny and lacking in clarity, the sepia-toned original, housed in the Berg Collection at New York Public Library, is stunning. The photo is mounted

FIGURE 24. "Maori Women in Feather Robes," *Following the Equator.* Courtesy of the Henry W. and Albert A. Berg Collection of English and American Literature, New York Public Library.

on dark, heavy paper upon which an elaborate decorative border has been hand-painted—perhaps the "delightful finish" alluded to by Clara. Close inspection of the image itself, however, reveals the inaccuracy of Bliss' title—for standing amidst the native women is a white female. Dressed in typical Victorian attire—a dark, high-collared, mutton-sleeved dress—her flowered bonnet is adorned with a single white feather, identical to those worn by the others. Since feathers traditionally denoted status in Maori culture, the plume confers honor upon this anonymous figure and simultaneously signifies her symbolic acceptance into the group.[64] But who is she? Where, when, and under what circumstances was the photo taken? And why would Kinsey have sent it to the Clemenses?

The location depicted in the image is difficult to pinpoint; the carved backdrop suggests the porch of a *whare runanga*, in all likelihood somewhere on the North Island where the majority of the native population lived. A small number of Maori did, however, live in the vicinity of Canterbury, making it possible that the Clemenses visited this site in the company of Mr. and Mrs. Kinsey. As Clara recalled in *My Father, Mark*

Twain, she and her parents "became acquainted with a family of Maori" somewhere in New Zealand. Although she does not specify where this encounter occurred, the next sentence of her account—"After leaving the city of Christchurch, we went to Napier"—implies a chronology placing it there. This surmise is substantiated by the fact that the mysterious white woman at the center of the image bears a strong resemblance to Joseph Kinsey's wife, Sarah. If she is the person in the photo, its ethnographic value—illustrating both the Maoris' skill with ornamental carving and the same type of feather cloaks appropriated as "costumes" by the colonial officers of the Christchurch Savage Club—is potentially enhanced by its personal associations. While Kinsey's purpose in sending the photo to Twain is unclear, its inclusion in the text reflects his influence in shaping the writer's views about the Maori.

"A CLOSE FRIEND OF MANY CHIEFS"

The favorable impressions Clemens formulated about New Zealand's native peoples during his tour of the South Island deepened in Auckland, where he met John Logan Campbell, one of the city's founding fathers. Campbell had arrived in March 1840, just weeks after the signing of the historic Treaty of Waitangi, which formally proclaimed British sovereignty over the islands. As one of the island's earliest European inhabitants, Campbell was a bona fide "Old Settler." Although trained as a physician, he abandoned medicine to pursue the adventurous life of a pioneer. He lived amicably with the Maori for a period of three months, familiarizing himself with their language and customs, eventually purchasing land from them and becoming a trader. Over time, Campbell acquired a timber mill, established a brewery, and founded a thriving import-export firm. In 1881, he published a memoir entitled *Poenamo*—"a mutilated but musical version of the Maori word for greenstone"[65]—that recounts his early interactions with the region's indigenous tribes. Livy met the 78-year-old Campbell at a reception on 25 November, where he presented her with an autographed copy: "To Mrs. Clemens/POENAMO is presented by the author/Logan Campbell, Kilbryde, Auckland."[66] Below the inscription, he jotted a note requesting that she invite her husband to visit his home for a smoke on the veranda.

Clemens evidently accepted this offer, remarking in chapter 33 of *Following the Equator*, "Kauri gum ... is the sap of the Kauri tree. Dr. Campbell of Auckland told me he sent a cargo of it to England fifty years ago, but nothing came of the venture" (FE, 311). Their conversation also included discussion of Campbell's life among the local tribes and his friendship with

Frederick Maning, the celebrated "Pakeha Maori" author of *Old New Zealand*—one of the "very valuable books" Malcolm Ross had given the writer in Dunedin. Unlike Hocken and Kinsey, who had arrived in New Zealand in the 1860s and 70s, respectively, Campbell represented the vanguard of settler colonialism, providing Clemens with a firsthand glimpse of the Maori as a proud, vibrant, as yet unconquered people. In *Poenamo*, he praises the "high chivalrous honour" of the natives' character, declaring them "unique in the history of the races of the world."[67] Campbell's admiration for the Maori persisted throughout his long life; in his will he left five thousand British pounds for the creation of a "towering obelisk" at the summit of One Tree Hill, the large estate he bequeathed to the city of Auckland as a public park to honor "the great Maori race."[68] Although Clemens's meeting with Campbell was brief, he is mentioned by name three times in *Following the Equator*—in other words, far more often than Ross, Hocken, or Kinsey— suggesting the writer's recognition of his venerable status: "The highest class white men who lived among the Maoris in the earliest time had a high opinion of them and a strong affection for them. Among the whites of this sort was the author of 'Old New Zealand' [Frederick Maning]; and Dr. Campbell of Auckland was another. Dr. Campbell was a close friend of several chiefs, and has many pleasant things to say of their fidelity, their magnanimity, and their generosity" (FE, 319–20).

Despite the obvious similarity between Campbell's idealized representation of the Maori and the noble savages Twain satirized in Cooper's *Leatherstocking Tales*, he neither questions the realism of the physician's assessment nor draws any connection with American Indians. His suppression of this transnational parallel becomes more evident in a subsequent passage he quotes from *Poenamo* concerning the Maoris' "quaint notions about the white man's queer civilization": "One of them thought the missionary had got everything wrong end first and upside down. 'Why, he wants us to stop worshiping and supplicating the evil gods, and go to worshiping and supplicating the Good One! There is no sense in that. A *good* god is not going to do us any harm'" (FE, 320). This dualistic notion of a good and bad god is identical to the Cheyenne belief that had fascinated the writer more than a decade earlier in Richard Irving Dodge's *Our Wild Indians*, one of his major sources for "Huck Finn and Tom Sawyer among the Indians." Like Campbell, Twain's fictional protagonist Brace Johnson had also lived among native peoples but found little to admire in them. He resolutely denies the Indians' humanity, yet paradoxically adopts their "sensible" religion, informing Tom and Huck that "the Injuns hadn't only but two Gods, a good one and a bad one, and they never paid no attention to the good one, nor ever prayed to him or worried about him at all, but only tried their level best to flatter up the bad god and keep on the good side of him" (HFTS, 61).[69] Clemens, however, makes no mention of Indians in this instance, perhaps realizing that the comparison would undermine his insistence on the exceptionalism of New Zealand's indigenous peoples—a fact of which he had become thoroughly convinced through the mentoring of his colonial hosts.

A WISH FULFILLED

By the time the Clemenses reached Wanganui[70] on the North Island on 3 December, their education about the Maori had entered a new, experiential phase. They were now on their own, largely unescorted, and confident enough in the knowledge they had acquired during their stay to begin formulating independent impressions of both the colony's history and indigenous inhabitants. Not surprisingly, most of their opinions—articulated in private correspondence and *Following the Equator* alike—bear the unmistakable imprint of their local mentors' influence. In the travelogue, for example, Twain reports seeing "lots of Maoris" in the city, noting that "the faces and bodies of some of the old ones [were] very tastefully frescoed" (FE, 318)—an expression of aesthetic approval doubtlessly influenced by his having been introduced to the practice of *moko* several weeks earlier in Dr. Hocken's Dunedin home. Far more telling, however, are the occasional aberrations in this pattern—instances in which Sam, Livy, or Clara misconstrue what they are seeing and expose the limits of their cross-cultural understanding.

Their stay in Wanganui offers a case in point. Clemens lectured in the city on 3 and 4 December, then left early the next morning for two additional performances in Hawera and New Plymouth, one hundred miles to the north. Livy and Clara remained behind, awaiting his return on the seventh. On the afternoon of 4 December, the writer took advantage of some free time to "see something of Maori character and customs for himself," just as Malcolm Ross had hoped, making a solitary excursion to a "Maori Council House across the river." Although Twain does not identify the place by name in *Following the Equator*, its location on the riverbank opposite the modern city suggests that he is referring to Putiki Pa, the region's principal native settlement. Moreover, the structure he describes visiting—"large, strong, carpeted from end to end with matting, and decorated with elaborate wood carvings, artistically executed" (FE, 318)—was not a moribund museum specimen, removed from its original setting and reassembled in a colonized space like the Maori House exhibit in Christchurch. Rather, it was in situ and actively in use. He also mentions meeting and interacting with Maori people for the first time in the travelogue, noting that he found them "very polite" (FE, 318).[71] This understated, almost anticlimactic, acknowledgment of indigenous civility reflects the efficacy of Twain's tutelage; informed at every turn that the Maori were not savages, he finds their gracious demeanor no surprise.

In addition to satisfying his own curiosity about the Maori, Clemens seems to have been conducting informal reconnaissance on this excursion in advance of his wife and daughter's visit to the same council house the following day. Livy provides a detailed account of the experience in a letter to Susy on 5 December:

> This afternoon Clara and I took a drive . . . away down the Wanganui River to a Maori settlement. When we got there we met . . . an old man in shawls and mats, ragged and soiled looking; he asked if we would like to go into the meeting house. This is not a house for religious meetings but a sort of council chamber, a gathering place for consultation, they use it between times for sleeping in. There are always some interesting curious carvings over the door and about the building. This one was a building I should think 200 ft. long by perhaps 20 or 25 wide, it was divided into three alleys like, the two outside ones with ferns and mats thrown down on the floor to make the beds. There are two large posts in the middle to support the building—in the best buildings these are carved—at one end [is] the door and one or two windows at the other. . . . It does not make it a very light building. When Clara and I started to step into the building the old man said something which of course we could not understand but we thought it meant dirt—as the floor did not look very clean, however we stepped in and looked about. When we got back to the carriage we began to feel the result of being in a dirty place as we had evidently many insects about us. Since we came back we have killed seven fleas, of course that does not begin to represent the number that we have seen. In fact since I have been writing one has hopped onto my paper but of course he was gone before I could capture him.
>
> I have been very much interested in the Maoris since we came here, and have been anxious to see more of them, now I have had enough, I shall not seek their dwellings any more. By the way, as we went toward the meeting house there joined us a Maori woman with her lips all tattooed.[72]

Numerous details in this letter attest to the knowledge Livy had gained about the Maori through her acquaintance with Thomas Hocken and Joseph Kinsey; she patiently explains that despite its name, the building she and

Clara visited was not used for religious purposes but rather for consultation and sleeping. These traditional structures, she confidently notes, "always [have] carvings" above the door; however, only the "best" contain carved support posts in the middle. While much of Livy's narrative—her description of the building's estimated size and complex interior layout—strives for objectivity, her diction unconsciously conveys a state of cultural unease. She reacts with disdain to the "ragged and soiled looking" appearance of the man who greets them hospitably at the settlement entrance, and presumes—in the absence of a translator—that his statement is a warning about unsanitary conditions inside the Council House rather than an expression of welcome. Upon entering the living space of this exotic Other, Livy finds herself literally and metaphorically "in a dirty place" from which she recoils in disgust after discovering her clothing infested with fleas. The interest she had previously professed in Maori culture is abruptly foreclosed by this unpleasant experience; "now," she grimly declares, "I have had enough." In contrast to Twain's references to the aesthetics of *moko* in *Following the Equator*, the sight of the Maori woman "with her lips all tattooed" at the council house revolts Livy. Clara unfortunately did not record her impressions of the visit, although her letter to Joseph Kinsey on 12 December announces—much like a student proudly reporting back to a former teacher—"We enjoyed Wanganui extremely & saw two Whares there & plenty of Maoris, & found them pleasant & interesting."[73]

Judging from Clemens's notebook entries, his visit to the Council House served to deepen his fascination with Maori culture. On the train back to Wanganui from Hawera and New Plymouth, he sat in a compartment full of natives and eavesdropped on their conversation, marveling at their "smooth & liquid speech." He also observed, "Some at my lecture last night—one of <u>these</u>. 'No good.'"[74] The quotation marks around this phrase suggest that one of the Maoris addressed these words to Twain, who interpreted them as a critique of his performance. A cancelled passage of the Berg manuscript describes his response to this perceived slight: "I could go on & say many pleasant things about the Maoris, but I think I won't. One of them put on his clothes and came to my lecture last night, and because he didn't understand English he said it was 'no good.' Such things wound me. For I am an orphan that has not had time to learn to know his loss; I have been an orphan more than fifty years. And am getting so that I cannot bear it."[75] Twain's reaction is oddly defensive; one man's discourteous remark dampens his admiration for the entire Maori race, prompting the suppression of other "pleasant things" about them. In much the same way that Huck reverts to racial stereotypes when Jim trumps his argument about the

French in chapter 14 of the novel, announcing "You can't learn a nigger to argue," Twain undercuts the legitimacy of the nameless Maori's remark by emphasizing his primitivism. He describes his critic as ignorant ("he didn't understand English") and habitually naked (donning the camouflage of Victorian attire in order to enter the privileged colonial space of the lecture hall), while simultaneously casting himself in the sympathetic, emotionally vulnerable role of "orphan." But why would the approval of an inconsequential stranger even remotely matter to a world-renowned celebrity like Mark Twain? The underlying issue seems to be a lack of reciprocity—the implicit expectation that the high regard in which he held the Maori would be returned in kind. For this reason, the passage raises—but does not resolve—the possibility of kinship across racial and cultural lines.

Upon Clemens's return to Wanganui, he and his family spent Sunday, 8 December touring local sites before departing the next day for Wellington, where Clemens would present his last two "At Homes" in New Zealand. One of their stops was Moutoa Gardens, a public park established on the site of a traditional Maori marketplace, where trade goods were exchanged before European contact. There, set amidst the flower beds and manicured lawns, stood a historic landmark—the colony's first war memorial, erected to commemorate the 1864 battle of nearby Moutoa Island between two Maori *iwi* (tribes): the upriver Hauhau, "whose expressed goal was to expel all Europeans from the country,"[76] and downriver Wanganui, known as "kupapa," who were natives loyal to the British crown. The monument, a personification of grief depicting a weeping woman with an infant cradled in her arms, honors the kupapas killed in this conflict.

Clemens's description of this monument—one of *Following the Equator's* most passionate denunciations of imperialism—also reveals that he misunderstood several key facts about the battle. He claims, for example, that the combatants were Maori and British, and that the monument marks the burial site of the conflict's colonial casualties, when in fact no one at all is buried there. These errors, which would no doubt have been corrected by a well-informed local host had one been present, offer insight into Twain's evolving political views. In characterizing the British as "alien oppressors" and the Maori as valiant defenders of "their fatherland,"[77] he displays an awareness of—and more importantly, a newfound respect for—indigenous landrights and self-determination. His tutelage about the Maori reaches its apogee at Moutoa Gardens.

Clemens's confusion originated with the bilingual inscriptions on the monument's base, which he did not realize were English and Maori versions of the same text. Believing these words paid homage to two discrete groups of men, he concluded that he was viewing "a couple of curious war-monuments" rather than one. The first, he claimed, had been raised "in honor of white men 'who fell in defence of law and order against fanaticism and barbarism'" (FE 321), although the skirmish in fact produced only one European casualty— a missionary identified as "Lay Brother Euloge." The writer was especially troubled by the biased language of the dedication itself, fuming in his notebook, "This is the most comical monument in the whole earth. Try to imagine the humorless deeps of stupidity of the idiot who composed that inscription—& the dullness of the people who can't see the satire."[78]

Twain's reaction to what he termed the "other monument . . . erected by white men to Maoris who fell fighting with the whites and *against their own people*, in the Maori war" was even harsher (FE, 322). "Pull it down," he demanded, for "it is a disgrace to both parties—the traitors & those who praise them."[79] Revisiting his notebook entry a year later during the composition of *Following the Equator*, he elaborated on these objections, pondering the interrelation of discourse and political ideology in the monument's inscription:

> Fanaticism. We Americans are English in blood, English in speech, English in religion, English in the essentials of our governmental system, English in the essentials of our civilization; and so, let us hope . . . that that word got there through lack of heedfulness, and will not be suffered to remain. If you carve it at Thermopylae, or where Winkelried died, or upon Bunker Hill monument, and read it again— 'who fell in defence of law and order against fanaticism'— you will perceive what that word means, and how mischosen it is. Patriotism is Patriotism. Calling it Fanaticism cannot degrade it; nothing can degrade it. Even though it be a political mistake, and a thousand times a political mistake, that does not affect it; it is honorable—always honorable, always noble—and privileged to hold its head up and look the nations in the face. It is right to praise these brave white men who fell in the Maori war—they deserve it; but the presence of that word detracts from the dignity of their cause and their deeds, and makes them appear to have spilt their blood in a conflict with ignoble men, men not worthy of that costly sacrifice. But the men *were* worthy. It was no shame to fight them. They fought for their homes, they fought for their country; they bravely fought and bravely fell; and it would take nothing from the honor of the brave Englishmen who lie under the monument, but *add* to it, to say that they died in defense of English laws and English homes against men worthy of the sacrifice—the Maori patriots. (FE, 321–22)

This meditation on patriotism reflects a new relativistic understanding of the legitimacy of native patrimony. Twain denounces the charges of "barbarism" and "fanaticism" leveled against the Hauhau, comparing their defense of their homeland to celebrated acts of resistance against imperial aggression throughout Western history—the Greeks at Thermopylae who defended their land from the incursions of Xerxes and the Persian Empire; the fourteenth-century Swiss folk hero Arnold Winkelried who flung himself upon the pikes of Austrian invaders to prevent his country's annexation by the Hapsburgs; and, most familiarly, the Americans who battled their British oppressors at Bunker Hill. From this perspective, the Maori who fought against their own kin in defense of colonial hegemony are traitors, undeserving of gratitude and public commemoration:

> The other monument cannot be rectified. Except with dynamite. . . . It is a monument erected by white men to Maoris who fell fighting with the whites and *against their own people*, in the Maori war. "Sacred to the memory of the brave men who fell on the 14th of May, 1864," etc. On one side are the names of about twenty Maoris. It is not a fancy of mine; the monument exists. I saw it. It is an object-lesson to the rising generation. It invites to treachery, disloyalty, unpatriotism. Its lesson, in frank terms is, "Desert your flag, slay your people, burn their homes, shame your nationality—we honor such." (FE, 322)

Twain's critique of the Moutoa Gardens war memorial proved prophetic. A century after his visit, almost two hundred natives occupied the park for seventy-nine days to protest a proposal by the New Zealand government to establish a one billion dollar cap for the "full and final settlement of all outstanding Maori land claims."[80] The activists chose the park—called Pakaitore in Maori—"as a symbol of past grievances," much in the same way that members of the American Indian Movement selected Wounded Knee, South Dakota, as their place of occupation in 1973. The Maori claimed that Pakaitore had never been ceded to the British by treaty; they also objected to the monument's offensive characterization of indigenous resistance to colonial incursion as "fanaticism and barbarism." Declaring *tino rangatiratanga* —absolute sovereignty—they established a large encampment, built a wooden fence, and publicly demanded the return of not only the park but all ancestral lands. Although the Maori did not achieve these goals, extensive media coverage of the occupation—like that of Alcatraz Island by the "Indians of All Tribes" from 1969 to 1971—helped to raise global consciousness about the injustices faced by contemporary indigenous peoples.

In 2010, Twain's remarks on the Moutoa Gardens war memorial inspired a work of experimental theater by New Zealand playwright David Geary called *Mark Twain & Me in Maoriland*. The production, which premiered at that year's annual International Arts Festival in Auckland, interweaves "historical fact with magical realism." According to the festival program guide, the play "sparks from the true account of Mark Twain's Australasian lecture tour, which came to an abrupt halt when the outspoken writer . . . shocked the colonials when he [stated that] a Moutoa monument, honouring Maori loyal to the English, should be blown up for encouraging natives to become traitors to their own race. He also claimed the rebel Maori, slandered as barbarians and fanatics, were in fact the country's true patriots."[81] Geary's foundational premise—that the writer extemporaneously vented his ire about the Moutoa Gardens monument during a public performance—while intriguing, is not supported by any contemporary sources.[82] Nonetheless, this creative revisioning of history—particularly the eruption of colonial "wrath" that allegedly ensued in the wake of the writer's comments—underscores both the relevance and radical nature of his views. More than a century after the publication of *Following the Equator*, Twain's words still offer a touchstone for exploring the effects of colonialism on the Maori in the twenty-first century.

INDIGENOUS DINING

Clemens's tour of New Zealand concluded with two triumphant performances in the colonial capital of Wellington on 10 and 11 December 1895. Before the first of these engagements, he paid a visit to Lord David Glasgow, the governor general, who attended that evening's lecture with his wife. While no records exist of the two men's conversation, etiquette dictates that the writer's impressions of New Zealand would have been solicited and duly received. In this context, he perhaps mentioned his interest in the Maori, laying the groundwork for a most unusual dinner invitation that materialized the next day. Clemens was routinely feted, wined and dined by local dignitaries throughout the world lecture tour; most of these events receive only superficial mention in his notebook, such as the entry for 10 December stating, "Supper at Wellington Club." This venue—New Zealand's oldest, most exclusive private men's club, chartered by Queen Victoria in 1841—catered to high-ranking members of the colonial aristocracy, yet Twain offers no indication of who sponsored the affair or attended it. In contrast, the dinner at which he was honored the following evening was extraordinary enough to warrant the following description:

> After lecture, supper at the Club Hotel, given by Mr. Carroll (half-caste)
> Minister for Maori Affairs. Present, young Honi-Heke, grand-nephew
> of the Maori hero and one of the 4 permitted Maori representatives—71

white—Reese, Minister; Ward, do.; an editor; Smythe, I—& one [or] 2 others—9 of us—Modesty Club.[83]

The host of this intimate dinner was the mixed blood politician James Carroll (1857–1926)—Irish on his father's side and Maori on his mother's—who served on Prime Minister Richard Seddon's Executive Council as a representative of the native race. Although Twain refers to him as the "Minister for Maori Affairs," the title is a misnomer since this cabinet-level post did not exist before 1899. Carroll nonetheless moved in the privileged inner circle of New Zealand's political elite and was a paradigm of successful assimilation. Fluent in both Maori and English, he was a superb orator and a staunch advocate for aboriginal rights. But above all, Carroll was a skilled diplomat—a culture broker able to bridge the often-contentious divide between whites and Aboriginals. Indeed, his base of appeal was so broad that in 1893 the European constituents of his district elected him to the New Zealand Parliament as their representative.

The care with which Clemens identifies the other individuals who attended the dinner suggests the importance he ascribed to this unique occasion. The entry itself, like others in the same notebook, is written in pencil. Numerals were subsequently added above each name in black ink, however, indicating that while no mention of the event occurs either in the manuscript or published text, he revisited it while composing *Following the Equator* in London. Moreover, the writer's oblique reference to the "Modesty Club" is a private joke attesting to the camaraderie he enjoyed with these new acquaintances. The name alludes to a fictitious organization—"THE MODEST CLUB of the United States of America"—so exclusive that he was its only member, which he invited William Dean Howells to join in an 1880 letter. Membership in the organization, he explains, "is consonant with yourself, for it is refined, cultured, more than ordinarily talented, & of exceptionally high character." Regarding other potential candidates for admission, he asserts,

> I do not know that we can find any others, though I have had some thought of Hay, Warner, Twichell, Aldrich, Osgood, Fields, Higginson, & a few more—together with Mrs. Howells, Mrs. Clemens, & certain others of the sex. . . . I have long felt that there ought to be an organized gang *of our kind.*

He also appends an extensive list of bylaws, specifying that fellowship—the communal pleasure of sharing good food and stimulating conversation—was the club's raison d'être:

The object of the Club shall be, to eat & talk.

Qualification for membership shall be, aggravated modesty, unobtrusiveness, native humility; learning, talent, intelligence; and unassailable character. . . .

Any member may call a meeting, when & where he or she may choose.

Two members shall constitute a quorum; & a meeting thus inaugurated shall be competent to eat & talk.

There shall be no fees or dues. There shall be no regular place of meeting.

There shall be no officers, except a President; & any member who has anything to eat & talk about, may constitute himself President for the time being, & call in any member or members he pleases, to help him devour & expatiate. (MTHL, 308–9)

Unlike the homogeneous association of writers, editors, and publishers envisioned in Twain's 1880 letter, linked not only by profession but also race and social class, the Wellington iteration of the "Modesty Club" was a diverse, multicultural gathering of influential politicians. "Reese," in all likelihood, was William Pember Reeves, the New Zealand minister of labor, and "Ward" was the minister of finance, who eleven years later became the colony's prime minister. But the most striking name on Twain's list is "young Hone-Heke," also known as Ngapua, the twenty-six-year-old grand-nephew of the celebrated warrior who led a rebellion against British rule in the 1840s. Although he and Carroll were initially allies, their relationship eventually grew strained over the question of Maori self-determination.[84] Ngapua, elected to Parliament in 1893, steadfastly championed this cause, introducing a controversial Native Rights Bill in 1897, which although vetoed was instrumental in the establishment of the Young Maori Party later that same year. The significance of Ngapua's presence at the club hotel dinner may best be understood in a comparative cultural context—it was akin to Twain breaking bread with a descendant of Red Cloud, Crazy Horse, or Sitting Bull. Unlike the writer's brief visit to the Maori Council House near Wanganui, where he exchanged polite formalities with a local chief, this occasion offered him an unprecedented opportunity to "devour & expatiate" with two leading representatives of the "rising generation" of natives—men of "learning, talent, [and] intelligence," whom he regarded not as inferior "Others" but peers and "brothers."

The dinner was apparently a leisurely affair that continued into the early hours of the next morning—as Clemens jotted in his notebook, "Finished at 1:30am"—unusually late given the poor state of his health. At some point during the evening, he made a short speech, which unfortunately has not been preserved. The substance of the men's conversation is similarly cloaked in mystery; neither Carroll nor Ngapua even mentions meeting the writer in their diaries. And yet, given the intensity of Twain's response to the Moutoa Gardens war memorial just three days earlier, it seems possible—if not inevitable—that he broached the subject. This conjecture raises a tantalizing question: how might Carroll and Ngapua have responded to the moral outrage of their distinguished American guest? As members of the colonial Parliament, their loyalty to the British Crown was expected; however, as Maoris, they would surely have been gratified by this powerful validation of indigenous patrimony. Two details in Clemens's notebook entry corroborate these speculations. First, his characterization of the assembled guests as the "Modesty Club" implies a bond of interracial solidarity, perhaps fostered—at least in part—by the expression of ideological sympathies. The second, more compelling, detail—a politically fraught lesson in Maori etymology—suggests that native-white relations were among the topics discussed at table: "Pakeha—white man (equivalent to <u>foreigner</u>). Genesis of it: pakepakeha, <u>white fairy</u>—the fairies were white. When the white man came, they took him for a kind of fairy because of his complexion.[85] He transcribes this information without commentary; however, its relevance to his own circumstances is unmistakable. Although the writer had—in the imperial prerogative of his white skin—declared himself "At Home" in lecture halls throughout the colony, he was on this occasion politely reminded of his status as a foreigner by his native hosts.

Clemens's epiphany about indigenous landrights—spurred largely by his viewing of the Moutoa Gardens memorial—infuses his concluding remarks about New Zealand in *Following the Equator:* "The sturdy Maoris made the settlement of the country by the whites rather difficult. Not at first—but later. At first they welcomed the whites, and were eager to trade with them—particularly for muskets. . . . In the early days things went well enough. The natives sold land without clearly understanding the terms of exchange, and the whites bought it without being much disturbed about the native's confusion of mind" (FE, 322–23). This thumbnail history—the hospitable reception of European newcomers who exploit the natives' interest in new technologies as a means of defrauding them of ancestral lands—echoes the pattern of North American colonial conquest. In both instances, amicable interracial relations devolve into violence, yet Twain champions the spirited resistance of the Maori rather than denouncing them as savages: "By and by the Maori began to comprehend that he was being wronged; then there was trouble, for he was not a man to swallow a wrong and go aside and cry about it. He had the Tasmanian's spirit and endurance, and a notable share of military science besides; and so he rose against the oppressor, did this gallant 'fanatic,' and started a war that was not brought to a definite end until more than a generation had sped."

In the Berg manuscript, Twain placed an asterisk after the term *fanatic*, adding a footnote omitted from the published text that states, "He is so named on a monument at Wanganui by some man with an ignoble heart or a shallow mind. The Maoris were patriots—patriots of the first order."[86] The writer then tore the chapter "Land Disputes and Final Settlement" from J. S. Laurie's 1896 book, *The Story of Australasia,* and clipped it to the manuscript to support his argument. Like the lengthy passages from James Bonwick's *The Lost Tasmanian Race* that he planned to incorporate into his discussion of Australia's Aboriginals, these pages were apparently part of the "raft of reprint matter" later excised by editor Andrew Chatto. Laurie's thesis—that "the integrity of property rights is paramount" among all human beings—discusses the dispossession of the Maori in relation to other indigenous peoples, thereby rendering explicit the cross-cultural analogy that is suppressed in Twain's text:

> It is an egregious mistake to suppose that the Maori or any other semi-barbarous race, not strictly nomadic, may be pronounced indifferent to land because he, in ignorance of value, is, or was, willing to barter a hundred acres for an old musket. Even the wretched Australian aborigine, or infinitely more sternly, the American Red Indian, appreciates the paramount importance of his hunting-grounds, and stands ready, as we have seen, from the date of Botany Bay, to resent foreign intrusion on his territory.[87]

Despite Twain's marginalia in Bonwick's text linking the British slaughter of native Tasmanians to "our own modern dealings with the Indians," he never acknowledged the parallel between Indians and Aboriginals in either his published work or private correspondence. While the reasons for his silence are ultimately unknowable, a notebook entry made after viewing Dr. Hocken's grotesque lignified caterpillar offers a clue:

> Idiots argue that Nature is kind & fair to us if we are loyal & obey her laws. . . . How then are these people going to excuse Nature for afflicting that helpless and ignorant creature [?] It would save those people a world of uncomfortable shuffling if they would recognize one plain fact—a fact which a man willing to see can be blind to— viz., that there is nothing kindly, nothing beneficent, nothing friendly in Nature toward <u>any</u> creature, except by capricious fits & starts; & that Nature's attitude toward all life is profoundly vicious, treacherous & malignant.[88]

Human beings, he observes, are willing to engage "plain facts" only up to a point; when confronting a truth too distressing to bear, however, they avert their gaze in denial. Throughout his life, Clemens was, without question, a man ever "willing to see"—alert, inquisitive, insightful—and yet, as this instance demonstrates, he too could be "blind," unable to forthrightly acknowledge the shameful legacy of America's imperial past.

Conclusion

Education consists mainly in what we have unlearned.
                                        1897 Notebook Entry

In February 1896, a Calcutta reporter interviewed Clemens about his first impressions of India. His remarks—lauding the many benefits of British colonial rule—indicate that the fleeting connections he had made several months earlier between the condition of indigenous peoples in the Southern Hemisphere and American Indians remained percolating in his consciousness. The "English [race]," he asserts, is "vigorous, prolific, and enterprising. Above all it is composed of merciful people, the best kind for colonizing the globe. Look, for instance, at Canada."[1] To illustrate this point, the writer chooses a curious example—the disparate treatment of natives north and south of the US border. In Canada, he notes, "the Indians are peaceful and contented enough," while in the United States "there are continual rows with the Government, which invariably end in the red man being shot down." Clemens's explanation of this difference, though oversimplified and not entirely factual, is telling:

> I attribute it to the greater humanity with which the Indians are treated in Canada. In the States we shut them off into a reservation, which we frequently encroached upon. Then ensued trouble. The red men killed settlers, and of course the Government had to order out troops and put them down. If an Indian kills a white man he is sure to lose his life, but if a white man kills a redskin he never suffers according to law.[2]

This reflection on comparative North American colonial histories, perhaps inspired by "Governor Davey's Proclamation" board—the idealized image of reciprocal racial justice that the writer had recently seen in Tasmania—demonstrates his awareness that genocidal violence was not an inevitable corollary of imperial conquest. In contrast to earlier works, such as "The Noble Red Man" and "Huck Finn and Tom Sawyer among the Indians," in which the horrific bloodshed that plagued the Western frontier is attributed to the innate savagery of native peoples, he now acknowledges the federal government's culpability in fomenting a destructive pattern of escalating attacks and reprisals. But most significantly, his response briefly—almost wistfully—acknowledges the prospect of an alternate scenario wherein American settlers and Indians might have harmoniously coexisted—if only the "greater humanity" that characterized Canada's relations with its First Nations tribes had been extended to them. This sentiment echoes the "yearning myth" that D.H. Lawrence posits at the heart of Cooper's *Leatherstocking Tales*—a "dream beyond democracy . . . [of] the nucleus of a new society" embodied in the interracial friendship of Natty Bumppo and Chingachgook.[3]

A year later, however, this retrospective expression of regret was all but forgotten as Twain penned the conclusion of *Following the Equator*. While still conceding the inevitability of colonial conquest—that "all the savage lands in the world are going to be brought under subjection to the Christian governments of Europe" (FE, 625)—he represents Indians not as dispossessed victims but as imperialist aggressors:

> All the territorial possessions of all the political establishments in the earth—including America, of course—consist of pilferings from other people's wash. No tribe, however insignificant, and no nation, howsoever mighty, occupies a foot of land that was not stolen. When the English, the French, and the Spaniards reached America, the Indian tribes had been raiding each other's territorial clothes-lines for ages, and every acre of ground in the continent had been stolen and re-stolen 500 times. The English, the French, and the Spaniards went to work and stole it all over again; and when that was satisfactorily accomplished they went diligently to work and stole it from each other. (FE, 623)

According to John Carlos Rowe, Twain's stolen-laundry metaphor treats "different peoples, regions, and histories . . . reductively (and inaccurately). [It also] ignores the fact that some societies, notably native American, are not structured around property ownership either by the community or the individual."[4] The writer's failure to distinguish between the indigeneity of Indians—and the hereditary landrights conferred by millennia of continuous habitation—and the foreignness of European colonizers further compromises the logic of his analogy. His inclusion of their dispossession as an example of the universal "law of custom [which] supersedes all other forms of law" (FE, 624) rationalizes the doctrine of Manifest Destiny, allowing him to sidestep any overt acknowledgment of national guilt.

Between 1901 and 1910, Clemens's involvement with the American Anti-Imperialist League, many of whose members (such as Herbert Welsh and Carl Schurz) had been prominent advocates of native rights earlier in their careers, fostered a reconsideration of this view. Filtered through yet another international lens—the US occupation of the Philippines and suppression of the islanders' resistance—he finally recognized the primacy of Indian land title, a fact Orion had championed a half century earlier. In a 1907 interview published in the *Baltimore News*, he states, "It makes my blood boil to think of the titled robbers of Europe who could give a man a piece of paper granting him vast estates not yet stolen from their real owners, but just about to be stolen. Think of Calvert in Maryland, Penn in Pennsylvania, and the rest—freebooters of the worst type—coming into a country, with no right but the right of superior force, and daring to claim possession of whole States!"[5] Twain's 1902 dialogue "The Dervish and the Offensive Stranger" also addresses this topic, claiming that the European settlers of the New World "hunted and harried the original owners of the soil, and robbed them, beggared them, drove them from their homes, and exterminated them, root and branch"; yet inexplicably, he chose not to publish it (CT2, 548). As Lou Budd observed, the writer "was never to focus directly on the dark agony of the American Indian, a subject fit for his most trenchant insights."[6]

Occasional flickers of recognition occur in private documents: Henry Parker Willis's declaration that it is the "manifest mission of the Teutonic nations . . . to organiz[e] the world politically [through] interference in the affairs of populations not wholly barbaric" in his 1905 volume, *Our Philippine Problem: A Study of American Colonial Policy*, prompts Twain to comment, "Our Indians, for instance?"[7] Similarly, in his autobiographical dictation of 12 January 1906, the writer offers a sardonic account of native genocide in a passage concerning the origins of Thanksgiving Day:

> Thanksgiving Day . . . originated in New England two or three centuries ago when those people recognized that they really had something to be thankful for—annually, not oftener—if they had succeeded in exterminating their neighbors, the Indians, during the previous twelve months instead of getting exterminated by their neighbors the Indians. Thanksgiving Day became a habit, for the reason that in the course of time, as the years drifted on, it was perceived that the exterminating had ceased to be mutual and was all on the white man's side, consequently on the Lord's side, consequently it was proper to thank the Lord for it and extend the usual annual compliments. The original reason for a Thanksgiving Day has long ago ceased to exist—the Indians have long ago been comprehensively and satisfactorily exterminated and the account closed with Heaven, with the thanks due. But, from old habit, Thanksgiving Day has remained with us. (A1, 267–68)[8]

The selectivity of Twain's published anti-imperial critiques—denouncing US expansion and aggression abroad while largely ignoring it at home—suggests that he considered the dispossession of indigenous peoples a fait accompli. Discomfited by the fulfillment of the "vanishing Indian" myth he had internalized as a child, he perhaps found the topic too painful—and ultimately futile—too confront. "The woes of the wronged & the unfortunate poison my life," he told Herbert Welsh in 1906, "& make it so undesirable that pretty often I wish I were 90 instead of 70."[9] This explanation, while poignant, is nonetheless unsatisfactory; as an avid reader of newspapers, the writer unquestionably knew that Indians had neither "vanished" nor been "exterminated, root and branch."

During the years Clemens resided in New York City, the annual Lake Mohonk Conference, established in 1883 by the Friends of the Indian, attracted hundreds of participants who met to discuss the assimilation, land-drights, and eventual citizenship of native peoples. Moreover, tribal resistance to federal policies continued to flare up sporadically in the West, particularly in Oklahoma's Indian Territory, stoking fears of a potential uprising. In the arena of sports, the Carlisle Indian School's football team, featuring future Olympian Jim Thorpe in the position of halfback, played—and often trounced—Penn, Harvard, Princeton, and West Point. President Teddy Roosevelt himself acknowledged Indians as a political entity, inviting six prominent native leaders, among them, the Apache chief Geronimo, Quanah Parker of the Comanche, and American Horse of the Lakota, to participate in his 1905 inaugural parade. The men accepted, riding on horseback in traditional regalia through the streets of the nation's capital; in return, they were granted an audience with Roosevelt and the opportunity to advocate firsthand for the welfare of their people.[10] Twain's inattention to these widespread reports about Indians implies either disinterest or a foreclosed mindset. His gaze was in a sense farsighted—keenly focused on international phenomena, such as King Leopold's abuses in the Congo, while those in closer proximity remained blurred and indistinct—as illustrated by his response to one of the nation's most enduring forms of popular entertainment.

BUFFALO BILL REDUX

On 2 April 1901, about six months after the Clemens family returned to New York after nearly a decade abroad, William F. Cody opened the eighteenth consecutive season of his legendary Wild West at Madison Square Garden. The cavernous arena was "packed to the roof" with a capacity crowd, its ringside box seats occupied by an array of eminent figures—politicians and high-ranking military men,[11] many of whom were grizzled veterans of the Indian Wars—as well as the writer, his wife, and his daughter.[12] In the seventeen years since he had seen and effusively admired Cody's spectacle at the Elmira Driving Park, its scope and content had significantly changed. Renamed "The Wild West and Congress of the Rough Riders of the World" in 1893, the extravaganza now celebrated not only the conquest of the American frontier but also the exploits of Western imperial powers abroad. While the show's 1901 iteration still featured a number of familiar set pieces, such as "Attack on the Deadwood Stagecoach" and "Buffalo Hunt," along with the marksmanship of Annie Oakley, the "Grand Review" had a decidedly global character. It included Cossacks, Arabs, a "Commando of Transvaal Boers," and "Baden-Powell's Defenders of Mafeking"—the British soldiers who defeated the Boers in South Africa—marching alongside cowboys and Indians.[13]

The most striking addition to the 1901 program, however, was its jingoistic climax, "The Battle of Tien-Tsin." This piece reenacted the June 1900 siege in which rebellious Boxers, played by Indians garbed as Chinamen—one group of indigenous "heathens" conveniently standing in for another[14]—were defeated by an international force, the so-called Eight Nation Alliance, of Britain, Japan, France, Russia, Germany, Italy, the Austro-Hungarian Empire, and the United States. Designed to "rouse patriotism to an effervescent degree,"[15] the skit presented the assault on the Peking citadel as an archetypal contest between the "proudly defiant Royal Standard of Paganism" and the "Christian World," and concluded with the triumphant hoisting of the "BANNERS OF CIVILIZATI/ON."[16] According to the *New York Times,* the finale was "full of stirring action, all very successfully done . . . and will probably prove more popular even than did the capture of San Juan Hill, which was so important a part of last year's Wild West."[17]

Numerous reporters in attendance at the event—doubtlessly familiar with "To the Person Sitting in Darkness," Clemens's scathing denunciation of US imperialism in China and the Philippines, published two months earlier in the *North American Review*—eagerly observed his response to Cody's political pageantry. The *New York Telegram,* for example, described him looking "sour as a German pickle" throughout the show and clapping "feebly" when the impresario bowed directly in front of his box.[18] The *New York Press* commented that when the "Rough Riders of the World" were introduced during the "Grand Review," he "ignored those fighting for extending England's empire and applauded loudly for the Boers."[19] By the time "The Battle of Tien Tsin" began, Clemens apparently had had enough. He stood up and abruptly exited the garden, thereby signaling "his disapproval of our foreign policy" in the estimation of several journalists.[20] Although the writer never acknowledged his departure as an act of political protest, his solidarity with the Boxer cause is apparent in a speech he made to the New York Public Education Association later that year: "When it comes to a settlement of the immigrant question I am with the Boxer every time. The Boxer is a patriot; he is the only patriot China has. The Boxer believes in driving us out of his country. I wish him success. I am a Boxer myself."[21]

"WHITE BOXERS AND PAWNEES"

Clemens's ardent sympathy for the Boxers did not, however, extend to the native actors who played them onstage. Despite the proximity of his ringside seat, he seems not to have registered their identity or the ironic implications of the performance itself. Although invisible as Indians, the verisimilitude of their defeat as Boxers rankled the writer for months, resurfacing in a December 1901 notebook entry: "Second Advent. Begins triumphal march around the globe at Tien Tsin preceded by Generals, Warships, cavalry, infantry, artillery, who clear the road & pile the dead for 'propagation of the Gospel,' followed by looting [and] singing 'where every prospect pleases & only man is vile.' Christ arrives in a vast war-fleet furnished by the Great Powers."[22]

This statement echoes the argument of "To the Person Sitting in Darkness," which does in fact address the subject of Indians, though in a strained, peripheral manner. Enraged at the exorbitant indemnities collected by the American Board of Foreign Missions as compensation for the Christian lives and property lost during the Boxer Rebellion, Twain insists that missionaries should embody not only "the grace and gentleness and charity and loving kindness of our religion" but also "the American spirit"—a quality he explicitly identifies with the continent's earliest inhabitants (CT2, 459). The analogy he constructs to illustrate this point is strangely counter-intuitive; ignoring the parallel between the coercive tactics used to convert indigenous peoples in both settings, he equates the missionaries, rather than the Boxers, with Indians, imaginatively recasting these allegedly civilized soldiers of Christ as savages.

The terms of Twain's comparison are problematic. His statement, "The oldest Americans are the Pawnees," arbitrarily asserts the historical primacy of this one tribe above all others; yet his recent reading of Marquis de

Nadaillac's *Pre-Historic America*, a study of the continent's Paleolithic peoples, demonstrates that he knew this to be untrue.[23] The name Pawnee apparently amused the writer; earlier in his career, he had invoked them as quintessentially stereotypical savages on several occasions—spoofing a reformer who served in the role of president of the "Pawnee Educational Society" in the 1867 sketch "Female Suffrage" and lamenting that he and his companions aboard their westward-bound stagecoach in *Roughing It* had "no swallow-tail coats and white kid gloves to wear at Pawnee receptions in the Rocky Mountains" (RI, 4). Moreover, the authoritative "evidence" he cites to support his analogy derives from a fictitious source, *Macallum's History:*

> When a white Boxer kills a Pawnee and destroys his property, the other Pawnees do not trouble to seek *him* out, they kill any white person that comes along; also, they make some white village pay deceased's heirs the full cash value of deceased, together with full cash value of the property destroyed; they also make the village pay, in addition, *thirteen times* the value of that property into a fund for the dissemination of the Pawnee religion, which they regard as the best of all religions for the softening and humanizing of the heart of man. It is their idea that it is only fair and right that the innocent should be made to suffer for the guilty, and that it is better that ninety and nine innocent should suffer than that one guilty person should escape. (CT2, 459)

Twain's oxymoron "white Boxer" effects a double displacement, transposing the categories of both race and indigeneity. The Christian missionaries are "Pawnees" because of the indiscriminate manner in which they exact vengeance against "Others" who have wronged them—killing innocent civilians rather than seeking out the actual perpetrators. Rather than following Christ's injunction to "turn the other cheek" when confronted with violence, they embrace the notion of collective responsibility, which the writer characterized in *Following the Equator* as "the primary law of savage life" (FE, 209). His analogy thus reveals an enduring perception of native peoples as the embodiment of barbaric violence.

James McNutt's observation that Twain "never totally refrained from using the Indian's savagery as a club wherever convenient"[24] is corroborated by the gratuitous racial slur he employs in an October 1907 autobiographical dictation to condemn Teddy Roosevelt's inhumane hunting practice of "slaughtering helpless bears" at a private game preserve: "The President of the United States ought to hire a squaw and a comb and get at it" (A3, 162). He impugns the uncivilized character of the nation's commander in chief by likening him to a native chieftain whose lice-infested body requires the grooming of a subservient "squaw." This repulsive imagery strongly echoes the writer's 1862 description of the fictitious Washoe chief Hoop-de-doodle do, who "sheds vermin . . . of prodigious size" as he walks, then promptly eats them, suggesting a persistent imaginative association between dirt and Indian depravity.

"OUT OF HISTORY OF YESTERDAY'S DATE"

Six months before his death, Clemens returned to the interrelated themes of savagery, violence, and collective responsibility in an unpublished theological screed called "Letters from the Earth." Raging against the hypocritical Christian notion of God as a benign "Father of Mercy," he recounts a paradigmatic example of "root and branch extinction"—the Israelite slaughter of the Midianites (Num. 31:1–18) in which *all* the virgins, *all* the men, *all* the babies, *all* 'creatures that breathe,' *all* houses, [and] *all* cities" (CT2, 926) were destroyed in retaliation for an unspecified (and in his estimation, presumably minor) offense. The remorseless sweep of God's vengeance, he writes, "makes no distinction between innocent and guilty. . . what the insane Father required was blood and misery; he was indifferent as to who furnished it" (CT2, 925).

Although Twain initially claims that the Midianite massacre has no parallel in "either savage or civilized history," he concedes a few sentences later that other, equally appalling, incidents can be found in the "history made by the red Indian of America," citing the 1862 Dakota uprising in Minnesota. He had made this same comparison more than three decades earlier in a passage written for—and subsequently omitted from—*The Innocents Abroad:*

> Ordered by Joshua, by the prophet Samuel & by Moses, these people committed the most astounding atrocities; they utterly exterminated not only the helpless women & children of vanquished foes, but even the irresponsible dumb brutes of the field & the pasture. The Indians of Minnesota massacred the whites precisely in the same way a few years ago; but they spared the dumb animals. Israel said God commanded their massacres. The Indians will say the Great Spirit commanded theirs. All savage peoples harbor the engaging vanity that they are the chosen of God. They imagine that all their journeyings are superintended by the Deity in person & all their little performances suggested by him.[25]

In "Letters from the Earth," Twain extrapolates on this same idea, anchoring it within the gruesome context of a specific incident:

Twelve Indians broke into a farm house at daybreak and captured the family. It consisted of the farmer and his wife and four daughters, the youngest age fourteen and the eldest eighteen. They crucified the parents; that is to say, they stood them stark naked against the wall of the living room and nailed their hands to the wall. Then they stripped the daughters bare, stretched them upon the floor in front of their parents, and repeatedly ravished them. Finally they crucified the girls against the wall opposite the parents, and cut off their noses and their breasts. They also—but I will not go into that. There is a limit. There are indignities so atrocious that the pen cannot write them. One member of that poor crucified family—the father—was still alive when help came two days later. (CT2, 927)

According to Paul Baender's explanatory notes on "Letters from the Earth" in *What is Man?* (WIM), the likely source of this story is Richard Irving Dodge's 1877 book *The Plains of North America and Their Inhabitants*. Clemens owned not one but two copies of this text—the first purchased soon after its original publication and a second sent at his request to Elmira during the summer of 1884 in preparation for writing "Huck Finn and Tom Sawyer among the Indians." He also commended Dodge to Howells in 1877 as "a man who knows all about Indians, & yet has some humanity in him" and expressed hope that the newly elected President Rutherford B. Hayes would appoint him "head of the Indian Department" (MTHL, 172). This respect doubtlessly influenced his uncritical acceptance of the story's veracity, despite Dodge's own caveat about hearing it thirdhand in the mid-1870s from an anonymous "gentleman" who journeyed to Minnesota after the fighting had ended. In fact, while instances of extreme violence did occur on both sides during the Dakota uprising, most have never been confirmed. The collective hysteria that existed among the region's Anglo-American settlers in the late summer of 1862 makes it difficult to separate fiction from reality; as Minnesota's first governor Colonel Henry H. Sibling, who commanded the state militia during the conflict, informed his wife in a letter on 21 August 1862, "Do not believe the thousand extravagant reports you hear. People are absolutely crazy with excitement and [heed] every absurdity."[26]

When the writer first encountered the tale in 1877, its iconic qualities—unsuspecting settlers beset at daybreak inside the security of their home—likely reminded him of Jane Clemens's harrowing tale of the Montgomery Massacre, rekindling his early aversion to Indians. His account in "Letters from the Earth," however, is not a verbatim extract from Dodge but an impressionistic re-creation more than a quarter century later, suggesting that its horrors were deeply imprinted in his memory. In this regard,

Twain's divergences from the original source—all of which amplify the grotesque violence inflicted upon the family—are revealing. He states that there were four daughters rather than three, the oldest of whom was eighteen not twenty—underscoring the victims' vulnerability and innocence. He also uses the verb "crucified" three times, although it never appears in Dodge, and erroneously claims that all six members of the family suffered this appalling fate. Additionally, the sole surviving member of the household in his account is not one of the daughters but the father—whose inability to protect his loved ones from sexual defilement at the hands of these implacable savages parallels the emasculating helplessness Brace Johnson experiences upon discovering evidence that his fiancée has been gang raped by her Sioux captors in the unfinished sequel.

In much the same way that Peggy Mills's fate is rendered unspeakable in "Huck Finn and Tom Sawyer among the Indians," the halting syntax of Twain's statement, "They also—but I will not go into that," invokes the boundaries of Victorian propriety to explain why the "atrocious indignities" inflicted upon the girls cannot be described. His refusal to address the subject of sexual violence not only reflects the high cultural value—or "sacrality," as Christopher Castiglia terms it—of female chastity and virtue in nineteenth-century American society but also affirms his superiority to the savages who committed these heinous acts.[27] Underscoring the moral inviolability of this taboo, he states, "There is a limit," beyond which "the pen cannot write."— Twain had used this same rhetorical strategy almost forty years earlier at the end of "The Noble Red Man," describing an Indian attack in which *"Children were burned alive in the presence of their parents. Wives were ravished before their husbands' eyes. Husbands were mutilated, tortured, and scalped, and their wives compelled to look on."* He then challenges readers of the *Galaxy* to imagine even more unfathomable atrocities, explaining, "But their favorite mutilations cannot be put into print" (CT1, 446). These statements—respective bookends from the beginning and end of the writer's career—demonstrate that he never relinquished the notion of Indians as lustful, barbarous creatures intent upon the destruction of white womanhood.

Twain also claims that the 1862 attack was not an isolated anomaly but simply *"one* incident of the Minnesota massacre. I could give you fifty. They would cover all the different kinds of cruelty the brutal human talent has ever invented" (CT2, 927). He thus insinuates that the Dakota embody the lowest, most abhorrent traits of human behavior. And yet, when placed within the comparative context of the Midianite massacre, he ultimately deems the Indians' actions "more merciful" than the Father of Mercies'. "Having been deeply wronged and treacherously treated by the government of the United States," the Indians' vengeance was rooted in a justifiable cause. Moreover, the scale of their destruction was not nearly as comprehensive: they burned some, but not all, of their enemies' homes; stole livestock but killed none; and "sold no virgins into slavery." Most importantly, according to Twain, they killed the women after raping them, "charitably ma[king] their subsequent sufferings brief, ending them with the precious gift of death" (CT2, 927). This indictment demolishes any distinction between civilization and savagery, implying that human nature—regardless of race, ethnicity, culture, or creed—is universally brutal and debased.

"INDIAN EVE"

In a 1903 essay entitled "Instructions in Art," published in the *New Metropolitan* magazine, Twain explored the notion of common humanity from a more lighthearted, humorous perspective. Posing as an "exalted" portraitist whose subjects are impossible to identify, he uses a series of original sketches to dispense inane advice, such as do not "paint in installments—the head on one canvas and the bust on another." Twain also parodies the pretentious jargon of art critics, describing one of his portraits—a nude—as both a "still-life" and "an impressionist picture, done in distemper, with a chiaroscuro motif modified by monochromatic technique."[28] To demonstrate his versatility, the author incorporates illustrations of a wide variety of subjects, from Proserpine and Chauncey Depew to an obscure, empty-handed fisherman named "Joseph Jefferson." But "the best and most winning and eloquent portrait my brush has ever produced," he immodestly claims, is "a lady in the style of Raphael" (fig. 25):

> Originally I started it out for Queen Elizabeth, but was not able to do the lace hopper her head projects out of, therefore I tried to turn it into Pocahontas, but was again baffled, and was compelled to make further modifications, this time achieving success. By spiritualizing it and turning it into the noble mother of our race and throwing into the countenance the sacred joy which her first tailor-made outfit infuses into her spirit, I was enabled to add to my gallery.[29]

The notations Twain inscribed on this illustration reveal that the figure's metamorphosis was more complex than he acknowledges. As the subject evolves, owing to the limitations of his draftsmanship, it transcends not

FIGURE 25.   "Indian Eve," "Instructions in Art." Public domain.

only time and space but also the categories of race, ethnicity, and gender.
Twain's "joke," of course, is that the finished portrait is not Eve—or even
female—but rather, as the words in the upper-left corner indicate, a likeness
of Sitting Bull, the famed Lakota veteran of the Battle of the Little Big
Horn, whose assassination on 15 December 1890 was a precipitating factor

in the Wounded Knee massacre two weeks later. Sitting Bull was one of the most photographed native leaders of the nineteenth century; moreover, his iconic appearance—prominent cheekbones, braided hair, aquiline nose, and direct, defiant gaze—made him instantly recognizable in the pages of periodicals like *Harper's Weekly* and *Frank Leslie's Illustrated Newspaper.* The chief had briefly toured with Buffalo Bill's Wild West in 1885; his notoriety was such that even after his death, Cody continued to reproduce the photograph in souvenir programs, including the edition produced for the 1901 performance Clemens attended. While Twain's drawing cannot be explicitly linked to one particular photograph, the fringed buckskin at his shoulders and distinctive floral design of the ceremonial sash across his breast bear close resemblance to the promotional image taken with Cody in 1885.

The evolution of the portrait's identity reflects the relativistic quality of Twain's late thinking about race. His changes, moving progressively backward through time from Sitting Bull and Pocahontas to the mother of us all, trace a symbolic genealogy of the human family. Like the speaker in Whitman's "Song of Myself," Twain's composite image is "maternal as well as paternal," representing "every hue . . . every caste and religion, / Not merely of the New World but of Africa Europe or Asia . . . a wandering savage."[30] In dissolving the binaries that have traditionally separated groups and cultures, the portrait underscores the commonality of all peoples.

"Indian Eve" also anticipates Twain's remarks in a 1909 letter to one of his Juggernaut Club pen pals, a young French woman named Helene Pickard. Knowing of the writer's great admiration for Joan of Arc, Miss Pickard had sent him an image that depicted her as "fair and comely, and sweet, and refined." This pleased him, he wrote, since most artists represent the saint as "coarse and clumsy . . . [believing] that because she was a peasant she couldn't have been otherwise." Twain then points out an aesthetic irony—that representations of another peasant, the Virgin Mary, traditionally portray her as "fair, and comely, and sweet, and refined—and white. Which she wasn't." According to the letter's postscript, Jean, who was then serving as her father's secretary, demanded that he delete this sacrilegious statement. He refused, explaining that in ancient times only one-tenth of the population was white; Mary therefore must have been darkskinned. The writer then adds, "To my mind one color is just as respectable as another; there is nothing important, nothing essential, about a complexion. I mean, to *me*. But with the Deity it is different. He doesn't think much of white people. He prefers the colored. Andrea del Sarto's pink-and-lily Madonnas revolt Him, my child. That is, they would, but He never looks at them."[31]

JEAN, GEORGE DE FOREST BRUSH, AND "A HORSE'S TALE"

Twain's relativistic thinking about Indians deepened during the summers of 1905 and 1906, as the result of his extended stay in the mountains of Dublin, New Hampshire. The village was a thriving art colony, founded in 1888 by the painter Abbott Thayer (1849–1921), which attracted an eclectic array of artists, writers, intellectuals, and political figures. At the turn of the century, two of Thayer's close associates, the painters Joseph Lindon Smith (1863–1950) and George de Forest Brush (1855–1941), purchased property in the area, becoming year-round residents. The colony's social center was Loon Point, a rambling compound of houses, studios, and open-air theaters built by Smith and his wife, Corinna, a native rights activist. Throughout the summer months, the Smiths—affectionately known as the "King and Queen of Dublin"—hosted elaborate theatricals on their property, "drawing visitors like Mark Twain, Henry Adams, and Augustus St. Gaudens, and sometimes enticing them onto the stage."[32]

As Katy Leary explains in *A Lifetime with Mark Twain*, the Dublin art colony offered Clemens a respite from the loneliness he experienced in the aftermath of Livy's death: "A lot of their friends was there, and [he] thought it would be nice."[33] The atmosphere was relaxed and convivial. According to Karen Lystra, "The Dubliners regularly amused themselves on summer evening by playing charades, with two teams that mixed adults and children. Generally Twain and the artist George de Forest Brush were team captains."[34] Clemens's camaraderie with Brush and Smith is also illustrated by the nonsensical mock debate they staged at the Dublin Lake Club in September 1906 on the topic "If it were decreed that one of the sexes must be exterminated, which one could best be spared?" For over an hour, the three men delighted their audience with "a stream of earnest and incoherent words interrupted at intervals by an illustrative good anecdote which does not illustrate anything" (A2, 214–15).

A young muralist named Barry Faulkner (1881–1966), then studying and living with Thayer in his Dublin home, remembers Jean Clemens inviting a number of young people to supper, after which her father "put on a fine show... entertain[ing] us by reading aloud his essay on 'Fennimore Cooper's Literary Offences'.... at the time I thought he had just written the piece, and that he was jubilant over his new baby, but it had been written ten years previous and the woods and dry twigs of the Dublin underbrush may have reminded him so forcibly of Cooper's 'delicate art of the forest' that he had dug out the old piece for his and our enjoyment."[35] Twain's reading selection was not, as Faulkner surmised, a response to the colony's bucolic setting but rather its residents' abiding fascination with Indians. While in Dublin, Jean became close friends with Nancy and Gerry Brush, two of the artist's older children, who introduced her to an unconventional domestic milieu that reflected their father's formative experiences living among various tribes in the West. As Jean discovered when she and Katy Leary first journeyed to New Hampshire during the winter of 1905 to view their rental quarters, the Brush children wore moccasins rather than conventional shoes and traipsed through the woods on snowshoes—an experience Nancy later recalled as "wonderful fun, glid[ing] softly over the high drifts, feeling as self-reliant as an Indian."[36] In addition to a farmhouse filled with indigenous artifacts, the Brush property included a tepee encampment created by the artist, where the family often slept in all seasons. Nancy's 1970 biography of her father fondly attests to his prowess not only as a builder but as a teacher: "Papa knew how to cut and sew a tepee, how to set up the slim poles into a pyramid and wind the tent around it, and how to leave at the top the extra long pole with a little flap of material, like a sail, which was movable and adjusted the draft in the top opening. This was the chimney for the rock-lined fire hole in the center of the earthen floor. We spread blankets and pillows under the [tepee's] low sloping roof."[37] The artist also paddled a birchbark canoe around Dublin Lake, patching and mending it with traditional techniques he learned from the Penobscot Indians.[38] As these details suggest, "playing Indian" was an integral part of daily life in the Brush family home.

The artist's interest in native cultures had developed largely as a matter of chance. After studying traditional portraiture at L'Ecole des Beaux Arts in Paris during the 1870s, he returned to the United States in 1880 at age twenty-five uncertain of his career path. When a business opportunity for his older brother Alfred arose in Wyoming in the spring of 1882, George accompanied him, much as Clemens had followed Orion to Nevada Territory in 1861. Brush's initial encounter with native peoples in the West was, like that of the writer, disillusioning; in an 1885 essay "An Artist among the Indians," published in *Century Magazine,* he describes feeling "deceived" by the contrast between the impoverished individuals seen on the streets of little railroad towns and the "false charms" ascribed to them in his early reading.[39] Unlike Clemens, however, Brush did not avert his gaze. He was curious to learn more, realizing he had found a uniquely American subject for his work. Brush moved to Fort Washakie and spent the summer living with the Arapahoe and Shoshone, at one point disguising himself as an Indian to observe a Sun Dance. He often repeated this story to his children, emphasizing that the government's subsequent ban on the ceremony "showed deep ignorance and rudeness, as [did] all their dealings with these people."[40] From Wyoming, Brush traveled north to the Crow reservation in Montana for the winter, living in one tepee and setting up a studio and woodstove in another, where he sketched scenes of tribal life. During these years in the West, he became—in the words of his eldest daughter—"well accustomed to [Indian] ways, acquiring much knowledge from them, and growing to love them."[41]

Returning to the East in the autumn of 1883, Brush often chose to live and work outdoors rather than in conventional houses. While teaching at the Art Students League in Manhattan a year later, for example, he rented land from a farmer in Hastings-on-Hudson and set up a tepee, cooking meals over an open fire. Similarly, the sculptor Augustus St. Gaudens notes in his memoir that the artist and his new wife, Mittie, spent several months in 1887 living in a tepee "on the edge of our woods, near a ravine, about five hundred yards from the house" in Cornish, New Hampshire, "for he had camped with the Indians for years and knew their habits."[42] Between 1883 and 1889, Brush also embarked upon a series of paintings based on his experiences and observations in the West. "In choosing Indians as subjects for art," he wrote, "I do not paint from the historian's or antiquary's point of view; I do not care to represent them in any curious habits which could not be comprehended by us; I am interested in those habits and deeds in which we have feelings in common."[43] This statement, as art historian Nancy Anderson explains, reveals that Brush had no interest in serving as an ethnologist; rather, "he saw in the subject of the Indian an opportunity to explore the universal, the essential, human experience."[44] In this respect, she argues, "Brush's images are anomalies—even contradictions—for their often stunningly beautiful surfaces deny the reality of contemporary Indian life in America." His intent was not to portray the misery and poverty of reservation life but the humanity of native peoples, as illustrated in his 1885 portrait "Mourning Her Brave": "I witnessed this custom daily among the Crows. I know that we do not mourn in this manner, but death and grief we are all acquainted with."[45]

As Barry Faulkner recalls, Brush retained "his Indian ways and habits"[46] long after leaving the West. At charade parties in Dublin, "there were sure to be demands for the Dog Dance, and then Brush would slip into the wild Indian rhythms he had learned on the Crow reservation. Soft, doggy yelps punctuated the sinuous grace of his movements, and the beautifully modulated monotony of the dance transported us to Indian tepees, and the mountains of Montana."[47] The artist's penchant for performing native dances is

FIGURE 26. Jean Clemens, "Indian Play." Courtesy of the Mark Twain Project, The Bancroft Library, University of California, Berkeley.

reflected in a series of photos—simply labeled "Indian play"—that Jean took in Dublin during the summer of 1905 (fig. 26).

Although the exact date of this event is unknown, an article published in the *Peterboro Transcript* on 24 August describes a pageant, directed by Joseph Lindon Smith, that was held on the estate of George Bridge Leighton and featured Brush "perform[ing] a snake dance costumed as an Indian."[48] The images reveal that Jean was positioned at the rear of a sizable audience of well-dressed men and women intently watching the movements of at least ten actors dressed in elaborate feathered headdresses and fringed moccasins. A painted tepee—also likely the handiwork of Brush—occupies the center stage. This scenario of "playing Indian," however ethnographically inaccurate, reflects the colony's interest in the plight of native peoples and a superficial appreciation of their traditional lifeways.

Although Clemens was not in the audience that day—having traveled to Norfolk, Connecticut, to visit Clara, only to have his return to Dublin delayed by a painful case of gout—Jean likely told him about the pageant and shared her photographs, perhaps influencing the uncharacteristically idyllic representation of tribal life he created several weeks later in "A Horse's Tale." On 20 September 1905, actress Minnie Maddern Fiske contacted him in Dublin requesting assistance with her campaign against bullfighting in Spain. He agreed, and penned the story—set primarily in and around Fort Paxton, a fictitious Western military installation—in eight days. Narrated by Buffalo Bill's horse, Soldier Boy, the text focuses on a spirited young orphan, Cathy Alison, who is sent to live with her uncle, the fort's commander. Cathy's charms captivate not only the soldiers and scouts but also the local Indians. Rechristened "Firefly," she is taken to visit White Cloud's camp, set in "a great shut-in meadow, full of Indian lodges and dogs and squaws and everything that is interesting." She enthusiastically describes the tranquil, intergenerational domesticity of the scene in a letter to her Aunt Mercedes in Rouen:

> Young Indians and girls romping and laughing and carrying on . . . the squaws busy at work, and the bucks busy resting, and the old men sitting in a bunch smoking, and passing the pipe not to the left but the right. . . . [Chief] Thunder-Bird put on his Sunday-best war outfit to let me see him, and he was splendid to look at, with his face painted red and bright and intense like a fire-coal and a valance of eagle feathers from the top of his head all down his back, and he had his tomahawk too, and his pipe, which has a stem which is longer than my arm.[49]

Twain's description of the chief may be indebted to the traditional regalia George de Forest Brush often donned for theatrical performances in Dublin. Moreover, although the writer increasingly came to associate Cathy with his deceased eldest daughter, Susy—even to the point of sending her photo to *Harper's* editor Frederick Duneka to use as the basis of one of the story's illustrations—the protagonist's fascination with native culture also links her with Jean. In a diary entry dated 6 August 1906, during the family's second summer in Dublin, for example, she reports:

> This morning quite early, Nancy drove home to get another dress to wear to Joe Smith's play tonight . . . [she] got back about ten o'clock. . . . We talked for a while and then I read aloud to her several of Charles _____ charming Indian-animal tales. One was, the Great Cat's Nursery, which is a delightful story about a puma and her young kittens and her struggles against the hardships of life. That story is one of my favorites and I like the entire book, in fact there is something beautifully poetic about almost every _____ in it.[50]

This account suggests that Jean's bond with Nancy, who was nearly a decade her junior, was rooted in a shared appreciation of indigenous culture. The specificity of her description reveals that the text in question is *Red Hunters and the Animal People*, a 1904 collection of stories from the ancient Dakota oral tradition published by Charles Eastman—who coincidentally would attend Twain's seventieth birthday celebration at Delmonico's a year later. As Eastman explains in the volume's preface, these stories illustrate the spirituality of the traditional Indian worldview—an animate universe in which the "four-footed tribes" of animals are brothers to human beings, to be killed "only as necessity and the exigencies of

life demand, and not wantonly." The Indian," he writes, is a natural philosopher who

> considered it a sacrilege to learn the secrets of an animal and then use
> this knowledge against him. If you wish to know his secrets you must
> show him that you are sincere, your spirit and his spirit must meet on
> common ground, and that is impossible until you have abandoned for
> the time being your habitation, your weapons, and thoughts of the
> chase, and entered into perfect accord with the wild creatures. Such
> were some of the most sacred beliefs of the Red man.[51]

Judging from the detailed nature of her account, Jean was particularly
intrigued by "The Dance of the Little People," which she characterizes as
"an exquisite tale about the moon-dance of the meadow-mice on a lake-
shore in the bright moonlight, and how it is watched & the mice protected
by several Indian boys." The material and spiritual seamlessly coexist in
this universe, and humans safeguard rather than exert dominion over
smaller creatures. The dance itself is a ceremony through which the mice
express their "respect and love" for the Creator—whom Eastman refers to
as the "Great Mystery"—seeking to restore the harmony they previously
disrupted by "nibbling off the edges of the moon" long ago.

Jean's interest in Indians persisted for the rest of her tragically short life.
On 7 August 1907, she records an unpleasant incident that occurred during
her stay at Dr. Peterson's sanitarium in Katonah, New York: "After supper
I was dreadfully upset by an argument with Bantam, concerning our treatment of the Indians & breaking of our treaties with them. He tho't civilization must advance & that it was all right. I really feel dreadfully that he
should so regard frank dishonor & injustice."[52] While these views may
have predated Jean's association with the Brush family in Dublin, her
friendship with them deepened her political awareness of the wrongs native
peoples had suffered. George de Forest Brush was very fond of Jean and
took an active interest in her health, visiting her on several occasions at the
sanitarium when business took him to New York City. In February 1908 he
wrote to his daughter Nancy, "Poor dear Jean Clemens is very ill. I have
been to see her and I am trying to help her, but it is so difficult. However, I
hope that I have induced her to give up civilized life this summer and go
with her friends with whom she is living to lead a wild camp life at Lovell
Center. I have every reason to think that she will go. I think she could get
well."[53] This allusion to "Lovell" refers to Camp Wo-He-Lo on Sebago
Lake, Maine—the precursor of the Campfire Girls organization—founded
in 1907 by the educator and social reformer Dr. Luther Halsey Gulick. Its
name, an Indian-sounding acronym for the tenets of "Work, Health, and

Love," suggests the centrality of tribal lore in the camp's programming and philosophy. Campers would learn indigenous crafts, choose names "culled from the lexicons of various native languages," and design their own ceremonial dresses and headbands.[54] Brush was thus, in essence, enjoining Jean to "play Indian"—much as he and the members of his immediate family routinely did—in order to recover her health. Although the letter indicates her receptivity to the idea, Jean was unable to escape civilization for the Maine wilderness during the summer of 1908, but instead vacationed at the seaside resort of Gloucester, Massachusetts.

As Katy Leary remembers, Jean was "always talking about what a cruel thing it was the way the Americans treated the Indians in the early days. She felt terrible about that, and used to talk about it to her father ... she felt it was very cruel to kind of push the Indians back out of the way. She thought the Government ought to do something more about it than they had done."[55] Jean's progressive views echo those of other native rights champions whom Clemens had encountered over the course of his long career—Orion, Dan De Quille, Joaquin Miller, Sara Thomsen Kinney, Kate Foote, and George de Forest Brush. Much as Orion had in his letters of protest to the treasury secretary regarding the treatment of Great Basin tribes in the 1860s, Jean publicly voiced her disapproval of federal Indian policy in a letter to the editor of the *New York Times*, published under the heading "Mediaeval Torture," on 5 April 1909. Her impetus was an article entitled "Indians in Revolt; Six Whites Killed" that had appeared on the newspaper's front page a week earlier. The "revolt" concerned a group of Creek Indians in Oklahoma led by Chitto Harjo, also known as chief Crazy Snake, who opposed the federal government's division of their reservation lands under the terms of the General Allotment Act. Refusing to accept or pay taxes on the individual parcels of land they had been assigned, the Creeks remained in their old homes and declared their intention to fight rather than surrender. Troops sent to arrest Crazy Snake were met with gunfire; although the chief escaped, his twenty-two-year-old son, a graduate of the Carlisle Indian School, was captured. According to the *Times*, the young man—who "retain[ed] all his native instincts" despite his education and Christianization—"cursed his foes and vehemently refused to tell them anything about his father's whereabouts"; in response, the sheriff ordered him strung up in a tree, threatening, "Tell us where your father is, or you'll hang there until you die. No fooling about this." Gasping for breath, finally he relented: "Let down. Tell—all—know."[56]

Jean's outrage over the inhumane treatment of Crazy Snake's son at the hands of supposedly civilized law enforcement officials parallels her father's impulsive reaction to the 1886 article in the *Hartford Daily Courant* concerning the New Mexico bounty on Apache scalps. Her letter begins with a series of scorching rhetorical questions:

> Is it possible that in this civilized land today a Deputy Sheriff can with impunity torture a prisoner? Though the son of Crazy Snake is but an Indian, how is it that the Sheriff could threaten him with death by half hanging him in order to extort revelations concerning his father and his friends?
>
> Is such brutality to pass without punishment merely because the prisoner is not a citizen?
>
> If we, considering ourselves one of the most civilized nations of the world, permit our officers to make use of the methods of the middle ages—without counting our wholesale robbery of the Indians' lands—then they who make less pretense of being civilized should be expected to murder and burn on all occasions.[57]

Jean's letter reveals that she was remarkably well informed on the subject of indigenous rights. Noting the irony that the continent's oldest inhabitants were not US citizens, she criticizes the doctrine of Manifest Destiny as "wholesale robbery" and also challenges the binary of civilization and savagery by pointing out the brutality of the sheriff's actions. According to Michael Shelden's biography, *Mark Twain: Man in White*, Jean proudly informed her father and sister of the letter's publication in a telephone conversation. While Clemens's response to the substance of her argument is unknown, Shelden writes that this "powerful protest" raised the question of "why such a vibrant young woman wasn't living in her own home,"[58] suggesting that the document's existence was an integral factor in Jean's coming to live at Stormfield three weeks later. Writing to Clara in July, he pronounced his youngest daughter "a surprise & a wonder . . . [with] plenty of wisdom, judgment, penetration, practical good sense—like her mother—& character, courage...a humane spirit, charity, kindliness . . . [and] high ideals."[59] If they did discuss the issue of native dispossession during those last few months of Jean's life, the writer inexplicably left no account of it in either public or private. His last known depiction of Indians—the nightmare scenario of the Dakota massacre in "Letters from the Earth"—bears no mark of her mitigating influence.

"BORN FOR A SAVAGE"

The erratic, deeply conflicted views Mark Twain expressed about American Indians over a period of nearly sixty years defy easy explanation. Rather than conforming to a coherent linear trajectory that culminates in a redemptive epiphany, his representation of native peoples remains paradoxical and inconsistent up until the time of his death. In Twain's imagination, Indians are the dualistic incarnation of a loathsome racial Other and his truest, natural Self. In "Conversations with Satan," an unpublished story written in Vienna in 1897–98, the devil smokes companionably with the writer in his hotel room, explaining that "the early American Indians introduced [tobacco] in Sheol twenty or thirty thousand years ago, and out of gratitude he is never severe on that race."[60] Seeking to curry favor with *Durchlaucht* (Your Highness), he contemplates "indicat[ing] in an unobtrusive way that by rights I was an Indian, though changed in the cradle through no fault of my own." This ideation—which dates back to descriptions of himself in the early 1860s as an "ignorant half-breed" and representative of "red men"—persists until the end of Clemens's life. Reflecting on the honorary doctorate he was awarded by Oxford University in a 1907 autobiographical dictation, he states, "I take the same childlike delight in a new degree that an Indian takes in a fresh scalp, and I take no more pains to conceal my joy than the Indian does" (A3, 53). Several months later, he donned his Oxford robe after speaking at a Lotos Club banquet given in his honor. Amidst the cheers of the assembled company, he gazed down at his resplendent regalia and observed, "I like that gown. I always did like red. The redder it is the better I like it. I was born for a savage. Now whoever saw any red like this? There is no red outside the arteries of an archangel that could compare."[61] Twain's appreciation of the garment's rich hue is not simply a matter of aesthetics but is also an unselfconscious admission of his essential identity—primitive and sublimely celestial, an Indian and archangel combined. The vaguely biblical syntax of his assertion, "I was born for a savage"—evoking the proverb "A friend loveth at all times, and a brother is born for adversity"—suggests that "savagery" is the intrinsic state of all peoples. As he wrote in "Concerning the Jews," "All that I care to know is that a man is a human being—that is enough for me; he can't be any worse" (CT2, 355). Despite the incontestable progress in the writer's opinions regarding many of the key ideological debates of his time, Indians remained an enigma for him—objects of pity, loathing, and confused fascination—until the end.

Notes

Full catalog information regarding Clemens's unpublished correspondence can be found at marktwainproject.org using the UUCL numbers in the notes below.

INTRODUCTION

1. See O. Larson, *American Infidel*, 251–52.
2. Quoted in the *Cambridge Tribune* 11, no. 16, 23 June 1888, 5.
3. "A Grand Display," *Hartford Times*, 11 June 1888.
4. "4 Paw and Wild West Combined," advertisement, *Hartford Daily Courant*, 8 June 1888.
5. Slout, *Olympians*, 72.
6. Intercircus rivalry likely played a part in Davis's plan. In September 1884, Clemens had attended two consecutive performances of Buffalo Bill's Wild West in Elmira, NY. For years afterward—as the agent must have known—Cody shamelessly used the writer's enthusiastic letter of praise about the show's verisimilitude for advertising purposes, sending it to local newspapers in advance of the Wild West's appearance and featuring it in the official souvenir program from 1887 through the early 1890s. See chapter 5 for an extended discussion of this topic.
7. "Indians and Mark Twain," *New York Herald*, 13 January 1895, 7.
8. Thompson, *On the Road*, 233. The anecdote about Twain and the Forepaugh Circus Indians appears on pages 245–47.
9. Foner, *Mark Twain: Social Critic*, 238.
10. Budd, *Mark Twain: Social Philosopher*, 45.
11. Ibid., 122–23.
12. Harris, "Mark Twain's Response," 495.
13. See chapter 6 for an extended discussion of the circumstances surrounding the composition of this letter.
14. Foner, 237–38.
15. Geismar, *Mark Twain*, 317.
16. Ibid., 285.
17. Denton, "Mark Twain," 1.
18. Ibid., 2.
19. Budd, *Mark Twain: Social Philosopher*, 189.

20. Ibid., 46.
21. Ibid., 107.
22. McNutt, "Mark Twain," 238, 240.
23. Steinbrink, *Getting*, 125.
24. Kolb, *Mark Twain*, 66.
25. Blackhawk, *Violence over the Land*, 275.
26. Messent, "Racial and Colonial Discourse," 70.

CHAPTER ONE. THE ROMANCE AND TERROR OF INDIANS

1. See McNutt, "Mark Twain," and Coulombe, *Mark Twain*.
2. Dippie, *Vanishing American*, 15.
3. Fatout, *Mark Twain Speaking*, 440–41.
4. Faragher, "More Motley than Mackinaw," 305.
5. Unrau, *Mixed Bloods*, 14.
6. Faragher, "More Motley than Mackinaw," 305.
7. Flint, *Recollections*, 119–20.
8. Benton, *Thirty Years View*, 27.
9. "Proposition to Extinguish Indian Title to Lands in Missouri, 14 May 1824," in Kappler, *Indian Affairs*, 512.
10. Aron, *American Confluence*, 210.
11. Ibid., 186.
12. Benton, *Thirty Years View*, 28.
13. "Treaty with the Sauk and Foxes, 1824," in Kappler, *Indian Affairs*, 207.
14. Ibid., 209.
15. "Treaty with the Oto, 1836," in Kappler, *Indian Affairs*, 479.
16. Haines, *Callaghan Mail*, 31.
17. Ibid., 45.
18. Ibid., 29, 31.
19. Holcombe, *History of Marion County*, 896.
20. *Hannibal Messenger*, 28 July 1859, 1.
21. Arnold, "Shelley," in *Essays in Criticism*, 252.
22. Unpublished draft of "In Defence of Harriet Shelley," MTP, 2–3.
23. Powers, *Dangerous Water*, 39–40.
24. Orion Clemens, "Jane Lampton MS," MTP. The essay was likely written in November–December 1890, just after Jane's death.
25. Collins, *History of Kentucky*, 473. Charles Lambert's 1962 biography, *Benjamin Logan*, states that Collins obtained this information from Jane Casey directly in a personal interview conducted shortly before her 1844 death (122).
26. At the time of the attack, Jane's mother and youngest sister were visiting at Logan's Fort. According to Collins, two of her older brothers—Thomas and Robert—"were absent spying" as well (*History of Kentucky*, 472).
27. Collins, *History of Kentucky*, 472.
28. Trabue, *Westward into Kentucky*, 198n71.
29. Ibid., 151.

30. Collins, *History of Kentucky,* 472.

31. Ibid.

32. Ibid.

33. In *Jane Clemens,* Rachel M. Varble describes William Casey as a "gentle, dark Irishman" who once killed two Indians—a chief drinking from a spring, the other walking on a trail—then "buried them decently, never boasting of his deeds" (6).

34. Ibid., 13.

35. "Col. Wm. Casey, of Ky. From his daughter, Mrs. Ann Montgomery, Columbia, Ky., 1844," Draper Manuscripts 12C, Wisconsin Historical Society.

36. Varble, *Jane Clemens,* 36–37.

37. Ibid., 42.

38. Ibid., 70.

39. Slotkin, *Regeneration through Violence,* 158.

40. Friend, *Kentucke's Frontier,* xix.

41. Matt. 5:44, King James Version.

42. "O. Clemens, Mark Twain's Brother: He Possesses Many Gifts Which Have Made His Relative Famous," *Chicago Tribune,* 15 May 1892. The lyric was composed for an amateur "tableau of civilization" performed in Keokuk on 5 May. MTP Scrapbook #26 (1891–1896), 73–74.

43. Powers, *Mark Twain: A Life,* 23–24.

44. The complete lyrics of "The Blue Juniata" can be found at the Library of Congress website, http://memory.loc.gov.

45. Teetor, *Past and Present,* 79.

46. Ibid.

47. Coggeshall, *Poets and Poetry,* 144.

48. Unpublished and untitled manuscript, "Draft A," 1–5, a continuation of "Fenimore Cooper's Literary Offences," MTP.

49. Unpublished and untitled manuscript, "Various Drafts," 21–22, a continuation of "Fenimore Cooper's Literary Offences," MTP

50. Cooper, *The Last of the Mohicans,* 414.

51. Dippie, *Vanishing American,* 22.

52. McNutt, "Mark Twain," 235.

53. Lorch, "Orion Clemens," 365–66.

54. Fanning, *Mark Twain and Orion,* 31–32.

55. Benjamin Drake was the author of *The Life and Adventures of Black Hawk* (1851); John Frost authored *Indian Wars of the United States* (1852); the other sources Orion cites are *A History of Illinois* (1854) and *Annals of the West* (1850), by Thomas Ford and John Mason Peck, respectively.

56. O. Clemens, *City of Keokuk,* 32.

57. Mahoney, *Provincial Lives,* 93.

58. Kalter, "A Savagist Abroad," 37.

59. O. Clemens, *City of Keokuk,* 31.

60. Ibid., 37.

61. Ibid., 38.

62. Ibid., 41.

63. Ibid., 33.

64. Ibid.

65. Kalter hypothesizes that Twain was involved in the sketch's production "in at least one of several ways: reading and discussion of the source materials prior to the publication of the pamphlet; reading, editing, and proofreading for Orion; setting the print; reading the pamphlet after its publication, possibly after leaving Keokuk; and least likely, acting as a ghost writer of parts of the text" ("A Savagist Abroad," 37). In my estimation, the writer's role was far more tangential.

66. Fanning, *Mark Twain and Orion*, xvi.

67. Turner, *Significance of the Frontier*, 3.

68. Wecter, *Sam Clemens of Hannibal*, 151.

69. Fishkin, *Lighting Out*, 43.

70. Ibid., 43.

71. "The Characters Mark Used in His Writing," *Twainian* 10, no. 5 (September–October 1951): 4. According to the journal's editors, the interview with Doc Brown piece was reprinted from an old undated newspaper entitled *Grit*.

72. See Fishkin, *Lighting Out*, 46–48.

73. "Tom Sawyer Characters in Hannibal," *St. Louis Post Dispatch*, 2 June 1902, 5. My thanks to both Victor Fischer and Bob Hirst for providing me with the full text of this article.

74. *Oxford English Dictionary*, online edition 2012.

75. Ibid.

76. Faragher, "More Motley than Mackinaw," 305.

77. Kalter describes Joe's Spanish disguise as "dramatic choreography" that "reveals an aspect of his fuller identity" ("A Savagist Abroad," 34).

78. Parkman, *Oregon Trail*, 362.

79. Scheick, *Half-Blood*, 18.

80. Ibid., 2.

81. Quoted in H. Brown, *Injun Joe's Ghost*, 101.

82. Melville, *Confidence Man*, 148.

83. Revard, "Why Mark Twain," 335.

84. Baender, *Adventures of Tom Sawyer*, 714. Twain revised his original wording to make Joe's intentions less gruesome, amending the manuscript to read, "You go for her looks. You slit her nostrils—you notch her ears like a sow's!"

85. Lawrence, *Studies*, 40.

86. Hsu, *Sitting in Darkness*, 59.

87. Cox, *Muting White Noise*, xi.

88. Hsu, *Sitting in Darkness*, 60.

89. Revard, "Why Mark Twain," 336, 340.

90. Kalter, "A Savagist Abroad," 35.

91. Deloria, *Playing Indian*, 5.

92. Ibid., 120.

93. Ibid., 184.

94. Baender, *Adventures of Tom Sawyer*, 447. The later interpolation is numbered "447A-C." Twain also renumbered the beginning of chapter 17 as "447D."

95. Fischer, *A Well-Executed Failure*, 2.

96. Bishop, "End of the Iroquois," 77. The plaque at the base of the granite obelisk erected at the battle site in 1912 similarly praises General Sullivan for "Destroying the Iroquois Confederacy / Ending attacks on our settlements / And thereby Opening / Westward the pathway of Civilization."

97. The number of scalps taken varies from eight to twelve in different accounts. See Mann, *George Washington's War*, 211n398.

98. Cook, *Journals*, 8; Mann, *George Washington's War*, 205.

99. Cook, *Journals*, 279.

100. Deloria, *Playing Indian*, 184.

101. Ibid., 3.

102. Ford Madox Hueffer as quoted in A. Moody, *Ezra Pound, Poet*, 113.

CHAPTER TWO. BLIND IN NEVADA

1. Governor James W. Nye to Hon. Caleb B. Smith, 14 August 1861, *House Executive Documents*, 719.

2. Marsh, *Letters from Nevada Territory*, 119.

3. Governor James W. Nye to Hon. Caleb B. Smith, 14 August 1861, *House Executive Documents*, 719.

4. *Gold Hill Daily News*, 2 June 1864.

5. Nevada did not achieve statehood until 31 October 1864, some nine months after the column was published.

6. Marsh, *Letters from Nevada Territory*, 370.

7. Marsh and Clemens, *Reports*, 403. This volume compiles minutes recorded during the sessions by convention secretary William M. Gillespie, with published reports that appeared in two Virginia City newspapers, the *Territorial Enterprise* and the *Daily Union*. According to the editors, the official convention reporters were Andrew Marsh for the *Enterprise* and Amos Bowman for the *Union;* however, Clemens himself was also in attendance, ostensibly to "transcribe Marsh's shorthand notes." The extent of his role remains unclear—and may have involved editing and preparing the final copy for these reports. For further information see Smith and Anderson, *Mark Twain*, 10–12.

8. Ibid., 404.

9. This surmise is corroborated by Twain's coy allusion to the legislative debate in a letter published in the *Enterprise* on 4 January 1864: "Well, somebody proposed as a substitute for the pictorial Great Seal, a figure of a jackass-rabbit reposing in the shade of his native sage-brush, with the motto '*Volens* enough, but not so d____d *Potens.*' Possibly that had something to do with the

rejection of one of the proposed mottoes by the Convention" (cited in Smith and Anderson, *Mark Twain,* 123). That "somebody," in all likelihood, was Clemens. Two years earlier, in his 20 March 1862 letter to Jane Lampton Clemens, he privately proposed an even more grotesque alternative to Orion's design—a buzzard "standing solemnly on a decomposed ox ... with his head canted to one side, his left leg advanced to steady himself, and chewing a fragrant thing of entrails with their ends dangling about his portly bosom. I ask you in all candor, Madam ... wouldn't it make a bully coat-of-arms for the Territory?—neat and appropriate, and all that? And wouldn't it look gay on the great seal?" (L1, 176).

10. SLC to Jacob H. Burrough, 1 November 1876 (UCCL, 01384).

11. Scharnhorst, *Bret Harte,* 12–13. See also Tarnoff, *Bohemians,* 24–26.

12. Tarnoff, 25.

13. Lorch, "Mark Twain's Early Views," 2.

14. Blackhawk, *Violence over the Land,* 11.

15. Hattori, "Acculturation," 229–30. See also Hattori, *Northern Paiutes,* 8; Knack and Stewart, *River Shall Run,* 18–21.

16. Rowlandson, *Sovereignty and Goodness,* 79.

17. Moody, *Western Carpetbagger,* 54.

18. Weisenberger, *Idol of the West,* 21–22.

19. Smith and Anderson, *Mark Twain,* 21.

20. This phrase is the title of chapter 36 of De Quille's *The Big Bonanza.*

21. This obituary is quoted—without citation—in George Williams III, *Mark Twain,* 58.

22. De Quille, *Washoe Rambles,* 30–31.

23. Ibid., 105.

24. Ibid., 35.

25. Ibid.,10.

26. De Quille, "Salad Days," 26.

27. Hopkins, *Life among the Piutes,* 71.

28. My narration of these events is compiled from a variety of sometimes conflicting sources: Dan De Quille's 1876 history of the Comstock Lode, *The Big Bonanza;* Myron Angel's 1881 *History of Nevada;* Sarah Winnemucca Hopkins's 1883 autobiography, *Life among the Piutes;* William Miller's 1957 essay, "The Pyramid Lake Indian War of 1860"; Ferol Egan's *Sand in a Whirlwind: The Paiute Indian War of 1860,* and Sally Zanjani, *Devils Will Reign: How Nevada Began.*

29. Angel, *History of Nevada,* 153.

30. "Death of Major Ormsby," *Territorial Enterprise,* 19 May 1860, 2.

31. According to Angel, when Ormsby pleaded for his life, Numaga's reply was "No use now ... too late, and [he] sent an arrow flying through the stomach and another through the face of his late friend, who sinking to the ground, was rolled from the ridge dying into the gully below" (*History of Nevada,* 157). According to Ferol Egan, however, Ormsby was not killed by Numaga, but by another Paiute warrior in the confusion of battle.

32. Hopkins, *Life among the Piutes,* 72.

33. Dan De Quille, "Letter from Washoe," *Golden Era* [San Francisco], 5 May 1861. I would like to thank Lawrence Berkove for bringing this piece, along with numerous others on the subject of Indians by De Quille, to my attention.

34. Marsh, *Letters from Nevada Territory,* 101.

35. Ibid., 232.

36. Ibid., 154.

37. Ibid.

38. Ibid., 125.

39. Ibid., 262.

40. Ibid., 118.

41. Ibid., 146.

42. Ibid., 280.

43. Gianella, "Site of Williams Station," 5. See also *Roughing It,* 792.

44. Gianella, "Site of Williams Station," 7.

45. Delaney, "Truth," 3.

46. Ibid.

47. Knack and Stewart, *River Shall Run,* 94.

48. James W. Nye to Honorable Caleb B. Smith, secretary of the Interior, 13 July 1861. *House Executive Documents,* series 1117, 723.

49. Angel, *History of Nevada,* 165. "Hickory" was a rugged cotton twill fabric similar to denim, commonly used in the nineteenth century for work shirts and coveralls.

50. Warren Wasson to James W. Nye, 13 July 1861, *House Executive Documents,* series 1117, 724. *Fancy articles* was a generic term for special apparel—such as beads, jewelry, and red bunting that could be cut into strip and tied into the hair—not intended for everyday use.

51. James W. Nye to Hon. Caleb B. Smith, 19 July 1861, *House Executive Documents,* series 1117, 721.

52. Ibid., 717, 721.

53. The *Enterprise* article of 3 August is reprinted in "Governor Nye's Doings," *Marysville Daily Appeal,* 8 August 1861, 3.

54. "Hoop-de-Dooden-Doo," *Marysville Daily Appeal,* 8 August 1861, 2. My thanks to Robert H. Hirst, general editor of the Mark Twain Project, for supplying me with copies of both these items.

55. Knack and Stewart, *River Shall Run,* 21.

56. De Quille, "Uncle Bob," 4–5.

57. Ibid.

58. Dan De Quille, "Shooting a Frog-Eater," n.d.

59. Fatout, *Mark Twain Speaking,* 64.

60. McCullough and McIntire-Strasburg, *Mark Twain,* 231–32.

61. Fatout, *Mark Twain Speaking,* 64.

62. De Quille, *Big Bonanza,* 196.

63. De Quille, *Washoe Rambles,* 84.

64. Ibid., 35–36.

65. De Quille, *Big Bonanza*, 196.

66. James and James, *Virginia City*, 68.

67. Ibid., 196.

68. Pope, *Essay on Man*, 18.

69. Greeley, *Overland Journey*, 151–52.

70. Ibid., 154–55.

71. "First Annual Fair of the Washoe Agricultural, Mining and Mechanical Society," *Daily Union* (Virginia, N.T.), 13 October 1863. Orion Clemens Scrapbook #2, 1861–63 (MTP).

72. *Galena Daily Gazette* 1, no. 59 (25 April 1864), 2.

73. "Communicated," *Colorado Weekly Chieftain* (Pueblo, CO), 17 September 1868.

74. Zanjani, *Sarah Winnemucca*, 69.

75. De Quille, *Big Bonanza*, 214.

76. *House Executive Documents*, series 1117, 1862, 369.

77. Fanning, *Mark Twain*, 70.

78. *House Executive Documents*, series 1117, 1862, 370–71.

79. *Esmeralda Star*, 17 May 1862, quoted in Robert W. Ellison, *Long Beard*, 60.

80. Dan De Quille, "Talking Indian," San Francisco *Golden Era* [San Francisco], 8 June 1862, 2.

81. Philip Fanning describes the leadership Orion displayed in these negotiations as his "finest hour." "Not only did he bring the rule of law to an important and particularly unstable corner of the West . . . but he [also] enforced the peace" (*Mark Twain*, 82).

82. Orion Clemens, Letterpress Copybook, 3 February 1863, Nevada State Archives, Carson City.

83. *Gold Hill Daily News*, 19 December 1863.

84. Gribben, foreword, x.

85. Orion Clemens to Honorable William P. Dole, 2 July 1863, Letterpress Copybook.

86. "O. Clemens, Mark Twain's Brother: He Possesses Many of the Gifts which have made His Relative Famous," *Chicago Tribune*, 15 May 1892. According to the article, the lyric was composed for an amateur "tableau of civilization" performed in Keokuk, Iowa, on 5 May 1892. MTP, Scrapbook #26 (1891–96), 73–74.

87. Orion Clemens to U.S. Treasury Auditor, 10 March 1863, Letterpress Copybook.

88. Crosby, *Ecological Imperialism*, 199. Before the onset of European colonization, diseases like smallpox, measles, typhoid, cholera, and others were unknown in the Americas; lacking immunity to these pathogens, native populations were devastated by so-called virgin soil epidemics, which Crosby claims produced mortality rates of "up to one-fourth, one-half, or more." A particularly virulent strain of smallpox nearly eradicated the Mandans, a Northern Plains tribe, in 1837–38.

CHAPTER THREE. INDIANS IMAGINED, 1862–1872

1. Mark Twain's *Letter from Washington*, 9, published in the Virginia City *Territorial Enterprise* on 7 March 1868. See www.twainquotes.com.

2. According to Edgar Marquess Branch and Robert H. Hirst, "Of the twelve California and Nevada papers that are known to have reprinted 'Petrified Man,' eight of them gave no sign whatever that they doubted the truth of the story. San Francisco newspapers were shrewd enough: the *Alta* called it a 'sell' and the *Evening Bulletin* 'A Washoe Joke.' But the *Sacramento Bee* asserted more tentatively that it was 'probably a hoax,' and the *Bulletin* reported that 'the interior journals seem to be copying [it] in good faith'" (ETS1, 158).

3. D. Morgan, *Shoshonean Peoples*, 85.

4. Michelson, *Mark Twain on the Loose*, 16.

5. Blackhawk, *Violence over the Land*, 249; see also Crum, *Road*, 21.

6. Blackhawk, *Violence over the Land*, 249.

7. The details of this 1861 massacre, as described by a local trader named Charles Stebbins, can be found in Angel, *History of Nevada*, 178.

8. The *Bancroft Scraps*, acquired by the University of California at Berkeley in 1905, are a collection of 113 scrapbooks containing nineteenth-century newspaper clippings grouped by subject matter (e.g., "California Fisheries," "Pacific Coast Telegraph"). They were used by historian Hubert Howe Bancroft (1832–1918) in preparing his *History of California* (1886–1890) and *History of Nevada, Colorado, and Wyoming* (1890). While the collection offers a diverse range of journalistic perspectives on Nevada's native peoples, only a few of the newspapers from which these articles were clipped are identified by name; the handwritten dating is unreliable as well. I have deduced that this particular item appeared in a Unionville newspaper on the basis of the following statement: "Gravelly Ford is about one hundred miles easterly of this point" (23).

9. Madsen, *Shoshoni Frontier*, 166.

10. "Mysterious and Terrible Murder," Sacramento *Union*, 12 September 1862, 2.

11. Ibid.

12. *Bancroft Scraps*, vol. 93, *Nevada Indians*.

13. Madsen, *Shoshoni Frontier*, 143.

14. Ibid., 167.

15. Patrick Connor to General George Wright, quoted in Madsen, *Glory Hunter*, 63.

16. Ibid.

17. See Paine, *Mark Twain*, 1:205; Powers, *Mark Twain*, 110. Since Clemens's first local items for the *Enterprise* are dated 1 October, he must have arrived in Virginia City several days earlier.

18. "A Terrible Massacre," *Red Bluff Beacon*, 18 September 1862; "By State Telegraph," *Daily Alta California*, 16 September 1862; and "The Massacre on the Plains," *Marysville Daily Appeal*, 20 September 1862—all available online at the California Digital Newspaper Collection, https://cdnc.ucr.edu.

19. Fatout, *Mark Twain Speaking*, 58. See also chapter 42 of *Roughing It*.

20. *San Francisco Daily Morning Call*, 15 July 1863, reprinted in *Twainian* (January–February 1953), 2–3.

21. The *Galaxy* sketch, entitled "A Couple of Sad Experiences," contains two discrete pieces, "The Petrified Man" and "My Famous 'Bloody Massacre,'" which were later reprinted in *Sketches, New and Old* (1875)—without the introductory passage—as two separate texts, "The Petrified Man" and "My Bloody Massacre."

22. This note appears in *The Choice Humorous Works of Mark Twain*, 433. The revised book is now in MTP.

23. Michelson, *Printer's Devil*, 69.

24. For additional information on the acrimony between Clemens and Sewall, see ETS1, 155–57 and L1, 170.

25. G.T. Sewall to Governor James W. Nye, 31 January 1862. Quoted with the permission of the Nevada State Library and Archives.

26. G.T. Sewall to Governor James W. Nye, 30 July 1862, Nevada State Library and Archives.

27. Marsh, *Letters from Nevada Territory*, 603.

28. Wolfe, "Settler Colonialism," 387.

29. *Territorial Enterprise*, December 1862, reprinted in Effie Mona Mack, *Mark Twain in Nevada*, 224–27. "Colonel" J.G. Howard was not in fact a military officer but an attorney. He was also one of the organizers of the Democratic Party in Nevada Territory and was likely the politician disparaged for making "piute gabble his platform" in the *Gold Hill News*. See Marsh, *Letters from Nevada Territory*, 698n353.

30. "That Piute Idea," Gold Hill *Daily News* 1:20, 4 November 1863.

31. Deloria, *Playing Indian*, 65. The Improved Order of Red Men spread across the nation during the nineteenth century, eventually claiming more than half a million members. The organization still exists today, although it is greatly diminished in size; additional information is available on the group's website, http://redmen.org.

32. Ibid.

33. "Original Occupants," Gold Hill *Daily News* 1:28, 12 November 1863.

34. Smith and Anderson, *Mark Twain*, 99.

35. This slang term etymologically derives from the Chinook jargon phrase "hayo makamak," meaning "plenty to eat." It first appeared in print circa 1856, in reference to a self-important person.

36. Michno, *Deadliest Indian War*, 93.

37. Egan, *Sand in a Whirlwind*, 92.

38. Because only a small fraction of Clemens's early western journalism survives, it is possible he used "Digger" in print before June 1864; however, this is the first instance I have found in the texts that have been recovered.

39. T. Kroeber, *Ishi in Two Worlds*, 19.

40. Lonnberg, "Digger Indian Stereotype," 215.

41. Heizer, *They Were Only Diggers*, xiv–xv.

42. Lonnberg, " Digger Indian Stereotype," 216.

43. Day, *Mark Twain's Letters*, 36.

44. Twain, "The Californian's Tale," in Neider, *Complete Short Stories*, 272.

45. See Paine, *Mark Twain*, 1:268–69.

46. SLC to W.R. Ward, 8 September 1887 (UCCL, 03773).

47. Ibid.

48. SLC to William Wright (Dan De Quille), 28 January 1876 (UCCL, 01304).

49. Angel, *History of Nevada*, 169.

50. William Wright (Dan De Quille) to SLC, 7 February 1876 (UCLC, 35604).

51. Gillis, *Memories of Mark Twain*, 89.

52. *Territorial Enterprise*, 8 February 1876.

53. Letter 25, 5 June 1867, in Franklin and Dane, *Mark Twain's Travels*, 264.

54. Ibid., 265–66.

55. Ibid., 264–65.

56. Ibid., 266.

57. Madsen, *Glory Hunter*, 140.

58. "Cruelty to Indians," quoted in Hays, *A Race at Bay*, 133.

59. Madsen, *Glory Hunter*, 154. Twain's admiration for Connor is also evident in a sketch called "The Coming Man," published in his January 1871 column in the *Galaxy:* "General P. Edward O'Connor [*sic*] has done the highest and faithfullest and best military service in Mormondom, that ever has been rendered there for our country. For about seven years or such a matter he has made both Brigham and the Indians reasonably civil and polite ... Colonel O'Connor flew to arms and put down the Indians and the Mormons and *kept* them down for years." Quoted in McElderry, *Mark Twain's Contributions*, 120.

60. W.T. Sherman to U.S. Grant, 27 May 1867, quoted in Fellman, *Citizen Sherman*, 264.

61. "Local Intelligence: The Reason General Sherman will not go to Europe," *New York Times*, 31 May 1867, 2.

62. Ganzel, *Mark Twain Abroad*, 23. Ganzel's book does not reveal the source of this information, and the editors at the Mark Twain Project have not been able to confirm its accuracy.

63. Obenzinger, *American Palestine*, 193. See also Amy Kaplan's (*Anarchy of Empire*, 76–77) discussion of Twain's allusion to Sherman in his letters from Hawaii.

64. McKeithan, *Traveling*, 227.

65. Obenzinger, *American Palestine*, 190.

66. Fragment No. 10, "Christ and the Patriarchs," in Jean Webster-McKinney Family Papers, Vassar College.

67. Percy Bysshe Shelley to Thomas Love Peacock, 20 April 1818, in Ingpen, *Letters*, 593.

68. "The Washoe: First People of the Lake," www.fs.usda.gov.

69. Kroeber, *Handbook of the Indians*, 252, 301, 313, 452.

70. Hoffman, "Cremation," 415.

71. In January 1859, James Mason Hutchings (1820–1902), the editor of *Hutchings's Illustrated California Magazine,* published an article entitled "The Way the Digger Indians Bury their Dead," which explains, "When the body is consumed, they carefully collect the ashes, and after mixing a portion of them with some pitch, with which to cover their faces and go into mourning, they are buried" (322). Hutchings also popularized "pictorial letter sheets," featuring woodcuts accompanied by a brief descriptive text, which were commonly used by pioneers corresponding with their families in the East. "The California Indians," one of the designs commonly available in the early 1860s, featured an illustration of "Indians Burning Their Dead," reproduced in Madley, *An American Genocide,* 176.

72. McNutt, 223–24. The various iterations of "Stormfield" make the date of its composition difficult to determine. In a 23 March 1878 letter to Orion, Clemens explains, "Nine years ago I mapped out my 'Journey to Heaven.' . . . After a year or more, I wrote it up. . . . Five years ago I wrote it again, altering the plan. That MS is at my elbow now" (UCCL, 01547). In his 1862 and 1865 travels through the eastern Sierras, Clemens does not seem to have ventured as far south as California's Tulare County, the traditional homeland of Southern Paiute tribes, such as the Monos and Tule Rivers, who did in fact practice cremation.

73. Kaplan, *Anarchy of Empire,* 74.

74. Budd, *Mark Twain: Social Philosopher,* 45.

75. Wolfe, "Settler Colonialism," 388.

76. See Fulton, *Reconstruction of Mark Twain,* 57.

77. Deloria, *Playing Indian,* 3.

78. Angel, *History of Nevada,* 151.

79. The earliest publication of the squib I have located is in the 26 July 1876 *Somerset Herald* (PA); it also appeared in the 31 July 1876 *Reading Times* (PA), and the 23 August 1876 *Abbeville Press and Banner* (SC). Numerous newspapers also reprinted the article with the more neutral headline, "Mark Twain on the Indians."

80. *Record of the Year,* 2:2, August 1876, 4.

81. "Indian Peace Commission Report to the President, January 7, 1868," *Annual Report of the Commissioner of Indian Affairs for the Year 1868* (Washington, DC: Government Printing Office, 1868), 45.

82. One of Mark Twain's newspaper colleagues in Washington, George Alfred Townsend, reported on 11 March that before sailing for California Clemens "had written several hundred MS. pages of a book for one of the Hartford publishing houses, expecting to make his letters to the *Alta Californian* [sic] useful for the bulk of the book." "G.A.T.," *Cleveland Leader,* 17 March 1868, 2.

83. *Oakland News,* 15 August 1868, 3.

84. Dubinsky, *Second Greatest Disappointment,* 61.

85. *Harper's Weekly* 21:1067, 9 June 1877, 441. The text accompanying the illustration confirms the ubiquity of native vendors at Niagara Falls: "It is hard

to keep from buying carvings and trinkets of Indian workmanship. At every step one is pestered by peddlers. . . . They dog one's footsteps everywhere."

86. Porter, *Niagara*, 71–72.

87. Dubinsky, *Second Greatest Disappointment*, 66.

88. Steinbrink, *Getting*, 48.

89. *New York Times*, "Fenian Mass Meeting in Buffalo—Address by General O'Neil," 2 February 1868, 1.

90. *New York Tribune*, 13 July 1865.

91. Limerick, *Something in the Soil*, 63.

92. Slotkin, *Regeneration through Violence*, 158.

93. Orion Clemens to Honorable William P. Dole, 2 July 1863, Nevada State Archives.

94. Byrd, *Transit of Empire*, 24–25.

95. Wood, *Uncivilized Races of Men*, 1331–32.

96. Cronise, *Natural Wealth of California*, 21.

97. Ibid., 21–22.

98. Richardson, *Beyond the Mississippi*, 495. See also David, *Mark Twain*, 133.

99. D. Morgan, *Shoshonean Peoples*, 243.

100. Rasmussen, *Dear Mark Twain*, 153.

101. Ibid.

102. Ibid., 154.

103. Martin Griffith, "Racism Claim Dooms Bid to Honor Mark Twain in Nevada," Associated Press, 18 May 2014.

104. Darrel Cruz letter to Linda Newman, chair of the Nevada State Board of Geographic Names, 17 March 2014. My thanks to Mr. Cruz for providing me with a copy of this document and granting me permission to cite it.

105. Martin Griffith, "Racism Claim Dooms Bid to Honor Mark Twain in Nevada," Associated Press, 18 May 2014.

106. The minutes of all Nevada State Geographic Board of Names meetings are available online at www.nbmg.unr.edu/geonames.

107. Darrel Cruz to Jeff Kintop, 23 May 2014. Quoted with Mr. Cruz's permission.

108. Personal communication, 23 June 2016.

CHAPTER FOUR. THE ROOTS OF RACIAL ANIMUS IN
"THE NOBLE RED MAN"

1. Florence King, "The Noble White Man," 50–51.

2. This tendency, previously mentioned in relation to the scholarship of Joseph Coulombe and James McNutt, is also evident in Elizabeth Hanson's "Mark Twain's Indians Re-examined," 11.

3. Krause, *Mark Twain as Critic*, 136.

4. Ibid., 139.

5. Steinbrink, *Getting*, 125.

6. See Stormfront.org/forum. See also Dao and Kovaleski, "Music Style," A12.

7. Though the Piegan Massacre was instrumental in reshaping government Indian policy, it has been eclipsed by other, better-known military atrocities, such as the Sand Creek (1864) and Wounded Knee (1890) massacres, and warrants only a footnote in most historical studies of the West.

8. *New York Times*, 9 March 1870, 1.

9. Welch, *Killing Custer*, 35.

10. *New York Times*, 8 March 1870, 1.

11. Mardock, *Reformers*, 67.

12. Ibid.

13. *American Annual Cyclopedia* 10 (1870): 713.

14. Welch, *Killing Custer*, 35.

15. Ibid., 504.

16. McElderry, *Mark Twain's Contributions*, 59.

17. Steinbrink, *Getting*, 126.

18. In June 1870, Utah representative William Henry Hooper argued in congress that, if indigenous peoples were treated justly, there would be no Indian wars: "The Mormons have sent more than eighty thousand persons, with their property, through the Indian country, across the plains, in the last twenty-two years, and have never lost a life, an animal, or a bale of goods by Indian depredation" (*New York Evening Post*, 13 June 1870).

19. Coulombe, *Mark Twain*, 106.

20. *New York Times*, 13 June 1870, 4.

21. According to Francis Paul Prucha's *American Indian Treaties*, "Of the 367 treaties that were ratified, 69 were negotiated and signed in Washington, DC. Tribal delegates, together with interpreters and agents, came to the capital to speak with the Great Father and to negotiate agreements with the government. On such occasions they usually had pictures taken in their best attire" (272).

22. Poole, *Among the Sioux*, xxxviii.

23. *Harper's Weekly*, 18 June 1870, 385.

24. *New York Times*, "Washington: Special Dispatch," 1 June 1870, 4.

25. Poole, *Among the Sioux*, 170.

26. *New York Herald*, 12 June 1870, 4.

27. *New York Times*, "Washington: Special Dispatch," 2 June 1870, 4.

28. Frank Goodyear's *Red Cloud* reports that the leader "posed before the camera on at least forty-five occasions over a period of almost forty years. The total number of different photographs taken of Red Cloud is at least 128, making him the most photographed nineteenth-century Native American" (1). In June 1870, however, he declined Mathew Brady's invitation to be photographed in both his Washington and New York studios.

29. American painter and illustrator Charles Stanley Reinhart (1844–96) contributed engravings to many leading nineteenth-century periodicals, publishing over two hundred images in *Harper's Weekly* alone. As John

Coward observes in *The Newspaper Indian,* "The accuracy of [most Indian] illustrations in *Leslie's* and *Harper's* was problematic. At their best, such images might capture some sense of reality, at least from the (white) artist's point of view.... Artists and engravers had every incentive to improve reality, to make their images as interesting and exciting as possible. Such images might depart from the literal truth, but they could be justified as emotionally true" (128).

30. The *Harper's* article is entitled "On the Warpath," ironically undercutting the pacific intentions of the Lakota depicted in the illustration.

31. Larson, *Red Cloud,* 129.

32. Ibid.

33. *New York Times,* 3 June 1870, 1.

34. Larson, *Red Cloud,* 131.

35. *New York Tribune,* 9 June 1870. Twain was well acquainted with this kind of social reportage and parodied it in "A Fashion Item," published in the *Chicago Republican* on 8 February 1868.

36. Dee Brown, *Bury My Heart,* 79.

37. *New York Times,* 8 June 1870, 1.

38. *New York Times,* 13 June 1870, 4.

39. The *New York Evening Post* of 8 June 1870 offered a different perspective, praising the rhetorical skill of Red Cloud's speech while decrying the "idle" and "absurd" futility of his attempts to halt technological progress ("The Last of the Ogallalas," 2).

40. *New York Times,* 13 June 1870, 1.

41. *New York Times,* 17 June 1870, 1.

42. *Nation,* vol. 10, no. 260, 23 June 1870, 396.

43. "The Last Appeal of Red Cloud," in Hays, *A Race at Bay,* 101.

44. *Nation,* 10:260, 23 June 1870, 396.

45. "Red Cloud's Influence for Peace on Returning Home," *Philadelphia Evening Telegraph,* 22 July 1870, quoted in the *Second Annual Report of the Board of Indian Commissioners to the Secretary of the Interior, 1870* (Washington: Government Printing Office, 1871), 49.

46. *Buffalo Morning Express,* 3 June 1870.

47. *Buffalo Morning Express,* 14 June 1870.

48. Coward, *Newspaper Indian,* 100.

49. *Buffalo Morning Express,* 8 June 1870.

50. *Buffalo Morning Express,* 10 June 1870.

51. According to the *Oxford English Dictionary,* the word *demonstration* has a specialized military meaning that is germane to its usage in the 1870 *Buffalo Morning Express* article. The term denotes "a show of military force or offensive movement, especially in the course of active hostilities to engage the enemy's attention while other operations are ongoing elsewhere, or in a time of peace to indicate readiness for active hostilities" (187).

52. *Punchinello,* vol. 1 (12), 18 June 1870, 189.

53. See Schmidt, "'Hy Slocum' Identified," www.twainquotes.com.

54. "'Lo' at the Capitol" is a previously unidentified Slocum piece, countering Joseph B. McCullough's statement that "the final Slocum sketch [was published] in the *Express* on October 8, 1869" "Mark Twain," 45.

55. For the details of Twain's ill-fated 1864 attempt to collaboratively write a novel with Fitch and several other territorial writers, see chapter 51 of *Roughing It*, 339–47.

56. For details of this infamous attack, see Welch, *Killing Custer*, 61–64.

57. *Buffalo Morning Express*, 18 June 1870.

58. Twain's description is found in an editorial entitled "The Ticket— Explanation," published in the *Buffalo Morning Express* on 30 September 1869, reprinted in McCullough and McIntire-Strasburg, *Mark Twain*, 59–60.

59. Considerable controversy exists to this day over whether Sheridan actually uttered these hateful words. Dee Brown alleges that he did (*Bury My Heart*, 166); twenty-four years later, in *Killing Custer*, James Welch concurs (29). The most detailed analysis of the aphorism's origin is Wolfgang Mieder's "'The Only Good Indian Is a Dead Indian,'" 38–60.

60. *Buffalo Morning Express*, 20 June 1870.

61. Ibid.

62. The brief contains at least one other error. Red Cloud and Spotted Tail did not travel together, either en route to Washington or back to their western reservation. Spotted Tail's delegation left New York City several days before Red Cloud's party; the article is therefore mistaken in placing the two men together on the Central Depot platform.

63. *New York Evening Post*, 17 June 1870.

64. Larson, *Red Cloud*, 136.

65. Steinbrink, *Getting*, 200–201.

66. Ibid., 122.

67. *Congressional Globe*, 29 June 1870, 4958.

68. *Congressional Globe*, 11 July 1870, 5449.

69. Ibid.

70. Ibid.

71. *Sacramento Daily Union*, 23 July 1870, 1. I wish to thank Eric Moody, former director of the Nevada State Historical Society, for bringing this article to my attention.

72. McElderry, *Mark Twain's Contributions*, 78.

73. Ibid., 77–78.

74. According to the University of California editors of *Mark Twain's Letters*, vol. 4, the writer "planned and completed drafts of the first four chapters [of *Roughing It*], which were clearly dependent on [Orion's] memorandum book, between 28 August and 2 September" [1870]," 186–87.

75. Baetzhold and McCullough, *Bible*, 101.

76. Ibid., 288, 296.

77. Ibid., 101.

78. Ibid.,102. In their introduction to "Extracts from Methuselah's Diary," Baetzhold and McCullough misdate this note, claiming that Twain's "mention

of Custer and Howard moved [its] frame of reference forward several years. Custer's war against the Sioux in 1876 had culminated in the Little Big Horn massacre on 22 June [the battle actually took place on 25 and 26 June]. The linking of the two generals suggests, however, that Mark Twain was specifically inspired by events in 1877" (94). My thanks to Vic Fischer of the Mark Twain Project, who examined the watermark of the page on which the note is written and determined that it is a type of paper used by Clemens only in 1873.

79. Madley, *American Genocide*, 336.

80. Cothran, *Remembering the Modoc War*, 29.

81. Ibid., 52. As historian Robert M. Utley explains in *The Indian Frontier 1846–1890*, Canby had the "dubious distinction" of being "the only regular army general slain by Indians in the entire history of the Indian Wars" (169).

82. W.T. Sherman quoted in Madley, 342.

83. Ibid., 344.

84. Marberry, *Splendid Poseur*, 82. According to Marberry, Miller experienced a precipitous fall from grace in London after negative reviews of his 1873 volume of poetry, *Songs from the Sun-Lands*, prompting his departure for Italy.

85. Ibid., 116.

86. Ibid., 82.

87. Ibid., 124.

88. Miller, *Romantic Life*, vi.

89. Miller, *Life amongst the Modocs*, 7.

90. Ibid., 397.

91. Ibid., 401.

92. Fatout, *Mark Twain Speaking*, 75.

93. Miller, *Life amongst the Modocs*, 381.

94. Ibid., 385.

95. Ibid., 388.

CHAPTER FIVE. "HOW MUCH HIGHER AND FINER IS THE INDIAN'S GOD"

1. In "A Record of the Small Foolishnesses of Susie and 'Bay' Clemens (Infants)," published in *A Family Sketch and Other Private Writings*, Twain presents a slightly different version of this anecdote. He dates the incident to 1881, when Susy was nine, and remembers her prayer in more emphatic terms: "Well, mamma, I don't know that I can make you understand; but you know, the Indians thought they knew: and they had a great many gods. We know, now, that they were wrong. By and by, maybe it will be found out that *we* are wrong, too. So, now, I only pray *that there may be a God—and a heaven—*OR SOMETHING BETTER" (82).

2. Mark Twain, "From the Manuscript of *A Tramp Abroad* (1879): 'The French and the Comanches,'" in *Letters from the Earth*, 146.

3. SLC to OLC, 28 November 1881 (UCCL, 02103).

4. SLC to OLC, 28 November 1881 (UCCL, 02103).

5. Three of the volumes at the Mark Twain Papers contain inscriptions on the flyleaf: the text in *Count Frontenac*, signed in ink, reads, "2/ S.L. Clemens/~/ Hartford, 1881"; *The Jesuits*, also signed in ink, reads, "3/ S. L. Clemens/~/ Hartford, 1881"; the flyleaf of *The Oregon Trail*, however, is signed in pencil and contains no numeral (apparently a reference to the volume's number in the set) or date. The two volumes of *The Conspiracy of Pontiac*, bound in green cloth and part of a set, are unsigned and contain no marginalia.

6. SLC to OLC, 29, November 1881 (UCCL, 02105).

7. Paine, *Mark Twain*, 3:1538.

8. Notebook no. 42, 50. Quoted in Gribben, *Mark Twain's Library*, 527.

9. SLC to John W. Sanborn, 1 October 1879 (UCCL, 10422).

10. Marginalia in Clemens's copy of Parkman's *The Jesuits in North America*, lxxxviii–ix, MTP.

11. Ibid., lxxxii–iii.

12. Ibid., lxxviii.

13. Ibid., lxxx.

14. Ibid., lxxxii.

15. Ibid., lxxviii.

16. Ibid., lxxxix.

17. Ibid., 29.

18. Ibid., 93.

19. Ibid., 107.

20. Ibid., 124.

21. Ibid., 144.

22. Ibid., 162–63.

23. Ibid., 163.

24. SLC to Charles Hopkins Clark, 6 March 1880 (UCCL, 08597).

25. Clemens's copy of *The Jesuits*, 254–55.

26. Ibid., 31.

27. Twain, *Complete Interviews*, 519.

28. Clemens's copy of *The Jesuits in North America*, 135.

29. Ibid., lxxvi–vii.

30. Kime, "Huck among the Indians," 333.

31. Clemens's copy of *The Oregon Trail*, MTP, 14, 26, 80, 109, 117.

32. SLC to Charles L. Webster, 6 July 1884, quoted in Webster, *Mark Twain, Business Man*.

33. Budd, *Mark Twain: Social Philosopher*, 67.

34. Gribben, *Mark Twain's Library*, 197.

35. Clemens's copy of Richard Irving Dodge, *The Plains of the Great West and Their Inhabitants* (New York: G. P. Putnam's Sons, 1877), 428, 431, Mark Twain Library, Redding, CT.

36. Ibid., 440.

37. Ibid.

38. SLC to Charles L. Webster, 24 July 1884 (UCCL, 02155). According to an invoice from James R. Osgood and Company housed in the Mark Twain Papers, the writer purchased a copy of *The Plains of the Great West* in November 1877. He apparently did not have that copy in hand while summering in Elmira seven years later, however, and thus requested that his nephew secure another. Walter Blair indicates that "late in life" Twain gave a copy of Dodge's book to the public library in Redding, CT (HHT, 85). On the basis of topical political references to Schuyler Colfax, Secretary Belknap, and Sitting Bull in Twain's marginalia, I believe that the Redding Library volume, rather than the one Webster provided in 1884, is the copy that was purchased in 1877.

39. Webster, *Mark Twain, Business Man*, 270. See also Alan Gribben's reconstruction of the SLC-Charles Webster correspondence (*Mark Twain's Library*, 197).

40. Dodge, *Our Wild Indians*, 651.

41. Ibid., 652.

42. Gribben, *Mark Twain's Library*, 197–98.

43. Marginalia inscribed on page 109 of Twain's copy of *Our Wild Indians*, as reproduced in *Neufeld Collection*, 63. I would like to express gratitude to Kevin MacDonnell of MacDonnell Rare Books of Austin, Texas, for assisting me in tracking down the provenance of the Dodge book and supplying me with copies of these pages from the Christie's catalog on *Our Wild Indians*.

44. Ibid.

45. Dodge, *Our Wild Indians*, 100.

46. Dodge, *Our Wild Indians*, 100–101.

47. *Neufeld Collection*, 63.

48. *Neufeld Collection*, 63.

49. Dodge, *Our Wild Indians*, 109.

50. Ibid., 108.

51. *Neufeld Collection*, 63.

52. Kime, "Huck among the Indians," 324.

53. Kime, Introduction, 33.

54. Dodge alludes to female prisoners becoming the property of their captors, and thus "victims to the brutality of every one of the party," but offers no concrete details regarding the practice of gang rape or use of wooden stakes to pin the woman to the ground (*Our Wild Indians*, 529–30).

55. Dodge, *Plains of the Great West*, 334–35.

56. Axtell, *Invasion Within*, 310. See also Block, *Rape and Sexual Power*, 221–26.

57. Gwynne, *Empire*, 44–45.

58. "Message of the President of the United States in Answer to a Resolution ... in Relation to the Indian Barbarities in Minnesota," Senate Executive Document no. 7, 37th Congress, 3rd Session, 11 December 1862, 3–4.

59. Ebersole, *Captured by Texts*, 218.

60. Ibid.

61. Castiglia, *Bound and Determined*, 123.

62. Wilcox, *Custer and Other Poems*, 129.

63. Kasson, *Marble Queens and Captives*, 74.

64. Ibid., 79.

65. B. Brown, *Reading the West*, 34.

66. Ibid.

67. In Walter Blair, introduction to HHT, 88.

68. *Neufeld Collection*, 63.

69. Clemens's copy of *The Oregon Trail*, 151.

70. Ibid., 152–53.

71. Ibid., 153.

72. Stoneley, *Mark Twain*, 114.

73. Paine, *Mark Twain*, 2:899.

74. Stoneley, *Mark Twain*, 115.

75. Webster, *Mark Twain, Business Man*, 274.

76. Frank Richmond, the so-called Cicero of the Ring, was a sonorous-voiced actor who served for many years as the master of ceremonies in Buffalo Bill's Wild West.

77. William F. Cody to SLC, 8 August [actually September] 1884 (UCCL, 42273).

78. Cody originally sent four complimentary tickets to Clemens, presumably so that Livy and his two eldest daughters could accompany him to the performance. He attended alone, however, apparently as the result of a scare the children had experienced at Quarry Farm several days earlier. In a 7 September 1884 letter to Howells, Clemens explains the circumstances: "My whole interest, now, is centred in the task of hunting up, capturing, & sending to the penitentiary a drunken ruffian who ... drew a revolver on Susie and Clara last Wednesday when they were down the road a piece & without a protector" (MTHL, 504).

79. John M. Burke to SLC, 9 September 1884, Elmira, NY.

80. Display advertisement for Buffalo Bill's Wild West, Elmira *Sunday Tidings*, 3:43, 31 August 1884.

81. "The Wild West: Exciting Scenes of Prairie Life—Good Shooting and Varied Attractions," *Hartford Daily Courant*, 18 July 1885.

82. Reddin, *Wild West Shows*, 81.

83. Warren, *Buffalo Bill's America*, 362.

84. Ibid.

85. Neider, *Complete Short Stories*, 530.

86. Reddin, *Wild West Shows*, 81.

87. See "Did Buffalo Bill Visit your Town?," a compilation of all the show's extant route books that identify the dates and locations where the Wild West performed in both the United States and Europe, www.buffalobill.org.

88. Display advertisement, Elmira *Sunday Tidings*, 3:44, 7 September 1884.

89. Although the issue of the *Advertiser* in which Spooner's letter appeared is no longer extant, portions of it were reprinted in an article entitled "Sabbath Breaking," *Sunday Tidings* 3:45, 14 September 1884.

90. Ibid.

91. SLC to William F. Cody, 10 September 1884 (UCCL, 12811).

92. Display advertisement for Buffalo Bill's Wild West, Elmira *Sunday Tidings* 3:43, 31 August 1884.

93. White, "Frederick Jackson Turner," 29.

94. In *Buffalo Bill: Scout, Showman, Visionary,* Steve Friesen explains that the Wild West's verisimilitude was of paramount importance to Cody; for this reason, "the term *show* was never used in its title nor in any official materials. . . . Members of the *Wild West* who used the word were fired. It was an authentic portrayal of the West, not a common melodrama or medicine show" (48).

95. P. Deloria, *Indians in Unexpected Places,* 60.

96. White, "Frederick Jackson Turner," 35.

97. Ibid., 27.

98. Warren, *Buffalo Bill's America,* 30.

99. Reddin, *Wild West Shows,* 61.

100. "Mark Twain and the Wild West," *Hartford Daily Courant,* 16 July 1885, 2.

101. See Joy Kasson, *Buffalo Bill's Wild West;* Paul Reddin, *Wild West Shows;* and L.G. Moses, *Wild West Shows,* among others.

102. Thanks to Mary Robinson, director of the McCracken Research Library, Buffalo Bill Historical Center, Cody, WY, for providing me with a copy of Twain's testimonial from the 1887 Wild West program.

103. 1884 Program, Buffalo Bill's Wild West, provided courtesy of Buffalo Bill Historical Center, Cody, WY.

104. Warren, *Buffalo Bill's America,* 251.

105. Ibid., 30.

106. SLC to Joseph H. Twichell, 16 September 1884 (UCCL, 01327).

107. SLC to OLC, 9 February 1894 (UCCL, 04690).

108. Fillmore, "Study of Indian Music," 620.

109. Ibid., 619.

110. Fillmore, "Study of Indian Music," 623. See also McNutt, "Mark Twain," 237.

CHAPTER SIX. THE CURIOUS TALE OF THE CONNECTICUT INDIAN ASSOCIATION

1. Andrews, *Nook Farm,* 3.

2. Ibid., 129.

3. Johnson, "Historical Sketch," 9.

4. Ibid., 3.

5. Harriet Beecher Stowe to Sara Thomson Kinney, 16 March 1883, TKC.

6. Harriet Beecher Stowe to Sara Thomson Kinney, 25 January 1884, TKC.

7. Johnson, "Historical Sketch," 17.

8. "Helping the Indian," *Hartford Daily Courant,* 11 September 1888, 4.

9. Clippings Scrapbook, vol.1, TKC.

10. Johnson, "Historical Sketch," 10.

11. Gibson, *American Indian*, 448.

12. While admission to the association's annual business meetings was free, collections were routinely taken up after presentations by guest speakers; the meetings thus served as fund-raising opportunities as well.

13. "Connecticut Indian Association: Fifth Annual Meeting," *Hartford Daily Courant*, 26 January 1888, 3; *Hartford Post*, 14 February 1888.

14. "Connecticut Indian Civilization: Fifth Annual Meeting," *Hartford Daily Courant*, 6 November 1889, 2.

15. Ibid.

16. S. C. Armstrong to Sara Thomson Kinney, 8 November 1890, TKC.

17. "The Honorable C. W. Depew To-Night," *Hartford Times*, 15 May 1885, 2.

18. Handwritten copy of 9 May 1885 letter, "To the Ladies of the Connecticut Indian Association," TKC.

19. "Chauncey M. Depew's Lecture: A Complimentary Letter," *Hartford Daily Courant*, 12 May 1885, 2.

20. Andrews, *Nook Farm*, 129.

21. Ibid., 103.

22. Webster, Mark Twain, Business Man, 324. The original letter contains not one but two cancelled inscriptions. The message to Bunce is written on the back of page 2 of Clemens's letter to Webster; the other, which is incomplete, is inscribed upside down at the bottom of the back of page 1. The latter message is also addressed to a member of the Friday Evening Club—Henry C. Robinson: "Wednesday | Dr Bro Robinson—| Billiards *tomorrow* night, on a." It is likely unfinished because Clemens realized in the process of writing it that Robinson had also agreed to be seated on the Opera House platform at Depew's lecture. My thanks to Bob Hirst, general editor of the Mark Twain Papers, for this clarification.

23. Andrews, *Nook Farm*, 259.

24. According to a speech Depew gave for Twain's sixty-seventh birthday in 1902, the two men had been "friends for something more than a quarter of a century"; however, 1882 is the earliest record I can find of their meeting. See Depew, "Birthday and Anniversary Addresses," 239. In *My Memories of Eighty Years* (291–95), Depew offers a detailed account of an enjoyable visit with the Clemenses and Twichells at Bad Nauheim, Germany, in August 1892. The men also corresponded occasionally until the end of Twain's life.

25. The irreverence of some of Depew's witticisms, such as "A pessimist is a man who thinks all women are bad. An optimist is one who hopes they are," would no doubt have appealed to Twain. Regarding Clemens's plan to publish a collection of the orator's speeches, see NBJ3, 376n45.

26. According to the *Courant*, a total of nine men—Hawley, Twichell, Parker, Clemens, Trumbull, Robinson, Warner, Bulkeley, and Hyde—were seated on the stage along with the speaker ("The Lecture by Mr. Depew," 16 May 1885, 1), whereas the *Hartford Times* mentions only six ("Mr. Depew's Lecture," 16 May 1885, 2). The two reviews differ in tone as well: the *Courant* praises Depew's "fascinating" speech, recounting its content in great detail, but

laments that the audience, "while fair in size, [was] much too small for the occasion." The *Times*, on the other hand, critiques the speaker's gestures as "not elocutionarily correct" and describes the talk as filled with "heavy historical and literary padding" and lacking in originality, concluding, "It was all in good taste—but it was all so well known!"

27. Depew, *My Memories*, 72.

28. Ibid., 72–73.

29. Johnson, "Historical Sketch," 5.

30. Ibid., 15.

31. "Connecticut Indian Association: Fourth Annual Meeting," *Hartford Daily Courant*, 2 February 1886, 1.

32. Connecticut Indian Association Minutes Book, 1881–87, TKC.

33. Connecticut Indian Association Scrapbooks (box 3), TKC.

34. Indian Letters (box 4), TKC.

35. SLC to Sara T. Kinney, 13 February 1886 (UCCL, 10551).

36. See Kent Rasmussen's *Dear Mark Twain* for numerous examples of such "begging" letters.

37. The total amount of Clemens's philanthropic contributions to Gerhardt is uncertain. An 1882 letter (UCCL, 02282) specifies the total dollar amount as twenty-eight hundred to three thousand dollars distributed over a period of five years. A subsequent letter, however, dated 14–25 June 1883 (UCCL, 02881) mentions Clemens sent the "final instalment of the stipulated $4500." A third, on 1 August 1883 (UCCL, 02818), discusses Livy's suggestion to add "one thousand dollars to the stipulated sum to continue your studies another year." Letters written in 1885 also indicate that the Clemenses' support of Gerhardt continued after the couple's return to Hartford from Paris. The contemporary value of Clemens's forty-five hundred dollar contribution to the Gerhardts' support was derived by means of the calculation tool "Seven Ways to Compute the Relative Value of a U.S. Dollar Amount, 1774 to Present," www.measuringworth.com.

38. The exact dates of Porter's study abroad are difficult to pinpoint. The Mark Twain Papers contain just two letters, dated 1 March 1882 (UCLC, 41048) and 4 April 1883 (UCLC, 41514), which the painter wrote to Clemens from Paris. On this basis, it can be surmised that Porter spent at least thirteen months in France; however, his residency abroad may in fact have been longer.

39. See Fishkin, *Lighting Out*, 98.

40. SLC to Isabella Beecher Hooker, 27 May 1884 (UCCL, 10482). Quoted with the permission of the Harriet Beecher Stowe Research Center, Hartford, CT.

41. SLC to Francis Wayland, 24 December 1885 (UCCL, 11278).

42. SLC to Karl and Hattie Gerhardt, 1 and 3 May 1883 (UCCL, 02380).

43. Kinney's disappointment can be inferred from the fact that she did not reach out to Clemens later during the summer of 1886, when the Connecticut Indian Association began soliciting donations for a new undertaking—financing the medical school tuition of the first female Native American physician, Susan LaFlesche of the Omaha tribe.

44. Ibid.

45. *Hartford Daily Courant*, 23 February 1886, 2.

46. Ibid.

47. US Department of Agriculture, Studies of Family Living in the United States and Other Countries (Washington, DC), 138. In 1886, $250 would have equaled roughly $6,200 today.

48. Wayland accepted a position on the association's advisory board in the mid-1880s and continued in this role until his death in 1904.

49. The text is found in volume 1 of the Connecticut Indian Association Scrapbook, TKC. The handwritten date at the top of the clipping, 24 August 1886, is apparently incorrect, since the piece does not appear in that issue of the *Hartford Daily Courant*.

50. "About a Blackbird," *Hartford Daily Courant*, 16 November 1886, 1.

51. The obituary of her husband, Major John Coddington Kinney, which appeared in the *Courant* a day after his death on 22 April 1891, states that he served as the secretary of the Mohonk Indian Conference; thus, both Kinneys played leadership roles within this liberal national organization.

52. Emily Whitman was the wife of Henry A. Whitman, vice president of the Hartford Life and Annuity Insurance Company.

53. "Blackbird Again," *Hartford Daily Courant*, 23 November 1886, 2.

54. "News from the Indian, 'Blackbird,'" *Hartford Daily Courant*, 3 May 1887, 2.

55. Karamanski, *Blackbird's Song*, xiii.

56. "For the Benefit of Indians," *Hartford Daily Courant*, 8 October 1890, 1.

57. Ten years after Twain's death, Burton played a pivotal role in the local campaign to preserve the writer's home. In "Save Clemens's Home for Our Own Honor, Says Burton," published on the front page of the *Hartford Daily Courant*, 18 April 1920, he described Clemens as "the man who lived in my backyard."

58. Burton, "Mark Twain," 5.

59. Ibid.

60. "Henry [sic] Ibsen: The First Lecture in the Course by Mr. R. E. Burton," *Hartford Daily Courant*, 24 October 1890, 3; "Sidney Lanier: Mr. Burton's Lecture Yesterday Afternoon," *Hartford Daily Courant*, 1 November 1890, 3.

61. The configuration of the home's first floor suggests the rooms in question were likely the library and dining room—a combined space that could easily accommodate an audience of seventy-five to a hundred people. If, however, Burton's lectern had been set up in the dining room rather than the library, people could also have been seated in the drawing room.

62. Burton, *Mark Twain*, 5.

63. SLC to Sara T. Kinney, 23 April 1891, quoted in the *Hartford Daily Courant*, 27 April 1891, 1 (UCCL, 13004),

64. Carter, "Meaning," 436.

65. Ibid.

66. Parkman, *Count Frontenac,* 150. Clemens's annotated copy of this volume is housed at the MTP. See Slotkin, *Fatal Environment,* 524.

67. Twain, *Letters from the Earth,* 146.

68. William Lecky's *Spirit of Rationalism,* quoted in Fulton, *Mark Twain,* 35–36.

69. Parkman, *Jesuits in North America,* 255.

70. Leon, *Mark Twain,* 94–95.

71. Slotkin, *Fatal Environment,* 529.

72. Fulton, *Mark Twain,* 80.

73. Beard, *Hardly a Man,* 336.

74. "Historiated letters" differ from both "ornamented letters," which are characterized by elaborately intertwined foliage patterns, and "inhabited letters," which contain humans, animals, or fantastic beasts that climb through the vegetation. See "The Decorated Letter" (www.getty.edu).

75. SLC to L.E. Parkhurst, Hartford, CT, 20 December 1889 (UCCL, 03991).

76. Sylvester Baxter, "Mark Twain's Masterpiece," *Boston Sunday Herald,* 15 December 1889, 17.

77. Ibid.

78. Clemens expressed his gratitude for Baxter's insightful review in a note to the journalist on 19 December 1889 that begins, "It was an admirable notice, & I cannot thank you enough. And I am so glad you said the appreciative word for Beard's excellent pictures" (UCCL, 02705).

79. Kate Foote to Hattie (Harriet) and Mary Foote, 8 October 1868, Harriet Beecher Stowe Research Center.

80. Kate Foote to Alice Hooker Day, 2 February 1891, Harriet Beecher Stowe Research Center.

81. Kate Foote to SLC, 17 October 1890 (UCCL, 45262).

82. Howells, "Editor's Study," 319.

83. Kate Foote to SLC, 6 November 1890 (UCCL, 45299).

84. Ibid.

85. SLC to OLC, 13 January 1891 (UCCL, 04157).

86. SLC to Kate Foote, 16 January 1891 (UCCL, 04160).

87. Kate Foote, "Our Washington Letter," *Independent,* 22 January 1891. Clippings Scrapbook, Foote Collection, Harriet Beecher Stowe Research Center.

88. Kate Foote, "Our Washington Letter," *Independent,* 18 December 1891.

89. "Friends of the Indian: Annual Conference of Indian Commissioners and Missionaries," *Washington Post,* 9 January 1891, 6.

90. "The Sioux Powwow: Indian Chiefs Tell Secretary Noble What They Want," *Washington Post,* 8 February 1891, 2.

91. "Hard on the Soldiers: Indian Chiefs Describe the Fight at Wounded Knee," *Washington Post,* 12 February 1891, 5

92. Kate Foote, "Our Washington Letter," *Independent,* 19 February 1891.

93. Ibid.

94. Ibid.

95. "The Fight at Wounded Knee—What an Educated Indian Says about It," *Hartford Daily Courant*, 9 January 1891, 1.

96. Jane Lampton Clemens died in Keokuk on 27 October 1890; Olivia Lewis Langdon died in Elmira a month later on 28 November 1890.

97. Ohio Society Banquet," *New York Times*, 7 February 1891, 1.

98. Messent, *Short Works*, 168–69.

CHAPTER SEVEN. INDIGENES ABROAD

1. Welland, *Mark Twain in England*, 170.

2. Ibid.

3. The *More Tramps Abroad* manuscript, housed in the New York Public Library's Berg Collection of English and American Literature, contains annotations by both Chatto and Bliss, and thus literally bears the marks of being repeatedly shuttled back and forth across the Atlantic.

4. Welland, *Mark Twain in England*, 181–82.

5. SLC to Francis E. Bliss, 2 July 1897 (UCCL, 05249). Page 722 of the Berg manuscript contains the following note, presumably by Andrew Chatto to his typesetters: "OMIT all this reprint. 3,100 words in this text. 4,000 [words of] reprint in this chapter altogether."

6. *More Tramps Abroad* manuscript, 722.

7. Bonwick, *Tasmanian Race*, 44–47.

8. Ibid., 45.

9. *More Tramps Abroad* manuscript, 728.

10. Eastman, *From the Deep Woods*, 111.

11. *More Tramps Abroad* manuscript, 733. A facsimile of this page is reproduced in Isaac Gewirtz's *Mark Twain, A Skeptic's Progress*, 100.

12. *More Tramps Abroad* manuscript, 720.

13. Messent, "Racial and Colonial Discourse," 80.

14. Twain, *Complete Interviews*, 353.

15. Notebook no. 35, 24–25.

16. Ibid., 30.

17. Wolfe, "Elimination," 387–88.

18. This folk etymology must have been provided to Clemens by one of his local hosts. "Tacoma" has been translated variously as "the place where the waters begin," "white sentinel," or "large breast."

19. This association is corroborated when the image is considered in conjunction with the facsimile of a heavily edited page from Twain's notebook, which appears at the beginning of chapter 3 in both editions. Featuring a series of scribbles, strikethroughs, and numerous rejected drafts of the same sentence, the document illustrates the labor and frustration of the writing process. The author finally writes perpendicularly across his text, "Give it up. Am sorry he [the man who invented the cuckoo clock] died" (FE, 49).

20. Twain explores these perceived similarities between Americans and Australia's colonists at even greater length in the manuscript of *More Tramps*

Abroad, speculating that the phenomenon is attributable to politics rather than immigration (398).

21. The same "space-annihilating power of thought" recurs later on the tour when Clemens sees a "burly German" strike a native in Bombay. The incident instantly reminds him of how his father "every now and then" cuffed the family's "harmless slave boy, Lewis, for trifling little blunders and awkwardnesses" (FE, 352).

22. Wolfe, *Settler Colonialism,* 2.

23. Wolfe, "Elimination," 388.

24. Notebook no. 35, 68–70.

25. These reminders of Clemens's mining days in the West persisted throughout the world lecture tour. As Coleman O. Parsons recounts in "Mark Twain: Paid Performer in South Africa," "In Johannesburg, gold miners would rush forward to shake Clemens's hand at the end of each performance, referring to shared experiences in Nevada or California. 'Put it there, old man! Don't you remember me?—don't you remember Bill Bloodgood that night in Jim Dusenberry's cabin? And that Chinaman who poured our whiskey into the oilcan? Dear old Mark, those were happy days!'" (10).

26. Crosby, *Ecological Imperialism,* 196–97. See also Diamond, *Guns, Germs, and Steel.*

27. Messent, "Racial and Colonial Discourse," 70.

28. Kaplan, *Anarchy of Empire,* 75.

29. Rosaldo, "Imperialist Nostalgia," 87.

30. Twain, *Complete Interviews,* 227.

31. Messent, "Racial and Colonial Discourse," 71.

32. D. Brown, *Bury My Heart,* 89.

33. Messent, "Racial and Colonial Discourse," 71.

34. Snaith, *Theological Word Book,* 136–37.

35. Kaplan, *Anarchy of Empire,* 75.

36. McCarthy, *Exhibiting Maori,* 19–20.

37. Notebook no. 35, 59.

38. Rosaldo, "Imperialist Nostalgia," 69–70.

39. Gilpin, *Observations,* 140.

40. Mark Twain House and Museum archives.

41. Quoted with the permission of the Mark Twain House and Museum, Hartford, CT.

42. *More Tramps Abroad* manuscript.

43. Ibid.

44. *Following the Equator* typescript, Berg, 219.

45. Broome, *Aboriginal Victorians,* 170.

46. Messent, "Racial and Colonial Discourse," 75.

47. OLC to Susan L. Crane, 3 November 1895 (UCCL, 04970).

48. Edmonds, "'Failing in Every Endeavor,'" 203.

49. "George Frankland," in Kerr, *Dictionary of Australian Artists,* 273.

50. Edmonds, "Imperial Objects," 81.

51. Manderson, "Law of the Image," 157.

52. The album been digitized by the National Library of Australia: "Album of the Boileau Family's Voyage from England to Australia, 1894–95," www.nla .gov.au.

53. Twain's points are largely paraphrased from Bonwick's description of the proclamation board's panels in *The Lost Tasmanian Race*, 55.

54. The text of this letter, found on page 86 of Alexander Morton's 1894–98 Scrapbook, is reproduced with the permission of the Tasmanian Museum and Art Gallery. I would also like to express my gratitude to the museum's research officer, Joanne Huxley, for providing me with a copy of this unpublished letter.

55. The "Minutes of the June 1867 Meeting," published in the *Papers and Proceedings of the Royal Society of Tasmania* (1875), records this bequest under the subheading "Presentations to the Museum": "From Mr. Bolter— Governor Davey's Proclamation (pictorial) to the Aborigines of Tasmania," 18.

56. Cato, *Story of the Camera*, 83.

57. SLC to Frank Bliss, 3–5 May 1897 (UCCL, 05511).

58. Edmonds, "'Failing in Every Endeavor,'" 205.

59. Edmonds, "Imperial Objects," 82.

60. Ibid.

61. Bonwick, *Lost Tasmanian Race*, 147.

62. Ibid., 206.

63. Once again, Twain's information is deeply indebted to Bonwick, who states that the natives' lives in the settlements consisted of "school lessons, catechizings in abstruse doctrines of faith, with long prayers and sermons" (*Tasmanian Race*, 206).

64. Bonwick, *Lost Tasmanian Race*, 10.

65. Ibid.

66. Miller and Johnson, *Puritans*, 100–101.

CHAPTER EIGHT. THE MAORI

1. Twain, *Complete Interviews*, 248.

2. OLC to OSC, 2–5 December 1895 (UCCL, 04979).

3. C. Clemens, *My Father, Mark Twain*, 149.

4. Spencer, *On Social Evolution*, 13.

5. Notebook no. 34, 32.

6. Smythe, "Real Mark Twain," 30.

7. According to *Te Ara: The Encyclopedia of New Zealand*, "In the past many believed that the Maori name for Mt. Cook, Aorangi, meant 'the cloud-piercer.' But Aorangi was a person. According to tradition, when the canoe in which he and his brothers were voyaging in the southwest Pacific was wrecked, he scrambled to the highest point of the canoe's upturned hull. One early name for the South Island is Te Waka o Aoraki, meaning Aoraki's canoe" (www.teara .govt.nz).

8. Notebook no. 34, 29–30.

9. Ibid., 32.

10. Horatio G. Robley, in *Moko, or Maori Tattooing*, translates this term as a "white man blackwashed" (105).

11. Gribben, *Mark Twain's Library*, 449.

12. The use of native cultural names for settler homes was a fashionable trend among affluent New Zealanders in the late nineteenth and early twentieth centuries. See Petersen, "European Use," 58.

13. Anson, "Thomas Morland Hocken," 87; 89.

14. Kerr, *Hocken, Prince of Collectors*, 95. Hocken corresponded extensively with Major-General Horatio Robley, who used two *moko* signatures from the doctor's personal collection as illustrations in his 1896 study of Maori tattooing.

15. Fenwick, "Memoir," n.p.

16. Anson, "Thomas Morland Hocken," 96.

17. Ibid.

18. Hocken, "Introduction," 157.

19. Ibid.

20. Anson, "Thomas Morland Hocken," 96.

21. Ibid.

22. Petersen, "European Use," 64, 57.

23. Notebook no. 34, 30.

24. Twain, *Complete Interviews*, 250.

25. Notebook no. 34, 32.

26. A nineteenth-century photo of Atahapara's interior shows three of Merrett's paintings—"The Warrior Chieftains of New Zealand," "Group of Maoris," and "Maori Man in Cloak"—displayed next to a monumental carved rafter from the porch of a Maori meetinghouse. (Hocken Collection, University of Otago, Dunedin).

27. Robley, *Moko, or Maori Tattooing*, 57. Robley describes the *aweto hotete* as a native plant of New Zealand, which exists on the borderline between the "vegetal and animal kingdoms." Clemens's description of the process whereby the caterpillar becomes the plant's host in *Following the Equator* is uncannily similar to Robley's, suggesting a direct line of transmission from this printed source to Hocken to the writer.

28. Smythe, "Real Mark Twain," 31.

29. Notebook no. 34, 37.

30. *Otago Daily Times*, 11 November 1895, 3, www.paperspast.natlib .govt.nz.

31. Lummis, "Ukiyo-e," 23.

32. Woodward, "Sir Joseph Kinsey," specifically identifies Malcolm Ross as a close friend, with whom Kinsey shared a keen interest in mountaineering and photography, "two delights which so often seem to go together" (92).

33. *Otago Daily Times*, "The Early History, Maori, and South Seas Court," 3 December 1889, 4.

34. SLC to Sarah G. Kinsey, 23 November 1895 (UCCL, 04975).

35. OLC to Joseph Kinsey, 21 November 1895 (UCCL, 04974).

36. Walker, "'Maori House,'" 8.

37. Ibid., 6.

38. Stack, "Account of the Maori House," 178.

39. Gribben, *Mark Twain's Library*, 507.

40. Thomas, *Entangled Objects*, 139.

41. Hutton, *Guide to the Collections*, 204.

42. McCarthy, *Exhibiting Maori*, 42.

43. Ibid.

44. "First Letter," George Augustus Sala, 8 October 1857, www.savageclub .com.

45. Watson, *Savage Club*, 21.

46. Ibid., 235.

47. SLC to Ralph Waldo Emerson with copies to Oliver Wendell Holmes and Henry Wadsworth Longfellow, 27 December 1877 (UCCL, 01184).

48. My thanks to Allan Smith, the current secretary of the Christchurch Savage Club, for his kindness in fielding my questions about the various protocols involved in the group's meetings. In his recollection, the tradition of officers wearing Maori feather cloaks persisted until the 1990s.

49. Fatout, *Mark Twain Speaking*, 302.

50. Ibid., 304.

51. Ibid., 302.

52. SLC to William L. Webster, 30 March 1888 (UCCL, 12210).

53. OLC to Joseph Kinsey, 21 November 1895 (UCCL, 04974).

54. McCarthy, *Exhibiting Maori*, 26.

55. Personal correspondence with Roger Fyfe, senior curator of anthropology, Canterbury Museum, Christchurch, New Zealand, 7 October 2012.

56. Keane, "Pounamu."

57. Mitira, "Explaining," 37.

58. Hutton, *Guide to the Collections*, 219.

59. OLC to Susan L. Crane, 24 November 1895 (UCCL, 04976).

60. Notebook no. 34, 40.

61. According to Joan Woodward, Kinsey had a unique photographic vision: "Not for Kinsey the usual family album stuff! His style was to create a good joke; it is easy to imagine his gleeful preparation as he organizes a tableau, arranging his subjects and setting up the props. The veranda and garden at *Warrimoo* were the scene for much of this photographic hilarity, and the darkroom on the grounds must have rocked with laughter" ("Sir Joseph Kinsey," 92–93).

62. SLC to Joseph Kinsey, 12 December 1895 (UCCL, 04980); Clara Clemens to Joseph Kinsey, 12 December 1895 (UCCL, 04981); OLC to Joseph Kinsey, 13 December 1895 (UCCL, 04982).

63. SLC to Francis E. Bliss, 3–5 May 1897 (UCCL, 05511).

64. According to Paul Moon, senior lecturer in Maori studies at the Auckland University of Technology, "One clue about the location [of the meetinghouse seen in the photo] is the white feather (Te Raukura) worn by the women in their hair. These were worn almost exclusively—from the second

half of the 19th century—by those Maori living in the Taranaki region [in the western part of the North Island] and particularly by followers of the prophet and leader Te Whiti" (personal correspondence, 17 July 2014).

65. Cowan, "Sir John Logan Campbell."

66. Gribben, *Mark Twain's Library*, 126. This entry indicates that the book is housed in the archives of the Mark Twain House and Museum in Hartford, Connecticut; however, it unfortunately cannot be located.

67. Campbell, *Poenamo*, 138.

68. R. Stone, *Father and His Gifts*, 252–53.

69. See chapter 5 for an extended discussion of this topic.

70. In 2009, the New Zealand Board of Geographic Names voted to restore the original Maori spelling "Whanganui" for both the city and river on which it is set. Local residents, however, overwhelmingly opposed the measure, which led to a subsequent decision deeming either spelling officially acceptable.

71. Clemens's description of this visit in his notebook is even more terse than in the published travelogue: "Lectured, Wanganui, again. Went to see a chief & a Maori pah—or rather a council house—beautiful carving" (Notebook no. 34, 47). Striving to use the accurate term for the structure he visited, he quickly realizes that *pa* (a fortified village) is incorrect. What he means is "council house," but he cannot recollect the Maori word *whare*.

72. OLC to OSC, 2–5 December 1895 (UCCL, 04979).

73. Clara Clemens to Joseph Kinsey, 12 December 1895 (UCCL, 04981).

74. Notebook no. 34, 50.

75. *More Tramps* manuscript, 939.

76. Moon, "History of Moutoa Gardens," 356.

77. Notebook no. 34, 51.

78. Ibid.

79. Ibid.

80. "Indigenous Maoris in New Zealand Occupy Pakaitore to Claim Their Sovereignty, 1995," *Global Nonviolent Action Database*, http://nvdatabase .swarthmore.edu.

81. David Geary's *Mark Twain & Me in Maoriland* was performed at the International Arts Festival in Auckland in July 2010.

82. In *At Home Abroad: Mark Twain in Australasia*, Miriam Shillingsburg quotes from enthusiastic reviews of Twain's lectures, published in the *Wanganui Herald* and *Wanganui Chronicle*, which contain no intimation of such editorializing (168–70).

83. Ibid., 52.

84. For a detailed discussion of Ngapua's political career and the issues that arose in his relationship with Carroll as a result, see Moon, *Ngapua: The Political Life of Hone Heke Ngapua, MHR.*

85. Notebook no. 34, 52.

86. *More Tramps* manuscript, 969.

87. Laurie, *Story of Australasia*, 355.

88. Notebook no. 34, 31.

CONCLUSION

1. Twain, *Complete Interviews,* 287.

2. Ibid.

3. Lawrence, *Studies,* 59.

4. Rowe, "Mark Twain's Critique," 113.

5. Twain, *Complete Interviews,* 591.

6. Budd, *Mark Twain: Social Philosopher,* 107.

7. Willis, *Our Philippine Problem,* 2. Quoted with the permission of the Mark Twain Library, Redding, CT.

8. Although part of the 12 January 1906 dictation was published in the *North American Review* in April 1907, this passage was not included. See Kiskis, *Mark Twain's Own,* 143–50.

9. SLC per Isabel V. Lyon to Herbert Welsh, on or after 15 December 1906, New York, NY (UCCL, 07594).

10. Binkovitz, "Who Were the Six?"

11. The *New York Telegraph* named the following army officers in attendance: Adjutant General H. C. Corbin; Brigadier General W. H. Penrose; General Michael V. Sheridan, whose brother Philip was perhaps the most infamous of the nineteenth-century Indian fighters; Colonel Samuel Reber, along with the family of General Nelson A. Miles; and Major General Wesley Merritt, who had served as the first American governor of the Philippines in 1898 ("Buffalo Bill Is Warmly Greeted," 3 April 1901).

All reviews cited of this premier 1901 performance can be found in vol. 10 of Nate Salsbury's scrapbooks, provided courtesy of the Denver Public Library. These archival clippings unfortunately include no pagination.

12. "Age Can't Wither 'Buffalo Bill,'" *New York Press,* 3 April 1901, states that Clemens was accompanied by his wife and daughter but does not specify if it was Clara or Jean.

13. Official Programme, *Buffalo Bill's Wild West and Congress of the Rough Riders of the World,* 1901.

14. "Buffalo Bill's Wild West," *New York Times,* 3 April 1901, 9. According to Paul Reddin's study *Wild West Shows,* Cody's use of native actors as stand-ins for the Boer rebels was also reported in the *New York Journal* and *New York Telegraph* (257).

15. "Age Can't Wither 'Buffalo Bill,'" *New York Press,* 3 April 1901.

16. Official Programme, *Buffalo Bill's Wild West.*

17. *Buffalo Bill's Wild West.*

18. *Evening Sun* (New York), 3 April 1901, Nate Salsbury Scrapbook.

19. Nate Salsbury Scrapbook, quoted in Reddin, 136.

20. *New York Press,* 4 April 1901, quoted in Reddin, *Wild West Shows,* 136.

21. Fatout, *Mark Twain Speaking,* 361–62.

22. Notebook no. 44, 20.

23. See Gribben, *Mark Twain's Library,* 497.

24. McNutt, "Mark Twain," 238.

25. Unpublished manuscript, "Christ and the Patriarchs" (June 1868) in the Jean Webster-McKinney Family Papers, Vassar College.

26. Carley, "Sioux Campaign of 1862," 101. I also consulted the eminent Western historian Robert Utley about the account's authenticity; he pronounced it "pure fantasy. That doesn't mean there were no atrocities, on both sides, but not that extreme" (personal correspondence, 5 September 2014).

27. Castiglia, *Bound and Determined*, 218.

28. Mark Twain, "Instructions in Art," *New Metropolitan*, April–May 1903.

29. Ibid.

30. Walt Whitman, *Leaves of Grass* (1855), lines 343–44.

31. Barbara Schmidt, "Mark Twain's Juggernaut Correspondence," www.twainquotes.com.

32. W. Morgan, *Monadnock Summer*, 65.

33. Lawton, *Lifetime with Mark Twain*, 247.

34. Lystra, *Dangerous Intimacy*, 62.

35. Faulkner, "Mark Twain in Dublin," 1–2.

36. Bowditch, *George de Forest Brush*, 67.

37. Ibid., 66.

38. Ibid., 129.

39. Brush, "Artist among the Indians," 54.

40. Brush quoted in Bowditch, *George de Forest Brush*, 23.

41. Ibid.

42. Ibid.

43. Brush, "Artist among the Indians," 57.

44. Anderson, "Layered Fiction," 17.

45. Brush, "Artist among the Indians," 57.

46. Faulkner, "George de Forest Brush," 13.

47. Ibid., 4.

48. My thanks to Lisa Foote, archivist of the Dublin (NH) Historical Society. On the basis of Jean's photos, she was able to identify the location of the event from the distinctive ridgeline of the mountains in the background. She also kindly provided me with the *Peterboro Transcript* article, 24 August 1905, 2.

49. Neider, *Complete Short Stories*, 529–30.

50. JLC Diary, 6 August 1906, MTP.

51. Eastman, *Red Hunters*, v–vi.

52. JLC Diary, 7 August 1907, MTP.

53. Bush quoted in Bowditch, *George de Forest Brush*, 103–4.

54. Deloria, *Playing Indian*, 111.

55. Lawton, *Lifetime with Mark Twain*, 293.

56. "Indians in Revolt; Six Whites Killed," *New York Times*, 29 March 1909, 1–2.

57. Jean L. Clemens, "Mediaeval Torture," *New York Times*, 5 April 1909, 6.

58. Shelden, *Mark Twain*, 344.

59. SLC to CLC, 18 July 1909, UCCL, 08435. 1909 (UCCL, 08435).

60. Hirst, *Who Is Mark Twain?*, 37.

61. Mark Twain, *Plymouth Rock and the Pilgrims and Other Speeches,* 320. Paul Fatout's version of the speech in *Mark Twain Speaking* contains slight variations on the wording Neider reports (610).

Bibliography

ARCHIVAL SOURCES

Bancroft Scraps. 23 vols. Bancroft Library. University of California, Berkeley. n.d.

Berg Collection of American Literature. New York Public Library.

Canterbury Museum. Christchurch, New Zealand.

Connecticut Indian Association Archives. Thomson-Kinney Collection. Connecticut State Library, Hartford, CT.

Draper Manuscripts. Wisconsin Historical Society. Madison.

Harriet Beecher Stowe Research Center, Hartford, CT

Hocken Collections, University of Otago, Dunedin, New Zealand

Mark Twain House and Museum. Hartford, CT.

Mark Twain Library. Redding, CT.

Mark Twain Papers. University of California, Berkeley.

Orion Clemens. Letterpress Copybook. Nevada State Archives. Carson City.

Papers of Nevada Territorial Governor James W. Nye, 1861–1864. Nevada State Archives. Carson City.

Scrapbooks of Alexander Morton. Tasmanian Museum and Art Gallery. Hobart.

Smithsonian Archives of American Art. Washington, DC.

PRIMARY AND SECONDARY SOURCES

American Annual Cyclopedia and Register of Important Events of the Year., Vol 10. New York: D. Appelton, 1870.

American State Papers: Indian Affairs. Buffalo: W. S. Hein, 1998.

Anderson, Nancy K. "Layered Fiction: The Indian Paintings." In *George de Forest Brush: The Indian Paintings,* edited by Nancy K. Anderson, 7–33. Washington, DC: National Gallery of Art, 2008.

Andrews, Kenneth R. *Nook Farm: Mark Twain's Hartford Circle.* Cambridge, MA: Harvard University Press, 1950.

Angel, Myron. *History of Nevada.* Oakland, CA: Thompson and West, 1881.

Anson, Dimitri. "Thomas Morland Hocken: Collector of Maori Artifacts." *Tribal Art* 12–3, no. 48 (Spring 2008): 86–101.

Arnold, Matthew. *Essays in Criticism.* 2nd ser. London: MacMillan, 1888.

Aron, Steven. *American Confluence: The Missouri Frontier from Borderland to Border State.* Bloomington: Indiana University Press, 2009.

Axtell, James. *The Invasion Within: The Contest of Cultures in Colonial North America.* New York: Oxford University Press, 1985.

Baender, Paul, ed. *The Adventures of Tom Sawyer: A Facsimile of the Author's Holographic Manuscript.* 2 vol. Frederick, MD: University Publications of America, 1982.

Baetzhold, Howard, and Joseph B. McCullough, eds. *The Bible According to Mark Twain.* New York: Touchstone Books, 1996.

Baxter, Sylvester. "Mark Twain's Masterpiece." *Boston Sunday Herald,* 15 December 1889, 17.

Beard, Daniel Carter. *Hardly a Man Is Now Alive.* New York: Doubleday, 1998.

Benton, Thomas Hart. *Thirty Years View, or a History of the Working of the American Government from 1820–1850.* New York: D. Appleton, 1883.

Binkovitz, Leah. "Who Were the Six Indian Chiefs in Teddy Roosevelt's Inaugural Parade?" *Smithsonian Magazine,* 16 January 2013.

Bishop, Morris. "The End of the Iroquois." *American Heritage* 20, no. 6 (October 1969): 28–33, 77–81.

Blackhawk, Ned. *Violence over the Land: Indians and Empires in the Early American West.* Cambridge, MA: Harvard University Press, 2006.

Block, Sharon. *Rape and Sexual Power in Early America.* Chapel Hill: University of North Carolina Press, 2006.

Bonwick, James. *The Lost Tasmanian Race.* London: Sampson Low, Marston, Searle, and Rivington, 1884.

Bowditch, Nancy Douglas. *George de Forest Brush: Recollections of a Joyous Painter.* Peterborough, NH: Noone House, 1970.

Broome, Richard. *Aboriginal Victorians: A History since 1800.* Melbourne: Allen and Unwin, 2005.

Brown, Bill, ed. *Reading the West: An Anthology of Dime Westerns.* Boston: Bedford Books, 1997.

Brown, Dee. *Bury My Heart at Wounded Knee: An Indian History of the American West.* New York: Holt, Reinhart and Winston, 1970.

Brown, Harry J. *Injun Joe's Ghost: The Indian Mixed-Blood in American Writing.* Columbia: University of Missouri Press, 2004.

Brush, George de Forest. "An Artist among the Indians." *Century Magazine,* 30 May 1885, 54–57.

Budd, Louis J. *Mark Twain: Social Philosopher.* 2nd edition. Columbia: University of Missouri Press, 2001.

Burton, Richard. "Mark Twain in the Hartford Days." *Mark Twain Quarterly* 1, no. 4 (Summer 1937): 5.

Byrd, Jodi. *The Transit of Empire.* Minneapolis: University of Minnesota Press, 2011.

Campbell, John Logan. *Poenamo: Sketches of the Early Days in New Zealand.* Auckland: Golden Press, 1980.

Carley, Kenneth. "The Sioux Campaign of 1862: Sibley's Letters to His Wife." *Minnesota History* 38, no. 3 (September 1962): 99–114.

Carter, Everett. "The Meaning of *a Connecticut Yankee*": Norton Critical Edition, *A Connecticut Yankee in King Arthur's Court,* edited by Allison R. Ensor, 434–52. New York: W.W. Norton, 1982.

Castiglia, Christopher. *Bound and Determined.* Chicago: University of Chicago Press, 1996.

Cato, Jack. *The Story of the Camera in Australia.* 3rd ed. Melbourne: Institute of Australian Photography, 1979.

Clemens, Clara. *My Father, Mark Twain.* New York: Harper and Brothers, 1931.

Clemens, Orion. *City of Keokuk in 1856.* Keokuk, IA: Orion Clemens, 1856.

Coggeshall, William Turner, ed. *The Poets and Poetry of the West.* With Biographical and Critical Notes. New York: Follet, Foster, 1860.

Collins, Lewis. *History of Kentucky.* Covington, KY: Collins, 1882.

Cook, Frederick, ed. *Journals of the Military Expedition of Major John Sullivan against the Six Nations of Indians with Records of Centennial Celebrations.* Auburn, NY: Knapp, Peck, and Thomson, 1887.

Cooper, James Fenimore. *The Last of the Mohicans.* New York: Signet Classics, 1962.

Cothran, Boyd. *Remembering the Modoc War: Redemptive Violence and the Making of American Innocence.* Chapel Hill: University of North Carolina Press, 2014.

Coulombe, Joseph. *Mark Twain and the American West.* Columbia: University of Missouri Press, 2003.

Cowan, James. "Sir John Logan Campbell: The Father of Auckland." *New Zealand Railways Magazine* 8, no. 7 (November 1933): 17–21. New Zealand Electronic Text Collection. www.nzetc.victoria.ac.nz.

Coward, John. *The Newspaper Indian: Native American Identity in the Press, 1820–1890.* Urbana: University of Illinois Press, 1999.

Cox, James H. *Muting White Noise: Native American and European Novel Traditions.* Norman: University of Oklahoma Press, 2006.

Cronise, Titus. *The Natural Wealth of California.* San Francisco: H.H. Bancroft, 1868.

Crosby, Alfred W. *Ecological Imperialism: The Biological Expansion of Europe, 900–1900.* Cambridge: Cambridge University Press, 2004.

Crum, Steven J. *The Road on Which We Came: A History of the Western Shoshone.* Salt Lake City: University of Utah Press, 1994.

Dao, James, and Serge Kovaleski. "Music Style Is Called Supremacist Recruiting Tool." *New York Times,* 8 August 2012.

David, Beverly. *Mark Twain and His Illustrators.* Vol. 1, *1869–1875.* Troy, NY: Whitston, 1986.

Davis, Chester. "Mark's New Zealand." *Twainian* 34–37 (July–August 1978): 2–4.

Day, A. Grove., ed. *Mark Twain's Letters from Hawaii*. Honolulu: University of Hawaii Press, 1975.

Delaney, Wesley A. "The Truth about That Humboldt Trip as Told by Gus Oliver to A.B. Paine." *Twainian* 7, no. 3 (May–June 1948): 1–3.

Deloria, Philip. *Indians in Unexpected Places*. Lawrence: University of Kansas Press, 2004.

———. *Playing Indian*. New Haven, CT: Yale University Press, 1998.

Denton, Lynn W. "Mark Twain and the American Indian." *Mark Twain Journal* 16, no. 1 (Winter 1971–72): 1–3.

Depew, Chauncy M. "Birthday and Anniversary Addresses." In *Orations, Addresses, and Speeches of Chauncy M. Depew*. Vol. 3, edited by John Denison Champlin. New York: privately printed, 1910.

———. *My Memories of Eighty Years*. New York: Scribner's Sons, 1921.

De Quille Dan [William Wright]. *The Big Bonanza*. New York: Alfred A. Knopf, 1947.

———"How Uncle Bob 'Got' His 'First Injun.'" *Golden Era*, 20 April 1862, 4–5.

———"Letter from Washoe." *Golden Era*, 5 May 1861.

———"Salad Days of Mark Twain." In *Twain in His Own Time*, edited by Gary Scharnhorst. Iowa City: University of Iowa Press, 2010. First published 1893.

———"Shooting a Frog Eater—A Story of the Plains." *Salt Lake City Tribune*, n.d.

———*Washoe Rambles*. Los Angeles: Westernlore Press, 1963.

Diamond, Jared. *Guns, Germs, and Steel: The Fates of Human Societies*. New York: W. W. Norton, 1999.

Dippie, Brian. *The Vanishing American: White Attitudes and U.S. Indian Policy*. Lawrence: University Press of Kansas, 1982.

Dodge, Richard Irving. *Our Wild Indians: Thirty-Three Years' Personal Experience among the Red Men of the Great West*. New York: Archer House, 1959.

———*The Plains of the Great West and Their Inhabitants*. Newark: University of Delaware Press, 1989.

———. *The Plains of North America and Their Inhabitants*. Newark: University of Delaware Press, 1989.

Dubinsky, Karen. *The Second Greatest Disappointment: Honeymooning and Tourism at Niagara Falls*. New Brunswick, NJ: Rutgers University Press, 1999.

Eastman, Charles A. *From the Deep Woods to Civilization*. Lincoln: University of Nebraska Press, 1977.

———. *Red Hunters and the Animal People*. New York: Harper and Brothers, 1905.

Ebersole, Gary. *Captured by Texts: Puritan to Post-modern Images of Indian Captivity*. Charlottesville: University of Virginia Press, 1995.

Edmonds, Penelope. "'Failing in Every Endeavor to Conciliate': Governor Arthur's Proclamation Boards to the Aborigines, Australian Conciliation

Narratives, and Their Transnational Connections." *Journal of Australian Studies* 35, no. 2 (June 2011): 201–18.

―――. "Imperial Objects, Truths and Fictions: Reading Nineteenth-Century Australian Colonial Objects as Historical Sources." In *Rethinking Colonial Histories: New And Alternative Approaches*, edited by Penelope Edmonds and Samuel Furphy, 73–87. Melbourne: University of Melbourne Department of History, 2006.

Effgen, Alex Brink. "Mark Twain's Defense of Virtue from the Offense of English Literature." *Mark Twain Annual* 11 (2013): 77–95.

Egan, Ferol. *Sand in a Whirlwind: The Paiute Indian War of 1860*. 2nd ed. Reno: University of Nevada Press, 2003.

Ellison, Robert W. *Long Beard: Warren Wasson—Nevada Pioneer, Indian Agent, U.S. Marshal, Inventor & Enigma*. Minden, NV: Hot Springs Mountain Press, 2008.

Fanning, Philip. *Mark Twain and Orion Clemens: Brothers, Partners, Strangers*. Tuscaloosa: University of Alabama Press, 2006.

Faragher, John Mack. "More Motley than Mackinaw: From Ethnic Mixing to Ethnic Cleansing on the Frontier of the Lower Mississippi." In *Contact Points: American Frontiers from the Mohawk Valley to the Mississippi*, edited by Andrew R.L. Clayton and Fredrika J. Teute, 304–26. Chapel Hill: University of North Carolina Press, 1998.

Fatout, Paul, ed. *Mark Twain Speaking*. Iowa City: University of Iowa Press, 1976.

Faulkner, Barry. "George de Forest Brush." Unpublished manuscript. Faulkner Papers, Smithsonian Archives of American Art.

―――. "Mark Twain in Dublin." Unpublished manuscript. Faulkner Papers, Smithsonian Archives of American Art.

Fellman, Michael. *Citizen Sherman*. Lawrence: University Press of Kansas, 1995.

Fenwick, George. "Memoir: Dr. Thomas Morland Hocken." In *The Early History of New Zealand*. Wellington: John MacKay (Government Printer), 1914.

Fillmore, John Comfort. "A Study of Indian Music." *Century Magazine* 47, no. 4 (February 1894): 616–23.

Fischer, Joseph R. *A Well-Executed Failure: The Sullivan Campaign against the Iroquois, July-September 1779*. Columbia: University of South Carolina Press, 1997.

Fishkin, Shelley Fisher. *Lighting Out for the Territory: Reflections on Mark Twain and American Culture*. New York: Oxford University Press, 1997.

Flint, Timothy. *Recollections of the Last Ten Years in the Valley of the Mississippi*. Edited by George R. Brooks. Carbondale: Southern Illinois University Press, 1968.

Foner, Philip. *Mark Twain: Social Critic*. New York: International, 1958.

Foote, Kate. "Our Washington Letter." *Independent*, 18 December 1890, 22 January 1891, 19 February 1891.

Friend, Craig Thompson. *Kentucke's Frontier.* Bloomington: Indiana University Press, 2010.

Friesen, Steve. *Buffalo Bill: Scout, Showman, Visionary.* Golden, CO: Fulcrum, 2010.

Fulton, Joe B. *Mark Twain in the Margins: The Quarry Farm Marginalia and A Connecticut Yankee in King Arthur's Court.* Tuscaloosa: University of Alabama Press, 2007.

———. *The Reconstruction of Mark Twain: How a Confederate Bushwhacker Became the Lincoln of Our Literature.* Baton Rouge: Louisiana State University Press, 2010.

Ganzel, Dewey. *Mark Twain Abroad: The Cruise of the Quaker City.* Chicago: University of Chicago Press, 1968.

Geismar, Maxwell. *Mark Twain: An American Prophet.* Boston: Houghton Mifflin, 1970.

"George Frankland." *The Dictionary of Australian Artists: Painters, Sketchers, Photographers, and Engravers to 1870.* Edited by Joan Kerr. Melbourne: Oxford University Press, 1992.

Gewirtz, Isaac. *Mark Twain, A Skeptic's Progress.* New York: New York Public Library, 2010.

Gianella, Vincent P. "The Site of Williams Station, Nevada." *Nevada Historical Society Quarterly* 3, no. 4 (October–December 1960): 5–10.

Gibson, Arrell Morgan. *The American Indian: Prehistory to the Present.* Lexington, MA: Heath, 1980.

Gillis, William R. *Memories of Mark Twain and Steve Gillis.* Sonora, CA: Banner, 1924.

Gilpin, William. *Observations on the River Wye.* London: Cadell and Davies, 1880.

Goodyear, Frank. *Red Cloud: Photographs of a Lakota Chief.* Lincoln: University of Nebraska Press, 2003.

Greeley, Horace. *An Overland Journey from New York to San Francisco in the Summer of 1859.* Lincoln: University of Nebraska Press, 1999.

Gribben, Alan. Foreword to *Mark Twain and Orion Clemens: Brothers, Partners, Strangers,* by Philip Fanning. Tuscaloosa: University of Alabama Press, 2006.

———. *Mark Twain's Library: A Reconstruction.* 2 vol. Boston: G.K. Hall, 1980.

Gwynne, S.C. *Empire of the Summer Moon.* New York: Scribner, 2011.

Haines, Harold H., ed. *The Callaghan Mail, 1821–1859, Featuring the Lives of William Callaghan, the Pioneer, and His Educated Slave, Isaac Crawford, Indians, Big Game, Gold, and Old Letters.* Hannibal, MO, 1946.

Hanson, Elizabeth. "Mark Twain's Indians Re-examined." *Mark Twain Journal* 20, no. 4 (1981): 11–12.

Harris, Helen L. "Mark Twain's Response to the Native American." *American Literature* 46, no. 4 (January 1975): 495–505.

Hattori, Eugene. "'And Some of Them Swear Like Pirates': Acculturation of American Indian Women in Nineteenth Century Virginia City." In

Comstock Women: The Making of a Mining Community, edited by Ronald M. James and C. Elizabeth Raymond, 229–45. Reno: University of Nevada Press, 1998.

———. *Northern Paiutes on the Comstock: Archaeology and Ethnohistory of an American Indian Population in Virginia City, Nevada*. Carson City: Nevada State Museum, 1975.

Hays, Robert G., ed. *A Race at Bay: New York Times Editorials on "the Indian Problem," 1860–1900*. Carbondale: Southern Illinois University Press, 1997.

Heizer, Robert F., ed. *They Were Only Diggers: A Collection of Articles from California Newspapers, 1851–1866, on Indian and White Relations*. Ramona, CA: Ballena Press, 1974.

Hirst, Robert H., ed. *Who Is Mark Twain?* New York: Harper Studio, 2009.

Hocken, Thomas M. "Introduction: Early History, Maori, and South Seas Court." *Official Catalogue of the Exhibits*. Dunedin: Exhibition Commissioners, 1889.

Hoffman, Walter James. "Cremation among the Digger Indians." *Proceedings of the American Philosophical Society* 14. no. 94 (1875).

Holcombe, R.I. *History of Marion County, Missouri*. St. Louis: E. F. Perkins, 1884.

Hopkins, Sarah Winnemucca. *Life among the Piutes*. Reno: University of Nevada Press, 1994.

Howells, William Dean. "Editor's Study." *Harper's Monthly* 80, January 1890, 319–21.

Hsu, Hsuan L. *Sitting in Darkness: Mark Twain's Asia and Comparative Racialization*. New York: New York University Press, 2015.

Hutton, F.W. *Guide to the Collections in the Canterbury Museum, Christchurch, New Zealand*. Christchurch: Lyttleton Times, 1895.

"Indian Peace Commission Report to the President, January 7, 1868." *Annual Report of the Commissioner of Indian Affairs for the Year 1868*. Washington, DC: Government Printing Office, 1868.

Ingpen, Roger, ed. *The Letters of Percy Bysshe Shelley*. London: Sir Isaac Pitman and Sons, 1909.

James, Ronald M., and Susan A. James. *Virginia City and the Big Bonanza*. Charleston: Arcadia, 2009.

Johnson, Ellen Terry. "Historical Sketch of the Connecticut Indian Association from 1881 to 1888." Hartford: Fowler and Miller Press, 1888.

Kalter, Susan. "A Savagist Abroad: Anti-colonial Theory and the Quiet Violence of Twain's Western Oeuvre." *Texas Studies in Literature and Language* 53, no. 1 (Spring 2011): 26–113.

Kaplan. Amy. *The Anarchy of Empire in the Making of U.S. Culture*. Cambridge, MA: Harvard University Press, 2002.

Kappler, Charles, ed. *Indian Affairs: Laws and Treaties*, Vol. 2. Washington: Government Printing Office, 1904.

Karamanski, Theodore J. *Blackbird's Song: Andrew J. Blackbird and the Odawa People*. East Lansing: Michigan State University Press, 2012.

Kasson, Joy S. *Buffalo Bill's Wild West: Celebrity, Memory, and Popular History.* New York: Hill and Wang, 2000.

———. *Marble Queens and Captives: Women in Nineteenth-Century American Sculpture.* New Haven, CT: Yale University Press, 1990.

Keane, Basil. "Pounamu." *Te Ara: The Encyclopedia of New Zealand.* www.teara.govt.nz

Kerr, Donald. *Hocken, Prince of Collectors.* Dunedin, New Zealand: Otago University Press, 2015.

Kime, Wayne. "Huck among the Indians: Mark Twain and Richard Irving Dodge's *The Plains of the Great West and Their Inhabitants.*" *Western American Literature* 24, no. 4 (Winter 1990): 321–33.

———. Introduction to *The Plains of the Great West and Their Inhabitants,* by Richard Irving Dodge. Newark: University of Delaware Press, 1989.

King, Florence. "The Noble White Man." Review of *Mark Twain's Collected Tales, Sketches, Speeches, & Essays. National Review* 45, no. 1, 18 January 1993.

Kiskis, Michael J. *Mark Twain's Own Autobiography: The Chapters from the North American Review.* Madison: University of Wisconsin Press, 1990.

Knack, Martha, and Omer C. Stewart. *As Long as the River Shall Run: An Ethnohistory of the Pyramid Lake Indian Reservation Today.* Berkeley: University of California Press, 1984.

Kolb, Harold H. *Mark Twain: The Gift of Humor.* New York: University Press of America, 2015.

Krause, Sydney. *Mark Twain as Critic.* Baltimore: Johns Hopkins University Press, 1967.

Kroeber, Alfred L. *Handbook of the Indians of California.* San Francisco: Filmer Brothers Press, 1967.

Kroeber, Theodora. *Ishi in Two Worlds.* 50th Anniversary Edition. Berkeley: University of California Press, 2011.

Lambert, Charles. *Benjamin Logan.* Lexington: University Press of Kentucky, 1962.

Larson, Orvin. *American Infidel: Robert G. Ingersoll.* Madison, WI: Freedom from Religion Foundation, 1993.

Larson, Robert. *Red Cloud: Warrior-Statesman of the Lakota Sioux.* Norman: University of Oklahoma Press, 1999.

Laurie, J.S. *The Story of Australasia: Its Discovery, Colonisation and Development.* London: Osgood, McIlvaine, 1896.

Lawrence, D.H. *Studies in Classic American Literature.* New York: Penguin Books, 1978.

Lawton, Mary. *A Lifetime with Mark Twain: The Memories of Katy Leary, for Thirty Years His Faithful and Devoted Servant.* New York: Haskell House, 1972.

Leon, Philip. *Mark Twain at West Point.* Toronto: ECW Press, 1996.

Limerick, Patricia Nelson. *Something in the Soil: Legacies and Reckonings in the New West.* New York: W.W. Norton, 2000.

Lonnberg, Allan. "The Digger Indian Stereotype in California." *Journal of California and Great Basin Anthropology* 3, no. 2 (1981): 215–23.

Lorch, Fred. "Mark Twain's Early Views on Western Indians." *Twainian* 4, no. 7 (1945): 1–2.

———. "Orion Clemens." *Palimpsest* 10, no. 10 (October 1929): 353–88.

Lummis, Geraldine. "Ukiyo-e and the Canterbury Museum." Master's thesis, University of Canterbury, 2011.

Lystra, Karen. *Dangerous Intimacy: The Untold Story of Mark Twain's Final Years.* Berkeley: University of California Press, 2004.

Mack, Effie Mona. *Mark Twain in Nevada.* New York: Charles Scribner's Sons, 1947.

Madley, Benjamin. *An American Genocide: The United States and the California Indian Catastrophe, 1846–1873.* New Haven, CT: Yale University Press, 2016.

Madsen, Brigham D. *Glory Hunter: A Biography of Patrick Edward Connor.* Salt Lake City: University of Utah Press, 1990.

———. *The Shoshoni Frontier and the Bear River Massacre.* Salt Lake City: University of Utah Press, 1985.

Mahoney, Timothy. *Provincial Lives: Middle-Class Experience in the Antebellum Middle West.* New York: Cambridge University Press, 1999.

Manderson, Desmond. "The Law of the Image and the Image of the Law: Colonial Representations of the Rule of Law." *New York Law School Law Review* 57 (2012–13): 153–68.

Mann, Barbara Alice. *George Washington's War on Native America.* Lincoln: University of Nebraska Press, 2009.

Marberry, M. M. *Splendid Poseur: Joaquin Miller—American Poet.* New York: Thomas Y. Crowell, 1953.

Mardock, Robert W. *Reformers and the American Indian.* Columbia: University of Missouri Press, 1971.

Marsh, Andrew. *Letters from Nevada Territory, 1861–1862.* Edited by William C. Miller, Russell W. McDonald, and Ann Rollins. Carson City: Nevada Legislative Counsel Bureau, 1972.

Marsh, Andrew, and Samuel L. Clemens. *Reports of the 1863 Constitutional Convention of the Territory of Nevada.* Edited by William C. Miller and Eleanor Bushnell. Carson City: State of Nevada Legislative Counsel Bureau, 1972.

McCarthy, Conal. *Exhibiting Maori: A History of Colonial Cultures of Display.* Oxford: Berg, 2007.

McCullough, Joseph. "Mark Twain and the Hy Slocum-Carl Byng Controversy." *American Literature* 43 (March 1971): 42–59.

McCullough, Joseph, and Janice McIntire-Strasburg, eds. *Mark Twain at the Buffalo Express.* Dekalb: Northern Illinois University Press, 1999.

McElderry, Bruce R., ed. *Mark Twain's Contributions to the* Galaxy, *1868–1871.* New York: Scholars' Facsimiles and Reprints, 1961.

McKeithan, Daniel Morley, ed. *Traveling with the Innocents Abroad: Mark Twain's Original Reports from Europe and the Holy Land.* Norman: University of Oklahoma Press, 1958.

McNutt, James. "Mark Twain and the American Indian: Earthly Realism and Heavenly Idealism." *American Indian Quarterly* 4, no. 3 (August 1978): 223–42.

Melville, Herman. *The Confidence Man.* Evanston: Northwestern University Press, 1984.

"Message of the President of the United States in Answer to a Resolution . . . in Relation to the Indian Barbarities in Minnesota." Senate Executive Document no. 7, 37th Cong., 3rd sess., 11 December 1862: 3–4.

Messent, Peter. "Racial and Colonial Discourse in Mark Twain's *Following the Equator.*" *Essays in Arts and Sciences* 22 (October 1993): 67–84.

———. *The Short Works of Mark Twain: A Critical Study.* Philadelphia: University of Pennsylvania Press, 2001.

Michelson, Bruce. *Mark Twain on the Loose.* Amherst: University of Massachusetts Press, 1995.

———. *Printer's Devil: Mark Twain and the American Publishing Revolution.* Berkeley: University of California Press, 2006.

Michno, Gregory. *The Deadliest Indian War in the West: The Snake Conflict, 1864–1868.* Caldwell, ID: Caxton Press, 2007.

Mieder, Wolfgang. "The Only Good Indian Is a Dead Indian: History and Meaning of a Proverbial Stereotype." *Journal of American Folklore* 106, no. 419 (1993): 38–60.

Miller, Joaquin. *Life amongst the Modocs: Unwritten History.* Berkeley: Heyday Books/Urion Press, 1996.

———. *Romantic Life amongst the Red Indians: An Autobiography.* London: Saxon, 1890.

Miller, Perry, and Thomas H. Johnson, eds. *The Puritans: A Sourcebook of Their Writings.* Vol. 1. New York: Harper Torchbooks, 1963.

Miller, William Charles, ed. "The Pyramid Lake Indian War of 1860." Pts. 1 and 2. *Nevada Historical Society Quarterly* 1, no. 1 (Summer 1957): 37–53; 1, no. 2 (Fall 1957): 100–13.

Mitira, Tiaki Hikawera. "Explaining the Meaning and Purpose of Tapu." *Takitimu,* 37–39. Wellington: Read, 1972. New Zealand Electronic Text Collection. www.nzetc.victoria.ac.nz.

Moody, A. David. *Ezra Pound, Poet.* Vol. 1, *The Young Genius, 1885–1920.* New York: Oxford University Press, 2007.

Moody, Eric, ed. *Western Carpetbagger: The Extraordinary Memoirs of "Senator" Thomas Fitch.* Reno: University of Nevada Press, 1979.

Moon, Paul. "The History of Moutoa Gardens and Claims of Ownership." *Journal of the Polynesian Society* 105, no. 3 (1996): 347–65.

———. *Ngapua: The Political Life of Hone Heke Ngapua, MHR.* Auckland: David Ling, 2006.

Morgan, Dale L. *Shoshonean Peoples and the Overland Trails: Frontiers of the Utah Superintendency of Indian Affairs, 1849–1869.* Logan: Utah State University Press, 2007.

Morgan, William. *Monadnock Summer: The Architectural Legacy of Dublin, New Hampshire.* Boston: David Godine, 2011.

Moses, L.G. *Wild West Shows and the Images of American Indians, 1883–1933.* Albuquerque: University of New Mexico Press, 1996.

Neider, Charles, ed. *The Complete Short Stories of Mark Twain.* New York: Doubleday, 1957.

Obenzinger, Hilton. *American Palestine: Melville, Twain, and Holy Land Mania.* Princeton, NJ: Princeton University Press, 1999.

Paine, Albert Bigelow. *Mark Twain: A Biography.* 3 vols. New York: Chelsea House, 1997.

Parkman, Francis. *Count Frontenac and New France under Louis XIV.* Boston: Little, Brown, 1880.

———. *The Jesuits in North America in the Seventeenth Century.* Boston: Little, Brown, 1880.

———. *The Oregon Trail.* Boston: Little, Brown, 1880.

Parsons, Coleman O. "Mark Twain: Paid Performer in South Africa." *Mark Twain Journal* 19, no. 2 (1978): 2–11.

Petersen, Anna K.C. "The European Use of Maori Art in New Zealand Homes c. 1890–1914." In *At Home in New Zealand: Houses, History, People,* edited by Barbara Brookes, 57–72. Wellington: Bridge Williams Books, 2000.

Philip M. Neufeld Collection of Manuscripts and Printed Books. Part 1, 25 April 1995. New York: Christies' Auction House, 1995. Auction catalog.

Poole, D.C. *Among the Sioux of Dakota: Eighteen Months' Experience as an Indian Agent, 1869–1870.* St. Paul: Minnesota Historical Society Press, 1988.

Pope, Alexander. *An Essay on Man, Moral Essays, and Satires.* London: Cassel, 1905.

Porter, Peter. *Niagara: An Aboriginal Center of Trade.* Niagara Falls: privately printed, 1906.

Powers, Ron. *Dangerous Water: A Biography of the Boy Who Became Mark Twain.* Cambridge, MA: Da Capo Press, 1999.

———. *Mark Twain: A Life.* New York: Free Press, 2005.

Prucha, Francis Paul. *American Indian Treaties: The History of a Political Anomaly.* Berkeley: University of California Press, 1994.

Rasmussen, Kent, ed. *Dear Mark Twain: Letters from His Readers.* Berkeley: University of California Press, 2013.

Reddin, Paul. *Wild West Shows.* Urbana: University of Illinois Press, 1999.

Reports of the 1863 Constitutional. Convention of the Territory of Nevada. Edited by William C. Miller and Eleanor Bushnell. Carson City, NV: Legislative Counsel Bureau, 1972.

Revard, Carter. "Why Mark Twain Murdered Injun Joe—and Will Never Be Indicted": Norton Critical Edition, *The Adventures of Tom Sawyer*, edited by Beverly Lyon Clark, 332–52. New York: W. W. Norton, 2007.

Richardson, Albert D. *Beyond the Mississippi*. Hartford: American Publishing Company, 1867.

Robley, Horatio G. *Moko, or Maori Tattooing*. Mineola, NY: Dover, 2003.

Rosaldo, Renato. "Imperialist Nostalgia." In *Culture and Truth: The Remaking of Social Analysis*. Boston: Beacon Press, 1989.

Rowe, John Carlos. "Mark Twain's Critique of Globalization (Old and New) in *Following The Equator, A Journey Around the World* (1897)." *Arizona Quarterly* 61, no. 1 (Spring 2005): 109–35.

Rowlandson, Mary. *The Sovereignty and Goodness of God, Together with the Faithfulness of His Promises Displayed: Being a Narrative of the Captivity and Restoration of Mrs. Mary Rowlandson*. Edited by Neal Salisbury. New York: Bedford/St. Martin's Press, 1997.

Scharnhorst, Gary. *Bret Harte: Opening the American Literary West*. Norman: University of Oklahoma Press, 2000.

———, ed. *Mark Twain in His Own Time*. Iowa City: University of Iowa Press, 2010.

Scheick, William J. *The Half-Blood: A Cultural Symbol in 19th Century American Fiction*. Lexington: University Press of Kentucky, 1979.

Schmidt, Barbara. "'Hy Slocum' Identified." www.twainquotes.com.

———. "Mark Twain's Juggernaut Club Correspondence: The Helene Pickard Letters." www.twainquotes.com.

Shelden, Michael. *Mark Twain: Man in White*. New York: Random House, 2010.

Shillingsburg, Miriam. *At Home Abroad: Mark Twain in Australasia*. Jackson: University Press of Mississippi, 1988.

Slotkin, Richard. *The Fatal Environment: The Myth of the Frontier in the Age of Industrialization 1800–1890*. New York: Harper Perennial, 1994.

———. *Regeneration through Violence: The Mythology of the American Frontier, 1600–1860*. Middletown, CT: Wesleyan University Press, 1973.

Slout, William L. *Olympians of the Sawdust Circle: A Biographical Dictionary of the Nineteenth Century American Circus*. Rockville, MD: Borgo Press, 2009.

Smith, Henry Nash, and Frederick Anderson, eds. *Mark Twain of the Enterprise: Newspaper Articles and Other Documents, 1862–1864*. Berkeley: University of California Press, 1957.

Smythe, Carlyle. "The Real Mark Twain." *Pall Mall Magazine* 16, no. 65 (September 1898): 29–36.

Snaith, Norman H. *A Theological Word Book of the Bible*. Edited by Alan Richardson. New York: Macmillan, 1951.

Spencer, Herbert. *On Social Evolution*. Edited by J.D.Y. Peel. Chicago: University of Chicago Press, 1972.

Stack, James W. "An Account of the Maori House, Attached to the Christchurch Museum." *Transactions and Proceedings of the Royal Society of New Zealand* 8 (1875): 172–76.

Steinbrink, Jeffrey. *Getting to Be Mark Twain.* Berkeley: University of California Press, 1991.

Stone, Albert E. *The Innocent Eye: Childhood in Mark Twain's Imagination.* New York: Archon Books, 1970.

Stone, R.C.J. *The Father and His Gift: John Logan Campbell's Later Years.* Auckland: Auckland University Press, 1987.

Stoneley, Peter. *Mark Twain and the Feminine Aesthetic.* Cambridge: Cambridge University Press, 1992.

Tarnoff, Ben. *The Bohemians: Mark Twain and the San Francisco Writers Who Invented American Literature.* New York: Penguin Press, 2014.

Teetor, Henry. *The Past and Present of Mill Creek Valley.* Cincinnati: Cohen, 1882.

Thomas, Nicholas. *Entangled Objects: Exchange, Material Culture, and Colonialism in the Pacific.* Cambridge, MA: Harvard University Press, 1991.

Thompson, William Carter. *On the Road with a Circus.* New York: New Amsterdam, 1905.

Trabue, Daniel. *Westward into Kentucky: The Narrative of Daniel Trabue.* Edited by Chester Raymond. Lexington: University Press of Kentucky, 1981.

Twain, Mark. *The Adventures of Tom Sawyer.* Berkeley: University of California Press, 1980.

———. *The American Claimant.* New York: Oxford University Press, 1996.

———. *Autobiography of Mark Twain.* Vol. 1. Edited by Harriet Elinor Smith, with associate editors Benjamin Griffin, Victor Fischer, Michael B. Frank, Sharon K. Goetz, and Leslie Diane Myrick. Berkeley: University of California Press, 2010.

———. *Autobiography of Mark Twain.* Vol. 2. Edited by Benjamin Griffin and Harriet Elinor Smith, with associate editors Victor Fischer, Michael B. Frank, Sharon K. Goetz, and Leslie Diane Myrick. Berkeley: University of California Press, 2013.

———. *Autobiography of Mark Twain.* Vol. 3. Edited by Benjamin Griffin and Harriet Elinor Smith, with associate editors Victor Fischer, Michael B. Frank, Amanda Gagel, Sharon K. Goetz, Leslie Diane Myrick, and Christopher M. Ohge. Berkeley: University of California Press, 2015.

———. *The Choice Humorous Works of Mark Twain.* Revised and corrected by the author. London: Chatto and Windus, 1874.

———. *Collected Tales, Sketches, Speeches, & Essays 1852–1890.* Edited by Louis J. Budd. New York: Library of America, 1992.

———. *Collected Tales, Sketches, Speeches, & Essays 1891–1910.* Edited by Louis J. Budd. New York: Library of America, 1992.

———. *A Connecticut Yankee in King Arthur's Court.* Edited by Bernard L. Stein. Berkeley: University of California Press, 1983.

———. *Early Tales & Sketches.* Vol. 1, *1851–1864.* Edited by Edgar Marquess Branch and Robert H. Hirst. Berkeley: University of California Press, 1979.

———. *Early Tales & Sketches.* Vol. 2, *1864–1865.* Edited by Edgar Marquess Branch and Robert H. Hirst. Berkeley: University of California Press, 1981.

———. *Following the Equator.* New York: Oxford University Press, 1996.

———. "Huck Finn and Tom Sawyer among the Indians and Other Unfinished Stories." Berkeley: University of California Press, 1989.

———. *The Innocents Abroad.* New York: Oxford University Press, 1996.

———. *Letters.* Vol. 1, *1853–1866.* Edited by Edgar Marquess Branch, Michael B. Frank, and Kenneth M. Sanderson, with associate editors Harriet Elinor Smith, Lin Salamo, and Richard Bucci. Berkeley: University of California Press, 1988.

———. *Letters.* Vol. 2, *1867–1868.* Edited by Harriet Elinor Smith and Richard Bucci, with associate editor Lin Salamo. Berkeley: University of California Press, 1990.

———. *Letters,.* Vol. 3, *1869.* Edited by Victor Fischer and Michael B. Frank, with associate editor Dahlia Armon. Berkeley: University of California Press, 1992.

———. *Letters.* Vol. 4, *1870–1871.* Edited by Victor Fischer and Michael B. Frank, with associate editor Lin Salamo. Berkeley: University of California Press, 1995.

———. *Letters.* Vol. 5, *1872–1873.* Edited by Lin Salamo and Harriet Elinor Smith. Berkeley: University of California Press, 1997.

———. *Letters.* Vol. 6, *1874–1875.* Edited by Michael B. Frank and Harriet Elinor Smith. Berkeley: University of California Press, 2002.

———. *Letters from the Earth.* Edited by Bernard DeVoto. New York: Harper and Row, 1974.

———. *Life on the Mississippi.* New York: Oxford University Press, 1996.

———. *Mark Twain: The Complete Interviews.* Edited by Gary Scharnhorst. Tuscaloosa: University of Alabama Press, 2006.

———. *Mark Twain-Howells Letters: The Correspondence of Samuel L. Clemens and William D. Howells, 1872–1910.* 2 vols. Edited by Henry Nash Smith and William M. Gibson. Cambridge: Belknap Press of Harvard University Press, 1960.

———. *Mark Twain's (Burlesque) Autobiography and First Romance.* New York: Sheldon, 1871.

———. *Mark Twain's Hannibal, Huck & Tom.* Edited by Walter Blair. Berkeley: University of California Press, 1969.

———. *More Tramps Abroad.* London: Chatto and Windus, 1897.

———. *Plymouth Rock and the Pilgrims and Other Speeches.* Edited by Charles Neider. New York: Cooper Square Press, 2000.

———. *Pudd'nhead Wilson* and *Those Extraordinary Twins.* Edited by Sidney E. Berger. New York: W. W. Norton & Co., 2005.

———. *Roughing It.* Edited by Harriet Elinor Smith and Edgar Marquess Branch, with associate editors Lin Salamo and Robert Pack Browning. Berkeley: University of California Press, 1993.

———. *Sketches, New and Old.* New York: Oxford University Press, 1996.

———. *What Is Man? And Other Philosophical Writings.* Edited by Paul Baender. Berkeley: University of California Press, 1973.

Turner, Frederick Jackson. *The Significance of the Frontier in American History* Edited by Harold P. Simonson. New York: Frederick Ungar, 1963.

Unrau, William E. *Mixed Bloods and Tribal Dissolution: Charles Curtis and the Quest for Indian Identity.* Lawrence: University Press of Kansas, 1989.

Utley, Robert. *The Indian Frontier 1846–1890.* Rev. ed. Albuquerque: University of New Mexico Press, 2003.

Varble, Rachel M. *Jane Clemens: The Story of Mark Twain's Mother.* Garden City, NY: Doubleday, 1964.

Walker, Franklin, and G. Ezra Dane, eds. *Mark Twain's Travels with Mr. Brown.* New York: Alfred A. Knopf, 1940.

Walker, Paul. "The 'Maori House' at the Canterbury Museum." *Interstices* 4 (1991): 1–11.

Warren, Louis S. *Buffalo Bill's America: William Cody and the Wild West Show.* New York: Alfred A. Knopf, 2005.

Watson, Aaron. *The Savage Club: A Medley of History, Anecdote, and Reminiscence, with a Chapter by Mark Twain.* London: T. Fisher Unwin, 1907.

Webster, Samuel Charles, ed. *Mark Twain, Business Man.* Boston: Little, Brown, 1946.

Wecter, Dixon. *Sam Clemens of Hannibal.* Boston: Houghton Mifflin, 1952.

Weisenberger, Francis Phelps. *Idol of the West: The Fabulous Career of Rollin Mallory Daggett.* Syracuse: Syracuse University Press, 1965.

Welch, James. *Killing Custer.* With Paul Stekler. New York: Penguin Books, 1994.

Welland, Dennis. *Mark Twain in England.* London: Chatto and Windus, 1978.

White, Richard. "Frederick Jackson Turner and Buffalo Bill." In *The Frontier in American Culture,* edited by James R. Grossman, 7–65. Berkeley: University of California Press, 1994.

Wilcox, Ella Wheeler. *Custer and Other Poems.* Chicago: W. B. Conkey, 1896.

Williams, George III. *Mark Twain: His Life in Virginia City, Nevada.* Carson City, NV: Tree by the River Publishing Trust, 2007.

Willis, Nathaniel Parker. *Our Philippine Problem: A Study of American Colonial Policy.* New York: Henry Holt, 1905.

Wolfe, Patrick. "Settler Colonialism and the Elimination of the Native." *Journal of Genocide Research* 8, no. 4 (December 2006): 387–409.

———. *Settler Colonialism and the Transformation of Anthropology.* London: Cassell, 1999.

Wood, J. G. *The Uncivilized Races of Men.* Hartford: J. B. Burr and Hyde, 1870.

Woodward, Joan. "Sir Joseph Kinsey (1852–1936)." *Art New Zealand* 53 (Summer 1989–1990): 92–95.

Zanjani, Sally. *Devils Will Reign: How Nevada Began.* Reno: University of Nevada Press, 2006.

———. *Sarah Winnemucca Hopkins.* Lincoln: University of Nebraska Press, 2001.

Index

Page references in italics refer to illustrations.

Buffalo Bill's Wild West *(continued)*
European tour of, 222; Indian camp at, 218, *219*; influence on "Huck Finn and Tom Sawyer among the Indians," 223–24; Manifest Destiny and, 222; mythic narrative of, 224; re-enactments at, 222–24; religious rituals in, 220; route books of, 220, 390nn78,87; savagery in, 224; Sioux in, 218–19, 224; Sitting Bull in, 361; somatic sensation at, 221; sweat lodges at, 219; triumph of civilization in, 222, 224. *See also* Cody, William F.; The Wild West and Congress of the Rough Riders of the World
Buffalo Jim (Paiute warrior), 109
Buffalo Morning Express (newspaper): Clemens's association with, 147, 159; Lakota delegation coverage, 159–68; on military demonstration, 162, 385n51; native rhetoric in, 161–62, 163; New Books column, 164, 165–66; *Sheridan's Troopers* review, 164–67
buffalo robes, Plains Indians', 255
Bunce, Ned, 235, 392n22
Bunker Hill, battle of, 342
Burke, John M., 218
Burrough, Jacob, 57, 78
Burton, Nathaniel J.: in Connecticut Indian Association, 229; *Yale Lectures on Preaching and Other Writings*, 246
Burton, Richard E.: "For the Benefit of Indians" lectures, 245–47, 260, 394n61; "Mark Twain in the Hartford Days," 246; preservation campaign of, 394n57
Bushmen, South African: Diggers and, 136–37
Bushnell, D.E., 96, 98
Byrd, Jodi: *The Transit of Empire*, 136

Caciques, Indian, 306
"The Californian's Tale" (Twain), 111; savagery in, 271; white womanhood in, 10

California Trail, violence on, 95–96
Callaghan, William: *The Callaghan Mail*, 17–18
Campbell, John Logan, 312, 313; *Poenamo*, 226, 335, 336; residence among Maori, 335–36
Camp Grant massacre (1871), 241–42
Camp Independence (Nevada Territory), 86
Camp Wo-He-Lo (Sebago Lake, Maine), 367–68
Canada, treatment of Indians in, 349, 350
Canby, Edward R.S.: murder of, 178, 387n81
captivity narratives, 202
Carlisle Indian School, 228, 352, 369
Carroll, James, 345, 401n84; at Wellington Club dinner, 344
Carter, Everett, 250
Cary, William de la Montagne: "Scalp Dance," 47, *48*
Casey, Anne, 22
Casey, Jane Montgomery: in "Montgomery Massacre," 20–22, 372n25; stress disorder of, 22
Casey, William, 22, 373n33
Castiglia, Christopher, 358
Catholicism, Clemens on, 191, 248
Catlin, George, 201
Caw (Kansa) tribe, migration of, 18–19
Chadwick, Jocelyn: *The Jim Dilemma*, 3–4
Chapin, Samuel, 57
Charles L. Webster and Company, revenues from, 268
Chase, Salmon, 55
Chatto, Andrew, 273, 274, 293; excisions by, 347
Chauncey, Philip: *Notes and Anecdotes of the Aborigines of Australia*, 289
Cheney, Susan, 230
Cheyenne: murder of, 285–86; spirituality of, 11, 336
Chiricahua, federal treaty with, 177